8080/8085 Assembly Language Subroutines

8080/8085 Assembly Language Subroutines

Lance A. Leventhal
Winthrop Saville

Osborne/McGraw-Hill
Berkeley, California

Disclaimer of Warranties and Limitation of Liabilities

The authors have taken due care in preparing this book and the programs in it, including research, development, and testing to ascertain their effectiveness. The authors and the publisher make no expressed or implied warranty of any kind with regard to these programs or the supplementary documentation in this book. In no event shall the authors or the publisher be liable for incidental or consequential damages in connection with or arising out of the furnishing, performance, or use of any of these programs.

IBM is a registered trademark of IBM.

Teletype is a registered trademark of Teletype Corp.

CP/M is a registered trademark of Digital Research.

Published by
Osborne/McGraw-Hill
2600 Tenth Street
Berkeley, California 94710
U.S.A.

For information on translations and book distributors outside of the U.S.A., please write to Osborne/ McGraw-Hill at the above address.

8080/8085 ASSEMBLY LANGUAGE SUBROUTINES

1234567890 DODO 89876543

ISBN 0-931988-58-6

Cover design by Jean Lake˙

Text design by Paul Butzler

Contents

This book is dedicated to my mother, Ruby Moore

LAL

Preface

This book is intended to serve as a source and a reference for the assembly language programmer. It contains an overview of assembly language programming for a particular microprocessor and a collection of useful subroutines. In the subroutines, a standard format, documentation package, and parameter passing techniques were used. The rules of the most popular assemblers have been followed and the purpose, procedure, parameters, results, execution time, and memory usage of each routine have been described.

The overview sections summarize assembly language programming for those who do not have the time or need for a complete textbook; the Assembly Language Programming series provides more extensive discussions. Chapter 1 introduces assembly language programming for the particular processor and summarizes the major features that make this processor different from other microprocessors and minicomputers. Chapter 2 shows how to implement instructions and addressing modes that are not explicitly available. Chapter 3 describes common programming errors.

The collection of subroutines emphasizes common tasks that occur in many applications. These tasks include code conversion, array manipulation, arithmetic, bit manipulation, shifting functions, string manipulation, sorting, and searching. We have also provided examples of I/O routines, interrupt service routines, and initialization routines for common family chips such as parallel interfaces, serial interfaces, and timers. You should be able to use these programs as subroutines in actual applications and as starting points for more complex programs.

This book is intended for the person who wants to use assembly language immediately, rather than just learn about it. The reader could be

- An engineer, technician, or programmer who must write assembly language programs for a design project.

- A microcomputer user who wants to write an I/O driver, a diagnostic program, a utility, or a systems program in assembly language.

vii

· An experienced assembly language programmer who needs a quick review of techniques for a particular microprocessor.

· A systems designer who needs a specific routine or technique for immediate use.

· A high-level language programmer who must debug or optimize programs at the assembly level or must link a program written in a high-level language to one written in assembly language.

· A maintenance programmer who must understand quickly how specific assembly language programs work.

· A microcomputer owner who wants to understand the operating system for a particular computer, or who wants to modify standard I/O routines or systems programs.

· A student, hobbyist, or teacher who wants to see examples of working assembly language programs.

This book can also serve as a supplement for students of the Assembly Language Programming series.

This book should save the reader time and effort. The reader should not have to write, debug, test, or optimize standard routines, or search through a textbook for particular examples. The reader should instead be able to obtain easily the specific information, technique, or routine that he or she needs. This book has been organized and indexed for rapid use and reference.

Obviously, a book with such an aim demands feedback from its readers. Although all the programs have been thoroughly tested and carefully documented, please inform the publisher if you find any errors. If you have suggestions for better methods or for additional topics, routines, programming hints, or index entries, please tell us about them. We have used our programming experience to develop this book, but your help is needed to improve it. We would greatly appreciate your comments, criticisms, and suggestions.

NOMENCLATURE

We have used the following nomenclature in this book to describe the architecture of the 8080 and 8085 processors, to specify operands, and to represent general values of numbers and addresses.

8080 and 8085 Architecture

Byte-length registers include

A (accumulator)
B
C
D
E
H
L
M (memory location addressed via registers H and L)
F (flags)
I (interrupt mask, 8085 only)

Of these, the user registers are the first seven: A, B, C, D, E, H, and L. The F (flag) and I (interrupt mask) registers consist of a set of bits with independent functions and meanings. The F register is organized as shown in Figure P-1.

The I register (8085 only) has two different forms, one when read (with the RIM instruction) and one when written (with the SIM instruction). The two versions are organized as shown in Figures P-2 and P-3.

Register pairs and word-length registers include

B or BC   (registers B and C, B most significant)
D or DE   (registers D and E, D most significant)
H or HL   (registers H and L, H most significant)
PC   (program counter)
PSW   (processor status word, accumulator and flags; accumulator most significant)
SP or S   (stack pointer)

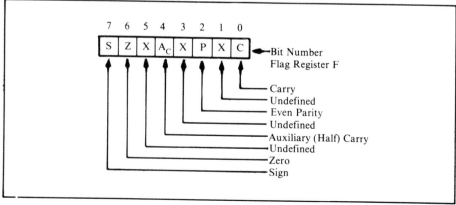

Figure P-1. The flag (F) register

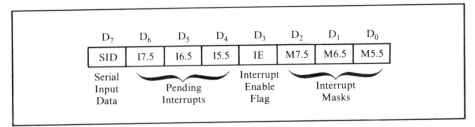

Figure P-2. The interrupt mask (I) register (as read by
a RIM instruction)

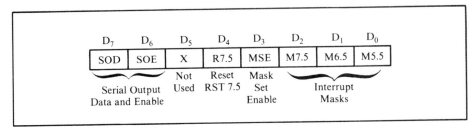

Figure P-3. The interrupt mask (I) register (as written by
a SIM instruction)

Special 8085 facilities include

IE	Interrupt enable flag
I5.5	Pending interrupt flag for RST 5.5 input
I6.5	Pending interrupt flag for RST 6.5 input
I7.5	Pending interrupt flag for RST 7.5 input
MSE	Mask set enable
M5.5	Mask bit for RST 5.5 input
M6.5	Mask bit for RST 6.5 input
M7.5	Mask bit for RST 7.5 input
Reset RST 7.5	Bit used to reset RST 7.5 flip-flop
SID	Serial input data line
SOD	Serial output data line
SOE	Serial output enable

These bits are arranged in the I register as shown previously.

Flags include

Auxiliary (Half) Carry (A_C)
Carry (C)
Parity (P)
Sign (S)
Zero (Z)

These flags are arranged in the F register as shown previously.

8080/8085 Assembler

Delimiters include

:	After a label, except for EQU, SET, and MACRO, which require a space
space	After an operation code
,	Between operands in the operand (address) field
;	Before a comment

Pseudo-operations include

DB	Define byte; place byte-length data in memory
DS	Define storage; allocate bytes of memory
DW	Define word; place word-length data in memory
END	End of program
EQU	Equate; define the attached label
ORG	Set origin; place subsequent object code starting at the specified address

Designations include

Number Systems:

B (suffix)	Binary
D (suffix)	Decimal
H (suffix)	Hexadecimal
Q (suffix)	Octal

The default mode is decimal; hexadecimal numbers must start with a digit (that is, you must add a leading zero if the number starts with a letter).

Others:

' ' or " "	ASCII (character surrounded by single or double quotation marks)
$	Current value of location (program) counter

General Nomenclature

ADDR	A 16-bit address in data memory
BASE	A constant 16-bit address in data memory
BICON	An 8-bit data item in binary format
DEST	A 16-bit address in program memory, the destination for a jump instruction
HIGH	A 16-bit data item
INDIR	A 16-bit address in data memory, the starting address for an indirect address. The indirect address is stored in memory locations INDIR and INDIR+1.
IPORT	An 8-bit device (port) address
LOW	A 16-bit data item
MASK	An 8-bit number used for masking
NTEMP	A 16-bit data item
NTIMES	An 8-bit data item
NTIML	An 8-bit data item
NTIMM	An 8-bit data item
NUM	A 16-bit data item
NUM1	A 16-bit address in data memory
NUM2	A 16-bit address in data memory

OFFSET	A 16-bit data item
OPER	A 16-bit address in data memory
OPER1	A 16-bit address in data memory
OPER2	A 16-bit address in data memory
OPORT	An 8-bit device (port) address
reg	A user register (A, B, C, D, E, H, or L)
reg1	Another user register, not the same as reg
RETPT	A 16-bit address in program memory
rp	A register pair (B, D, or H)
rph	The more significant byte of rp
rpl	The less significant byte of rp
rp1	Another register pair, not the same as rp
rp1h	The more significant byte of rp1
rp1l	The less significant byte of rp1
rp2	Another register pair, not the same as rp1
rp2h	The more significant byte of rp2
rp2l	The less significant byte of rp2
SPTR	A 16-bit address in data memory
STRNG	A 16-bit address in data memory
SUM	A 16-bit address in data memory
VAL16	A 16-bit data item
VAL16H	The more significant byte of VAL16
VAL16L	The less significant byte of VAL16
VALUE	An 8-bit data item

Chapter 1 **General Programming Methods**

This chapter describes general methods for writing assembly language programs for the 8080 and 8085 microprocessors. It presents techniques for performing the following operations:

- Loading and saving registers
- Storing data in memory
- Arithmetic and logical functions
- Bit manipulation
- Bit testing
- Testing for specific values
- Numerical comparisons
- Looping (repeating sequences of operations)
- Array processing and manipulation
- Table lookup
- Character code manipulation
- Code conversion
- Multiple-precision arithmetic
- Multiplication and division
- List processing
- Processing of data structures.

Special sections describe passing parameters to subroutines, general methods for writing I/O drivers and interrupt service routines, and techniques for making programs run faster or use less memory.

The operations described are required in such applications as instrumentation, test equipment, computer peripherals, communications equipment, industrial control, process control, business equipment, aerospace and military systems, and consumer products. Microcomputer users will employ these operations in writing I/O drivers, utility programs, diagnostics, and systems software and in understanding, debugging, and improving programs written in high-level languages. This chapter provides a brief guide to 8080 and 8085 assembly language programming for those who have an immediate application in mind.

QUICK SUMMARY FOR EXPERIENCED PROGRAMMERS

For those who are familiar with assembly language programming on other computers, here is a brief review of the peculiarities of the 8080 and 8085 processors. Being aware of these features can save a lot of time and trouble.

1. Arithmetic and logical operations are allowed only between the accumulator and a byte of immediate data or between the accumulator and a general-purpose register. However, one general-purpose register is really a memory location; register M actually refers to the memory address in registers H and L. Thus, for example, the instruction ADD M means *add to the accumulator the contents of the byte of memory addressed through registers H and L.* Arithmetic and logical instructions do *not* allow direct addressing.

2. The accumulator and registers H and L are special. They are the only registers that can be loaded or stored directly. The accumulator is the only register that can be complemented, shifted, loaded indirectly from the address in register pair B or D, stored indirectly at the address in register pair B or D, or used in IN and OUT instructions.

H and L are the only register pair that can be used indirectly in arithmetic or logical instructions, in storing immediate data, or in loading or storing registers other than the accumulator. H and L are also the only register pair that can be transferred to the program counter or stack pointer. Furthermore, these registers serve as a double-length accumulator for 16-bit addition (DAD). Registers D and E are rather special in that a single instruction (XCHG) can exchange them with registers H and L. Thus the 8080 and 8085's registers are highly asymmetric and the programmer must choose carefully which data and addresses go into which registers.

3. There are often several names for the same physical register. Many instructions use A, B, C, D, E, H, or L as 8-bit registers. Other instructions use B and C (B more significant), D and E (D more significant), or H and L (H more significant) as 16-bit register pairs. The terms *register pair B, registers B and C,* and *register pair BC* all have the same meaning; there are similar variations for registers D and E and H and L. Note that the register pair and the two single registers are identical physically and cannot be used for separate purposes at the same time.

In fact, H and L are almost always used to hold an indirect address because of the availability of instructions that access register M as well as special instructions such as SPHL, PCHL, XTHL, and XCHG. Registers D and E are used for a second address in preference to B and C because of the XCHG instruction. Registers B and C are generally used as separate 8-bit registers for temporary data storage.

4. The effects of instructions on flags are extremely inconsistent. Some particularly unusual effects are: (a) Logical instructions clear the Carry, (b) Shift instructions affect no flags other than the Carry, (c) Load, store, move, increment register pair, and decrement register pair instructions affect no flags at all, and (d) 16-bit addition (DAD) affects only the Carry flag. You can use Table A-1 to determine how an instruction affects the flags.

5. There is no indirect addressing through memory locations and no indexing. The lack of indirect addressing through memory is overcome by loading the indirect address into registers H and L. Thus, true indirect addressing is a two-step process. One could also load the indirect address into registers B and C or D and E if one only wanted to use it to load or store the accumulator.

The lack of indexed addressing is overcome by adding register pairs explicitly with DAD. DAD adds a register pair to H and L. Thus, indexing requires several steps: (a) Load the index into a register pair, (b) Load the base address into another pair (one pair must be H and L), (c) Add the two pairs explicitly using DAD, and (d) Use the sum as an indirect address (by referring to register M). Indexing on the 8080 or 8085 processor is a long, awkward process.

6. There is no two's complement overflow flag, so one must detect two's complement overflow in software. Handling signed numbers is therefore difficult.

7. Many common instructions are missing but can easily be simulated with register operations. Examples are clearing the accumulator (use SUB A or XRA A), logical left shift accumulator (use ADD A), clearing the Carry (use ANA A or ORA A), and testing the accumulator (use ANA A or ORA A). Either ANA A or ORA A clears Carry and sets the other flags according to the contents of the accumulator. Remember, loading a register does not affect any flags.

8. There are no relative branches. In fact, the only jump instruction that does not require an absolute address is PCHL, which loads the program counter from registers H and L and thus provides an indirect jump.

9. There are two separate sets of increment and decrement instructions. DCR and INR apply to 8-bit registers and affect all flags except Carry. DCX and INX apply to 16-bit register pairs and affect no flags at all. You can use a 16-bit register pair as an ordinary counter, but the only way to test the pair for 0 is to logically OR the two registers together in the accumulator.

10.   There are no arithmetic or logical shifts. The only shift instructions are rotations with and without the Carry flag. Other shifts must be simulated with the rotate instructions (RRC, RLC, RAR, and RAL) and addition instructions (ADD A, ADC A, and DAD H). The Carry flag can be set with STC and cleared with ANA A (or ORA A).

11.   The accumulator is the only register that can be shifted, complemented, or used for input or output. The only instructions that operate directly on general-purpose registers are MOV (transfer to or from another register), MVI (load immediate), DCR (decrement by 1), and INR (increment by 1). These instructions can also operate on register M, the byte of memory addressed through registers H and L.

12.   Only register pairs can be moved to or from the stack. One pair is the Processor Status Word (PSW), which consists of the accumulator (more significant byte) and the flags (less significant byte). The CALL and RETURN instructions transfer addresses to or from the stack.

13.   The 8080 lacks a readable Interrupt Status flag. This creates difficulties if the original state of the interrupt system must be restored after executing a section of code that must run with interrupts disabled. The solution is to maintain a copy of the interrupt status in RAM. The 8085, on the other hand, has a readable Interrupt Enable flag.

14.   The 8080 and 8085 use the following common conventions:

· All 16-bit addresses are stored with the less significant byte first (that is, at the lower address). The order of the bytes in an address is the same as in the Z80 and 6502 microprocessors, but the opposite of that used in the 6800 and 6809.

· The stack pointer contains the lowest address actually occupied by the stack. This convention is also used in the Z80 and 6809 microprocessors, but the obvious alternative (next available address) is used in the 6502 and 6800. All 8080/8085 instructions store data in the stack using predecrementing (subtracting 1 from the stack pointer before storing a byte) and load data from the stack using postincrementing (adding 1 to the stack pointer after loading a byte).

· The Interrupt Enable flag (in the 8085 only) is 1 to allow interrupts and 0 to disallow them. This convention is the same as in the Z80, but the opposite of that used in the 6502, 6800, and 6809.

REGISTER SET

8080/8085 assembly language programming is complicated by the asymmetry of the processors' instruction sets. Many instructions apply only to particular registers, register pairs, or sets of registers. Almost every register has unique features, and almost every instruction has peculiarities. Table 1-1 lists the byte-length registers and the instructions that operate on them. Table 1-2 lists the register pairs (or word-length registers) and the instructions that operate on them (of course, all instructions change the program counter implicitly). Table 1-3 lists the indirect addresses contained in register pairs and the instructions that use those addresses. Table 1-4 lists the instructions that apply only to the accumulator and Table 1-5 lists the instructions that apply only to particular register pairs. Table 1-6 lists the instructions that apply to the stack.

The general uses of the registers are as follows:

· The accumulator is the center of data processing; it is the source of one operand and the destination of the result in most arithmetic and logical operations.

Table 1-1. 8-Bit Registers and Applicable Instructions

Register	Instructions
A	ACI, ADC, ADD, ADI, ANA, ANI, CMA, CMP, CPI, DAA, DCR, IN, INR, LDA, LDAX, MOV, MVI, ORA, ORI, OUT, RAL, RAR, RIM (8085 only), RLC, RRC, SBB, SBI, SIM (8085 only), STA, STAX, SUB, SUI, XRA, XRI
B,C,D,E,H,L	ADC, ADD, ANA, CMP, DCR, INR, MOV, MVI, ORA, SBB, SUB, XRA
F (flags)	CMC, STC (see also PSW register pair)
I (interrupt mask, 8085 only)	RIM, SIM (8085 only)

Table 1-2. Register Pairs and Applicable Instructions

Register Pair	Instructions
B (B and C)	DAD, DCX, INX, LXI, POP, PUSH
D (D and E)	DAD, DCX, INX, LXI, POP, PUSH, XCHG
H (H and L)	DAD, DCX, INX, LHLD, LXI, PCHL, POP, PUSH, SHLD, SPHL, XCHG, XTHL
PSW (A and flags)	POP, PUSH
Program Counter	CALL instructions, JUMP instructions, PCHL, RETURN instructions, RST
Stack Pointer	CALL instructions, DAD, DCX, INX, LXI, POP, PUSH, RETURN instructions, RST, SPHL

Table 1-3. Indirect Addresses and Applicable Instructions

Location of Address	Instructions
Register pair B (B and C)	LDAX,STAX
Register pair D (D and E)	LDAX,STAX
Register pair H (H and L)	ADC,ADD,ANA,CMP,DCR,INR, MOV,MVI,ORA,SBB,SUB,XRA
Stack pointer	CALL instructions, POP,PUSH, RETURN instructions, RST,XTHL

Table 1-4. Instructions that Apply Only to the Accumulator

Instruction	Function	Instruction	Function
ACI	Add with Carry immediate	RAL	Rotate left through Carry
ADI	Add immediate	RAR	Rotate right through Carry
ANI	Logical AND immediate	RIM	Read interrupt mask (8085 only)
CMA	Complement (logical)	RLC	Rotate left
CPI	Compare immediate	RRC	Rotate right
DAA	Decimal adjust (correction)	SBI	Subtract with borrow immediate
IN	Input	SIM	Set interrupt mask (8085 only)
LDA	Load direct	STA	Store direct
LDAX	Load indirect	STAX	Store indirect
ORI	Logical OR immediate	SUI	Subtract immediate
OUT	Output	XRI	Logical EXCLUSIVE OR immediate

Table 1-5. Instructions that Apply to Only One or Two Register Pairs

Instruction	Register Pairs	Function
LDAX	B or D	Load accumulator indirect
LHLD	H	Load H and L direct
PCHL	H, PC	Transfer H and L to PC
SHLD	H	Store H and L direct
STAX	B or D	Store accumulator indirect
XCHG	D, H	Exchange HL with DE
XTHL	H	Exchange HL with top of stack

Table 1-6. Instructions that Use the Stack

Instruction	Function
CALL instructions	Jump and save program counter in stack
POP	Load register pair from stack
PUSH	Store register pair in stack
RETURN instructions	Load program counter from stack
RST	Jump to vector address and save PC in stack
XTHL	Exchange H and L with top of stack

· Registers H and L (register pair H) form the primary memory address register. Instructions that refer to register M are actually referring to the memory address in that register pair.

· Registers D and E (register pair D) form the secondary memory address register because the programmer can exchange their contents with H and L using XCHG.

· Registers B and C (register pair B) are general-purpose registers with no special features, although the instructions LDAX (load accumulator indirect) and STAX (store accmulator indirect) can use them as address registers. Programmers generally use B and C for counters and temporary data storage.

We may describe the special features of particular registers as follows:

· **Accumulator.** The only byte-length register that can be loaded or stored directly. The only register that can be shifted, complemented, or decimal adjusted with a single instruction. The only register that can be loaded or stored using the addresses in register pairs B or D. The only register that can be stored in an output port (using OUT) or loaded from an input port (using IN). The source and destination for all arithmetic and logical instructions except DAD, DCR, DCX, INR, and INX. The only register that can be loaded from the interrupt mask register (RIM) or stored in the interrupt mask register (SIM). (Only the 8085 processor has an interrupt mask register.)

· **Registers H and L.** The only register pair that can be used indirectly (by referring to register M) in the instructions ADC, ADD, ANA, CMP, DCR, INR, MOV, MVI, ORA, SBB, SUB, and XRA. The only register pair that can be loaded or stored directly. The source and destination for the DAD instruction. The only register pair that can be exchanged with D and E or with the top of the stack. The only register pair that can be moved to the stack pointer (using SPHL) or to the program counter (using PCHL). The only register pair that can be shifted with a single instruction (DAD H).

· **Registers D and E.** The only register pair that can be exchanged with H and L (using XCHG).

· **Stack pointer.** The only address register that provides autoincrementing (postincrement) and autodecrementing (predecrement). Can only be loaded using LXI or SPHL. Value can be determined only by loading H and L with 0 and using DAD SP. The only register pair that can be used to transfer other register pairs to or from memory (using PUSH and POP) or to transfer the program counter to or from memory (CALL and RETURN instructions).

· **Processor Status Word (PSW).** Consists of the accumulator (more significant byte) and the flags (less significant byte). Can only be transferred to and from the stack using PUSH and POP.

Note the following:

· Only the accumulator or H and L can be loaded directly from memory or stored directly in memory. There are no equivalents of LDA, STA, LHLD, or SHLD for the other registers or register pairs.

· Only the address in H and L (register M) can be used to do anything except load or store the accumulator. Only the address in H and L can be used in transferring data to or from other registers or in arithmetic and logical instructions.

· Only DCR, DCX, DAD, INR, and INX perform arithmetic operations without involving the accumulator (both DCR and INR may be applied to the accumulator). Of these instructions, only DCR, DAD, and INR affect any flags; DCR and INR affect all flags except Carry, whereas DAD affects only Carry.

Register Transfers

MOV can transfer any 8-bit general-purpose register (A, B, C, D, E, H, or L) to any other 8-bit general-purpose register. The flag (F) register can only be transferred to or from the stack along with the accumulator (using PUSH PSW and POP PSW). The interrupt mask register (8085 only) can only be transferred to or from the accumulator using RIM or SIM. XCHG exchanges register pairs D and H.

The common transfer instructions are:

· MOV A,reg transfers the contents of reg to the accumulator.

· MOV reg,A transfers the contents of the accumulator to reg.

· MOV reg,M loads reg with the contents of the memory address in registers H and L.

· MOV M,reg stores reg at the memory address in registers H and L.

· XCHG exchanges register pair D (registers D and E) with register pair H (registers H and L).

The destination is the first operand in MOV. That is, MOV reg1,reg2 transfers the contents of reg2 to reg1, the opposite of the convention proposed in IEEE Standard 694 for assembly language instructions.[1] MOV changes the destination register, but does not affect the source register. XCHG changes four registers (D,E,H, and L); it is thus equivalent to four MOVs plus some intermediate instructions that save one byte of data while transferring another. Neither MOV nor XCHG affects the flags.

LOADING REGISTERS FROM MEMORY

The 8080 and 8085 microprocessors have four addressing modes that can be used to load registers from memory. These are: direct (from a specific memory address), immediate (with a specific value), indirect (from an address stored in a register pair), and stack (from the top of the stack).[2]

Direct Loading of Registers

Only the accumulator or registers H and L (register pair H) can be loaded from memory using direct addressing.

Examples

1. LDA 2050H

This instruction loads the accumulator (register A) from memory location 2050_{16}.

2. LHLD 0A000H

This instruction loads register L from memory location $A000_{16}$ and register H from memory location $A001_{16}$. Note the standard 8080/8085 format for storing 16-bit numbers with the less significant byte first, followed by the more significant byte at the next higher address.

Immediate Loading of Registers

Immediate addressing can be used to load any register or register pair. The register pairs include the stack pointer.

Examples

1. MVI C,6

This instruction loads register C with the value 6. The 6 is an 8-bit data item, not a 16-bit address; do not confuse the number 6 with the address 0006_{16}.

2. LXI D,15E3H

This instruction loads register D with 15_{16} and register E with $E3_{16}$.

Indirect Loading of Registers

The instruction MOV reg,M can load any register from the address in registers H and L. The instruction LDAX can load the accumulator using the address in register pair B or D. Note that no instruction loads a register pair indirectly.

Examples

1. MOV D,M

This instruction loads register D from the memory address in registers H and L. The assembly language instruction has the form MOV destination register, source register; the order of the registers is the opposite of that proposed for IEEE Standard 694.[3]

2. LDAX B

This instruction loads the accumulator from the memory address in registers B and C. The instruction MOV A,M has the same effect, but it uses the address in registers H and L. Note, however, that you cannot use B and C or D and E to load any register indirectly except the accumulator.

Stack Loading of Registers

The instruction POP rp loads a register pair from the top of the stack and adjusts the stack pointer appropriately. One register pair for POP is the Processor Status Word (PSW), which consists of the accumulator (MSB) and the flags (LSB). No instructions load single registers from the stack or use the stack pointer indirectly without changing it (although XTHL has no net effect on the stack pointer since it transfers data both to and from the stack).

Example

POP D

This instruction loads registers D and E from the top of the stack and increments the stack pointer by 2. Register E is loaded first in accordance with the standard 8080/8085 format for 16-bit numbers.

The stack has the following special features:

· The stack pointer contains the address of the most recently occupied location (the lowest occupied address). The stack can be anywhere in memory.

· Data is stored in the stack using predecrementing. That is, instructions decrement the stack pointer by 1 *before* storing each byte. Data is loaded from the stack using postincrementing. That is, instructions increment the stack pointer by 1 *after* loading each byte.

· As is typical with microprocessors, there are no overflow or underflow indicators.

STORING REGISTERS IN MEMORY

Three addressing modes can be used to store registers in memory: direct (at a specific memory address), indirect (at an address stored in a register pair), and stack (at the top of the stack).

Direct Storage of Registers

Direct addressing can be used only to store the accumulator or the H and L registers.

Examples

1. STA 35C8H

This instruction stores the accumulator in memory location $35C8_{16}$.

2. SHLD 203AH

This instruction stores register L in memory location $203A_{16}$ and register H in memory location $203B_{16}$ in the usual upside-down manner.

Indirect Storage of Registers

The instruction MOV M,reg can store any register at the address in registers H and L. The instruction STAX can store the accumulator at the address in register pair B or D. Note that there is no instruction that stores a register pair indirectly.

Examples

1. MOV M,C

This instruction stores register C at the address contained in registers H and L. The form is *move to M from C*.

2. STAX D

This instruction stores the accumulator at the memory address in registers D and E. The instruction MOV M,A has the same effect, except that it uses the address in registers H and L. Note, however, that the accumulator is the only register that can be stored indirectly using registers D and E or B and C.

Stack Storage of Registers

The instruction PUSH rp stores a register pair at the top of the stack and adjusts the stack pointer appropriately. One register pair is the Processor Status Word (PSW), consisting of the accumulator (MSB) and the flags (LSB). No instruction stores a single register in the stack.

Example

PUSH B

This instruction stores registers B and C at the top of the stack and decrements the stack pointer by 2. Register B is stored first, so C ends up at the top of the stack.

OTHER LOADING AND STORING OPERATIONS

Other loading and storing operations require more than one instruction. Typical examples are:

1. Direct loading of a register other than A

```
        LDA      ADDR
        MOV      reg,A
```

or

```
        LXI      H,ADDR
        MOV      reg,M
```

The second approach leaves A unchanged, but ties up H and L. Of course, the address in H and L would then be available for later use.

2. Indirect loading of a register (from the address in memory locations INDIR and INDIR+1)

```
        LHLD     INDIR     ;GET INDIRECT ADDRESS
        MOV      reg,M     ;LOAD DATA INDIRECTLY
```

3. Direct loading of a register pair other than H and L

· Registers D and E

```
        LHLD     ADDR      ;MOVE DATA TO HL
        XCHG               ;AND THEN TO DE
```

XCHG specifically exchanges register pair D with register pair H.

· Registers B and C

```
        LHLD     ADDR       ;MOVE DATA TO HL
        MOV      B,H        ;AND THEN TO BC, BYTE AT A TIME
        MOV      C,L
```

· Stack pointer

```
        LHLD     ADDR       ;MOVE DATA TO HL
        SPHL                ;AND THEN TO SP
```

SPHL transfers H and L to the stack pointer.

4. Direct storage of a register other than A

```
        MOV      A,reg
        STA      ADDR
```

or

```
        LXI      H,ADDR
        MOV      M,reg
```

5. Indirect storage of a register (at the address in memory locations INDIR and INDIR+1)

```
        LHLD     INDIR      ;GET THE INDIRECT ADDRESS
        MOV      M,reg      ;STORE DATA THERE
```

6. Direct storage of a register pair other than H and L

· Registers D and E

```
        XCHG                ;MOVE DE TO HL
        SHLD     ADDR       ;AND THEN TO MEMORY
```

· Registers B and C

```
        MOV      H,B        ;MOVE BC TO HL, BYTE AT A TIME
        MOV      L,C
        SHLD     ADDR       ;AND THEN TO MEMORY
```

· Stack pointer

```
        LXI      H,0        ;MOVE SP TO HL
        DAD      SP
        SHLD     ADDR       ;AND THEN TO MEMORY
```

There is no counterpart to SPHL for moving data in the other direction.

STORING VALUES IN RAM

The usual ways to initialize RAM locations are either through the accumulator or directly or indirectly using registers H and L.

Examples

1. Store an 8-bit item (VALUE) at address ADDR.

```
MVI     A,VALUE
STA     ADDR
```

or

```
LXI     H,ADDR
MVI     M,VALUE
```

In the first approach, MVI A,VALUE can be replaced with SUB A or XRA A if VALUE = 0. Note, however, that SUB A or XRA A affects the flags, whereas MVI A,0 does not.

2. Store a 16-bit item (VAL16) in addresses ADDR and ADDR+1 (MSB in ADDR+1).

```
LXI     H,VAL16
SHLD    ADDR
```

3. Store an 8-bit item (VALUE) at the address in memory locations INDIR and INDIR+1.

```
LHLD    INDIR     ;GET INDIRECT ADDRESS
MVI     M,VALUE   ;STORE VALUE INDIRECTLY
```

ARITHMETIC AND LOGICAL OPERATIONS

Most arithmetic and logical operations (addition, subtraction, AND, OR, EXCLUSIVE OR, and comparison) can only be performed between the accumulator and an 8-bit register or a byte of immediate data. The result (if any) is placed in the accumulator. If the register is M, the processor obtains the operand from the memory address in registers H and L.

Examples

1. Add register B to the accumulator.

```
ADD     B
```

The sum ends up in the accumulator.

2. Logically AND the accumulator with the binary value BICON.

```
ANI     BICON
```

Immediate addressing requires a special operation code.

3. Logically OR the accumulator with the data at the address in registers H and L.

```
ORA        M
```

Register M actually refers to the data at the address in H and L.

Other operations require more than one instruction. Here are some typical examples.

· Add memory locations OPER1 and OPER2, place sum in SUM.

```
LDA        OPER1        ;OBTAIN FIRST OPERAND
MOV        B,A
LDA        OPER2        ;OBTAIN SECOND OPERAND
ADD        B
STA        SUM          ;SAVE SUM
```

or

```
LXI        H,OPER1      ;OBTAIN FIRST OPERAND
MOV        A,M
LXI        H,OPER2      ;ADD SECOND OPERAND
ADD        M
LXI        H,SUM        ;SAVE SUM
MOV        M,A
```

The second alternative can be shortened considerably if the operands and the sum occupy consecutive memory addresses. If, for example, OPER2 = OPER1 + 1 and SUM = OPER2 + 1, the result is

```
LXI        H,OPER1
MOV        A,M          ;OBTAIN FIRST OPERAND
INX        H
ADD        M            ;ADD SECOND OPERAND
INX        H
MOV        M,A          ;SAVE SUM
```

· Add a constant (VALUE) to memory location OPER.

```
LDA        OPER
ADI        VALUE
STA        OPER
```

or

```
LXI        H,OPER
MOV        A,M
ADI        VALUE
MOV        M,A
```

If VALUE = 1 or −1, we can replace the last three instructions with INR M or DCR M. Neither instruction affects the accumulator.

BIT MANIPULATION

The programmer can set, clear, complement, or test bits by using logical operations with appropriate masks. Shift and complement instructions can operate only on the accumulator, but arithmetic and logical instructions can supplement the limited collection of shifts. Chapter 7 contains additional examples of bit manipulation.

Individual bits in the accumulator can be operated on as follows:

· Set them by logically ORing with 1s in the appropriate positions

· Clear them by logically ANDing with 0s in the appropriate positions

· Invert (complement) them by logically EXCLUSIVE ORing with 1s in the appropriate positions

· Test them (for all 0s) by logically ANDing with 1s in the appropriate positions.

Examples

1. Set bit 6 of the accumulator.

```
ORI    01000000B ;SET BIT 6 BY ORING WITH 1
```

Logically ORing a bit with 0 leaves it unchanged.

2. Clear bit 3 of the accumulator.

```
ANI    11110111B ;CLEAR BIT 3 BY ANDING WITH 0
```

Logically ANDing a bit with 1 leaves it unchanged.

3. Invert (complement) bit 2 of the accumulator.

```
XRI    00000100B ;INVERT BIT 2 BY XORING WITH 1
```

Logically EXCLUSIVE ORing a bit with 0 leaves it unchanged.

4. Test bit 5 of the accumulator. Clear the Zero flag if bit 5 is 1 and set the Zero flag if bit 5 is 0.

```
ANI    00100000B ;TEST BIT 5 BY ANDING WITH 1
```

Note the inversion here; the Zero flag is set to 1 if the bit is 0.

You can change more than 1 bit at a time by using the appropriate mask.

5. Set bits 4 and 5 of the accumulator.

```
ORI    00110000B ;SET BITS 4 AND 5 BY ORING WITH 1
```

6. Invert (complement) bits 0 and 7 of the accumulator.

```
XRI    10000001B ;INVERT BITS 0 AND 7 BY XORING WITH 1
```

The only general way to manipulate bits in other registers or in memory is by moving the values to the accumulator.

· Set bit 4 of register C.

```
MOV   A,C
ORI   00010000B
MOV   C,A
```

· Clear bit 1 of memory location ADDR.

```
LDA   ADDR
ANI   11111101B
STA   ADDR
```

An occasionally handy shortcut to manipulating bit 0 of a register or memory location is to use INR or DCR. Either complements bit 0; that is, either INR or DCR sets bit 0 if it was 0, and clears it if it was 1. These shortcuts are useful if the register or memory location contains only a single 1-bit flag.

The instructions RAL and RAR rotate the accumulator and the Carry flag together as if they formed a 9-bit register. Figures 1-1 and 1-2 show the effects of RAL and RAR. The instructions RLC and RRC rotate the accumulator alone as shown in Figures 1-3 and 1-4; the bit shifted off the end appears both in the Carry flag and in the bit at the other end. Adding the accumulator to itself provides other shift instructions as follows:

· ADD A shifts the accumulator left logically one position as shown in Figure 1-5, clearing bit 0.

· ADC A rotates the accumulator and Carry flag left one position. ADC A differs from RAL only in that it affects all the flags, whereas RAL affects only the Carry flag.

Note that RAL, ADC A, and RAR preserve the old Carry (in either bit 0 or bit 7), whereas RLC, RRC, and ADD A destroy it.

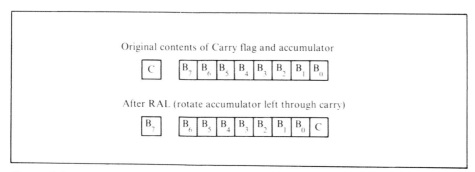

Figure 1-1. The RAL (rotate accumulator left through carry) instruction

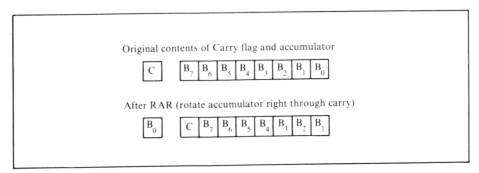

Figure 1-2. The RAR (rotate accumulator right through carry) instruction

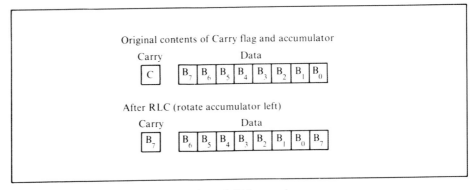

Figure 1-3. The RLC (rotate accumulator left) instruction

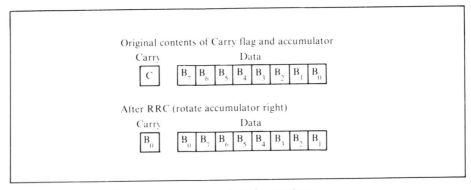

Figure 1-4. The RRC (rotate accumulator right) instruction

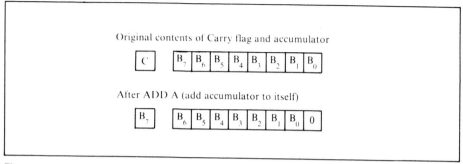

Figure 1-5. The ADD A (add accumulator to itself) instruction

Examples

1. Rotate accumulator right two positions without the Carry.

```
RRC
RRC
```

2. Shift accumulator left logically two positions.

```
ADD   A
ADD   A
```

You can implement arithmetic or logical shifts by using the Carry flag. STC sets the Carry, while either ANA A or ORA A clears it without changing the accumulator. Registers or memory locations can be shifted by moving their contents to the accumulator. The only shortcut is DAD H, which performs a 16-bit logical left shift of register pair H.

Examples

1. Shift register C right logically one position.

```
MOV   A,C
ANA   A       ;CARRY = 0
RAR           ;SHIFT RIGHT, MOVING 0 INTO MSB
MOV   C,A
```

2. Shift memory location ADDR right one position, preserving the sign bit (bit 7). Shifting while preserving the sign bit results in what is called *sign extension*. A shift that operates in this manner is called an *arithmetic shift*, since it preserves the sign of a two's complement number. It can therefore be used to divide or normalize signed numbers.

```
LDA   ADDR
RLC                   ;COPY THE SIGN BIT TO CARRY AND BIT 0
RAR                   ;SHIFT COPIES RIGHT TWICE
RAR
STA   ADDR
```

This sequence depends on RLC moving bit 7 both to the Carry and to bit 0 of the accumulator, as shown in Figure 1-3. The result is two copies of bit 7, exactly what sign extension requires.

MAKING DECISIONS

Decision-making procedures can be categorized as follows:

· Branching if a bit is set (a logic 1) or cleared (a logic 0)

· Branching if two values are equal or not equal

· Branching if one value is greater than another or less than it.

The first category allows the processor to sense the value of a flag, switch, status line, or other binary (ON/OFF) input. The second category allows the processor to determine whether an input or a result has a specific value (e.g., an input is a specific command character or terminator, or a result is 0). The third category allows the processor to determine whether a value is above or below a numerical threshold (e.g., a value is valid or invalid, or is above or below a warning level or setpoint). Assuming that the primary value is in the accumulator and the secondary value (if needed) is in a register or memory location, the procedures are as follows.

Branching Set or Cleared Bit

· Determine if a bit is set or cleared by logically ANDing the accumulator with a 1 in the specified bit position and 0s elsewhere. The Zero flag then reflects the bit value and can be used for branching.

Examples

1. Branch to DEST if bit 5 of the accumulator is 1.

```
ANI   00100000B       ;MASK FOR BIT 5
JNZ   DEST
```

The Zero flag is set to 1 if and only if bit 5 of the accumulator is 0.

2. Branch to DEST if bit 2 of the accumulator is 0.

```
ANI   00000100B      ;MASK FOR BIT 2
JZ    DEST
```

There are shortcuts for bits 0, 6, and 7.

3. Branch to DEST if bit 7 of the accumulator is 1.

```
ANA   A              ;ESTABLISH SIGN FLAG FROM A
JM    DEST
```

4. Branch to DEST if bit 6 of the accumulator is 0.

```
ADD   A              ;ESTABLISH SIGN FLAG FROM BIT 6
JP    DEST
```

5. Branch to DEST if bit 0 of the accumulator is 1.

```
RAR                  ;MOVE BIT 0 TO CARRY
JC    DEST
```

Branching Based on Equality

Determine if the value in the accumulator is equal to another value by subtraction. Subtracting sets the Zero flag to 1 if the values are equal, and to 0 if they are not. Compare instructions (CMP or CPI) are more useful than subtract instructions (SBC, SBI, SUB, or SUI) because compares preserve the accumulator for later operations.

Examples

1. Branch to DEST if the accumulator contains the number VALUE.

```
CPI   VALUE          ;IS DATA = VALUE?
JZ    DEST           ;YES, BRANCH
```

2. Branch to DEST if the contents of the accumulator are not equal to the contents of memory location ADDR.

```
LXI   H,ADDR
CMP   M              ;IS DATA = VALUE IN MEMORY?
JNZ   DEST           ;NO, BRANCH
```

There are shortcuts if VALUE is 0, 1, or FF_{16}.

3. Branch to DEST if the accumulator contains 0.

```
ANA   A              ;ESTABLISH ZERO FLAG FROM A
JZ    DEST           ;BRANCH IF A CONTAINS ZERO
```

4. Branch to DEST if the accumulator does not contain FF_{16}.

```
INR  A                    ;ESTABLISH ZERO FLAG
JNZ  DEST                 ;BRANCH IF A WAS NOT FF
```

This procedure applies to any 8-bit register or to the memory address in H and L.

5. Branch to DEST if the accumulator contains 1.

```
DCR  A                    ;ESTABLISH ZERO FLAG
JZ   DEST                 ;BRANCH IF A CONTAINED 1
```

6. Branch to DEST if memory location ADDR contains 0.

```
LXI  H,ADDR
INR  M                    ;ESTABLISH ZERO FLAG FROM ADDR
DCR  M
JZ   DEST                 ;BRANCH IF ADDR CONTAINS ZERO
```

The increment/decrement procedure also applies to any general-purpose register.

Branching Based on Magnitude Comparisons

· Determine if the contents of the accumulator are greater than or less than some other value by subtraction. If, as is typical, the values are unsigned, the Carry flag indicates which is larger. In general,

· Carry = 1 if the value subtracted is larger than the contents of the accumulator (that is, if a borrow is necessary).

· Carry = 0 if the contents of the accumulator are larger or if the two values are equal (that is, if no borrow is necessary).

Since subtracting equal values clears Carry, the alternatives (considering the accumulator as the primary operand) are

· Primary operand less than secondary operand (Carry set)

· Primary operand greater than or equal to secondary operand (Carry cleared).

If the required alternatives are *less than or equal to* and *greater than*, simply exchange the primary and secondary operands (that is, form $Y - X$ instead of $X - Y$). Another approach is to handle the equality case with a separate conditional jump.

Examples

1. Branch to DEST if the contents of the accumulator are greater than or equal to the number VALUE.

```
CPI  VALUE                ;IS DATA ABOVE VALUE?
JNC  DEST                 ;YES, BRANCH
```

2. Branch to DEST if the contents of memory address OPER1 are less than the contents of address OPER2.

```
LDA  OPER1          ;GET FIRST OPERAND
LXI  H,OPER2
CMP  M              ;IS IT LESS THAN SECOND OPERAND?
JC   DEST           ;YES, BRANCH
```

If the values are signed, subtraction may cause two's complement overflow; that is, the difference may not fit into 7 bits and may therefore affect the sign bit. However, overflow cannot occur in the following cases, so the Sign flag may be used instead of the Carry flag for branching.

· If the two numbers have the same sign, then the difference is smaller in magnitude than the larger operand (in magnitude), and overflow cannot occur. It is easy to determine if two numbers have the same sign by EXCLUSIVE ORing them together and checking the Sign flag. Remember, the EXCLUSIVE OR of two bits is 1 if and only if they have different values.

```
XRI  VALUE          ;COULD OVERFLOW OCCUR?
JP   NOOVF          ;NOT IF SIGNS ARE THE SAME
```

· If the value you are comparing with is 0, then set and examine the Sign flag.

Examples

1. Jump to DEST if the accumulator contains a signed positive number.

```
ANA  A              ;SET FLAGS FROM VALUE IN A
JP   DEST
```

2. Jump to DEST if a register contains a signed negative number.

```
INR  reg            ;SET FLAGS FROM VALUE IN REGISTER
DCR  reg
JM   DEST
```

This sequence does not affect the accumulator or the register.

3. Jump to DEST if memory location ADDR contains a signed positive number.

```
LXI  H,ADDR         ;POINT TO DATA IN MEMORY
INR  M              ;SET FLAGS FROM MEMORY CONTENTS
DCR  M
JP   DEST
```

This sequence does not affect the accumulator or the memory location.

If overflow could occur, you can test for it by comparing the signs of the result and the original value in the accumulator. If a number with a different sign is subtracted from the accumulator and no overflow occurs, obviously the sign of the difference should be the same as the original sign of the accumulator. To check if the two signs are the same, use the following sequence, subtracting B from A and using C for temporary storage:

```
MOV   C,A            ;SAVE ORIGINAL VALUE IN C
SUB   B              ;PERFORM COMPARISON
XRA   C              ;DID SIGN CHANGE?
JP    NOOVF          ;NO, OVERFLOW DID NOT OCCUR
```

This sequence is awkward because several cases must be considered. In addition, the original variables and the difference must be either retained or recalculated. The procedure for handling overflow after addition is different because then overflow can occur only if the operands have the same sign.

Tables 1-7 and 1-8 summarize the common instruction sequences for making decisions with the 8080 or 8085 microprocessor. Table 1-7 lists the sequences that depend only on the value in the accumulator; Table 1-8 lists the sequences that depend on numerical comparisons between the value in the accumulator and a specific number or the contents of a register. If the register is M, the comparison is actually with a memory location addressed via registers H and L.

Table 1-7. Decision Sequences Depending on the Accumulator Alone

Condition	Flag-Setting Instruction	Conditional Jump
Any bit = 0	ANI mask (1 in bit position)	JZ
Any bit = 1	ANI mask (1 in bit position)	JNZ
Bit 7 = 0	RAL, RLC, or ADD A	JNC
Bit 7 = 1	RAL, RLC, or ADD A	JC
Bit 6 = 0	ADD A	JP
Bit 6 = 1	ADD A	JM
Bit 0 = 0	RAR or RRC	JNC
Bit 0 = 1	RAR or RRC	JC
(A) = 0	ANA A or ORA A	JZ
(A) ≠ 0	ANA A or ORA A	JNZ
(A) positive (MSB = 0)	ANA A or ORA A	JP
(A) negative (MSB = 1)	ANA A or ORA A	JM

Table 1-8. Decision Sequences Depending on Numerical Comparisons

Condition	Flag-Setting Instruction	Conditional Jump
(A) = VALUE	CPI VALUE	JZ
(A) ≠ VALUE	CPI VALUE	JNZ
(A) ≥ VALUE (unsigned)	CPI VALUE	JNC
(A) < VALUE (unsigned)	CPI VALUE	JC
(A) = (reg)	CMP reg	JZ
(A) ≠ (reg)	CMP reg	JNZ
(A) ≥ (reg) (unsigned)	CMP reg	JNC
(A) < (reg) (unsigned)	CMP reg	JC

LOOPING

The simplest way to implement a loop (that is, repeat a sequence of instructions) on the 8080 or 8085 microprocessor is as follows:

1. Load a general-purpose register with the number of times the sequence is to be executed.

2. Execute the sequence.

3. Decrement the register by 1.

4. Return to Step 2 if the result of Step 3 is not 0.

Typical programs look like this:

```
            MVI   reg,NTIMES      ;COUNT = NUMBER OF REPETITIONS
LOOP:       .
            .
            .   instructions to be repeated
            .
            DCR   reg
            JNZ   LOOP
```

Nothing except clarity stops us from counting up (using INR) instead of counting down; of course, the initialization must be changed appropriately. In any case, the instructions to be repeated must not interfere with the counting of the repetitions. The counter can be stored in any general-purpose register, but most programmers use either B or C for a counter, since H and L generally serve as the primary memory address register and D and E as the secondary memory address register.

So typical loops look like this:

```
            MVI   B,NTIMES
LOOP:       .
            .
            .   instructions to be repeated
            .
            DCR   B
            JNZ   LOOP
```

The 8-bit length of register B limits this simple loop to 256 repetitions. The programmer can provide larger numbers of repetitions by nesting single-register loops or by using a register pair as illustrated in the following examples:

· Nested loops

```
            MVI   B,NTIMM         ;START OUTER COUNTER
LOOPO:      MVI   C,NTIML         ;START INNER COUNTER
LOOPI:      .
            .
            .   instructions to be repeated
            .
```

```
        DCR   C                ;DECREMENT INNER COUNTER
        JNZ   LOOPI
        DCR   B                ;DECREMENT OUTER COUNTER
        JNZ   LOOPO
```

The outer loop restores the inner counter (register C) to its starting value (NTIML) after each decrement of the outer counter (register B). The nesting produces a multiplicative factor—the processor repeats the instructions starting at LOOPI NTIMM × NTIML times.

· 16-bit counter in a register pair

```
        LXI   B,NTIMES         ;INITIALIZE 16-BIT COUNTER
LOOP:   .
        .
        .   instructions to be repeated
        .
        DCX   B
        MOV   A,B              ;TEST 16-BIT COUNTER FOR ZERO
        ORA   C
        JNZ   LOOP
```

The extra steps are necessary because DCX does not affect the Zero flag (so there is no way of telling if the count has reached 0). The simplest way to determine if a register pair contains 0 is to logically OR the two registers. The result is 0 if and only if all bits in both registers are 0s. Check this procedure to be sure that it works. One problem is that the logical OR uses the accumulator, thus requiring you to save its old contents if they are needed in the next iteration.

ARRAY MANIPULATION

The simplest way to access a particular element of an array is by placing its address in registers H and L. One can then

· Manipulate the element by referring to it as register M.

· Access the succeeding element (at the next higher address) by using INX to increment registers H and L or the preceding element (at the next lower address) by using DCX to decrement H and L.

· Access an arbitrary element by loading another register pair with the element's distance from the address in HL and using the DAD (16-bit addition) instruction.

Typical array manipulation procedures are easy to program if the array is one-dimensional and the elements each occupy one byte. Some examples are:

· Add an element of an array to the accumulator. Assume that the address of the element is in registers H and L. Update H and L so that they contain the address of the succeeding 8-bit element.

```
ADD    M              ;ADD CURRENT ELEMENT
INX    H              ;ADDRESS NEXT ELEMENT
```

· Check to see if an element of an array is 0 and add 1 to register B if it is. Assume that the element's address is in registers H and L. Update H and L so that they contain the address of the preceding 8-bit element.

```
        MOV    A,M              ;OBTAIN CURRENT ELEMENT
        ANA    A                ;IS CURRENT ELEMENT ZERO?
        JNZ    UPDDT
        INR    B                ;YES, ADD 1 TO COUNT OF ZEROS
UPDDT:  DCX    H                ;ADDRESS PRECEDING ELEMENT
```

· Load the accumulator with the 35th element of an array. Assume that H and L contain the base address of the array.

```
LXI    D,35             ;GET OFFSET FOR 35TH ELEMENT
DAD    D                ;CALCULATE ELEMENT'S ADDRESS
MOV    A,M              ;OBTAIN THE ELEMENT
```

DAD performs a 16-bit addition, using H and L as a 16-bit accumulator. The 16-bit offset in D and E can be either positive or negative.

Manipulating array elements becomes more difficult if more than one element is needed during each iteration (as in a sort that requires interchanging of elements), if the elements are more than one byte long, or if the elements are themselves addresses (as in a table of starting addresses). The basic problems are the lack of explicit indexing (which would allow the processor to calculate an indexed address during an instruction cycle) and the lack of instructions that access 16-bit items indirectly. Some examples of more general array manipulation are:

· Load registers D and E with a 16-bit element of an array (stored LSB first). Assume that H and L contain the starting address of the element. Update H and L so that they contain the starting address of the succeeding 16-bit element.

```
MOV    E,M              ;GET LSB OF ELEMENT
INX    H
MOV    D,M              ;GET MSB OF ELEMENT
INX    H                ;ADDRESS NEXT ELEMENT
```

· Exchange an element of an array with its successor if the two are not already in descending order. Assume that the elements are 8-bit unsigned numbers, and that the address of the current element is in H and L. Update H and L so they contain the address of the successor element.

```
MOV    A,M              ;GET CURRENT ELEMENT
INX    H
CMP    M                ;IS IT LESS THAN SUCCESSOR?
JNC    DONE             ;NO, NO INTERCHANGE NECESSARY
MOV    B,M              ;YES, START THE INTERCHANGE
MOV    M,A              ;CURRENT ELEMENT TO NEW POSITION
DCX    H
```

```
               MOV  M,B           ;SUCCESSOR ELEMENT TO NEW POSITION
               INX  H
DONE:          NOP
```

This procedure is awkward because the processor can address only one element at a time using registers H and L. Clearly, the problem would be even more serious if the two elements were more than one position apart.

· Load the accumulator from the 12th indirect address in a table. Assume that the base address of the table is in registers H and L.

```
               LXI  D,24          ;GET DOUBLED OFFSET FOR ELEMENT
               DAD  D             ;CALCULATE STARTING ADDRESS OF ELEMENT
               MOV  E,M           ;GET LSB OF INDIRECT ADDRESS
               INX  H
               MOV  D,M           ;GET MSB OF INDIRECT ADDRESS
               LDAX D             ;OBTAIN DATA FROM INDIRECT ADDRESS
```

Note that the index must be doubled to handle tables containing addresses, since each 16-bit address occupies two bytes of memory.

Some ways to simplify array processing are:

· Keep the base address of the table or array in registers D and E (or B and C), so DAD does not destroy it.

· Use ADD A to double an index in the accumulator. The doubled index can then be used to handle arrays or tables consisting of 16-bit elements.

· Use XCHG to move addresses to and from registers H and L.

Chapters 5 and 9 contain further examples of array manipulation.

TABLE LOOKUP

Since the 8080 and 8085 processors lack indexing, the address calculations required for table lookup must be performed explicitly using DAD. As with array manipulation, table lookup is simple if the table consists of 8-bit data items; it is more complex if the table contains longer items or addresses. The instructions XCHG, PCHL, and SPHL can be useful, but require the programmer to place the results in specific pairs of registers. Some examples are:

· Load the accumulator with an element from a table. Assume that the base address of the table is BASE (a constant) and the 16-bit index is in memory locations INDEX and INDEX + 1 (MSB in INDEX + 1).

```
               LXI  D,BASE        ;GET BASE ADDRESS
               LHLD INDEX         ;GET INDEX
               DAD  D             ;CALCULATE ADDRESS OF ELEMENT
               MOV  A,M           ;OBTAIN THE ELEMENT
```

Note that the roles of register pairs D and H cannot be reversed conveniently, since there is no instruction that loads register pair D directly.

· Load the accumulator with an element from a table. Assume that the base address of the table is BASE (a constant) and the index is in the accumulator.

```
MOV   L,A             ;EXTEND INDEX TO 16 BITS IN HL
MVI   H,0
LXI   D,BASE          ;GET BASE ADDRESS
DAD   D               ;CALCULATE ADDRESS OF ELEMENT
MOV   A,M             ;OBTAIN THE ELEMENT
```

· Load registers D and E with a 16-bit element from a table. Assume that the base address of the table is BASE (a constant) and the index is in the accumulator.

```
ADD   A               ;DOUBLE INDEX FOR 16-BIT ELEMENTS
MOV   L,A             ;EXTEND INDEX TO 16 BITS
MVI   H,0
LXI   B,BASE          ;GET BASE ADDRESS
DAD   B               ;CALCULATE START ADDRESS OF ELEMENT
MOV   E,M             ;GET LSB OF ELEMENT
INX   H
MOV   D,M             ;GET MSB OF ELEMENT
```

DAD H can also be used to double the index; it is slower than ADD A but it automatically handles cases in which the doubled index is too large for 8 bits.

· Transfer control (jump) to a 16-bit address obtained from a table. Assume that the base address of the table is BASE (a constant) and the index is in the accumulator.

```
ADD   A               ;DOUBLE INDEX FOR 16-BIT ELEMENTS
MOV   L,A             ;EXTEND INDEX TO 16 BITS
MVI   H,0
LXI   B,BASE          ;GET BASE ADDRESS
DAD   B               ;CALCULATE START ADDRESS OF ELEMENT
MOV   A,M             ;GET LSB OF DESTINATION
INX   H
MOV   H,M             ;GET MSB OF DESTINATION
MOV   L,A
PCHL                  ;JUMP TO DESTINATION
```

The common uses of jump tables are to implement CASE statements (multi-way branches used in languages such as FORTRAN, Pascal, and PL/I) to decode commands from a keyboard, and to respond to function keys on a terminal.

CHARACTER MANIPULATION

The easiest way to manipulate characters on the 8080 or 8085 processor is to treat them as unsigned 8-bit numbers. The letters and digits form ordered subsequences of the ASCII character set (for example, the ASCII representation of the letter A is one less than the ASCII representation of B). Appendix C contains a complete ASCII character set.

Examples

· Branch to address DEST if the accumulator contains ASCII E.

```
        CPI   'E'        ;IS DATA ASCII E?
        JZ    DEST       ;YES, BRANCH
```

· Search a string starting at address STRNG until a non-blank character is found.

```
        LXI   H,STRNG    ;POINT TO START OF STRING
EXAMC:  MOV   A,M        ;GET NEXT CHARACTER
        CPI   ' '        ;IS IT A BLANK?
        JNZ   DONE       ;NO, DONE
        INX   H          ;YES, PROCEED TO NEXT CHARACTER
        JMP   EXAMC
DONE:   NOP
```

or

```
        LXI   H,STRNG-1  ;POINT TO BYTE BEFORE STRING
EXAMC:  INX   H
        MOV   A,M        ;GET NEXT CHARACTER
        CPI   ' '        ;IS IT A BLANK?
        JZ    EXAMC      ;YES, KEEP LOOKING
```

Either version could be made to execute faster by placing the blank character in a general-purpose register (for example, register C) and comparing each character to that register (using CMP C) rather than with an immediate data value.

· Branch to address DEST if the accumulator contains a letter between C and F, inclusive.

```
        CPI   'C'        ;IS DATA BELOW C?
        JC    DONE       ;YES, DONE
        CPI   'F'+1      ;IS DATA F OR BELOW?
        JC    DEST       ;YES, MUST BE BETWEEN C AND F
DONE:   NOP
```

Chapter 8 contains further examples of string manipulation.

CODE CONVERSION

Data can be converted from one code to another using arithmetic or logical operations (if the relationship is simple) or lookup tables (if the relationship is complex).

Examples

1. Convert an ASCII digit to its binary-coded-decimal (BCD) equivalent.

```
SUI   '0'        ;CONVERT ASCII TO BCD
```

Since the ASCII digits form an ordered subsequence of the code, it is only necessary to subtract the offset (ASCII 0).

Bits 4 and 5 can be cleared with the instruction:

```
ANI   11001111B ;CONVERT ASCII TO BCD
```

Either the arithmetic instruction or the logical instruction will, for example, convert ASCII 0 (30_{16}) to decimal 0 (00_{16}).

2. Convert a binary-coded-decimal (BCD) digit to its ASCII equivalent.

```
ADI   '0'        ;CONVERT BCD TO ASCII
```

The inverse conversion is equally simple. You can also set bits 4 and 5 with the instruction

```
ORI   00110000B ;CONVERT BCD TO ASCII
```

Either the arithmetic instruction or the logical instruction will, for example, convert decimal 6 (06_{16}) to ASCII 6 (36_{16}).

3. Convert one 8-bit code to another using a lookup table. Assume that the lookup table starts at address NEWCD and is indexed by the value in the original code (for example, the 27th entry is the value in the new code corresponding to 27 in the original code). Assume that the data is in the accumulator.

```
MOV   L,A        ;EXTEND INDEX TO 16 BITS
MVI   H,O
LXI   D,NEWCD    ;GET BASE ADDRESS
DAD   D          ;CALCULATE ADDRESS OF ELEMENT
MOV   A,M        ;GET THE ELEMENT
```

Chapter 4 contains further examples of code conversion.

MULTIPLE-PRECISION ARITHMETIC

Multiple-precision arithmetic requires a series of 8-bit operations. One must

· Clear the Carry initially, since there is never a carry into or borrow from the least significant bytes.

· Use the Add with Carry (ADC) or Subtract with Borrow (SBB) instruction to perform an 8-bit operation that includes the carry or borrow from the previous operation.

A typical 64-bit addition program is

```
        MVI   B,8         ;NUMBER OF BYTES = 8
        ANA   A           ;CLEAR CARRY INITIALLY
        LXI   H,NUM1      ;POINT TO START OF NUMBERS
        LXI   D,NUM2
ADD8:   LDAX  D           ;GET A BYTE OF ONE OPERAND
        ADC   M           ;ADD A BYTE OF THE OTHER OPERAND
        MOV   M,A         ;STORE THE 8-BIT SUM
        INX   D
        INX   H
        DCR   B           ;COUNT BYTE OPERATIONS
        JNZ   ADD8
```

Chapter 6 contains further examples.

MULTIPLICATION AND DIVISION

There are many ways to implement multiplication. One approach is to convert multiplication by a small integer into a specific short sequence of additions and left shifts.

Examples

1. Multiply the accumulator by 2.

```
        ADD   A           ;DOUBLE A
```

2. Multiply the accumulator by 5.

```
        MOV   B,A
        ADD   A           ;A TIMES 2
        ADD   A           ;A TIMES 4
        ADD   B           ;A TIMES 5
```

Both examples assume that no carries ever occur. DAD H could be used similarly to produce a 16-bit result.

This approach is often handy in determining the locations of elements of two-dimensional arrays. For example, assume that a set of temperature readings has been taken at four different positions in each of three different storage tanks. The readings are organized as a two-dimensional array T(I,J), where I is the tank number (1, 2, or 3) and J identifies the position in the tank (1, 2, 3, or 4). The readings are stored in consecutive memory addresses as follows, starting with the reading at position 1 of tank 1:

BASE	T(1,1)	Reading at tank 1, position 1
BASE+1	T(1,2)	Reading at tank 1, position 2
BASE+2	T(1,3)	Reading at tank 1, position 3
BASE+3	T(1,4)	Reading at tank 1, position 4
BASE+4	T(2,1)	Reading at tank 2, position 1
BASE+5	T(2,2)	Reading at tank 2, position 2

```
BASE+6      T(2,3)    Reading at tank 2, position 3
BASE+7      T(2,4)    Reading at tank 2, position 4
BASE+8      T(3,1)    Reading at tank 3, position 1
BASE+9      T(3,2)    Reading at tank 3, position 2
BASE+10     T(3,3)    Reading at tank 3, position 3
BASE+11     T(3,4)    Reading at tank 3, position 4
```

In general, the reading T(I,J) is located at address $BASE + 4 \times (I - 1) + (J - 1)$. If I is in the accumulator and J is in register B, we can load the accumulator with T(I,J) as follows:

```
DCR   A         ;CALCULATE OFFSET FOR TANK I
ADD   A         ;2 X (I-1)
ADD   A         ;4 X (I-1)
ADD   B         ;ADD OFFSET FOR POSITION J
DCR   A         ;4 X (I-1) + (J-1)
MOV   L,A       ;EXTEND INDEX TO 16 BITS
MVI   H,0
LXI   D,BASE    ;GET BASE ADDRESS OF READINGS
DAD   D         ;ACCESS DESIRED READING
MOV   A,M       ;FETCH DESIRED READING
```

This approach can be extended to multidimensional arrays as shown in Chapter 5.

We can implement division by a power of 2 as a series of right logical shifts.

Example

Divide the accumulator by 4.

```
ANA   A         ;CLEAR CARRY
RAL             ;DIVIDE A BY 2
ANA   A         ;CLEAR CARRY
RAL             ;DIVIDE A BY 2 AGAIN
```

or

```
RAL                       ;ROTATE RIGHT TWICE
RAL
ANI   000111111B          ;AND CLEAR TWO LEADING BITS
```

If signed numbers are being multiplied or divided, care must be taken to separate the signs from the magnitudes. Logical shifts must be replaced with arithmetic shifts that preserve the sign bit.

Other approaches to multiplication and division include algorithms involving shifts and additions (multiplication) or shifts and subtractions (division) as described in Chapter 6, and lookup tables as discussed previously in this chapter.

LIST PROCESSING

Additional information on the following material can be found in an article by K.S. Shankar published in *IEEE Computer*.[4]

Lists can be processed like arrays if the elements are stored in consecutive addresses. If the elements are queued or chained, however, the limitations of the instruction set are evident in that

· No indexing is provided.

· No indirect addressing is available, except through register pairs.

· Addresses in register pairs can only be used to retrieve or store 8-bit data.

Examples

1. Retrieve an address stored starting at the address in registers H and L. Place the retrieved address in H and L.

```
MOV  E,M      ;GET MSB OF LINK
INX  H
MOV  D,M      ;GET LSB OF LINK
XCHG          ;REPLACE CURRENT POINTER WITH LINK
```

This procedure allows movement from one element to another in a linked list.

2. Retrieve data from the address in memory locations INDIR and INDIR+1 (MSB in INDIR+1) and increment that address by 1.

```
LHLD INDIR    ;GET POINTER FROM MEMORY
MOV  A,M      ;GET DATA USING POINTER
INX  H        ;UPDATE POINTER BY 1
SHLD INDIR
```

This procedure allows the address in memory to be used as a pointer to the next available location in a buffer.

3. Store an address from DE starting at the address in registers H and L. Increment H and L by 2.

```
MOV  M,E      ;STORE LSB OF POINTER
INX  H
MOV  M,D      ;STORE MSB OF POINTER
INX  H        ;COMPLETE UPDATING OF H AND L
```

This procedure allows one to form a list of addresses. Such a list could be used, for example, to write threaded code in which each routine concludes by transferring control to its successor. The list could also contain the starting addresses of a series of test procedures or tasks or the addresses of memory locations or I/O devices assigned by the operator to particular functions.

GENERAL DATA STRUCTURES

Additional information on the following material can be found in the book *Data Structures Using Pascal* by A. Tenenbaum and M. Augenstein.[5]

More general data structures can be processed using the procedures described for array manipulation, table lookup, and list processing. The key limitations in the instruction set are the same ones mentioned in the discussion of list processing.

Examples

1. Queues or linked lists. Assume that there is a queue header consisting of the base address of the first element in memory locations HEAD and HEAD+1. If the queue is empty, HEAD and HEAD+1 both contain 0. The first two locations in each element contain the base address of the next element or 0 if there is no next element.

· Add an element to the head of the queue. Assume that the element's base address is in registers D and E.

```
LXI   H,HEAD      ;REPLACE HEAD, SAVING OLD VALUE
MOV   A,M         ;MOVE LESS SIGNIFICANT BYTES
MOV   M,E
INX   H
MOV   B,M         ;MOVE MORE SIGNIFICANT BYTES
MOV   M,D
STAX  D           ;NEW HEAD POINTS TO OLD HEAD
MOV   A,B         ; INCLUDING MORE SIGNIFICANT BYTES
INX   D
STAX  D
```

· If the queue is empty, set the Zero flag and exit. Otherwise, remove an element from the head of the queue, place its base address in registers D and E, and clear the Zero flag.

```
       LXI   H,HEAD      ;OBTAIN HEAD OF QUEUE
       MOV   E,M         ;LESS SIGNIFICANT BYTE
       INX   H
       MOV   D,M         ;MORE SIGNIFICANT BYTE
       MOV   A,D
       ORA   E           ;ANY ELEMENTS IN QUEUE?
       JZ    DONE        ;NO, DONE
       INX   D           ;YES, MAKE NEXT ELEMENT NEW HEAD
       LDAX  D
       MOV   M,A         ;MORE SIGNIFICANT BYTE
       DCX   D
       DCX   H
       LDAX  D
       MOV   M,A         ;LESS SIGNIFICANT BYTE
DONE:  NOP
```

Since no instruction after ORA E affects any flags, the final value of the Zero flag indicates whether the queue was empty.

2. Stacks. Assume that there is a software stack consisting of 8-bit elements. The address of the next empty location is in addresses SPTR and SPTR+1. The lowest address that the stack can occupy is LOW and the highest address is HIGH. Note that this software stack grows up in memory (toward higher addresses), whereas the microprocessor's hardware stack grows down (toward lower addresses).

· If the stack overflows, set the Carry flag and exit. Otherwise, store the accumulator in the stack and increase the stack pointer by 1. Overflow means that the stack has expanded beyond its assigned area.

```
        LHLD SPTR          ;GET STACK POINTER
        XCHG
        LXI  H,-(HIGH+1)   ;CHECK FOR STACK OVERFLOW
        DAD  D             ;SET CARRY IF STACK OVERFLOWS
        JC   DONE
        XCHG
        MOV  M,A           ;STORE ACCUMULATOR IN STACK
        INX  H             ;UPDATE STACK POINTER
        SHLD SPTR
DONE:   NOP
```

· If the stack underflows, set the Carry flag and exit. Otherwise, decrease the stack pointer by 1 and load the accumulator from the stack. Underflow means that you have attempted to remove data from an empty stack.

```
        LHLD SPTR          ;GET STACK POINTER
        XCHG
        LXI  H,-(LOW+1)    ;CHECK FOR STACK UNDERFLOW
        DAD  D             ;CLEAR CARRY IF STACK UNDERFLOWS
        JNC  DONE
        XCHG
        DCX  H             ;UPDATE STACK POINTER
        MOV  A,M           ;LOAD ACCUMULATOR FROM STACK
        SHLD SPTR          ;RESTORE STACK POINTER
DONE:   CMC                ;SET CARRY IF STACK UNDERFLOWS
```

Both example programs utilize the fact that DAD affects only the Carry flag. Note also that DCX and INX do not affect any flags.

PARAMETER PASSING TECHNIQUES

The most common ways to pass parameters on the 8080 or 8085 microprocessor are:

1. In registers. Seven 8-bit general-purpose registers (A, B, C, D, E, H, and L) are available, and the three register pairs (B, D, and H) may be used to pass addresses. This approach is adequate in simple cases, but it lacks generality and can handle only a limited number of parameters. The programmer must remember the normal uses of the registers in assigning parameters. In other words,

· The accumulator is the obvious place to put a single 8-bit parameter.

· Register pair H is the obvious place to put the primary address-length (16-bit) parameter.

· Register pair D is a better place to put a secondary address-length parameter than is register pair B because of the XCHG instruction.

This approach is reentrant as long as the interrupt service routines save and restore all registers.

2. In an assigned area of memory. The easiest way to implement this approach is to place the base address of the assigned area in registers H and L. The calling routine must store the parameters in memory and load the base address into registers H and L before transferring control to the subroutine. This approach is general and can handle any number of parameters, but it requires a lot of management. If a different area of memory is assigned for each call, a stack is being created. If a common area of memory is used, reentrancy is lost. In this method, the programmer is responsible for assigning areas of memory, avoiding interference between routines, and saving and restoring the pointers required to resume routines after subroutine calls or interrupts.

3. In program memory immediately following the subroutine call. If you use this approach, be sure to remember the following:

· The base address of the memory area is at the top of the stack. That is, the base address is the normal return address, the location immediately following the call. The base address can be moved to registers H and L by popping the stack with

```
POP    H              ;RETRIEVE BASE ADDRESS OF PARAMETER AREA
```

· All parameters must be fixed for a given call, since the program memory is typically read-only.

· The subroutine must calculate the actual return address (the address immediately following the parameter area) and place it on top of the stack before executing a RETURN instruction.

Example

Assume that subroutine SUBR requires an 8-bit parameter and a 16-bit parameter. Show a main program that calls SUBR and contains the required parameters. Also show the initial part of the subroutine that retrieves the parameters, storing the 8-bit item in the accumulator and the 16-bit item in registers H and L, and places the correct return address at the top of the stack.

Subroutine call

```
CALL   SUBR           ;EXECUTE SUBROUTINE
DB     PAR8           ;8-BIT PARAMETER
DW     PAR16          ;16-BIT PARAMETER
...next instruction...
```

Subroutine

```
SUBR:    POP   H           ;POINT TO START OF PARAMETER AREA
         MOV   A,M         ;GET 8-BIT PARAMETER
         INX   H
         MOV   E,M         ;GET LSB OF 16-BIT PARAMETER
         INX   H
```

```
MOV   D,M        ;GET MSB OF 16-BIT PARAMETER
INX   H          ;POINT TO NEXT INSTRUCTION
PUSH  H          ;RESTORE ADJUSTED RETURN ADDRESS
XCHG             ;MOVE 16-BIT PARAMETER TO HL
  .
  .
  ...remainder of subroutine...
  .
RET              ;RETURN TO CALLING PROGRAM
```

The initial POP H instruction loads registers H and L with the return address that CALL SUBR saved at the top of the stack. In fact, the return address does not contain an instruction; instead, it contains the first parameter (PAR8). The three INX H instructions leave H and L containing the address of the next executable instruction in the calling program. PUSH H then places that address at the top of the stack so that the final RET transfers control back to the instruction following the parameters.

This approach allows parameter lists of any length. However, obtaining the parameters from memory and adjusting the return address is awkward at best; it becomes a longer and slower process as the number of parameters increases.

4. In the stack. If you use this approach, be sure to remember the following:

· CALL stores the return address at the top of the stack. The parameters that the calling routine placed in the stack begin at address ssss + 2, where ssss is the contents of the stack pointer. The 16-bit return address occupies the top two locations of the stack, and the stack pointer itself always refers to the lowest (last) occupied address, not the highest (next) empty one.

· The only way for the subroutine to determine the value of the stack pointer (that is, the location of the parameters) is by using the sequence

```
LXI   H,0        ;MOVE STACK POINTER TO HL
DAD   SP
```

This sequence places the stack pointer in registers H and L (the opposite of SPHL).

· The calling program must place the parameters in the stack before calling the subroutine. The subroutine should remove the parameters from the stack and place the results there before returning control. Having the subroutine handle most of the overhead (often referred to as *cleaning the stack*) reduces the amount of overhead involved in each call.

· Complete reentrancy can be achieved by allocating stack locations dynamically for temporary storage with the sequence

```
LXI   H,-NTEMP   ;LEAVE ROOM FOR TEMPORARIES
DAD   SP
SPHL             ;A GENERAL WAY TO ADJUST SP
```

This sequence leaves NTEMP empty locations at the top of the stack as shown in

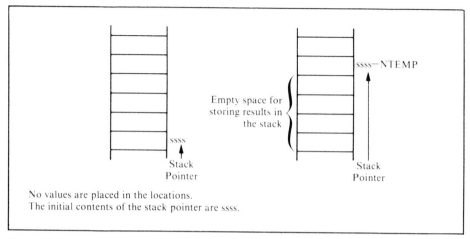

Figure 1-6. The stack before and after assigning NTEMP empty locations
for temporary storage

Figure 1-6. Of course, if NTEMP is small, simply executing DCX SP NTEMP times
will be much faster and shorter.

Example

Assume that subroutine SUBR requires an 8-bit parameter and a 16-bit parameter
and that it produces two 8-bit results. Show a call of SUBR, the placing of the
parameters in the accumulator and registers H and L, and the storing of the results
from memory locations RESLT and RESLT+1 into the stack before the return.
Figure 1-7 shows the appearance of the stack initially, after the subroutine call, and
after the return from the subroutine. If you always use the stack for parameters and
results, you will generally keep the parameters at the top of the stack in the proper
order.

Calling program

```
        LHLD PAR16      ;GET 16-BIT PARAMETER
        PUSH H          ;MOVE 16-BIT PARAMETER TO STACK
        LDA  PAR8       ;GET 8-BIT PARAMETER
        PUSH PSW        ;8-BIT PARAMETER TO STACK, WASTE A BYTE
        CALL SUBR       ;EXECUTE SUBROUTINE
        NOP             ;RESULTS ARE NOW AT TOP OF STACK
```

Subroutine

```
SUBR:   POP  B          ;SAVE RETURN ADDRESS IN BC
        POP  PSW        ;GET 8-BIT PARAMETER
        POP  H          ;GET 16-BIT PARAMETER
        PUSH B          ;PUT RETURN ADDRESS BACK IN STACK
```

```
         .
         ...remainder of subroutine
         .
         .
         LHLD RESLT       ;GET RESULTS
         XTHL             ;RESULTS TO STACK, RETURN ADD. TO HL
         PCHL             ;RETURN TO MAIN PROGRAM
```

XTHL places the results in the stack and loads the return address into HL. Note that you can only transfer 16-bit register pairs to or from the stack; the easiest ways to handle 8-bit parameters are either to pair them or to simply waste a byte of the stack each time.

SIMPLE INPUT/OUTPUT

Simple input/output can be performed using either 8-bit device addresses or full 16-bit memory addresses. The advantages of device addresses are that they are short and provide a separate address space for I/O ports. The disadvantages are that only

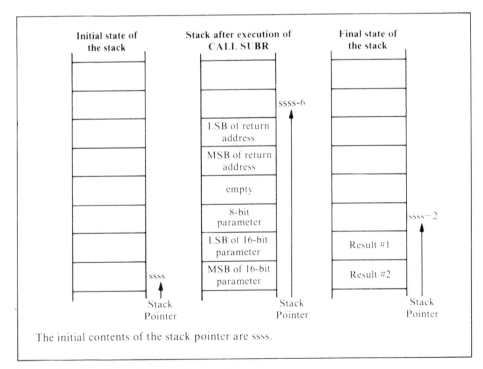

Figure 1-7. The effect of a subroutine on the stack

the IN and OUT instructions use device addresses, and they allow only direct addressing. That is, IN and OUT instructions require specific addresses; there is no simple way to allow the I/O addresses to be parameters, thus permitting a single I/O routine to handle many different devices. If, on the other hand, I/O ports occupy memory addresses, any instruction that references memory can also perform I/O. The problems with this approach are that it is non-standard, makes it difficult for a reader to differentiate I/O transfers from memory transfers, and requires that some memory address space be reserved for I/O devices.

Examples

1. Load the accumulator from input port 2.

```
        IN    2           ;READ FROM PORT 2
```

The device address (02_{16}) is part of the program memory. It therefore cannot be changed easily to accommodate a different set of I/O ports or variable I/O devices.

2. Load the accumulator from the input port assigned to the memory address in registers H and L.

```
        MOV   A,M         ;READ DATA FROM INPUT PORT
```

Here the same input routine can obtain data from any memory address. Of course, that memory address is no longer available for normal use, thus reducing the actual memory capacity of the computer.

3. Store the accumulator in output port 6.

```
        OUT   6           ;WRITE DATA TO PORT 6
```

The 6 is part of the program memory and cannot be changed easily to accommodate a different set of I/O ports or variable I/O devices.

4. Store the accumulator in the output port assigned to the memory address in registers H and L.

```
        MOV   M,A         ;SEND DATA TO OUTPUT PORT
```

Here the same output routine can send data to any memory address. The actual address can be a parameter, thus allowing the routine to handle multiple I/O devices attached to a single computer or variable addresses corresponding to different configurations or models.

5. Load the accumulator from a memory address obtained from a device table. The table starts in address IOTBL and the device number is in the accumulator.

```
        ADD   A           ;DOUBLE INDEX FOR 16-BIT ENTRIES
        MOV   L,A         ;MAKE INDEX INTO 16 BITS IN HL
        MVI   H,0
        LXI   D,IOTBL     ;GET BASE ADDRESS OF DEVICE TABLE
        DAD   D           ;INDEX TO DEVICE ADDRESS
```

```
MOV  E,M        ;GET LSB OF DEVICE ADDRESS
INX  H
MOV  D,M        ;GET MSB OF DEVICE ADDRESS
LDAX D          ;READ DATA FROM INPUT DEVICE
```

Here again it is assumed that the device occupies a memory address.

An I/O device table allows us to distinguish between actual I/O addresses (*physical devices*) and the device numbers to which a program refers (*logical devices*). A systems program uses the I/O device table to convert device numbers into actual I/O addresses. The operator or programmer can then vary the assignments without understanding the conversion process or the underlying I/O hardware.

For example, a program written in a high-level language may refer to input device #2 and output device #5. For testing purposes, an operator may assign devices #2 and #5 to be the input and output ports, respectively, of his or her console. For normal stand-alone operation the operator may assign device #2 to be an analog input unit and device #5 the system printer. For operation by remote control, the operator may assign devices #2 and #5 to be communications units used for input and output. In real applications, the device table generally contains the starting addresses of I/O subroutines (*drivers*) rather than actual memory addresses.

Chapter 10 contains additional examples of I/O routines.

STATUS AND CONTROL

Status and control signals can be handled like any other data. The only special problem is that the processor may not be able to read output ports; if the current contents of an output port must be known, you must retain a copy in RAM of the data stored there.

Examples

1. Branch to address DEST if bit 3 of input port 6 is 1.

```
IN   6          ;READ STATUS FROM PORT 6
ANI  00001000B  ;TEST BIT 3
JNZ  DEST
```

2. Branch to address DEST if bits 4, 5, and 6 of input port STAT are 5 (101 binary).

```
IN   STAT       ;READ STATUS
ANI  01110000B  ;MASK OFF BITS 4, 5, AND 6
CPI  01010000B  ;IS STATUS FIELD = 5?
JZ   DEST       ;YES, BRANCH TO DEST
```

3. Set bit 5 of output port CNTL to 1. Assume that a copy of the data is in a table starting at address OUTP.

```
LXI   H,OUTP+CNTL    ;GET COPY OF DATA
MOV   A,M
ORI   00100000B      ;SET BIT 5 OF PORT
OUT   CNTL           ;SEND DATA TO OUTPUT PORT
MOV   M,A             ;UPDATE COPY OF DATA
```

The copy must be updated every time you change the data.

4. Set bits 2, 3, and 4 of output port CNTL to 6 (110 binary). Assume that a copy of the data is in a table starting at address OUTP.

```
LXI   H,OUTP+CNTL    ;GET COPY OF DATA
MOV   A,M
ANI   11100011B      ;CLEAR BITS 2, 3, AND 4
ORI   00011000B      ;SET CONTROL FIELD TO 6
OUT   CNTL           ;SEND DATA TO OUTPUT PORT
MOV   M,A             ;UPDATE COPY OF DATA
```

Retaining copies of the data in memory (or using values stored in a latched, buffered output port) lets part of the data be changed without affecting other parts that may have unrelated meanings. For example, the state of one indicator light (such as a light that indicated either local or remote operation) could be changed without affecting other indicator lights attached to the same port. Similarly, one control line (for example, a line that determined whether an object was moving in the positive or negative X-direction) could be changed without affecting other control lines attached to the same port.

PERIPHERAL CHIPS

The most common peripheral chips in 8080/8085 systems are the 8251 serial interface, the 8253 programmable timer, and the 8255 parallel interface. All these devices can perform a variety of functions, much like the microprocessor itself. Of course, peripheral chips perform fewer different functions than processors and the range of functions is much more limited.

The idea behind programmable peripheral chips is that each chip contains many useful circuits; designers select the one they want to use by storing arbitrary codes in control registers, much as one selects circuits from a designer's casebook by specifying arbitrary page numbers or other designations. The advantages of programmable chips are that a single board containing such devices can handle many applications, and changes or corrections can be made by changing selection codes rather than by redesigning circuit boards. The disadvantages of programmable chips are the lack of standards and the difficulty of learning and explaining how specific chips operate.

Chapter 10 contains typical initialization routines for the 8251, 8253, and 8255 devices. Only a brief overview of the 8255 device will be provided here.

8255 Parallel Interface (Programmable Peripheral Interface)

The 8255 Programmable Peripheral Interface (PPI) contains two 8-bit parallel I/O ports (A and B) and two 4-bit ports (port C, bits 0-3 and bits 4-7). It has three major operating modes, selected by the contents of a write-only control register shown in Figure 1-8. Table 1-9 describes the addressing of the 8255's ports and control register. The key features of the operating modes are as follows:

1. In mode 0, all four ports act independently and the user can select each to be either an input port or an output port. Outputs are latched but inputs are not.

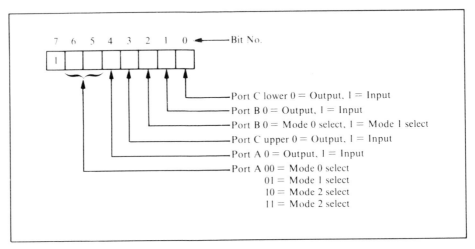

Figure 1-8. Control bytes that select operating modes and directions for an 8255 parallel interface

Table 1-9. 8255 Port Addresses

Address Inputs		Port Selected	Name in Examples
A_1 A_0			
0 0		Port A	PORTA
0 1		Port B	PORTB
1 0		Port C	PORTC
1 1		Control Register*	CNTLP
*Note that the 8255 control register is write-only			

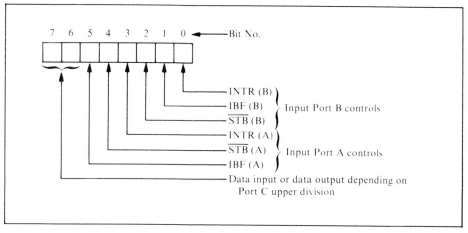

Figure 1-9. Input control signals at 8255 Port C in Mode 1

2. In mode 1, three bits of port C act as status and control signals for port A and three bits act similarly for port B. This is essentially a handshaking mode. If the data port (A or B) is input, the status and control signals are defined as follows and as shown in Figure 1-9.

· STB (strobe)—a 0 from the peripheral loads data into the input latch.

· IBF (input buffer full)—a 1 indicates that data has been loaded into the input latch but the processor has not yet read it.

· INTR (interrupt request)—a 1 indicates that data has been loaded into the input latch but has not yet been read by the processor, and that the interrupt for the port is enabled. This signal can be used to interrupt the processor.

If the data port is output, the status and control signals are defined as follows and as shown in Figure 1-10.

· ACK (acknowledge)—a 0 (from the peripheral) indicates that it has accepted the most recent output data and is ready for more. ACK thus serves as a Peripheral Ready signal.

· OBF (output buffer full)—a 0 indicates that the processor has stored data in the port, but the peripheral has not yet accepted it.

· INTR (interrupt request)—a 1 indicates that the peripheral has accepted the most recent output data and is ready for more. Also, the interrupt for the port is enabled. This signal can be used to interrupt the processor.

Each part of port C also has an interrupt enable bit, which can be set or reset. Setting the bit enables the interrupts from the data port (via INTR) and clearing the bit disables them. Interrupt-driven operation of an 8255 device will be discussed later.

3. In mode 2, port A is a bidirectional port and five bits of port C act as control signals for it. This mode will not be discussed any further, since it is not nearly as common as modes 0 and 1.

The user should be aware of the following special features of the 8255 device in its common operating modes:

· In selecting directions, the user must make an entire 4- or 8-bit port input or output. Individual bits are not selectable.

· The convention for selecting directions is 1 for input and 0 for output. Be careful; other 8080/8085 family devices such as the 8155 RAM/I/O/timer use the opposite convention.

· Port C allows the setting or clearing of any bit by sending a special command byte to the control port (that is, by executing OUT PORTC with bit 0 of the data cleared). Figure 1-11 shows the required format. This procedure is convenient for enabling or disabling interrupts and for changing the logic levels of control lines attached to the port.

· Outputs are latched in both mode 0 and mode 1. Inputs are latched in mode 1 only.

· Reset makes all ports inputs, clears the control register, and disables all interrupts.

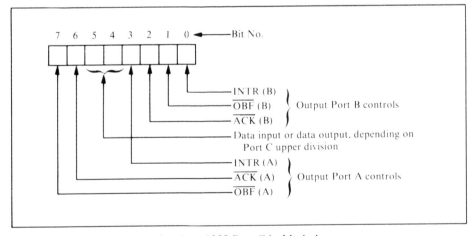

Figure 1-10. Output control signals at 8255 Port C in Mode 1

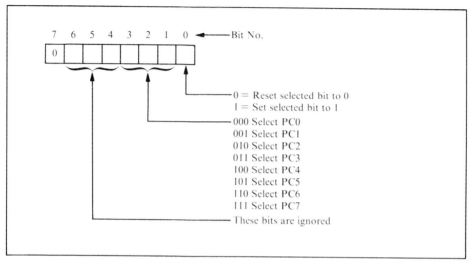

Figure 1-11. Control bytes that set or clear a bit of 8255 Port C

• The control register cannot be read, so a copy of its contents must be kept in RAM if they are needed.

The following examples assume the addresses for the 8255 ports given by the rightmost column of Table 1-9.

• Place all ports in operating mode 0. Make port A input, port B output, bits 0-3 of port C input, and bits 4-7 of port C output.

```
MVI   A,10010001B
OUT   CNTLP
```

The bit values have the following significance:

> Bit 7 = 1 to assign modes and directions
> Bit 6 = 0 and bit 5 = 0 to place port A in mode 0
> Bit 4 = 1 to make port A input
> Bit 3 = 0 to make bits 4-7 of port C output
> Bit 2 = 0 to place port B in mode 0
> Bit 1 = 0 to make port B output
> Bit 0 = 1 to make bits 0 through 3 of port C output

Check these values by referring to Figure 1-8.

• Place port A in operating mode 1 (handshaking) and port B in mode 0. Make port A output, port B input, bits 0-3 of port C input, and bits 4-7 of port C output.

```
MVI   A,10100011B
OUT   CNTLP
```

Here, when bit 6 = 0 and bit 5 = 1, port A is in mode 1. Bit 4 = 0, making port A output, and bit 1 = 1, making port B input. The directions for port C apply only to bits 0 through 2 (lower half) and bits 4 and 5 (upper half), since bits 3, 6, and 7 are used for port A handshaking signals as shown in Figure 1-10.

· Place ports A and B both in operating mode 1 (handshaking). Make port A input, port B output, and bits 6 and 7 of port C output.

```
        MVI   A,10110100B
        OUT   CNTLP
```

Here bit 4 = 1, making port A input; bit 2 = 1, placing port B in mode 1; and bit 1 = 1, making port B input. The directions for port C apply only to bits 6 and 7, since bits 0 through 5 are all used for handshaking signals, as shown in Figures 1-9 (port A) and 1-10 (port B).

· Wait for port A Input Buffer Full to go high and then read the data from port A into memory location INDAT. Assume that A is an input port in mode 1.

```
WAITR:  IN    PORTC           ;IS INPUT DATA AVAILABLE?
        ANI   00100000B
        JZ    WAITR           ;NO, WAIT
        IN    PORTA           ;YES, READ THE DATA
        STA   INDAT           ;SAVE DATA IN MEMORY
```

The port A Input Buffer Full signal is bit 5 of port C (see Figure 1-9) if A is an input port in operating mode 1.

· Wait for port B Acknowledge to go low and then send the data from memory location OUTDAT to port B. Assume that B is an output port in mode 1.

```
WAITR:  IN    PORTC           ;IS PERIPHERAL READY?
        ANI   00000100B
        JNZ   WAITR           ;NO, WAIT
        LDA   OUTDAT          ;YES, GET DATA FROM MEMORY
        OUT   PORTB           ;SEND DATA TO OUTPUT PORT
```

The port B Acknowledge (Peripheral Ready) signal is bit 2 of port C (see Figure 1-10) if B is an output port in mode 1.

· Set bit 5 of port C to 1 without changing any other bits.

```
        MVI   A,00001011B     ;SET BIT 5 OF PORT C
        OUT   CNTLP
```

Here bit 7 = 0 to perform a bit set or reset operation; bits 3, 2, and 1 are 101_2 (5_{10}) to select bit 5 of port C; and bit 0 = 1 to set the bit. You can check the bit values by referring to Figure 1-11.

· Clear bit 0 of port C without changing any other bits.

```
        SUB   A               ;CLEAR BIT 0 OF PORT C
        OUT   CNTLP
```

Here bits 3, 2, and 1 are 000_2 (0_{10}) to select bit 0 of port C, and bit $0 = 0$ to clear the bit.

Note the following problems encountered in using the 8255 device:[2]

· When either port A or port B is assigned as an output port, individual pins may be initialized either high or low by writing data to the I/O port before making the directional assignments. When either or both halves of port C are assigned as an output port, all signals will initially be low.

· When operating in mode 0, beware of assigning the upper and lower halves of port C to input and output. Some users have reported that reading from port C may alter output signal levels, and writing into port C may change the input buffer and thus modify bit settings created by the input signal. This problem does not always occur.

· In modes 1 and 2, the control byte shown in Figure 1-11 must be used to write to port C, one bit at a time. A byte cannot simply be written directly to port C. Also in modes 1 and 2, all control signals must be initialized by writing the appropriate bits of port C using the appropriate control bytes.

WRITING INTERRUPT-DRIVEN PROGRAMS

Most 8080 and 8085 interrupt systems[6,7] use the RST instructions and inputs, which transfer control to the specific memory addresses listed in Table 1-10. All RST instructions and inputs save the old program counter at the top of the stack, but do

Table 1-10. Restart Instructions and Inputs

Mnemonic Form	Binary Form	Hexadecimal Form	Destination Address (Hex)
RST 0	11000111	C7	0000
RST 1	11001111	CF	0008
RST 2	11010111	D7	0010
RST 3	11011111	DF	0018
RST 4	11100111	E7	0020
RST 5	11101111	EF	0028
RST 6	11110111	F7	0030
RST 7	11111111	FF	0038
TRAP(RST 4.5)*			0024
RST 5.5*			002C
RST 6.5*			0034
RST 7.5*			003C
*8085 only (separate inputs)			

not save any other registers automatically. The following sequence saves all the user registers.

```
PUSH PSW        ;SAVE ALL REGISTERS
PUSH B
PUSH D
PUSH H
```

PSW consists of the accumulator (MSB) and the flags (LSB). The opposite sequence restores the user registers.

```
POP   H         ;RESTORE REGISTERS
POP   D
POP   B
POP   PSW
```

Interrupts must be reenabled explicitly with EI immediately before the RET instruction that terminates the service routine. EI delays the actual enabling of interrupts for one instruction cycle to avoid unnecessary stacking of return addresses (that is, an RET instruction can remove the return address from the stack before a pending interrupt is recognized).

Be careful to save any write-only registers that may have to be restored at the end of the routine. For example, the 8214 priority interrupt control unit has a write-only priority register. A copy of this register must be saved in RAM and restored from the stack.

```
PUSH PSW        ;SAVE REGISTERS
PUSH B
PUSH D
PUSH H
LDA  PRTY       ;SAVE OLD PRIORITY
PUSH PSW
MVI  A,NPRTY    ;GET NEW PRIORITY
OUT  PPORT      ;PLACE IT IN EXTERNAL PRIORITY REGISTER
STA  PRTY       ;STORE COPY OF NEW PRIORITY IN RAM
```

The restoration procedure must recover the previous priority as well as the original contents of the registers.

```
POP   PSW       ;RESTORE OLD PRIORITY
OUT   PPORT     ;PLACE IT IN EXTERNAL PRIORITY REGISTER
STA   PRTY      ;SAVE COPY OF PRIORITY IN RAM
POP   H         ;RESTORE REGISTERS
POP   D
POP   B
POP   PSW
```

To achieve general reentrancy, the stack must be used for all temporary storage beyond that provided by the registers. As noted in the discussion of parameter passing, space can be assigned on the stack (NTEMP bytes) with the sequence

```
LXI  H,-NTEMP   ;ASSIGN NTEMP EMPTY BYTES ON STACK
DAD  SP
SPHL            ;A GENERAL WAY TO ADJUST SP
```

Later, of course, the temporary storage area can be removed with the sequence

```
LXI   H,NTEMP    ;REMOVE NTEMP EMPTY BYTES FROM STACK
DAD   SP
SPHL              ;A GENERAL WAY TO ADJUST SP
```

If NTEMP is small, replace these sequences with NTEMP DCX SP or INX SP instructions to save time and memory. Chapter 11 contains examples of simple interrupt service routines.

8255 PPI Interrupts

To use an 8255 parallel interface in an interrupt-driven system, the device's interrupt enable bits must be set. Figure 1-11 describes the outputs that the program must send to the 8255's write-only control register. The interrupt enables are bit 2 for port B and either bit 4 or bit 6 for port A, depending on whether that port is input or output. Setting an interrupt enable bit enables interrupts; clearing the bit disables interrupts. The following examples assume that the 8255 is in operating mode 1 and its control register is output port CNTLP.

Examples

1. Enable the input interrupt from port A.

```
MVI   A,00001001B
OUT   CNTLP
```

Bit 7 is 0 to perform a set/reset function; bits 3, 2, and 1 are 100_2 (4_{10}) to select bit 4 (interrupt enable A when A is an input port); bit 0 is 1 to set the enable and thus enable interrupts. Bits 4, 5, and 6 are not used.

2. Enable the output interrupt from port B.

```
MVI   A,00000101B
OUT   CNTLP
```

Bits 3, 2, and 1 are 010_2 (2_{10}) to select bit 2 (interrupt enable B).

3. Disable the output interrupt from port A.

```
MVI   A,00001100B
OUT   CNTLP
```

Bits 3, 2, and 1 are 110_2 (6_{10}) to select bit 6 (interrupt enable A when A is an output port), and bit 0 is 0 to clear the enable and thus disable interrupts.

An interrupting output port starts up with its interrupt active, since the peripheral has obviously accepted the most recent data (there was none). Thus, it will generally be necessary to send the output device a *null* (meaningless) output to force it into the inactive state (or else disable its interrupt initially). This problem does not occur with input ports, since the input buffer starts out empty.

The 8255's interrupt logic must be enabled. In modes 1 and 2, the processor may send interrupt requests via INTRA and INTRB (pins 3 and 0, respectively, of I/O port C). These interrupt requests will occur only if these bits are first made 1s using the appropriate control bytes (see Figure 1-11).

MAKING PROGRAMS RUN FASTER

In general, a program can be made to run substantially faster[8] only by determining where it is spending its time. This requires determining which loops (other than delay routines) the processor is executing most often. Reducing the execution time of a frequently executed loop will have a major effect because of the multiplying factor. It is thus critical to determine how often instructions are being executed and to work on loops in the order of their frequency of execution.

Once it has been determined which loops are executed most frequently, their execution times can be reduced using the following techniques:

· Eliminate redundant operations. These may include a constant that is being added during each iteration or a special case that is being tested repeatedly. They may also include a constant or a memory address that is being fetched from memory each time rather than being stored in a register or register pair.

· Reorganize the loop to reduce the number of jump instructions. Branches can often be eliminated by changing the initial conditions, reversing the order of operations, or combining operations. In particular, it can be helpful to start everything one step back, thus making the first iteration the same as all the others. Reversing the order of operations can be helpful if numerical comparisons are involved, since the equality case may not have to be handled separately. Reorganization may also allow the user to combine condition checking inside the loop with the overall loop control.

· Use in-line code rather than subroutines. This will save at least a CALL and a RETURN.

· Use the stack rather than specific memory addresses for temporary storage. Remember that XTHL exchanges the top of the stack with registers H and L and thus can both restore an old value and save the current one.

· Assign registers to take maximum advantage of such specialized instructions as SHLD, LHLD, XCHG, XTHL, and PCHL. In particular, always try to place addresses in register pair D (because of XCHG) rather than register pair B.

· Use the 16-bit instructions (LHLD, SHLD, INX, DCX, DAD, PUSH, POP, XCHG, XTHL, PCHL, and SPHL) whenever possible to manipulate 16-bit data.

· Use the instructions MVI M, INR M, and DCR M to manipulate data in memory without having to save and restore a register.

· Use the instructions MOV, MVI, INR, DCR, INX, DCX, SHLD, LHLD, XCHG, XTHL, PUSH, POP, PCHL, and SPHL to manipulate data in registers without having to save and restore the accumulator.

· Use RST, PCHL, or RET as short jump instructions. Of course, the required addresses must be either unused (RST) or needed anyway for other purposes (PCHL or RET). Note that PCHL and RET will take extra time if you must load the destination address into H and L or put it on the stack, but they will save time if the destination address is already available in the required place.

· Organize sequences of conditional jumps to minimize average execution time. Branches that are often taken should come before ones that are seldom taken. For example, one should check for a result being negative (true 50% of the time if the value is random) before checking for it to be 0 (true less than 1% of the time if the value is random).

· Test for conditions under which a sequence has no effect and branch around it if the conditions hold. This will be profitable if the sequence is long and frequently does not change the result. A typical example is the propagation of carries through higher order bytes. If a carry seldom occurs, it will be faster on the average to test for it rather than simply propagate a 0.

A general way to reduce execution time is to replace long sequences of instructions with tables. A single table lookup can perform the same operation as a sequence of instructions if there are no special exits or program logic involved. The cost is extra memory, but that may be justified if the memory is available. If enough memory is available, a lookup table may be a reasonable approach even if many of its entries are the same. Besides its speed, table lookup is also general, easy to program, and easy to change.

MAKING PROGRAMS USE LESS MEMORY

A program can be made to use significantly less memory simply by identifying common sequences of instructions and replacing those sequences with subroutines. The result is a single copy of the sequences instead of numerous copies; the cost is the extra execution time of the CALL and RET instructions. The more instructions that can be placed in subroutines, the more memory is saved. Of course, such subroutines are typically not general and may be difficult to understand or use. Some sequences may even be available in a monitor or other systems program; those sequences can then be replaced with calls to the system program as long as the return is handled properly.

Some methods that reduce execution time also reduce memory usage. In particular, eliminating redundant operations, reorganizing loops, using the stack, organizing the use of registers, using the 16-bit instructions, operating directly on memory or registers, and using specialized jump instructions reduce both memory usage and execution time. Of course, using in-line code rather than loops and subroutines reduces execution time but increases memory usage.

Lookup tables generally use extra memory but save execution time. Some ways to reduce their memory requirements are by eliminating intermediate values and interpolating the results, eliminating redundant values with special tests, and reducing the range of input values.[9,10] Often a few prior tests or restrictions will greatly reduce the size of the required table.

REFERENCES

1. Fischer, W.P., "Microprocessor Assembly Language Draft Standard," *IEEE Computer*, December 1979, pp. 96-109. Further discussions of the standard appear on pp. 79-80 of *IEEE Computer*, April 1980, and on pp. 8-9 of *IEEE Computer*, May 1981. See also Duncan, F.G., "Level-Independent Notation for Microcomputer Programs," *IEEE Micro*, May 1981, pp. 47-56.

2. Osborne, A., *An Introduction to Microcomputers: Volume 1—Basic Concepts*, 2nd ed., Berkeley, Calif.: Osborne/McGraw-Hill, 1980.

3. Fischer, W.P., *op. cit.*

4. Shankar, K.S., "Data Structures, Types, and Abstractions," *IEEE Computer*, April 1980, pp. 67-77.

5. Tenenbaum, A. and M. Augenstein, *Data Structures Using Pascal*, Englewood Cliffs, N.J.: Prentice-Hall, 1981. There are several versions of this book by the same authors for different languages and computers.

6. Weller, W.J. et al., *Practical Microcomputer Programming: The Intel 8080*, Evanston, Ill.: Northern Technology Books, 1976.

7. Leventhal, L.A. and W.C. Walsh, *Microcomputer Experimentation with the Intel SDK-85*, Englewood Cliffs, N.J.: Prentice-Hall, 1980.

8. Dollhoff, T., "Microprocessor Software: How to Optimize Timing and Memory Usage. Part One: Techniques for the Intel 8080 and Motorola 6800," *Digital Design*, November 1976, pp. 56-69.

9. Seim, T.A., "Numerical Interpolation for Microprocessor-Based Systems," *Computer Design*, February 1978, pp. 111-16.

10. Abramovich, A. and T.R. Crawford, "An Interpolating Algorithm for Control Applications on Microprocessors," Proceedings of the 1978 Conference on Industrial Applications of Microprocessors, Philadelphia, Penn., pp. 195-201. The proceedings are available from IEEE, 445 Hoes Lane, Piscataway, N.J. 08854.

Chapter 2 **Implementing Additional Instructions and Addressing Modes**

This chapter shows how to implement instructions and addressing modes that are not included in the 8080 or 8085 instruction set. Of course, no instruction set can ever include all possible combinations. Designers must choose a set based on how many operation codes are available, how easily an additional combination could be implemented, and how often it would be used. A description of additional instructions and addressing modes does not imply that the basic instruction set is incomplete or poorly designed.

Our attention will be given to additional instructions and addressing modes that are

- Obvious parallels to those included in the instruction set.
- Described in the draft Microprocessor Assembly Language Standard.[1]
- Discussed in Volume 1 of *An Introduction to Microcomputers.*[2]
- Implemented on other microprocessors, especially ones that are closely related or partly compatible.[3]

This chapter should be of particular interest to those who are familiar with the assembly languages of other computers.

INSTRUCTION SET EXTENSIONS

Extensions to the instruction set are described according to the organization suggested in the draft standard for IEEE Task P694.[4] Instructions are divided into the following groups (listed in the order in which they are discussed): arithmetic, logical, data transfer, branch, skip, subroutine call, subroutine return, and miscellaneous. For each type of instruction, types of operands are discussed in the following order: byte (8-bit), word (16-bit), decimal, bit, nibble or digit, and multiple. In describing addressing modes, the following order is used: direct, indirect, immediate, indexed, register, autopreincrement, autopostincrement, autopredecrement, autopostdecrement, indirect preindexed (also called preindexed or indexed indirect), and indirect postindexed (also called postindexed or indirect indexed).

ARITHMETIC INSTRUCTIONS

In this group are included addition, addition with Carry, subtraction, subtraction in reverse, subtraction with Carry (borrow), increment, decrement, multiplication, division, comparison, two's complement (negate), and extension. Instructions that do not clearly fall into a particular category are repeated for convenience.

Addition Instructions (Without Carry)

1. Add memory location ADDR to accumulator.

```
LXI  H,ADDR   ;POINT TO DATA
ADD  M        ;THEN ADD IN DATA
```

2. Add Carry to accumulator.

```
ACI  0        ;(A) = (A) + CARRY
```

3. Decimal add Carry to accumulator.

```
ACI  0        ;(A) = (A) + CARRY
DAA           ; IN DECIMAL
```

4. Decimal add VALUE to accumulator.

```
ADI  VALUE    ;(A) = (A) + VALUE
DAA           ; IN DECIMAL
```

5. Decimal add register to accumulator.

```
ADD  reg      ;(A) = (A) + (REG)
DAA           ; IN DECIMAL
```

6. Add 16-bit number to HL.

```
LXI  rp,VAL16
DAD  rp       ;HL = HL + VAL16
```

rp can be either B and C or D and E.

7. Add memory locations ADDR and ADDR+1 (MSB in ADDR+1) to HL.

```
XCHG          ;OPERAND 1 TO DE
LHLD ADDR     ;FETCH OPERAND 2
DAD  D        ;ADD OPERANDS
```

The operand in memory is stored in the usual 8080/8085 format with the less significant byte at the lower address.

8. Add memory locations ADDR and ADDR+1 (MSB in ADDR+1) to memory locations SUM and SUM+1 (MSB in SUM+1).

```
LHLD  SUM          ;GET CURRENT SUM
XCHG
LHLD  ADDR         ;ADD ELEMENT
DAD   D
SHLD  SUM          ;SAVE UPDATED SUM
```

9. Add the 16-bit number VAL16 to memory locations ADDR and ADDR+1 (MSB in ADDR+1).

```
LHLD  ADDR         ;GET CURRENT SUM
LXI   rp,VAL16     ;ADD ELEMENT
DAD   rp
SHLD  ADDR         ;SAVE UPDATED SUM
```

rp can be either B and C or D and E.

Addition Instructions (With Carry)

1. Add memory location ADDR to accumulator with Carry.

```
LXI   H,ADDR       ;POINT TO DATA
ADC   M            ;THEN ADD IN DATA WITH CARRY
```

2. Add Carry to accumulator.

```
ACI   0            ;A = A + CARRY
```

3. Decimal add VALUE to accumulator with Carry.

```
ACI   VALUE        ;A = A + VALUE + CARRY
DAA                ;IN DECIMAL
```

4. Decimal add register to accumulator with Carry.

```
ADC   reg          ;A = A + REG + CARRY
DAA                ;IN DECIMAL
```

5. Add register pair to HL with Carry.

```
MOV   A,L          ;ADD LSB'S
ADC   rpl
MOV   L,A
MOV   A,H          ;THEN ADD MSB'S
ADC   rph
MOV   H,A
```

or

```
        JNC   NOCRY      ;IS CARRY 1?
        INX   H          ;YES, ADD AN EXTRA 1
NOCRY:  DAD   rp         ;ADD 16 BITS
```

Here rph is the more significant byte of rp and rpl is the less significant byte.

Subtraction Instructions (Without Borrow)

1. Subtract memory location ADDR from accumulator.

```
        LXI   H,ADDR     ;POINT TO DATA
        SUB   M          ;THEN SUBTRACT IT
```

2. Subtract borrow (Carry) from accumulator.

```
        SBI   0          ;A = A - CARRY
```

3. Decimal subtract VALUE from accumulator.

```
        MOV   reg,A      ;SAVE MINUEND
        MVI   A,9AH      ;CALCULATE 100 - SUBTRAHEND
        SUI   VALUE
        ADD   reg        ;ADD MINUEND BACK
        DAA              ;CORRECT FOR DECIMAL RESULT
```

Carry is an inverted borrow; that is, Carry = 1 if the subtraction does not require a borrow and 0 if it does.

4. Decimal subtract register from accumulator.

```
        MOV   reg1,A     ;SAVE MINUEND
        MVI   A,9AH      ;CALCULATE 100 - SUBTRAHEND
        SUB   reg
        ADD   reg1       ;ADD MINUEND BACK
        DAA              ;CORRECT FOR DECIMAL RESULT
```

Carry is an inverted borrow.

5. Subtract 16-bit number from HL.

```
        LD    rp,-VAL16  ;HL = HL - VAL16
        DAD   rp
```

Carry is an inverted borrow.

6. Subtract register pair from HL.

```
        MOV   A,L        ;SUBTRACT LSB'S
        SUB   rpl
        MOV   L,A
        MOV   A,H        ;SUBTRACT MSB'S WITH BORROW
        SBB   rph
        MOV   H,A
```

Subtraction in Reverse Instructions

1. Subtract accumulator from VALUE and place difference in accumulator.

```
CMA             ;NEGATE A
INR   A
ADI   VALUE     ;FORM - A + VALUE
```

or

```
MOV   reg,A     ;CALCULATE VALUE - A
MVI   A,VALUE
SUB   reg
```

Carry is an inverted borrow in the first method and a true borrow in the second method.

2. Subtract accumulator from register and place difference in accumulator.

```
CMA             ;NEGATE A
INR   A
ADD   reg       ;FORM - A + REG
```

or

```
MOV   reg1,A    ;CALCULATE REG - A
MOV   A,reg
SUB   reg1
```

Carry is an inverted borrow in the first method and a true borrow in the second method.

3. Decimal subtract accumulator from VALUE and place difference in accumulator.

```
MOV   reg,A
MVI   A,9AH     ;CALCULATE 100 - SUBTRAHEND
SUB   reg
ADI   VALUE     ;ADD MINUEND
DAA             ;CORRECT FOR DECIMAL RESULT
```

4. Decimal subtract accumulator from register and place difference in accumulator.

```
MOV   reg1,A
MVI   A,9AH     ;CALCULATE 100 - SUBTRAHEND
SUB   reg1
ADD   reg       ;ADD MINUEND
DAA             ;CORRECT FOR DECIMAL RESULT
```

Subtraction with Borrow (Carry) Instructions

1. Subtract memory location ADDR from accumulator with borrow.

```
LXI   H,ADDR     ;POINT TO DATA
SBB   M          ;THEN SUBTRACT WITH BORROW
```

2. Subtract borrow (Carry) from accumulator.

```
SBI   0
```

3. Decimal subtract inverted borrow from accumulator (Carry = 1 if no borrow was generated, 0 if a borrow was generated).

```
ACI   99H        ;ADD 99 PLUS CARRY
DAA              ;MAKE RESULT DECIMAL
```

The final Carry is 0 if the subtraction generates a borrow and 1 if it does not.

4. Decimal subtract VALUE from accumulator with inverted borrow.

```
MOV   reg,A      ;SAVE MINUEND
MVI   A,99H      ;CALCULATE 100 - SUBTRAHEND - (1-CARRY)
ACI   0
SUI   VALUE
ADD   reg        ;ADD MINUEND
DAA              ;MAKE RESULT DECIMAL
```

The Carry is an inverted borrow.

5. Decimal subtract register from accumulator with inverted borrow.

```
MOV   reg1,A     ;SAVE MINUEND
MVI   A,99H      ;CALCULATE 100 - SUBTRAHEND - (1-CARRY)
ACI   0
SUB   reg
ADD   reg1       ;ADD MINUEND
DAA              ;MAKE RESULT DECIMAL
```

6. Subtract 16-bit number from HL with borrow.

```
        JNC   NOCRY       ;FORM HL - CARRY
        DCX   H
NOCRY:  LXI   rp,-VALUE   ;HL = HL - CARRY - VALUE
        DAD   rp
```

The final Carry is an inverted borrow.

7. Subtract register pair from HL with borrow.

```
MOV   A,L        ;SUBTRACT LSB'S WITH BORROW
SBB   rpl
MOV   L,A
MOV   A,H        ;SUBTRACT MSB'S WITH BORROW
SBB   rph
MOV   H,A
```

Increment Instructions

1. Increment memory location ADDR.

```
LXI   H,ADDR
INR   M
```

2. Increment accumulator, setting the Carry flag if the result is 0.

```
ADI   1
```

Remember that INR does not affect Carry, although it does affect the Zero flag.

3. Decimal increment accumulator (add 1 to A in decimal).

```
ADI   1
DAA
```

INR cannot be used here, since it does not affect the Carry.

4. Increment memory locations ADDR and ADDR+1 (MSB in ADDR+1).

```
LHLD ADDR
INX  H          ;16-BIT INCREMENT
SHLD ADDR
```

or

```
      LXI   H,ADDR
      INR   M          ;ADD 1 TO LSB
      JNZ   DONE
      INX   H          ;ADD CARRY TO MSB
      INR   M
      DCX   H
DONE: NOP
```

The second alternative leaves ADDR in H and L for later use.

5. Increment register pair, setting the Zero flag if the result is 0.

```
INX   rp      ;16-BIT INCREMENT
MOV   A,rpl   ;TEST 16-BIT RESULT FOR ZERO
ORA   rph
```

This sequence changes the accumulator and the other flags (remember that ORA clears Carry).

Decrement Instructions

1. Decrement memory location ADDR.

```
LXI  H,ADDR
DCR  M
```

2. Decrement accumulator, setting Carry flag if a borrow is generated.

```
SUI  1
```

3. Decrement accumulator, setting Carry flag if no borrow is generated.

```
ADI  0FFH
```

4. Decimal decrement accumulator (subtract 1 from A in decimal).

```
ADI  99H        ;ADD 99 DECIMAL TO SUBTRACT 1
DAA
```

The Carry here is an inverted borrow; it is cleared if a borrow is generated and set otherwise.

5. Decrement memory locations ADDR and ADDR+1 (MSB in ADDR+1).

```
LHLD ADDR
DCX  H          ;16-BIT DECREMENT
SHLD ADDR
```

6. Decrement register pair, setting the Zero flag if the result is 0.

```
DCX  rp         ;16-BIT DECREMENT
MOV  A,rpl      ;TEST REGISTER PAIR FOR ZERO
ORA  rph
```

This sequences destroys the old contents of the accumulator and changes the other flags (remember that ORA clears Carry).

Multiplication Instructions

1. Multiply accumulator by 2.

```
ADD  A
```

2. Multiply accumulator by 3 (using reg for temporary storage).

```
MOV  reg,A      ;SAVE A
ADD  A          ;2 X A
ADD  reg        ;3 X A
```

3. Multiply accumulator by 4.

```
ADD  A          ;2 X A
ADD  A          ;4 X A
```

Cases 1, 2, and 3 can easily be extended to perform multiplication by other small integers.

4. Multiply registers H and L by 2.

```
DAD   H
```

This approach to multiplication by a small integer produces a 16-bit result.

5. Multiply registers H and L by 3 (using rp for temporary storage).

```
MOV   rph,H
MOV   rpl,L
DAD   H           ;2 X HL
DAD   rp          ;3 X HL
```

Note that XCHG cannot be used here, since it destroys the old contents of HL.

Division Instructions

1. Divide accumulator by 2 unsigned.

```
ANA   A           ;CLEAR CARRY
RAR               ;DIVIDE BY 2, CLEARING SIGN
```

2. Divide accumulator by 4 unsigned.

```
ANA   A           ;CLEAR CARRY
RAR               ;DIVIDE BY 2, CLEARING SIGN
ANA   A           ;CLEAR CARRY AND DIVIDE BY 2 AGAIN
RAR
```

or

```
RAR               ;SHIFT RIGHT TWICE
RAR
ANI   00111111B   ;THEN CLEAR 2 MSB'S
```

Eventually it becomes faster to clear the MSBs with a logical AND at the end, rather than clear Carry each time.

3. Divide accumulator by 2 signed.

```
RLC               ;COPY SIGN BIT IN BIT 0, CARRY
RAR               ;DIVIDE BY 2, EXTENDING SIGN
RAR
```

RLC produces two copies of bit 7, one in the Carry and one in bit 0 of the accumulator. This is known as an *arithmetic shift*, since it preserves the sign of the number while reducing its magnitude. The fact that the sign bit is copied to the right is known as *sign extension*.

4. Divide memory locations ADDR and ADDR+1 (MSB in ADDR+1) by 2 unsigned.

```
ANA   A           ;CLEAR CARRY
LXI   H,ADDR+1
MOV   A,M         ;GET MSB
RAR               ;SHIFT MSB RIGHT LOGICALLY
MOV   M,A
DCX   H
MOV   A,M         ;MOVE CARRY OVER TO LSB
RAR
MOV   M,A
```

5. Divide memory locations ADDR and ADDR+1 (MSB in ADDR+1) by 2 signed.

```
LXI   H,ADDR+1
MOV   A,M         ;SHIFT MSB RIGHT ARITHMETICALLY
RLC
RAR
RAR
MOV   M,A
DCX   H
MOV   A,M         ;MOVE CARRY OVER TO LSB
RAR
MOV   M,A
```

6. Divide register pair by 2 unsigned.

```
ANA   A           ;CLEAR CARRY
MOV   A,rph       ;SHIFT MSB RIGHT LOGICALLY
RAR
MOV   rph,A
MOV   A,rpl       ;MOVE CARRY OVER TO LSB
RAR
MOV   rpl,A
```

7. Divide register pair by 2 signed.

```
MOV   A,rph       ;SHIFT MSB RIGHT ARITHMETICALLY
RLC
RAR
RAR
MOV   rph,A
MOV   A,rpl       ;MOVE CARRY OVER TO LSB
RAR
MOV   rpl,A
```

Comparison Instructions

1. Compare VALUE with accumulator bit by bit, setting each bit position that is different.

```
XRI   VALUE
```

Remember, the EXCLUSIVE OR of two bits is 1 if and only if the bits are different.

2. Compare register with accumulator bit by bit, setting each bit position that is different.

```
          XRA   reg
```

3. Compare register pairs. Set Carry if rp1 is larger (in the unsigned sense) than rp2 and clear Carry otherwise. Set the Zero flag if the two pairs are equal and clear the Zero flag otherwise.

```
          MOV   A,rp2h      ;COMPARE MSB'S
          CMP   rp1h
          JNZ   DONE        ;DONE UNLESS MSB'S EQUAL
          MOV   A,rp2l      ;MSB'S EQUAL, COMPARE LSB'S
          CMP   rp1l        ;SET CARRY IF RP1 LARGER
DONE:     NOP
```

4. Compare register pairs (rp1 and rp2). Set Carry if rp1 is larger (in the unsigned sense) than rp2 and clear Carry otherwise.

```
          MOV   A,rp2l      ;SET BORROW FROM LSB'S
          CMP   rp1l
          MOV   A,rp2h      ;THEN COMPARE MSB'S WITH BORROW
          SBB   rp1h
```

SBB is used on the more significant bytes to include the borrow from the less significant bytes. The Zero flag reflects only the second subtraction; that is, the Zero flag is set to 1 if rp2 is larger than rp1 but the difference is less than 100_{16}.

5. Compare register pair with 16-bit number. Set Carry if the 16-bit number is less than or equal to the register pair (in the unsigned sense) and clear Carry otherwise. Assume that the register pair is not H and L.

```
          LXI   H,-VAL16   ;GET COMPLEMENTED CONSTANT
          DAD   rp
```

For comparisons with H and L, we can use

```
          LXI   D,-VAL16   ;GET COMPLEMENTED CONSTANT
          DAD   D
```

6. Block comparison (as on Z80 microprocessor). Compare accumulator with memory bytes starting at the address in registers H and L. Continue either until a match is found (indicated by Carry = 0) or until the byte counter (register B) is decremented to 0 (indicated by Carry = 1).

```
CMPBYT:   CMP   M           ;CHECK CURRENT BYTE
          JZ    DONE        ;DONE IF MATCH FOUND
          INX   H           ;OTHERWISE, PROCEED TO NEXT BYTE
          DCR   B
          JNZ   CMPBYT      ;IF THERE ARE ANY LEFT
          STC               ;IF NOT, EXIT SETTING CARRY
DONE:     NOP
```

Remember, comparing two equal numbers clears the Carry.

Two's Complement (Negate) Instructions

1. Negate accumulator.

```
CMA                ;ONES COMPLEMENT
INR   A            ;TWOS COMPLEMENT
```

The two's complement is the one's complement plus 1.

2. Negate register.

```
SUB   A            ;FORM 0 - REG
SUB   reg
MOV   reg,A
```

3. Negate memory location ADDR.

```
LXI   H,ADDR
SUB   A            ;FORM 0 - (ADDR)
SUB   M
MOV   M,A
```

4. Negate register pair.

```
MOV   A,rph        ;ONES COMPLEMENT
CMA
MOV   rph,A
MOV   A,rpl
CMA
MOV   rpl,A
INX   rp           ;ADD 1 FOR TWOS COMPLEMENT
```

5. Nine's complement accumulator (that is, replace (A) with 99 − (A)).

```
MOV   reg,A
MVI   A,99H
SUB   reg
```

No DAA is necessary, since 99 − (A) is always a valid BCD number if the accumulator originally contained a valid BCD number.

6. Ten's complement accumulator (that is, replace (A) with 100 − (A)).

```
MOV   reg,A        ;FORM NINES COMPLEMENT
MVI   A,99H
SUB   reg
ADI   1            ;THEN ADD 1 DECIMAL
DAA
```

Remember that DAA works correctly only after addition instructions.

Extend Instructions

1. Extend accumulator to a 16-bit unsigned number in a register pair.

```
MOV   rpl,A      ;8-BIT MOVE
MVI   rph,0      ;EXTEND 8 BITS TO 16 BITS
```

This procedure allows you to use the value in the accumulator as an index. DAD will then add the index to the base.

2. Extend accumulator to a 16-bit signed number in a register pair.

```
MOV   rpl,A      ;8-BIT MOVE
ADD   A          ;MOVE SIGN BIT TO CARRY
SBB   A          ;SUBTRACT SIGN BIT FROM ZERO
MOV   rph,A      ;EXTEND 8 BITS TO 16 BITS SIGNED
```

SBB A produces 00 if Carry is 0 and FF_{16} if Carry is 1. It thus extends Carry across the entire accumulator.

3. Extend memory location ADDR to a 16-bit signed number in memory locations ADDR (LSB) and ADDR+1 (MSB).

```
LXI   H,ADDR     ;FETCH NUMBER
MOV   A,M
ADD   A          ;MOVE SIGN BIT TO CARRY
SBB   A          ;FORM SIGN BYTE (00 OR FF)
INX   H          ;STORE SIGN BYTE
MOV   M,A
```

4. Extend bit 0 of accumulator across entire accumulator; that is, make (A) = 00 if bit 0 = 0 and FF_{16} if bit 0 = 1.

```
RAR              ;MOVE BIT 0 TO CARRY
SBB   A          ;FORM 0 - BIT 0
```

5. Sign function. Replace the value in the accumulator by 00 if it is positive and by FF_{16} if it is negative.

```
ADD   A          ;MOVE SIGN BIT TO CARRY
SBB   A          ;FORM 0 - SIGN BIT
```

LOGICAL INSTRUCTIONS

This group includes logical AND, logical OR, logical EXCLUSIVE OR, logical NOT (complement), shift, rotate, and test instructions. It also includes arithmetic instructions (such as adding the accumulator to itself) that perform logical functions.

Logical AND Instructions

1. Clear bits of accumulator.

```
ANI    MASK        ;CLEAR BIT BY MASKING
```

MASK has 0s in the bit positions to be cleared and 1s in the positions to be left unchanged. For example:

```
ANI    11011011B ;CLEAR BITS 2 AND 5
```

Remember, logically ANDing a bit with 1 leaves it unchanged.

2. Bit test — set the flags as if accumulator had been logically ANDed with a register or memory location, but do not change the accumulator.

```
MOV    reg1,A       ;SAVE ACCUMULATOR
ANA    reg          ;PERFORM LOGICAL AND
MOV    A,reg1       ;RESTORE ACCUMULATOR
```

This sequence depends on the fact that MOV does not affect any flags.

3. Test bits of accumulator.

```
ANI    MASK        ;TEST BITS BY MASKING
```

MASK has 1s in the bit positions to be tested and 0s elsewhere. The Zero flag is set to 1 if all the tested bit positions are 0s and to 0 otherwise. JZ or JNZ can then force a branch depending on the tested bits. For example:

```
ANI    01000000B ;TEST BIT 6
```

The result is 0 if bit 6 of A is 0 and 01000000_2 if bit 6 of A is 1. The Zero flag ends up containing the logical complement of bit 6.

4. Logical AND immediate with flags (condition codes). Logically AND a byte of immediate data with the flag register, clearing those flags that are logically ANDed with 0s.

```
PUSH PSW          ;MOVE PSW TO A REGISTER PAIR
POP    rp
MVI    A,MASK      ;CLEAR FLAGS
ANA    rp1
MOV    rp1,A
PUSH rp            ;RESTORE PSW WITH FLAGS CLEARED
POP    PSW
```

This sequence changes a register pair (B, D, or H).

Logical OR Instructions

1. Set bits of accumulator.

```
ORI   MASK       ;SET BITS BY MASKING
```

MASK has 1s in the bit positions to be set and 0s elsewhere. For example:

```
ORI   00010010B ;SET BITS 1 AND 4
```

Remember, logically ORing a bit with 0 leaves it unchanged.

2. Test a register pair for 0. Set the Zero flag if both halves of a register pair are 0.

```
MOV   A,rph       ;TEST REGISTER PAIR FOR ZERO
ORA   rpl
```

The Zero flag is set if and only if both bytes of the register pair are 0. The accumulator and the other flags are also changed.

3. Logical OR immediate with flags (condition codes). Logically OR a byte of immediate data with the flag register, setting those flags that are logically ORed with 1s.

```
PUSH PSW          ;MOVE PSW TO A REGISTER PAIR
POP  rp
MVI  A,MASK       ;SET FLAGS
ORA  rpl
MOV  rpl,A
PUSH rp           ;RESTORE PSW WITH FLAGS SET
POP  PSW
```

This sequence changes a register pair (B, D, or H).

Logical EXCLUSIVE OR Instructions

1. Complement bits of accumulator.

```
XRI   MASK        ;COMPLEMENT BITS BY MASKING
```

MASK has 1s in the bit positions to be complemented and 0s in the positions that are to be left unchanged. For example:

```
XRI   11000000B ;COMPLEMENT BITS 6 AND 7
```

Remember, logically EXCLUSIVE ORing a bit with 0 leaves it unchanged.

2. Complement accumulator, setting flags.

```
XRI   11111111B ;INVERT A AND SET FLAGS
```

Logically EXCLUSIVE ORing with all 1s inverts all the bits. This instruction differs from CMA only in that it affects all the flags, whereas CMA does not affect any flags.

3. Compare register with accumulator bit by bit, setting each bit position that is different.

```
XRA    reg          ;BIT-BY-BIT COMPARISON
```

The EXCLUSIVE OR function is the same as a "not equal" function. Note that the Sign flag is 1 if the two operands have different values in bit 7.

4. Add register to accumulator logically (i.e., without any carries between bit positions).

```
XRA    reg          ;LOGICAL ADDITION
```

The EXCLUSIVE OR function is also the same as a bit-by-bit sum with no carries. Logical sums are often used to form checksums and error-detecting or error-correcting codes.

Logical NOT Instructions

1. Complement accumulator, setting flags.

```
XRI    11111111B ;INVERT A AND SET FLAGS
```

Logically EXCLUSIVE ORing with all 1s inverts all the bits. This instruction differs from CMA only in that it affects the flags, whereas CMA does not.

2. Complement bits of accumulator.

```
XRI    MASK         ;COMPLEMENT BITS BY MASKING
```

MASK has 1s in the bit positions to be complemented and 0s in the positions that are to be left unchanged. For example:

```
XRI    01010001B ;COMPLEMENT BITS 0, 4, AND 6
```

Remember, logically EXCLUSIVE ORing a bit with 0 leaves it unchanged.

3. Complement memory location ADDR.

```
LXI    H,ADDR
MOV    A,M          ;OBTAIN DATA
CMA                 ;COMPLEMENT
MOV    M,A          ;RESTORE RESULT
```

CMA applies only to the accumulator.

4. Complement bit 0 of a register.

```
INR    reg
```

or

```
DCR    reg
```

Either instruction may, of course, affect the other bits in the register. The final value of bit 0 will surely be 0 if it was originally 1 and 1 if it was originally 0.

5. Complement bit 0 of a memory location.

```
LXI   H,ADDR
INR   M
```

or

```
LXI   H,ADDR
DCR   M
```

6. Complement digit of accumulator.

· Less significant digit

```
XRI   00001111B ;COMPLEMENT LESS SIGNIFICANT DIGIT
```

· More significant digit

```
XRI   11110000B ;COMPLEMENT MORE SIGNIFICANT DIGIT
```

These procedures are useful if the accumulator contains a decimal digit in negative logic, such as the input from a typical ten-position rotary or thumbwheel switch.

Shift Instructions

1. Shift accumulator right logically.

```
ANA   A         ;CLEAR CARRY
RAR             ;SHIFT RIGHT LOGICALLY
```

ANA A (or ORA A) clears the Carry without affecting the accumulator. An alternative is

```
RAR             ;ROTATE RIGHT
```

2. Shift accumulator right arithmetically, preserving the sign bit.

```
RLC             ;COPY SIGN BIT IN BIT 0, CARRY
RAR             ;THEN SHIFT BACK TWICE
RAR
```

RLC sets both the Carry flag and bit 0 of the accumulator to the old value of bit 7.

3. Shift accumulator left logically.

```
ADD   A         ;SHIFT LEFT LOGICALLY
```

Adding the accumulator to itself is equivalent to a logical left shift.

4. Shift registers H and L left logically.

```
DAD   H         ;SHIFT HL LEFT LOGICALLY
```

Adding registers H and L to themselves is equivalent to a 16-bit logical left shift.

    5. Shift register pair right logically.

```
        ANA   A           ;CLEAR CARRY
        MOV   A,rph       ;SHIFT MSB RIGHT LOGICALLY
        RAR
        MOV   rph,A
        MOV   A,rpl       ;ROTATE LSB RIGHT, PICKING UP CARRY
        RAR
        MOV   rpl,A
```

The key point here is that the less significant byte must be rotated to pick up the Carry from the logical shift of the more significant byte.

    6. Shift register pair right arithmetically.

```
        MOV   A,rph       ;SHIFT MSB RIGHT ARITHMETICALLY
        RLC
        RAR
        RAR
        MOV   rph,A
        MOV   A,rpl       ;ROTATE LSB RIGHT
        RAR
        MOV   rpl,A
```

The shift of the LSB is the same as in the logical shift.

    7. Digit swap accumulator. That is, exchange the four least significant bits with the four most significant bits.

```
        RLC               ;DIGIT SHIFT = 4 ROTATES
        RLC
        RLC
        RLC
```

or

```
        RRC               ;DIGIT SHIFT = 4 ROTATES
        RRC
        RRC
        RRC
```

    8. Normalize accumulator. That is, shift the accumulator left until its most significant bit is 1. Do not shift at all if the accumulator contains 0.

```
        ANA   A           ;TEST ACCUMULATOR
        JM    DONE        ;EXIT IF ALREADY NORMALIZED
        JZ    DONE        ;EXIT IF ZERO
SHIFT:  ADD   A           ;OTHERWISE, SHIFT A LEFT 1 BIT
        JP    SHIFT       ;KEEP SHIFTING UNTIL NORMALIZED
DONE:   NOP
```

Rotate Instructions

1. Rotate register pair right.

```
MOV   A,rpl      ;MOVE BIT 0 TO CARRY
RAR
MOV   A,rph      ;ROTATE MSB RIGHT
RAR
MOV   rph,A
MOV   A,rpl      ;ROTATE LSB RIGHT
RAR
MOV   rpl,A
```

The first two instructions move bit 0 of the register pair to the Carry.

2. Rotate register pair right.

```
MOV   A,rph      ;MOVE BIT 15 TO CARRY
RAL
MOV   A,rpl      ;ROTATE LSB LEFT
RAL
MOV   rpl,A
MOV   A,rph      ;ROTATE MSB LEFT
RAL
MOV   rph,A
```

The first two instructions move bit 15 of the register pair to the Carry.

3. Rotate accumulator left through Carry, setting flags.

```
ADC   A          ;ROTATE LEFT, SETTING FLAGS
```

This instruction is the same as RAL, except that it affects all the flags whereas RAL affects only Carry.

4. Rotate register pair right through Carry.

```
MOV   A,rph      ;ROTATE MSB RIGHT WITH CARRY
RAR
MOV   rph,A
MOV   A,rpl      ;ROTATE LSB RIGHT
RAR
MOV   rpl,A
```

5. Rotate register pair left through Carry.

```
MOV   A,rpl      ;ROTATE LSB LEFT WITH CARRY
RAL
MOV   rpl,A
MOV   A,rph      ;ROTATE MSB LEFT
RAL
MOV   rph,A
```

Test Instructions

1. **Test accumulator.** Set flags according to the value in the accumulator without changing that value.

```
        ANA  A              ;TEST ACCUMULATOR
```
or
```
        ORA  A              ;TEST ACCUMULATOR
```
Both alternatives clear the Carry.

2. **Test register.** Set flags according to the value in a register without changing that value.
```
        INR  reg            ;TEST A REGISTER
        DCR  reg
```
This sequence does not affect the Carry flag or the accumulator.

3. **Test memory location.** Set flags according to the value in a memory location without changing that value.

```
        LXI  H,ADDR         ;TEST MEMORY LOCATION ADDR
        INR  M
        DCR  M
```
This sequence does not affect the Carry flag or the accumulator.

4. **Test register pair.** Set the Zero flag according to the value in a register pair without changing that value.

```
        MOV  A,rph          ;TEST REGISTER PAIR
        ORA  rpl
```
This sequence changes the accumulator and the other flags.

5. **Test bits of accumulator.** Set the Zero flag if all the tested bit are 0s and clear the Zero flag otherwise.

```
        ANI  MASK           ;TEST BIT BY MASKING
```
MASK has 1s in the bit positions to be tested and 0s elsewhere. The Zero flag is set to 1 if the tested bits are all 0s and to 0 otherwise. The Zero flag can then be used as a branch condition. For example:

```
        ANI  00001000B ;TEST BIT 3
```
The result is 0 if bit 3 of A is 0 and 00001000_2 if bit 3 of A is 1. So the Zero flag ends up containing the logical complement of bit 3.

6. **Compare register with accumulator bit by bit.** Set each bit position that is different to 1.

```
XRA   reg        ;BIT-BY-BIT COMPARISON
```

The EXCLUSIVE OR function is the same as a "not equal" function.

7. **Bit test.** Set flags as if the accumulator had been logically ANDed with a register or memory location, but do not change the accumulator.

```
MOV   reg1,A     ;SAVE ACCUMULATOR
ANA   reg        ;PERFORM LOGICAL AND
MOV   A,reg1     ;RESTORE ACCUMULATOR
```

DATA TRANSFER INSTRUCTIONS

This group includes load, store, move, exchange, input, output, clear, and set instructions. Also included are arithmetic instructions (such as subtracting the accumulator from itself) that move a specific value or the contents of a register to the accumulator or other destination without changing any data.

Load Instructions

1. Load register direct.

```
LDA   ADDR
MOV   reg,A
```

or

```
LXI   H,ADDR
MOV   reg,M
```

The first alternative uses the accumulator, whereas the second alternative uses registers H and L.

2. Load accumulator indirect.

· From address in HL

```
MOV   A,M
```

· From address in BC or DE

```
LDAX rp
```

3. Load register indirect.

· From address in HL

```
MOV   reg,M
```

· From address in BC or DE

```
LDAX rp
MOV   reg,A
```

4. Load register pair direct.

· H and L

```
LHLD ADDR
```

· D and E

```
LHLD ADDR
XCHG
```

· B and C

```
LHLD ADDR
MOV  B,H
MOV  C,L
```

5. Load stack pointer direct.

```
LHLD ADDR
SPHL
```

6. Load registers H and L indirect from address in HL.

```
MOV  A,M      ;LOAD LSB
INX  H
MOV  H,M      ;LOAD MSB
MOV  L,A
```

7. Load register pair (B or D) indirect from address in HL.

```
MOV  rpl,M    ;LOAD LSB
INX  H
MOV  rph,M    ;LOAD MSB
DCX  H        ;RETURN HL TO ORIGINAL VALUE
```

8. Load flag register direct.

```
LHLD ADDR     ;LOAD L FROM ADDR
PUSH H        ;HL TO STACK, L ON TOP
POP  PSW      ;HL TO PSW WITH L TO FLAGS
```

This procedure allows a user to initialize the flag register for debugging or testing purposes. Note that it changes the accumulator and the less significant half of a register pair.

9. Load flag register with the 8-bit number VALUE.

```
MVI  rpl,VALUE ;PUT VALUE IN LSB OF REGISTER PAIR
PUSH rp        ;MOVE TO FLAGS THROUGH STACK
POP  PSW
```

The limitation of pushing and popping register pairs complicates this sequence.

10. Load interrupt masks (I register) direct (8085 only).

```
LDA  ADDR     ;GET VALUE
SIM           ;SET INTERRUPT MASKS
```

11. Load interrupt masks (I register) with the 8-bit number VALUE (8085 only).

```
MVI  A,VALUE      ;GET VALUE
SIM               ;SET INTERRUPT MASKS
```

12. Load memory locations PTR and PTR+1 with ADDR (MSB in PTR+1).

```
LXI  H,ADDR       ;GET INDIRECT ADDRESS
SHLD PTR          ;SAVE INDIRECT ADDRESS IN MEMORY
```

Store Instructions

1. Store register direct.

```
MOV  A,reg
STA  ADDR
```

or

```
LXI  H,ADDR
MOV  M,reg
```

The first alternative uses the accumulator, whereas the second alternative uses registers H and L.

2. Store accumulator indirect.

· At address in HL

```
MOV  M,A
```

· At address in BC or DE

```
STAX rp
```

3. Store register indirect.

· At address in HL

```
MOV  M,reg
```

· At address in DE or BC

```
MOV  A,reg
STAX rp
```

4. Store register pair direct.

· H and L

```
SHLD ADDR
```

· D and E

```
XCHG
SHLD ADDR
```

· B and C

```
MOV   H,B
MOV   L,C
SHLD  ADDR
```

5. Store stack pointer direct.

```
LXI   H,0
DAD   SP
SHLD  ADDR
```

The only way to determine the value of the stack pointer is to add it to H and L.

6. Store register pair (B or D) indirect at address in HL.

```
MOV   M,rpl        ;STORE LSB
INX   H
MOV   M,rph        ;STORE MSB
DCX   H            ;RETURN HL TO ORIGINAL VALUE
```

The register pair is stored in memory in the usual upside-down format.

7. Store flag register direct.

```
PUSH PSW           ;F TO TOP OF STACK
POP  H             ;F TO L
SHLD ADDR          ;F TO ADDR, DESTROY ADDR + 1
```

or

```
PUSH PSW           ;F TO TOP OF STACK
POP  H             ;F TO L
MOV  A,L           ;F TO A
STA  ADDR          ;F TO ADDR
```

8. Store interrupt masks (I register) direct (8085 only).

```
RIM                ;GET INTERRUPT MASKS
STA  ADDR          ;STORE I REGISTER IN MEMORY
```

Note that the I register as read by RIM differs from the I register as written by SIM.

Move Instructions

1. Transfer accumulator to flag register.

```
MOV   rpl,A
PUSH  rp
POP   PSW
```

The flag register is the less significant byte of the Processor Status Word (PSW). This sequence also changes the accumulator and the less significant half of a register pair. The accumulator can be preserved by adding MOV rph,A to the beginning of the routine.

2. Transfer flag register to accumulator.

```
PUSH PSW
POP  rp
MOV  A,rp1
```

This sequence changes both halves of register pair rp.

3. Move register pair 1 to register pair 2.

```
MOV  rp2l,rp1l
MOV  rp2h,rp1h
```

This sequence transfers the contents of register pair rp1 to rp2 without changing rp1. Remember, XCHG exchanges register pairs D and H specifically.

4. Move HL to stack pointer.

```
SPHL
```

5. Move stack pointer to HL.

```
LXI  H,0
DAD  SP
```

6. Move HL to program counter.

```
PCHL
```

7. Block move (as on Z80 microprocessor with a 16-bit byte counter in BC).[5,6] Transfer data from addresses starting at the one in registers H and L to addresses starting at the one in registers D and E. The number of bytes to be transferred is in registers B and C.

```
MOVBYT:   MOV  A,M      ;GET A BYTE OF DATA
          STAX D        ;AND MOVE IT
          INX  D        ;INCREMENT BUFFER POINTERS
          INX  H
          DCX  B        ;COUNT BYTES
          MOV  A,B
          ORA  C
          JNZ  MOVBYT
```

8. Move multiple (fill). Place the contents of the accumulator in successive memory locations starting at the address in registers H and L. The number of bytes to be filled (one or more) is in register B.

```
FILBYT:   MOV  M,A      ;FILL A MEMORY LOCATION
          INX  H        ;POINT TO NEXT LOCATION
          DCR  B        ;COUNT BYTES
          JNZ  FILBYT
```

This routine can initialize an array or buffer. If you want to fill more than 256 bytes, the procedure becomes more complex. If register E is used for temporary storage and the the number of bytes to be filled is in registers B and C, the program is

```
         MOV  E,A        ;SAVE FILL VALUE
FILBYT:  MOV  M,E        ;FILL A MEMORY LOCATION
         INX  H          ;POINT TO NEXT LOCATION
         DCX  B          ;COUNT BYTES, SAVING DATA
         MOV  A,B
         ORA  C
         JNZ  FILBYT
```

Remember that MOV does not affect the flags.

Exchange Instructions

1. Exchange registers using the accumulator.

```
         MOV  A,reg1
         MOV  reg1,reg2
         MOV  reg2,A
```

2. Exchange register pairs.

· DE with HL

```
         XCHG
```

· BC with HL

```
         PUSH B          ;BC TO TOP OF STACK
         XTHL            ;BC TO HL, HL TO TOP OF STACK
         POP  B          ;HL TO BC
```

XTHL exchanges HL with the top of the stack.

· General, rp1 with rp2

```
         PUSH rp1        ;PUT RP1, RP2 IN STACK
         PUSH rp2
         POP  rp1        ;EXCHANGE BY POPPING IN WRONG ORDER
         POP  rp2
```

3. Exchange stack pointer with HL.

```
         XCHG            ;HL TO DE
         LXI  H,0        ;SP TO HL
         DAD  SP
         XCHG            ;SP TO DE, RESTORE HL
         SPHL            ;HL TO SP
         XCHG            ;SP TO HL
```

This procedure can be employed to differentiate between a user stack and the operating system or monitor stack.

Input Instructions

1. Place serial input (SID) in Carry (8085 only).

```
        RIM                     ;FETCH SERIAL INPUT
        RAL                     ;MOVE SID TO CARRY
```

RIM places the serial input in bit 7 of the accumulator.

2. Block input (as on Z80 microprocessor). Move a block of data from input port IPORT to memory starting at the address in H and L.

· 8-bit byte counter in register B

```
BLKIN:  IN    IPORT             ;READ A BYTE
        MOV   M,A               ;SAVE INPUT BYTE IN MEMORY
        INX   H                 ;POINT TO NEXT MEMORY LOCATION
        DCR   B                 ;COUNT BYTES
        JNZ   BLKIN
```

· 16-bit byte counter in registers B and C

```
BLKIN:  IN    IPORT             ;READ A BYTE
        MOV   M,A               ;SAVE INPUT BYTE IN MEMORY
        INX   H                 ;POINT TO NEXT MEMORY LOCATION
        DCX   B                 ;COUNT BYTES
        MOV   A,B               ;TEST BYTE COUNTER FOR ZERO
        ORA   C
        JNZ   BLKIN
```

The register pair must be tested for 0 since DCX does not affect any flags.

Output Instructions

1. Perform serial output through SOD (8085 only).

In order to change the SOD (serial output data) line, the serial output enable (bit 6 of the I register) must be set. You must also clear the mask set enable (bit 3 of the I register) to avoid changing the interrupt masks.

· Send Carry as serial output data (SOD)

```
        MVI   A,10000000B       ;SET BIT 7 BEFORE SHIFTING
        RAR                     ;MOVE CARRY TO SOD, MAKE SOE 1
        SIM                     ;SEND CARRY ON SOD LINE
```

· Make SOD 1

```
        MVI   A,11000000B       ;SET SOD, SOD ENABLE
        SIM                     ;MAKE SOD 1
```

· Make SOD 0

```
        MVI   A,01000000B       ;CLEAR SOD, SET SOD ENABLE
        SIM                     ;MAKE SOD 0
```

2. Block output (as on Z80 microprocessor). Move a block of data from memory (starting at the address in H and L) to output port OPORT.

· 8-bit byte counter in register B

```
BLKOUT:   MOV   A,M        ;FETCH A BYTE FROM MEMORY
          OUT   OPORT      ;SEND BYTE TO OUTPUT PORT
          INX   H          ;POINT TO NEXT MEMORY LOCATION
          DCR   B          ;COUNT BYTES
          JNZ   BLKOUT
```

· 16-bit byte counter in registers B and C

```
BLKOUT:   MOV   A,M        ;FETCH A BYTE FROM MEMORY
          OUT   OPORT      ;SEND BYTE TO OUTPUT PORT
          INX   H          ;POINT TO NEXT MEMORY LOCATION
          DCX   B          ;COUNT BYTES
          MOV   A,B        ;TEST 16-BIT COUNTER FOR ZERO
          ORA   C
          JNZ   BLKOUT
```

Clear Instructions

1. Clear the accumulator.

```
        SUB   A
```
or
```
        XRA   A
```
or
```
        MVI   A,0
```

The third alternative executes more slowly and occupies more memory than the other two, but does not affect the flags.

2. Clear a register.

```
        MVI   reg,0
```

3. Clear a memory location.

```
        SUB   A
        STA   ADDR
```
or
```
        LXI   H,ADDR
        MVI   M,0
```

The second alternative executes more slowly than the first but does not affect the accumulator or the flags. Of course, it does use registers H and L.

4. Clear a register pair.

```
LXI   rp,0
```

5. Clear memory locations ADDR and ADDR+1.

```
LXI   H,0
SHLD  ADDR
```

6. Clear Carry flag.

```
ANA   A
```

or

```
ORA   A
```

Any logical instruction except CMA will clear Carry, but these two are convenient since they do not change the accumulator. Remember, ANDing or ORing a bit with itself does not affect its value. To clear Carry without affecting the other flags, use

```
STC               ;FIRST SET CARRY
CMC               ;THEN CLEAR IT BY COMPLEMENTING
```

This approach is useful when Carry indicates the occurrence of an error or exception.

7. Clear bits of accumulator.

```
ANI   MASK        ;CLEAR BITS BY MASKING
```

MASK has 0s in the bit positions to be cleared and 1s in the positions that are to be left unchanged. For example:

```
ANI   10111110B ;CLEAR BITS 0 AND 6
```

Logically ANDing a bit with 1 leaves it unchanged.

Set Instructions

1. Set the accumulator to FF_{16} (all 1s in binary).

```
MVI   A,0FFH
```

or

```
SUB   A
DCR   A
```

2. Set a register to FF_{16}.

```
MVI   reg,0FFH
```

3. Set a memory location to FF_{16}.

```
MVI   A,0FFH
STA   ADDR
```

or

```
LXI   H,ADDR
MVI   M,0FFH
```

4. Set bits of accumulator.

```
ORI   MASK        ;SET BITS BY MASKING
```

MASK has 1s in the bit positions to be set and 0s elsewhere. For example:

```
ORI   10000000B ;SET BIT 7 (SIGN BIT)
```

Logically ORing a bit with 0 leaves it unchanged.

BRANCH (JUMP) INSTRUCTIONS

Unconditional Branch Instructions

1. Jump indirect.

· To address in H and L

```
PCHL
```

· To address at the top of the stack

```
RET
```

Note that RET is just an ordinary indirect jump that obtains its destination from the top of the stack. RET can be used for purposes other than returning from a subroutine.

· To address in D and E

```
XCHG
PCHL
```

· To address in B and C

```
MOV   H,B
MOV   L,C
PCHL
```

or

```
PUSH BC
RET
```

The second alternative is much slower than the first, but does not change HL.

· To address in memory locations ADDR and ADDR+1

```
LHLD ADDR        ;FETCH INDIRECT ADDRESS
PCHL             ;AND BRANCH TO IT
```

2. Jump indexed, assuming that the base of the address table is in registers H and L and the index is in the accumulator.

```
ADD   A          ;DOUBLE INDEX FOR 2-BYTE ENTRIES
MOV   E,A        ;EXTEND INDEX TO 16 BITS
MVI   D,O
DAD   D          ;CALCULATE ADDRESS OF ELEMENT
MOV   E,M        ;FETCH ELEMENT FROM ADDRESS TABLE
INX   H
MOV   D,M
XCHG             ;JUMP TO ADDRESS OBTAINED FROM TABLE
PCHL
```

It has been assumed that the address table (jump table) consists of as many as 128 2-byte entries stored in the usual 8080/8085 format with the less significant bytes first. A typical table would be

```
JTAB:   DW    ROUTO    ;STARTING ADDRESS FOR ROUTINE O
        DW    ROUT1    ;STARTING ADDRESS FOR ROUTINE 1
        DW    ROUT2    ;STARTING ADDRESS FOR ROUTINE 2
```

3. Jump and link. That is, transfer control to address DEST, saving the current value of the program counter in registers H and L.

```
        LXI   H,HERE   ;LOAD HL WITH LINK
HERE:   JMP   DEST     ;TRANSFER CONTROL
```

This procedure can provide a subroutine capability that does not use the stack. The subroutine can return control by adjusting the link and executing PCHL. For example, to return control to the instruction immediately following JMP DEST, the subroutine would have to add 3 to H and L (since JMP DEST occupies three bytes).

Conditional Branch Instructions

1. Branch if 0.

· Branch if accumulator contains 0

```
        ANA   A        ;TEST ACCUMULATOR
        JZ    DEST
```

· Branch if a register contains 0

```
        INR   reg      ;TEST REGISTER
        DCR   reg
        JZ    DEST
```

· Branch if a memory location contains 0

```
        LXI   H,ADDR   ;TEST MEMORY LOCATION
        INR   M
        DCR   M
        JZ    DEST
```

or

```
        LDA   ADDR     ;TEST MEMORY LOCATION
        ANA   A
        JZ    DEST
```

· Branch if a register pair contains 0

```
MOV   A,rph      ;TEST REGISTER PAIR
ORA   rpl
JZ    DEST
```

· Branch if a bit of the accumulator is 0

```
ANI   MASK       ;TEST BIT OF ACCUMULATOR
JZ    DEST
```

MASK has a 1 in the position to be tested and 0s elsewhere. Note the inversion here; if the bit in A is 0, the result is 0 and the Zero flag is set to 1. Special cases are

· Branch if bit 7 of the accumulator is 0

```
RAL              ;MOVE BIT 7 TO CARRY
JNC   DEST       ;AND TEST CARRY
```

You can replace RAL with RLC, ADD A, or ADC A.

· Branch if bit 6 of the accumulator is 0

```
ADD   A          ;SET SIGN FROM BIT 6
JP    DEST       ;AND THEN TEST SIGN FLAG
```

· Branch if bit 0 of the accumulator is 0

```
RAR              ;MOVE BIT 0 TO CARRY
JNC   DEST       ;AND TEST CARRY
```

· Branch if the serial input (SID) is 0 (8085 only)

```
RIM              ;FETCH SERIAL INPUT (SID)
RAL              ;MOVE SID TO CARRY
JNC   DEST
```

or

```
RIM              ;FETCH SERIAL INPUT (SID)
ANA   A          ;SET SIGN FLAG FROM SID
JP    DEST
```

· Branch if the interrupt enable (bit 3 of the I register) is 0 (8085 only)[7]

```
RIM              ;READ INTERRUPT MASK REGISTER
ANI   00001000B  ;TEST INTERRUPT ENABLE FLAG
JZ    DEST
```

This sequence can be used to save the current interrupt status before executing a routine that must run with interrupts disabled. That status can then be restored afterward.

· Branch if there are no pending interrupts (I7.5, I6.5, and I5.5 are all 0, 8085 only)

```
RIM              ;READ INTERRUPT MASK REGISTER
ANI   01110000B  ;MASK PENDING INTERRUPT BITS
JZ    DEST       ;BRANCH IF THEY ARE ALL ZERO
```

The pending interrupt bits (I7.5, I6.5, and I5.5) are bits 6, 5, and 4 of the interrupt mask (I) register, respectively.

2. Branch if not 0.

· Branch if accumulator does not contain 0

```
ANA   A          ;TEST ACCUMULATOR
JNZ   DEST
```

· Branch if a register does not contain 0

```
INR   reg        ;TEST REGISTER
DCR   reg
JNZ   DEST
```

· Branch if a memory location does not contain 0

```
LXI   H,ADDR      ;TEST MEMORY LOCATION
INR   M
DCR   M
JNZ   DEST
```

or

```
LDA   ADDR        ;TEST MEMORY LOCATION
ANA   A
JNZ   DEST
```

· Branch if a register pair does not contain 0

```
MOV   A,rph       ;TEST REGISTER PAIR
ORA   rpl
JNZ   DEST
```

· Branch if a bit of the accumulator is 1

```
ANI   MASK        ;TEST BIT OF ACCUMULATOR
JNZ   DEST
```

MASK has a 1 in the bit position to be tested and 0s elsewhere. Note the inversion here; if the bit of A is 1, the result is not 0 and the Zero flag is cleared. Special cases are

· Branch if bit 7 of the accumulator is 1

```
RAL              ;MOVE BIT 7 TO CARRY
JC    DEST       ;AND TEST CARRY
```

RAL can be replaced with RLC, ADD A, or ADC A.

· Branch if bit 6 of the accumulator is 1

```
ADD   A          ;SET SIGN FROM BIT 6
JM    DEST       ;AND THEN TEST SIGN FLAG
```

· Branch if bit 0 of the accumulator is 1

```
RAR              ;MOVE BIT 0 TO CARRY
JC    DEST       ;AND TEST CARRY
```

· Branch if the serial input (SID) is 1 (8085 only)

```
RIM              ;FETCH SERIAL INPUT (SID)
RAL              ;MOVE SID TO CARRY
JC    DEST
```

or

```
RIM                 ;FETCH SERIAL INPUT (SID)
ANA   A             ;SET SIGN FLAG FROM SID
JM    DEST
```

· Branch if the interrupt enable (bit 3 of the I register) is 1 (8085 only)[8]

```
RIM                 ;READ INTERRUPT MASK REGISTER
ANI   00001000B     ;TEST INTERRUPT ENABLE FLAG
JNZ   DEST
```

This sequence can be used to save the current interrupt status before executing a routine that must run with interrupts disabled. That status can then be restored afterward.

· Branch if there are pending interrupts (I7.5, I6.5, and I5.5 are not all 0, 8085 only)

```
RIM                 ;READ INTERRUPT MASK REGISTER
ANI   01110000B     ;MASK PENDING INTERRUPT BITS
JNZ   DEST          ;BRANCH IF INTERRUPT IS PENDING
```

I7.5, I6.5, and I5.5 (the pending interrupt bits) are bits 6, 5, and 4 of the interrupt mask (I) register, respectively.

3. Branch if Equal.

· Branch if (A) = VALUE

```
CPI   VALUE         ;COMPARE BY SUBTRACTING
JZ    DEST
```

The following two special cases apply to any register or to a memory location addressed via H and L (register M):

· Branch if (reg) = 1

```
DCR   reg           ;CHECK BY DECREMENTING
JZ    DEST          ;AND SEEING IF THE RESULT IS ZERO
```

· Branch if (reg) = FF_{16}

```
INR   reg           ;CHECK BY INCREMENTING
JZ    DEST          ;AND SEEING IF THE RESULT IS ZERO
```

· Branch if (A) = (reg)

```
CMP   reg           ;COMPARE BY SUBTRACTING
JZ    DEST
```

· Branch if (A) = (ADDR)

```
LXI   H,ADDR        ;COMPARE BY SUBTRACTING
CMP   M
JZ    DEST
```

· Branch if (rp) = VAL16

```
        MOV   A,rph      ;CHECK MSB
        CPI   VAL16H
        JNZ   DONE
        MOV   A,rpl      ;CHECK LSB'S ONLY IF MSB'S EQUAL
        CPI   VAL16L
        JZ    DEST       ;BRANCH IF BOTH BYTES ARE EQUAL
DONE:   NOP
```

or

```
        LXI   H,-VAL16   ;HL = RP - VAL16
        DAD   rp
        MOV   A,H        ;TEST HL FOR ZERO
        ORA   L
        JZ    DEST
```

DAD is difficult to use here, since it does not affect the Zero flag. HL must be tested for 0 explicitly. If rp is HL, the first instruction should be LXI rp1, −VAL16 and the second DAD rp1.

· Branch if (rp1) = (rp2)

```
        MOV   A,rp1h     ;COMPARE MSB'S
        CMP   rp2h
        JNZ   DONE
        MOV   A,rp1l     ;COMPARE LSB'S ONLY IF MSB'S EQUAL
        CMP   rp2l
        JZ    DEST       ;BRANCH IF BOTH BYTES ARE EQUAL
DONE:   NOP
```

Note: You should not use either of the next two sequences to test for stack overflow or underflow, since intervening operations could change the stack pointer by more than 1.

· Branch if (SP) = VAL16

```
        LXI   H,-VAL16   ;FORM STACK POINTER - VAL16
        DAD   SP
        MOV   A,H        ;TEST DIFFERENCE FOR ZERO
        ORA   L
        JZ    DEST
```

· Branch if (SP) = (rp)

```
        LXI   H,0        ;MOVE STACK POINTER TO HL
        DAD   SP
        MOV   A,H        ;COMPARE MSB'S
        CMP   rph
        JNZ   DONE
        MOV   A,L        ;COMPARE LSB'S ONLY IF MSB'S EQUAL
        CMP   rpl
        JZ    DEST
DONE:   NOP
```

4. Branch if Not Equal.

· Branch if (A) ≠ VALUE

```
CPI   VALUE        ;COMPARE BY SUBTRACTING
JNZ   DEST
```

The following two special cases apply to any register or to a memory location addressed via H and L (register M):

· Branch if (reg) ≠ 1

```
DCR   reg          ;CHECK BY DECREMENTING
JNZ   DEST         ;AND TESTING RESULT FOR ZERO
```

· Branch if (reg) ≠ FF_{16}

```
INR   reg          ;CHECK BY INCREMENTING
JNZ   DEST         ;AND TESTING RESULT FOR ZERO
```

· Branch if (A) ≠ (reg)

```
CMP   reg          ;COMPARE BY SUBTRACTING
JNZ   DEST
```

· Branch if (A) ≠ (ADDR)

```
LXI   H,ADDR       ;COMPARE BY SUBTRACTING
CMP   M
JNZ   DEST
```

· Branch if (rp) ≠ VAL16

```
MOV   A,rph        ;COMPARE MSB'S
CPI   VAL16H
JNZ   DEST         ;BRANCH IF MSB'S NOT EQUAL
MOV   A,rpl        ;COMPARE LSB'S ONLY IF MSB'S EQUAL
CPI   VAL16L
JNZ   DEST         ;BRANCH IF LSB'S NOT EQUAL
```

or

```
LXI   H,-VAL16     ;HL = RP - VAL16
DAD   rp
MOV   A,H          ;TEST DIFFERENCE FOR ZERO
ORA   L
JNZ   DEST
```

DAD is difficult to use here, since it does not affect the Zero flag. You must test HL for 0 explicitly. If rp is HL, the first instruction should be LXI rp1,−VAL16 and the second DAD rp1.

· Branch if (rp1) ≠ (rp2)

```
MOV   A,rp1h       ;COMPARE MSB'S
CMP   rp2h
JNZ   DEST         ;BRANCH IF MSB'S ARE NOT EQUAL
MOV   A,rp1l       ;COMPARE LSB'S ONLY IF MSB'S EQUAL
CMP   rp2l
JNZ   DEST         ;BRANCH IF LSB'S ARE NOT EQUAL
```

Note: Do not use either of the next two sequences to test for stack overflow or underflow, since intervening operations could change the stack pointer by more than 1.

· Branch if (SP) ≠ VAL16

```
LXI   H,-VAL16   ;FORM STACK POINTER - VAL16
DAD   SP
MOV   A,H        ;TEST DIFFERENCE FOR ZERO
ORA   L
JNZ   DEST
```

· Branch if (SP) ≠ (rp), where rp is either B and C or D and E

```
LXI   H,0        ;MOVE SP TO HL
DAD   SP
MOV   A,H        ;COMPARE MSB'S
CMP   rph
JNZ   DEST       ;BRANCH IF MSB'S ARE NOT EQUAL
MOV   A,L        ;COMPARE LSB'S ONLY IF MSB'S EQUAL
CMP   rpl
JNZ   DEST
```

5. Branch if Positive.

· Branch if contents of accumulator are positive

```
ANA   A          ;TEST ACCUMULATOR
JP    DEST
```

· Branch if contents of a register are positive

```
INR   reg        ;TEST REGISTER
DCR   reg
JP    DEST
```

· Branch if contents of a memory location are positive

```
LXI   H,ADDR     ;TEST MEMORY LOCATION
INR   M
DCR   M
JP    DEST
```

or

```
LDA   ADDR       ;TEST MEMORY LOCATION VIA A
ANA   A
JP    DEST
```

· Branch if contents of a register pair are positive

```
INR   rph        ;TEST SIGN BIT IN MORE SIGNIFICANT BYTE
DCR   rph
JP    DEST
```

· Branch if 16-bit number in memory locations ADDR and ADDR+1 (MSB in ADDR+1) is positive

```
LDA   ADDR+1     ;TEST SIGN BIT IN MORE SIGNIFICANT BYTE
ANA
JP    DEST
```

6. Branch if Negative

· Branch if contents of accumulator are negative

```
ANA   A              ;TEST ACCUMULATOR
JM    DEST
```

· Branch if contents of a register are negative

```
INR   reg            ;TEST REGISTER
DCR   reg
JM    DEST
```

· Branch if contents of a memory location are negative

```
LXI   H,ADDR         ;TEST MEMORY LOCATION
INR   M
DCR   M
JM    DEST
```

or

```
LDA   ADDR           ;TEST MEMORY LOCATION VIA A
ANA   A
JM    DEST
```

· Branch if contents of a register pair are negative

```
INR   rph            ;TEST SIGN BIT IN MORE SIGNIFICANT BYTE
DCR   rph
JM    DEST
```

· Branch if 16-bit number in memory locations ADDR and ADDR+1 (MSB in ADDR+1) is negative

```
LDA   ADDR+1         ;TEST SIGN BIT IN MORE SIGNIFICANT BYTE
ANA
JM    DEST
```

7. Signed Branches.

We assume here that two's complement overflow is treated as discussed in Chapter 1. The initial comparison is always either CPI VALUE (for an 8-bit data item) or CMP reg (where reg is either a register or the data byte at the address in H and L).

· Branch if accumulator is greater than VALUE (signed)

```
      CPI   VALUE      ;COMPARE BY SUBTRACTING
      JM    DONE       ;NOT GREATER THAN IF NEGATIVE
      JNZ   DEST       ;OR IF RESULT IS ZERO
DONE: NOP
```

or

```
      CPI   VALUE+1    ;COMPARE BY SUBTRACTING VALUE + 1
      JP    DEST
```

Note that comparing equal numbers clears the Sign flag.

· Branch if accumulator is greater than register or memory location (signed)

```
        CMP  reg              ;COMPARE BY SUBTRACTING
        JM   DONE             ;NOT GREATER THAN IF NEGATIVE
        JNZ  DEST             ;OR IF RESULT IS ZERO
DONE:   NOP
```

or

```
        MOV  reg1,A           ;FORM REG - A
        MOV  A,reg
        CMP  reg1
        JM   DEST             ;BRANCH IF REG - A IS NEGATIVE
```

or

```
        INR  reg              ;FORM A - REG - 1
        CMP  reg
        JP   DEST             ;BRANCH IF DIFFERENCE IS POSITIVE
```

The problem here is avoiding a branch if the operands are equal. The third alternative changes the register; we could equally well change the accumulator by replacing INR reg with DCR A.

· Branch if accumulator is greater than or equal to VALUE (signed)

```
        CPI  VALUE            ;COMPARE BY SUBTRACTING
        JP   DEST             ;BRANCH IF DIFFERENCE POSITIVE
```

· Branch if accumulator is greater than or equal to register or memory location (signed)

```
        CMP  reg              ;COMPARE BY SUBTRACTING
        JP   DEST             ;BRANCH IF DIFFERENCE POSITIVE
```

· Branch if accumulator is less than VALUE (signed)

```
        CPI  VALUE            ;COMPARE BY SUBTRACTING
        JM   DEST             ;BRANCH IF DIFFERENCE NEGATIVE
```

· Branch if accumulator is less than register or memory location (signed)

```
        CMP  reg              ;COMPARE BY SUBTRACTING
        JM   DEST             ;BRANCH IF DIFFERENCE NEGATIVE
```

· Branch if accumulator is less than or equal to VALUE (signed)

```
        CPI  VALUE            ;COMPARE BY SUBTRACTING
        JM   DEST             ;BRANCH IF DIFFERENCE NEGATIVE
        JZ   DEST             ; OR ZERO
```

or

```
        CPI  VALUE+1          ;COMPARE BY SUBTRACTING VALUE+1
        JM   DEST             ;BRANCH IF DIFFERENCE NEGATIVE
```

· Branch if accumulator is less than or equal to register or memory location (signed)

```
        CMP  reg              ;COMPARE BY SUBTRACTING
        JM   DEST             ;BRANCH IF DIFFERENCE NEGATIVE
        JZ   DEST             ; OR ZERO
```

or

```
        MOV   reg1,A          ;FORM REG - A
        MOV   A,reg
        CMP   reg1
        JP    DEST            ;BRANCH IF REG - A IS POSITIVE
```

or

```
        INR   reg             ;FORM A - REG - 1
        CMP   reg
        JM    DEST            ;BRANCH IF DIFFERENCE NEGATIVE
```

In the last alternative, we could replace INR reg with DCR A, thus changing the accumulator instead of the register.

8. Branch if Higher (Unsigned).

That is, branch if the operands being compared are not equal and the comparison does not require a borrow.

The special problem here is avoiding a branch when the operands are equal.

· Branch if (A) > VALUE (unsigned)

```
        CPI   VALUE           ;COMPARE BY SUBTRACTING
        JC    DONE            ;NO BRANCH IF BORROW NEEDED
        JNZ   DEST            ;BRANCH IF NO BORROW, NOT EQUAL
DONE:   NOP
```

Comparing equal numbers clears Carry.

An alternative is

```
        CPI   VALUE+1         ;COMPARE BY SUBTRACTING VALUE+1
        JNC   DEST            ;BRANCH IF NO BORROW NEEDED
```

· Branch if (A) > (reg) (unsigned)

```
        CMP   reg             ;COMPARE BY SUBTRACTING
        JC    DONE            ;NO BRANCH IF BORROW NEEDED
        JNZ   DEST            ;BRANCH IF NO BORROW, NOT EQUAL
DONE:   NOP
```

or

```
        MOV   reg1,A          ;FORM REG - A
        MOV   A,reg
        CMP   reg1
        JC    DEST            ;BRANCH IF BORROW NEEDED
```

or

```
        INR   reg             ;FORM A - REG - 1
        CMP   reg
        JNC   DEST            ;BRANCH IF NO BORROW NEEDED
```

In the third alternative, we could replace INR REG with DCR A, thus changing the accumulator instead of the register.

· Branch if (A) > (ADDR) (unsigned)

```
        LXI    H,ADDR
        CMP    M               ;COMPARE BY SUBTRACTING
        JC     DONE            ;NO BRANCH IF BORROW NEEDED
        JNZ    DEST            ;BRANCH IF NO BORROW, NOT EQUAL
 DONE:  NOP
```

or

```
        MOV    reg,A           ;FORM (ADDR) - A
        LDA    ADDR
        CMP    reg
        JC     DEST            ;BRANCH IF BORROW NEEDED
```

· Branch if (HL) > VAL16 (unsigned)

```
        LXI    rp,-(VAL16+1)   ;FORM HL - VAL16 - 1
        DAD    rp
        JC     DEST            ;BRANCH IF NO BORROW NEEDED
```

· Branch if (HL) > (rp) (unsigned)

```
        MOV    A,rpl           ;SET BORROW FROM LSB'S
        CMP    L
        MOV    A,rph           ;THEN COMPARE MSB'S WITH BORROW
        SBB    H
        JC     DEST
```

· Branch if (SP) > VAL16 (unsigned)

```
        LXI    H,-(VAL16+1)    ;FORM SP - VAL16 - 1
        DAD    SP
        JC     DEST            ;BRANCH IF NO BORROW GENERATED
```

· Branch if (SP) > (rp) (unsigned)

```
        LXI    H,0             ;MOVE SP TO HL
        DAD    SP
        MOV    A,rpl           ;SET BORROW FROM LSB'S
        CMP    L
        MOV    A,rph           ;THEN COMPARE MSB'S WITH BORROW
        SBB    H
        JC     DEST
```

9. Branch if Not Higher (Unsigned).

That is, branch if the operands being compared are equal or if the comparison requires a borrow.

The special problem here is forcing a branch if the operands are equal.

· Branch if (A) ≤ VALUE (unsigned)

```
        CPI    VALUE           ;COMPARE BY SUBTRACTING
        JC     DEST            ;BRANCH IF BORROW NEEDED
        JZ     DEST            ; OR IF OPERANDS EQUAL
```

or

```
        CPI    VALUE+1         ;COMPARE BY SUBTRACTING VALUE+1
        JC     DEST            ;BRANCH IF BORROW NEEDED
```

· Branch if (A) ≤ (reg) (unsigned)

```
CMP   reg              ;COMPARE BY SUBTRACTING
JC    DEST             ;BRANCH IF BORROW NEEDED
JZ    DEST             ; OR IF OPERANDS EQUAL
```

or

```
MOV   reg1,A           ;FORM (REG) - (A)
MOV   A,reg
CMP   reg1
JNC   DEST             ;BRANCH IF NO BORROW NEEDED
```

or

```
INR   reg              ;FORM A - REG - 1
CMP   reg
JC    DEST             ;BRANCH IF BORROW NEEDED
```

In the third alternative, we could replace INR reg with DCR A, thus changing the accumulator instead of the register.

· Branch if (A) ≤ (ADDR) (unsigned)

```
LXI   H,ADDR
CMP   M                ;COMPARE BY SUBTRACTING
JC    DEST             ;BRANCH IF BORROW NEEDED
JZ    DEST             ; OR IF OPERANDS EQUAL
```

or

```
MOV   reg,A            ;FORM (ADDR) - (A)
LDA   ADDR
CMP   reg
JNC   DEST             ;BRANCH IF NO BORROW NEEDED
```

· Branch if (HL) ≤ VAL16 (unsigned)

```
LXI   rp,-(VAL16+1)    ;FORM HL - VAL16 - 1
DAD   rp
JNC   DEST             ;BRANCH IF BORROW NEEDED
```

· Branch if (HL) ≤ (rp) (unsigned)

```
MOV   A,rpl            ;SET BORROW FROM LSB'S
CMP   L
MOV   A,rph            ;THEN COMPARE MSB'S WITH BORROW
SBB   H
JNC   DEST
```

· Branch if (SP) ≤ VAL16 (unsigned)

```
LXI   H,-(VAL16+1)     ;FORM SP - VAL16 - 1
DAD   SP
JNC   DEST             ;BRANCH IF BORROW NEEDED
```

· Branch if (SP) ≤ (rp) (unsigned)

```
        LXI   H,0           ;MOVE SP TO HL
        DAD   SP
        MOV   A,rpl         ;SET BORROW FROM LSB'S
        CMP   L
        MOV   A,rph         ;THEN COMPARE MSB'S WITH BORROW
        SBB   H
        JNC   DEST
```

10. Branch if Lower (Unsigned).

That is, branch if the unsigned comparison requires a borrow.

· Branch if (A) < VALUE (unsigned)

```
        CPI   VALUE         ;COMPARE BY SUBTRACTING
        JC    DEST          ;BRANCH IF BORROW NEEDED
```

· Branch if (A) < (reg) (unsigned)

```
        CMP   reg           ;COMPARE BY SUBTRACTING
        JC    DEST          ;BRANCH IF BORROW NEEDED
```

· Branch if (A) < (ADDR) (unsigned)

```
        LXI   H,ADDR
        CMP   M             ;COMPARE BY SUBTRACTING
        JC    DEST          ;BRANCH IF BORROW NEEDED
```

· Branch if (HL) < VAL16 (unsigned)

```
        LXI   rp,-VAL16     ;FORM HL - VAL16
        DAD   rp
        JNC   DEST          ;BRANCH IF BORROW NEEDED
```

· Branch if (HL) < (rp) (unsigned)

```
        MOV   A,L           ;SET BORROW FROM LSB'S
        CMP   rpl
        MOV   A,H           ;THEN COMPARE MSB'S WITH BORROW
        SBB   rph
        JC    DEST
```

· Branch if (SP) < VAL 16 (unsigned)

```
        LXI   H,-VAL16      ;FORM SP - VAL16
        DAD   SP
        JNC   DEST          ;BRANCH IF BORROW NEEDED
```

· Branch if (SP) < (rp) (unsigned)

```
        LXI   H,0           ;MOVE SP TO HL
        DAD   SP
        MOV   A,L           ;SET BORROW FROM LSB'S
        CMP   rpl
        MOV   A,H           ;THEN COMPARE MSB'S WITH BORROW
        SBB   rph
        JC    DEST
```

11. Branch if Not Lower (Unsigned).

That is, branch if the unsigned comparison does not require a borrow.

· Branch if (A) ≥ VALUE (unsigned)

```
CPI   VALUE            ;COMPARE BY SUBTRACTING
JNC   DEST             ;BRANCH IF NO BORROW NEEDED
```

· Branch if (A) ≥ (reg) (unsigned)

```
CMP   reg              ;COMPARE BY SUBTRACTING
JNC   DEST             ;BRANCH IF NO BORROW NEEDED
```

· Branch if (A) ≥ (ADDR) (unsigned)

```
LXI   H,ADDR           ;COMPARE BY SUBTRACTING
CMP   M
JNC   DEST             ;BRANCH IF NO BORROW NEEDED
```

· Branch if (HL) ≥ VAL16 (unsigned)

```
LXI   rp,-VAL16        ;FORM HL - VAL16
DAD   rp
JC    DEST             ;BRANCH IF NO BORROW NEEDED
```

· Branch if (HL) ≥ (rp) (unsigned)

```
MOV   A,L              ;SET BORROW FROM LSB'S
CMP   rpl
MOV   A,H              ;THEN COMPARE MSB'S WITH BORROW
SBB   rph
JNC   DEST
```

· Branch if (SP) ≥ VAL16 (unsigned)

```
LXI   H,-VAL16         ;FORM SP - VAL16
DAD   SP
JC    DEST             ;BRANCH IF NO BORROW NEEDED
```

· Branch if (SP) ≥ (rp) (unsigned)

```
LXI   H,0              ;MOVE SP TO HL
DAD   SP
MOV   A,L              ;SET BORROW FROM LSB'S
CMP   rpl
MOV   A,H              ;THEN COMPARE MSB'S WITH BORROW
SBB   rph
JNC   DEST
```

SKIP INSTRUCTIONS

A skip instruction on the 8080 or 8085 microprocessor can be implemented by using a jump instruction with the proper destination. That destination should be one instruction beyond the one that follows the jump sequentially. The actual number of bytes skipped will vary, since 8080/8085 instructions may be one to three bytes long.

SUBROUTINE CALL INSTRUCTIONS

Unconditional Call Instructions

An indirect call can be implemented on the 8080 or 8085 microprocessor by calling a routine that jumps indirectly to a subroutine. An RET instruction at the end of the subroutine will then transfer control back to the original calling point. The main program performs

```
CALL TRANS
```

where subroutine TRANS transfers control to the ultimate destination. Note that TRANS ends with a jump, not with a return. Typical TRANS routines are

· To address in H and L

```
TRANS:   PCHL            ;ENTRY POINT IN HL
```

· To address in D and E

```
TRANS:   XCHG            ;ENTRY POINT IN DE
         PCHL
```

· To address in B and C

```
TRANS:   MOV  H,B        ;ENTRY POINT IN BC
         MOV  L,C
         PCHL
```

or

```
TRANS:   PUSH B          ;ENTRY POINT IN BC
         RET
```

The second alternative is slower than the first, but it leaves H and L unchanged.

· To address in memory locations ADDR and ADDR+1

```
TRANS:   LHLD ADDR       ;ENTRY POINT AT ADDR
         PCHL
```

· To address at the top of the stack. Here we want to exchange the return address with the top of the stack. This can be done in the main program as follows:

```
         LXI  H,RETPT    ;GET RETURN POINT ADDRESS
         XTHL            ;PUT RETURN ADDRESS ON STACK
         PCHL            ;AND JUMP TO OLD TOP OF STACK
```

The exchange can allow later resumption of a suspended program or provide a special exit to an error-handling routine.

Indexed calls can be implemented in the same way as indirect calls. The CALL instruction transfers control to a routine that performs an indexed jump. That routine ends with a JUMP instruction (typically PCHL) which does not affect the stack. An RET instruction at the end of the actual subroutine will transfer control back to the original calling point.

If the main program executes CALL JMPIND with the index in the accumulator and the starting address of the jump table in registers H and L, the indexed jump routine is

```
JMPIND: ADD   A          ;DOUBLE INDEX FOR 2-BYTE ENTRIES
        MOV   E,A        ;EXTEND INDEX TO 16 BITS
        MVI   D,0
        DAD   D          ;CALCULATE ADDRESS OF ELEMENT
        MOV   E,M        ;FETCH ELEMENT FROM JUMP TABLE
        INX   H
        MOV   D,M
        XCHG             ;AND JUMP TO IT
        PCHL
```

One problem with indexed and indirect calls is that the transfer routines may interfere with the actual subroutines. For example, the indexed jump routine JMPIND changes the accumulator, registers D and E, registers H and L, and the flags. Thus, none of these registers can be used to pass parameters to the subroutine. The programmer must always remember that the intermediate transfer routines are interposed between the main program and the actual subroutine. A similar interposition occurs when operating system routines transfer control from one task to another or from a main program to an I/O driver or an interrupt service routine.

Conditional Call Instructions

A conditional call on the 8080 or 8085 microprocessor can be implemented by using the sequences shown earlier for conditional branches. The only change is that jumps to the actual destination must be replaced with calls (for example, replace JNZ DEST with CNZ DEST or JP DEST with CP DEST).

SUBROUTINE RETURN INSTRUCTIONS

Unconditional Return Instructions

RET returns control automatically to the address saved at the top of the stack. If the return address is saved elsewhere (for example, in a register pair or in two fixed memory locations), control can be transferred to it by performing an indirect jump.

Conditional Return Instructions

Conditional returns on the 8080 or 8085 microprocessor can be implemented by using the sequences shown earlier for conditional branches. The only change is that jumps to the actual destination be replaced with returns (for example, replace JNC DEST with RNC or JM DEST with RM).

Return with Skip Instructions

· Add a fixed offset to the address at the top of the stack before returning control to it. This sequence allows the programmer to transfer control past parameters, data, and other non-executable items.

```
POP   D            ;GET RETURN ADDRESS
LXI   H,OFFSET     ;ADD OFFSET TO RETURN ADDRESS
DAD   D
PCHL               ;RETURN WITH SKIP
```

· Change the return address to RETPT. Assume that the current return address is stored at the top of the stack.

```
LXI   H,RETPT      ;CHANGE RETURN ADDRESS TO RETPT
XTHL
```

XTHL exchanges HL with the top of the stack. This procedure can force a special exit to an error routine or exception-handling program without changing the logic of the subroutine or losing track of the original return address.

Return from Interrupt Instructions

If the initial portion of the interrupt service routine saves all the registers with the sequence

```
PUSH PSW           ;SAVE ALL REGISTERS
PUSH B
PUSH D
PUSH H
```

a standard return sequence (at the end of the routine) is

```
POP   H            ;RESTORE ALL REGISTERS
POP   D
POP   B
POP   PSW
EI                 ;REENABLE INTERRUPTS
RET
```

Registers must be restored in the opposite order from that in which they were saved. EI must come immediately before RET to avoid unnecessary stacking of return addresses.

MISCELLANEOUS INSTRUCTIONS

This category includes no operations, push, pop, halt, wait, trap (break or software interrupt), decimal adjust, enabling and disabling of interrupts, translation (table lookup), and other instructions that do not fall into previous categories.

1. No Operation Instructions.

Like NOP itself, any MOV instruction with the same source and destination does nothing except advance the program counter. These additional no-ops are

```
MOV   A,A
MOV   B,B
MOV   C,C
MOV   D,D
MOV   E,E
MOV   H,H
MOV   L,L
```

There is no MOV M,M instruction.

2. Push Instructions.

· Push a single register (A, B, D, or H)

```
PUSH rp           ;PUSH THE DOUBLE REGISTER
INX  SP           ;BUT DROP THE LSB
```

rp can be PSW, the processor status word (consisting of the accumulator and the flags). Programmers generally prefer to combine byte-length operands or simply waste a byte of the stack rather than attempt to push a single register.

· Push the interrupt mask (I) register (8085 only)

```
RIM               ;MOVE I TO A
PUSH PSW          ;PUSH I AND F INTO STACK
INX  SP           ;DROP F FROM STACK
```

This sequence allows you to save the interrupt enable flag (bit 3 of register I) for later restoration.

· Push memory location ADDR

```
LDA  ADDR         ;OBTAIN DATA FROM MEMORY
PUSH PSW          ;SAVE DATA, FLAGS
INX  SP           ;THEN DROP THE FLAGS
```

ADDR could be an external priority or control register (or a copy of an external register).

· Push memory locations ADDR and ADDR+1

```
LHLD ADDR         ;PUSH MEMORY LOCATIONS
PUSH H
```

3. Pop (Pull) Instructions.

· Pop a single register (A, B, D, or H), assuming that it has been saved as shown previously

```
DCX  SP           ;BACK UP THE STACK POINTER
POP  rp           ;POP THE DOUBLE REGISTER
```

This sequence changes the less significant half of the register pair unpredictably.

· Pop the interrupt mask (I) register (8085 only), assuming that it has been saved at the top of the stack

```
DCX  SP          ;BACK UP THE STACK POINTER
POP  PSW         ;POP A AND FLAGS
```

A SIM instruction at this point will not restore the I register, since that register as written differs from the one RIM reads. The value popped from the stack can be used as follows:

Restore the interrupt masks (bits 0, 1, and 2).

```
ANI  00000111B ;MASK OFF THE INTERRUPT MASK BITS
ORI  00001000B ;SET INTERRUPT MASK ENABLE
SIM            ;RESTORE INTERRUPT MASK BITS
```

Note that bit 3 (the mask set enable) must be set to change the interrupt masks.

Enable interrupts if they were previously enabled (bit 3 = 1).

```
       ANI  00001000B ;WERE INTERRUPTS PREVIOUSLY ENABLED?
       JZ   DONE
       EI              ;YES, REENABLE THEM
DONE:  NOP
```

· Pop memory location ADDR, assuming that it has been saved at the top of the stack

```
DCX  SP          ;BACK UP THE STACK POINTER
POP  PSW         ;POP ACCUMULATOR AND FLAGS
STA  ADDR        ;RESTORE DATA TO MEMORY
```

This sequence changes the flags unpredictably. ADDR could be an external priority or control register (or a copy of an external register).

· Pop memory locations ADDR and ADDR+1, assuming that they were saved as shown previously

```
POP  H           ;POP MEMORY LOCATIONS
SHLD ADDR
```

Sometimes it is necessary to push and pop key memory locations and other values besides the registers.

Wait Instructions

The simplest way to implement a wait on the 8080 or 8085 microprocessor is to use an endless loop such as

```
HERE:   JMP  HERE       ;WAIT IN PLACE
```

The processor will execute JMP until it is interrupted and will resume executing it after the interrupt service routine returns control. On the 8080, interrupts must have been enabled with EI or the processor will execute the loop endlessly. On the 8085 a TRAP (non-maskable) interrupt will be recognized without any enabling.

Trap Instructions

The common 8080/8085 traps (also called breaks or software interrupts) are the RST instructions (see the list in Table 1-10). RST n calls the subroutine starting at address 8 × n. Thus, for example, RST 0 transfers control to memory address 0000 after saving the program counter in the stack. Similarly, RST 6 transfers control to memory address 0030_{16} after saving the program counter in the stack. The interrupt system generally uses the RST instructions, but the programmer can dedicate unused ones to common subroutines, error traps, or supervisor entry points. RST then serves as a 1-byte call.

Adjust Instructions

1. Branch if accumulator does not contain a valid decimal (BCD) number.

```
MOV   reg,A       ;SAVE A
ADI   0           ;DECIMAL ADJUST A AFTER ADDING ZERO
DAA
CMP   reg         ;DID DECIMAL ADJUST CHANGE A?
JNZ   DEST        ;YES, THEN A COULD NOT HAVE BEEN VALID
```

2. Decimal increment accumulator (add 1 to A in decimal).

```
ADI   1
DAA
```

3. Decimal decrement accumulator (subtract 1 from A in decimal).

```
ADI   99H
DAA
```

The Carry flag is an inverted borrow.

Enable Interrupt Instructions

1. Enable interrupts if bit 3 of saved I register is 1 (8085 only).

```
        POP   PSW        ;RESTORE SAVED I REGISTER
        ANI   00001000B  ;WERE INTERRUPTS ENABLED?
        JZ    DONE
        EI               ;YES, REENABLE THEM
DONE:   NOP
```

This sequence allows interrupts to be reenabled after the processor has executed a sequence during which they had to be disabled. The problem here is to avoid accidentally enabling interrupts at the end when they were not enabled originally.

One problem in programming 8080-based interrupt systems is that the 8080 lacks a readable interrupt enable flag.[9] The programmer can solve this problem by creating an Interrupt Enable flag in a RAM location. If this location is called IFLAG, the sequences

```
DI                          ;DISABLE INTERRUPTS
LXI    H,IFLAG              ;AND CLEAR INTERRUPT ENABLE IN RAM
MVI    M,O
```

and

```
LXI    H,IFLAG              ;SET INTERRUPT ENABLE IN RAM
MVI    M,1
EI                          ;AND ENABLE INTERRUPTS
```

must be used instead of the normal DI and EI, respectively. Now IFLAG can be used to determine whether interrupts are currently enabled or disabled. A routine that must run with interrupts disabled (but can be entered with interrupts enabled or disabled) must save IFLAG and disable the interrupts initially, restore IFLAG afterward, and reenable the interrupts if IFLAG shows that they were enabled previously. Note that IFLAG is set and cleared while the interrupts are disabled.

2. Unmask (allow) interrupts RST 5.5, RST 6.5, and RST 7.5—8085 only.

· Unmask RST 5.5

```
MVI    A,00001110B         ;UNMASK RST 5.5
SIM
```

or

```
RIM                        ;READ OLD INTERRUPT MASKS
ANI    00000110B           ;RETAIN RST 6.5, RST 7.5
ORI    00001000B           ;SET MASK SET ENABLE
SIM                        ;UNMASK RST 5.5
```

The second sequence preserves the other interrupt masks.

· Unmask RST 6.5

```
MVI    A.00001101B         ;UNMASK RST 6.5
SIM
```

or

```
REM                        ;READ OLD INTERRUPT MASKS
ANI    00000101B           ;RETAIN RST 5.5, RST 7.5
ORI    00001000B           ;SET MASK SET ENABLE
SIM                        ;UNMASK RST 6.5
```

The second sequence preserves the other interrupt masks.

· Unmask RST 7.5

```
MVI    A,00001011B         ;UNMASK RST 7.5
SIM
```

or

```
RIM                        ;READ OLD INTERRUPT MASKS
ANI    00000011B           ;RETAIN RST 5.5, RST 6.5
ORI    00001000B           ;SET MASK SET ENABLE
SIM                        ;UNMASK RST 7.5
```

The second sequence preserves the other interrupt masks.

Disable Interrupt Instructions

1. Mask (disallow) interrupts RST 5.5, RST 6.5, and RST 7.5—8085 only.

· Mask RST 5.5

```
        MVI   A,00001111B    ;MASK RST 5.5
        SIM
```
or
```
        RIM                  ;READ OLD INTERRUPT MASKS
        ANI   00000111B      ;SEPARATE OUT MASK BITS
        ORI   00001001B      ;SET MASK SET ENABLE, RST 5.5
        SIM                  ;MASK RST 5.5
```

The second sequence preserves the other interrupt masks.

· Mask RST 6.5

```
        MVI   A,00001111B    ;MASK RST 6.5
        SIM
```
or
```
        RIM                  ;READ OLD INTERRUPT MASKS
        ANI   00000111B      ;SEPARATE OUT MASK BITS
        ORI   00001010B      ;SET MASK SET ENABLE, RST 6.5
        SIM                  ;MASK RST 6.5
```

The second sequence preserves the other interrupt masks.

· Mask RST 7.5

```
        MVI   A,00001111B    ;MASK RST 7.5
        SIM
```
or
```
        RIM                  ;READ OLD INTERRUPT MASKS
        ANI   00000111B      ;SEPARATE OUT MASK BITS
        ORI   00001100B      ;SET MASK SET ENABLE, RST 7.5
        SIM                  ;MASK RST 7.5
```

The second sequence preserves the other interrupt masks.

· Clear (reset) RST 7.5

```
        MVI   A,00010000B    ;RESET RST 7.5 FLIP-FLOP
```

A positive (rising) edge on RST 7.5 always sets the RST 7.5 flip-flop, even if the interrupt has been masked or disabled.

· Clear (reset) RST 7.5 if it is active (pending)

```
        RIM                  ;READ INTERRUPT MASKS
        ANI   01000000B      ;IS RST 7.5 PENDING?
        JZ    DONE
        MVI   A,00010000B    ;YES, RESET RST 7.5
        SIM
DONE:   NOP
```

RST 7.5 is reset by performing a SIM instruction with bit 4 of the accumulator set. Since bits 3 and 6 of the accumulator are both 0, this SIM does not affect the interrupt masks or the serial output (SOD).

Translate Instructions

1. Translate the accumulator into the corresponding entry in a table starting at the address in registers H and L.

```
MOV   E,A        ;EXTEND OPERAND TO 16-BIT INDEX
MVI   D,0
DAD   D          ;USE OPERAND TO ACCESS TABLE
MOV   A,M        ;REPLACE OPERAND WITH TABLE ENTRY
```

This procedure can be used to convert data from one code to another.

2. Translate the accumulator into the corresponding 16-bit entry in a table starting at the address in registers H and L. Place the entry in H and L.

```
XCHG             ;MOVE BASE ADDRESS TO DE
MOV   L,A        ;EXTEND OPERAND TO 16-BIT INDEX
MVI   H,0
DAD   H          ;DOUBLE INDEX FOR 2-BYTE ENTRIES
DAD   D          ;CALCULATE INDEXED ADDRESS
MOV   E,M        ;OBTAIN ENTRY
INX   H
MOV   D,M
XCHG             ;MOVE ENTRY TO HL
```

Using DAD H to double the operand allows it take on any 8-bit value (using ADD A would limit us to values below 128).

Miscellaneous Instructions

1. Allocate space on the stack; decrease the stack pointer to provide NUM empty locations at the top.

```
LXI   H,-NUM     ;ADD NUM BYTES TO TOP OF STACK
DAD   SP
SPHL             ;SP = SP - NUM
```

An alternative is a series of DCX SP instructions.

2. Deallocate space from the stack; increase the stack pointer to remove NUM temporary locations from the top.

```
LXI   H,NUM      ;REMOVE NUM BYTES FROM TOP OF STACK
DAD   SP
SPHL             ;SP = SP + NUM
```

An alternative is a series of INX SP instructions.

ADDITIONAL ADDRESSING MODES

· **Indirect Addressing.** Indirect addressing can be provided on the 8080 and 8085 processors by loading the indirect address into registers H and L with LHLD. Then addressing with register M provides the equivalent of indirect addressing. This is always a two-step process. Register pairs B and D can also be employed in the instructions LDAX and STAX.

Examples

1. Load the accumulator indirectly from the address in memory locations ADDR and ADDR+1.

```
        LHLD ADDR           ;FETCH INDIRECT ADDRESS
        MOV  A,M            ;FETCH DATA INDIRECTLY
```

2. Store the accumulator indirectly at the address in memory locations ADDR and ADDR+1.

```
        LHLD ADDR           ;FETCH INDIRECT ADDRESS
        MOV  M,A            ;STORE DATA INDIRECTLY
```

3. Load the accumulator indirectly from the address in registers H and L (that is, from the address stored starting at the address in H and L).

```
        MOV  E,M            ;FETCH INDIRECT ADDRESS
        INX  H
        MOV  D,M
        LDAX D             ;FETCH DATA INDIRECTLY
```

4. Store the accumulator indirectly at the address in registers H and L (that is, at the address stored starting at the address in H and L).

```
        MOV  E,M            ;FETCH INDIRECT ADDRESS
        INX  H
        MOV  D,M
        STAX D             ;STORE DATA INDIRECTLY
```

5. Jump indirectly to the address in memory locations ADDR and ADDR+1.

```
        LHLD ADDR           ;FETCH INDIRECT ADDRESS
        PCHL               ;AND JUMP TO IT
```

Indirection can be repeated indefinitely to produce multilevel indirect addressing. For example, the following routine uses the indirect address indirectly to load the accumulator.

```
        MOV  E,M            ;FETCH FIRST INDIRECT ADDRESS
        INX  H
        MOV  D,M
        XCHG
        MOV  E,M            ;USE INDIRECT ADDRESS INDIRECTLY
        INX  H
        MOV  D,M
        LDAX D             ;FETCH DATA INDIRECTLY
```

Indirect addresses should be stored in memory in the usual 8080/8085 format—that is, with the less significant byte first (at the lower address).

· **Indexed Addressing.** Indexed addressing can be provided by using DAD to add the base and the index. Obviously, the explicit addition requires extra execution time.

Examples

1. Load the accumulator from an indexed address obtained by adding the accumulator to a fixed base address.

```
LXI   D,BASE       ;GET BASE ADDRESS
MOV   L,A          ;EXTEND INDEX TO 16 BITS
MVI   H,0
DAD   D            ;CALCULATE INDEXED ADDRESS
MOV   A,M          ;FETCH DATA FROM INDEXED ADDRESS
```

2. Load the accumulator from an indexed address obtained by adding the accumulator to memory locations BASE and BASE+1.

```
LHLD  BASE         ;GET BASE ADDRESS
MOV   E,A          ;EXTEND INDEX TO 16 BITS
MVI   D,0
DAD   D            ;CALCULATE INDEXED ADDRESS
MOV   A,M          ;FETCH DATA FROM INDEXED ADDRESS
```

3. Load the accumulator from an indexed address obtained by adding memory locations INDEX and INDEX+1 to registers H and L.

```
XCHG               ;SAVE BASE IN DE
LHLD  INDEX        ;GET INDEX FROM MEMORY
DAD   D            ;CALCULATE INDEXED ADDRESS
MOV   A,M          ;FETCH DATA FROM INDEXED ADDRESS
```

4. Jump indexed to a jump instruction in a list. The index is in the accumulator and the base address of the list is in registers H and L.

```
MOV   B,A          ;TRIPLE INDEX FOR 3-BYTE JUMPS
ADD   A
ADD   B
MOV   C,A          ;EXTEND TRIPLED INDEX TO 16 BITS
MVI   B,0
DAD   B            ;CALCULATE INDEXED ADDRESS
PCHL               ;AND TRANSFER CONTROL THERE
```

The list would appear as follows, starting at address BASE:

```
BASE:   JMP   SUB0       ;JUMP TO SUBROUTINE 0
        JMP   SUB1       ;JUMP TO SUBROUTINE 1
        JMP   SUB2       ;JUMP TO SUBROUTINE 2
        ...
```

Since each JMP instruction occupies three bytes, we must multiply the index by 3 before adding it to the base address. If the list is more than 256 bytes long, we can use the following procedure to multiply the index by 3:

```
XCHG                    ;SAVE BASE IN DE
MOV   L,A               ;EXTEND INDEX TO 16 BITS
MVI   H,0
MOV   B,L               ;COPY INDEX INTO BC
MOV   C,H
DAD   H                 ;DOUBLE INDEX
DAD   B                 ;TRIPLE INDEX
DAD   D                 ;CALCULATE INDEXED ADDRESS
PCHL                    ; AND JUMP TO IT
```

· **Autopreincrementing.** In autopreincrementing, the address register is incremented automatically before it is used. Autopreincrementing can be provided on the 8080 or 8085 processor by incrementing a register pair before using it as an address.

Examples

1. Load the accumulator using autopreincrementing on registers H and L.

```
INX   H                 ;AUTOPREINCREMENT H AND L
MOV   A,M               ;FETCH DATA
```

2. Store the accumulator using autopreincrementing on registers D and E.

```
INX   D                 ;AUTOPREINCREMENT D AND E
STAX  D                 ;STORE DATA
```

3. Load registers D and E starting at the address 2 larger than the contents of registers H and L.

```
INX   H                 ;AUTOPREINCREMENT H AND L BY 2
INX   H
MOV   E,M               ;FETCH LSB
INX   H
MOV   D,M               ;FETCH MSB
```

Autoincrementing by 2 is essential in handling arrays of addresses or 16-bit data items.

4. Store the accumulator using autopreincrementing on memory locations ADDR and ADDR+1.

```
LHLD ADDR               ;AUTOPREINCREMENT INDIRECT ADDRESS
INX   H
MOV   M,A               ;STORE DATA
SHLD ADDR               ;UPDATE INDIRECT ADDRESS
```

Autopreincrementing can be combined with indirection. Here memory locations ADDR and ADDR+1 could point to the last occupied location in a buffer.

5. Transfer control to the address stored starting at an address 2 larger than the contents of memory locations NXTPGM and NXTPGM+1.

```
LHLD NXTPGM             ;GET POINTER
INX   H                 ;AUTOPREINCREMENT POINTER
INX   H
SHLD NXTPGM             ;UPDATE POINTER
MOV   E,M               ;FETCH STARTING ADDRESS USING POINTER
```

```
        INX   H
        MOV   D,M
        XCHG                ;AND TRANSFER CONTROL TO IT
        PCHL
```

Here NXTPGM and NXTPGM + 1 point to the starting address of the routine that the processor has just executed. Initially, NXTPGM and NXTPGM+1 would contain BASE − 2, where BASE is the starting address of a table of routines. A typical table would be

```
BASE:   DW    ROUT0         ;STARTING ADDRESS OF ROUTINE 0
        DW    ROUT1         ;STARTING ADDRESS OF ROUTINE 1
        DW    ROUT2         ;STARTING ADDRESS OF ROUTINE 2
        DW    ROUT3         ;STARTING ADDRESS OF ROUTINE 3
        ...
```

· **Autopostincrementing.** In autopostincrementing, the address register is incremented after it is used. Autopostincrementing can be provided on the 8080 or 8085 processor by incrementing a register pair after using it as an address. Note that the processor autopostincrements the stack pointer when it executes POP and RET.

Examples

1. Load the accumulator using autopostincrementing on registers H and L.

```
        MOV   A,M           ;FETCH DATA
        INX   H             ;AUTOPOSTINCREMENT H AND L
```

2. Store the accumulator using autopostincrementing on registers D and E.

```
        STAX  D             ;STORE DATA
        INX   D             ;AUTOPOSTINCREMENT D AND E
```

3. Load registers D and E starting at the address in registers H and L. Afterward, increment registers H and L by 2.

```
        MOV   E,M           ;FETCH LSB
        INX   H
        MOV   D,M           ;FETCH MSB
        INX   H
```

Autoincrementing by 2 is essential in handling arrays of addresses or 16-bit data items. Note that postincrementing is generally simpler and more natural than preincrementing.

4. Store the accumulator using autopostincrementing on memory locations ADDR and ADDR+1.

```
        LHLD  ADDR          ;FETCH INDIRECT ADDRESS
        MOV   M,A           ;STORE DATA
        INX   H             ;AUTOPOSTINCREMENT INDIRECT ADDRESS
        SHLD  ADDR
```

Autopostincrementing can be combined with indirection. Here memory locations ADDR and ADDR+1 could point to the next empty location in a buffer.

5. Transfer control to the address stored at the address in memory locations NXTPGM and NXTPGM+1. Then increment those locations by 2.

```
LHLD NXTPGM
MOV  E,M        ;FETCH STARTING ADDRESS USING POINTER
INX  H
MOV  D,M
INX  H          ;COMPLETE AUTOPOSTINCREMENT
SHLD NXTPGM
XCHG            ;TRANSFER CONTROL TO STARTING ADDRESS
PCHL
```

Here NXTPGM and NXTPGM+1 point to the starting address of the next routine the processor is to execute. Initially, NXTPGM and NXTPGM+1 would contain BASE, the starting address of a table of routines. A typical table would be

```
BASE:   DW   ROUTO    ;STARTING ADDRESS OF ROUTINE 0
        DW   ROUT1    ;STARTING ADDRESS OF ROUTINE 1
        DW   ROUT2    ;STARTING ADDRESS OF ROUTINE 2
        DW   ROUT3    ;STARTING ADDRESS OF ROUTINE 3
        ...
```

· **Autopredecrementing.** In autopredecrementing, the address register is decremented automatically before it is used. Autopredecrementing on the 8080 or 8085 processor can be provided by decrementing a register pair before using it as an address. Note that the processor autopredecrements the stack pointer when it executes PUSH and CALL.

Examples

1. Load the accumulator using autopredecrementing on registers H and L.

```
DCX  H          ;AUTOPREDECREMENT H AND L
MOV  A,M        ;FETCH DATA
```

2. Store the accumulator using autopredecrementing on registers D and E.

```
DCX  D          ;AUTOPREDECREMENT D AND E
STAX D          ;STORE DATA
```

3. Load registers D and E starting at the address 2 smaller than the contents of registers H and L.

```
DCX  H          ;FETCH MSB
MOV  D,M
DCX  H          ;FETCH LSB
MOV  E,M
```

Autodecrementing by 2 is essential in handling arrays of addresses or 16-bit data items. Note that predecrementing is generally simpler and more natural than postdecrementing.

4. Store the accumulator using autopredecrementing on memory locations ADDR and ADDR+1.

```
LHLD  ADDR        ;AUTOPREDECREMENT INDIRECT ADDRESS
DCX   H
MOV   M,A         ;STORE DATA
SHLD  ADDR        ;UPDATE INDIRECT ADDRESS
```

Autopredecrementing can be combined with indirection. Here memory locations ADDR and ADDR+1 could point to the last occupied location in a stack.

5. Transfer control to the address stored at an address 2 smaller than the contents of memory locations NXTPGM and NXTPGM+1.

```
LHLD  NXTPGM      ;FETCH STARTING ADDRESS USING POINTER
DCX   H
MOV   D,M
DCX   H
MOV   E,M
SHLD  NXTPGM      ;STORE AUTOPREDECREMENTED POINTER
XCHG              ;TRANSFER CONTROL TO STARTING ADDRESS
PCHL
```

Here NXTPGM and NXTPGM+1 point to the starting address of the most recently executed routine in a list. Initially, NXTPGM and NXTPGM+1 would contain FINAL+2, where FINAL is the address of the last entry in a table of routines. A typical table would be

```
        DW    ROUT0     ;STARTING ADDRESS OF ROUTINE 0
        DW    ROUT1     ;STARTING ADDRESS OF ROUTINE 1
        .
        .
        .
FINAL:  DW    ROUTL     ;STARTING ADDRESS OF LAST ROUTINE
```

Work through the table backward. This approach is useful in evaluating mathematical formulas entered from a keyboard. If, for example, the computer must evaluate the expression

```
Z = LN (A x SIN (B x EXP (C x Y)))
```

it must work backward. That is, the order of operations is

1. Calculate $C \times Y$
2. Calculate $EXP (C \times Y)$
3. Calculate $B \times EXP (C \times Y)$
4. Calculate $A \times SIN (B \times EXP (C \times Y))$
5. Calculate $LN (A \times SIN (B \times EXP (C \times Y)))$.

Working backward is convenient when the computer cannot start a task until it has received an entire line or command. It must then work back to the beginning.

· **Autopostdecrementing.** In autopostdecrementing, the address register is decremented automatically after it is used. Autopostdecrementing on the 8080 or 8085 processor can be implemented by decrementing a register pair after using it as an address.

Examples

1. Load the accumulator using autopostdecrementing on registers H and L.

```
MOV   A,M          ;FETCH DATA
DCX   H            ;AUTOPOSTDECREMENT H AND L
```

2. Store the accumulator using autopostdecrementing on registers D and E.

```
STAX  D            ;STORE DATA
DCX   D            ;AUTOPOSTDECREMENT D AND E
```

3. Load registers D and E starting at the address in H and L. Afterward, decrement H and L by 2.

```
INX   H            ;FETCH MSB
MOV   D,M
DCX   H            ;FETCH LSB
MOV   E,M
DCX   H            ;AUTOPOSTDECREMENT HL BY 2
DCX   H
```

Autodecrementing by 2 is essential in handling arrays of addresses or 16-bit data items.

4. Store the accumulator using autopostdecrementing on memory locations ADDR and ADDR+1.

```
LHLD ADDR          ;FETCH INDIRECT ADDRESS
MOV   M,A          ;STORE DATA
DCX   H            ;AUTOPOSTDECREMENT INDIRECT ADDRESS
SHLD ADDR
```

Autopostdecrementing can be combined with indirection. Here memory locations ADDR and ADDR+1 could point to the next empty location in a stack.

5. Transfer control to the address stored at the address in memory locations NXTPGM and NXTPGM+1. Then decrement those locations by 2.

```
LHLD NXTPGM        ;FETCH POINTER
INX   H            ;FETCH STARTING ADDRESS
MOV   D,M
DCX   H
MOV   E,M
DCX   H            ;AUTOPOSTDECREMENT POINTER
DCX   H
SHLD NXTPGM
XCHG               ;JUMP TO STARTING ADDRESS
PCHL
```

Here NXTPGM and NXTPGM+1 point to the address of the next routine the processor is to execute. Initially, NXTPGM and NXTPGM+1 would contain FINAL, the address of the last entry in a table of routines. A typical table would be

```
       DW    ROUT0     ;STARTING ADDRESS OF ROUTINE 0
       DW    ROUT1     ;STARTING ADDRESS OF ROUTINE 1
       .
       .
       .
FINAL: DW    ROUTL     ;STARTING ADDRESS OF LAST ROUTINE
```

Here the computer works through the table backward. This approach is useful in interpreting commands entered in the normal left-to-right manner from a keyboard. For example, assume that the operator of a process controller enters the command SET TEMP (POSITION 2) = MEAN (TEMP (POSITION 1), TEMP (POSITION 3)). The controller program must execute the command working right to left and starting from inside the inner parentheses as follows:

· Determine the index corresponding to POSITION 1.

· Obtain TEMP (POSITION 1) from a table of temperature readings.

· Determine the index corresponding to POSITION 3.

· Obtain TEMP (POSITION 3) from a table of temperature readings.

· Evaluate MEAN (TEMP (POSITION 1), TEMP (POSITION 3)) by executing the MEAN program with the two entries as parameters.

· Determine the index corresponding to POSITION 2.

· Execute the SET function, which presumably involves setting controls and parameters to achieve the desired value of TEMP(POSITION 2).

The operator enters the command working left to right and from outer parentheses to inner parentheses. The computer, on the other hand, must execute it inside out (starting from the inner parenthesis) and right to left. Autodecrementing is obviously a handy way to implement this reversal.

· **Indirect preindexed addressing (preindexing).** In preindexing, the processor must first calculate an indexed address and then use that address indirectly. Since the indexed table must consist of 2-byte indirect addresses, the indexing must involve a multiplication by 2.

Examples

· Load the accumulator using preindexing. The base address is in registers H and L and the index is in the accumulator.

```
ADD   A         ;DOUBLE INDEX FOR 2-BYTE ENTRIES
MOV   E,A       ;EXTEND INDEX TO 16 BITS
MVI   D,O
DAD   D         ;CALCULATE INDEXED ADDRESS
MOV   E,M       ;OBTAIN INDIRECT ADDRESS
INX   H
MOV   D,M
LDAX  D         ;OBTAIN DATA INDIRECTLY
```

· Store the accumulator using preindexing. The base address is in memory locations ADDR and ADDR+1 and the index is in memory location INDEX.

```
LHLD ADDR        ;FETCH BASE ADDRESS
MOV  B,A         ;SAVE DATA
LDA  INDEX       ;FETCH INDEX
ADD  A           ;DOUBLE INDEX FOR 2-BYTE ENTRIES
MOV  E,A         ;EXTEND INDEX TO 16 BITS
MVI  D,O
DAD  D           ;CALCULATE INDEXED ADDRESS
MOV  E,M         ;OBTAIN INDIRECT ADDRESS
INX  H
MOV  D,M
XCHG             ;STORE DATA INDIRECTLY
MOV  M,B
```

· Transfer control (jump) to the address obtained indirectly from the table starting at address JTAB. The index is in the accumulator.

```
ADD  A           ;DOUBLE INDEX FOR 2-BYTE ENTRIES
MOV  E,A         ;EXTEND INDEX TO 16 BITS
MVI  D,O
LXI  H,JTAB      ;GET BASE ADDRESS
DAD  D           ;CALCULATE INDEXED ADDRESS
MOV  E,M         ;OBTAIN INDIRECT ADDRESS
INX  H
MOV  D,M
XCHG             ;TRANSFER CONTROL TO INDIRECT ADDRESS
PCHL
```

The table starting at address JTAB would appear as follows:

```
JTAB:  DW    ROUTO     ;STARTING ADDRESS OF ROUTINE 0
       DW    ROUT1     ;STARTING ADDRESS OF ROUTINE 1
       DW    ROUT2     ;STARTING ADDRESS OF ROUTINE 2
       ...
```

· **Indirect postindexed addressing (postindexing).** In postindexing, the processor must first obtain an indirect address and then apply indexing with that address as the base. Thus, the indirect address tells the processor where the table or array starts.

Examples

· Load the accumulator using postindexing. The base address is in memory locations ADDR and ADDR+1 and the index is in the accumulator.

```
LHLD ADDR        ;OBTAIN BASE ADDRESS INDIRECTLY
MOV  E,A         ;EXTEND INDEX TO 16 BITS
MVI  D,O
DAD  D           ;CALCULATE INDEXED ADDRESS
MOV  A,M
```

· Store the accumulator using postindexing. The base address is in memory locations ADDR and ADDR+1 and the index is in memory location INDEX.

```
LHLD ADDR        ;OBTAIN BASE ADDRESS INDIRECTLY
MOV  B,A         ;SAVE DATA
LDA  INDEX       ;OBTAIN INDEX
MOV  E,A         ;EXTEND INDEX TO 16 BITS
```

```
MVI    D,0
DAD    D          ;CALCULATE INDEXED ADDRESS
MOV    M,B        ;STORE DATA
```

By changing the contents of memory locations ADDR and ADDR+1, this routine can be made to operate on many different arrays.

· Transfer control (jump) to the address obtained by indexing from the base address in memory locations ADDR and ADDR+1. The index is in the accumulator.

```
MOV    B,A        ;TRIPLE INDEX FOR 3-BYTE JUMPS
ADD    A
ADD    B
MOV    E,A        ;EXTEND INDEX TO 16 BITS
MVI    D,0
LHLD   ADDR       ;OBTAIN BASE ADDRESS INDIRECTLY
DAD    D          ;CALCULATE INDEXED ADDRESS
PCHL              ;AND TRANSFER CONTROL TO IT
```

The table contains 3-byte JMP instructions; a typical example is

```
BASE:  JMP    ROUT0      ;TRANSFER TO ROUTINE 0
       JMP    ROUT1      ;TRANSFER TO ROUTINE 1
       JMP    ROUT2      ;TRANSFER TO ROUTINE 2
       . . .
```

The address BASE must be placed in memory locations ADDR and ADDR+1.

REFERENCES

1. Fischer, W.P., "Microprocessor Assembly Language Draft Standard," *IEEE Computer,* December 1979, pp. 96-109. *See also* Distler, R.J. and M.A. Shaver, "Trial Implementation Reveals Errors in IEEE Standard," *IEEE Computer,* July 1982, pp. 76-77.

2. Osborne, A., *An Introduction to Microcomputers. Volume 1: Basic Concepts,* 2nd ed., Berkeley, Calif.: Osborne/McGraw-Hill, 1980.

3. Leventhal, L.A., *Z80 Assembly Language Programming.* Berkeley, Calif.: Osborne/McGraw-Hill, 1979, pp. 3-164 through 3-169.

4. Fischer, *loc. cit.*

5. Taylor, C.L., "Data-Block Transfer Program Is Efficient and Flexible," *Electronics,* June 21, 1979, p. 147.

6. Leventhal, L.A., "Take Advantage of 8080 and 6800 Data-Manipulation Capabilities," *Electronic Design,* April 12, 1977, pp. 90-97.

7. Caplan, G., "Special Techniques Handle Critical Sections," *EDN,* March 5, 1980, p. 90.

8. *Ibid.*

9. *Ibid.*

Chapter 3 **Common Programming Errors**

This chapter describes common errors in 8080 and 8085 assembly language programs. The final section describes common errors in input/output drivers and interrupt service routines. The chapter's aims are the following:

· To warn programmers of potential trouble spots and sources of confusion.

· To describe likely causes of programming errors.

· To emphasize the techniques and warnings presented in Chapters 1 and 2.

· To inform maintenance programmers of likely places to look for errors and misinterpretations.

· To provide the beginner with a starting point in the difficult process of locating and correcting errors.

Of course, no list of errors can be complete. The most common mistakes have been emphasized, but the infrequent or subtle errors that frustrate even the experienced programmer have not been described. However, most errors are remarkably obvious once uncovered, and this discussion should help the reader debug most programs.

CATEGORIZATION OF PROGRAMMING ERRORS

Common 8080/8085 programming errors can be divided into the following categories:

· Reversing the order of operands or parts of operands. Typical errors include reversing source and destination in move instructions, inverting the format in which 16-bit quantities are stored, and inverting the direction of subtractions or comparisons.

· Using the flags improperly. Typical errors include using the wrong flag (such as Sign instead of Carry), branching after instructions that do not affect a particular flag inverting the branch conditions (particularly when the Zero flag is involved), branching incorrectly in equality cases, and changing a flag accidentally before branching.

· Confusing registers and register pairs. A typical error is operating on a register (B, D, or H) instead of on the similarly named register pair.

· Confusing addresses and data. Typical errors include using immediate addressing instead of direct addressing, or vice versa, and confusing registers with the memory locations addressed via register pairs.

· Using the wrong formats. Typical errors include using BCD (decimal) instead of binary, or vice versa, and using binary or hexadecimal instead of ASCII.

· Handling arrays incorrectly. The usual problem is going outside the array's boundaries.

· Ignoring implicit effects. Typical errors include using the accumulator, a register pair, the stack pointer, flags, or memory locations without considering the effects of intervening instructions. Most errors arise from instructions that have unexpected, implicit, or indirect effects.

· Failing to provide proper initial conditions for particular routines or for the microcomputer as a whole. Most routines require the initialization of counters, indirect addresses, base addresses, registers, flags, and temporary storage locations. The microcomputer as a whole requires the initialization of all global RAM addresses (note particularly indirect addresses and counters).

· Organizing the program incorrectly. Typical errors include skipping or repeating initialization routines, failing to update counters or address registers, and forgetting to save intermediate or final results.

A common source of errors that is beyond the scope of this discussion is conflict between the user program and systems programs. A simple example of conflict is for a user program to save data in memory locations that a systems program needs for storage. The user program data thus changes whenever the systems program is executed.

More complex sources of conflict include the interrupt system, input/output ports, the stack, and the flags. After all, the systems programs must employ the same resources as user programs. Systems programs generally attempt to save and restore the user's environment, but they often have subtle or unexpected effects. Making an operating system transparent to the user is a problem comparable to devising a set of regulations, laws, or tax codes that have no loopholes or side effects.

REVERSING THE ORDER OF OPERANDS

The following instructions and conventions are the most common sources of errors:

· MOV R1,R2 moves the contents of register R2 to register R1. Reversing the source and the destination in MOV instructions is probably the single most common error in 8080/8085 assembly language programs. The best way to avoid this problem is to use the operator notation described by Duncan.[1]

· 16-bit addresses and data items are assumed to be stored with their less significant bytes first (that is, at the lower address). This convention becomes particularly confusing in instructions that load or store register pairs or use the stack.

· CMP REG subtracts its operand from the accumulator, not the other way around. Similarly, CPI DATA subtracts the value DATA from the accumulator.

Examples

1. MOV A,B
This instruction loads the accumulator from register B. Since it does not change B, the instruction acts like *copy B into A*.

2. MOV M,A
This instruction stores the accumulator at the memory address in registers H and L. Since it does not change the accumulator, the instruction acts like *copy A into memory addressed by H and L*.

3. LDA 2040H
The address 2040_{16} occupies the two bytes of program memory immediately following the operation code; 40_{16} comes first and 20_{16} last. This order is particularly important to remember if an address is entered or changed at the object code level during debugging.

4. PUSH H
This instruction stores registers H and L in memory at the addresses immediately below the initial contents of the stack pointer (that is, at addresses S−1 and S−2 if the stack pointer initially contains S). Register H is stored at address S−1 and L at address S−2 in the usual upside-down format.

5. LHLD 2050H
This instruction loads register L from memory address 2050_{16} and H from 2051_{16}.

6. SHLD 3600H
This instruction stores register L in memory address 3600_{16} and H in address 3601_{16}.

7. CMP B

This instruction sets the flags as if register B had been subtracted from the accumulator.

8. CPI 25H

This instruction sets the flags as if the number 25_{16} had been subtracted from the accumulator.

USING THE FLAGS INCORRECTLY

8080/8085 instructions have widely varying effects on the flags. There are few general rules, and even instructions with similar meanings may operate differently. Cases that require special caution are

· Data transfer instructions such as MOV, MVI, LDA, STA, LDAX, LXI, LHLD, SHLD, XCHG, and XTHL do not affect any flags. An otherwise superfluous arithmetic or logical instruction (such as ANA A, DCR, INR, or ORA A) may be needed to set the flags.

· The Carry flag acts as a borrow after a CMP, CPI, SBC, SBI, SUB, or SUI instruction; that is, the Carry is set if the 8-bit unsigned subtraction would require a borrow. If, however, the programmer implements subtraction by adding the two's or ten's complement of the subtrahend, the Carry is an inverted borrow; that is, the Carry is cleared if the 8-bit unsigned subtraction would require a borrow.

· After a comparison (CMP or CPI), the Zero flag indicates whether the operands are equal; it is set if the operands are equal and cleared if they are not. There is an obvious source of confusion here—JZ means *jump if the result is 0*, that is, *jump if the Zero flag is 1*. JNZ, of course, has the opposite meaning.

· In comparing unsigned numbers, the Carry flag indicates which number is larger. CMP or CPI sets Carry if the accumulator is less than the other operand and clears it if the accumulator is greater than or equal to the other operand. Note that the Carry is cleared if the operands are equal. If this division of cases (*greater than or equal* and *less than*) is not what you want (that is, you want the division to be *greater than* and *less than or equal*), you can reverse the subtraction, subtract 1 from the accumulator, or add 1 to the other operand.

· In comparing signed numbers, the Sign flag indicates which operand is larger unless two's complement overflow occurs (see Chapter 1). CMP or CPI sets the Sign flag if the accumulator is less than the other operand and clears it if the accumulator is greater than or equal to the other operand. Note that comparing equal operands clears the Sign flag. As with unsigned numbers, the equality case can be handled in the opposite way by adjusting either operand or reversing the subtraction.

· All logical instructions except CMA clear the Carry flag. ANA A or ORA A is, in fact, a quick, simple way to clear Carry without affecting any registers. CMA affects no flags at all (XRI 0FFH is an equivalent instruction that affects the flags).

· The common way to execute code only if a condition is true is to branch around it if the condition is false. For example, to increment register B if Carry is 1, use the sequence

```
        JNC   NEXT
        INR   B
NEXT:   NOP
```

The branch occurs if Carry is 0.

· The 16-bit arithmetic instructions have little effect on the flags. INX and DCX do not affect any flags at all; DAD affects only the Carry flag. The limited effects on the flags show that these instructions are intended for address arithmetic, not for the processing of 16-bit data.

· INR and DCR do not affect the Carry flag. This allows them to be used for counting in loops that perform multiple-byte arithmetic (the Carry is needed to transfer carries or borrows between bytes). INR and DCR do, however, affect the Zero and Sign flags, and those effects can be used to determine whether a carry or borrow occurred.

· Shift instructions (RAL, RAR, RRC, RLC) affect only the Carry flag.

· Special-purpose arithmetic and logical instructions such as ADD A (logical left shift accumulator), ADC A (rotate left accumulator), SUB A (clear accumulator), and ANA A or ORA A (test accumulator) affect all the flags.

· PUSH and POP instructions do not affect the flags, except for POP PSW, which changes all the flags. Remember, the Processor Status Word (PSW) consists of the accumulator (MSB) and the flags (LSB).

Examples

1. The sequence

```
        LDA   2040H
        JZ    DONE
```

has unpredictable results, since LDA does not affect the flags. To produce a jump if memory location 2040_{16} contains 0, use

```
        LDA   2040H
        ANA   A              ;TEST ACCUMULATOR
        JZ    DONE
```

ORA A may be used instead of ANA A.

2. The sequence

```
MOV   A,E
JP    DEST
```

has unpredictable results, since MOV does not affect the flags. Either of the following sequences forces a branch if register E is positive:

```
MOV   A,E
ANA   A
JP    DEST
```

or

```
SUB   A
ORA   E
JP    DEST
```

3. The instruction CPI 25H sets the Carry flag as follows:

Carry = 1 if the contents of A are between 00 and 24_{16}.

Carry = 0 if the contents of A are between 25_{16} and FF_{16}.

The Carry flag is set if A contains an unsigned number less than the other operand and cleared if A contains an unsigned number greater than or equal to the other operand.

If you want to set Carry when the accumulator contains 25_{16}, use CPI 26H instead of CPI 25H. This results in

```
CPI   25H
JC    LESS      ;BRANCH IF (A) LESS THAN 25
```

or

```
CPI   26H
JC    LESSEQ    ;BRANCH IF (A) 25 OR LESS
```

4. The sequence

```
RAL
JP    DONE
```

has unpredictable results, since RAL does not affect the Sign flag. The correct sequence (producing a circular shift that affects the flags) is

```
ADC   A         ;SHIFT CIRCULAR, SETTING FLAGS
JP    DONE
```

Of course, one can also use the somewhat slower

```
RAL
RAL
JC    DONE
```

5. The sequence

```
INR   B
JC    OVRFLW
```

has unpredictable results, since INR does not affect the Carry flag. The correct sequence is

```
INR   B
JZ    OVRFLW
```

since INR does affect the Zero flag.

6. The sequence

```
DCR   B
JC    OVRFLW
```

has unpredictable results, since DCR does not affect the Carry flag. If B cannot contain a number larger than 80_{16} (unsigned), use

```
DCR   B
JM    OVRFLW
```

since DCR does affect the Sign flag. Note, however, that an erroneous branch will occur if B initially contains 81_{16}.

A longer but more general sequence is

```
INR   B               ;TEST REGISTER B
DCR   B
JZ    OVRFLW          ;BRANCH IF B CONTAINS ZERO
DCR   B
```

Note that register B will contain 0 (not FF_{16}) if the program branches to address OVRFLW.

7. The sequence

```
DCX   B
JNZ   LOOP
```

has unpredictable results, since DCX does not affect any flags. The correct sequence for decrementing and testing a 16-bit counter in register pair B is

```
DCX   B
MOV   A,C             ;CHECK IF BC HAS ANY 1 BITS
ORA   B
JNZ   LOOP            ;BC CANNOT BE ZERO IF ANY BITS ARE 1
```

This sequence affects the accumulator and all the flags, including Carry (which ORA clears).

8. ANA A or ORA A clears Carry without affecting any registers. To clear Carry without affecting the other flags, use the sequence

```
STC                  ;FIRST SET THE CARRY FLAG
CMC                  ;THEN CLEAR IT BY COMPLEMENTING
```

9. SUB A or XRA A clears the accumulator, the Carry flag, and the Sign flag (and sets the Zero flag). To clear the accumulator without affecting the flags, use MVI A,0.

10. The sequence

```
LXI   D,-VAL16
DAD   D
JZ    BNDRY
```

has unpredictable results, since DAD does not affect the Zero flag. To force a branch if H and L contain VAL16, test H and L explicitly as follows:

```
LXI   D,-VAL16
DAD   D
MOV   A,H          ;TEST H AND L FOR ZERO
ORA   L
JZ    BNDRY
```

CONFUSING REGISTERS AND REGISTER PAIRS

The rules to remember are

· MOV, LDAX, STAX, and MVI affect single registers.

· LHLD, LXI, POP, PUSH, XCHG, and XTHL affect register pairs.

· Register M refers to the byte of memory located at the address in registers H and L. It does not refer to either register H or register L by itself.

Typical errors are using MOV A,H instead of MOV A,M or vice versa, using LDAX instead of MOV, and using MVI instead of LXI or vice versa. The use of register pairs to hold addresses means that certain transfers are uncommon. For example, MOV L,M would load register L from the address in H and L; H and L would then contain one byte of an address (in H) and one byte of data (in L). While this is legal, it is seldom useful.

Examples

1. MOV A,H
This instruction moves register H to the accumulator. It does not change register H or any memory location.

2. LDAX B
This instruction loads the accumulator from the memory address in registers B and C. It does not affect either register B or register C.

3. MVI H,0
This instruction places 0 in register H. It does not affect memory.

4. MOV M,A
This instruction stores the accumulator in the memory location addressed by regis-

ters H and L. It does not affect either H or L. A sequence that loads H and L with an address indirectly is

```
MOV   E,M        ;GET LSB OF INDIRECT ADDRESS
INX   H
MOV   D,M        ;GET MSB OF INDIRECT ADDRESS
XCHG             ;PUT INDIRECT ADDRESS IN HL
```

To employ only a single temporary register (the accumulator), load the more significant byte directly into H as follows:

```
MOV   A,M        ;GET LSB OF INDIRECT ADDRESS
INX   H
MOV   H,M        ;GET MSB OF INDIRECT ADDRESS
MOV   L,A        ;MOVE LSB OF ADDRESS TO L
```

This takes the same number of clock cycles as the previous sequence, but uses A instead of D and E for temporary storage.

5. LXI H,2050H

This instruction loads 2050_{16} into register pair HL (20_{16} into H and 50_{16} into L).

6. ADD M

This instruction adds the memory byte addressed via registers H and L to the accumulator. It does not affect either H or L.

7. DAD H

This instruction adds register pair H to itself, thus shifting H and L left one bit logically. It does not affect the accumulator or access data from memory.

CONFUSING ADDRESSES AND DATA

The rules to remember are

· The instructions LDA, STA, LHLD, JMP, and CALL require an address as an operand.

· The instructions MVI and LXI require data.

The addressing terminology for jumps and calls is somewhat confusing. Although they are said to use direct addressing, they treat their operands more as LXI does than as LHLD does. For example, JMP 2040H loads 2040_{16} into the program counter, much as LXI H,2040H loads 2040_{16} into register pair H. LHLD 2040H loads the contents of memory locations 2040_{16} and 2041_{16} into register pair H.

Examples

1. MVI A,40H loads the number 40_{16} into the accumulator. LDA 40H loads the contents of memory location 0040_{16} into the accumulator.

2. LXI H,0C00H loads $0C00_{16}$ into registers H and L ($0C_{16}$ into H and 00_{16} into L). LHLD 0C00H loads the contents of memory locations $0C00_{16}$ and $0C01_{16}$ into register pair H (the contents of $0C00_{16}$ into L and the contents of $0C01_{16}$ into H).

Confusing addresses and their contents is a common error in handling data structures. For example, the queue of tasks to be executed by a piece of test equipment might consist of a block of information for each task. That block might contain the

· Starting address of the test routine

· Number of seconds for which the test is to run

· Address in which the result is to be saved

· Upper and lower thresholds against which the result is to be compared

· Base address of the next block in the queue.

Thus, the block contains data, direct addresses, and indirect addresses. Typical errors that a programmer could make are

· Transferring control to the memory locations containing the starting address of the test routine, rather than to the actual starting address.

· Storing the result in the block rather than at the address specified in the block.

· Using the thresholds as an address rather than as data.

· Assuming that the next block starts in the current block, rather than at the base address given in the current block.

Jump tables are another common source of errors. The following are alternative implementations:

· Form a table of jump instructions and transfer control to the correct element (for example, to the third jump instruction).

· Form a table of destination addresses and transfer control to the contents of the correct element (for example, to the address in the third element).

Problems will surely occur if the processor uses jump instructions as addresses or vice versa.

FORMAT ERRORS

The rules to remember for the standard 8080/8085 assembler are

· An H at the end of a number indicates hexadecimal and a B indicates binary.

· The default mode for numbers is decimal. That is, the assembler assumes all numbers to be decimal unless they are specifically marked otherwise.

· A hexadecimal number that starts with a letter digit (A, B, C, D, E, or F) must be preceded by 0 (for example, 0CFH instead of CFH) for the assembler to interpret it correctly. Of course, the leading 0 does not affect the value of the number.

· All arithmetic and logical operations are binary, except DAA, which corrects the result of an 8-bit binary addition to the proper BCD value.

Beware of the following common errors:

· Omitting the H from a hexadecimal operand. The assembler will assume it to be decimal if it contains no letter digits and a name if it starts with a letter. The assembler will indicate an error only if it cannot interpret the operand as either a decimal number or a name.

· Omitting the B from a binary operand. The assembler will assume it to be decimal.

· Confusing decimal (BCD) representations with binary representations. Remember, 10 is not an integral power of 2, so the binary and BCD representations are not the same beyond 9. BCD constants must be designated as hexadecimal numbers, not as decimal numbers.

· Confusing binary or decimal representations with ASCII representations. An ASCII input device produces ASCII characters and an ASCII output device responds to ASCII characters.

Examples

1. LDA 2000
This instruction loads the accumulator from memory address 2000_{10} ($07D0_{16}$), not address 2000_{16}. The assembler will not indicate an error, since 2000 is a valid decimal number.

2. ANI 00000011
This instruction logically ANDs the accumulator with the decimal number 11 (1011_2), not with the binary number 11 (3_{10}). The assembler will not indicate an error, since 00000011 is a valid decimal number despite its unusual form.

3. ADI 40
This instruction adds the number 40_{10} to the accumulator. Note that 40_{10} is not the same as BCD 40, which is 40_{16}; $40_{10} = 28_{16}$. The assembler will not indicate an error, since 40 is a valid decimal number.

4. MVI A,3
This instruction loads the accumulator with the number 3. If this value is now sent to an ASCII output device, the device will respond as if it had received the character ETX (03_{16}), not the character 3 (33_{16}). The correct version is

```
MVI   A,'3'      ;GET AN ASCII 3
```

5. If memory location 2040_{16} contains a single decimal digit, the sequence

```
LDA   2040H
OUT   DEVCE
```

will not print that digit on an ASCII output device. The correct sequence is

```
LDA   2040H    ;GET DECIMAL DIGIT
ADI   '0'      ;ADJUST TO ASCII
OUT   DEVCE
```

6. If input port INDEV contains a single ASCII decimal digit, the sequence

```
IN    INDEV
STA   2040H
```

will not store the actual digit in memory location 2040_{16}. Instead, it will store the ASCII version, which is the actual digit plus 30_{16}. The correct sequence is

```
IN    INDEV    ;GET ASCII DIGIT
SUI   '0'      ;ADJUST TO DECIMAL
STA   2040H
```

Performing decimal arithmetic on 8080/8085 processors is awkward, since DAA works only after 8-bit addition instructions (ACI, ADC, ADD, and ADI). It does not work properly after subtraction, increment, decrement, or double add. Chapter 6 contains programs for decimal arithmetic operations. Since DAA does not work properly after DCR or INR, the following sequences are necessary to perform decimal increment and decrement by 1:

· Add 1 to the accumulator in decimal.

```
ADI   1
DAA
```

· Subtract 1 from the accumulator in decimal.

```
ADI   99H
DAA
```

The Carry is an inverted borrow.

HANDLING ARRAYS INCORRECTLY

The most common problem here is executing an extra iteration or stopping one short. Remember, memory locations BASE through BASE+N contain N+1 bytes, not N bytes. It is easy to forget the last entry or drop the first one. On the other hand, if there are N entries, they will occupy memory locations BASE through BASE+N−1; now it is easy to find yourself working beyond the end of the array.

IMPLICIT EFFECTS

Some implicit effects to remember are

· The clearing of Carry by all logical operations except CMA.

· The changing of both halves of a register pair by such instructions as LXI, LHLD, INX, DCX, and XCHG.

· The use of the memory address one larger than the one specified by LHLD and SHLD.

· The changing of the stack pointer by POP, PUSH, CALL, RET, and RST.

· The saving of the return address in the stack by CALL and RST.

· The use of the address in H and L by any instruction involving register M.

· The changing of H and L by DAD.

· The use of the accumulator by IN, LDAX, OUT, RIM, SIM, and STAX. RIM and SIM are available only on the 8085.

Examples

1. ANI 00001111B

This instruction clears Carry as well as performing a logical operation.

2. INX H

This instruction adds 1 to register pair H, not to register H or L individually. In fact, INX H adds 1 to register L and then adds the Carry, if there is one, to register H. Remember, INR and DCR are 8-bit operations, whereas INX and DCX are 16-bit operations.

3. LXI D,2050H

This instruction changes both register D (to 20_{16}) and register E (to 50_{16}).

4. LHLD 16EFH

This instruction uses memory addresses $16EF_{16}$ and $16F0_{16}$. It loads register L from address $16EF_{16}$ and H from address $16F0_{16}$.

5. PUSH H

This instruction not only saves registers H and L in memory, but it also decrements the stack pointer by 2.

6. RET

This instruction not only loads the program counter from the top two locations in the stack, but it also increments the stack pointer by 2.

7. INR M

This instruction adds 1 to the contents of the memory location addressed by register pair H. Note that it is not the same as INR H (which adds 1 to register H), INR L (which adds 1 to register L), or INX H (which adds 1 to register pair H).

8. DAD D

This instruction adds the 16-bit number in register pair D to the 16-bit number in register pair H and saves the result in register pair H. The old contents of register pair H are lost, but register pair D is unchanged.

9. IN 20H

This instruction loads the accumulator from port 20_{16}. The old contents of the accumulator are lost.

10. RIM

This instruction (8085 only) loads the accumulator with the interrupt masks. The old contents of the accumulator are lost.

INITIALIZATION ERRORS

Initialization routines must perform the following tasks for the microcomputer system as a whole and for particular routines:

· Load all RAM locations with initial values. This includes indirect addresses and other temporary storage. You cannot assume that a memory location contains 0 just because it has not been used.

· Load all registers and flags with initial values. Reset initializes only the interrupt system (by disabling it). The startup program must, for example, initialize the stack pointer using either LXI SP or the sequence LHLD, SPHL.

· Initialize all counters and indirect addresses. Note particularly register pairs that are being used as address registers. Remember that register pair H must be loaded with an address before using instructions that refer to register M.

ORGANIZING THE PROGRAM INCORRECTLY

The following problems are the most common:

· Accidentally reinitializing a register, register pair, flag, memory location, counter, or indirect address. Be sure that the branches do not result in the repetition of initialization instructions.

· Failing to update a counter or indirect address. A problem here may be a path that branches around the updating instructions or that changes values before executing those instructions.

· Forgetting to save results. It is remarkably easy to calculate a result and then load something else into the accumulator. Identifying errors like this is frustrating and time-consuming, since all the instructions that calculate the result work properly and yet the result itself is being lost. For example, a branch may transfer control to an instruction that writes over the result.

· Forgetting to branch around instructions that should not be executed in a particular path. Remember, the computer will execute instructions consecutively unless told to do otherwise. Thus, the computer may fall through to a section of a program that it was only expected to reach via a branch. An unconditional jump instruction will force a branch around the section that should not be executed.

ERROR RECOGNITION BY ASSEMBLERS

Most assemblers will recognize some common errors immediately, such as

· Undefined operation code (usually a misspelling or the omission of a colon after a label).

· Undefined name (often a misspelling or an omitted definition).

· Illegal character (for example, a 2 in a binary number or a B in a decimal number).

· Illegal format (for example, an incorrect delimiter or the wrong operands).

· Illegal value (usually a number too large for 8 or 16 bits).

· Missing operand.

· Double definition (two different values assigned to one name).

· Illegal label (for example, a label attached to a pseudo-operation that does not allow a label).

· Missing label (for example, on an EQU pseudo-operation that requires one).

These errors are annoying but easy to correct. The only problem comes when an error (such as omitting the semicolon from a comment line) confuses the assembler completely and results in a series of meaningless error messages.

There are, however, many simple errors that assemblers will not recognize. The programmer should be aware that his or her program may contain such errors even if the assembler does not report them. Typical examples are

· Omitted lines. Obviously, the assembler cannot tell that a line has been omitted completely unless it contains a label or definition that is used elsewhere. The easiest lines to omit are ones that are repetitious or seem unnecessary. Typical repetitions are a series of shifts, branches, increments, or decrements. Instructions that often appear unnecessary include ANA A, DCX H, INX H, ORA A, and SUB A.

· Omitted designations. The assembler cannot tell if an operand is meant to be hexadecimal or binary unless the omission results in an illegal character (such as C in a decimal number). Otherwise, the assembler will assume all numbers to be decimal. Problems often occur with hexadecimal numbers that contain no letter digits (such as 44 or 2050) and with binary numbers (such as 00000110).

· Misspellings that are still valid. Typical examples are typing AND or ADC instead of ADD, ORA instead of XRA, D instead of B (as a register or register pair), or D instead of E (as a register). Unless the misspelling is invalid, the assembler has no way of sensing an error. Valid misspellings are a frequent problem if a programmer uses names that look alike, such as XXX and XXXX, L121 and L112, or VAR11 and VARII.

· Designating instructions as comments. If a semicolon is placed at the start of an instruction line, the assembler will treat the line as a comment. This can be a perplexing error, since the line appears in the listing but is not assembled into code.

Sometimes an assembler can be confused by entering completely invalid instructions. An assembler may accept them simply because its developer never anticipated such mistakes. The results can be unpredictable, much like the result of accidentally entering your Social Security number instead of your credit card number on a form. Some cases in which an 8080/8085 assembler can go wrong are

· If a single register is specified in an instruction that operates on register pairs. Some assemblers will accept instructions like INX L, DAD C, or LXI E,2040H. They will produce meaningless object code without any indication of error.

· If an invalid digit is entered, such as X in a decimal or hexadecimal number or 7 in a binary number. Some assemblers will assign arbitrary values to such invalid digits.

· If an invalid operand is entered such as 8 in RST, PSW in LXI, or SP in PUSH or POP. Some assemblers will accept these and generate meaningless code.

The assembler will only recognize errors that its developer anticipated. Programmers are often able to make mistakes the developer never imagined, much as automobile drivers are often capable of getting into predicaments no highway engineer or traffic policeman ever thought possible. Note that only a line-by-line hand check of the program will find errors that the assembler does not recognize.

COMMON ERRORS IN I/O DRIVERS

Since most errors in I/O drivers involve both hardware and software, they are difficult to categorize. Some things to watch for are

· Confusing input ports and output ports. Input port 20_{16} and output port 20_{16} are different in most systems. Even when the two ports are the same physically, it may still be impossible to read back output data unless the port is latched and buffered.

· Attempting to perform operations that are physically impossible. Reading data from an output device (such as a display) or sending data to an input device (such as a keyboard) makes no physical sense. However, accidentally using the wrong port number will cause no assembly errors; the port, after all, exists, and the assembler has no way of knowing that certain operations cannot be performed on it. Similarly, a program may attempt to save data in an unassigned address or in a ROM.

· Forgetting implicit hardware effects. Transferring data to or from a port sometimes changes the status lines automatically (as in operating mode 1 of the 8255 parallel interface). Even reading or writing the port while debugging a program will change the status lines. When using memory-mapped I/O, be particularly careful of comparisons; they read a memory address even though they do not change any registers. Similarly, instructions like DCR M and INR M both read and write a memory address. Automatic port operations can save parts and simplify programs, but be sure to remember how they work and when they occur.

· Reading or writing without checking status. Many devices can only accept or provide data when a status line indicates they are ready. Transferring data to or from them at other times will have unpredictable results.

· Ignoring the differences between input and output. Remember that an input device normally starts out *not ready* — it has no data available although the computer is ready to accept data. On the other hand, an output device normally starts out *ready* — that is, it could accept data but the computer usually has none to send it. In many situations (particularly when using 8155, 8156, or 8255 programmable I/O devices) it may be necessary to send a null character (something that has no effect) to each output port just to change its state from *ready* to *not ready* initially.

· Failing to keep a copy of output data. Remember that it will not generally be possible to read it back from an output port. If you need it later to repeat a transmission that was received incorrectly, change part of it (as in turning on or off one of several indicator lights attached to the same port), or save it as part of the interrupted status (the data is the current priority level), you must save a copy of it in memory. The copy must be updated every time the actual data is changed.

· Reading data before it is stable or while it is changing. It is imperative to understand exactly when the data from the input device is guaranteed to be stable. In the case of switches that bounce, the program can sample them twice (more than a debouncing time apart) before taking any action. In the case of keys that bounce, the program may act only when they are released rather than when they are pressed. Acting on release also forces the operator to release the key rather than holding it down. In the case of persistent data (such as in serial I/O), be sure to center the reception (that is, read the data near the centers of the pulses rather than at the edges where the values may be changing).

· Forgetting to reverse the polarity of data being transferred to or from devices that operate in negative logic. Many simple I/O devices, such as switches and displays, use negative logic; a logic 0 means that a switch is closed or a display is lit. Common ten-position switches or dials also often produce data in negative logic, as do many encoders. The solution is simple: Complement the data using CMA after reading it or before sending it.

· Confusing actual I/O ports with registers that are inside I/O chips. Programmable I/O devices, such as the 8251, 8253, 8255, and 8279, typically have control or command registers (which determine how the device operates) and status registers (which reflect the current state of the device or the transfer). These registers are inside the chips; they are not connected to peripherals. Transferring data to or from these registers is not the same as transferring data to or from actual I/O ports.

· Using bidirectional ports improperly. Many devices, such as the 8155, 8156, 8255, 8355, and 8755, have bidirectional I/O ports that can be used either for input or for output. Normally, resetting the computer makes these ports inputs to avoid initial transients, so the program must explicitly change them to outputs if necessary. Be particularly careful of instructions that read bits or ports that are designated as outputs or that write into bits or ports that are designated as inputs. The only way to determine what will happen is to read the documentation for the specific device.

· Forgetting to clear status after performing an I/O operation. Once the processor has read data from a port or written data into a port, that port should revert to the *not ready* state. Some I/O devices change the status of their ports automatically after input or output operations, but others either do not or change status automatically only after input. Leaving the status set can result in an endless loop or erratic operation.

COMMON ERRORS IN INTERRUPT SERVICE ROUTINES

Many interrupt-related errors involve both hardware and software, but some common mistakes are the following:

· Failing to reenable interrupts. The 8080 and 8085 processors disable interrupts automatically after accepting one, but do not reenable interrupts unless they execute EI.

· Failing to save registers. Neither the 8080 nor the 8085 saves any registers besides the program counter automatically. Any registers that the service routine uses must be saved in the stack explicitly.

· Saving or restoring registers in the wrong order. Registers must be restored in the opposite order from that in which they were saved.

· Enabling interrupts before initializing priorities and other parameters of the interrupt system.

· Forgetting that the response to an interrupt includes saving the program counter at the top of the stack. The return address will thus be on top of whatever else is in the stack.

· Not disabling the interrupt during multi-byte transfers or instruction sequences that cannot be interrupted. In particular, watch for partial updating of data (such as time) that an interrupt service routine may use.

· Failing to reenable interrupts after a sequence that must run with interrupts disabled. A problem here is that interrupts should not be enabled afterward if they were not enabled originally. This is difficult to do on the 8080 since its interrupt enable is not readable, as it is on the 8085. A solution is to keep a flag in memory that indicates whether interrupts are currently enabled or disabled. Of course, this flag must be updated after every DI instruction and before every EI instruction.[2]

· Failing to clear the signal that caused the interrupt. The service routine must clear the interrupt even if no I/O operations are necessary. For example, even when the processor has no data to send to an interrupting output device, it still must either clear or disable the interrupt. Otherwise, the processor will get caught in an endless loop. Similarly, even though a real-time clock typically requires no servicing other than an updating of time, the service routine still must clear the interrupt. This clearing may involve reading a register in a programmable timer.

· Failing to communicate with the main program. The main program will not know that an interrupt has been serviced unless it is informed explicitly. The usual way to inform the main program is to have the service routine change a flag. The main program can tell from the flag's value that the service routine has been executed. This procedure is comparable to the practice of a postal patron raising a flag to indicate that there is mail to be picked up. The mail carrier lowers the flag after picking up the mail. In this simple procedure, the main program must examine the flag often enough to avoid missing changes in its value. Of course, the programmer can always provide a buffer that can hold many data items.

· Failing to save and restore priority. The priority of an interrupt is often held in a write-only register or in a memory location. That priority must be saved just like an ordinary register and restored properly at the end of the service routine. If the priority register is write-only (as in the 8214 interrupt control unit), every program that changes it must save a copy of its contents in memory.

The 8085 microprocessor has a more complex interrupt system than the 8080. New problems that arise from the additional features of the 8085 include

· Failing to enable the additional hardware inputs (RST 5.5, RST 6.5, and RST 7.5) by clearing the mask bits in the I register. Be careful; these bits are masks, not enables. A mask bit must be cleared to allow interrupts and set to disable them. The interrupt mask bits thus have the opposite polarity from the interrupt enable flag. Even if the interrupt mask bits have been cleared, the interrupt enable flag still must be set (with EI) to allow maskable interrupts to be recognized. The 8085 also has a nonmaskable hardware interrupt (TRAP or RST 4.5), which is often used to indicate an impending loss of power.

· Misusing the enable bits in SIM. SIM has two distinct functions: setting or clearing the interrupt masks, and placing a value on the SOD (serial output data) line. The mask set enable (bit 3) and the serial output enable (bit 6) allow the programmer to perform one function without affecting the other. That is, by setting bit 3 and clearing bit 6, the programmer can change the interrupt masks without changing the serial output. Similarly, by clearing bit 3 and setting bit 6, the programmer can change the serial output without changing the interrupt masks. The enable bits are necessary because the 8085's designers decided to use one register for two unrelated functions.

Note also that the 8085's I register as written by SIM is different from the I register as read by RIM.

REFERENCES

1. Duncan, F.G., "Level-Independent Notation for Microcomputer Programs," *IEEE Micro*, May 1981, pp. 47-56.

2. Caplan, G., "Special Techniques Handle Critical Sections," *EDN*, March 5, 1980, p. 90.

Introduction to the Program Section

The program section contains sets of assembly language subroutines for the 8080 and 8085 microprocessors. Each subroutine is documented with an introductory section and comments; each is followed by at least one example of its use. The introductory material contains the following information: the purpose of the routine; its procedure and the registers that are used; the execution time, program size, and data memory required for the routine; as well as special cases, entry conditions, and exit conditions.

Each routine has been made as general as possible. This is difficult in the case of the input/output (I/O) and interrupt service routines described in Chapters 10 and 11, since in practice these routines are always computer-dependent. In such cases the computer dependence has been limited to generalized input and output handlers and interrupt managers. Specific examples have been drawn there from computers based on the popular CP/M operating systems, but the general principles are applicable to other 8080-or 8085-based computers as well.

In all routines, the following parameter passing techniques have been used:

1. A single 8-bit parameter is passed in the accumulator. A second 8-bit parameter is passed in register B, and a third in register C.

2. A single 16-bit parameter is passed in registers H and L with the more significant byte in H. A second 16-bit parameter is passed in registers D and E with the more significant byte in D.

3. Larger numbers of parameters are passed in the stack, either directly or indirectly. It is assumed that subroutines are entered via a CALL instruction that places the return address at the top of the stack, and hence on top of the parameters.

141

Where there has been a choice between execution time and memory usage, the preference has been to minimize execution time. For example, it was decided to duplicate loops rather than to transfer addresses between the stack and a register pair.

In addition, the approach that minimizes the number of repetitive calculations was selected. For example, in the case of array indexing, the number of bytes between the starting addresses of elements differing only by one in a particular subscript (known as the *size* of that subscript) depends only on the number of bytes per element and the bounds of the array. Thus, the sizes of the various subscripts can be calculated as soon as the bounds of the array are known. The sizes are therefore used as parameters for the indexing routines, so that they need not be calculated each time a particular array is indexed.

The execution time was specified for most short routines. For longer routines an approximate execution time was given. The execution time of programs involving many branches will obviously depend on which path the computer follows in a particular case. This is further complicated for the 8085 by the fact that conditional jump instructions themselves require different numbers of clock cycles depending on whether the branch is taken. Thus, a precise execution time is often impossible to define. The documentation always contains at least one typical example showing an approximate or maximum execution time.

Error indicators and special cases must be considered as follows:

1. Routines should provide an easily tested indicator (such as the Carry flag) of whether any errors or exceptions have occurred.

2. Trivial cases, such as no elements in an array or strings of zero length, should result in immediate exits with minimal effect on the underlying data.

3. Misspecified data (such as a maximum string length of zero or an index beyond the end of an array) should result in immediate exits with minimal effect on the underlying data.

4. The documentation should include a summary of errors and exceptions (under the heading of "Special Cases").

5. Exceptions that may actually be convenient for the user (such as deleting more characters than could possibly be left in a string rather than counting the precise number) should be handled in a reasonable way, but should still be indicated as errors.

Obviously, no method of handling errors or exceptions can ever be completely consistent or well suited to all applications. One approach is that a reasonable set of subroutines deal with this issue, rather than ignoring it or assuming that the user will always provide data in the proper form.

The subroutines are listed as follows:

Bit Manipulation and Shifts

String Manipulation

Array Operations

Input/Output

Interrupts

Binary to BCD Conversion (BN2BCD)

Converts one byte of binary data to two bytes of BCD data.

Procedure: The program subtracts 100 repeatedly from the original data to determine the hundreds digit, then subtracts 10 repeatedly from the remainder to determine the tens digit, and finally shifts the tens digit left four positions and combines it with the ones digit.

Registers Used: AF, C, HL

Execution Time: 491 cycles maximum; depends on the number of subtractions required to determine the tens and hundreds digits

Program Size: 29 bytes

Data Memory Required: None

Entry Conditions

Binary data in A

Exit Conditions

Hundreds digit in H

Tens and ones digits in L

Examples

1. Data: $(A) = 6E_{16}$ (110 decimal)

   Result: $(H) = 01_{16}$ (hundreds digit)
   $(L) = 10_{16}$ (tens and ones digits)

2. Data: $(A) = B7_{16}$ (183 decimal)

   Result: $(H) = 01_{16}$ (hundreds digit)
   $(L) = 83_{16}$ (tens and ones digits)

```
;                                                            ;
;                                                            ;
;                                                            ;
;                                                            ;
;       Title:          Binary to BCD Conversion             ;
;       Name:           BN2BCD                               ;
;                                                            ;
;                                                            ;
;                                                            ;
;                                                            ;
;       Purpose:        Convert one byte of binary data to two ;
;                       bytes of BCD data                    ;
;                                                            ;
;       Entry:          Register A = Binary data             ;
;                                                            ;
;       Exit:           Register H = High byte of BCD data   ;
```

147

```
;                       Register L = Low  byte of BCD data        ;
;                                                                 ;
;          Registers used: AF,C,HL                                ;
;                                                                 ;
;          Time:           491 cycles maximum                     ;
;                                                                 ;
;          Size:           Program 29 bytes                       ;
;                                                                 ;
;                                                                 ;

BN2BCD:
          ;CALCULATE 100´S DIGIT
          ;DIVIDE DATA BY 100
          ; H = QUOTIENT
          ; A = REMAINDER
          MVI     H,OFFH              ;START QUOTIENT AT -1
D100LP:
          INR     H                   ;ADD 1 TO QUOTIENT
          SUI     100                 ;SUBTRACT 100
          JNC     D100LP              ;JUMP IF A IS STILL LARGER THAN 0
          ADI     100                 ;IF NOT, ADD THE LAST 100 BACK

          ;CALCULATE 10´S AND 1´S DIGITS
          ;DIVIDE REMAINDER OF THE 100´S DIGIT BY 10
          ; L = 10´S DIGIT
          ; A = 1´S DIGIT
          MVI     L,OFFH              ;START QUOTIENT AT -1
D10LP:
          INR     L                   ;ADD 1 TO QUOTIENT
          SUI     10                  ;SUBTRACT 10
          JNC     D10LP               ;JUMP IF DIFFERENCE STILL POSITIVE
          ADI     10                  ;IF NOT, ADD THE LAST 10 BACK

          ;COMBINE 1´S AND 10´S DIGITS
          MOV     C,A                 ;SAVE 1´S DIGIT IN C
          MOV     A,L
          RLC                         ;MOVE 10´S TO HIGH NIBBLE OF A
          RLC
          RLC
          RLC
          ORA     C                   ;OR IN THE 1´S DIGIT

          ;RETURN WITH L = LOW BYTE, H = HIGH BYTE
          MOV     L,A
          RET


;                                                                 ;
;                                                                 ;
;          SAMPLE EXECUTION                                       ;
;                                                                 ;
;                                                                 ;

SC4A:
          ;CONVERT 0A HEXADECIMAL TO 10 BCD
          MVI     A,OAH
```

```
CALL    BN2BCD              ;H = 0, L = 10H

;CONVERT FF HEXADECIMAL TO 255 BCD
MVI     A,OFFH
CALL    BN2BCD              ;H = 02H, L = 55H

;CONVERT 0 HEXADECIMAL TO 0 BCD
MVI     A,0
CALL    BN2BCD              ;H = 0, L = 0

JMP     SC4A

END
```

Converts one byte of BCD data to one byte of binary data.

Procedure: The program masks off the more significant digit and multiplies it by 10 using shifts ($10 = 8 + 2$, and multiplying by 8 or by 2 is equivalent to three or one left shifts, respectively). Then the program adds the product to the less significant digit.

Registers Used: AF, BC
Execution Time: 60 cycles
Program Size: 14 bytes
Data Memory Required: None

Entry Conditions

BCD data in A

Exit Conditions

Binary data in A

Examples

1. Data: $(A) = 99_{16}$

   Result: $(A) = 63_{16} = 99_{10}$

2. Data: $(A) = 23_{16}$

   Result: $(A) = 17_{16} = 23_{10}$

```
;
;
;
;
;       Title:      BCD to Binary Conversion
;       Name:       BCD2BN
;
;
;
;       Purpose:    Convert one byte of BCD data to one
;                   byte of binary data
;
;       Entry:      Register A = BCD data
;
;       Exit:       Register A = Binary data
;
;       Registers used: AF,BC
;
```

```
;           Time:           60 cycles                                    ;
;                                                                        ;
;           Size:           Program 14 bytes                            ;
;                                                                        ;
;                                                                        ;

BCD2BN:
            ;MULTIPLY UPPER NIBBLE BY 10 AND SAVE IT
            ; UPPER NIBBLE * 10 = UPPER NIBBLE * (8 + 2)
            MOV     B,A             ;SAVE ORIGINAL BCD VALUE IN B
            ANI     0F0H            ;MASK OFF UPPER NIBBLE
            RRC                     ;SHIFT RIGHT 1 BIT
            MOV     C,A             ;C = UPPER NIBBLE * 8
            RRC                     ;SHIFT RIGHT 2 MORE TIMES
            RRC                     ;A = UPPER NIBBLE * 2
            ADD     C
            MOV     C,A             ;C = UPPER NIBBLE * (8 + 2)

            ;GET LOWER NIBBLE AND ADD IT TO
            ; BINARY EQUIVALENT OF UPPER NIBBLE
            MOV     A,B             ;GET ORIGINAL BCD VALUE BACK
            ANI     0FH             ;MASK OFF UPPER NIBBLE
            ADD     C               ;ADD TO BINARY UPPER NIBBLE
            RET


;                                                                        ;
;                                                                        ;
;           SAMPLE EXECUTION                                             ;
;                                                                        ;
;                                                                        ;

SC4B:

            ;CONVERT 0 BCD TO 0 HEXADECIMAL
            MVI     A,0
            CALL    BCD2BN          ;A = 0H

            ;CONVERT 99 BCD TO 63 HEXADECIMAL
            MVI     A,099H
            CALL    BCD2BN          ;A = 63H

            ;CONVERT 23 BCD TO 17 HEXADECIMAL
            MVI     A,23H
            CALL    BCD2BN          ;A = 17H

            JMP     SC4B

            END
```

Binary to Hexadecimal ASCII
Conversion (BN2HEX)

Converts one byte of binary data to two ASCII characters corresponding to the two hexadecimal digits.

Procedure: The program masks off each hexadecimal digit separately and converts it to its ASCII equivalent. This involves a simple addition of 30_{16} if the digit is decimal. If the digit is non-decimal, an additional 7 must be added to bridge the gap between ASCII 9 (39_{16}) and ASCII A (41_{16}).

Registers Used: AF, B, HL

Execution Time: 162 cycles plus seven extra cycles for each non-decimal digit (8080) or 160 cycles plus four extra cycles for each non-decimal digit (8085)

Program Size: 29 bytes

Data Memory Required: None

Entry Conditions

Binary data in A

Exit Conditions

ASCII version of more significant hexadecimal digit in H

ASCII version of less significant hexadecimal digit in L

Examples

1. Data: (A) = FB_{16}

   Result: (H) = 46_{16} (ASCII F)
            (L) = 42_{16} (ASCII B)

2. Data: (A) = 59_{16}

   Result: (H) = 35_{16} (ASCII 5)
            (L) = 39_{16} (ASCII 9)

```
;
;
;
;
;        Title:          Binary to Hex ASCII
;        Name:           BN2HEX
;
;
;
;        Purpose:        Convert one byte of binary data to
;                        two ASCII characters
;
```

```
;
;       Entry:              Register A = Binary data
;
;       Exit:               Register H = ASCII more significant digit
;                           Register L = ASCII less significant digit
;
;       Registers used: AF,B,HL
;
;       Time:               Approximately 160 cycles
;
;       Size:               Program 29 bytes
;
;

BN2HEX:
        ;CONVERT HIGH NIBBLE TO ASCII
        MOV     B,A             ;SAVE ORIGINAL BINARY VALUE
        ANI     0F0H            ;GET HIGH NIBBLE
        RRC                     ;MOVE HIGH NIBBLE TO LOW NIBBLE
        RRC
        RRC
        RRC
        CALL    NASCII          ;CONVERT HIGH NIBBLE TO ASCII
        MOV     H,A             ;RETURN HIGH NIBBLE IN H

        ;CONVERT LOW NIBBLE TO ASCII
        MOV     A,B
        ANI     0FH             ;GET LOW NIBBLE
        CALL    NASCII          ;CONVERT LOW NIBBLE TO ASCII
        MOV     L,A             ;RETURN LOW NIBBLE IN L
        RET


        ;-------------------------------------
        ;SUBROUTINE NASCII
        ;PURPOSE:    CONVERT A HEXADECIMAL DIGIT TO ASCII
        ;ENTRY: A = BINARY DATA IN LOWER NIBBLE
        ;EXIT:   A = ASCII CHARACTER
        ;REGISTERS USED: A,F
        ;-------------------------------------
NASCII:
        CPI     10
        JC      NAS1            ;JUMP IF HIGH NIBBLE < 10
        ADI     7               ;ELSE ADD 7 SO AFTER ADDING '0' THE
                                ; CHARACTER WILL BE IN 'A'..'F'

NAS1:
        ADI     '0'             ;ADD ASCII 0 TO MAKE A CHARACTER
        RET


;
;
;       SAMPLE EXECUTION
;
;
```

```
SC4C:
        ;CONVERT 0 TO ´00´
        MVI     A,0
        CALL    BN2HEX          ;H=´0´=30H, L=´0´=30H

        ;CONVERT FF HEX TO ´FF´
        MVI     A,0FFH
        CALL    BN2HEX          ;H=´F´=46H, L=´F´=46H

        ;CONVERT 23 HEX TO ´23´
        MVI     A,23H
        CALL    BN2HEX          ;H=´2´=32H, L=´3´=33H

        JMP     SC4C

        END
```

Hexadecimal ASCII to Binary
Conversion (HEX2BN) 4D

Converts two ASCII characters (representing two hexadecimal digits) to one byte of binary data.

Procedure: The program converts each ASCII character separately to a hexadecimal digit. This involves a simple subtraction of 30_{16} (ASCII 0) if the digit is decimal. If the digit is non-decimal, another 7 must be subtracted to account for the break between ASCII 9 (39_{16}) and ASCII A (41_{16}). The program then shifts the more significant digit left four bits and combines it with the less significant digit. The program does not

check the validity of the ASCII characters (that is, whether they are indeed the ASCII representations of hexadecimal digits).

Registers Used: AF, B

Execution Time: 147 cycles plus seven extra cycles for each non-decimal digit (8080) or 146 cycles plus four extra cycles for each non-decimal digit (8085)

Program Size: 25 bytes

Data Memory Required: None

Entry Conditions

More significant ASCII digit in H, less significant digit in L

Exit Conditions

Binary data in A

Examples

1. Data: (H) = 44_{16} (ASCII D)
            (L) = 37_{16} (ASCII 7)

   Result: (A) = $D7_{16}$

2. Data: (H) = 31_{16} (ASCII 1)
            (L) = 42_{16} (ASCII B)

   Result: (A) = $1B_{16}$

```
;
;
;
;
;       Title:          Hex ASCII to Binary
;       Name:           HEX2BN
;
;
;
;       Purpose:        Convert two ASCII characters to one
;                       byte of binary data
```

```
;
;          Entry:           Register H = ASCII more significant digit
;                           Register L = ASCII less significant digit
;
;          Exit:            Register A = Binary data
;
;          Registers used: AF,B
;
;          Time:            Approximately 147 cycles
;
;          Size:            Program 25 bytes
;
;

HEX2BN:
           MOV       A,L                 ;GET LOW CHARACTER
           CALL      A2HEX               ;CONVERT IT TO HEXADECIMAL
           MOV       B,A                 ;SAVE HEX VALUE IN B
           MOV       A,H                 ;GET HIGH CHARACTER
           CALL      A2HEX               ;CONVERT IT TO HEXADECIMAL
           RLC                           ;SHIFT HEX VALUE TO UPPER 4 BITS
           RLC
           RLC
           RLC
           ORA       B                   ;OR IN LOW HEX VALUE
           RET


           ;---------------------------------------
           ;SUBROUTINE: A2HEX
           ;PURPOSE: CONVERT ASCII DIGIT TO A HEX DIGIT
           ;ENTRY: A = ASCII HEXADECIMAL DIGIT
           ;EXIT:  A = BINARY VALUE OF ASCII DIGIT
           ;REGISTERS USED: A,F
           ;---------------------------------------
A2HEX:
           SUI       'O'                 ;SUBTRACT ASCII OFFSET
           CPI       10
           JC        A2HEX1              ;BRANCH IF A IS A DECIMAL DIGIT
           SUI       7                   ;ELSE SUBTRACT OFFSET FOR LETTERS
A2HEX1:
           RET


;
;
;          SAMPLE EXECUTION
;
;

SC4D:
           ;CONVERT 'C7' TO C7 HEXADECIMAL
           MVI       H,'C'
           MVI       L,'7'
           CALL      HEX2BN              ;A=C7H

           ;CONVERT '2F' TO 2F HEXADECIMAL
```

```
        MVI     H,'2'
        MVI     L,'F'
        CALL    HEX2BN                  ;A = 2FH

        ;CONVERT '2A' TO 2A HEXADECIMAL
        MVI     H,'2'
        MVI     L,'A'
        CALL    HEX2BN                  ;A = 2AH

        JMP     SC4D

        END
```

Conversion of a Binary Number to
Decimal ASCII (BN2DEC) 4E

Converts a 16-bit signed binary number into an ASCII string. The string consists of the length of the number in bytes, an ASCII minus sign (if needed), and the ASCII digits. Note that the length is a binary number, not an ASCII number.

Procedure: The program takes the absolute value of the number if it is negative. The program then keeps dividing the absolute value by 10 until the quotient becomes 0. It converts each digit of the quotient to ASCII by adding ASCII 0 and concatenates the digits along with

an ASCII minus sign (in front) if the original number was negative.

Registers Used: All

Execution Time: Approximately 8400 cycles

Program Size: 124 bytes

Data Memory Required: Four bytes anywhere in memory for the buffer pointer (two bytes starting at address BUFPTR), the length of the buffer (one byte at address CURLEN), and the sign of the original value (one byte at address NGFLAG). This data memory does not include the output buffer, which should be seven bytes long.

Entry Conditions

Base address of output buffer in H and L
Value to convert in D and E

Exit Conditions

Order in buffer:
  Length of the string in bytes (a binary number)
  ASCII − (if original number was negative)
  ASCII digits (most significant digit first)

Examples

1. Data: Value to convert = $3EB7_{16}$

   Result (in output buffer):
       05 (number of bytes in buffer)
       31 (ASCII 1)
       36 (ASCII 6)
       30 (ASCII 0)
       35 (ASCII 5)
       35 (ASCII 5)
       That is, $3EB7_{16} = 16{,}055_{10}$

2. Data: Value to convert = $FFC8_{16}$

   Result (in output buffer):
       03 (number of bytes in buffer)
       2D (ASCII −)
       35 (ASCII 5)
       36 (ASCII 6)
       That is, $FFC8_{16} = -56_{10}$, when considered as a signed two's complement number

```
;
;                                                                        ;
;                                                                        ;
;                                                                        ;
;          Title:           Binary to Decimal ASCII                      ;
;          Name:            BN2DEC                                       ;
;                                                                        ;
;                                                                        ;
;                                                                        ;
;          Purpose:         Convert a 16-bit signed binary number        ;
;                           to ASCII data                                ;
;                                                                        ;
;          Entry:           Register H = High byte of output buffer address ;
;                           Register L = Low byte of output buffer address  ;
;                           Register D = High byte of value to convert   ;
;                           Register E = Low byte of value to convert    ;
;                                                                        ;
;          Exit:            The first byte of the buffer is the length,  ;
;                           followed by the characters.                  ;
;                                                                        ;
;          Registers used: All                                          ;
;                                                                        ;
;          Time:            Approximately 8,400 cycles                   ;
;                                                                        ;
;          Size:            Program 124 bytes                            ;
;                           Data      4 bytes                            ;
;                                                                        ;
;

BN2DEC:
         ;SAVE PARAMETERS
         SHLD    BUFPTR              ;STORE THE BUFFER POINTER
         XCHG                        ;HL = VALUE TO CONVERT
         MVI     A,0
         STA     CURLEN              ;CURRENT BUFFER LENGTH IS 0
         MOV     A,H
         STA     NGFLAG              ;SAVE SIGN OF VALUE
         ORA     A                   ;SET FLAGS
         JP      CNVERT              ;JUMP IF VALUE IS POSITIVE
         SUB     A                   ;ELSE TAKE ABSOLUTE VALUE (0 - VALUE)
         SUB     L
         MOV     L,A
         SBB     A                   ;PROPOGATE BORROW
         SUB     H
         MOV     H,A


         ;CONVERT VALUE TO A STRING
CNVERT:
         ;HL := HL DIV 10   (DIVIDEND,QUOTIENT)
         ;DE := HL MOD 10   (REMAINDER)
         MVI     E,0                 ;REMAINDER = 0
         MVI     B,16                ;16 BITS IN DIVIDEND
         ORA     A                   ;CLEAR CARRY TO START
DVLOOP:
         ;SHIFT NEXT BIT OF QUOTIENT INTO BIT 0 OF DIVIDEND
```

```
        ;SHIFT NEXT MOST SIGNIFICANT BIT OF DIVIDEND INTO
        ; LEAST SIGNIFICANT BIT OF REMAINDER
        ;HL HOLDS BOTH DIVIDEND AND QUOTIENT. QUOTIENT IS SHIFTED
        ; IN AS THE DIVIDEND IS SHIFTED OUT
        ;E IS THE REMAINDER

        ;DO A 24-BIT SHIFT LEFT, SHIFTING
        ; CARRY TO L, L TO H, H TO E
        MOV     A,L
        RAL                         ;CARRY (NEXT BIT OF QUOTIENT) TO BIT 0,
        MOV     L,A                 ; BIT 7 TO CARRY
        MOV     A,H
        RAL                         ;SHIFT OTHER BYTE OF DIVIDEND
        MOV     H,A                 ; AND QUOTIENT
        MOV     A,E
        RAL                         ;SHIFT NEXT BIT OF DIVIDEND
        MOV     E,A                 ; INTO REMAINDER

        ;IF REMAINDER IS 10 OR MORE, NEXT BIT OF
        ; QUOTIENT IS 1 (THIS BIT IS PLACED IN CARRY)
        SUI     10                  ;SUBTRACT 10 FROM REMAINDER
        CMC                         ;COMPLEMENT CARRY
                                    ; (THIS IS NEXT BIT OF QUOTIENT)
        JNC     DECCNT              ;JUMP IF REMAINDER IS LESS THAN 10
        MOV     E,A                 ;OTHERWISE MAKE REMAINDER = DIFFERENCE
                                    ; BETWEEN PREVIOUS REMAINDER AND 10

DECCNT:
        DCR     B
        JNZ     DVLOOP              ;CONTINUE UNTIL ALL BITS ARE DONE

        ;SHIFT LAST CARRY INTO QUOTIENT
        RAL                         ;LAST BIT OF QUOTIENT TO BIT 0
        ANI     1                   ;REMOVE ALL OTHER BITS
        DAD     H                   ;SHIFT QUOTIENT LEFT
        ORA     L                   ;OR IN BIT 0
        MOV     L,A                 ;MOVE BACK TO L

        ;INSERT THE NEXT CHARACTER
CHINS:
        MOV     A,E
        ADI     '0'                 ;CONVERT 0..9 TO ASCII '0'..'9'
        CALL    INSERT

        ;IF QUOTIENT IS NOT 0, KEEP DIVIDING
        MOV     A,H                 ;TEST QUOTIENT
        ORA     L
        JNZ     CNVERT

EXIT:
        LDA     NGFLAG
        ORA     A
        JP      POS                 ;BRANCH IF ORIGINAL VALUE WAS POSITIVE
        MVI     A,'-'               ;ELSE
        CALL    INSERT              ; PUT A MINUS SIGN IN FRONT
```

```
POS:
        RET

        ;-----------------------------------
        ;SUBROUTINE: INSERT
        ;PURPOSE: INSERT THE CHARACTER IN REGISTER A AT THE
        ;         FRONT OF THE BUFFER
        ;ENTRY: CURLEN = LENGTH OF BUFFER
        ;       BUFPTR = CURRENT ADDRESS OF LAST CHARACTER IN BUFFER
        ;EXIT:  REGISTER A INSERTED IMMEDIATELY AFTER LENGTH BYTE
        ;REGISTERS USED: AF,B,C,D,E
        ;-----------------------------------
INSERT:
        PUSH    H               ;SAVE HL
        MOV     C,A             ;SAVE CHARACTER IN C

        ;MOVE THE BUFFER RIGHT ONE CHARACTER
        LHLD    BUFPTR          ;GET BUFFER POINTER
        MOV     D,H             ;DE = SOURCE (CURRENT END OF BUFFER)
        MOV     E,L
        INX     H               ;HL = DESTINATION (CURRENT END + 1)
        SHLD    BUFPTR          ;STORE NEW BUFFER POINTER
        LDA     CURLEN
        ORA     A               ;TEST FOR CURLEN = 0
        JZ      EXITMR          ;JUMP IF ZERO (NOTHING TO  MOVE)
                                ; JUST STORE CHARACTER
        MOV     B,A             ;B = LOOP COUNTER
MVELP:
        XCHG                    ;HL = SOURCE
        MOV     A,M             ;GET NEXT CHARACTER
        XCHG
        MOV     M,A             ;STORE IT
        DCX     H               ;DECREMENT DESTINATION
        DCX     D               ;DECREMENT SOURCE
        DCR     B               ;DECREMENT COUNTER
        JNZ     MVELP           ;CONTINUE UNTIL ALL BYTES MOVED

EXITMR:
        MOV     A,C             ;GET CHARACTER TO INSERT
        MOV     M,A             ;INSERT CHARACTER AT FRONT OF BUFFER
        LDA     CURLEN          ;INCREMENT CURRENT LENGTH BY 1
        INR     A
        STA     CURLEN
        DCX     H               ;POINT TO LENGTH BYTE OF BUFFER
        MOV     M,A             ;UPDATE IT
        POP     H               ;RESTORE HL
        RET

        ;DATA
BUFPTR: DS      2               ;ADDRESS OF LAST CHARACTER IN BUFFER
CURLEN: DS      1               ;CURRENT LENGTH OF BUFFER
NGFLAG: DS      1               ;SIGN OF ORIGINAL VALUE
```

```
;                                                             ;
;                                                             ;
;          SAMPLE EXECUTION                                   ;
;                                                             ;
;                                                             ;
SC4E:
          ;CONVERT 0 TO '0'
          LXI    H,BUFFER           ;HL = BASE ADDRESS OF BUFFER
          LXI    D,0                ;DE = 0
          CALL   BN2DEC             ;CONVERT
                                    ; BUFFER SHOULD = '0'

          ;CONVERT 32767 TO '32767'
          LXI    H,BUFFER           ;HL = BASE ADDRESS OF BUFFER
          LXI    D,32767            ;DE = 32767
          CALL   BN2DEC             ;CONVERT
                                    ; BUFFER SHOULD = '32767'

          ;CONVERT -32768 TO '-32768'
          LXI    H,BUFFER           ;HL = BASE ADDRESS OF BUFFER
          LXI    D,-32768           ;DE = -32768
          CALL   BN2DEC             ;CONVERT
                                    ; BUFFER SHOULD = '-32768'

          JMP    SC4E

BUFFER: DS       7                  ;7-BYTE BUFFER

          END
```

Conversion of ASCII Decimal to Binary (DEC2BN)

Converts an ASCII string consisting of the length of the number (in bytes), a possible ASCII − or + sign, and a series of ASCII digits to two bytes of binary data. Note that the length is an ordinary binary number, not an ASCII number.

Procedure: The program sets a flag if the first ASCII character is a minus sign and skips over a leading plus sign. It then converts each subsequent digit to decimal by subtracting ASCII 0, multiplies the previous digits by 10 (using the fact that $10 = 8 + 2$, so a multiplication by 10 can be reduced to left shifts and additions), and adds the new digit to the product. Finally, the program subtracts the result from 0 if the original number was negative. The program exits immediately, setting the Carry flag, if it finds something other than a leading sign or a decimal digit in the string.

Registers Used: All

Execution Time: Approximately 160 cycles per byte plus a maximum of 201 cycles overhead

Program Size: 88 bytes

Data Memory Required: One byte anywhere in RAM (address NGFLAG) for a flag indicating the sign of the number

Special Cases:

1. If the string contains something other than a leading sign or a decimal digit, the program returns with the Carry flag set to 1. The result in HL is invalid.

2. If the string contains only a leading sign (ASCII + or ASCII −), the program returns with the Carry flag set to 1 and a result of 0.

Entry Conditions

Base address of string in H and L

Exit Conditions

Binary value in H and L

The Carry flag is 0 if the string was valid; the Carry flag is 1 if the string contained an invalid character.

Note that the result is a signed two's complement 16-bit number.

Examples

1. Data: String consists of
   04 (number of bytes in string)
   31 (ASCII 1)
   32 (ASCII 2)
   33 (ASCII 3)
   34 (ASCII 4)
   That is, the number is $+1234_{10}$

   Result: $(H) = 04_{16}$ (more significant byte of binary data)
   $(L) = D2_{16}$ (less significant byte of binary data)
   That is, the number $+1234_{10} = 04D2_{16}$

2. Data: String consists of
                06 (number of bytes in string)
                2D (ASCII −)
                33 (ASCII 3)
                32 (ASCII 2)
                37 (ASCII 7)
                35 (ASCII 5)
                30 (ASCII 0)
             That is, the number is $-32,750_{10}$

    Result: $(H) = 80_{16}$ (more significant byte of binary
                 data)
               $(L) = 12_{16}$ (less significant byte of binary
                 data)
               That is, the number $-32,750_{10} = 8012_{16}$

```
;                                                              ;
;                                                              ;
;                                                              ;
;                                                              ;
;          Title:          Decimal ASCII to Binary             ;
;          Name:           DEC2BN                              ;
;                                                              ;
;                                                              ;
;                                                              ;
;          Purpose:        Convert ASCII characters to two bytes of binary ;
;                          data                                ;
;                                                              ;
;          Entry:          Register H = High byte of input buffer address ;
;                          Register L = Low byte of input buffer address ;
;                                                              ;
;          Exit:           Register H = High byte of value     ;
;                          Register L = Low byte of value      ;
;                          if no errors then                   ;
;                           Carry = 0                          ;
;                          else                                ;
;                           Carry = 1                          ;
;                                                              ;
;      Registers used: All                                     ;
;                                                              ;
;          Time:           Approximately 160 cycles per byte plus ;
;                          a maximum of 201 cycles overhead    ;
;                                                              ;
;          Size:           Program  88 bytes                   ;
;                          Data      1 byte                    ;
;                                                              ;
;                                                              ;


DEC2BN:
        ;INITIALIZE - SAVE LENGTH, CLEAR SIGN AND VALUE
        MOV     A,M             ;SAVE LENGTH IN B
        MOV     B,A
        INX     H               ;POINT TO BYTE AFTER LENGTH
        SUB     A
        STA     NGFLAG          ;ASSUME NUMBER IS POSITIVE
        LXI     D,0             ;START WITH VALUE = 0
```

```
        ;CHECK FOR EMPTY BUFFER
        ORA     B               ;IS BUFFER LENGTH ZERO?
        JZ      EREXIT          ;YES, EXIT WITH VALUE = O

        ;CHECK FOR MINUS OR PLUS SIGN IN FRONT
INIT1:
        MOV     A,M             ;GET FIRST CHARACTER
        CPI     ´-´             ;IS IT A MINUS SIGN?
        JNZ     PLUS            ;NO, BRANCH
        MVI     A,OFFH          ;YES, MAKE SIGN NEGATIVE
        STA     NGFLAG
        JMP     SKIP            ;SKIP OVER MINUS SIGN

PLUS:
        CPI     ´+´             ;IS FIRST CHARACTER A PLUS SIGN?
        JNZ     CHKDIG          ;YES, START CONVERSION
SKIP:   INX     H               ;SKIP OVER THE SIGN BYTE
        DCR     B               ;DECREMENT COUNT
        JZ      EREXIT          ;ERROR EXIT IF ONLY A SIGN IN BUFFER

        ;CONVERSION LOOP
        ; CONTINUE UNTIL BUFFER IS EMPTY
        ; OR A NON-NUMERIC CHARACTER IS FOUND
CNVERT:
        MOV     A,M             ;GET NEXT CHARACTER
CHKDIG: SUI     ´O´
        JC      EREXIT          ;ERROR IF < ´O´ (NOT A DIGIT)
        CPI     9+1
        JNC     EREXIT          ;ERROR IF > ´9´ (NOT A DIGIT)
        MOV     C,A             ;CHARACTER IS DIGIT, SAVE IT

        ;VALID DECIMAL DIGIT SO
        ;   VALUE := VALUE * 10
        ; = VALUE * (8 + 2)
        ; = (VALUE * 8) + (VALUE * 2)
        PUSH    H               ;SAVE BUFFER POINTER
        XCHG                    ;HL = VALUE
        DAD     H               ; * 2
        MOV     E,L             ;SAVE TIMES 2 IN DE
        MOV     D,H
        DAD     H               ; * 4
        DAD     H               ; * 8
        DAD     D               ;VALUE = VALUE * 10

        ;ADD IN THE NEXT DIGIT
        ; VALUE := VALUE + DIGIT
        MOV     E,C             ;MOVE NEXT DIGIT TO E
        MVI     D,O             ; HIGH BYTE IS O
        DAD     D               ;ADD DIGIT TO VALUE
        XCHG                    ;DE = VALUE
        POP     H               ;POINT TO NEXT CHARACTER
        INX     H
        DCR     B
        JNZ     CNVERT          ;CONTINUE CONVERSION

        ;CONVERSION IS COMPLETE, CHECK SIGN
```

```
            XCHG                    ;HL = VALUE
            LDA       NGFLAG
            ORA       A
            JP        OKEXIT        ;JUMP IF THE VALUE WAS POSITIVE
            SUB       A             ;ELSE REPLACE RESULT WITH -RESULT
            SUB       L
            MOV       L,A
            SBB       A             ;PROPOGATE BORROW
            SUB       H
            MOV       H,A

            ;NO ERRORS, EXIT WITH CARRY CLEAR
OKEXIT:
            ORA       A             ;CLEAR CARRY TO INDICATE NO ERROR
            RET
            ;AN ERROR, EXIT WITH CARRY SET
EREXIT:
            XCHG                    ;HL = VALUE
            STC                     ;SET CARRY TO INDICATE ERROR
            RET

            ;DATA
NGFLAG:     DS        1             ;SIGN OF NUMBER


;                                                                   ;
;                                                                   ;
;           SAMPLE EXECUTION                                        ;
;                                                                   ;
;                                                                   ;

SC4F:
            ;CONVERT '1234' TO 04D2 HEX
            LXI       H,S1          ;HL = BASE ADDRESS OF S1
            CALL      DEC2BN

                                    ;H = 04, L = D2 HEX

            ;CONVERT '+32767' TO 7FFF HEX
            LXI       H,S2          ;HL = BASE ADDRESS OF S2
            CALL      DEC2BN

                                    ;H = 7F HEX, L = FF HEX

            ;CONVERT '-32768' TO 8000 HEX
            LXI       H,S3          ;HL = BASE ADDRESS OF S3
            CALL      DEC2BN

                                    ;H = 80 HEX, L = 00 HEX

            JMP       SC4F

S1:         DB        4,'1234'
S2:         DB        6,'+32767'
S3:         DB        6,'-32768'

            END
```

Lower-Case to Upper-Case Translation (LC2UC)

Converts an ASCII lower-case letter to its upper-case equivalent.

Procedure: The program uses comparisons to determine whether the data is an ASCII lower-case letter. If it is, the program subtracts 20_{16} from it, thus converting it to its upper-case equivalent. If it is not, the program leaves it unchanged.

Registers Used: AF

Execution Time: 51 cycles if the original character is a lower-case letter, fewer cycles otherwise

Program Size: 13 bytes

Data Memory Required: None

Entry Conditions

Character in A

Exit Conditions

If an ASCII lower-case letter is present in A, then its upper-case equivalent is returned in A. In all other cases, A is unchanged.

Examples

1. Data: (A) = 62_{16} (ASCII b)

   Result: (A) = 42_{16} (ASCII B)

2. Data: (A) = 54_{16} (ASCII T)

   Result: (A) = 54_{16} (ASCII T)

```
;                                                                      ;
;                                                                      ;
;                                                                      ;
;       Title:      Lower-Case to Upper-Case Translation              ;
;       Name:       LC2UC                                             ;
;                                                                      ;
;                                                                      ;
;                                                                      ;
;       Purpose:    Convert one ASCII character to upper-case from    ;
;                   lower-case if necessary                           ;
;                                                                      ;
;       Entry:      Register A = Lower-case ASCII character           ;
;                                                                      ;
;       Exit:       Register A = Upper-case ASCII character if A      ;
;                               is lower-case, else A is unchanged    ;
```

167

```
;          Registers used: AF                                              ;
;                                                                          ;
;                                                                          ;
;          Time:           51 cycles if A is lower-case, less otherwise    ;
;                                                                          ;
;          Size:           Program 13 bytes                                ;
;                          Data    none                                    ;
;                                                                          ;
;                                                                          ;

LC2UC:
          CPI       'a'
          JC        EXIT            ;BRANCH IF < 'a' (NOT LOWER-CASE)
          CPI       'z'+1
          JNC       EXIT            ;BRANCH IF > 'z' (NOT LOWER-CASE)
          SUI       'a'-'A'         ;CHANGE 'a'..'z' into 'A'..'Z'
EXIT:
          RET


;                                                                          ;
;                                                                          ;
;          SAMPLE EXECUTION                                                ;
;                                                                          ;
;                                                                          ;

SC4G:
          ;CONVERT LOWER-CASE E TO UPPER-CASE
          MVI       A,'e'
          CALL      LC2UC               ;A='E'=45H

          ;CONVERT LOWER-CASE Z TO UPPER-CASE
          MVI       A,'z'
          CALL      LC2UC               ;A='Z'=5AH

          ;CONVERT UPPER-CASE A TO UPPER-CASE A
          MVI       A,'A'
          CALL      LC2UC               ;A='A'=41H
          JMP       SC4G

          END
```

ASCII to EBCDIC Conversion (ASC2EB)

Converts an ASCII character to its EBCDIC equivalent.

Procedure: The program uses a simple table lookup with the data as the index and address EBCDIC as the base. A printable ASCII character with no EBCDIC equivalent is translated to an EBCDIC space (40_{16}); a non-printable ASCII character with no EBCDIC equivalent is translated to an EBCDIC NUL (00_{16}).

Registers Used: AF, DE, HL

Execution Time: 55 cycles

Program Size: 11 bytes, plus 128 bytes for the conversion table

Data Memory Required: None

Entry Conditions

ASCII character in A

Exit Conditions

EBCDIC equivalent in A

Examples

1. Data: (A) = 35_{16} (ASCII 5)

   Result: (A) = $F5_{16}$ (EBCDIC 5)

2. Data: (A) = 77_{16} (ASCII w)

   Result: (A) = $A6_{16}$ (EBCDIC w)

3. Data: (A) = $2A_{16}$ (ASCII *)

   Result: (A) = $5C_{16}$ (EBCDIC *)

```
;                                                            ;
;                                                            ;
;                                                            ;
;                                                            ;
;       Title:          ASCII to EBCDIC Conversion           ;
;       Name:           ASC2EB                               ;
;                                                            ;
;                                                            ;
;                                                            ;
;                                                            ;
;       Purpose:        Convert an ASCII character to its    ;
;                       corresponding EBCDIC character       ;
;                                                            ;
;                                                            ;
```

```
;       Entry:          Register A = ASCII character          ;
;                                                             ;
;       Exit:           Register A = EBCDIC character         ;
;                                                             ;
;       Registers used: AF,DE,HL                              ;
;                                                             ;
;       Time:           55 cycles                             ;
;                                                             ;
;       Size:           Program 11 bytes                      ;
;                       Data   128 bytes for the table        ;
;                                                             ;
;                                                             ;

ASC2EB:
        LXI     H,EBCDIC        ;GET BASE ADDRESS OF EBCDIC TABLE
        ANI     01111111B       ;BE SURE BIT 7 = 0
        MOV     E,A             ;USE ASCII AS INDEX INTO EBCDIC TABLE
        MVI     D,0
        DAD     D
        MOV     A,M             ;GET EBCDIC
        RET

;ASCII TO EBCDIC TABLE
; A PRINTABLE ASCII CHARACTER WITH NO EBCDIC EQUIVALENT IS
; TRANSLATED TO AN EBCDIC SPACE (040H), A NON-PRINTABLE ASCII CHARACTER
; WITH NO EQUIVALENT IS TRANSLATED TO AN EBCDIC NUL (000H)
EBCDIC:
        ;       NUL  SOH  STX  ETX  EOT  ENQ  ACK  BEL        ;ASCII
        DB      000H,001H,002H,003H,037H,02DH,02EH,02FH       ;EBCDIC
        ;       BS   HT   LF   VT   FF   CR   SO   SI          ;ASCII
        DB      016H,005H,025H,00BH,00CH,00DH,00EH,00FH       ;EBCDIC
        ;       DLE  DC1  DC2  DC3  DC4  NAK  SYN  ETB         ;ASCII
        DB      010H,011H,012H,013H,03CH,03DH,032H,026H       ;EBCDIC
        ;       CAN  EM   SUB  ESC  IFS  IGS  IRS  IUS         ;ASCII
        DB      018H,019H,03FH,027H,01CH,01DH,01EH,01FH       ;EBCDIC
        ;       SPACE !    "    #    $    %    &    '          ;ASCII
        DB      040H,05AH,07FH,07BH,05BH,06CH,050H,00DH       ;EBCDIC
        ;       (    )    *    +    ,    _    .    /           ;ASCII
        DB      04DH,05DH,05CH,04EH,06BH,060H,04BH,061H       ;EBCDIC
        ;       0    1    2    3    4    5    6    7           ;ASCII
        DB      0F0H,0F1H,0F2H,0F3H,0F4H,0F5H,0F6H,0F7H       ;EBCDIC
        ;       8    9    :    ;    <    =    >    ?           ;ASCII
        DB      0F8H,0F9H,07AH,05EH,04CH,07EH,06EH,06FH       ;EBCDIC
        ;       @    A    B    C    D    E    F    G           ;ASCII
        DB      07CH,0C1H,0C2H,0C3H,0C4H,0C5H,0C6H,0C7H       ;EBCDIC
        ;       H    I    J    K    L    M    N    O           ;ASCII
        DB      0C8H,0C9H,0D1H,0D2H,0D3H,0D4H,0D5H,0D6H       ;EBCDIC
        ;       P    Q    R    S    T    U    V    W           ;ASCII
        DB      0D7H,0D8H,0D9H,0E2H,0E3H,0E4H,0E5H,0E6H       ;EBCDIC
        ;       X    Y    Z    [    \    ]    ^    _           ;ASCII
        DB      0E7H,0E8H,0E9H,040H,0E0H,040H,040H,06DH       ;EBCDIC
        ;       `    a    b    c    d    e    f    g           ;ASCII
        DB      009H,081H,082H,083H,084H,085H,086H,087H       ;EBCDIC
        ;       h    i    j    k    l    m    n    o           ;ASCII
        DB      088H,089H,091H,092H,093H,094H,095H,096H       ;EBCDIC
        ;       p    q    r    s    t    u    v    w           ;ASCII
```

```
        DB      097H, 098H, 099H, 0A2H, 0A3H, 0A4H, 0A5H, 0A6H              ;EBCDIC
        ;          x    y    z    {    ¦.   }    ~    DEL                    ;ASCII
        DB      0A7H, 0A8H, 0A9H, 0C0H, 06AH, 0D0H, 0A1H, 007H              ;EBCDIC


;                                                                           ;
;                                                                           ;
;       SAMPLE EXECUTION                                                    ;
;                                                                           ;
;                                                                           ;

SC4H:
        ;CONVERT ASCII 'A' TO EBCDIC
        MVI     A,'A'               ;ASCII 'A'
        CALL    ASC2EB              ;EBCDIC 'A' = 0C1H

        ;CONVERT ASCII '1' TO EBCDIC
        MVI     A,'1'               ;ASCII '1'
        CALL    ASC2EB              ;EBCDIC '1' = 0F1H

        ;CONVERT ASCII 'a' TO EBCDIC
        MVI     A,'a'               ;ASCII 'a'
        CALL    ASC2EB              ;EBCDIC 'a' = 081H

        JMP     SC4H

        END
```

Converts an EBCDIC character to its ASCII equivalent.

Procedure: The program uses a simple table lookup with the data as the index and address ASCII as the base. A printable EBCDIC character with no ASCII equivalent is translated to an ASCII space (20_{16}); a non-printable EBCDIC character with no ASCII equivalent is translated to an ASCII NUL (00_{16}).

Registers Used: AF, DE, HL

Execution Time: 48 cycles

Program Size: Nine bytes, plus 256 bytes for the conversion table

Data Memory Required: None

Entry Conditions

EBCDIC character in A

Exit Conditions

ASCII equivalent in A

Examples

1. Data: (A) = 85_{16} (EBCDIC e)

   Result: (A) = 65_{16} (ASCII e)

2. Data: (A) = $4E_{16}$ (EBCDIC +)

   Result: (A) = $2B_{16}$ (ASCII +)

```
;
;
;
;
;        Title:      EBCDIC to ASCII Conversion
;        Name:       EB2ASC
;
;
;
;        Purpose:    Convert an EBCDIC character to its
;                    corresponding ASCII character
;
;        Entry:      Register A = EBCDIC character
;
;        Exit:       Register A = ASCII character
;
;        Registers used: AF,DE,HL
```

172

```
;                                                                     ;
;       Time:               48 cycles                                 ;
;                                                                     ;
;       Size:               Program 9 bytes                           ;
;                           Data  256 bytes for the table             ;
;                                                                     ;
;                                                                     ;

EB2ASC:
        LXI     H,ASCII         ;GET BASE ADDRESS OF ASCII TABLE
        MOV     E,A             ;USE EBCDIC AS INDEX
        MVI     D,0
        DAD     D
        MOV     A,M             ;GET ASCII CHARACTER
        RET

;EBCDIC TO ASCII TABLE
; A PRINTABLE EBCDIC CHARACTER WITH NO ASCII EQUIVALENT IS
; TRANSLATED TO AN ASCII SPACE (020H), A NON-PRINTABLE EBCDIC CHARACTER
; WITH NO EQUIVALENT IS TRANSLATED TO AN ASCII NUL (000H)
ASCII:
;       NUL  SOH  STX  ETX       HT        DEL          ;EBCDIC
DB      000H,001H,002H,003H,000H,009H,000H,07FH         ;ASCII
;                      VT   FF   CR   SO   SI           ;EBCDIC
DB      000H,000H,000H,00BH,00CH,00DH,00EH,00FH         ;ASCII
;       DLE  DC1  DC2  DC3            BS                ;EBCDIC
DB      010H,011H,012H,013H,000H,000H,008H,000H         ;ASCII
;       CAN  EM             IFS  IGS  IRS  IUS          ;EBCDIC
DB      018H,019H,000H,000H,01CH,01DH,01EH,01FH         ;ASCII
;                                LF   ETB  ESC          ;EBCDIC
DB      000H,000H,000H,000H,000H,00AH,017H,01BH         ;ASCII
;                                ENQ  ACK  BEL          ;EBCDIC
DB      000H,000H,000H,000H,000H,005H,006H,007H         ;ASCII
;                 SYN                      EOT          ;EBCDIC
DB      000H,000H,016H,000H,000H,000H,000H,004H         ;ASCII
;                           DC4  NAK       SUB          ;EBCDIC
DB      000H,000H,000H,000H,014H,015H,000H,01AH         ;ASCII
;       SPACE                                           ;EBCDIC
DB      ' ' ,000H,000H,000H,000H,000H,000H,000H         ;ASCII
;                 ¢    .    <    (    +    |            ;EBCDIC
DB      000H,000H,' ' ,'.' ,'<' ,'(' ,'+' ,' '          ;ASCII
;        &                                              ;EBCDIC
DB      '&' ,000H,000H,000H,000H,000H,000H,000H         ;ASCII
;                 !    $    *    )    ;    ¬            ;EBCDIC
DB      000H,000H,'!' ,'$' ,'*' ,')' ,';' ,' '          ;ASCII
;        _    /                                         ;EBCDIC
DB      '_' ,'/' ,000H,000H,000H,000H,000H,000H         ;ASCII
;                 ¦    ,    %    -    >    ?            ;EBCDIC
DB      000H,000H,'¦' ,',' ,'%' ,'-' ,'>' ,'?'          ;ASCII
;                                                       ;EBCDIC
DB      000H,000H,000H,000H,000H,000H,000H,000H         ;ASCII
;            `    :    #    @    '    =    "            ;EBCDIC
DB      000H,'`' ,':' ,'#' ,'@' ,'''',' =' ,'"'         ;ASCII
;            a    b    c    d    e    f    g            ;EBCDIC
DB      000H,'a' ,'b' ,'c' ,'d' ,'e' ,'f' ,'g'          ;ASCII
;        h    i                                         ;EBCDIC
```

```
        DB      'h' ,'i' ,000H,000H,000H,000H,000H,000H        ;ASCII
        ;         j    k    l    m    n    o    p               ;EBCDIC
        DB      000H,'j' ,'k' ,'l' ,'m' ,'n' ,'o' ,'p'         ;ASCII
        ;         q    r                                        ;EBCDIC
        DB      'q' ,'r' ,000H,000H,000H,000H,000H,000H        ;ASCII
        ;              ~    s    t    u    v    w    x           ;EBCDIC
        DB      000H,'~' ,'s' ,'t' ,'u' ,'v' ,'w', 'x'         ;ASCII
        ;         y    z                                        ;EBCDIC
        DB      'y' ,'z' ,000H,000H,000H,000H,000H,000H        ;ASCII
        ;                                                        ;EBCDIC
        DB      000H,000H,000H,000H,000H,000H,000H,000H        ;ASCII
        ;                                                        ;EBCDIC
        DB      000H,000H,000H,000H,000H,000H,000H,000H        ;ASCII
        ;              {    A    B    C    D    E    F    G      ;EBCDIC
        DB      '{' ,'A' ,'B' ,'C' ,'D' ,'E' ,'F' ,'G'         ;ASCII
        ;         H    I                                        ;EBCDIC
        DB      'H' ,'I' ,000H,000H,000H,000H,000H,000H        ;ASCII
        ;         }    J    K    L    M    N    O    P           ;EBCDIC
        DB      '}' ,'J' ,'K' ,'L' ,'M' ,'N' ,'O' ,'P'         ;ASCII
        ;         Q    R                                        ;EBCDIC
        DB      'Q' ,'R' ,000H,000H,000H,000H,000H,000H        ;ASCII
        ;         \         S    T    U    V    W    X           ;EBCDIC
        DB      '\' ,000H,'S' ,'T' ,'U' ,'V' ,'W', 'X'         ;ASCII
        ;         Y    Z                                        ;EBCDIC
        DB      'Y' ,'Z' ,000H,000H,000H,000H,000H,000H        ;ASCII
        ;         0    1    2    3    4    5    6    7           ;EBCDIC
        DB      '0' ,'1' ,'2' ,'3' ,'4' ,'5' ,'6' ,'7'         ;ASCII-
        ;         9                                             ;EBCDIC
        DB      '9' ,000H,000H,000H,000H,000H,000H,000H        ;ASCII


;                                                              ;
;                                                              ;
;       SAMPLE EXECUTION                                       ;
;                                                              ;
;                                                              ;

SC4I:
        ;CONVERT EBCDIC 'A' TO ASCII
        MVI     A,0C1H          ;EBCDIC 'A'

        CALL    EB2ASC          ;ASCII 'A' = 041H

        ;CONVERT EBCDIC '1' TO ASCII
        MVI     A,0F1H          ;EBCDIC '1'
        CALL    EB2ASC          ;ASCII '1' = 031H

        ;CONVERT EBCDIC 'a' TO ASCII
        MVI     A,081H          ;EBCDIC 'a'
        CALL    EB2ASC          ;ASCII 'a' = 061H

        JMP     SC4I

        END
```

Memory Fill (MFILL)

Places a specified value in each byte of a memory area of known size, starting at a given address.

Procedure: The program simply fills the memory area with the value one byte at a time.

Registers Used: AF, C, DE, HL

Execution Time: Approximately 36 cycles per byte plus 14 cycles overhead (8080) or approximately 37 cycles per byte plus 11 cycles overhead (8085)

Program Size: 10 bytes

Data Memory Required: None

Special Cases:

1. A size of 0000_{16} is interpreted as 10000_{16}. It therefore causes the program to fill 65,536 bytes with the specified value.

2. Filling areas occupied or used by the program itself will cause unpredictable results. Obviously, filling the stack area requires special caution, since the return address is saved there.

Entry Conditions

Base address of memory area in H and L
Area size (number of bytes) in D and E
Value to be placed in memory in A

Exit Conditions

The area from the base address through the number of bytes given by the area size is filled with the specified value. The area thus filled starts at BASE and continues through BASE + SIZE -1 (BASE is the base address and SIZE is the area size).

Examples

1. Data: Value = FF_{16}
   Area size (in bytes) = 0380_{16}
   Base address = $1AE0_{16}$

   Result: FF_{16} placed in addresses $1AE0_{16}$ through $1E5F_{16}$

2. Data: Value = 00_{16} (8080/8085 operation code for NOP)
   Area size (in bytes) = $1C65_{16}$
   Base address = $E34C_{16}$

   Result: 00_{16} placed in addresses $E34C_{16}$ through $FFB0_{16}$

```
;                                                                    ;
;                                                                    ;
;                                                                    ;
;           Title:         Memory Fill                               ;
;           Name:          MFILL                                     ;
;                                                                    ;
;                                                                    ;
;                                                                    ;
;           Purpose:       Fill an area of memory with a value       ;
;                                                                    ;
;           Entry:         Register H = High byte address of base    ;
;                          Register L = Low byte address of base     ;
;                          Register D = High byte of area size       ;
;                          Register E = Low byte of area size        ;
;                          Register A = Value to be placed in memory ;
;                                                                    ;
;                          NOTE: A size of 0 is interpreted as 65536 ;
;                                                                    ;
;           Exit:          Area filled with value                    ;
;                                                                    ;
;           Registers used: AF,C,DE,HL                               ;
;                                                                    ;
;           Time:          8080 - 36 cycles per byte plus 14 cycles  ;
;                          overhead                                  ;
;                          8085 - 37 cycles per byte plus 11 cycles  ;
;                          overhead                                  ;
;                                                                    ;
;           Size:          Program 10 bytes                          ;
;                          Data    None                              ;
;                                                                    ;
;                                                                    ;
;
MFILL:
        MOV     C,A                 ;C = VALUE TO STORE
LOOP:
        MOV     M,C                 ;FILL ONE BYTE WITH VALUE
        INX     H                   ;POINT TO NEXT BYTE
        DCX     D                   ;DECREMENT COUNTER
        MOV     A,E
        ORA     D
        JNZ     LOOP                ;CONTINUE UNTIL COUNTER = 0
        RET


;                                                                    ;
;                                                                    ;
;           SAMPLE EXECUTION                                         ;
;                                                                    ;
;                                                                    ;


SC5A:
        ;FILL BF1 THROUGH BF1+15 WITH 00
        LXI     H,BF1               ;BASE ADDRESS
```

```
        LXI     D,SIZE1             ;NUMBER OF BYTES
        MVI     A,0                 ;VALUE TO FILL WITH
        CALL    MFILL              ;FILL MEMORY

        ;FILL BF2 THROUGH BF2+1999 WITH FF
        LXI     H,BF2              ;BASE ADDRESS
        LXI     D,SIZE2            ;NUMBER OF BYTES
        MVI     A,OFFH             ;VALUE TO FILL WITH
        CALL    MFILL              ;FILL MEMORY

        JMP     SC5A

SIZE1   EQU     16                 ;SIZE OF BUFFER 1 (10 HEX)
SIZE2   EQU     2000               ;SIZE OF BUFFER 2 (07D0 HEX)
BF1:    DS      SIZE1              ;BUFFER 1
BF2:    DS      SIZE2              ;BUFFER 2

        END
```

Moves a block of data from a source area to a destination area.

Procedure: The program determines if the base address of the destination area is within the source area. If it is, then working up from the starting address would overwrite some source data. To avoid overwriting, the program works down from highest address (sometimes called a *move right*). If the base address of the destination area is not within the source area, the program simply moves the data starting from the lowest address (sometimes called a *move left*). An area size (number of bytes to move) of 0000_{16} causes an exit with no memory changed. The program provides automatic address wraparound mod 64K.

Registers Used: All

Execution Time: 48 cycles per byte (8080) or 50 cycles per byte (8085) plus 97 cycles overhead (8080) or 96 cycles overhead (8085) if data can be moved starting from the lowest address (i.e., left); or 134 cycles overhead (8080) or 141 cycles overhead (8085) if data must be moved starting from the highest address (i.e., right) because of overlap

Program Size: 53 bytes

Data Memory Required: None

Special Cases:

1. A size (number of bytes to move) of 0 causes an immediate exit with no memory changed.

2. Moving data to or from areas occupied or used by the program itself or by the stack will have unpredictable results.

Entry Conditions

Base address of source area in H and L
Base address of destination area in D and E
Number of bytes to move in registers B and C

Exit Conditions

The block of memory is moved from the source area to the destination area. If the number of bytes to be moved is NBYTES, the base address of the destination area is DEST, and the base address of the source area is SOURCE, then the data in addresses SOURCE through SOURCE + NBYTES − 1 is moved to addresses DEST through DEST + NBYTES − 1.

Examples

1. Data: Number of bytes to move $= 0200_{16}$
   Base address of destination area $=$
      $05D1_{16}$
   Base address of source area $= 035E_{16}$

   Result: The contents of locations $035E_{16}$ through $055D_{16}$ are moved to $05D1_{16}$ through $07D0_{16}$.

2. Data: Number of bytes to move $= 1B7A_{16}$
   Base address of destination area $= C946_{16}$
   Base address of source area $= C300_{16}$

   Result: The contents of locations $C300_{16}$ through $DE79_{16}$ are moved to $C946_{16}$ through $E4BF_{16}$.

Note that Example 2 is a more difficult problem than Example 1 because the source and destination areas overlap. If, for instance, the program were simply to move data to the destination area starting from the lowest address, it would initially move the contents of $C300_{16}$ to $C946_{16}$. This would destroy the old contents of $C946_{16}$, which are needed later in the move. The solution to this problem is to move the data starting from the highest address if the destination area is above the source area but overlaps it.

```
;
;
;
;
;
;       Title:          Block Move                              ;
;       Name:           BLKMOV                                  ;
;                                                               ;
;                                                               ;
;                                                               ;
;       Purpose:        Move data from source to destination    ;
;                                                               ;
;       Entry:          Register H = High byte of source address ;
;                       Register L = Low byte of source address  ;
;                       Register D = High byte of destination address ;
;                       Register E = Low byte of destination address ;
;                       Register B = High byte of number of bytes to ;
;                         move                                  ;
;                       Register C = Low byte  of number of bytes to ;
;                         move.                                 ;
;                                                               ;
;       Exit:           Data moved from source to destination   ;
;                                                               ;
;       Registers used: All                                    ;
;                                                               ;
;       Time:           8080 - 48 cycles per byte              ;
;                       8085 - 50 cycles per byte              ;
;                       Overhead is: 8080 - 101 cycles if no   ;
;                         problem with overlap, 157 cycles if  ;
;                         overlap; 8085 - 96 cycles if no      ;
;                         problem with overlap, 141 cycles if  ;
;                         overlap                              ;
;                                                               ;
;       Size:           Program 53 bytes                       ;
;                                                               ;
;

BLKMOV:
        MOV     A,B             ;IS SIZE OF AREA 0?
        ORA     C
        RZ                      ;YES, RETURN WITH NOTHING MOVED

;DETERMINE IF DESTINATION AREA IS ABOVE SOURCE AREA AND OVERLAPS
; IT (OVERLAP CAN BE MOD 64K). OVERLAP OCCURS IF
; STARTING DESTINATION ADDRESS MINUS STARTING SOURCE ADDRESS
```

```
            ;(MOD 64K) IS LESS THAN NUMBER OF BYTES TO MOVE
            PUSH    H               ;SAVE SOURCE
            MOV     A,E             ;CALCULATE DESTINATION - SOURCE
            SUB     L
            MOV     L,A             ;SAVE LOW BYTE OF DIFFERENCE
            MOV     A,D
            SBB     H
            MOV     H,A             ;SAVE HIGH BYTE OF DIFFERENCE
            MOV     A,L             ;COMPARE WITH NUMBER OF BYTES TO MOVE
            SUB     C
            MOV     A,H
            SBB     B
            POP     H               ;RESTORE SOURCE

            JNC     DOLEFT          ;JUMP IF NO PROBLEM WITH OVERLAP

            ;DESTINATION AREA IS ABOVE SOURCE AREA AND OVERLAPS IT
            ;MOVE FROM HIGHEST ADDRESS TO AVOID DESTROYING DATA
            MOV     A,L             ;SOURCE PTR = SOURCE PTR + LENGTH
            ADD     C
            MOV     L,A
            MOV     A,H
            ADC     B
            MOV     H,A
            MOV     A,E             ;DEST PTR = DEST PTR + LENGTH
            ADD     C
            MOV     E,A
            MOV     A,D
            ADC     B
            MOV     D,A

            ;MOVE BLOCK STARTING AT HIGHEST ADDRESS
RHTLP:
            DCX     H               ;DECREMENT SOURCE POINTER
            DCX     D               ;DECREMENT DESTINATION POINTER
            MOV     A,M             ;GET NEXT BYTE FROM SOURCE
            STAX    D               ;MOVE IT TO DESTINATION
            DCX     B               ;DECREMENT COUNTER
            MOV     A,B
            ORA     C
            JNZ     RHTLP           ;CONTINUE UNTIL COUNTER = 0
            RET

            ;ORDINARY MOVE STARTING AT LOWEST ADDRESS
DOLEFT:
            MOV     A,M             ;GET NEXT BYTE FROM SOURCE
            STAX    D               ;MOVE IT TO DESTINATION
            INX     H               ;INCREMENT SOURCE POINTER
            INX     D               ;INCREMENT DESTINATION POINTER
            DCX     B               ;DECREMENT COUNTER
            MOV     A,B
            ORA     C
            JNZ     DOLEFT          ;CONTINUE UNTIL COUNTER = 0

EXIT:
            RET
```

```
;                                                                    ;
;                                                                    ;
;          SAMPLE EXECUTION                                          ;
;                                                                    ;
;                                                                    ;
SOURCE    EQU      2000H              ;BASE ADDRESS OF SOURCE AREA
DEST      EQU      2010H              ;BASE ADDRESS OF DESTINATION AREA
LEN       EQU      11H                ;NUMBER OF BYTES TO MOVE

          ;MOVE 11 HEX BYTES FROM 2000-2010 HEX TO 2010-2020 HEX
SC5B:
          LXI      H,SOURCE
          LXI      D,DEST
          LXI      B,LEN
          CALL     BLKMOV             ;MOVE DATA FROM SOURCE TO DESTINATION

          JMP      SC5B

          END
```

Two-Dimensional Byte Array
Indexing (D2BYTE) 5C

Calculates the address of an element of a two-dimensional byte-length array, given the base address of the array, the two subscripts of the element, and the size of a row (that is, the number of columns). The array is assumed to be stored in row major order (that is, by rows) and both subscripts are assumed to begin at 0.

Procedure: The program multiplies the row size (number of columns in a row) times the row subscript (since the elements are stored by rows) and adds the product to the column subscript. It then adds the sum to the base address. The

Registers Used: All

Execution Time: Approximately 1500 cycles, depending mainly on the amount of time required to perform the multiplication

Program Size: 48 bytes

Data Memory Required: Four bytes anywhere in memory to hold the return address (two bytes starting address RETADR) and the column subscript (two bytes starting at address SS2)

program performs the multiplication using a standard shift-and-add algorithm (see Subroutine 6B).

Entry Conditions

Order in stack (starting from the top):

Less significant byte of return address
More significant byte of return address

Less significant byte of column subscript
More significant byte of column subscript

Less significant byte of the size of a row (in bytes)
More significant byte of the size of a row (in bytes)

Less significant byte of row subscript
More significant byte of row subscript

Less significant byte of base address of array
More significant byte of base address of array

Exit Conditions

Address of element in H and L

Examples

1. Data: Base address = $3C00_{16}$
   Column subscript = 0004_{16}
   Size of row (number of columns) = 0018_{16}
   Row subscript = 0003_{16}

   Result: Element address = $3C00_{16} + 0003_{16} *$
   $0018_{16} + 0004_{16} = 3C00_{16} + 0048_{16} +$
   $0004_{16} = 3C4C_{16}$
   That is, the address of ARRAY(3,4) is
   $3C4C_{16}$.

2. Data: Base address = $6A4A_{16}$
Column subscript = 0035_{16}
Size of row (number of columns) = 0050_{16}
Row subscript = 0002_{16}

Result: Element address = $6A4A_{16} + 0002_{16} *$
$0050_{16} + 0035_{16} = 6A4A_{16} + 00A0_{16} +$
$0035_{16} = 6B1F_{16}$
That is, the address of ARRAY(2,35) is
$6B1F_{16}$.

Note that all subscripts are hexadecimal ($35_{16} = 53_{10}$).

The general formula is

ELEMENT ADDRESS = ARRAY BASE
ADDRESS + ROW SUBSCRIPT * ROW SIZE +
COLUMN SUBSCRIPT

Note that we refer to the *size* of the row subscript; the size is the number of consecutive memory addresses for which the subscript has the same value. This is also the number of bytes from the starting address of an element to the starting address of the element with the same column subscript but a row subscript one larger.

```
;                                                                    ;
;                                                                    ;
;                                                                    ;
;                                                                    ;
;        Title:          Two-Dimensional Byte Array Indexing         ;
;        Name:           D2BYTE                                      ;
;                                                                    ;
;                                                                    ;
;                                                                    ;
;        Purpose:        Given the base address of a byte array, two ;
;                        subscripts 'I' and 'J', and the size of the ;
;                        first subscript in bytes, calculate the address ;
;                        of A[I,J]. The array is assumed to be stored in ;
;                        row major order (A[0,0], A[0,1],..., A[K,L]), ;
;                        and both dimensions are assumed to begin at ;
;                        zero as in the following Pascal declaration: ;
;                          A:ARRAY[0..2,0..7] OF BYTE;               ;
;                                                                    ;
;        Entry:          TOP OF STACK                                ;
;                          Low byte of return address               ;
;                          High byte of return address              ;
;                          Low byte of second subscript (column element) ;
;                          High byte of second subscript (column element);
;                          Low byte of first subscript size, in bytes ;
;                          High byte of first subscript size, in bytes ;
;                          Low byte of first subscript (row element) ;
;                          High byte of first subscript (row element) ;
;                          Low byte of array base address           ;
;                          High byte of array base address          ;
;                        NOTE:                                       ;
;                        The first subscript size is the length of a ;
;                        row in bytes.                               ;
;                                                                    ;
;        Exit:           Register H = High byte of element address   ;
;                        Register L = Low byte of element address    ;
```

```
;
;           Registers used: All                                      ;
;                                                                    ;
;           Time:           Approximately 1500 cycles                ;
;                                                                    ;
;           Size:           Program 48 bytes                         ;
;                           Data    4 bytes                          ;
;                                                                    ;
;                                                                    ;

D2BYTE:
          ;SAVE RETURN ADDRESS
          POP     H
          SHLD    RETADR

          ;GET SECOND SUBSCRIPT
          POP     H
          SHLD    SS2

          ;GET SIZE OF FIRST SUBSCRIPT (ROW LENGTH), FIRST SUBSCRIPT
          POP     D               ;GET LENGTH OF ROW
          POP     B               ;GET FIRST SUBSCRIPT

          ;MULTIPLY FIRST SUBSCRIPT * ROW LENGTH USING SHIFT AND ADD
          ; ALGORITHM. PRODUCT IS IN HL
          LXI     H,0             ;PRODUCT = 0
          MVI     A,15            ;COUNT = BIT LENGTH - 1
MLP:
          PUSH    PSW             ;SAVE COUNT
          ORA     D               ;SIGN FLAG = MSB OF MULTIPLIER
                                  ; (BIT 7 OF COUNT IS ALWAYS ZERO)
          JP      MLP1            ;JUMP IF MSB OF MULTIPLIER = 0
          DAD     B               ;ADD MULTIPLICAND TO PARTIAL PRODUCT
MLP1:     DAD     H               ;SHIFT PARTIAL PRODUCT
          XCHG
          DAD     H               ;SHIFT MULTIPLIER
          XCHG
          POP     PSW             ;RESTORE COUNT
          DCR     A
          JNZ     MLP             ;CONTINUE THROUGH 15 BITS

          ;DO LAST ADD IF MSB OF MULTIPLIER IS 1
          ORA     D               ;SIGN FLAG = MSB OF MULTIPLIER
          JP      MLP2
          DAD     B               ;ADD IN MULTIPLICAND IF SIGN = 1

          ;ADD IN SECOND SUBSCRIPT
MLP2:     XCHG
          LHLD    SS2
          DAD     D

          ;ADD BASE ADDRESS TO FORM FINAL ADDRESS
          POP     D               ;GET BASE ADDRESS OF ARRAY
          DAD     D               ;ADD BASE TO INDEX

          ;RETURN TO CALLER
```

```
        PUSH    H                       ;RESTORE RETURN ADDRESS TO STACK
        LHLD    RETADR
        XTHL
        RET

        ;DATA
RETADR: DS      2                       ;TEMPORARY FOR RETURN ADDRESS
SS2:    DS      2                       ;TEMPORARY FOR SECOND SUBSCRIPT


;
;
;       SAMPLE EXECUTION
;
;

SC5C:
        LXI     H,ARY                   ;PUSH BASE ADDRESS OF ARRAY
        PUSH    H
        LHLD    SUBS1                   ;PUSH FIRST SUBSCRIPT
        PUSH    H
        LHLD    SSUBS1                  ;PUSH SIZE OF FIRST SUBSCRIPT
        PUSH    H
        LHLD    SUBS2                   ;PUSH SECOND SUBSCRIPT
        PUSH    H
        CALL    D2BYTE                  ;CALCULATE ADDRESS
                                        ;FOR THE INITIAL TEST DATA
                                        ;HL = ADDRESS OF ARY(2,4)
                                        ;   = ARY + (2*8) + 4
                                        ;   = ARY + 20 (CONTENTS ARE 21)
                                        ;NOTE BOTH SUBSCRIPTS START AT 0

        JMP     SC5C

        ;DATA
SUBS1:  DW      2                       ;SUBSCRIPT 1
SSUBS1: DW      8                       ;SIZE OF SUBSCRIPT 1
SUBS2:  DW      4                       ;SUBSCRIPT 2

;THE ARRAY (3 ROWS OF 8 COLUMNS)
ARY:    DB      1 ,2 ,3 ,4 ,5 ,6 ,7 ,8
        DB      9 ,10,11,12,13,14,15,16
        DB      17,18,19,20,21,22,23,24

        END
```

Two-Dimensional Word Array
Indexing (D2WORD)

Calculates the starting address of an element of a two-dimensional word-length (16-bit) array, given the base address of the array, the two subscripts of the element, and the size of a row in bytes. The array is assumed to be stored in row major order (that is, by rows), and both subscripts are assumed to begin at 0.

Procedure: The program multiplies the row size (in bytes) times the row subscript (since the elements are stored by row), adds the product to the doubled column subscript (doubled because each element occupies two bytes), and

Registers Used: All

Execution Time: Approximately 1500 cycles, depending mainly on how long it takes to multiply row size times row subscript

Program Size: 49 bytes

Data Memory Required: Four bytes anywhere in memory to hold the return address (two bytes starting at address RETADR) and the column subscript (two bytes starting at address SS2)

adds the sum to the base address. The program uses a standard shift-and-add algorithm (see Subroutine 6B) to multiply.

Entry Conditions

Order in stack (starting at the top):

Less significant byte of return address
More significant byte of return address
Less significant byte of column subscript
More significant byte of column subscript
Less significant byte of size of rows (in bytes)
More significant byte of size of rows (in bytes)
Less significant byte of row subscript
More significant byte of row subscript
Less significant byte of base address of array
More significant byte of base address of array

Exit Conditions

Starting address of element in H and L
The element occupies the address in H and L and the next higher address.

Examples

1. Data: Base address = $5E14_{16}$
   Column subscript = 0008_{16}
   Size of a row (in bytes) = $001C_{16}$ (i.e., each row has 0014_{10} or $000E_{16}$ word-length elements)
   Row subscript = 0005_{16}

   Result: Element starting address = $5E14_{16} + 0005_{16} * 001C_{16} + 0008_{16} * 2 = 5E14_{16} + 008C_{16} + 0010_{16} = 5EB0_{16}$
   That is, the starting address of ARRAY(5,8) is $5EB0_{16}$ and the element occupies $5EB0_{16}$ and $5EB1_{16}$.

2. Data: Base address $= B100_{16}$
Column subscript $= 0002_{16}$
Size of a row (in bytes) $= 0008_{16}$ (i.e., each row has four word-length elements)
Row subscript $= 0006_{16}$

Result: Element starting address $= B100_{16} + 0006_{16} * 0008_{16} + 0002_{16} * 2 = B100_{16} + 0030_{16} + 0004_{16} = B134_{16}$
That is, the starting address of $ARRAY(6,2)$ is $B134_{16}$ and the element occupies $B134_{16}$ and $B135_{16}$.

The general formula is

ELEMENT STARTING ADDRESS =
ARRAY BASE ADDRESS + ROW SUBSCRIPT *
SIZE OF ROW + COLUMN SUBSCRIPT * 2

Note that one parameter of this routine is the size of a row in bytes. The size for word-length elements is the number of columns per row times 2 (the size of an element in bytes). The reason this parameter was chosen rather than the number of columns or the maximum column index is that this parameter can be calculated once (when the array bounds are determined) and used whenever the array is accessed. The alternative parameters (number of columns or maximum column index) would require extra calculations during each indexing operation.

```
;                                                              ;
;                                                              ;
;                                                              ;
;                                                              ;
;       Title:      Two-Dimensional Word Array Indexing        ;
;       Name:       D2WORD                                     ;
;                                                              ;
;                                                              ;
;                                                              ;
;                                                              ;
;       Purpose:    Given the base address of a word array, two;
;                   subscripts 'I' and 'J', and the size of the;
;                   first subscript in bytes, calculate the address ;
;                   of A[I,J]. The array is assumed to be stored in ;
;                   row major order (A[0,0], A[0,1],..., A[K,L]), ;
;                   and both dimensions are assumed to begin at ;
;                   zero as in the following Pascal declaration: ;
;                     A:ARRAY[0..2,0..7] OF WORD;              ;
;                                                              ;
;       Entry:      TOP OF STACK                               ;
;                     Low byte of return address              ;
;                     High byte of return address             ;
;                     Low byte of second subscript (column element) ;
;                     High byte of second subscript (column element);
;                     Low byte of first subscript size, in bytes ;
;                     High byte of first subscript size, in bytes ;
;                     Low byte of first subscript (row element) ;
;                     High byte of first subscript (row element) ;
;                     Low byte of array base address          ;
;                     High byte of array base address         ;
;                   NOTE:                                      ;
;                     The first subscript size is the length of a ;
;                     row in words * 2.                        ;
```

```
;                                                                          ;
;         Exit:           Register H = High byte of element address        ;
;                         Register L = Low byte of element address         ;
;                                                                          ;
;         Registers used: All                                              ;
;                                                                          ;
;         Time:           Approximately 1500 cycles                        ;
;                                                                          ;
;         Size:           Program 49 bytes                                 ;
;                         Data     4 bytes                                 ;
;                                                                          ;
;                                                                          ;

D2WORD:
          ;SAVE RETURN ADDRESS
          POP     H
          SHLD    RETADR

          ;GET SECOND SUBSCRIPT, MULTIPLY BY 2 FOR WORD-LENGTH ELEMENTS
          POP     H
          DAD     H               ;* 2
          SHLD    SS2

          ;GET SIZE OF FIRST SUBSCRIPT (ROW LENGTH), FIRST SUBSCRIPT
          POP     D               ;GET LENGTH OF ROW
          POP     B               ;GET FIRST SUBSCRIPT

          ;MULTIPLY FIRST SUBSCRIPT * ROW LENGTH USING SHIFT AND ADD
          ; ALGORITHM. PRODUCT IS IN HL
          LXI     H,0             ;PRODUCT = 0
          MVI     A,15            ;COUNT = BIT LENGTH - 1
MLP:
          PUSH    PSW             ;SAVE COUNT
          ORA     D               ;SIGN FLAG = MSB OF MULTIPLIER
                                  ; (BIT 7 OF COUNT IS ALWAYS ZERO)
          JP      MLP1            ;JUMP IF MSB OF MULTIPLIER = 0
          DAD     B               ;ADD MULTIPLICAND TO PARTIAL PRODUCT
MLP1:     DAD     H               ;SHIFT PARTIAL PRODUCT
          XCHG
          DAD     H               ;SHIFT MULTIPLIER
          XCHG
          POP     PSW             ;RESTORE COUNT
          DCR     A
          JNZ     MLP             ;CONTINUE THROUGH 15 BITS

          ;ADD MULTIPLICAND IN LAST TIME IF MSB OF MULTIPLIER IS 1
          ORA     D               ;SIGN FLAG = MSB OF MULTIPLIER
          JP      MLP2
          DAD     B               ;ADD IN MULTIPLICAND IF SIGN = 1

          ;ADD IN SECOND SUBSCRIPT
MLP2:     XCHG
          LHLD    SS2
          DAD     D

          ;ADD BASE ADDRESS TO FORM FINAL ADDRESS
```

```
            POP       D                   ;GET BASE ADDRESS OF ARRAY
            DAD       D                   ;ADD BASE TO INDEX

            ;RETURN TO CALLER
            PUSH      H                   ;RESTORE RETURN ADDRESS TO STACK
            LHLD      RETADR
            XTHL
            RET

            ;DATA
RETADR:     DS        2                   ;TEMPORARY FOR RETURN ADDRESS
SS2:        DS        2                   ;TEMPORARY FOR SECOND SUBSCRIPT


;                                                                            ;
;                                                                            ;
;           SAMPLE EXECUTION                                                 ;
;                                                                            ;
;                                                                            ;

SC5D:
            LXI       H,ARY               ;PUSH BASE ADDRESS OF ARRAY
            PUSH      H
            LHLD      SUBS1               ;PUSH FIRST SUBSCRIPT
            PUSH      H
            LHLD      SSUBS1              ;PUSH SIZE OF FIRST SUBSCRIPT
            PUSH      H
            LHLD      SUBS2               ;PUSH SECOND SUBSCRIPT
            PUSH      H
            CALL      D2WORD              ;CALCULATE ADDRESS
                                          ;FOR THE INITIAL TEST DATA
                                          ;HL = ADDRESS OF ARY(2,4)
                                          ;   = ARY + (2*16) + 4 * 2
                                          ;   = ARY + 40 (CONTENTS ARE 2100H)
                                          ;NOTE BOTH SUBSCRIPTS START AT 0

            JMP       SC5D

            ;DATA
SUBS1:      DW        2                   ;SUBSCRIPT 1
SSUBS1:     DW        16                  ;SIZE OF SUBSCRIPT 1
SUBS2:      DW        4                   ;SUBSCRIPT 2

;THE ARRAY (3 ROWS OF 8 COLUMNS)
ARY:        DW        0100H,0200H,0300H,0400H,0500H,0600H,0700H,0800H
            DW        0900H,1000H,1100H,1200H,1300H,1400H,1500H,1600H
            DW        1700H,1800H,1900H,2000H,2100H,2200H,2300H,2400H

            END
```

Calculates the starting address of an element of an N-dimensional array given the base address and N pairs of sizes and subscripts. The size of a dimension is the number of bytes from the starting address of an element to the starting address of the element with an index one larger in the dimension but the same in all other dimensions. The array is assumed to be stored in row major order (that is, organized so that subscripts to the right change before subscripts to the left).

Note that the size of the rightmost subscript is simply the size of the elements (in bytes); the size of the next subscript is the size of the elements times the maximum value of the rightmost subscript plus 1, and so on. All subscripts are assumed to begin at 0. Otherwise, the user must normalize the subscripts. (See the second example at the end of the listing.)

Procedure: The program loops on each dimension, calculating the offset in that dimension as the subscript times the size. If the size is an easy case (an integral power of 2), the program reduces the multiplication to left shifts. Otherwise, it performs each multiplication using the shift-and-add algorithm of Subroutine 6B. Once the program has calculated the overall offset, it adds that offset to the base address to obtain the starting address of the element.

Registers Used: All

Execution Time: Approximately 1700 cycles per dimension plus 170 cycles overhead (depends mainly on how much time is required to perform the multiplications)

Program Size: 130 bytes

Data Memory Required: Five bytes anywhere in memory to hold the return address (two bytes starting at address RETADR), the accumulated offset (two bytes starting at address OFFSET), and the number of dimensions (one byte at address NUMDIM)

Special Case: If the number of dimensions is 0, the program returns with the base address in H and L.

Entry Conditions

Order in stack (starting from the top)

Less significant byte of return address
More significant byte of return address

Less significant byte of number of dimensions
More significant byte of number of dimensions
   (not used)

Less significant byte of size of rightmost
   dimension
More significant byte of size of rightmost
   dimension

Less significant byte of rightmost subscript
More significant byte of rightmost subscript

.
.
.

Less significant byte of size of leftmost
   dimension
More significant byte of size of leftmost
   dimension

Less significant byte of leftmost subscript
More significant byte of leftmost subscript

Less significant byte of base address of array
More significant byte of base address of array

Exit Conditions

Starting address of element in H and L

The element occupies memory addresses START through START + SIZE − 1, where START is the calculated address and SIZE is the size of an element in bytes.

Examples

1. Data: Base address = $3C00_{16}$
   Number of dimensions = 03_{16}
   Rightmost subscript = 0005_{16}
   Rightmost size = 0003_{16} (3-byte entries)
   Middle subscript = 0003_{16}
   Middle size = 0012_{16} (six 3-byte entries)
   Leftmost subscript = 0004_{16}
   Leftmost size = $007E_{16}$ (seven sets of six 3-byte entries)

   Result: Element starting address = $3C00_{16}$ + $0005_{16} * 0003_{16} + 0003_{16} * 0012_{16} + 0004_{16} * 007E_{16} = 3C00_{16} + 000F_{16} + 0036_{16} + 01F8_{16} = 3E3D_{16}$
   That is, the element is ARRAY(4,3,5); it occupies addresses $3E3D_{16}$ through $3E3F_{16}$. (The maximum values of the various subscripts are 6 (leftmost) and 5 (middle), with each element occupying three bytes.)

The general formula is

STARTING ADDRESS = BASE ADDRESS +

$$\sum_{i=0}^{N-1} SUBSCRIPT_i * SIZE_i$$

where:

N is the number of dimensions
$SUBSCRIPT_i$ is the ith subscript
$SIZE_i$ is the size of the ith dimension

Note that the size of each dimension is used as a parameter to reduce the number of repetitive multiplications and to generalize the procedure. The sizes can be calculated and saved as soon as the bounds of the array are known. Those sizes can then be used whenever indexing is performed on that array. Obviously, the sizes do not change if the bounds are fixed, and they should not be recalculated as part of each indexing operation. The sizes are also general, since the elements can themselves consist of any number of bytes.

```
;                                                              ;
;                                                              ;
;                                                              ;
;                                                              ;
;       Title:        N-Dimensional Array Indexing             ;
;       Name:         NDIM                                     ;
;                                                              ;
;                                                              ;
;                                                              ;
```

```
;                                                                        ;
;       Purpose:        Calculate the address of an element in an        ;
;                       N-dimensional array given the base address,      ;
;                       N pairs of size in bytes and subscript, and the  ;
;                       number of dimensions of the array. The array is  ;
;                       assumed to be stored in row major order          ;
;                       (A[0,0,0],A[0,0,1],...,A[0,1,0],A[0,1,1],...).    ;
;                       Also, it is assumed that all dimensions begin     ;
;                       at 0 as in the following Pascal declaration:     ;
;                         A:ARRAY[0..10,0..3,0..5] OF SOMETHING          ;
;                                                                        ;
;       Entry:          TOP OF STACK                                     ;
;                         Low byte of return address                    ;
;                         High byte of return address                   ;
;                         Low byte of number of dimensions              ;
;                         High byte of number of dimensions (not used)  ;
;                         Low byte of dim N-1 size                      ;
;                         High byte of dim N-1 size                     ;
;                         Low byte of dim N-1 subscript                 ;
;                         High byte of dim N-1 subscript                ;
;                         Low byte of dim N-2 size                      ;
;                         High byte of dim N-2 size                     ;
;                         Low byte of dim N-2 subscript                 ;
;                         High byte of dim N-2 subscript                ;
;                                                                        ;
;                                     .                                  ;
;                                     .                                  ;
;                                     .                                  ;
;                         Low byte of dim 0 size                        ;
;                         High byte of dim 0 size                       ;
;                         Low byte of dim 0 subscript                   ;
;                         High byte of dim 0 subscript                  ;
;                         Low byte of array base address               ;
;                         High byte of array base address              ;
;                       NOTE:                                            ;
;                         All sizes are in bytes.                       ;
;                                                                        ;
;       Exit:           Register H = High byte of element's starting     ;
;                       address                                          ;
;                       Register L = Low byte  of element's starting     ;
;                       address                                          ;
;                                                                        ;
;       Registers used: All                                              ;
;                                                                        ;
;       Time:           Approximately 1700 cycles per dimension          ;
;                       plus 170 cycles overhead                        ;
;                                                                        ;
;       Size:           Program 130 bytes                               ;
;                       Data      5 bytes                               ;
;                                                                        ;
;                                                                        ;
NDIM:
        ;POP PARAMETERS
        POP     H               ;SAVE RETURN ADDRESS
        SHLD    RETADR
        ;OFFSET := 0
```

```
        LXI     H,0
        SHLD    OFFSET

        ;GET NUMBER OF DIMENSIONS AND TEST FOR 0
        POP     H
        MOV     A,L
        STA     NUMDIM          ;GET NUMBER OF DIMENSIONS
        ORA     A               ;TEST FOR 0
        JZ      ADBASE          ;RETURN WITH BASE ADDRESS IN HL
                                ; IF THERE ARE NO DIMENSIONS

        ;LOOP ON EACH DIMENSION
        ; DOING OFFSET := OFFSET + (SUBSCRIPT * SIZE)
LOOP:
        POP     D               ;GET SIZE
        POP     H               ;GET SUBSCRIPT
        CALL    NXTOFF          ;OFFSET := OFFSET + (SUBSCRIPT * SIZE)
        LXI     H,NUMDIM
        DCR     M               ;DECREMENT NUMBER OF DIMENSIONS
        JNZ     LOOP            ;CONTINUE THROUGH ALL DIMENSIONS

ADBASE:
        ;CALCULATE STARTING ADDRESS OF ELEMENT
        ;OFFSET = BASE + OFFSET
        LHLD    OFFSET
        POP     D               ;GET BASE ADDRESS
        DAD     D               ;SUM WITH OFFSET

        ;RESTORE RETURN ADDRESS AND EXIT
        XCHG
        LHLD    RETADR          ;RESTORE RETURN ADDRESS TO STACK
        PUSH    H
        XCHG
        RET


        ;--------------------------------
        ;SUBROUTINE NXTOFF
        ;PURPOSE: OFFSET := OFFSET + (SUBSCRIPT * SIZE);
        ;ENTRY: OFFSET = CURRENT OFFSET
        ;       DE = CURRENT SIZE OF THIS DIMENSION
        ;       HL = CURRENT SUBSCRIPT
        ;EXIT:  OFFSET = OFFSET + (SUBSCRIPT * SIZE);
        ;REGISTERS USED: ALL
        ;--------------------------------
NXTOFF:
        PUSH    H               ;SAVE CURRENT SUBSCRIPT ON THE STACK

        ;CHECK IF SIZE IS POWER OF 2 LESS THAN 256
        MOV     A,D
        ORA     A               ;HIGH BYTE = 0?

        JNZ     BIGSZ           ;JUMP IF SIZE IS LARGE

        MOV     A,E             ;A = LOW BYTE OF SIZE
        LXI     H,EASYAY        ;HL = BASE ADDRESS OF EASYAY
        MVI     B,SZEASY        ;B = SIZE OF EASY ARRAY
```

```
            MVI     C,0                     ;C = SHIFT COUNTER
EASYLP:
            CMP     M
            JZ      ISEASY                  ;JUMP IF SIZE IS POWER OF 2
            INX     H                       ;INCREMENT TO NEXT BYTE OF EASYAY
            INR     C                       ;INCREMENT SHIFT COUNTER
            DCR     B                       ;DECREMENT COUNT
            JNZ     EASYLP                  ;JUMP IF NOT THROUGH ALL EASY ELEMENTS
            JMP     BIGSZ                   ;JUMP IF SIZE IS NOT EASY

ISEASY:
            POP     H                       ;GET SUBSCRIPT
            MOV     A,C                     ;GET NUMBER OF SHIFTS
            ORA     A                       ;TEST FOR 0
            JZ      ADDOFF                  ;JUMP IF SHIFT FACTOR = 0

            ;ELEMENT SIZE * SUBSCRIPT REDUCES TO LEFT SHIFTS
            DAD     H                       ;MULTIPLY SUBSCRIPT BY 2
            DCR     A                       ;DECREMENT SHIFT COUNT
            JNZ     SHIFT                   ;CONTINUE UNTIL DONE
            JMP     ADDOFF                  ;DONE SO ADD OFFSET + SUBSCRIPT

BIGSZ:
            ;SIZE NOT POWER OF 2, MULTIPLY
            ; ELEMENT SIZE TIMES SUBSCRIPT THE HARD WAY
            POP     B                       ;GET SUBSCRIPT

            ;MULTIPLY FIRST SUBSCRIPT * ROW LENGTH USING SHIFT AND ADD
            ; ALGORITHM. PRODUCT IS IN HL
            ; BC = SUBSCRIPT (MULTIPLICAND)
            ; DE = SIZE (MULTIPLIER)
            LXI     H,0                     ;PRODUCT = 0
            MVI     A,15                    ;COUNT = BIT LENGTH - 1
MLP:
            PUSH    PSW                     ;SAVE COUNT
            ORA     D                       ;SIGN FLAG = MSB OF MULTIPLIER
                                            ; (BIT 7 OF COUNT IS ALWAYS ZERO)
            JP      MLP1                    ;JUMP IF MSB OF MULTIPLIER = 0
            DAD     B                       ;ADD MULTIPLICAND TO PARTIAL PRODUCT
MLP1:       DAD     H                       ;SHIFT PARTIAL PRODUCT
            XCHG
            DAD     H                       ;SHIFT MULTIPLIER
            XCHG
            POP     PSW                     ;RESTORE COUNT
            DCR     A
            JNZ     MLP                     ;CONTINUE THROUGH 15 BITS

            ;ADD IN MULTIPLICAND LAST TIME IF MSB OF MULTIPLIER IS 1
            ORA     D                       ;SIGN FLAG = MSB OF MULTIPLIER
            JP      ADDOFF
            DAD     B                       ;ADD IN MULTIPLICAND IF SIGN = 1

            ;ADD SUBSCRIPT * SIZE TO OFFSET


ADDOFF:
```

```
        XCHG
        LHLD      OFFSET              ;GET OFFSET
        DAD       D                   ;ADD PRODUCT OF SUBSCRIPT * SIZE
        SHLD      OFFSET              ;SAVE OFFSET
        RET

EASYAY:                               ;SHIFT FACTOR
        DB        1                   ;0
        DB        2                   ;1
        DB        4                   ;2
        DB        8                   ;3
        DB        16                  ;4
        DB        32                  ;5
        DB        64                  ;6
        DB        128                 ;7
SZEASY  EQU       $-EASYAY

        ;DATA
RETADR:           DS        2         ;TEMPORARY FOR RETURN ADDRESS
OFFSET:           DS        2         ;TEMPORARY FOR PARTIAL OFFSET
NUMDIM:           DS        1         ;NUMBER OF DIMENSIONS

;                                                                       ;
;                                                                       ;
;       SAMPLE EXECUTION                                                ;
;                                                                       ;
;                                                                       ;

SC5E:
        ;FIND ADDRESS OF AY1[1,3,0]
        ; SINCE LOWER BOUNDS OF ARRAY 1 ARE ALL ZERO IT IS NOT
        ; NECESSARY TO NORMALIZE THEM

        ;PUSH BASE ADDRESS OF ARRAY 1
        LXI       H,AY1
        PUSH      H

        ;PUSH SUBSCRIPT/SIZE FOR DIMENSION 1
        LXI       H,1                 ;SUBSCRIPT
        PUSH      H
        LXI       H,A1SZ1             ;SIZE
        PUSH      H

        ;PUSH SUBSCRIPT/SIZE FOR DIMENSION 2
        LXI       H,3                 ;SUBSCRIPT
        PUSH      H
        LXI       H,A1SZ2             ;SIZE
        PUSH      H

        ;PUSH SUBSCRIPT/SIZE FOR DIMENSION 3
        LXI       H,0                 ;SUBSCRIPT
        PUSH      H
        LXI       H,A1SZ3             ;SIZE
        PUSH      H

        ;PUSH NUMBER OF DIMENSIONS
```

```
        LXI     H,A1DIM         ;DIMENSIONS
        PUSH    H

        CALL    NDIM            ;CALCULATE ADDRESS
                                ;AY = STARTING ADDRESS OF ARY1(1,3,0)
                                ;   = ARY + (1*126) + (3*21) + (0*3)
                                ;   = ARY + 189

    ;CALCULATE ADDRESS OF AY2[-1,6]
    ; SINCE LOWER BOUNDS OF AY2 DO NOT START AT 0, SUBSCRIPTS
    ; MUST BE NORMALIZED

    ;PUSH BASE ADDRESS OF ARRAY 2
        LXI     H,AY2
        PUSH    H

    ;PUSH (SUBSCRIPT - LOWER BOUND)/SIZE FOR DIMENSION 1
        LXI     H,-1            ;SUBSCRIPT
        LXI     D,-A2D1L        ;NEGATIVE OF LOWER BOUND
        DAD     D               ;ADD NEGATIVE TO NORMALIZE TO 0
        PUSH    H
        LXI     H,A2SZ1         ;SIZE
        PUSH    H

    ;PUSH (SUBSCRIPT - LOWER BOUND)/SIZE FOR DIMENSION 2
        LXI     H,6             ;SUBSCRIPT
        LXI     D,-A2D2L        ;NEGATIVE OF LOWER BOUND
        DAD     D               ;ADD NEGATIVE TO NORMALIZE TO 0
        PUSH    H
        LXI     H,A2SZ2         ;SIZE
        PUSH    H

    ;PUSH NUMBER OF DIMENSIONS
        LXI     H,A2DIM
        PUSH    H

        CALL    NDIM            ;CALCULATE ADDRESS
                                ;AY = ADDRESS OF ARY1(-1,6)
                                ;   = ARY+(((-1)-(-5))*18)+((6-)*2)
                                ;   = ARY+80

        JMP     SC5E

;DATA
;AY1 : ARRAY[A1D1L..A1D1H,A1D2L..A1D2H,A1D3L..A1D3H] 3-BYTE ELEMENTS
;             [ 0 ..  3 ,  0 ..  5 ,  0 ..  6 ]
A1DIM:  EQU     3                           ;NUMBER OF DIMENSIONS
A1D1L:  EQU     0                           ;LOW BOUND OF DIMENSION 1
A1D1H:  EQU     3                           ;HIGH BOUND OF DIMENSION 1
A1D2L:  EQU     0                           ;LOW BOUND OF DIMENSION 2
A1D2H:  EQU     5                           ;HIGH BOUND OF DIMENSION 2
A1D3L:  EQU     0                           ;LOW BOUND OF DIMENSION 3
A1D3H:  EQU     6                           ;HIGH BOUND OF DIMENSION 3
A1SZ3:  EQU     3                           ;SIZE OF ELEMENT IN DIMENSION 3
A1SZ2:  EQU     ((A1D3H-A1D3L)+1)*A1SZ3 ;SIZE OF ELEMENT IN DIMENSION 2
A1SZ1:  EQU     ((A1D2H-A1D2L)+1)*A1SZ2 ;SIZE OF ELEMENT IN DIMENSION 1
```

```
AY1:      DS        ((A1D1H-A1D1L)+1)*A1SZ1 ;ARRAY
;AY2 : ARRAY[A1D1L..A1D1H,A1D2L..A1D2H] OF WORD
;           [  -5 ..  -1  ,  2  .. 10 ]
A2DIM:    EQU       2                       ;NUMBER OF DIMENSIONS
A2D1L:    EQU       -5                      ;LOW BOUND OF DIMENSION 1
A2D1H:    EQU       -1                      ;HIGH BOUND OF DIMENSION 1
A2D2L:    EQU       2                       ;LOW BOUND OF DIMENSION 2
A2D2H:    EQU       10                      ;HIGH BOUND OF DIMENSION 2
A2SZ2:    EQU       2                       ;SIZE OF ELEMENT IN DIMENSION 2
A2SZ1:    EQU       ((A2D2H-A2D2L)+1)*A2SZ2 ;SIZE OF ELEMENT IN DIMENSION 1
AY2:      DS        ((A2D1H-A2D1L)+1)*A2SZ1 ;ARRAY

          END
```

Subtracts two 16-bit numbers. The Carry flag acts as a borrow.

Procedure: The program simply subtracts the subtrahend from the minuend one byte at a time, starting with the less significant bytes. It includes the borrow when subtracting the more significant bytes. The subtraction of the more significant bytes sets the flags.

Registers Used: AF, DE, HL

Execution Time: 38 cycles (8080) or 34 cycles (8085)

Program Size: 7 bytes

Data Memory Required: None

Entry Conditions

Minuend in H and L
Subtrahend in D and E

Exit Conditions

Difference in H and L

Examples

1. Data: Minuend = $A45D_{16}$
   Subtrahend = $97E1_{16}$

   Result: Difference = $0C7C_{16}$
   Carry = 0 (no borrow)

2. Data: Minuend = $03E1_{16}$
   Subtrahend = $07E4_{16}$

   Result: Difference = $FBFD_{16}$
   Carry = 1 (borrow generated)

```
;                                                                    ;
;                                                                    ;
;                                                                    ;
;                                                                    ;
;       Title:          16-Bit Subtraction                           ;
;       Name:           SUB16                                        ;
;                                                                    ;
;                                                                    ;
;                                                                    ;
;       Purpose:        Subtract 2 16-bit signed or unsigned words and ;
;                       return a 16-bit signed or unsigned difference  ;
;                                                                    ;
;       Entry:          Register L = Low byte of minuend,            ;
;                       Register H = High byte of minuend,           ;
;                       Register E = Low byte of subtrahend,         ;
;                       Register D = High byte of subtrahend         ;
```

```
;
;        Exit:              Difference = Minuend - subtrahend        ;
;                           Register L = Low byte of difference,     ;
;                           Register H = High byte of difference     ;
;                                                                     ;
;        Registers used: AF,DE,HL                                     ;
;                                                                     ;
;        Time:              8080 = 38 cycles                          ;
;                           8085 = 34 cycles                          ;
;                                                                     ;
;        Size:              Program 7 bytes                           ;
;                                                                     ;
;
```

```
SUB16:
        MOV     A,L             ;SUBTRACT LOW BYTES
        SUB     E
        MOV     L,A
        MOV     A,H             ;SUBTRACT HIGH BYTES WITH BORROW
        SBB     D
        MOV     H,A
        RET
```

```
;                                                                     ;
;                                                                     ;
;        SAMPLE EXECUTION                                             ;
;                                                                     ;
;                                                                     ;
```

```
SC6A:
        ;SUBTRACT 1023 FROM 123
        LXI     H,123           ;HL = MINUEND
        LXI     D,1023          ;DE = SUBTRAHEND
        CALL    SUB16           ;123 - 1023 = -900 = 0FC7CH
                                ; REG L = 7CH, REG H = 0FCH
                                ; CARRY = 1 (BORROW GENERATED)

        JMP     SC6A

        END
```

Multiplies two 16-bit operands and returns the less significant (16-bit) word of the product.

Procedure: The program uses an ordinary shift-and-add algorithm, adding the multiplicand to the partial product each time it finds a 1 bit in the multiplier. The partial product and the multiplier are shifted left 15 times (the number of bits in the multiplier minus 1) to produce proper alignment. The more significant 16 bits of the product are lost.

Registers Used: All

Execution Time: Approximately 1003 to 1167 cycles (8080) or 1001 to 1065 cycles (8085), depending largely on the number of 1 bits in the multiplier.

Program Size: 26 bytes

Data Memory Required: None

Entry Conditions

Multiplicand in H and L
Multiplier in D and E

Exit Conditions

Less significant word of product in H and L

Examples

1. Data: Multiplier = 0012_{16}
   Multiplicand = $03D1_{16}$

   Result: Product = $44B2_{16}$
   The more significant word is 0.

2. Data: Multiplier = $37D1_{16}$
   Multiplicand = $A045_{16}$

   Result: Product = $AB55_{16}$
   This is actually the less significant 16-bit word of the 32-bit product $22F1AB55_{16}$.

Note that MUL16 returns only the less significant word of the product to maintain compatibility with other 16-bit arithmetic operations. The more significant word of the product is lost.

```
;
;
;
;
;       Title:      16-Bit Multiplication
;       Name:       MUL16
;
;
;
```

```
;
;          Purpose:          Multiply 2 signed or unsigned 16-bit words and      ;
;                            return a 16-bit signed or unsigned product          ;
;                                                                                ;
;          Entry:            Register L = Low byte of multiplicand               ;
;                            Register H = High byte of multiplicand              ;
;                            Register E = Low byte of multiplier                 ;
;                            Register D = High byte of multiplier                ;
;                                                                                ;
;          Exit:             Product = Multiplicand * multiplier                 ;
;                            Register L = Low byte of product                    ;
;                            Register H = High byte of product                   ;
;                                                                                ;
;          Registers used: All                                                   ;
;                                                                                ;
;          Time:             Approximately 1003 to 1167 cycles for 8080          ;
;                            Approximately 1001 to 1065 cycles for 8085          ;
;                                                                                ;
;          Size:             Program 26 bytes                                    ;
;                                                                                ;
;

          ;INITIALIZE PARTIAL PRODUCT, BIT COUNT
MUL16:
          MOV      C,L                  ;MOVE MULTIPLICAND TO BC
          MOV      B,H
          LXI      H,0                  ;PRODUCT = 0
          MVI      A,15                 ;COUNT = BIT LENGTH - 1

          ;SHIFT-AND-ADD ALGORITHM
          ;IF MSB OF MULTIPLIER IS 1, ADD MULTIPLICAND TO PARTIAL
          ; PRODUCT
          ;SHIFT PARTIAL PRODUCT, MULTIPLIER LEFT 1 BIT
MLP:
          PUSH     PSW                  ;SAVE COUNT
          ORA      D                    ;SIGN FLAG = MSB OF MULTIPLIER
                                        ; (BIT 7 OF COUNT IS ALWAYS ZERO)
          JP       MLP1                 ;JUMP IF MSB OF MULTIPLIER IS 0
          DAD      B                    ;ADD MULTIPLICAND TO PARTIAL PRODUCT
MLP1:     DAD      H                    ;SHIFT PARTIAL PRODUCT
          XCHG
          DAD      H                    ;SHIFT MULTIPLIER
          XCHG
          POP      PSW                  ;RESTORE COUNT
          DCR      A
          JNZ      MLP                  ;CONTINUE UNTIL COUNT = 0

          ;ADD MULTIPLICAND ONE LAST TIME IF MSB OF MULTIPLIER IS 1
          ORA      D                    ;SIGN FLAG = MSB OF MULTIPLIER
          RP                            ;RETURN IF MSB OF MULTIPLIER = 0
          DAD      B                    ;ELSE ADD MULTIPLICAND TO PRODUCT
          RET
;
;
;          SAMPLE EXECUTION                                                       ;
;                                                                                 ;
;
```

```
SC6B:
        LXI     H,-2                ;HL = MULTIPLICAND
        LXI     D,1023              ;DE = MULTIPLIER
        CALL    MUL16               ;16-BIT MULTIPLY
                                    ;RESULT OF 1023 * -2 = -2046 = 0F802H
                                    ; REGISTER L = 02H
                                    ;          H = F8H

        JMP     SC6B

        END
```

16-Bit Division (SDIV16, UDIV16)

Divides two 16-bit operands and returns the quotient and the remainder. There are two entry points: SDIV16 divides two 16-bit signed operands, whereas UDIV16 divides two 16-bit unsigned operands. If the divisor is 0, the Carry flag is set to 1 and both quotient and remainder are set to 0; otherwise, the Carry flag is cleared.

Procedure: If the operands are signed, the program determines the sign of the quotient and takes the absolute values of any negative operands. It must also retain the sign of the dividend, since that determines the sign of the remainder. The program then performs an unsigned division using a shift-and-subtract algorithm. It shifts the quotient and dividend left, placing a 1 bit in the quotient each time a trial subtraction is successful. If the operands are signed, the program must negate (that is, subtract from 0) the quotient or remainder if either

is negative. The Carry flag is cleared if the division is proper and set if the divisor is 0. A 0 divisor also causes a return with the quotient and remainder both set to 0.

> **Registers Used:** All
>
> **Execution Time:** Approximately 2630 to 3200 cycles (8080) or 2480 to 2950 cycles (8085), depending largely on how many trial subtractions are successful and thus require the replacement of the previous dividend by the remainder.
>
> **Program Size:** 136 bytes
>
> **Data Memory Required:** 3 bytes anywhere in RAM for the sign of the quotient (address SQUOT), the sign of the remainder (address SREM), and a divide loop counter (address COUNT)
>
> **Special Case:** If the divisor is 0, the program returns with the Carry set to 1, and both the quotient and the remainder set to 0.

Entry Conditions

Dividend in H and L
Divisor in D and E

Exit Conditions

Quotient in H and L
Remainder in D and E

If the divisor is non-zero, Carry = 0 and the result is normal.

If the divisor is 0, Carry = 1 and both quotient and remainder are 0000_{16}.

Examples

1. Data: Dividend = $03E0_{16}$
   Divisor = $00B6_{16}$

   Result: Quotient (from UDIV16) = 0005_{16}
   Remainder (from UDIV16) = 0052_{16}
   Carry = 0 (no divide-by-0 error)

2. Data: Dividend = $D73A_{16}$
   Divisor = $02F1_{16}$

   Result: Quotient (from SDIV16) = $FFF3_{16}$
   Remainder (from SDIV16) = $FD77_{16}$
   Carry = 0 (no divide-by-0 error)

The remainder of a signed division has been allowed to be either positive or negative. In this procedure, the remainder always takes the sign of the dividend. A negative remainder can easily be converted into one that is always positive.

Simply subtract 1 from the quotient and add the divisor to the remainder. The result of Example 2 is then

$$\text{Quotient} = FFF2_{16} = -14_{10}$$
$$\text{Remainder (always positive)} = 0068_{16}$$

```
;                                                                      ;
;                                                                      ;
;                                                                      ;
;                                                                      ;
;          Title:          16-Bit Division                            ;
;          Name:           SDIV16, UDIV16                             ;
;                                                                      ;
;                                                                      ;
;                                                                      ;
;          Purpose:        SDIV16                                     ;
;                             Divide 2 signed 16-bit words and return a ;
;                             16-bit signed quotient and remainder     ;
;                                                                      ;
;                          UDIV16                                     ;
;                             Divide 2 unsigned 16-bit words and return a;
;                             16-bit unsigned quotient and remainder   ;
;                                                                      ;
;          Entry:          Register L = Low byte of dividend          ;
;                          Register H = High byte of dividend         ;
;                          Register E = Low byte of divisor           ;
;                          Register D = High byte of divisor          ;
;                                                                      ;
;          Exit:           Register L = Low byte of quotient          ;
;                          Register H = High byte of quotient         ;
;                          Register E = Low byte of remainder         ;
;                          Register D = High byte of remainder        ;
;                                                                      ;
;                          If no errors then                          ;
;                            Carry := 0                               ;
;                          else                                       ;
;                            divide-by-zero error                     ;
;                            Carry := 1                               ;
;                            quotient := 0                            ;
;                            remainder := 0                           ;
;                                                                      ;
;          Registers used: All                                        ;
;                                                                      ;
;          Time:           Approximately 2630 to 3200 cycles for 8080 ;
;                          Approximately 2480 to 2950 cycles for 8085 ;
;                                                                      ;
;          Size:           Program 127 bytes                          ;
;                          Data       3 bytes                         ;
;                                                                      ;
;                                                                      ;
```

```
          ;SIGNED DIVISION
SDIV16:
          ;DETERMINE SIGN OF QUOTIENT BY EXCLUSIVE ORING HIGH BYTES
          ; OF DIVIDEND AND DIVISOR.  QUOTIENT IS POSITIVE IF SIGNS
          ; ARE THE SAME, NEGATIVE IF SIGNS ARE DIFFERENT
          ;
          ;REMAINDER HAS SAME SIGN AS DIVIDEND
          MOV     A,H              ;GET HIGH BYTE OF DIVIDEND
          STA     SREM             ;SAVE AS SIGN OF REMAINDER
          XRA     D                ;EXCLUSIVE OR WITH HIGH BYTE OF DIVISOR
          STA     SQUOT            ;SAVE SIGN OF QUOTIENT

          ;TAKE ABSOLUTE VALUE OF DIVISOR
          MOV     A,D
          ORA     A
          JP      CHKDE            ;JUMP IF DIVISOR IS POSITIVE
          SUB     A                ;SUBTRACT DIVISOR FROM ZERO
          SUB     L
          MOV     L,A
          SBB     A                ;PROPOGATE BORROW (A= FF IF BORROW)
          SUB     H
          MOV     D,A

          ;TAKE ABSOLUTE VALUE OF DIVIDEND
CHKDE:
          MOV     A,H
          ORA     A
          JP      DODIV            ;JUMP IF DIVIDEND IS POSITIVE
          SUB     A                ;SUBTRACT DIVIDEND FROM ZERO
          SUB     E
          MOV     E,A
          SBB     A                ;PROPOGATE BORROW (A = FF IF BORROW)
          SUB     D
          MOV     H,A

          ;DIVIDE ABSOLUTE VALUES
DODIV:    CALL    UDIV16
          RC                       ;EXIT IF DIVIDE-BY-ZERO

          ;NEGATE QUOTIENT IF IT IS NEGATIVE
          LDA     SQUOT
          ORA     A
          JP      DOREM            ;JUMP IF QUOTIENT IS POSITIVE
          MVI     A,0              ;SUBTRACT QUOTIENT FROM ZERO
          SUB     L
          MOV     L,A
          MVI     A,0
          SBB     H
          MOV     H,A

DOREM:
          ;NEGATE REMAINDER IF IT IS NEGATIVE
          LDA     SREM
          ORA     A
          RP                       ;RETURN IF REMAINDER IS POSITIVE
          SUB     A                ;SUBTRACT REMAINDER FROM ZERO
```

```
        SUB     E
        MOV     E,A
        SBB     A                   ;PROPOGATE BORROW (A = FF IF BORROW)
        SUB     D
        MOV     D,A
        RET


        ;UNSIGNED DIVISION
UDIV16:
        ;CHECK FOR DIVISION-BY-ZERO
        MOV     A,E                 ;TEST DIVISOR
        ORA     D
        JNZ     DIVIDE              ;BRANCH IF DIVISOR NON-ZERO
        LXI     H,0                 ;DIVIDE-BY-0 ERROR
        MOV     D,H
        MOV     E,L
        STC                         ;SET CARRY, INVALID RESULT
        RET

DIVIDE: MOV     C,L                 ;BC = DIVIDEND/QUOTIENT
        MOV     B,H
        LXI     H,0                 ;DE = REMAINDER
        MVI     A,16                ;16 BITS IN DIVIDEND
        ORA     A                   ;CLEAR CARRY TO START
DVLOOP:
        STA     COUNT               ;SAVE CURRENT COUNT VALUE

        ;SHIFT NEXT BIT OF QUOTIENT INTO BIT 0 OF DIVIDEND
        ;SHIFT NEXT MOST SIGNIFICANT BIT OF DIVIDEND INTO
        ; LEAST SIGNIFICANT BIT OF REMAINDER
        ;BC HOLDS BOTH DIVIDEND AND QUOTIENT. WHILE WE SHIFT A BIT
        ; FROM MSB OF DIVIDEND, WE SHIFT NEXT BIT OF QUOTIENT
        ; IN FROM CARRY
        ;HL HOLDS REMAINDER
        ;
        ;DO A 32-BIT LEFT SHIFT, SHIFTING
        ; CARRY TO C, C TO B, B TO L, L TO H
        MOV     A,C
        RAL                         ;CARRY (NEXT BIT OF QUOTIENT) TO BIT 0,
        MOV     C,A                 ; BIT 7 TO CARRY
        MOV     A,B
        RAL                         ;SHIFT OTHER BYTE OF DIVIDEND
        MOV     B,A                 ; AND QUOTIENT
        MOV     A,L
        RAL                         ;SHIFT NEXT BIT OF DIVIDEND
        MOV     L,A                 ; INTO REMAINDER
        MOV     A,H
        RAL                         ;SHIFT NEXT BIT OF DIVIDEND
        MOV     H,A                 ; INTO HIGH BYTE OF REMAINDER

        ;IF REMAINDER IS GREATER THAN OR EQUAL TO DIVISOR, NEXT
        ; BIT OF QUOTIENT IS 1. THIS BIT GOES TO CARRY.
        PUSH    H                   ;SAVE CURRENT REMAINDER
        MOV     A,L                 ;SUBTRACT DIVISOR FROM REMAINDER
        SUB     E
```

```
          MOV     L,A
          MOV     A,H
          SBB     D
          MOV     H,A
          CMC                     ;COMPLEMENT BORROW SO 1 INDICATES
                                  ; A SUCCESSFUL SUBTRACTION
                                  ; (THIS IS NEXT BIT OF QUOTIENT)
          JC      DROP            ;JUMP IF REMAINDER IS >= DIVIDEND
          XTHL                    ;OTHERWISE RESTORE REMAINDER
DROP:
          INX     SP              ;DROP REMAINDER FROM TOP OF STACK
          INX     SP
          LDA     COUNT
          DCR     A
          JNZ     DVLOOP          ;CONTINUE UNTIL ALL BITS DONE

          ;SHIFT LAST CARRY INTO QUOTIENT
          XCHG                    ;DE = REMAINDER
          MOV     A,C
          RAL                     ;LAST BIT OF QUOTIENT TO BIT 0
          MOV     L,A             ;QUOTIENT TO HL
          MOV     A,B
          RAL
          MOV     H,A
          ORA     A               ;CLEAR CARRY, VALID RESULT
          RET

          ;DATA
SQUOT:    DS      1               ;SIGN OF QUOTIENT
SREM:     DS      1               ;SIGN OF REMAINDER
COUNT:    DS      1               ;DIVIDE LOOP COUNTER


;                                                                   ;
;                                                                   ;
;         SAMPLE EXECUTION                                          ;
;                                                                   ;
;                                                                   ;

SC6C:
          ;SIGNED DIVIDE, -1023 / 123
          LXI     H,-1023         ;HL = DIVIDEND
          LXI     D,123           ;DE = DIVISOR
          CALL    SDIV16          ;QUOTIENT OF -1023 / 123 = -8
                                  ; L = F8H
                                  ; H = FFH
                                  ;REMAINDER OF -1023 / 123 = -39
                                  ; E = D9H
                                  ; D = FFH

          ;UNSIGNED DIVIDE, 64513 / 123
          LXI     H,64513
          LXI     D,123
          CALL    UDIV16          ;QUOTIENT OF 64513 / 123 = 524
                                  ; L = 0CH
```

```
                                    ; H = 02H
                                    ;REMAINDER OF 64513 / 123 = 61
                                    ; E = 3DH
                                    ; D = 00H

        JMP        SC6C

        END
```

Compares two 16-bit operands and sets the flags accordingly. The Zero flag always indicates whether the numbers are equal. If the operands are unsigned, the Carry flag indicates which is larger (Carry = 1 if subtrahend is larger and 0 otherwise). If the operands are signed, the Sign flag indicates which is larger (Sign = 1 if subtrahend is larger and 0 otherwise); two's complement overflow is considered and the Sign flag is inverted if it occurs.

Procedure: The program first checks if two's complement overflow could occur. This is possible only if the operands have different signs. If two's complement overflow is not possible, the program subtracts the less significant byte of the subtrahend from the minuend. If the less significant bytes are equal, it sets the flags from the subtraction of the more significant bytes. If the less significant bytes are not equal, the program must clear the Zero flag before exiting (by logically ORing with 1, but retaining the other flags). If two's complement overflow could occur, the program sets the Sign flag to the sign of the minuend. It does this by loading the more significant byte of the minuend into the accumulator before setting the Sign flag.

Registers Used: AF, DE, HL

Execution Time: Approximately 57 to 81 cycles (8080) or 51 to 69 cycles (8085)

Program Size: 36 bytes

Data Memory Required: None

Entry Conditions

Minuend in H and L
Subtrahend in D and E

Exit Conditions

Flags are set as if subtrahend had been subtracted from minuend, with a correction if two's complement overflow occurred.

Zero flag = 1 if the subtrahend and minuend are equal; 0 if they are not equal.

Carry flag = 1 if subtrahend is larger than minuend in the unsigned sense; 0 if it is less than or equal to the minuend.

Sign flag = 1 if subtrahend is larger than minuend in the signed sense; 0 if it is less than or equal to the minuend. This flag is corrected (inverted) if two's complement overflow occurs.

209

Examples

1. Data: Minuend (HL) = $03E1_{16}$
               Subtrahend (DE) = $07E4_{16}$

   Result: Carry = 1, indicating subtrahend is larger in unsigned sense
               Zero = 0, indicating operands are not equal
               Sign = 1, indicating subtrahend is larger in signed sense

2. Data: Minuend (HL) = $C51A_{16}$
               Subtrahend (DE) = $C51A_{16}$

   Result: Carry = 0, indicating subtrahend is not larger in unsigned sense
               Zero = 1, indicating operands are equal
               Sign = 0, indicating subtrahend is not larger in signed sense

3. Data: Minuend (HL) = $A45D_{16}$
               Subtrahend (DE) = $77E1_{16}$

   Result: Carry = 0, indicating subtrahend is not larger in unsigned sense
               Zero = 0, indicating operands are not equal
               Sign = 1, indicating subtrahend is larger in signed sense

In Example 3, the minuend is a negative two's complement number, whereas the subtrahend is a positive two's complement number.

```
;                                                                    ;
;                                                                    ;
;                                                                    ;
;                                                                    ;
;       Title:          16-Bit Compare                               ;
;       Name:           CMP16                                        ;
;                                                                    ;
;                                                                    ;
;                                                                    ;
;       Purpose:        Compare 2 16-bit signed or unsigned words and ;
;                       return the C,Z,S flags set or cleared        ;
;                                                                    ;
;       Entry:          Register L = Low byte of minuend             ;
;                       Register H = High byte of minuend            ;
;                       Register E = Low byte of subtrahend          ;
;                       Register D = High byte of subtrahend         ;
;                                                                    ;
;       Exit:           Flags returned based on minuend - subtrahend ;
;                       If both the minued and subtrahend are two's  ;
;                         complement numbers, then use the Z and S   ;
;                         flags;                                     ;
;                       Else use the Z and C flags.                  ;
;                         IF minuend = subtrahend THEN               ;
;                            Z=1,S=0,C=0                             ;
;                         IF minuend > subtrahend THEN               ;
;                            Z=0,S=0,C=0                             ;
;                         IF minuend < subtrahend THEN               ;
;                            Z=0,S=1,C=1                             ;
;       Registers used: AF,DE,HL                                     ;
```

```
;                                                                        ;
;         Time:              Approximately 57 to 81 cycles for 8080      ;
;                            Approximately 51 to 69 cycles for 8085      ;
;                                                                        ;
;         Size:              Program 36 bytes                            ;
;                                                                        ;
;                                                                        ;
          CHECK IF TWO'S COMPLEMENT OVERFLOW COULD OCCUR
          ONLY POSSIBLE IF SIGNS OF OPERANDS ARE DIFFERENT

CMP16:
          MOV       A,D
          XRA       H               ;ARE SIGNS OF OPERANDS DIFFERENT?
          JM        DIFF            ;JUMP IF SIGNS ARE DIFFERENT

          ;OVERFLOW NOT POSSIBLE - PERFORM UNSIGNED COMPARISON
          MOV       A,L             ;COMPARE LOW BYTES
          SUB       E
          JZ        EQUAL           ;JUMP IF LOW BYTES ARE EQUAL

          ;LOW BYTES NOT EQUAL, COMPARE HIGH BYTES
          ;REMEMBER, ZERO FLAG MUST BE CLEARED LATER
          MOV       A,H             ;COMPARE HIGH BYTES
          SBB       D
          JC        CYSET           ;EXIT WITH CARRY SET, ZERO FLAG = 0
          JNC       CYCLR           ;EXIT WITH CARRY CLEAR, ZERO FLAG = 0

          ;LOW BYTES ARE EQUAL, SET FLAGS BY COMPARING HIGH BYTES
          ; WITH BORROW
EQUAL:
          MOV       A,H
          SBB       D
          RET

          ;SIGNS OF OPERANDS ARE DIFFERENT, COMPARE BUT SET
          ; SIGN FLAG TO SIGN OF MINUEND
DIFF:
          MOV       A,L
          SUB       E               ;SUBTRACT LOW BYTES
          MOV       A,H
          SBB       D               ;SUBTRACT HIGH BYTES
          MOV       A,H             ;LOAD HIGH BYTE OF MINUEND
                                    ; TO OBTAIN PROPER SIGN
          JNC       CYCLR

          ;EXIT WITH CARRY SET AND ZERO FLAG = 0
          ;PROBLEM HERE IS THAT ORI ALWAYS CLEARS CARRY
CYSET:
          ORI       1               ;ZERO FLAG = 0, SIGN FLAG = BIT 7
          STC                       ;CARRY FLAG = 1
          RET

          ;EXIT WITH CARRY CLEAR AND ZERO FLAG = 0
CYCLR:    ORI       1               ;ZERO FLAG = 0, SIGN FLAG = BIT 7
                                    ; AND CARRY FLAG = 0
          RET
```

```
;                                                              ;
;                                                              ;
;       SAMPLE EXECUTION                                       ;
;                                                              ;
;                                                              ;

SC6D:
        ;COMPARE -32768 (8000 HEX) AND 1
        ;SINCE -32768 IS THE MOST NEGATIVE 16-BIT NUMBER,
        ; THIS COMPARISON WILL SURELY CAUSE OVERFLOW
        LXI     H,-32768
        LXI     D,1
        CALL    CMP16           ;CY = 0, Z = 0, S = 1

        ;COMPARE -4 (FFFC HEX) AND -1 (FFFF HEX)
        LXI     H,-4
        LXI     D,-1
        CALL    CMP16           ;CY = 1, Z = 0, S = 1

        ;COMPARE -1234 AND -1234
        LXI     H,-1234
        LXI     D,-1234
        CALL    CMP16           ;CY = 0, Z = 1, S = 0
        JMP     SC6D

        END
```

Multiple-Precision Binary Addition (MPBADD)

Adds two multi-byte unsigned binary numbers. Both numbers are stored with their least significant bytes at the lowest address. The sum replaces the addend. The length of the numbers (in bytes) is 255 or less.

Procedure: The program clears the Carry flag initially and adds the operands one byte at a time, starting with the least significant bytes. The final Carry flag reflects the addition of the most significant bytes. A length of 0 causes an immediate exit with no addition.

Registers Used: AF, B, DE, HL

Execution Time: 46 cycles per byte plus 24 cycles overhead (8080) or 47 cycles per byte plus 21 cycles overhead (8085)

Program Size: 13 bytes

Data Memory Required: None

Special Case: A length of 0 causes an immediate exit with the addend unchanged. The Carry flag is cleared.

Entry Conditions

Base address of addend in H and L
Base address of adder in D and E
Length of the operands in bytes in B

Exit Conditions

Addend replaced by addend plus adder

Example

1. Data: Length of operands (in bytes) = 6
   Addend = $19D028A193EA_{16}$
   Adder = $293EABF059C7_{16}$

   Result: Addend = $430ED491EDB1_{16}$
   Carry = 0

```
;                                                                    ;
;                                                                    ;
;                                                                    ;
;                                                                    ;
;        Title:       Multiple-Precision Binary Addition             ;
;        Name:        MPBADD                                         ;
;                                                                    ;
;                                                                    ;
;                                                                    ;
;        Purpose:     Add 2 arrays of binary bytes                   ;
```

```
;                       Array1 := Array1 + Array2                      ;
;                                                                      ;
;       Entry:          Registers H and L = Base address of array 1    ;
;                       Registers D and E = Base address of  array 2   ;
;                       Register B = Length of the arrays              ;
;                                                                      ;
;                          The arrays are unsigned binary numbers with a ;
;                          maximum length of 255 bytes, ARRAY[0] is the ;
;                          least significant byte, and ARRAY[LENGTH-1] ;
;                          the most significant byte.                  ;
;                                                                      ;
;       Exit:           Array1 := Array1 + Array2                      ;
;                                                                      ;
;       Registers used: AF,B,DE,HL                                     ;
;                                                                      ;
;       Time:           46 cycles per byte plus 24 cycles for 8080     ;
;                       47 cycles per byte plus 21 cycles for 8085     ;
;                                                                      ;
;       Size:           Program 13 bytes                               ;
;                                                                      ;
;                                                                      ;

MPBADD:
        ;CLEAR CARRY TO START, EXIT IF ARRAY LENGTH IS 0
        MOV     A,B
        ANA     A               ;CLEAR CARRY, TEST LENGTH
        RZ                      ;RETURN IF LENGTH = ZERO
LOOP:
        LDAX    D               ;GET NEXT BYTE
        ADC     M               ;ADD BYTES
        MOV     M,A             ;STORE SUM
        INX     H               ;INCREMENT ARRAY1 POINTER
        INX     D               ;INCREMENT ARRAY2 POINTER
        DCR     B
        JNZ     LOOP            ;CONTINUE UNTIL COUNTER = 0
        RET


;                                                                      ;
;                                                                      ;
;       SAMPLE EXECUTION                                               ;
;                                                                      ;
;                                                                      ;

SC6E:
        LXI     H,AY1           ;HL = BASE ADDRESS OF ARRAY 1
        LXI     D,AY2           ;DE = BASE ADDRESS OF ARRAY 2
        MVI     B,SZAYS         ;B = LENGTH OF ARRAYS IN BYTES
        CALL    MPBADD          ;SUM THE ARRAYS
                                ;               AY1+0 = 56H
                                ;               AY1+1 = 13H
                                ;               AY1+2 = CFH
                                ;               AY1+3 = 8AH
                                ;               AY1+4 = 67H
                                ;               AY1+5 = 45H
                                ;               AY1+6 = 23H
                                ;               AY1+7 = 01H
```

```
        JMP     SC6E

SZAYS   EQU     8           ;LENGTH OF ARRAYS IN BYTES
AY1:
        DB      0EFH
        DB      0CDH
        DB      0ABH
        DB      089H
        DB      067H
        DB      045H
        DB      023H
        DB      001H

AY2:
        DB      067H
        DB      045H
        DB      023H
        DB      001H
        DB      0
        DB      0
        DB      0
        DB      0

        END
```

Multiple-Precision Binary Subtraction (MPBSUB)

6F

Subtracts two multi-byte unsigned binary numbers. Both numbers are stored with their least significant bytes at the lowest address. The difference replaces the minuend. The length of the numbers (in bytes) is 255 or less.

Procedure: The program clears the Carry flag initially and subtracts the operands one byte at a time, starting with the least significant bytes. The final Carry flag reflects the subtraction of the most significant bytes. A length of 0 causes an immediate exit with no subtraction.

Registers Used: AF, B, DE, HL

Execution Time: 46 cycles per byte plus 28 cycles overhead (8080) or 47 cycles per byte plus 25 cycles overhead (8085)

Program Size: 14 bytes

Data Memory Required: None

Special Case: A length of 0 causes an immediate exit with the minuend unchanged (that is, the difference is equal to the minuend). The Carry flag is cleared.

Entry Conditions

Base address of minuend in H and L
Base address of subtrahend in D and E
Length of the operands in bytes in B

Exit Conditions

Minuend replaced by minuend minus subtrahend

Example

1. Data: Length of operands (in bytes) = 4
   Minuend = $2F5BA7C3_{16}$
   Subtrahend = $14DF35B8_{16}$

   Result: Minuend = $1A7C720B_{16}$
   The Carry flag is set to 0 since no borrow is necessary.

```
;
;
;
;
;                Title:      Multiple-Precision Binary Subtraction
;                Name:       MPBSUB
;
;
```

216

```
;                                                                    ;
;           Purpose:        Subtract 2 arrays of binary bytes        ;
;                           Minuend := Minuend - Subtrahend          ;
;                                                                    ;
;           Entry:          Registers H and L = Base address of minuend   ;
;                           Registers D and E = Base address of subtrahend ;
;                           Register B = Length of the arrays        ;
;                                                                    ;
;                           The arrays are unsigned binary numbers with a ;
;                           maximum length of 255 bytes, ARRAY[0] is the   ;
;                           least significant byte, and ARRAY[LENGTH-1]    ;
;                           the most significant byte.               ;
;                                                                    ;
;           Exit:           Minuend := Minuend - subtrahend          ;
;                                                                    ;
;           Registers used: AF,B,DE,HL                               ;
;                                                                    ;
;           Time:           46 cycles per byte plus 28 cycles for 8080   ;
;                           47 cycles per byte plus 25 cycles for 8085   ;
;                                                                    ;
;           Size:           Program 14 bytes                         ;
;                                                                    ;
;                                                                    ;

MPBSUB:
           ;CLEAR BORROW TO START, EXIT IF LENGTH IS 0
           MOV     A,B
           ANA     A                   ;CLEAR BORROW, TEST LENGTH
           RZ                          ;RETURN IF LENGTH = ZERO
           XCHG                        ;SWITCH ARRAY POINTERS
                                       ; SO HL POINTS TO SUBTRAHEND
LOOP:
           LDAX    D                   ;GET NEXT BYTE OF MINUEND
           SBB     M                   ;SUBTRACT BYTES
           STAX    D                   ;STORE DIFFERENCE
           INX     D                   ;INCREMENT MINUEND POINTER
           INX     H                   ;INCREMENT SUBTRAHEND POINTER
           DCR     B
           JNZ     LOOP                ;CONTINUE UNTIL COUNTER = 0
           RET


;                                                                    ;
;                                                                    ;
;           SAMPLE EXECUTION                                         ;
;                                                                    ;
;                                                                    ;


SC6F:
           LXI     H,AY1               ;HL = BASE ADDRESS OF MINUEND
           LXI     D,AY2               ;DE = BASE ADDRESS OF SUBTRAHEND
           MVI     B,SZAYS             ;B = LENGTH OF ARRAYS IN BYTES
           CALL    MPBSUB              ;SUBTRACT THE ARRAYS
                                       ;         AY1+0 = 88H
                                       ;         AY1+1 = 88H
```

```
                                    ;              AY1+2  =  88H
                                    ;              AY1+3  =  88H
                                    ;              AY1+4  =  67H
                                    ;              AY1+5  =  45H
                                    ;              AY1+6  =  23H
                                    ;              AY1+7  =  01H

            JMP       SC6F

SZAYS       EQU       8             ;LENGTH OF ARRAYS IN BYTES
AY1:
            DB        0EFH
            DB        0CDH
            DB        0ABH
            DB        089H
            DB        067H
            DB        045H
            DB        023H
            DB        001H

AY2:
            DB        067H
            DB        045H
            DB        023H
            DB        001H
            DB        0
            DB        0
            DB        0
            DB        0

            END
```

Multiple-Precision
Binary Multiplication (MPBMUL)   6G

Multiplies two multi-byte unsigned binary numbers. Both numbers are stored with their least significant byte at the lowest address. The product replaces the multiplicand. The length of the numbers (in bytes) is 255 or less. Only the less significant bytes of the product are returned to retain compatibility with other multiple-precision binary operations.

Procedure: The program uses an ordinary shift-and-add algorithm, adding the multiplier to the partial product each time it finds a 1 bit in the multiplicand. The partial product and the multiplicand are shifted through the bit length plus 1; the extra loop moves the final Carry into the product. The program maintains a full double-length unsigned partial product in memory locations starting at HIPROD (more significant bytes) and in the multiplicand (less significant bytes). The less significant bytes of the product replace the multiplicand as it is shifted

Registers Used: All

Execution Time: Depends on the length of the operands and on the number of 1 bits in the multiplicand (requiring actual additions). If the average number of 1 bits in the multiplicand is four per byte, the execution time is approximately $792 *$ $LENGTH^2 + 924 * LENGTH + 300$ cycles where LENGTH is the number of bytes in the operands.

Program Size: 116 bytes

Data Memory Required: 261 bytes anywhere in RAM. This is temporary storage for the more significant bytes of the product (255 bytes starting at address HIPROD), the loop counter (2 bytes starting at address COUNT), the address immediately following the most significant byte of the high product (2 bytes starting at address ENDHP), and the base address of the multiplier (2 bytes starting at address MLIER).

Special Case: A length of 0 causes an immediate exit with the product equal to the multiplicand. The Carry flag is cleared.

and examined for 1 bits. A 0 length causes an exit with no multiplication.

Entry Conditions

Base address of multiplicand in H and L
Base address of multiplier in D and E
Length of the operands in bytes in B

Exit Conditions

Multiplicand replaced by multiplicand times multiplier

Example

1. Data: Length of operands (in bytes) = 04
            Multiplicand = $0005D1F7_{16}$
            Multiplier = $00000AB1_{16}$

   Result: Multiplicand = $3E39D1C7_{16}$

Note that MPBMUL returns only the less significant bytes (that is, the number of bytes in the multiplicand and multiplier) of the product

to maintain compatibility with other multiple-precision arithmetic operations. The more significant bits of the product are available starting with their least significant byte at address HIPROD. The user may need to check those bytes for a possible overflow or extend the operands with additional zeros.

```
;                                                                    ;
;                                                                    ;
;                                                                    ;
;                                                                    ;
;         Title:         Multiple-Precision Binary Multiplication    ;
;         Name:          MPBMUL                                      ;
;                                                                    ;
;                                                                    ;
;                                                                    ;
;                                                                    ;
;         Purpose:       Multiply 2 arrays of binary bytes           ;
;                        Multiplicand := Multiplicand * multiplier   ;
;                                                                    ;
;         Entry:         Registers H and L = Base address of multiplicand;
;                        Registers D and E = Base address of multiplier  ;
;                        Register B = Length of arrays in bytes      ;
;                                                                    ;
;                        The arrays are unsigned binary numbers with a ;
;                        maximum length of 255 bytes, ARRAY[0] is the ;
;                        least significant byte, and ARRAY[LENGTH-1] ;
;                        the most significant byte.                  ;
;                                                                    ;
;         Exit:          Multiplicand := Multiplicand * multiplier   ;
;                                                                    ;
;         Registers used: All                                       ;
;                                                                    ;
;         Time:          Assuming the average number of 1 bits in multi- ;
;                        plicand is 4 * length then the time is approxi- ;
;                        mately:                                     ;
;                           (792 * length^2) + (924 * length) + 300 cycles ;
;                                                                    ;
;         Size:          Program 113 bytes                           ;
;                        Data    261 bytes                           ;
;                                                                    ;
;                                                                    ;
```

```
MPBMUL:
        ;EXIT IF LENGTH OF ARRAYS IS ZERO
        MOV     A,B
        ANA     A               ;IS LENGTH OF ARRAYS = 0?
        RZ                      ;YES, EXIT

        ;MAKE POINTERS POINT TO END OF ARRAYS
        MOV     C,B
        MVI     B,0             ;BC = LENGTH
        DAD     B               ;END = BASE + LENGTH
        XCHG                    ;DE POINTS TO END OF MULTIPLICAND
        SHLD    MLIER           ;SAVE ADDRESS OF MULTIPLIER
        LXI     H,HIPROD
        DAD     B
        SHLD    ENDHP           ;SAVE ADDRESS AT END OF HIPROD

        ;SET COUNT TO NUMBER OF BITS IN ARRAY PLUS 1
        ; COUNT := (LENGTH * 8) + 1
        MOV     L,C             ;MOVE LENGTH TO HL
        MOV     H,B
```

```
                DAD      H                  ;LENGTH * 8, SHIFT LEFT 3 TIMES
                DAD      H
                DAD      H
                INX      H                  ;ADD 1
                SHLD     COUNT              ;SAVE NUMBER OF BITS TO DO

                ;ZERO HIGH PRODUCT ARRAY
        ZEROPD:
                MOV      B,C                ;B = LENGTH IN BYTES
                LXI      H,HIPROD           ;GET ADDRESS OF HIPROD
        ZEROLP:
                MVI      M,O                ;CLEAR BYTE OF HIPROD
                INX      H
                DCR      B
                JNZ      ZEROLP             ;CONTINUE UNTIL HIPROD ARRAY IS ZERO

                ;MULTIPLY USING SHIFT-AND-ADD ALGORITHM
                ANA      A                  ;CLEAR CARRY FIRST TIME THROUGH
        LOOP:
                ;SHIFT CARRY INTO HIPROD ARRAY AND LEAST SIGNIFICANT
                ; BIT OF HIPROD ARRAY TO CARRY
                MOV      B,C                ;GET LENGTH
                LHLD     ENDHP              ;GET LAST BYTE OF HIPROD + 1
        SRPLP:
                DCX      H                  ;BACK UP TO NEXT BYTE
                MOV      A,M
                RAR                         ;ROTATE BYTE OF HIPROD ARRAY
                MOV      M,A                ;STORE IT
                DCR      B
                JNZ      SRPLP              ;CONTINUE UNTIL INDEX = O

                ;SHIFT CARRY (NEXT BIT OF LOWER PRODUCT) INTO MOST
                ; SIGNIFICANT BIT OF MULTIPLICAND.
                ; THIS ALSO SHIFTS NEXT BIT OF MULTIPLICAND TO CARRY
                MOV      L,E                ;HL = ADDRESS OF END OF MULTIPLICAND
                MOV      H,D
                MOV      B,C                ;B = LENGTH IN BYTES
        SRA1LP:
                DCX      H                  ;BACK UP TO NEXT BYTE
                MOV      A,M
                RAR                         ;ROTATE BYTE OF MULTIPLICAND
                MOV      M,A
                DCR      B
                JNZ      SRA1LP

                ;IF NEXT BIT OF MULTIPLICAND IS 1,
                ; ADD MULTIPLIER TO HIPROD ARRAY
                JNC      DECCNT             ;JUMP IF NEXT BIT IS ZERO

                ;ADD MULTIPLIER TO HIPROD
                PUSH     D                  ;SAVE ADDRESS OF MULTIPLICAND
                LHLD     MLIER              ;DE = ADDRESS OF MULTIPLIER
                XCHG
                LXI      H,HIPROD           ;HL = ADDRESS OF HIPROD
                MOV      B,C                ;B = LENGTH IN BYTES
                ANA      A                  ;CLEAR CARRY TO START
```

```
                                     ;ADD BYTE AT A TIME
ADDLP:
        LDAX    D                    ;GET NEXT MULTIPLIER BYTE
        ADC     M                    ;ADD TO HIPROD
        MOV     M,A                  ;STORE NEW HIPROD
        INX     D
        INX     H
        DCR     B
        JNZ     ADDLP                ;CONTINUE UNTIL DONE
        POP     D                    ;RESTORE ADDRESS OF MULTIPLICAND

        ;DECREMENT BIT COUNTER, EXIT IF DONE
        ; DOES NOT CHANGE CARRY!
DECCNT:
        LDA     COUNT                ;SUBTRACT 1 FROM BIT COUNTER
        DCR     A
        STA     COUNT
        JNZ     LOOP                 ;BRANCH IF LSB OF COUNT NOT ZERO
        PUSH    PSW                  ;SAVE CARRY
        LDA     COUNT+1              ;GET HIGH BYTE OF BIT COUNTER
        ANA     A
        JZ      EXIT                 ;BRANCH IF COUNT IS 0
        DCR     A                    ;DECREMENT HIGH BYTE OF COUNT
        STA     COUNT+1
        POP     PSW                  ;RESTORE CARRY
        JMP     LOOP

EXIT:
        POP     PSW                  ;DROP PSW FROM STACK
        RET

        ;DATA
COUNT:  DS      2                    ;TEMPORARY FOR LOOP COUNTER
ENDHP:  DS      2                    ;ADDRESS OF LAST BYTE OF HIPROD + 1
MLIER:  DS      2                    ;ADDRESS OF MULTIPLIER
HIPROD: DS      255                  ;HIGH PRODUCT BUFFER


;                                                                        ;
;                                                                        ;
;          SAMPLE EXECUTION                                              ;
;                                                                        ;
;                                                                        ;


SC6G:
        LXI     H,AY1                ;HL = ADDRESS OF MULTIPLICAND
        LXI     D,AY2                ;DE = ADDRESS OF MULTIPLIER
        MVI     B,SZAYS              ;B = LENGTH OF OPERANDS IN BYTES
        CALL    MPBMUL               ;MULTIPLE-PRECISION BINARY MULTIPLY
                                     ;RESULT OF 12345H * 1234H = 14B60404H
                                     ; IN MEMORY AY1     = 04H
                                     ;           AY1+1   = 04H
                                     ;           AY1+2   = B6H
                                     ;           AY1+3   = 14H
                                     ;           AY1+4   = 00H
```

```
                                      ;           AY1+5   = 00H
                                      ;           AY1+6   = 00H

          JMP       SC6G

SZAYS     EQU       7                 ;LENGTH OF OPERANDS IN BYTES
AY1:
          DB        045H
          DB        023H
          DB        001H
          DB        0
          DB        0
          DB        0
          DB        0

AY2:
          DB        034H
          DB        012H
          DB        0
          DB        0
          DB        0
          DB        0
          DB        0

          END
```

Divides two multi-byte unsigned binary numbers. Both numbers are stored with their least significant byte at the lowest address. The quotient replaces the dividend; the address of the least significant byte of the remainder is in H and L. The length of the numbers (in bytes) is 255 or less. The Carry flag is cleared if no errors occur; if a divide by 0 is attempted, the Carry flag is set to 1, the dividend is left unchanged, and the remainder is set to 0.

Procedure: The program divides with the usual shift-and-subtract algorithm, shifting quotient and dividend and placing a 1 bit in the quotient each time a trial subtraction is successful. An extra buffer holds the result of the trial subtraction; that buffer is simply switched with the buffer holding the dividend if the trial subtraction is successful. The program exits immediately, setting the Carry flag, if it finds the divisor to be 0. The Carry flag is cleared otherwise.

Registers Used: All

Execution Time: Depends on the length of the operands and on the number of 1 bits in the quotient (requiring a buffer switch). If the average number of 1 bits in the quotient is four per byte, the execution time is approximately $1240 * LENGTH^2 + 2046 * LENGTH + 515$ cycles where LENGTH is the number of bytes in the operands.

Program Size: 176 bytes

Data Memory Required: 522 bytes anywhere in RAM. This is temporary storage for the high dividend (255 bytes starting at address HIDE1), the result of the trial subtraction (255 bytes starting at address HIDE2), the base address of the dividend (2 bytes starting at address DVEND), the base address of the divisor (2 bytes starting at address DVSOR), pointers to the two temporary buffers for the high dividend (2 bytes starting at addresses HDEPTR and ODEPTR, respectively), a loop counter (2 bytes starting at address COUNT), and a subtraction loop counter (1 byte at address SUBCNT).

Special Cases:

1. A length of 0 causes an immediate exit with the Carry flag cleared, the quotient equal to the original dividend, and the remainder undefined.

2. A divisor of 0 causes an exit with the Carry flag set to 1, the quotient equal to the original dividend, and the remainder equal to 0.

Entry Conditions

Base address of dividend in H and L
Base address of divisor in D and E
Length of the operands in bytes in B

Exit Conditions

Dividend replaced by dividend divided by divisor
If the divisor is non-zero, Carry = 0 and the result is normal.
If the divisor is 0, Carry = 1, the dividend is unchanged, and the remainder is 0.
The remainder is stored starting with its least significant byte at the address in H and L.

Example

1. Data: Length of operands (in bytes) = 03
   Divisor = $000F45_{16}$
   Dividend = $35A2F7_{16}$

   Result: Dividend = 000383_{16}
   Remainder (starting at address in HL) =
      $0003A8_{16}$
   Carry flag is 0 to indicate no divide-by-0
      error.

```
;                                                                      ;
;                                                                      ;
;                                                                      ;
;                                                                      ;
;        Title:          Multiple-Precision Binary Division            ;
;        Name:           MPBDIV                                        ;
;                                                                      ;
;                                                                      ;
;                                                                      ;
;                                                                      ;
;        Purpose:        Divide 2 arrays of binary bytes               ;
;                        Dividend := Dividend / divisor                ;
;                                                                      ;
;        Entry:          Registers H and L = Base address of dividend  ;
;                        Registers D and E = Base address of divisor   ;
;                        Register B = Length of operands in bytes      ;
;                                                                      ;
;                        The arrays are unsigned binary numbers with a ;
;                        maximum length of 255 bytes, ARRAY[0] is the  ;
;                        least significant byte, and ARRAY[LENGTH-1]   ;
;                        the most significant byte.                    ;
;                                                                      ;
;        Exit:           Dividend := Dividend / divisor                ;
;                        Registers H and L = Base address of remainder ;
;                        If no errors then                             ;
;                          Carry := 0                                  ;
;                        else                                          ;
;                          divide-by-0 error                           ;
;                          Carry := 1                                  ;
;                          dividend unchanged                          ;
;                          remainder := 0                              ;
;                                                                      ;
;        Registers used: All                                          ;
;                                                                      ;
;        Time:           Assuming there are length/2 1 bits in the     ;
;                        quotient then the time is approximately       ;
;                        (1240 * length^2) + (2046 * length) + 515 cycles;
;                                                                      ;
;        Size:           Program 177 bytes                             ;
;                        Data    522 bytes                             ;
```

```
;
;
MPBDIV:
        ;TEST LENGTH OF OPERAND, INITIALIZE POINTERS
        MOV     A,B
        ORA     A               ;IS LENGTH OF ARRAYS = 0?
        JZ      OKEXIT          ;EXIT IF SO
        SHLD    DVEND           ;SAVE BASE ADDRESS OF DIVIDEND
        XCHG
        SHLD    DVSOR           ;SAVE BASE ADDRESS OF DIVISOR
        MOV     C,B             ;C = LENGTH OF OPERANDS

        ;SET COUNT TO NUMBER OF BITS IN THE ARRAYS
        ; COUNT := (LENGTH * 8) + 1
        MOV     L,C             ;HL = LENGTH IN BYTES
        MVI     H,0
        DAD     H               ;LENGTH * 2
        DAD     H               ;LENGTH * 4
        DAD     H               ;LENGTH * 8
        INX     H               ;LENGTH * 8 + 1
        SHLD    COUNT           ;SAVE BIT COUNT

        ;ZERO BOTH HIGH DIVIDEND ARRAYS
        LXI     H,HIDE1         ;HL = ADDRESS OF HIDE1
        LXI     D,HIDE2         ;DE = ADDRESS OF HIDE2
        MOV     B,C             ;B = LENGTH
        SUB     A               ;GET 0 FOR FILL
ZEROLP:
        MOV     M,A             ;ZERO BOTH DIVIDEND ARRAYS
        STAX    D
        INX     H
        INX     D
        DCR     B
        JNZ     ZEROLP

        ;SET HIGH DIVIDEND POINTER TO HIDE1
        LXI     H,HIDE1
        SHLD    HDEPTR

        ;SET OTHER HIGH DIVIDEND POINTER TO HIDE2
        LXI     H,HIDE2
        SHLD    ODEPTR

        ;CHECK IF DIVISOR IS ZERO BY LOGICALLY ORING ALL BYTES
        LHLD    DVSOR           ;HL = ADDRESS OF DIVISOR
        MOV     B,C             ;B = LENGTH IN BYTES
        SUB     A               ;START LOGICAL OR AT 0
CHKOLP:
        ORA     M               ;OR NEXT BYTE
        INX     H               ;INCREMENT TO NEXT BYTE
        DCR     B
        JNZ     CHKOLP          ;CONTINUE UNTIL ALL BYTES ORED
        ORA     A               ;SET FLAGS FROM LOGICAL OR
        JZ      EREXIT          ;ERROR EXIT IF DIVISOR IS 0
```

```
              ;DIVIDE USING TRIAL SUBTRACTION ALGORITHM
              ORA       A               ;CLEAR CARRY FIRST TIME THROUGH
LOOP:
              ;C = LENGTH
              ;DE = ADDRESS OF DIVISOR
              ;CARRY = NEXT BIT OF QUOTIENT
              ;SHIFT CARRY INTO LOWER DIVIDEND ARRAY AS NEXT BIT OF QUOTIENT
              ; AND MOST SIGNIFICANT BIT OF LOWER DIVIDEND TO CARRY
              MOV       B,C             ;B = NUMBER OF BYTES TO ROTATE
              LHLD      DVEND           ;HL = ADDRESS OF DIVIDEND
SLLP1:
              MOV       A,M
              RAL                       ;ROTATE BYTE OF DIVIDEND LEFT
              MOV       M,A
              INX       H               ;NEXT BYTE
              DCR       B
              JNZ       SLLP1           ;CONTINUE UNTIL ALL BYTES SHIFTED

              ;DECREMENT BIT COUNTER AND EXIT IF DONE
              ;CARRY IS NOT CHANGED!
DECCNT:
              LDA       COUNT           ;SUBTRACT 1 FROM BIT COUNTER
              DCR       A
              STA       COUNT
              JNZ       CONT            ;BRANCH IF LSB OF COUNT NON-ZERO
              LDA       COUNT+1         ;OTHERWISE, BORROW FROM MSB
              DCR       A
              STA       COUNT+1
              JM        OKEXIT          ;EXIT WHEN COUNT BECOMES NEGATIVE

              ;SHIFT CARRY INTO LSB OF UPPER DIVIDEND
CONT:
              LHLD      HDEPTR          ;HL = CURRENT HIGH DIVIDEND POINTER
              MOV       B,C             ;B = LENGTH IN BYTES
SLLP2:
              MOV       A,M
              RAL                       ;ROTATE BYTE OF UPPER DIVIDEND
              MOV       M,A
              INX       H               ;INCREMENT TO NEXT BYTE
              DCR       B
              JNZ       SLLP2           ;CONTINUE UNTIL ALL BYTES SHIFTED


              ;SUBTRACT DIVISOR FROM HIGH DIVIDEND. PLACE DIFFERENCE IN
              ; OTHER HIGH DIVIDEND ARRAY
              PUSH      B               ;SAVE LENGTH
              MOV       A,C
              STA       SUBCNT          ;SUBCNT = LENGTH IN BYTES
              LHLD      ODEPTR
              MOV       C,L             ;BC = OTHER DIVIDEND
              MOV       B,H
              LHLD      HDEPTR
              XCHG                      ;DE = HIGH DIVIDEND
              LHLD      DVSOR           ;HL = DIVISOR
              ORA       A               ;CLEAR CARRY INITIALLY
SUBLP:
```

```
        LDAX    D               ;NEXT BYTE OF HIGH DIVIDEND
        SBB     M               ;SUBTRACT BYTE OF DIVISOR
        STAX    B               ;SAVE IN OTHER HIGH DIVIDEND
        INX     H               ;INCREMENT POINTERS
        INX     D
        INX     B
        LDA     SUBCNT          ;DECREMENT COUNT
        DCR     A
        STA     SUBCNT
        JNZ     SUBLP           ;CONTINUE UNITL DIFFERENCE COMPLETE
        POP     B               ;RESTORE LENGTH

        ;IF CARRY IS 1, HIGH DIVIDEND IS LESS THAN DIVISOR
        ; SO NEXT BIT OF QUOTIENT IS 0. IF CARRY IS 0,
        ; NEXT BIT OF QUOTIENT IS 1 AND WE REPLACE DIVIDEND
        ; WITH REMAINDER BY SWITCHING POINTERS
        CMC                     ;COMPLEMENT CARRY SO IT MATCHES
                                ; NEXT BIT OF QUOTIENT
        JNC     LOOP            ;JUMP IF NEXT BIT OF QUOTIENT 0
        LHLD    HDEPTR          ;OTHERWISE EXCHANGE POINTERS
        XCHG
        LHLD    ODEPTR
        SHLD    HDEPTR
        XCHG
        SHLD    ODEPTR

        ;CONTINUE WITH NEXT BIT OF QUOTIENT 1 (CARRY = 1)
        JMP     LOOP

        ;SET CARRY TO INDICATE A DIVIDE-BY-ZERO ERROR
EREXIT:
        STC                     ;SET CARRY, INVALID RESULT
        JMP     EXIT

        ;CLEAR CARRY TO INDICATE NO ERRORS
OKEXIT:
        ORA     A               ;CLEAR CARRY, VALID RESULT

        ;ARRAY 1 IS QUOTIENT
        ;HDEPTR CONTAINS ADDRESS OF REMAINDER
EXIT:   LHLD    HDEPTR          ;HL = BASE ADDRESS OF REMAINDER
        RET

        ;DATA
DVEND:  DS      2               ;ADDRESS OF DIVIDEND
DVSOR:  DS      2               ;ADDRESS OF DIVISOR
HDEPTR: DS      2               ;ADDRESS OF CURRENT HIGH DIVIDEND ARRAY
ODEPTR: DS      2               ;ADDRESS OF OTHER HIGH DIVIDEND ARRAY
COUNT:  DS      2               ;TEMPORARY FOR LOOP COUNTER
SUBCNT: DS      1               ;SUBTRACT LOOP COUNT
HIDE1:  DS      255             ;HIGH DIVIDEND BUFFER 1
HIDE2:  DS      255             ;HIGH DIVIDEND BUFFER 2


;
;
```

```
;       SAMPLE EXECUTION                                                 ;
;                                                                        ;
;                                                                        ;
SC6H:
        LXI     H,AY1           ;HL = BASE ADDRESS OF DIVIDEND
        LXI     D,AY2           ;DE = BASE ADDRESS OF DIVISOR
        MVI     B,SZAYS         ;B = LENGTH OF ARRAYS IN BYTES
        CALL    MPBDIV          ;MULTIPLE-PRECISION BINARY DIVIDE
                                ;RESULT OF 14B60404H / 1234H = 12345H
                                ; IN MEMORY AY1     = 45H
                                ;            AY1+1  = 23H
                                ;            AY1+2  = 01H
                                ;            AY1+3  = 00H
                                ;            AY1+4  = 00H
                                ;            AY1+5  = 00H
                                ;            AY1+6  = 00H

        JMP     SC6H

SZAYS   EQU     7       ;LENGTH OF ARRAYS IN BYTES
AY1:
        DB      004H
        DB      004H
        DB      0B6H
        DB      014H
        DB      0
        DB      0
        DB      0

AY2:
        DB      034H
        DB      012H
        DB      0
        DB      0
        DB      0
        DB      0
        DB      0

        END
```

Multiple-Precision
Binary Comparison (MPBCMP)

Compares two multi-byte unsigned binary numbers and sets the Carry and Zero flags appropriately. The Zero flag is set to 1 if the operands are equal and to 0 if they are not equal. The Carry flag is set to 1 if the subtrahend is larger than the minuend; the Carry flag is cleared otherwise. Thus, the flags are set as if the subtrahend had been subtracted from the minuend.

Procedure: The program compares the operands one byte at a time, starting with the most significant bytes and continuing until it finds corresponding bytes that are not equal. If all the bytes are equal, it exits with the Zero flag set to 1. Note that the comparison works through the operands starting with the most significant bytes, whereas the subtraction (Subroutine 6F) starts with the least significant bytes.

Registers Used: All

Execution Time: 44 cycles per byte that must be examined plus approximately 45 cycles overhead (8080) or 46 cycles per byte that must be examined plus approximately 45 cycles overhead (8085). That is, the program continues until it finds corresponding bytes that are not the same; each pair of bytes it must examine requires 44 cycles (8080) or 46 cycles (8085). There is an additional 20 cycles overhead if all bytes are equal.

Examples:

  1. Comparing two 6-byte numbers that are equal
    $44 * 6 + 65 = 329$ cycles (8080)
    $46 * 6 + 65 = 341$ cycles (8085)

  2. Comparing two 8-byte numbers that differ in the next to most significant bytes
    $44 * 2 + 45 = 133$ cycles (8080)
    $46 * 2 + 45 = 137$ cycles (8085)

Program Size: 54 bytes

Data Memory Required: None

Special Case: A length of 0 causes an immediate exit with the Carry flag cleared and the Zero flag set to 1.

Entry Conditions

Base address of minuend in H and L
Base address of subtrahend in D and E
Length of the operands in bytes in B

Exit Conditions

Flags set as if subtrahend had been subtracted from minuend.

Zero flag = 1 if subtrahend and minuend are equal; 0 if they are not equal.

Carry flag = 1 if subtrahend is larger than minuend in the unsigned sense; 0 if it is less than or equal to the minuend.

Examples

1. Data: Length of operands (in bytes) = 6
            Subtrahend = $19D028A193EA_{16}$
            Minuend = $4E67BC15A266_{16}$

    Result: Zero flag = 0 (operands are not equal)
            Carry flag = 0 (subtrahend is not larger than minuend)

2. Data: Length of operands (in bytes) = 6
   Subtrahend = $19D028A193EA_{16}$
   Minuend = $19D028A193EA_{16}$

   Result: Zero flag = 1 (operands are equal)
   Carry flag = 0 (subtrahend is not larger than minuend)

3. Data: Length of operands (in bytes) = 6
   Subtrahend = $19D028A193EA_{16}$
   Minuend = $0F37E5991D7C_{16}$

   Result: Zero flag = 0 (operands are not equal)
   Carry flag = 1 (subtrahend is larger than minuend)

```
;                                                              ;
;                                                              ;
;                                                              ;
;                                                              ;
;                                                              ;
;   Title:         Multiple-Precision Binary Comparison        ;
;   Name:          MPBCMP                                       ;
;                                                              ;
;                                                              ;
;                                                              ;
;                                                              ;
;   Purpose:       Compare 2 arrays of binary bytes and return ;
;                  the Carry and Zero flags set or cleared     ;
;                                                              ;
;   Entry:         Registers H and L = Base address of minuend ;
;                  Registers D and E = Base address of subtrahend ;
;                  Register B = Length of operands in bytes    ;
;                                                              ;
;                  The arrays are unsigned binary numbers with a ;
;                  maximum length of 255 bytes, ARRAY[0] is the ;
;                  least significant byte, and ARRAY[LENGTH-1] ;
;                  the most significant byte.                  ;
;                                                              ;
;   Exit:          IF minuend = subtrahend THEN                ;
;                     C=0,Z=1                                  ;
;                  IF minuend > subtrahend THEN                ;
;                     C=0,Z=0                                  ;
;                  IF minuend < subtrahend THEN                ;
;                     C=1,Z=0                                  ;
;                                                              ;
;   Registers used: All                                        ;
;                                                              ;
;   Time:          44 cycles per byte that must be examined plus ;
;                  65 cycles overhead for the 8080.            ;
;                  46 cycles per byte that must be examined plus ;
;                  65 cycles overhead for the 8085.            ;
;                                                              ;
;   Size:          Program 20 bytes                            ;
;                                                              ;
;                                                              ;

MPBCMP:
        ;TEST LENGTH OF OPERANDS, SET POINTERS TO MSB'S
        MOV     A,B
        ORA     A               ;IS LENGTH OF ARRAYS = 0?
```

```
        RZ                          ;YES, EXIT WITH C=0, Z=1
        MOV     C,B                 ;BC = LENGTH
        MVI     B,0
        DAD     B
        XCHG                        ;DE POINTS TO END OF MINUEND
        DAD     B                   ;HL POINTS TO END OF SUBTRAHEND
        ORA     A                   ;CLEAR CARRY INITIALLY

        ;SUBTRACT BYTES, STARTING WITH MOST SIGNIFICANT
        ;EXIT WITH FLAGS SET IF CORRESPONDING BYTES NOT EQUAL
LOOP:
        DCX     H                   ;BACK UP TO LESS SIGNIFICANT BYTE
        DCX     D
        LDAX    D                   ;GET NEXT MINUEND BYTE
        SBB     M                   ;SUBTRACT BYTE OF SUBTRAHEND
        RNZ                         ;RETURN IF NOT EQUAL WITH FLAGS
                                    ; SET
        DCR     C
        JNZ     LOOP                ;CONTINUE UNTIL ALL BYTES COMPARED
        RET                         ;EQUAL, RETURN WITH C=0, Z=1


;                                                                    ;
;                                                                    ;
;       SAMPLE EXECUTION                                             ;
;                                                                    ;
;                                                                    ;

SC6I:
        LXI     H,AY1               ;HL = BASE ADDRESS OF MINUEND
        LXI     D,AY2               ;DE = BASE ADDRESS OF SUBTRAHEND
        MVI     B,SZAYS             ;B = LENGTH OF OPERANDS IN BYTES
        CALL    MPBCMP              ;MULTIPLE-PRECISION BINARY COMPARISON
                                    ;RESULT OF COMPARE(7654321H,1234567H) IS
                                    ; C=0,Z=0

        JMP     SC6I

SZAYS   EQU     7                   ;LENGTH OF OPERANDS IN BYTES
AY1:
        DB      021H
        DB      043H
        DB      065H
        DB      007H
        DB      0
        DB      0
        DB      0

AY2:
        DB      067H
        DB      045H
        DB      023H
        DB      001H
        DB      0
        DB      0
        DB      0

        END
```

Multiple-Precision Decimal Addition (MPDADD) 6J

Adds two multi-byte unsigned decimal numbers. Both numbers are stored with their least significant digits at the lowest address. The sum replaces the addend. The length of the numbers (in bytes) is 255 or less.

Procedure: The program first clears the Carry flag and then adds the operands one byte (two digits) at a time, starting with the least significant digits. The sum replaces the addend. A length of 0 causes an immediate exit with no addition. The final Carry flag reflects the addition of the most significant digits.

Registers Used: All

Execution Time: 50 cycles per byte plus 24 cycles overhead (8080) or 51 cycles per byte plus 21 cycles overhead (8085)

Program Size: 14 bytes

Data Memory Required: None

Special Case: A length of 0 causes an immediate exit with the operand unchanged and the Carry flag cleared.

Entry Conditions

Base address of addend in H and L
Base address of adder in D and E
Length of the operands in bytes in register B

Exit Conditions

Addend replaced by addend plus adder

Example

1. Data: Length of operands (in bytes) = 6
                 Addend = 196028819315_{16}
                 Adder = 293471605987_{16}

   Result: Addend = 489500425302_{16}
                 Carry = 0

```
;                                                              ;
;                                                              ;
;                                                              ;
;                                                              ;
;        Title:        Multiple-Precision Decimal Addition     ;
;        Name:         MPDADD                                  ;
;                                                              ;
;                                                              ;
;                                                              ;
```

```
;                                                                      ;
;        Purpose:        Add 2 arrays of BCD bytes                      ;
;                        Array1 := Array1 + Array2                      ;
;                                                                       ;
;        Entry:          Registers H and L = Base address of array 1    ;
;                        Registers D and E = Base address of array 2    ;
;                        Register B = Length of arrays in bytes         ;
;                                                                       ;
;                        The arrays are unsigned BCD numbers with a     ;
;                        maximum length of 255 bytes, ARRAY[0] is the    ;
;                        least significant byte, and ARRAY[LENGTH-1]     ;
;                        the most significant byte.                     ;
;                                                                       ;
;        Exit:           Array1 := Array1 + Array2                      ;
;                                                                       ;
;        Registers used: ALL                                           ;
;                                                                       ;
;        Time:           51 cycles per byte plus 21 cycles overhead for ;
;                          8085.                                        ;
;                        50 cycles per byte plus 24 cycles overhead for ;
;                          8080.                                        ;
;                                                                       ;
;        Size:           Program 14 bytes                               ;
;                                                                       ;
;                                                                       ;

MPDADD:
        ;TEST ARRAY LENGTH FOR 0, CLEAR CARRY
        MOV     A,B
        ANA     A                   ;TEST LENGTH, CLEAR CARRY
        RZ                          ;EXIT IF LENGTH IS 0

        ;ADD OPERANDS 2 DIGITS AT A TIME
        ; NOTE CARRY IS 0 INITIALLY
LOOP:
        LDAX    D
        ADC     M                   ;ADD NEXT BYTES
        DAA                         ;CHANGE TO DECIMAL
        MOV     M,A                 ;STORE SUM
        INX     H                   ;INCREMENT TO NEXT BYTE
        INX     D
        DCR     B
        JNZ     LOOP                ;CONTINUE UNTIL ALL BYTES SUMMED
        RET


;                                                                       ;
;                                                                       ;
;        SAMPLE EXECUTION                                               ;
;                                                                       ;
;                                                                       ;

SC6J:
        LXI     H,AY1               ;HL = BASE ADDRESS OF ARRAY 1
        LXI     D,AY2               ;DE = BASE ADDRESS OF ARRAY 2
        MVI     B,SZAYS             ;B = LENGTH OF ARRAYS IN BYTES
```

```
        CALL    MPDADD          ;MULTIPLE-PRECISION BCD ADDITION
                                ;RESULT OF 1234567 + 1234567 = 2469134
                                ; IN MEMORY AY1      = 34H
                                ;             AY1+1  = 91H
                                ;             AY1+2  = 46H
                                ;             AY1+3  = 02H
                                ;             AY1+4  = 00H
                                ;             AY1+5  = 00H
                                ;             AY1+6  = 00H

        JMP     SC6J

SZAYS:  EQU     7               ;LENGTH OF ARRAYS IN BYTES
AY1:
        DB      067H
        DB      045H
        DB      023H
        DB      001H
        DB      0
        DB      0
        DB      0

AY2:
        DB      067H
        DB      045H
        DB      023H
        DB      001H
        DB      0
        DB      0
        DB      0

        END
```

Multiple-Precision
Decimal Subtraction (MPDSUB)

Subtracts two multi-byte unsigned decimal numbers. Both numbers are stored with their least significant digits at the lowest address. The difference replaces the minuend. The length of the numbers (in bytes) is 255 or less.

Procedure: The program first clears the Carry flag and then subtracts the subtrahend from the minuend one byte (two digits) at a time, starting with the least significant digits. A length of 0 causes an immediate exit with no subtraction. The final Carry flag is an inverted borrow reflecting the subtraction of the most significant digits.

Registers Used: All

Execution Time: 73 cycles per byte plus 32 cycles overhead (8080) or 73 cycles per byte plus 29 cycles overhead (8085)

Program Size: 22 bytes

Data Memory Required: None

Special Case: A length of 0 causes an immediate exit with the minuend unchanged (that is, the difference is equal to the minuend). The Carry flag is cleared.

Entry Conditions

Base address of minuend in H and L
Base address of subtrahend in D and E
Length of the operands in bytes in B

Exit Conditions

Minuend replaced by minuend minus subtrahend

Example

1. Data: Length of operands (in bytes) = 6
   Minuend = 293471605987_{16}
   Subtrahend = 1960288193151_{16}

   Result: Minuend = 097442786672_{16}
   Carry = 1, since no borrow is necessary

```
;                                                              ;
;                                                              ;
;                                                              ;
;                                                              ;
;     Title:        Multiple-Precision Decimal Subtraction     ;
;     Name:         MPDSUB                                      ;
;                                                              ;
;                                                              ;
```

```
;                                                                    ;
;         Purpose:          Subtract 2 arrays of BCD bytes           ;
;                           Minuend := Minuend - subtrahend          ;
;                                                                    ;
;         Entry:            Registers H and L = Base address of minuend     ;
;                           Registers D and E = Base address of subtrahend  ;
;                           Register B = Length of arrays in bytes   ;
;                                                                    ;
;                           The arrays are unsigned BCD numbers with a      ;
;                           maximum length of 255 bytes, ARRAY[0] is the    ;
;                           least significant byte, and ARRAY[LENGTH-1]     ;
;                           the most significant byte.               ;
;                                                                    ;
;         Exit:             Minuend := Minuend - subtrahend          ;
;                                                                    ;
;         Registers used: A,B,DE,F,HL                                ;
;                                                                    ;
;         Time:             73 cycles per byte plus 29 cycles overhead for  ;
;                             8085.                                  ;
;                           73 cycles per byte plus 32 cycles overhead for  ;
;                             8080.                                  ;
;                                                                    ;
;         Size:             Program 22 bytes                         ;
;                                                                    ;
;                                                                    ;


MPDSUB:
        ;TEST ARRAY LENGTH FOR ZERO, SET INVERTED BORROW
        MOV     A,B
        ORA     A               ;TEST ARRAY LENGTH, CLEAR CARRY
        RZ                      ;EXIT IF LENGTH IS 0
        CMC                     ;SET CARRY TO FORM 10'S COMPLEMENT
        XCHG                    ;HL = SUBTRAHEND
                                ;DE = MINUEND

        ;SUBTRACT OPERANDS 2 DIGITS AT A TIME BY ADDING TEN'S
        ; COMPLEMENT OF SUBTRAHEND TO MINUEND
        ;CARRY IS INVERTED BORROW IN TEN'S COMPLEMENT ARITHMETIC
        ;NOTE THAT DAA WORKS ONLY AFTER ADDITION INSTRUCTIONS
        ;BYTE OF TEN'S COMPLEMENT = 99 HEX + INVERTED BORROW
        ; - BYTE OF SUBTRAHEND.  RESULT IS ALWAYS NON-NEGATIVE
        ; AND CARRY AND HALF CARRY ARE ALWAYS 0, SO NO PROBLEM
        ; WITH BCD OPERANDS
LOOP:
        MVI     A,99H           ;FORM A BYTE OF 10'S COMPLEMENT
        ACI     0               ; OF SUBTRAHEND
        SUB     M
        MOV     C,A
        LDAX    D               ;GET MINUEND
        ADD     C               ;ADD COMPLEMENTED SUBTRAHEND
        DAA                     ;CHANGE TO DECIMAL
        STAX    D               ;STORE DIFFERENCE
        INX     H               ;INCREMENT TO NEXT BYTE
        INX     D
        DCR     B
```

```
        JNZ     LOOP            ;CONTINUE UNTIL ALL BYTES SUBTRACTED
        RET


;                                                                       ;
;                                                                       ;
;       SAMPLE EXECUTION                                                ;
;                                                                       ;
;                                                                       ;
SC6K:
        LXI     H,AY1           ;HL = BASE ADDRESS OF MINUEND
        LXI     D,AY2           ;DE = BASE ADDRESS OF SUBTRAHEND
        MVI     B,SZAYS         ;B = LENGTH OF OPERANDS IN BYTES
        CALL    MPDSUB          ;MULTIPLE-PRECISION BCD SUBTRACTION
                                ;RESULT OF 2469134 - 1234567 = 1234567
                                ; IN MEMORY AY1     = 67H
                                ;           AY1+1   = 45H
                                ;           AY1+2   = 23H
                                ;           AY1+3   = 01H
                                ;           AY1+4   = 00H
                                ;           AY1+5   = 00H
                                ;           AY1+6   = 00H

        JMP     SC6K

SZAYS:  EQU     7               ;LENGTH OF OPERANDS IN BYTES
AY1:
        DB      034H
        DB      091H
        DB      046H
        DB      002H
        DB      0
        DB      0
        DB      0

AY2:
        DB      067H
        DB      045H
        DB      023H
        DB      001H
        DB      0
        DB      0
        DB      0

        END
```

Multiple-Precision Decimal Multiplication (MPDMUL)

Multiplies two multi-byte unsigned decimal numbers. Both numbers are stored with their least significant digits at the lowest address. The product replaces the multiplicand. The length of the numbers (in bytes) is 255 or less. Only the least significant bytes of the product are returned to retain compatibility with other multiple-precision decimal operations.

Procedure: The program handles each digit of the multiplicand separately. It masks the digit off, shifts it (if it is the upper nibble of a byte), and then uses it as a counter to determine how many times to add the multiplier to the partial product. The least significant digit of the partial product is saved as the next digit of the full product, and the partial product is shifted right four bits. The program uses a flag to determine whether it is currently working with the upper or lower digit of a byte. A length of 0 causes an exit with no multiplication.

Registers Used: All

Execution Time: Depends on the length of the operands and on the size of the digits in the multiplicand (since those digits determine how many times the multiplier must be added to the partial product). If the average digit in the multiplicand has a value of 5, then the execution time is approximately $726 * LENGTH^2 + 1603 * LENGTH + 151$ cycles (8080) or $730 * LENGTH^2 + 1503 * LENGTH + 139$ cycles (8085), where LENGTH is the number of bytes in the operands.

Program Size: 195 bytes

Data Memory Required: 520 bytes anywhere in RAM. This is temporary storage for the high bytes of the partial product (255 bytes starting at address PROD), the multiplicand (255 bytes starting at address MCAND), the length of the arrays (1 byte at address LEN), a digit counter indicating upper or lower digit (1 byte at address DCNT), a loop counter (1 byte at address LPCNT), an overflow byte (1 byte at address OVRFLW), pointers to the multiplicand and multiplier (2 bytes each starting at addresses MCADR and MPADR, respectively), and the next byte of the multiplicand (1 byte at address NBYTE).

Special Case: A length of 0 causes an immediate exit with the multiplicand unchanged. The more significant bytes of the product (starting at address PROD) are undefined.

Entry Conditions

Base address of multiplicand in H and L
Base address of multiplier in D and E
Length of the operands in bytes in B

Exit Conditions

Multiplicand replaced by multiplicand times multiplier

Example

1. Data: Length of operands (in bytes) = 04
   Multiplier = 00003518_{16}
   Multiplicand = 00006294_{16}

   Result: Multiplicand = 221422926_{16}

Note that MPDMUL returns only the less significant bytes of the product (that is, the number of bytes in the multiplicand and multiplier) to maintain compatibility with other multiple-

239

precision decimal arithmetic operations. The more significant bytes of the product are available starting with their least significant digits at address PROD. The user may need to check those bytes for a possible overflow or extend the operands with zeros.

```
;                                                                    ;
;                                                                    ;
;                                                                    ;
;                                                                    ;
;        Title:         Multiple-Precision Decimal Multiplication    ;
;        Name:          MPDMUL                                       ;
;                                                                    ;
;                                                                    ;
;                                                                    ;
;        Purpose:       Multiply 2 arrays of BCD bytes               ;
;                       Multiplicand := Multiplicand * multiplier    ;
;                                                                    ;
;        Entry:         Registers H and L = Base address of multiplicand;
;                       Registers D and E = Base address of multiplier ;
;                       Register B = Length of arrays in bytes       ;
;                                                                    ;
;                           The arrays are unsigned BCD numbers with a ;
;                           maximum length of 255 bytes, ARRAY[0] is the ;
;                           least significant byte, and ARRAY[LENGTH-1] ;
;                           the most significant byte.               ;
;                                                                    ;
;        Exit:          Multiplicand := Multiplicand * multiplier    ;
;                                                                    ;
;        Registers used: All                                         ;
;                                                                    ;
;        Time:          Assuming average digit value of multiplicand ;
;                       is 5 then the time is approximately          ;
;                       (726 * length^2) + (1603 * length) + 151 cycles;
;                       for 8080                                     ;
;                       (730 * length^2) + (1503 * length) + 139 cycles;
;                       for 8085                                     ;
;                                                                    ;
;        Size:          Program 195 bytes                            ;
;                       Data    520 bytes                            ;
;                                                                    ;
;                                                                    ;

MPDMUL:
        ;INITIALIZE COUNTERS AND POINTERS
        MOV     A,B             ;TEST LENGTH OF OPERANDS
        ORA     A
        RZ                      ;EXIT IF LENGTH IS 0
        STA     LEN             ;SAVE LENGTH
        STA     LPCNT           ;LOOP COUNTER = LENGTH IN BYTES
        SHLD    MCADR           ;SAVE MULTIPLICAND ADDRESS
```

```
        XCHG
        SHLD    MPADR               ;SAVE MULTIPLIER ADDRESS


        ;SAVE MULTIPLICAND IN TEMPORARY BUFFER (MCAND)
        ; CLEAR PARTIAL PRODUCT, CONSISTING OF UPPER BYTES
        ; STARTING AT PROD AND LOWER BYTES REPLACING
        ; MULTIPLICAND
        LXI     H,MCAND
        SHLD    NBYTE               ;NEXT BYTE = LOW BYTE OF
                                    ; MULTIPLICAND
        XCHG                        ;HL = ADDRESS OF MULTIPLICAND
                                    ;DE = ADDRESS OF TEMPORARY MULTIPLICAND
                                    ;B = LENGTH OF OPERANDS IN BYTES
        MVI     C,0                 ;GET 0 TO FILL PARTIAL PRODUCT
INITLP0:
        MOV     A,M                 ;GET NEXT BYTE OF MULTIPLICAND
        STAX    D                   ;STORE IN TEMPORARY BUFFER
        MOV     M,C                 ;CLEAR BYTE OF MULTIPLICAND
        INX     D
        INX     H
        DCR     B
        JNZ     INITLP0             ;CONTINUE UNTIL DONE


        ;CLEAR UPPER BYTES OF PARTIAL PRODUCT
        LXI     H,PROD              ;HL = BASE ADDRESS OF PRODUCT
        LDA     LEN
        MOV     B,A                 ;B = LENGTH OF OPERANDS IN BYTES
                                    ;C STILL HAS 0 FOR FILL
INITLP1:
        MOV     M,C                 ;ZERO BYTE OF PRODUCT
        INX     H
        DCR     B
        JNZ     INITLP1             ;CONTINUE UNTIL ALL BYTES ZERO


        ;LOOP THROUGH ALL BYTES OF MULTIPLICAND
LOOP:
        MVI     A,1
        STA     DCNT                ;START WITH LOWER DIGIT


        ;LOOP THROUGH 2 DIGITS PER BYTE
        ; DURING LOWER DIGIT DCNT = 1
        ; DURING UPPER DIGIT DCNT = 0
DLOOP:
        SUB     A                   ;CLEAR OVERFLOW BYTE
        STA     OVRFLW
        LDA     DCNT
        ORA     A                   ;TEST FOR LOWER DIGIT (Z = 0)
        LHLD    NBYTE               ;GET NEXT BYTE
        MOV     A,M
        JNZ     DLOOP1              ;JUMP IF LOWER DIGIT
        RRC                         ;SHIFT UPPER DIGIT RIGHT 4 BITS
        RRC
        RRC
        RRC
```

```
DLOOP1:
        ANI     OFH             ;KEEP ONLY NEXT DIGIT
        JZ      SDIGIT          ;BRANCH IF NEXT DIGIT IS ZERO
        MOV     C,A             ;C = NEXT DIGIT

        ;ADD MULTIPLIER TO PRODUCT NDIGIT TIMES
ADDLP:
        LHLD    MPADR           ;HL = BASE ADDRESS OF MULTIPLIER
        LXI     D,PROD          ;DE = BASE ADDRESS OF PRODUCT
        LDA     LEN
        MOV     B,A             ;B = LENGTH
        ORA     A               ;CLEAR CARRY INITIALLY

        ;ADD MULTIPLIER TO PRODUCT 1 BYTE AT A TIME
INNER:
        LDAX    D               ;GET NEXT BYTE OF PRODUCT
        ADC     M               ;ADD BYTE OF MULTIPLIER
        DAA                     ;DECIMAL ADJUST
        STAX    D               ;STORE SUM IN PRODUCT
        INX     H
        INX     D
        DCR     B
        JNZ     INNER           ;CONTINUE UNTIL ALL BYTES ADDED
        JNC     DECND           ;JUMP IF NO OVERFLOW FROM ADDITION
        LXI     H,OVRFLW        ;ELSE INCREMENT OVERFLOW BYTE
        INR     M
DECND:
        DCR     C
        JNZ     ADDLP           ;CONTINUE UNTIL DIGIT = 0

        ;STORE LEAST SIGNIFICANT DIGIT OF PRODUCT
        ; AS NEXT DIGIT OF MULTIPLICAND
SDIGIT:
        LDA     PROD            ;GET LOW BYTE OF PRODUCT
        ANI     OFH
        MOV     B,A             ;SAVE IN B
        LDA     DCNT
        ORA     A               ;TEST FOR LOWER DIGIT (Z=0)
        MOV     A,B             ;A = NEXT DIGIT
        JNZ     SD1             ;JUMP IF WORKING ON LOWER DIGIT
        RRC                     ;ELSE MOVE HIGH DIGIT TO LOW DIGIT
        RRC
        RRC
        RRC
SD1:
        LHLD    MCADR           ;PLACE NEXT DIGIT IN MULTIPLICAND
        ORA     M
        MOV     M,A

        ;SHIFT PRODUCT RIGHT 1 DIGIT (4 BITS)
        LDA     LEN
        MOV     B,A             ;B = LENGTH
        MOV     E,A
        MVI     D,O
        LXI     H,PROD
        DAD     D               ;HL POINTS BEYOND END OF PROD
```

```
          LDA       OVRFLW
          MOV       D,A              ;D = OVERFLOW BYTE
SHFTLP:
          DCX       H                ;DECREMENT, POINT TO NEXT BYTE
          MOV       A,M
          MOV       C,A              ;SAVE IN C TO USE LOW DIGIT LATER
          ANI       OFOH             ;CLEAR LOWER DIGIT
          ORA       D                ;COMBINE PRODUCT AND OVRFLW
          RRC                        ;SWAP DIGITS SO HIGH DIGIT IS FROM
          RRC                        ; OVRFLW AND LOW DIGIT IS FROM PRODUCT
          RRC
          RRC
          MOV       M,A              ;STORE DIGITS IN PRODUCT
          MOV       A,C              ;GET LOWER DIGIT BACK
          ANI       OFH
          MOV       D,A              ;SAVE IT FOR NEXT LOOP
          DCR       B
          JNZ       SHFTLP           ;CONTINUE UNTIL DONE

          ;CHECK IF DONE WITH BOTH DIGITS OF CURRENT BYTE
          LXI       H,DCNT           ;ON LOWER DIGIT?
          DCR       M
          JZ        DLOOP            ;YES, DO UPPER DIGIT OF BYTE

          ;INCREMENT TO NEXT BYTE AND SEE IF DONE
          LHLD      NBYTE            ;INCREMENT TO NEXT MULTIPLICAND BYTE
          INX       H
          SHLD      NBYTE
          LHLD      MCADR            ;INCREMENT TO NEXT RESULT BYTE
          INX       H
          SHLD      MCADR
          LXI       H,LPCNT          ;DECREMENT LOOP COUNTER
          DCR       M
          JNZ       LOOP
EXIT:
          RET

          ;DATA
LEN:                DS        1      ;LENGTH OF ARRAYS IN BYTES
DCNT:               DS        1      ;DIGIT COUNTER FOR BYTES IN ARRAYS
LPCNT:              DS        1      ;LOOP COUNTER
OVRFLW:             DS        1      ;OVERFLOW BYTE
MCADR:              DS        2      ;POINTER TO MULTIPLICAND
MPADR:              DS        2      ;POINTER TO MULTIPLIER
NBYTE:              DS        2      ;NEXT BYTE OF MULTIPLICNAD
PROD:               DS        255    ;PRODUCT BUFFER
MCAND:              DS        255    ;MULTIPLICAND BUFFER


;                                                                    ;
;                                                                    ;
;         SAMPLE EXECUTION                                           ;
;                                                                    ;
;                                                                    ;

SC6L:
          LXI       H,AY1            ;BASE ADDRESS OF MULTIPLICAND
```

```
        LXI     D,AY2           ;BASE ADDRESS OF MULTIPLIER
        MVI     B,SZAYS         ;LENGTH OF ARRAYS IN BYTES
        CALL    MPDMUL          ;MULTIPLE-PRECISION BCD MULTIPLICATION
                                ;RESULT OF 1234 * 1234 = 1522756
                                ; IN MEMORY AY1     = 56H
                                ;           AY1+1   = 27H
                                ;           AY1+2   = 52H
                                ;           AY1+3   = 01H
                                ;           AY1+4   = 00H
                                ;           AY1+5   = 00H
                                ;           AY1+6   = 00H

        JMP     SC6L

SZAYS   EQU     7               ;LENGTH OF ARRAYS IN BYTES
AY1:
        DB      034H
        DB      012H
        DB      0
        DB      0
        DB      0
        DB      0
        DB      0

AY2:
        DB      034H
        DB      012H
        DB      0
        DB      0
        DB      0
        DB      0
        DB      0

        END
```

Multiple-Precision Decimal Division (MPDDIV)

Divides two multi-byte unsigned decimal numbers. Both numbers are stored with their least significant digits at the lowest address. The quotient replaces the dividend; the remainder is not returned but its base address is in memory locations HDEPTR and HDEPTR+1. The length of the numbers (in bytes) is 255 or less. The Carry flag is cleared if no errors occur; if a divide by 0 is attempted, the Carry flag is set to 1, the dividend is unchanged, and the remainder is set to 0.

Procedure: The program divides by determining how many times the divisor can be subtracted from the dividend. It saves that number in the quotient, makes the remainder into the new dividend, and rotates the dividend and the quotient left one digit. The program exits immediately and sets the Carry flag if it finds the divisor to be 0. The Carry flag is cleared otherwise. The program subtracts using ten's complement arithmetic; this results in the divisor being replaced by its nine's complement to increase speed.

Registers Used: All

Execution Time: Depends on the length of the operands and on the size of the digits in the quotient (determining how many times the divisor must be subtracted from the dividend). If the average digit in the quotient has a value of 5, the execution time is approximately $1128 * \text{LENGTH}^2 + 2722 * \text{LENGTH} + 393$ cycles (8080) or $1150 * \text{LENGTH}^2 + 2647 * \text{LENGTH} + 354$ (8085), where LENGTH is the number of bytes in the operands.

Program Size: 214 bytes

Data Memory Required: 523 bytes anywhere in RAM. This is storage for the high dividend (255 bytes starting at address HIDE1), the result of the subtraction (255 bytes starting at address HIDE2), the length of the operands (1 byte at address LENGTH), the next digit in the array (1 byte at address NDIGIT), the counter for the subtraction loop (1 byte at address CNT), pointers to the dividend, divisor, current high dividend and remainder, and other high dividend (2 bytes each starting at addresses DVADR, DSADR, HDEPTR, and ODEPTR, respectively), and the divide loop counter (2 bytes starting at address COUNT).

Special Cases:

1. A length of 0 causes an immediate exit with the Carry flag cleared, the quotient equal to the original dividend, and the remainder undefined.

2. A divisor of 0 causes an exit with the Carry flag set to 1, the quotient equal to the original dividend, and the remainder equal to 0.

Entry Conditions

Base address of dividend in H and L
Base address of divisor in D and E
Length of the operands in bytes in B

Exit Conditions

Dividend replaced by dividend divided by divisor
If the divisor is non-zero, Carry = 0 and the result is normal.
If the divisor is 0, Carry = 1, the dividend is unchanged, and the remainder is 0.
The base address of the remainder (i.e., the address of its least significant digits) is in HDEPTR and HDEPTR+1.
The divisor is replaced by its nine's complement.

Example

1. Data: Length of operands (in bytes) = 04
              Dividend = 22142298_{16}
              Divisor = 00006294_{16}

   Result: Dividend = 00003518_{16}
              Remainder (base address in HDEPTR and
                HDEPTR + 1) = 00000006_{16}
              Carry flag is 0 to indicate no divide-by-0
              error.

```
;                                                                      ;
;                                                                      ;
;                                                                      ;
;                                                                      ;
;          Title:      Multiple-Precision Decimal Division             ;
;          Name:       MPDDIV                                          ;
;                                                                      ;
;                                                                      ;
;                                                                      ;
;          Purpose:    Divide 2 arrays of BCD bytes                    ;
;                      Quotient := Dividend / divisor                  ;
;                                                                      ;
;          Entry:      Registers H and L = Base address of dividend    ;
;                      Registers D and E = Base address of divisor     ;
;                      Register B = Length of operands in bytes        ;
;                                                                      ;
;                      The arrays are unsigned BCD numbers with a      ;
;                      maximum length of 255 bytes, ARRAY[0] is the    ;
;                      least significant byte, and ARRAY[LENGTH-1]     ;
;                      the most significant byte.                      ;
;                                                                      ;
;          Exit:       Dividend := dividend / divisor                  ;
;                      Dvbuf := remainder                              ;
;                      If no errors then                               ;
;                        Carry := 0                                    ;
;                      else                                            ;
;                        divide by 0 error                             ;
;                        Carry := 1                                    ;
;                        Dividend unchanged                            ;
;                        remainder := 0                                ;
;                                                                      ;
;          Registers used: All                                        ;
;                                                                      ;
;          Time:       Assuming the average digit value in the         ;
;                      quotient is 5 then the time is approximately     ;
;                      (1128 * length^2) + (2722 * length) + 393 cycles;
;                       for the 8080                                   ;
;                      (1150 * length^2) + (2647 * length) + 354 cycles;
;                       for the 8085                                   ;
;                                                                      ;
;          Size:       Program 214 bytes                               ;
;                      Data    523 bytes                               ;
;                                                                      ;
```

```
MPDDIV:
        ;SAVE PARAMETERS AND CHECK FOR ZERO LENGTH
        SHLD    DVADR               ;SAVE DIVIDEND ADDRESS
        XCHG
        SHLD    DSADR               ;SAVE DIVISOR ADDRESS
        MOV     A,B
        STA     LENGTH              ;SAVE LENGTH
        ORA     A                   ;TEST LENGTH
        JZ      OKEXIT              ;EXIT IF LENGTH = 0

        ;ZERO BOTH DIVIDEND BUFFERS
        ; AND SET UP THE DIVIDEND POINTERS
        LXI     H,HIDE2
        SHLD    ODEPTR              ;OTHER DIVIDEND POINTER = HIDE2
        XCHG                        ;DE = HIDE2
        LXI     H,HIDE1
        SHLD    HDEPTR              ;HIGH DIVIDEND PTR = HIDE1
        SUB     A                   ;GET 0 TO USE IN FILLING BUFFERS
                                    ;B = LENGTH IN BYTES

INITLP:
        MOV     M,A                 ;ZERO BYTE OF HIDE1
        STAX    D                   ;ZERO BYTE OF HIDE2
        INX     H                   ;INCREMENT TO NEXT BYTE
        INX     D
        DCR     B
        JNZ     INITLP              ;CONTINUE UNTIL DONE

        ;SET COUNT TO NUMBER OF DIGITS PLUS 1
        ; COUNT := (LENGTH * 2) + 1;
        LDA     LENGTH
        MOV     L,A
        MVI     H,0
        DAD     H                   ;LENGTH * 2
        INX     H                   ;LENGTH * 2 + 1
        SHLD    COUNT               ;COUNT = LENGTH * 2 + 1

        ;CHECK FOR DIVIDE BY ZERO
        ;LOGICALLY OR ENTIRE DIVISOR TO SEE IF ALL BYTES ARE 0
        LHLD    DSADR               ;HL = ADDRESS OF DIVISOR
        LDA     LENGTH
        MOV     B,A                 ;B = LENGTH OF ARRAYS IN BYTES
        SUB     A                   ;START LOGICAL OR WITH 0

DV01:
        ORA     M                   ;OR NEXT BYTE OF DIVISOR
        INX     H
        DCR     B
        JNZ     DV01
        ORA     A                   ;TEST FOR ZERO DIVISOR
        JZ      EREXIT              ;ERROR EXIT IF DIVISOR IS 0

        ;TAKE 9'S COMPLEMENT OF DIVISOR AS 8080 ONLY DOES
        ; DECIMAL ADJUST AFTER ADD
        LHLD    DSADR               ;HL POINTS TO DIVISOR
        LDA     LENGTH
```

```
        MOV     B,A                ;B = LENGTH IN BYTES
DO9S:
        MVI     A,99H              ;FORM 9'S COMPLEMENT OF A BYTE
        SUB     M
        MOV     M,A
        INX     H
        DCR     B
        JNZ     DO9S               ;CONTINUE THROUGH ALL BYTES

        SUB     A                  ;START NEXT DIGIT AT 0
        STA     NDIGIT

        ;PERFORM DIVISION BY REPEATED SUBTRACTIONS

DVLOOP:
        ;ROTATE LEFT LOWER DIVIDEND AND QUOTIENT:
        ; HIGH DIGIT OF NDIGIT BECOMES LEAST SIGNIFICANT DIGIT
        ; OF QUOTIENT (DIVIDEND ARRAY) AND MOST SIGNIFICANT DIGIT
        ; OF DIVIDEND ARRAY GOES TO HIGH DIGIT OF NDIGIT
        LHLD    DVADR
        CALL    RLARY              ;ROTATE LOW DIVIDEND

        ;IF COUNT = 0 THEN WE ARE DONE
        LHLD    COUNT              ;DECREMENT COUNT BY 1
        DCX     H
        SHLD    COUNT
        MOV     A,H                ;TEST 16-BIT COUNT FOR 0
        ORA     L
        JZ      OKEXIT             ;EXIT WHEN COUNT = 0

        ;ROTATE LEFT HIGH DIVIDEND, MOST SIGNIFICANT DIGIT
        ; OF HIGH DIVIDEND BECOMES HIGH DIGIT OF NDIGIT
        LHLD    HDEPTR
        CALL    RLARY              ;ROTATE HIGH DIVIDEND

        ;SEE HOW MANY TIMES DIVISOR GOES INTO HIGH DIVIDEND
        ; ON EXIT FROM THIS LOOP, HIGH DIGIT OF NDIGIT IS NEXT
        ; QUOTIENT DIGIT AND HIGH DIVIDEND IS REMAINDER
        SUB     A                  ;CLEAR NUMBER OF TIMES TO START
        STA     NDIGIT

SUBLP:
        LHLD    HDEPTR
        XCHG                       ;DE POINTS TO HIGH DIVIDEND
        LHLD    ODEPTR
        MOV     C,L
        MOV     B,H                ;BC = OTHER HIGH DIVIDEND
        LHLD    DSADR              ;HL = NINES COMPLEMENT OF DIVISOR
        LDA     LENGTH             ;COUNT = LENGTH IN BYTES
        STA     CNT
        STC                        ;SET CARRY FOR 10'S COMPLEMENT

        ;SUBTRACT DIVISOR FROM DIVIDEND BY ADDING 10'S COMPLEMENT
        ; (9'S COMPLEMENT PLUS 1)
        ;FINAL CARRY IS AN INVERTED BORROW
```

```
INNER:
        LDAX    D               ;GET NEXT BYTE OF DIVIDEND
        ADC     M               ;ADD 10'S COMPLEMENT OF DIVISOR
        DAA                     ;CHANGE TO DECIMAL
        STAX    B               ;STORE RESULT IN OTHER DIVIDEND
        INX     H               ;INCREMENT TO NEXT BYTE
        INX     D
        INX     B
        LDA     CNT             ;DECREMENT COUNTER BY 1
        DCR     A
        STA     CNT
        JNZ     INNER           ;CONTINUE THROUGH ALL BYTES
                                ; CARRY IS INVERTED BORROW
        JNC     DVLOOP          ;JUMP WHEN BORROW OCCURS AT WHICH TIME
                                ; NDIGIT IS NUMBER OF TIMES DIVISOR
                                ; GOES INTO ORIGINAL HIGH DIVIDEND AND
                                ; HIGH DIVIDEND CONTAINS REMAINDER.


        ;DIFFERENCE IS NOT NEGATIVE, SO ADD 1 TO
        ; NUMBER OF SUCCESSFUL SUBTRACTIONS IN UPPER
        ; DIGIT OF NDIGIT
        LDA     NDIGIT          ;NDIGIT = NDIGIT + 10 HEX
        ADI     10H
        STA     NDIGIT

        ;EXCHANGE POINTERS, THUS MAKING DIFFERENCE NEW DIVIDEND
        LHLD    HDEPTR
        XCHG
        LHLD    ODEPTR
        SHLD    HDEPTR
        XCHG
        SHLD    ODEPTR
        JMP     SUBLP           ;CONTINUE UNTIL DIFFERENCE NEGATIVE

        ;NO ERRORS, CLEAR CARRY
OKEXIT:
        ORA     A               ;CLEAR CARRY, VALID RESULT
        RET

        ;DIVIDE BY ZERO ERROR, SET CARRY
EREXIT:
        STC                     ;SET CARRY, INVALID RESULT
        RET

        ;***********************************
        ;SUBROUTINE: RLARY
        ;PURPOSE:    ROTATE LEFT AN ARRAY ONE DIGIT (4 BITS)
        ;ENTRY: HL = BASE ADDRESS OF ARRAY
        ;       HIGH DIGIT OF NDIGIT IS DIGIT TO ROTATE THROUGH
        ;EXIT:  ARRAY ROTATED LEFT THROUGH HIGH DIGIT OF NDIGIT
        ;REGISTERS USED: ALL
        ;***********************************
RLARY:
        ;SHIFT NDIGIT INTO LOW DIGIT OF ARRAY AND
        ; SHIFT ARRAY LEFT
```

```
        LDA     LENGTH
        MOV     B,A                 ;B = LENGTH IN BYTES
        LDA     NDIGIT
        MOV     E,A                 ;E = NDIGIT
                                    ;HL = BASE ADDRESS OF ARRAY

SHIFT:
        MOV     A,M                 ;GET NEXT BYTE
        MOV     D,A                 ;SAVE IN D
        ANI     OFH                 ;CLEAR HIGH DIGIT
        ORA     E                   ;COMBINE NDIGIT AND BYTE
        RRC                         ;MOVE LOW DIGIT TO HIGH DIGIT
        RRC
        RRC
        RRC
        MOV     M,A                 ;STORE LOW DIGIT IN ARRAY
        MOV     A,D
        ANI     OFOH                ;CLEAR LOW DIGIT
        MOV     E,A                 ;SAVE AS NEXT NDIGIT IN REGISTER E
        INX     H                   ;INCREMENT TO NEXT BYTE
        DCR     B                   ;DECREMENT COUNT
        JNZ     SHIFT               ;CONTINUE UNTIL ALL BYTES SHIFTED
        MOV     A,E
        STA     NDIGIT              ;STORE NDIGIT
        RET

        ;DATA
LENGTH: DS      1                   ;LENGTH OF ARRAYS IN BYTES
NDIGIT: DS      1                   ;NEXT DIGIT IN ARRAY
CNT:    DS      1                   ;COUNTER FOR SUBTRACT LOOP
DVADR:  DS      2                   ;DIVIDEND ADDRESS
DSADR:  DS      2                   ;DIVISOR ADDRESS
HDEPTR: DS      2                   ;HIGH DIVIDEND POINTER
ODEPTR: DS      2                   ;OTHER DIVIDEND POINTER
COUNT:  DS      2                   ;DIVIDE LOOP COUNTER
HIDE1:  DS      255                 ;HIGH DIVIDEND BUFFER 1
HIDE2:  DS      255                 ;HIGH DIVIDEND BUFFER 2


;
;
;       SAMPLE EXECUTION:
;
;

SC6M:
        LXI     H,AY1               ;BASE ADDRESS OF DIVIDEND
        LXI     D,AY2               ;BASE ADDRESS OF DIVISOR
        MVI     B,SZAYS             ;LENGTH OF ARRAYS IN BYTES
        CALL    MPDDIV              ;MULTIPLE-PRECISION BCD DIVISION
                                    ;RESULT OF 1522756 / 1234 = 1234
                                    ; IN MEMORY AY1      = 34H
                                    ;          AY1+1     = 12H
                                    ;          AY1+2     = OOH
                                    ;          AY1+3     = OOH
                                    ;          AY1+4     = OOH
```

```
;                         AY1+5    = OOH
;                         AY1+6    = OOH

          JMP      SC6M

SZAYS     EQU      7               ;LENGTH OF ARRAYS IN BYTES
AY1:
          DB       O56H
          DB       O27H
          DB       O52H
          DB       O1H
          DB       O
          DB       O
          DB       O

AY2:
          DB       O34H
          DB       O12H
          DB       O
          DB       O
          DB       O
          DB       O
          DB       O

          END
```

Multiple-Precision
Decimal Comparison

Compares two multi-byte unsigned decimal (BCD) numbers and sets the Carry and Zero flags appropriately. The Zero flag is set to 1 if the operands are equal and to 0 if they are not equal. The Carry flag is set to 1 if the subtrahend is larger than the minuend; the Carry flag is cleared otherwise. Thus the flags are set as if the subtrahend had been subtracted from the minuend.

Note: This program is exactly the same as Subroutine 6I, the multiple-precision binary comparison, since the form of the operands does not matter if they are only being compared. See Subroutine 6I for a listing and other details.

Examples

1. Data: Length of operands (in bytes) = 6
               Subtrahend = 196528719340_{16}
               Minuend = 456780153266_{16}

    Result: Zero flag = 0 (operands are not equal)
               Carry flag = 0 (subtrahend is not larger than minuend)

2. Data: Length of operands (in bytes) = 6
               Subtrahend = 196528719340_{16}
               Minuend = 196528719340_{16}

    Result: Zero flag = 1 (operands are equal)
               Carry flag = 0 (subtrahend is not larger than minuend)

3. Data: Length of operands (in bytes) = 6
               Subtrahend = 196528719340_{16}
               Minuend = 073785991074_{16}

    Result: Zero flag = 0 (operands are not equal)
               Carry flag = 1 (subtrahend is larger than minuend)

Bit Set (BITSET)

Sets a specified bit in a byte to 1.

Procedure: The program logically ORs the selected byte with a mask containing a 1 in the chosen bit position and 0s elsewhere. The masks with one 1 bit are in a table.

Registers Used: AF, BC, HL

Execution Time: 61 cycles (8080) or 59 cycles (8085)

Program Size: 20 bytes

Data Memory Required: None

Special Case: Bit positions above 7 are interpreted mod 8 (bit position 9 is equivalent to bit position 1).

Entry Conditions

Bit number to set in A
Data byte in B

Exit Conditions

Result (byte with bit set) in A

Examples

1. Data: $(B) = 6E_{16} = 01101110_2$ (data)
   $(A) = 4$ (bit position to set)

   Result: $(A) = 7E_{16} = 01111110_2$ (data with bit 4 set to 1)

2. Data: $(B) = 39_{16} = 00111001_2$ (data)
   $(A) = 2$ (bit position to set)

   Result: $(A) = 3D_{16} = 00111101_2$ (data with bit 2 set to 1)

```
;                                                                    ;
;                                                                    ;
;                                                                    ;
;                                                                    ;
;       Title:          Bit Set                                      ;
;       Name:           BITSET                                       ;
;                                                                    ;
;                                                                    ;
;                                                                    ;
;       Purpose:        Set a bit in a byte                          ;
;                                                                    ;
;       Entry:          Register A = Bit number to set               ;
;                       Register B = Data byte                       ;
;                                                                    ;
;       Exit:           Register A = Data byte with bit set          ;
;                                                                    ;
```

253

```
;       Registers used: AF,BC,HL                                              ;
;                                                                            ;
;       Time:           59 cycles for 8085, 61 cycles for 8080               ;
;                                                                            ;
;       Size:           Program 20 bytes                                     ;
;                                                                            ;
;


        ;SET BIT BY ORING WITH 1 IN APPROPRIATE POSITION
        ;OBTAIN MASK BY USING BIT NUMBER AS INDEX INTO BITMSK
BITSET:
        ANI     00000111B       ;LIMIT BIT NUMBER TO 0...7
        MOV     C,A
        MOV     A,B
        LXI     H,BITMSK        ;BASE ADDRESS OF BITMSK ARRAY
        MVI     B,0             ;EXTEND BIT NUMBER TO 16 BITS
        DAD     B               ;INDEX INTO BITMSK ARRAY
        ORA     M               ;SET THE BIT
        RET

        ;TABLE OF MASKS WITH 1 BIT SET
BITMSK: DB      00000001B       ;BIT 0 = 1
        DB      00000010B       ;BIT 1 = 1
        DB      00000100B       ;BIT 2 = 1
        DB      00001000B       ;BIT 3 = 1
        DB      00010000B       ;BIT 4 = 1
        DB      00100000B       ;BIT 5 = 1
        DB      01000000B       ;BIT 6 = 1
        DB      10000000B       ;BIT 7 = 1


;                                                                            ;
;                                                                            ;
;       SAMPLE EXECUTION                                                     ;
;                                                                            ;
;                                                                            ;

SC7A:
        MVI     B,0             ;REGISTER B = DATA
        MVI     A,3             ;REGISTER A = BIT NUMBER (0...7)
        CALL    BITSET          ;RESULT = DATA WITH BIT 3 SET

        JMP     SC7A            ;   = 00001000B (08H)

        END
```

Bit Clear (BITCLR)

Clears a specified bit in a byte.

Procedure: The program logically ANDs the data with a mask containing a 0 in the chosen bit position and 1s elsewhere. The masks with one 0 bit are in a table.

> **Registers Used:** AF, BC, HL
>
> **Execution Time:** 61 cycles (8080) or 59 cycles (8085)
>
> **Program Size:** 20 bytes
>
> **Data Memory Required:** None
>
> **Special Case:** Bit positions above 7 are interpreted mod 8 (bit position 12 is equivalent to bit position 4).

Entry Conditions

Bit number to clear in A
Data byte in B

Exit Conditions

Result (data with bit cleared) in A

Examples

1. Data: $(B) = 6E_{16} = 01101110_2$ (data)
   $(A) = 6$ (bit position to clear)

   Result: $(A) = 2E_{16} = 00101110_2$ (data with bit 6 cleared)

2. Data: $(B) = 39_{16} = 00111001_2$ (data)
   $(A) = 4$ (bit position to clear)

   Result: $(A) = 29_{16} = 00101001_2$ (data with bit 4 cleared)

```
;                                                            ;
;                                                            ;
;                                                            ;
;                                                            ;
;       Title:          Bit Clear                            ;
;       Name:           BITCLR                               ;
;                                                            ;
;                                                            ;
;                                                            ;
;       Purpose:        Clear a bit in a byte                ;
;                                                            ;
;       Entry:          Register A = Bit number to clear     ;
;                       Register B = Data byte               ;
;                                                            ;
;       Exit:           Register A = Data byte with bit cleared ;
;                                                            ;
```

```
;         Registers used: AF,BC,HL                                      ;
;                                                                       ;
;         Time:           59 cycles for 8085, 61 for 8080              ;
;                                                                       ;
;         Size:           Program 20 bytes                             ;
;                                                                       ;
;                                                                       ;

BITCLR:
        ANI     00000111B       ;LIMIT BIT NUMBER TO 0...7
        MOV     C,A
        MOV     A,B
        LXI     H,BITMSK        ;BASE ADDRESS OF BITMSK ARRAY
        MVI     B,0             ;EXTEND BIT NUMBER TO 16 BITS
        DAD     B               ;INDEX INTO BITMSK ARRAY
        ANA     M               ;CLEAR BIT
        RET

        ;TABLE OF MASKS WITH 1 BIT CLEARED
BITMSK: DB      11111110B       ;BIT 0 = 0
        DB      11111101B       ;BIT 1 = 0
        DB      11111011B       ;BIT 2 = 0
        DB      11110111B       ;BIT 3 = 0
        DB      11101111B       ;BIT 4 = 0
        DB      11011111B       ;BIT 5 = 0
        DB      10111111B       ;BIT 6 = 0
        DB      01111111B       ;BIT 7 = 0


;                                                                       ;
;                                                                       ;
;         SAMPLE EXECUTION                                              ;
;                                                                       ;
;                                                                       ;

SC7B:
        MVI     B,11111111B     ;REGISTER B = DATA
                                ;REGISTER A = BIT NUMBER (0...7)
        CALL    BITCLR          ;RESULT = DATA WITH BIT 3 CLEARED

        JMP     SC7B            ; = 11110111B = 0F7H

        END
```

Sets the Zero flag to the complement of the value of a specified bit in a byte.

Procedure: The program logically ANDs the data with a mask containing a 1 in the chosen bit position and 0s elsewhere. The result is zero if the tested bit is 0 and non-zero if the tested bit is 1. The Zero flag is therefore set to the complement of the tested bit.

Registers Used: AF, BC, HL

Execution Time: 61 cycles (8080) or 59 cycles (8085)

Program Size: 20 bytes

Data Memory Required: None

Special Case: Bit positions above 7 are interpreted mod 8 (bit position 10 is equivalent to bit position 2).

Entry Conditions

Bit position to test in A
Data byte in B

Exit Conditions

Zero flag is set to complement of specified bit position in data byte. (Zero flag is set if the bit is 0 and cleared if it is 1.)

Examples

1. Data: $(B) = 6E_{16} = 01101110_2$ (data)
   $(A) = 3$ (bit position to test)

   Result: Zero flag = 0 (complement of bit 3 of data)

2. Data: $(B) = 39_{16} = 00111001_2$ (data)
   $(A) = 6$ (bit position to test)

   Result: Zero flag = 1 (complement of bit 6 of data)

```
;                                                              ;
;                                                              ;
;                                                              ;
;                                                              ;
;       Title:          Bit Test                              ;
;       Name:           BITTST                                ;
;                                                              ;
;                                                              ;
;                                                              ;
;       Purpose:        Test a bit in a byte                  ;
;                                                              ;
;       Entry:          Register A = Bit number to test       ;
;                       Register B = Data byte                ;
;                                                              ;
;       Exit:           Z = 1 if the bit is 0                 ;
```

```
;                       Z = 0 if the bit is 1                    ;
;                                                                ;
;           Registers used: AF,BC,HL                             ;
;                                                                ;
;           Time:           59 cycles for 8085,  61 cycles for 8080  ;
;                                                                ;
;           Size:           Program 20 bytes                     ;
;                                                                ;
;                                                                ;

BITTST:
        ANI     00000111B       ;LIMIT BIT NUMBER TO 0...7
        MOV     C,A
        MOV     A,B
        LXI     H,BITMSK        ;BASE ADDRESS OF BITMSK ARRAY
        MVI     B,0             ;EXTEND BIT NUMBER TO 16 BITS
        DAD     B               ;INDEX INTO BITMSK ARRAY
        ANA     M               ;TEST BIT
        RET

        ;TABLE OF MASKS WITH 1 BIT SET
BITMSK: DB      00000001B       ;BIT 0 = 1
        DB      00000010B       ;BIT 1 = 1
        DB      00000100B       ;BIT 2 = 1
        DB      00001000B       ;BIT 3 = 1
        DB      00010000B       ;BIT 4 = 1
        DB      00100000B       ;BIT 5 = 1
        DB      01000000B       ;BIT 6 = 1
        DB      10000000B       ;BIT 7 = 1


;                                                                ;
;                                                                ;
;           SAMPLE EXECUTION                                     ;
;                                                                ;
;                                                                ;

SC7C:
        MVI     B,11110111B     ;REGISTER B = DATA BYTE
        MVI     A,3             ;REGISTER A = BIT NUMBER (0...7)

        CALL    BITTST          ;Z = 1 AS BIT 3 OF DATA = 0

        JMP     SC7C

        END
```

Bit Field Extraction (BFE)

Extracts a field of bits from a byte and returns the field in the least significant bit positions. The width of the field and its lowest bit position are parameters.

Procedure: The program obtains a mask with the specified number of 1 bits from a table, shifts the mask left to align it with the specified lowest bit position, and obtains the field by logically ANDing the mask with the data. It then normalizes the bit field by shifting it right so that it starts in bit 0.

Registers Used: All

Execution Time: 23 * LOWEST BIT POSITION plus 112 cycles overhead (8080) or 22 * LOWEST BIT POSITION plus 100 cycles overhead (8085). (The lowest bit position determines the number of times the mask must be shifted left and the bit field right.)

Program Size: 38 bytes

Data Memory Required: None

Special Cases:

1. Requesting a field that would extend beyond the end of the byte causes the program to return with only the bits through bit 7. That is, no wraparound is provided. If, for example, the user asks for a 6-bit field starting at bit 5, the program will return only 3 bits (bits 5 through 7).

2. Both the lowest bit position and the number of bits in the field are interpreted mod 8. That is, for example, bit position 11 is equivalent to bit position 3 and a field of 10 bits is equivalent to a field of 2 bits. Note, however, that the number of bits in the field is interpreted in the range 1 to 8. That is, a field of 16 bits is equivalent to a field of 8 bits, not to a field of 0 bits.

3. Requesting a field of width 0 causes a return with a result of 0.

Entry Conditions

Starting (lowest) bit position in the field (0 to 7) in A
Number of bits in the field (1 to 8) in D
Data byte in E

Exit Conditions

Bit field in A (normalized to bit 0)

Examples

1. Data: Data value $= F6_{16} = 11110110_2$
   Lowest bit position $= 4$
   Number of bits in the field $= 3$

   Result: Bit field $= 07_{16} = 00000111_2$
   Three bits, starting at bit 4, have been extracted (that is, bits 4 through 6).

2. Data: Data value $= A2_{16} = 10100010_2$
   Lowest bit position $= 6$
   Number of bits in the field $= 5$

   Result: Bit field $= 02_{16} = 00000010_2$
   Two bits, starting at bit 6, have been extracted (that is, bits 6 and 7); that was all that was available, although five bits were requested.

```
;                                                                    ;
;                                                                    ;
;                                                                    ;
;                                                                    ;
;          Title:          Bit Field Extraction                      ;
;          Name:           BFE                                       ;
;                                                                    ;
;                                                                    ;
;                                                                    ;
;          Purpose:        Extract a field of bits from a byte and   ;
;                          return the field normalized to bit 0      ;
;                          NOTE: IF THE REQUESTED FIELD IS TOO LONG,  ;
;                              ONLY THE BITS THROUGH BIT 7 WILL BE    ;
;                              RETURNED. FOR EXAMPLE, IF A 4-BIT FIELD IS;
;                              REQUESTED STARTING AT BIT 7, ONLY 1    ;
;                              BIT (BIT 7) WILL BE RETURNED.          ;
;                                                                    ;
;          Entry:          Register A = Starting (lowest) bit position in ;
;                              the field (0...7)                      ;
;                          Register D = Number of bits in the field (1...8);
;                          Register E = Data byte                    ;
;                                                                    ;
;          Exit:           Register A = Field                        ;
;                                                                    ;
;          Registers used: All                                       ;
;                                                                    ;
;          Time:           112 cycles overhead plus                  ;
;                              (23 * lowest bit position) cycles for 8080 ;
;                          100 cycles overhead plus                  ;
;                              (22 * lowest bit position) cycles for 8085 ;
;                                                                    ;
;          Size:           Program 38 bytes                          ;
;                                                                    ;
;                                                                    ;

BFE:
           ;SHIFT DATA TO NORMALIZE TO BIT 0
           ; NO SHIFTING NEEDED IF LOWEST POSITION IS ALREADY 0
           ANI      00000111B          ;LIMIT LOWEST BIT TO 0...7
           JZ       EXTR               ;JUMP IF LOWEST BIT 0, NO SHIFT
           MOV      C,A                ;NUMBER OF SHIFTS = LOWEST BIT
                                       ; POSITION IN FIELD

           MOV      A,E

SHFT:
           ORA      A                  ;CLEAR CARRY
           RAR                         ;SHIFT DATA RIGHT LOGICALLY
           DCR      C
           JNZ      SHFT               ;CONTINUE UNTIL NORMALIZED
           MOV      E,A                ;SAVE NORMALIZED DATA

           ;EXTRACT FIELD BY MASKING WITH 1S
EXTR:
           MOV      A,D                ;IS WIDTH OF FIELD 0?
           ORA      A
```

```
        RZ                          ;YES, EXIT WITH FIELD = 0
        DCR     A                   ;INDEX = WIDTH - 1
        ANI     00000111B           ;ONLY ALLOW 0 THROUGH 7
        MOV     C,A                 ;BC = INDEX INTO MASK ARRAY
        MVI     B,0
        LXI     H,MSKARY            ;HL = BASE OF MASK ARRAY
        DAD     B
        MOV     A,E                 ;GET DATA
        ANA     M                   ;MASK OFF UNWANTED BITS
        RET

        ;MASK ARRAY WITH 1 TO 8 ONE BITS
MSKARY:
        DB      00000001B
        DB      00000011B
        DB      00000111B
        DB      00001111B
        DB      00011111B
        DB      00111111B
        DB      01111111B
        DB      11111111B


;                                                               ;
;                                                               ;
;       SAMPLE EXECUTION                                        ;
;                                                               ;
;                                                               ;

SC7D:
        MVI     E,00011000B         ;REGISTER E = DATA BYTE
        MVI     D,3                 ;REGISTER D = NUMBER OF BITS
        MVI     A,2                 ;ACCUMULATOR = LOWEST BIT
        CALL    BFE                 ;EXTRACT 3 BITS STARTING WITH #2

        JMP     SC7D                ; RESULT = 00000110B

        END
```

Bit Field Insertion (BFI) 7E

Inserts a field of bits into a byte. The width of the field and its starting (lowest) bit position are parameters.

Procedure: The program obtains a mask with the specified number of 0 bits from a table. It then shifts the mask and the bit field left to align them with the specified lowest bit position. It logically ANDs the mask with the original data byte, thus clearing the required bit positions, and then logically ORs the result with the shifted bit field.

Registers Used: AF, BC, D, HL

Execution Time: 42 * LOWEST BIT POSITION plus 177 cycles overhead (8080) or 40 * LOWEST BIT POSITION plus 161 cycles overhead (8085). (The lowest bit position of the field determines how many times the mask and the field must be shifted left.)

Program Size: 52 bytes

Data Memory Required: None

Special Cases:

1. Attempting to insert a field that would extend beyond the end of the byte causes the program to insert only the bits through bit 7. That is, no wraparound is provided. If, for example, the user attempts to insert a 6-bit field starting at bit 4, only 4 bits (bits 4 through 7) are actually replaced.

2. Both the starting bit position and the width of the bit field (number of bits) are interpreted mod 8. That is, for example, bit position 11 is the same as bit position 3 and a 12-bit field is the same as a 4-bit field. Note, however, that the width of the field is mapped into the range 1 to 8. That is, for example, a 16-bit field is the same as an 8-bit field.

3. Attempting to insert a field of width 0 causes a return with a result of 0.

Entry Conditions

Data in A
Number of bits in the field (1 to 8) in B
Starting (lowest) bit position of field in C
Field to insert in E

Exit Conditions

Result in A
The result is the original data with the bit field inserted, starting at the specified bit position.

Examples

1. Data: Value = $F6_{16}$ = 11110110_2
   Lowest bit position = 4
   Number of bits in the field = 2
   Bit field = 01_{16} = 00000001_2

   Result: Value with bit field inserted = $D6_{16}$ = 11010110_2
   The 2-bit field has been inserted into the original value starting at bit 4 (into bits 4 and 5).

2. Data: Value = $B8_{16}$ = 10111000_2
   Lowest bit position = 1
   Number of bits in the field = 5
   Bit field = 15_{16} = 00010101_2

   Result: Value with bit field inserted = AA_{16} = 10101010_2
   The 5-bit field has been inserted into the original value starting at bit 1 (into bits 1 through 5), changing 11100_2 ($1C_{16}$) to 10101_2 (15_{16}).

```
;                                                                      ;
;                                                                      ;
;                                                                      ;
;                                                                      ;
;         Title:          Bit Field Insertion                         ;
;         Name:           BFI                                         ;
;                                                                      ;
;                                                                      ;
;                                                                      ;
;         Purpose:        Insert a field of bits into a byte and return ;
;                         the byte                                     ;
;                         NOTE: IF THE REQUESTED FIELD IS TOO LONG,    ;
;                               ONLY THE BITS THROUGH BIT 7 WILL BE    ;
;                               INSERTED. FOR EXAMPLE, IF A 4-BIT FIELD IS;
;                               TO BE INSERTED STARTING AT BIT 7,      ;
;                               ONLY 1 BIT (BIT 7) WILL BE INSERTED.   ;
;                                                                      ;
;         Entry:          Register A = Data byte                       ;
;                         Register B = Number of bits in the field (1...8);
;                         Register C = Starting (lowest) bit position in  ;
;                                      which the data will be inserted ;
;                                      (0...7)                         ;
;                         Register E = Field to insert                 ;
;                                                                      ;
;         Exit:           Register A = Data with field inserted        ;
;                                                                      ;
;         Registers used: AF,BC,D,HL                                   ;
;                                                                      ;
;         Time:           177 cycles overhead plus                     ;
;                         (42 * lowest bit position) cycles for 8080   ;
;                         161 cycles overhead plus                     ;
;                         (40 * lowest bit position) cycles for 8085   ;
;                                                                      ;
;         Size:           Program 52 bytes                             ;
;                                                                      ;
;                                                                      ;
;                                                                      ;
BFE:
        PUSH    PSW             ;SAVE DATA

;GET MASK WITH REQUIRED NUMBER OF 0 BITS
        PUSH    B               ;SAVE STARTING BIT POSITION
        LXI     H,MSKARY
        MOV     A,B             ;GET NUMBER OF BITS (FIELD WIDTH)
        ANA     A               ;TEST FIELD WIDTH
        RZ                      ;RETURN WITH 0 FIELD IF FIELD
                                ; WIDTH IS 0
        DCR     A               ;INDEX = FIELD WIDTH - 1
        ANI     00000111B       ;RESTRICT INDEX TO 0-7
        MOV     C,A
        MVI     B,0
        DAD     B               ;INDEX INTO MASK ARRAY
        MOV     D,M             ;D = MASK WITH ZEROS FOR CLEARING
        POP     B               ;RETRIEVE STARTING BIT
        MOV     L,C             ;L = STARTING BIT
```

```
            ;TEST IF STARTING BIT IS 0
            MOV     A,C                 ;NUMBER OF SHIFTS = STARTING
                                        ; BIT POSITION OF FIELD
            ANI     00000111B           ;RESTRICT STARTING BIT TO 0...7
            MOV     A,E                 ;A = FIELD TO INSERT
            JZ      INSRT               ;JUMP IF STARTING BIT 0
                                        ; NO ALIGNMENT IS NECESSARY

            ;ALIGN FIELD TO INSERT
SFIELD:
            ORA     A                   ;CLEAR CARRY
            RAL                         ;SHIFT FIELD LEFT LOGICALLY
            DCR     C
            JNZ     SFIELD              ;CONTINUE UNTIL ALIGNED
            MOV     E,A                 ;E = ALIGNED FIELD

            ;ALIGN MASK
            MOV     A,D                 ;GET MASK
            MOV     C,L                 ;NUMBER OF SHIFTS = STARTING BIT
                                        ; POSITION OF FIELD
SMASK:
            RLC                         ;ROTATE MASK LEFT
            DCR     C
            JNZ     SMASK               ;CONTINUE UNTIL ALIGNED
            MOV     D,A                 ;D = ALIGNED MASK

            ;INSERT FIELD
INSRT:
            POP     PSW                 ;GET DATA BACK
            ANA     D                   ;AND OFF MASK AREA
            ORA     E                   ;OR IN FIELD
            RET

            ;MASK ARRAY - 1 TO 8 ZERO BITS
MSKARY:
            DB      11111110B
            DB      11111100B
            DB      11111000B
            DB      11110000B
            DB      11100000B
            DB      11000000B
            DB      10000000B
            DB      00000000B


;                                                                       ;
;                                                                       ;
;           SAMPLE EXECUTION                                            ;
;                                                                       ;
;                                                                       ;


SC7E:
            MVI     A,0                 ;REGISTER A = DATA
            MVI     B,3                 ;REGISTER B = NUMBER OF BITS
            MVI     C,2                 ;REGISTER C = LOWEST BIT POSITION
```

```
        MVI     E,00000101B     ;REGISTER E = FIELD TO INSERT
        CALL    BFE             ;INSERT 3-BIT FIELD STARTING AT
        JMP     SC7E            ; BIT 2, RESULT = 00010100B

        END
```

Multiple-Precision Arithmetic
Shift Right (MPASR)

Shifts a multi-byte operand right arithmetically by a specified number of bit positions. The length of the operand (in bytes) is 255 or less. The Carry flag is set from the last bit shifted out of the rightmost bit position. The operand is stored with its least significant byte at the lowest address.

Procedure: The program obtains the sign bit from the most significant byte, saves that bit in the Carry, and then rotates the entire operand right one bit, starting with the most significant byte. It repeats the operation for the specified number of shifts.

Registers Used: All

Execution Time: NUMBER OF SHIFTS * (52 + 38 * LENGTH OF OPERANDS IN BYTES) + 65 cycles (8080) or NUMBER OF SHIFTS * (48 + 38 * LENGTH OF OPERANDS IN BYTES) + 62 cycles (8085)

Program Size: 29 bytes

Data Memory Required: None

Special Cases:

1. If the length of the operand is 0, the program exits immediately with the operand unchanged and the Carry flag cleared.

2. If the number of shifts is 0, the program exits immediately with the operand unchanged and the Carry flag cleared.

Entry Conditions

Base address of operand in H and L
Length of the operand in bytes in B
Number of shifts (bit positions) in C

Exit Conditions

Operand shifted right arithmetically by the specified number of bit positions. The original sign bit is extended to the right. The Carry flag is set from the last bit shifted out of the rightmost bit position. Carry is cleared if either the number of shifts or the length of the operand is 0.

Examples

1. Data: Length of operand (in bytes) = 08
   Operand = $85A4C719FE06741E_{16}$
   Number of shifts = 04

   Result: Shifted operand = $F85A4C719FE06741_{16}$
   This is the original operand shifted right four bits arithmetically; the four most significant bits all take the value of the original sign bit (1).
   Carry = 1, since the last bit shifted from the rightmost bit position was 1.

2. Data: Length of operand (in bytes) = 04
   Operand = $3F6A42D3_{16}$
   Number of shifts = 03

   Result: Shifted operand = $07ED485A_{16}$
   This is the original operand shifted right three bits arithmetically; the three most significant bits all take the value of the original sign bit (0).
   Carry = 0, since the last bit shifted from the rightmost bit position was 0.

```
;
;                                                                    ;
;                                                                    ;
;                                                                    ;
;       Title:          Multiple-Precision Arithmetic Shift Right    ;
;       Name:           MPASR                                        ;
;                                                                    ;
;                                                                    ;
;                                                                    ;
;                                                                    ;
;       Purpose:        Arithmetic shift right a multi-byte operand  ;
;                       N bits                                       ;
;                                                                    ;
;       Entry:          Registers H and L = Base address of operand  ;
;                       Register B = Length of operand in bytes      ;
;                       Register C = Number of bits to shift         ;
;                                                                    ;
;                         The operand is stored with ARRAY[0] as its ;
;                         least significant byte and ARRAY[LENGTH-1] ;
;                         its most significant byte, where ARRAY     ;
;                         is its base address                        ;
;                                                                    ;
;       Exit:           Operand shifted right with the most significant ;
;                       bit propagated                               ;
;                       Carry := Last bit shifted from least         ;
;                                 significant position               ;
;                                                                    ;
;       Registers used: All                                         ;
;                                                                    ;
;       Time:           65 cycles overhead plus                      ;
;                       ((38 * length) + 52) cycles per shift for the ;
;                       8080                                         ;
;                       62 cycles overhead plus                      ;
;                       ((38 * length) + 48) cycles per shift for the ;
;                       8085                                         ;
;                                                                    ;
;       Size:           Program 29 bytes                             ;
;                                                                    ;
;                                                                    ;

MPASR:
        ;EXIT IF NUMBER OF SHIFTS OR LENGTH OF OPERAND IS 0
        ;ORA CLEARS CARRY IN EITHER CASE
        MOV     A,B
        ORA     A
        RZ                      ;RETURN IF LENGTH OF OPERAND IS 0
        MOV     A,C
        ORA     A
        RZ                      ;RETURN IF NUMBER OF SHIFTS IS 0

        ;CALCULATE ADDRESS OF MOST SIGNIFICANT (LAST) BYTE
        MOV     E,B             ;E = LENGTH OF OPERAND
        MVI     D,0             ;ADDRESS OF MSB = BASE+LENGTH-1
        DAD     D
        DCX     H               ;HL = ADDRESS OF MSB
                                ;C = NUMBER OF SHIFTS
```

```
              ;LOOP ON NUMBER OF SHIFTS TO PERFORM
              ;INITIAL CARRY = MOST SIGNIFICANT BIT OF ENTIRE OPERAND
LOOP:
              MOV     A,M             ;GET MOST SIGNIFICANT BYTE
              RAL                     ;CARRY = MOST SIGNIFICANT BIT
              MOV     B,E
              PUSH    H               ;SAVE ADDRESS OF MSB

              ;ROTATE BYTES RIGHT STARTING WITH MOST SIGNIFICANT
ASRLP:
              MOV     A,M
              RAR                     ;ROTATE NEXT BYTE RIGHT
              MOV     M,A
              DCX     H               ;DECREMENT TO LESS SIGNIFICANT BYTE
              DCR     B
              JNZ     ASRLP
              POP     H               ;RESTORE ADDRESS OF MSB
              DCR     C               ;DECREMENT NUMBER OF SHIFTS
              JNZ     LOOP
              RET


;                                                                      ;
;                                                                      ;
;             SAMPLE EXECUTION                                         ;
;                                                                      ;
;                                                                      ;

SC7F:
              LXI     H,AY            ;BASE ADDRESS OF OPERAND
              MVI     B,SZAY          ;LENGTH OF OPERAND IN BYTES
              MVI     C,SHIFTS        ;NUMBER OF SHIFTS
              CALL    MPASR           ;ARITHMETIC SHIFT RIGHT
                      ;RESULT OF SHIFTING  EDCBA987654321H, 4 BITS IS
                      ;                     FEDCBA98765432H, C=0
                      ;  IN MEMORY AY    = 032H
                      ;           AY+1 = 054H
                      ;           AY+2 = 076H
                      ;           AY+3 = 098H
                      ;           AY+4 = 0BAH
                      ;           AY+5 = 0DCH
                      ;           AY+6 = 0FEH

              JMP     SC7F

              ;DATA SECTION
SZAY:    EQU      7               ;LENGTH OF OPERAND IN BYTES
SHIFTS:  EQU      4               ;NUMBER OF SHIFTS
AY:      DB       21H,43H,65H,87H,0A9H,0CBH,0EDH

              END
```

Multiple-Precision Logical
Shift Left (MPLSL)

Shifts a multi-byte operand left logically by a specified number of bit positions. The length of the operand (in bytes) is 255 or less. The Carry flag is set from the last bit shifted out of the left-most bit position. The operand is stored with its least significant byte at the lowest address.

Procedure: The program clears the Carry initially (to fill with a 0 bit) and then shifts the entire operand left one bit, starting with the least significant byte. It repeats the operation for the specified number of shifts.

Registers Used: AF, BC, E

Execution Time: NUMBER OF SHIFTS * (45 + 38 * LENGTH OF OPERAND IN BYTES) + 43 cycles (8080) or NUMBER OF SHIFTS * (41 + 38 * LENGTH OF OPERAND IN BYTES) + 39 cycles (8085)

Program Size: 24 bytes

Data Memory Required: None

Special Cases:

1. If the length of the operand is 0, the program exits immediately with the operand unchanged and the Carry flag cleared.

2. If the number of shifts is 0, the program exits immediately with the operand unchanged and the Carry flag cleared.

Entry Conditions

Base address of operand in H and L
Length of operand in bytes in B
Number of shifts (bit positions) in C

Exit Conditions

Operand shifted left logically by the specified number of bit positions. (The least significant bit positions are filled with 0s.) The Carry flag is set from the last bit shifted out of the leftmost bit position. Carry is cleared if either the number of shifts or the length of the operand is 0.

Examples

1. Data: Length of operand (in bytes) = 08
   Operand = $85A4C719FE06741E_{16}$
   Number of shifts = 04

   Result: Shifted operand = $5A4C719FE06741E0_{16}$
   This is the original operand shifted left four bits logically; the four least significant bits are all cleared.
   Carry = 0, since the last bit shifted from the leftmost bit position was 0.

2. Data: Length of operand (in bytes) = 04
   Operand = $3F6A42D3_{16}$
   Number of shifts = 03

   Result: Shifted operand = $FB521698_{16}$
   This is the original operand shifted left three bits logically; the three least significant bits are all cleared.
   Carry = 1, since the last bit shifted from the leftmost bit position was 1.

```
;                                                                      ;
;                                                                      ;
;                                                                      ;
;                                                                      ;
;          Title:           Multiple-Precision Logical Shift Left      ;
;          Name:            MPLSL                                      ;
;                                                                      ;
;                                                                      ;
;                                                                      ;
;                                                                      ;
;          Purpose:         Logical shift left a multi-byte operand    ;
;                           N bits                                     ;
;                                                                      ;
;          Entry:           Registers H and L = Base address of operand;
;                           Register B = Length of operand in bytes    ;
;                           Register C = Number of bits to shift        ;
;                                                                      ;
;                              The operand is stored with ARRAY[0] as its;
;                              least significant byte and ARRAY[LENGTH-1];
;                              its most significant byte, where ARRAY   ;
;                              is its base address.                     ;
;                                                                      ;
;          Exit:            Operand shifted left filling the least     ;
;                           significant bits with zeros                ;
;                           Carry := Last most significant position    ;
;                                                                      ;
;     Registers used: AF,BC,E                                          ;
;                                                                      ;
;          Time:            43 cycles overhead plus                    ;
;                           ((38 * length) + 45) cycles per shift for the;
;                           8080                                       ;
;                           39 cycles overhead plus                    ;
;                           ((38 * length) + 41) cycles per shift for the;
;                           8085                                       ;
;                                                                      ;
;          Size:            Program 24 bytes                           ;
;                                                                      ;
;                                                                      ;

MPLSL:
        ;EXIT IF NUMBER OF SHIFTS OR LENGTH OF OPERAND IS 0
        ;ORA CLEARS CARRY IN EITHER CASE
        MOV     A,B
        ORA     A
        RZ                      ;RETURN IF LENGTH OF OPERAND IS 0
        MOV     A,C
        ORA     A
        RZ                      ;RETURN IF NUMBER OF SHIFTS IS 0

        ;LOOP ON NUMBER OF SHIFTS TO PERFORM
        MOV     E,B             ;E = LENGTH OF OPERAND
                                ;C = NUMBER OF SHIFTS
                                ;HL = ADDRESS OF FIRST BYTE IN OPERAND

        ;CARRY = 0 INITIALLY FOR LOGICAL SHIFT
LOOP:
```

```
        PUSH    H               ;SAVE ADDRESS OF LSB
        MOV     B,E             ;B = LENGTH OF OPERAND
        ORA     A               ;CLEAR CARRY FOR LOGICAL SHIFT

        ;ROTATE BYTES STARTING WITH LEAST SIGNIFICANT
LSLLP:
        MOV     A,M
        RAL                     ;ROTATE NEXT BYTE LEFT
        MOV     M,A
        INX     H               ;MOVE TO MORE SIGNIFICANT BYTE
        DCR     B
        JNZ     LSLLP
        POP     H               ;RESTORE ADDRESS OF LSB
        DCR     C               ;DECREMENT NUMBER OF SHIFTS
        JNZ     LOOP
        RET


;                                                                  ;
;                                                                  ;
;       SAMPLE EXECUTION                                           ;
;                                                                  ;
;                                                                  ;

SC7G:
        LXI     H,AY            ;BASE ADDRESS OF OPERAND
        MVI     B,SZAY          ;LENGTH OF OPERAND IN BYTES
        MVI     C,SHIFTS        ;NUMBER OF SHIFTS
        CALL    MPLSL           ;LOGICAL SHIFT LEFT
                        ;RESULT OF SHIFTING  EDCBA987654321H, 4 BITS IS
                        ;                       DCBA9876543210H, C=0
                        ;   IN MEMORY AY    = 010H
                        ;            AY+1   = 032H
                        ;            AY+2   = 054H
                        ;            AY+3   = 076H
                        ;            AY+4   = 098H
                        ;            AY+5   = 0BAH
                        ;            AY+6   = 0DCH


        JMP     SC7G

        ;DATA SECTION
SZAY:   EQU     7               ;LENGTH OF OPERAND IN BYTES
SHIFTS: EQU     4               ;NUMBER OF SHIFTS
AY:     DB      21H,43H,65H,87H,0A9H,0CBH,0EDH

        END
```

Multiple-Precision Logical
Shift Right (MPLSR)

Shifts a multi-byte operand right logically by a specified number of bit positions. The length of the operand (in bytes) is 255 or less. The Carry flag is set from the last bit shifted out of the rightmost bit position. The operand is stored with its least significant byte at the lowest address.

Procedure: The program clears the Carry initially (to fill with a 0 bit) and then shifts the entire operand right one bit, starting with the most significant byte. It repeats the operation for the specified number of shifts.

Registers Used: All

Execution Time: NUMBER OF SHIFTS * (45 + 38 * LENGTH OF OPERAND IN BYTES) + 65 cycles (8080) or NUMBER OF SHIFTS * (41 + 38 * LENGTH OF OPERAND IN BYTES) + 62 cycles (8085)

Program Size: 28 bytes

Data Memory Required: None

Special Cases:

1. If the length of the operand is 0, the program exits immediately with the operand unchanged and the Carry flag cleared.

2. If the number of shifts is 0, the program exits immediately with the operand unchanged and the Carry flag cleared.

Entry Conditions

Base address of operand in H and L
Length of operand in bytes in B
Number of shifts (bit positions) in C

Exit Conditions

Operand shifted right logically by the specified number of bit positions. (The most significant bit positions are filled with 0s.)

The Carry flag is set from the last bit shifted out of the rightmost bit position. Carry is cleared if either the number of shifts or the length of the operand is 0.

Examples

1. Data: Length of operand (in bytes) = 08
   Operand = $85A4C719FE06741E_{16}$
   Number of shifts = 04

   Result: Shifted operand = $085A4C719FE06741_{16}$
   This is the original operand shifted right four bits logically; the four most significant bits are all cleared.
   Carry = 1, since the last bit shifted from the rightmost bit position was 1.

2. Data: Length of operand (in bytes) = 04
   Operand = $3F6A42D3_{16}$
   Number of shifts = 03

   Result: Shifted operand = $07ED485A_{16}$
   This is the original operand shifted right three bits logically; the three most significant bits are all cleared.
   Carry = 0, since the last bit shifted from the rightmost bit position was 0.

```
;                                                                    ;
;                                                                    ;
;                                                                    ;
;                                                                    ;
;         Title:          Multiple-Precision Logical Shift Right     ;
;         Name:           MPLSR                                      ;
;                                                                    ;
;                                                                    ;
;                                                                    ;
;         Purpose:        Logical shift right a multi-byte operand N bits ;
;                                                                    ;
;         Entry:          Registers H and L = Base address of operand ;
;                         Register B = Length of operand in bytes    ;
;                         Register C = Number of bits to shift       ;
;                                                                    ;
;                         The operand is stored with ARRAY[0] as its ;
;                         least significant byte and ARRAY[LENGTH-1] ;
;                         its most significant byte, where ARRAY     ;
;                         is its base address                        ;
;                                                                    ;
;         Exit:           Operand shifted right filling the most     ;
;                         significant bits with zeros                ;
;                         Carry := Last bit shifted from least       ;
;                                  significant position              ;
;                                                                    ;
;         Registers used: All                                        ;
;                                                                    ;
;         Time:           65 cycles overhead plus                    ;
;                         ((38 * length) + 45) cycles per shift for the ;
;                         8080                                       ;
;                         62 cycles overhead plus                    ;
;                         ((38 * length) + 41) cycles per shift for the ;
;                         8085                                       ;
;                                                                    ;
;         Size:           Program 28 bytes                           ;
;                                                                    ;
;                                                                    ;

MPLSR:
        ;EXIT IF NUMBER OF SHIFTS OR LENGTH OF OPERAND IS 0
        ;ORA CLEARS CARRY IN EITHER CASE
        MOV     A,B
        ORA     A
        RZ                      ;RETURN IF LENGTH OF OPERAND IS 0
        MOV     A,C
        ORA     A
        RZ                      ;RETURN IF NUMBER OF SHIFTS IS 0

        ;CALCULATE ADDRESS OF MOST SIGNIFICANT (LAST) BYTE
        MOV     E,B             ;E = LENGTH OF OPERAND
        MVI     D,0             ;ADDRESS OF MSB = BASE+LENGTH-1
        DAD     D
        DCX     H               ;HL = ADDRESS OF MSB
                                ;C = NUMBER OF SHIFTS
```

```
              ;LOOP ON NUMBER OF SHIFTS TO PERFORM
              ;START WITH CARRY = 0 FOR LOGICAL SHIFT
LOOP:
              ORA      A                  ;CLEAR CARRY FOR LOGICAL SHIFT
              MOV      B,E                ;B = LENGTH OF OPERAND
              PUSH     H                  ;SAVE ADDRESS OF MSB

              ;ROTATE BYTES STARTING WITH MOST SIGNIFICANT
LSRLP:
              MOV      A,M
              RAR                         ;ROTATE NEXT BYTE RIGHT
              MOV      M,A
              DCX      H                  ;MOVE TO LESS SIGNIFICANT BYTE
              DCR      B
              JNZ      LSRLP
              POP      H                  ;RESTORE ADDRESS OF MSB
              DCR      C                  ;DECREMENT NUMBER OF SHIFTS
              JNZ      LOOP
              RET


   ;                                                                    ;
   ;                                                                    ;
   ;          SAMPLE EXECUTION                                          ;
   ;                                                                    ;
   ;                                                                    ;

SC7H:
              LXI      H,AY               ;HL = BASE ADDRESS OF OPERAND
              MVI      B,SZAY             ;B = LENGTH OF OPERAND IN BYTES
              MVI      C,SHIFTS           ;C = NUMBER OF SHIFTS
              CALL     MPLSR              ;LOGICAL SHIFT RIGHT
                            ;RESULT OF SHIFTING  EDCBA987654321H, 4 BITS IS
                            ;                         0EDCBA98765432H, C=0
                            ;  IN MEMORY AY    = 032H
                            ;            AY+1 = 054H
                            ;            AY+2 = 076H
                            ;            AY+3 = 098H
                            ;            AY+4 = 0BAH
                            ;            AY+5 = 0DCH
                            ;            AY+6 = 00EH

              JMP      SC7H

              ;DATA SECTION
SZAY     EQU      7           ;LENGTH OF OPERAND IN BYTES
SHIFTS   EQU      4           ;NUMBER OF SHIFTS
AY:      DB       21H,43H,65H,87H,0A9H,0CBH,0EDH

              END
```

Multiple-Precision Rotate
Right (MPRR)

Rotates a multi-byte operand right by a specified number of bit positions as if the most significant bit and the least significant bit were connected. The length of the operand (in bytes) is 255 or less. The Carry flag is set from the last bit shifted out of the rightmost bit position. The operand is stored with its least significant byte at the lowest address.

Procedure: The program shifts bit 0 of the least significant byte of the operand to the Carry flag and then rotates the entire operand right one bit, starting with the most significant byte. It repeats the operation for the specified number of rotates.

Registers Used: All

Execution Time: NUMBER OF ROTATES * (65 + 38 * LENGTH OF OPERAND IN BYTES) + 99 cycles (8080) or NUMBER OF ROTATES * (61 + 38 * LENGTH OF OPERAND IN BYTES) + 97 cycles (8085)

Program Size: 38 bytes

Data Memory Required: 1 byte anywhere in RAM for the length of the operand (address LEN)

Special Cases:

1. If the length of the operand is 0, the program exits immediately with the operand unchanged and the Carry flag cleared.

2. If the number of rotates is 0, the program exits immediately with the operand unchanged and the Carry flag cleared.

Entry Conditions

Base address of operand in H and L
Length of operand in bytes in B
Number of rotates (bit positions) in C

Exit Conditions

Operand rotated right logically by the specified number of bit positions. (The most significant bit positions are filled from the least significant bit positions.) The Carry flag is set from the last bit shifted out of the rightmost bit position. The Carry is cleared if either the number of rotates or the length of the operand is 0.

Examples

1. Data: Length of operand (in bytes) = 08
         Operand = $85A4C719FE06741E_{16}$
         Number of rotates = 04

   Result: Rotated operand = $E85A4C719FE06741_{16}$
          This is the original operand rotated right four bits; the four most significant bits are equivalent to the original four least significant bits.
          Carry = 1, since the last bit shifted from the rightmost bit position was 1.

2. Data: Length of operand (in bytes) = 04
         Operand = $3F6A42D3_{16}$
         Number of rotates = 03

   Result: Rotated operand = $67ED485A_{16}$
          This is the original operand rotated right three bits; the three most significant bits are equivalent to the original three least significant bits.
          Carry = 0, since the last bit shifted from the rightmost bit position was 0.

```
;                                                                    ;
;                                                                    ;
;                                                                    ;
;                                                                    ;
;            Title:          Multiple-Precision Rotate Right         ;
;            Name:           MPRR                                    ;
;                                                                    ;
;                                                                    ;
;                                                                    ;
;                                                                    ;
;            Purpose:        Rotate right a multi-byte operand N bits ;
;                                                                    ;
;            Entry:          Registers H and L = Base address of operand ;
;                            Register B = Length of operand in bytes ;
;                            Register C = Number of bits to rotate   ;
;                                                                    ;
;                                The operand is stored with ARRAY[0] as its ;
;                                least significant byte and ARRAY[LENGTH-1] ;
;                                its most significant byte, where ARRAY ;
;                                is its base address.                ;
;                                                                    ;
;            Exit:           Operand rotated right                   ;
;                            Carry := Last bit shifted from least    ;
;                                    significant position            ;
;                                                                    ;
;            Registers used: All                                     ;
;                                                                    ;
;            Time:           99 cycles overhead plus                 ;
;                            ((38 * length) + 65) cycles per rotate for the ;
;                            8080                                    ;
;                            97 cycles overhead plus                 ;
;                            ((38 * length) + 61) cycles per rotate for the ;
;                            8085                                    ;
;                                                                    ;
;            Size:           Program 38 bytes                        ;
;                            Data    1 byte                          ;
;                                                                    ;
;                                                                    ;

MPRR:
        ;EXIT IF NUMBER OF ROTATES OR LENGTH OF OPERAND IS 0
        ;ORA CLEARS CARRY IN EITHER CASE
        MOV     A,B
        ORA     A
        RZ                      ;RETURN IF LENGTH OF OPERAND IS 0
        STA     LEN             ;SAVE LENGTH
        MOV     A,C
        ORA     A
        RZ                      ;RETURN IF NUMBER OF ROTATES IS 0

        ;CALCULATE ADDRESS OF MOST SIGNIFICANT (LAST) BYTE
        PUSH    H               ;SAVE ADDRESS OF FIRST BYTE
        MOV     E,B             ;E = LENGTH OF OPERAND
        MVI     D,0             ;ADDRESS OF MSB = BASE+LENGTH-1
        DAD     D
        DCX     H               ;HL = ADDRESS OF MSB
```

```
        POP      D                    ;DE = ADDRESS OF LSB
                                      ;C = NUMBER OF ROTATES

        ;LOOP ON NUMBER OF ROTATES TO PERFORM
        ;CARRY = LEAST SIGNIFICANT BIT OF ENTIRE OPERAND
LOOP:
        LDAX     D                    ;GET LOW BYTE (LSB)
        RAR                           ;CARRY = BIT 0 OF LOW BYTE
        LDA      LEN
        MOV      B,A                  ;B = LENGTH OF OPERAND
        PUSH     H                    ;SAVE ADDRESS OF MSB

        ;ROTATE BYTES RIGHT STARTING WITH MOST SIGNIFICANT
RRLP:
        MOV      A,M
        RAR                           ;ROTATE NEXT BYTE RIGHT
        MOV      M,A
        DCX      H                    ;PROCEED TO LESS SIGNIFICANT BYTE
        DCR      B
        JNZ      RRLP
        POP      H                    ;RESTORE ADDRESS OF MSB
        DCR      C                    ;DECREMENT NUMBER OF ROTATES
        JNZ      LOOP
        RET

LEN:    DS       1                    ;LENGTH OF OPERAND IN BYTES


;
;
;       SAMPLE EXECUTION
;
;

SC7I:
        LXI      H,AY                 ;BASE ADDRESS OF OPERAND
        MVI      B,SZAY               ;LENGTH OF OPERAND IN BYTES
        MVI      C,ROTATES            ;NUMBER OF ROTATES
        CALL     MPRR     ;ROTATE RIGHT
                         ;RESULT OF ROTATING  EDCBA987654321H 4 BITS IS
                         ;                    1EDCBA98765432H, C=0
                         ;  IN MEMORY AY   = 032H
                         ;             AY+1 = 054H
                         ;             AY+2 = 076H
                         ;             AY+3 = 098H
                         ;             AY+4 = 0BAH
                         ;             AY+5 = 0DCH
                         ;             AY+6 = 01EH

        JMP      SC7I

        ;DATA SECTION
SZAY    EQU      7            ;LENGTH OF OPERAND IN BYTES
SHIFTS  EQU      4            ;NUMBER OF SHIFTS
AY:     DB       21H,43H,65H,87H,0A9H,0CBH,0EDH

        END
```

Multiple-Precision Rotate
Left (MPRL)

Rotates a multi-byte operand left by a specified number of bit positions as if the most significant bit and least significant bit were connected. The length of the operand (in bytes) is 255 or less. The Carry flag is set from the last bit shifted out of the leftmost bit position. The operand is stored with its least significant byte at the lowest address.

Procedure: The program shifts bit 7 of the most significant byte of the operand to the Carry flag. It then rotates the entire operand left one bit, starting with the least significant byte. It repeats the operation for the specified number of rotates.

Registers Used: All

Execution Time: NUMBER OF ROTATES * (65 + 38 * LENGTH OF OPERAND IN BYTES) + 103 cycles (8080) or NUMBER OF ROTATES * (61 + 38 * LENGTH OF OPERAND IN BYTES) + 100 cycles (8085)

Program Size: 39 bytes

Data Memory Required: 1 byte anywhere in RAM for the length of the operand (address LEN)

Special Cases:

1. If the length of the operand is 0, the program exits immediately with the operand unchanged and the Carry flag cleared.

2. If the number of rotates is 0, the program exits immediately with the operand unchanged and the Carry flag cleared.

Entry Conditions

Base address of operand in H and L
Length of operand in bytes in B
Number of rotates (bit positions) in C

Exit Conditions

Operand rotated left by the specified number of bit positions. (The least significant bit positions are filled from the most significant bit positions.) The Carry flag is set from the last bit shifted out of the leftmost bit position. The Carry is cleared if either the number of rotates or the length of the operand is 0.

Examples

1. Data: Length of operand (in bytes) = 08
   Operand = $85A4C719FE06741E_{16}$
   Number of rotates = 04

   Result: Rotated operand = $5A4C719FE06741E8_{16}$
   This is the original operand rotated left four bits; the four least significant bits are equivalent to the original four most significant bits.
   Carry = 0, since the last bit shifted from the leftmost bit position was 0.

2. Data: Length of operand (in bytes) = 04
   Operand = $3F6A42D3_{16}$
   Number of rotates = 03

   Result: Rotated operand = $FB521699_{16}$
   This is the original operand rotated left three bits; the three least significant bits are equivalent to the original three most significant bits.
   Carry = 1, since the last bit shifted from the leftmost bit position was 1.

```
;
;
;
;
;         Title:          Multiple-Precision Rotate Left
;         Name:           MPRL
;
;
;
;
;         Purpose:        Rotate left a multi-byte operand N bits
;
;         Entry:          Registers H and L = Base address of operand
;                         Register B = Length of operand in bytes
;                         Register C = Number of bits to rotate
;
;                            The operand is stored with ARRAY[0] as its
;                            least significant byte and ARRAY[LENGTH-1]
;                            its most significant byte, where ARRAY
;                            is its base address.
;
;         Exit:           Operand rotated left
;                         Carry := Last bit shifted from most
;                                    significant position
;
;         Registers used: All
;
;         Time:           103 cycles overhead plus
;                         ((38 * length) + 65) cycles per rotate for the
;                         8080
;                         100 cycles overhead plus
;                         ((38 * length) + 61) cycles per rotate for the
;                         8085
;
;         Size:           Program 39 bytes
;                         Data    1 byte
;
;
MPRL:
        ;EXIT IF NUMBER OF ROTATES OR LENGTH OF OPERAND IS 0
        ;ORA CLEARS CARRY IN EITHER CASE
        MOV     A,B
        ORA     A
        RZ                      ;RETURN IF LENGTH OF OPERAND IS 0
        STA     LEN             ;SAVE LENGTH
        MOV     A,C
        ORA     A
        RZ                      ;RETURN IF NUMBER OF ROTATES IS 0

        ;CALCULATE ADDRESS OF MOST SIGNIFICANT (LAST) BYTE
        PUSH    H               ;SAVE ADDRESS OF FIRST BYTE
        MOV     E,B             ;E = LENGTH OF OPERAND
        MVI     D,0             ;ADDRESS OF MSB = BASE+LENGTH-1
        DAD     D
        XCHG
```

```
          DCX       D                   ;DE = ADDRESS OF LAST BYTE
          POP       H                   ;HL = ADDRESS OF FIRST BYTE
                                        ;C  = NUMBER OF ROTATES

          ;LOOP ON NUMBER OF ROTATES TO PERFORM
          ;CARRY = MOST SIGNIFICANT BIT OF ENTIRE OPERAND
LOOP:
          LDAX      D                   ;GET HIGH BYTE
          RAL                           ;CARRY = BIT 7 OF HIGH BYTE
          LDA       LEN
          MOV       B,A                 ;B = LENGTH OF OPERAND IN BYTES
          PUSH      H                   ;SAVE ADDRESS OF LSB

          ;ROTATE BYTES LEFT STARTING WITH LEAST SIGNIFICANT
RLLP:
          MOV       A,M
          RAL                           ;ROTATE NEXT BYTE LEFT
          MOV       M,A
          INX       H                   ;PROCEED TO MORE SIGNIFICANT BYTE
          DCR       B
          JNZ       RLLP
          POP       H                   ;RESTORE ADDRESS OF LSB
          DCR       C                   ;DECREMENT NUMBER OF ROTATES
          JNZ       LOOP
          RET

LEN:      DS        1                   ;LENGTH OF OPERAND IN BYTES

;                                                                      ;
;                                                                      ;
;         SAMPLE EXECUTION                                             ;
;                                                                      ;
;                                                                      ;

SC7J:
          LXI       H,AY                ;HL = BASE ADDRESS OF OPERAND
          MVI       B,SZAY              ;B = LENGTH OF OPERAND IN BYTES
          MVI       C,ROTATES           ;C = NUMBER OF ROTATES
          CALL      MPRL      ;ROTATE LEFT
                              ;RESULT OF ROTATING  EDCBA987654321H, 4 BITS IS
                              ;                       DCBA987654321EH, C=0
                              ;  IN MEMORY AY   = 01EH
                              ;            AY+1 = 032H
                              ;            AY+2 = 054H
                              ;            AY+3 = 076H
                              ;            AY+4 = 098H
                              ;            AY+5 = 0BAH
                              ;            AY+6 = 0DCH

          JMP       SC7J      ;ROTATE LEFT

          ;DATA SECTION
SZAY      EQU       7         ;LENGTH OF OPERAND IN BYTES
ROTATES   EQU       4         ;NUMBER OF ROTATES
AY:       DB        21H,43H,65H,87H,0A9H,0CBH,0EDH

          END
```

Compares two strings and sets the Carry and Zero flags appropriately. The Zero flag is set to 1 if the strings are identical and to 0 otherwise. The Carry flag is set to 1 if the string with the base address in D and E (string 2) is larger than the string with the base address in H and L (string 1). Otherwise, the Carry flag is set to 0. The strings are a maximum of 255 bytes long and the actual characters are preceded by a byte containing the length. If the two strings are identical through the length of the shorter, the longer string is considered to be larger.

Procedure: The program first determines which string is shorter from the lengths that precede the actual characters. It then compares the strings one byte at a time through the length of the shorter. The program exits with the flags set if it finds corresponding bytes that differ. If the strings are the same through the length of the shorter, the program sets the flags by comparing the lengths.

Registers Used: AF, B, DE, HL

Execution Time:

1. If the strings are not identical through the length of the shorter, the time is $80 + 50 *$ NUMBER OF CHARACTERS COMPARED (8080) or $76 + 52 *$ NUMBER OF CHARACTERS COMPARED (8085). If, for example, the routine compares five characters before finding a disparity, the execution time is

$80 + 50 * 5 = 80 + 250 = 330$ cycles (8080)
$76 + 52 * 5 = 76 + 260 = 336$ cycles (8085)

2. If the strings are identical through the length of the shorter, the time is $120 + 50 *$ LENGTH OF SHORTER STRING (8080) or $113 + 52 *$ LENGTH OF SHORTER STRING (8085). If, for example, the shorter string is eight bytes long, the execution time is

$120 + 50 * 8 = 120 + 400 = 520$ cycles (8080)
$113 + 52 * 8 = 113 + 416 = 529$ cycles (8085)

Program Size: 36 bytes

Data Memory Required: 2 bytes anywhere in RAM for the lengths of the strings (addresses LENS1 and LENS2)

Entry Conditions

Base address of string 2 in D and E
Base address of string 1 in H and L

Exit Conditions

Flags are set as if string 2 had been subtracted from string 1. If the strings are the same through the length of the shorter, the flags are set as if the length of string 2 had been subtracted from the length of string 1.

Zero flag = 1 if strings are identical; 0 if they are not.

Carry flag = 1 if string 2 is larger than string 1; 0 if they are identical or string 1 is larger. If the strings are the same through the length of the shorter, the longer one is considered to be larger.

Examples

1. Data: String 1 = 05'PRINT' (05 is the length of the string).
String 2 = 03'END' (03 is the length of the string).

   Result: Zero flag = 0 (strings are not identical).
Carry flag = 0 (string 2 is not larger than string 1).

2. Data: String 1 = 05'PRINT' (05 is the length of the string).
String 2 = 02'PR' (02 is the length of the string).

   Result: Zero flag = 0 (strings are not identical).
Carry flag = 0 (string 2 is not larger than string 1).

The longer string (string 1) is considered to be larger. To determine whether string 2 is an abbreviation of string 1, use Subroutine 8C (Find the Position of a Substring) and determine whether string 2 was part of string 1 and started at the first character.

3. Data: String 1 = 05'PRINT' (05 is the length of the string).
String 2 = 06'SYSTEM' (06 is the length of the string).

   Result: Zero flag = 0 (strings are not identical).
Carry flag = 1 (string 2 is larger than string 1).

It is assumed here that the strings consist of ASCII characters. Note that the byte preceding the actual characters contains a hexadecimal number (the length of the string), not a character. This byte has been represented as two hexadecimal digits in front of the string; the string itself is surrounded by single quotation marks.

This routine treats spaces like other characters. If, for example, the strings are ASCII, the routine will find that SPRINGMAID is larger than SPRING MAID, since an ASCII M ($4D_{16}$) is larger than an ASCII space (20_{16}).

```
;                                                                      ;
;                                                                      ;
;                                                                      ;
;                                                                      ;
;                                                                      ;
;                                                                      ;
;                                                                      ;
;                                                                      ;
;                                                                      ;
;         Title:        String Compare                                 ;
;         Name:         STRCMP                                         ;
;                                                                      ;
;                                                                      ;
;                                                                      ;
;                                                                      ;
;         Purpose:      Compare 2 strings and return C and Z flags set ;
;                       or cleared                                     ;
;         Entry:        Register pair H = Base address of string 1     ;
;                       Register pair D = Base address of string 2     ;
;                                                                      ;
;                       A string is a maximum of 255 bytes long plus   ;
;                       a length byte which precedes it.               ;
;                                                                      ;
;         Exit:         IF string 1 = string 2 THEN                    ;
;                          Z=1,C=0                                     ;
;                       IF string 1 > string 2 THEN                    ;
;                          Z=0,C=0                                     ;
```

```
;                    IF string 1 < string 2 THEN                     ;
;                       Z=0, C=1                                     ;
;                                                                    ;
;        Registers used: AF, B, DE, HL                              ;
;                                                                    ;
;        Time:            80 cycles overhead plus 50 cycles per byte plus ;
;                         40 cycles if the strings are equal for the 8080 ;
;                         76 cycles overhead plus 52 cycles per byte for the 8085 ;
;                         37 cycles if the strings are equal for the 8085 ;
;                                                                    ;
;        Size:            Program 36 bytes                           ;
;                         Data     2 bytes                           ;
;                                                                    ;
;                                                                    ;

STRCMP:
        ;DETERMINE WHICH STRING IS SHORTER
        ;LENGTH OF SHORTER = NUMBER OF BYTES TO COMPARE
        LDAX    D               ;GET LENGTH OF STRING 2
        STA     LENS2
        CMP     M               ;COMPARE TO LENGTH OF STRING 1
        JC      BEGCMP          ;JUMP IF STRING 2 IS SHORTER
        MOV     A,M             ;ELSE STRING 1 IS SHORTER


        ;COMPARE STRINGS THROUGH LENGTH OF SHORTER
        ;EXIT AS SOON AS CORRESPONDING CHARACTERS DIFFER
BEGCMP:
        ORA     A               ;TEST LENGTH OF SHORTER STRING
        JZ      CMPLEN          ;COMPARE LENGTHS IF SHORTER STRING
                                ;IS EMPTY
        MOV     B,A             ;B = NUMBER OF BYTES TO COMPARE
        XCHG                    ;DE = STRING 1
                                ;HL = STRING 2
        LDAX    D
        STA     LENS1           ;SAVE LENGTH OF STRING 1
CMPLP:
        INX     D               ;PROCEED TO NEXT BYTE OF STRINGS
        INX     H
        LDAX    D               ;GET A BYTE OF STRING 1
        CMP     M               ;COMPARE TO BYTE OF STRING 2
        RNZ                     ;RETURN WITH FLAGS SET IF BYTES
                                ; NOT EQUAL
        DCR     B
        JNZ     CMPLP

        ;STRINGS SAME THROUGH LENGTH OF SHORTER
        ;SO USE LENGTHS TO SET FLAGS
CMPLEN: LDA     LENS1           ;COMPARE LENGTHS
        LXI     H,LENS2
        CMP     M
        RET                     ;RETURN WITH FLAGS SET OR CLEARED

        ;DATA
LENS1   DS      1               ;LENGTH OF STRING 1
LENS2   DS      1               ;LENGTH OF STRING 2
```

```
;                                                                    ;
;                                                                    ;
;          SAMPLE EXECUTION                                          ;
;                                                                    ;
;                                                                    ;

SC8A:
          LXI     H,S1          ;BASE ADDRESS OF STRING 1
          LXI     D,S2          ;BASE ADDRESS OF STRING 2
          CALL    STRCMP        ;COMPARE STRINGS
                                ;COMPARING "STRING 1" AND "STRING 2"
                                ; RESULTS IN STRING 1 LESS THAN
                                ; STRING 2, SO Z=0,C=1

          JMP     SC8A          ;LOOP FOR ANOTHER TEST

S1        DB      20H,'STRING 1                              '
S2        DB      20H,'STRING 2                              '

          END
```

String Concatenation (CONCAT) 8B

Combines (concatenates) two strings, placing the second immediately after the first in memory. If the concatenation would produce a string longer than a specified maximum, the program concatenates only enough of string 2 to give the combined string its maximum length. The Carry flag is cleared if all of string 2 can be concatenated and is set to 1 if part of string 2 must be dropped. Both strings are a maximum of 255 bytes long and the actual characters are preceded by a byte containing the length.

Procedure: The program uses the length of string 1 to determine where to start adding characters and the length of string 2 to determine how many characters to add. If the sum of the lengths exceeds the maximum, the program indicates an overflow and reduces the number of characters it must add (the number is the maximum length minus the length of string 1). It then moves the appropriate number of characters from string 2 to the end of string 1, updates the length of string 1, and sets the Carry flag to indicate whether any characters were discarded.

Registers Used: All

Execution Time: Approximately 39 * NUMBER OF CHARACTERS CONCATENATED plus 279 cycles overhead (8080) or 40 * NUMBER OF CHARACTERS CONCATENATED plus 265 cycles overhead (8085). NUMBER OF CHARACTERS CONCATENATED is normally the length of string 2, but will be the maximum length of string 1 minus its current length if the combined string would be too long. If, for example, NUMBER OF CHARACTERS CONCATENATED is 14_{16} (20_{10}), the execution time is
$39 * 20 + 279 = 780 + 279 = 1059$ cycles (8080)
$40 * 20 + 265 = 800 + 265 = 1065$ cycles (8085)

Program Size: 83 bytes

Data Memory Required: 5 bytes anywhere in RAM for the base address of string 1 (2 bytes starting at address S1ADR), the lengths of the strings (ad-

dresses S1LEN and S2LEN), and a flag that indicates whether the combined strings overflowed (address STRGOV).

Special Cases:

1. If concatenating would make the string longer than its specified maximum length, the program concatenates only enough of string 2 to reach the maximum. If any of string 2 must be truncated, the Carry flag is set to 1.

2. If string 2 has a length of 0, the program exits with the Carry flag cleared (no errors) and string 1 unchanged. That is, a length of 0 for either string is interpreted as 0, not as 256.

3. If the original length of string 1 exceeds the specified maximum, the program exits with the Carry flag set to 1 (indicating an error) and string 1 unchanged.

Entry Conditions

Base address of string 2 in D and E
Base address of string 1 in H and L
Maximum length of string 1 in B

Exit Conditions

String 2 concatenated at the end of string 1 and the length of string 1 increased appropriately. If the resulting string would exceed the maximum length, only the part of string 2 that would give string 1 its maximum length is concatenated. If any part of string 2 must be dropped, the Carry flag is set to 1. Otherwise, the Carry flag is cleared.

Examples

1. Data: Maximum length of string 1 = $0E_{16} = 14_{10}$
String 1 = 07'JOHNSON' (07 is the length of the string).
String 2 = 05', DON' (05 is the length of the string).

   Result: String 1 = 0C'JOHNSON, DON' ($0C_{16} = 12_{10}$ is the length of the combined string with string 2 placed after string 1).
Carry = 0, since the concatenation did not produce a string exceeding the maximum length.

2. Data: String 1 = 07'JOHNSON' (07 is the length of the string).
String 2 = 09', RICHARD' (09 is the length of the string).

   Result: String 1 = 0E'JOHNSON, RICHA' ($0E_{16} = 14_{10}$ is the maximum length allowed, so the last two characters of string 2 have been dropped).
Carry = 1, since the concatenation produced a string longer than the maximum length.

Note that the initial byte (containing the length of the string) is represented as two hexadecimal digits in both examples.

```
;                                                                              ;
;                                                                              ;
;                                                                              ;
;                                                                              ;
;        Title:           String Concatenation                                ;
;        Name:            CONCAT                                              ;
;                                                                              ;
;                                                                              ;
;                                                                              ;
;        Purpose:         Concatenate 2 strings into one string              ;
;                                                                              ;
;        Entry:           Register pair H = Base address of string 1         ;
;                         Register pair D = Base address of string 2         ;
;                         Register B = Maximum length of string 1            ;
;                                                                              ;
;                         A string is a maximum of 255 bytes long plus       ;
;                         a length byte which precedes it.                   ;
;                                                                              ;
;        Exit:            String 1 := String 1 concatenated with string 2    ;
;                         If no errors then                                   ;
;                            Carry := 0                                       ;
;                         else                                                ;
;                            begin                                            ;
;                               Carry := 1                                    ;
;                               if the concatenation makes string 1 too      ;
;                               long concatenate only the part of string 2   ;
;                               which will result in string 1 having its     ;
;                               maximum length.                              ;
;                               if length(string1) > maximum length then     ;
;                                  no concatenation is done                  ;
;                            end;                                             ;
```

```
;                                                               ;
;            Registers used: All                                ;
;                                                               ;
;            Time:           Approximately 39 * (length of string 2) cycles  ;
;                            plus 279 cycles overhead for the 8080           ;
;                            Approximately 40 * (length of string 2) cycles  ;
;                            plus 265 cycles overhead for the 8085           ;
;                                                               ;
;            Size:           Program 89 bytes                   ;
;                            Data    5 bytes                    ;
;                                                               ;
;                                                               ;

CONCAT:
            ;DETERMINE WHERE TO START CONCATENATING
            ;CONCATENATION STARTS AT END OF STRING 1
            ;END OF STRING 1 = BASE 1 + LENGTH1 + 1, WHERE
            ; THE EXTRA 1 MAKES UP FOR THE LENGTH BYTE
            ;NEW CHARACTERS COME FROM STRING 2, STARTING AT
            ; BASE2+1 (SKIPPING OVER LENGTH BYTE)
            SHLD    S1ADR               ;SAVE ADDRESS OF STRING 1
            PUSH    B                   ;SAVE MAXIMUM LENGTH OF STRING 1
            MOV     A,M                 ;SAVE LENGTH OF STRING 1
            STA     S1LEN
            MOV     C,A                 ;END1 = BASE1 + LENGTH1
            MVI     B,0
            DAD     B                   ;HL = LAST CHARACTER IN STRING 1
            LDAX    D                   ;SAVE LENGTH OF STRING 2
            STA     S2LEN
            POP     B                   ;RESTORE MAXIMUM LENGTH

            ;DETERMINE HOW MANY CHARACTERS TO CONCATENATE
            ;THIS IS LENGTH OF STRING 2 IF COMBINED STRING WOULD
            ; NOT EXCEED MAXIMUM LENGTH
            ;OTHERWISE, IT IS THE NUMBER THAT WOULD BRING COMBINED
            ; STRING TO ITS MAXIMUM LENGTH - THAT IS, MAXIMUM LENGTH
            ; MINUS LENGTH OF STRING 1
            MOV     C,A                 ;C = LENGTH OF STRING 2
            LDA     S1LEN
            ADD     C                   ;ADD LENGTHS OF STRINGS
            JC      TOOLNG              ;JUMP IF SUM EXCEEDS 255
            CMP     B                   ;COMPARE TO MAXIMUM LENGTH
            JZ      LENOK               ;JUMP IF NEW STRING IS MAX LENGTH
            JC      LENOK               ; OR LESS

            ;COMBINED STRING IS TOO LONG
            ; INDICATE STRING OVERFLOW, STRGOV := 0FFH
            ; SET NUMBER OF CHARACTERS TO CONCATENATE =  MAXLEN - S1LEN
            ; SET LENGTH OF STRING 1 TO MAXIMUM LENGTH
TOOLNG:
            MVI     A,0FFH              ;INDICATE STRING OVERFLOW
            STA     STRGOV
            LDA     S1LEN               ;CALCULATE MAXLEN - S1LEN
            MOV     C,A
            MOV     A,B
            SUB     C
```

```
        RC                          ;EXIT IF ORIGINAL STRING TOO LONG
        STA     S2LEN               ;CHANGE S2LEN TO MAXLEN - S1LEN
        MOV     A,B                 ;LENGTH OF STRING 1 = MAX LENGTH
        STA     S1LEN
        JMP     DOCAT               ;PERFORM CONCATENATION

        ;COMBINED STRING IS NOT TOO LONG
        ; LENGTH OF STRING 1 = S1LEN + S2LEN
        ; INDICATE NO OVERFLOW, STRGOV := 0
        ; NUMBER OF CHARACTERS TO CONCATENATE = LENGTH OF STRING 2
LENOK:
        STA     S1LEN               ;SAVE SUM OF LENGTHS
        SUB     A
        STA     STRGOV              ;INDICATE NO OVERFLOW

        ;CONCATENATE STRINGS
DOCAT:
        LDA     S2LEN               ;GET NUMBER OF CHARACTERS
        ORA     A
        JZ      EXIT                ;EXIT IF NOTHING TO CONCATENATE
        MOV     B,A                 ;B = NUMBER OF CHARACTERS
                                    ;HL = DESTINATION
                                    ;DE = SOURCE
CATLP:
        INX     H                   ;INCREMENT TO NEXT CHARACTERS
        INX     D
        LDAX    D                   ;GET A CHARACTER FROM STRING 2
        MOV     M,A                 ;MOVE IT TO END OF STRING 1
        DCR     B
        JNZ     CATLP               ;CONTINUE THROUGH ALL CHARACTERS

EXIT:
        LDA     S1LEN               ;GET NEW LENGTH OF STRING 1
        LHLD    S1ADR               ;GET ADDRESS OF LENGTH OF STRING 1
        MOV     M,A                 ;SET LENGTH
        LDA     STRGOV
        RAR                         ;CARRY = 1 IF OVERFLOW, 0 IF NOT
        RET

        ;DATA
S1ADR:  DS      2                   ;BASE ADDRESS OF STRING 1
S1LEN:  DS      1                   ;LENGTH OF STRING 1
S2LEN:  DS      1                   ;LENGTH OF STRING 2
STRGOV: DS      1                   ;STRING OVERFLOW FLAG


;
;
;       SAMPLE EXECUTION
;
;

SC8B:
        LXI     H,S1                ;HL = BASE ADDRESS OF S1
        LXI     D,S2                ;DE = BASE ADDRESS OF S2
```

```
        MVI     B,20H           ;B = MAXIMUM LENGTH OF STRING 1
        CALL    CONCAT          ;CONCATENATE STRINGS

        JMP     SC8B            ;RESULT OF CONCATENATING
                                ; "LASTNAME" AND ", FIRSTNAME"
                                ; IS S1 = 13H,"LASTNAME, FIRSTNAME"


        ;TEST DATA, CHANGE FOR OTHER VALUES
S1:     DB      8H              ;LENGTH OF S1
        DB      'LASTNAME                      ' ;32-BYTE MAX LENGTH
S2:     DB      0BH             ;LENGTH OF S2
        DB      ', FIRSTNAME                   ' ;32-BYTE MAX LENGTH

        END
```

Searches for the first occurrence of a substring within a string. Returns the index at which the substring starts if it is found and 0 if it is not found. The string and the substring are both a maximum of 255 bytes long and the actual characters are preceded by a byte containing the length. Thus, if the substring is found, its starting index cannot be less than 1 or more than 255.

Procedure: The program searches the string for the substring until it finds the substring or until the remaining part of the string is shorter than the substring and hence cannot possibly contain it. If the substring is not in the string, the program clears the accumulator; otherwise, the program places the starting index of the substring in the accumulator.

Registers Used: All

Execution Time: Data-dependent, but the overhead is 165 cycles (8080) or 154 cycles (8085), each successful match of 1 character takes 59 cycles (8080) or 54 cycles (8085), and each unsuccessful match of 1 character takes 133 cycles (8080 or 8085). The worst case is when the string and substring always match except for the last character in the substring, such as

   String = 'AAAAAAAAAB'
   Substring = 'AAB'

The execution time in that case is

   (STRING LENGTH − SUBSTRING LENGTH + 1) * (59 * (SUBSTRING LENGTH − 1) + 133) + 165 (8080)
   (STRING LENGTH − SUBSTRING LENGTH + 1) * (54 * (SUBSTRING LENGTH − 1) + 133) + 154 (8085)

If, for example, STRING LENGTH = 9 and SUBSTRING LENGTH = 3 (as in the case shown), the execution time is

   (9 − 3 + 1) * (59 * (3 − 1) + 133) + 165 = 7 * 251 + 165 = 1757 + 165 = 1922 cycles (8080)
   (9 − 3 + 1) * (54 * (3 − 1) + 133) + 154 = 7 * 241 + 154 = 1687 + 154 = 1841 cycles (8085)

Program Size: 81 bytes

Data Memory Required: 7 bytes anywhere in RAM for the base address of the string (2 bytes starting at address STRING), the base address of the substring (2 bytes starting at address SUBSTG), the length of the string (address SLEN), the length of the substring (address SUBLEN), and the current starting index in the string (address INDEX)

Special Cases:

1. If either the string or the substring has a length of 0, the program exits with 0 in the accumulator, indicating that it did not find the substring.

2. If the substring is longer than the string, the program exits with 0 in the accumulator, indicating that it did not find the substring.

3. If the program returns an index of 1, the substring may be regarded as an abbreviation of the string. That is, the substring occurs in the string, starting at the first character. A typical example would be a string PRINT and a substring PR.

4. If the substring occurs more than once in the string, the program will return only the index to the first occurrence (the occurrence with the lowest starting index).

Entry Conditions

Base address of substring in D and E
Base address of string in H and L

Exit Conditions

A contains the index at which the first occurrence of the substring starts if it is found and contains 0 if it is not found.

Examples

1. Data: String = 1D'ENTER SPEED IN MILES PER HOUR' ($1D_{16} = 29_{10}$ is the length of the string).
   Substring = 05'MILES' (05 is the length of the substring).

   Result: A contains 10_{16} (16_{10}), the index at which the substring 'MILES' starts.

2. Data: String = 1B'SALES FIGURES FOR JUNE 1981' ($1B_{16} = 27_{10}$ is the length of the string).
   Substring = 04'JUNE' (04 is the length of the substring).

   Result: A contains 13_{16} (19_{10}), the index at which the substring 'JUNE' starts.

3. Data: String = 10'LET Y1 = X1 + R7' ($10_{16} = 16_{10}$ is the length of the string).
   Substring = 02'R4' (02 is the length of the substring).

   Result: A contains 0, since the substring 'R4' does not appear in the string LET Y1 = X1 + R7.

4. Data: String = 07'RESTORE' (07 is the length of the string).
   Substring = 03'RES' (03 is the length of the substring).

   Result: A contains 1, the index at which the substring 'RES' starts. An index of 1 indicates that the substring could be an abbreviation of the string. Interactive programs, such as BASIC interpreters and word processors, often use such abbreviations to save on typing and storage.

```
;                                              ;
;                                              ;
;                                              ;
;                                              ;
;   Title:      Find the Position of a Substring   ;
;   Name:       POS                            ;
;                                              ;
;                                              ;
;                                              ;
;                                              ;
;   Purpose:    Search for the first occurrence of a substring   ;
;               within a string and return its starting index.   ;
;               If the substring is not found a 0 is returned.   ;
;                                              ;
;   Entry:      Register pair H = Base address of string   ;
;               Register pair D = Base address of substring   ;
;                                              ;
;               A string is a maximum of 255 bytes long plus   ;
;               a length byte which precedes it.   ;
;                                              ;
;   Exit:       If the substring is found then   ;
;                 Register A = Its starting index   ;
;               else                           ;
;                 Register A = 0               ;
;                                              ;
;   Registers used: All                        ;
;                                              ;
;                                              ;
```

```
;       Time:                   Since the algorithm is so data-dependent,        ;
;                               a simple formula is impossible; but the          ;
;                               following statements are true, and a             ;
;                               worst case is given below.                       ;
;                                                                                ;
;                               165 cycles overhead                             ;
;                               Each match of 1 character takes 59 cycles.       ;
;                               A mismatch takes 133 cycles for the 8080.        ;
;                                                                                ;
;                               154 cycles overhead                             ;
;                               Each match of 1 character takes 54 cycles.       ;
;                               A mismatch takes 133 cycles for the 8085.        ;
;                                                                                ;
;                               Worst case timing will be when the              ;
;                               string and substring always match               ;
;                               except for the last character of the            ;
;                               substring, such as                              ;
;                                   string = 'AAAAAAAAAB'                        ;
;                                   substring = 'AAB'                            ;
;                                                                                ;
;       Size:                   Program 81 bytes                                ;
;                               Data    7 bytes                                 ;
;                                                                                ;
;                                                                                ;

POS:
        ;SET UP TEMPORARIES
        ;EXIT IF STRING OR SUBSTRING HAS ZERO LENGTH
        SHLD    STRING          ;SAVE STRING ADDRESS
        XCHG
        MOV     A,M             ;TEST LENGTH OF SUBSTRING
        ORA     A
        JZ      NOTFND          ;EXIT IF LENGTH OF SUBSTRING = 0
        INX     H               ;MOVE PAST LENGTH BYTE OF SUBSTRING
        SHLD    SUBSTG          ;SAVE SUBSTRING ADDRESS
        STA     SUBLEN
        MOV     C,A             ;C = SUBSTRING LENGTH
        LDAX    D
        ORA     A               ;TEST LENGTH OF STRING
        JZ      NOTFND          ;EXIT IF LENGTH OF STRING = 0

        ;NUMBER OF SEARCHES = STRING LENGTH - SUBSTRING LENGTH
        ; + 1.   AFTER THAT, NO USE SEARCHING SINCE THERE AREN'T
        ; ENOUGH CHARACTERS LEFT TO HOLD SUBSTRING
        ;
        ;IF SUBSTRING IS LONGER THAN STRING, EXIT IMMEDIATELY
        ; AND INDICATE SUBSTRING NOT FOUND
        SUB     C               ;A = STRING LENGTH - SUBSTRING LENGTH
        JC      NOTFND          ;EXIT IF STRING SHORTER THAN SUBSTRING
        INR     A               ;COUNT = DIFFERENCE IN LENGTHS + 1
        MOV     C,A             ;REGISTER C = COUNT
        SUB     A               ;INITIAL STARTING INDEX = 0
        STA     INDEX

        ;SEARCH UNTIL REMAINING STRING SHORTER THAN SUBSTRING
```

```
SLP1:
        LXI     H,INDEX         ;INCREMENT STARTING INDEX
        INR     M
        LDA     SUBLEN          ;B = LENGTH OF SUBSTRING
        MOV     B,A
        LHLD    SUBSTG
        XCHG                    ;DE = STARTING ADDRESS OF SUBSTRING
        LHLD    STRING
        INX     H               ;INCREMENT TO NEXT BYTE OF STRING
        SHLD    STRING          ;HL = NEXT ADDRESS IN STRING
                                ;C = CURRENT VALUE OF COUNT


        ;TRY TO MATCH SUBSTRING STARTING AT INDEX
        ;MATCH INVOLVES COMPARING CORRESPONDING CHARACTERS
        ; ONE AT A TIME
CMPLP:
        LDAX    D               ;GET A CHARACTER OF SUBSTRING
        CMP     M               ;COMPARE TO CHARACTER OF STRING
        JNZ     SLP2            ;JUMP IF NOT SAME
        DCR     B
        JZ      FOUND           ;JUMP IF SUBSTRING FOUND
        INX     H               ;PROCEED TO NEXT CHARACTERS
        INX     D
        JMP     CMPLP


        ;ARRIVE HERE IF MATCH FAILS, SUBSTRING NOT YET FOUND
SLP2:
        DCR     C
        JNZ     SLP1            ;TRY NEXT HIGHER INDEX IF
                                ; ENOUGH STRING LEFT
        JZ      NOTFND          ;ELSE EXIT NOT FOUND
        ;FOUND SUBSTRING, RETURN ITS STARTING INDEX
FOUND:
        LDA     INDEX           ;SUBSTRING FOUND, A = STARTING INDEX
        RET

        ;COULD NOT FIND SUBSTRING, RETURN 0 AS INDEX
NOTFND:
        SUB     A               ;SUBSTRING NOT FOUND, A = 0
        RET

        ;DATA
STRING: DS      2               ;BASE ADDRESS OF STRING
SUBSTG: DS      2               ;BASE ADDRESS OF SUBSTRING
SLEN:   DS      1               ;LENGTH OF STRING
SUBLEN: DS      1               ;LENGTH OF SUBSTRING
INDEX:  DS      1               ;CURRENT INDEX INTO STRING


;                                                          ;
;                                                          ;
;            SAMPLE EXECUTION                              ;
;                                                          ;
;                                                          ;
```

```
SC8C:
        LXI     H,STG           ;HL = BASE ADDRESS OF STRING
        LXI     D,SSTG          ;DE = BASE ADDRESS OF SUBSTRING
        CALL    POS             ;FIND POSITION OF SUBSTRING
                                ; SEARCHING "AAAAAAAAB" FOR "AAB"
                                ; RESULTS IN REGISTER A=8

        JMP     SC8C            ;LOOP FOR ANOTHER TEST

        ;TEST DATA, CHANGE FOR OTHER VALUES
STG:    DB      0AH             ;LENGTH OF STRING
        DB      'AAAAAAAAB                    ' ;32-BYTE MAX LENGTH
SSTG:   DB      3H              ;LENGTH OF SUBSTRING
        DB      'AAB                          ' ;32-BYTE MAX LENGTH

        END
```

Copy a Substring from a String (COPY) 8D

Copies a substring from a string, given a starting index and the number of bytes to copy. The strings are a maximum of 255 bytes long and the actual characters are preceded by a byte containing the length. If the starting index of the substring is 0 (that is, the substring would start in the length byte) or is beyond the end of the string, the substring is given a length of 0 and the Carry flag is set to 1. If the substring would exceed its maximum length or would extend beyond the end of the string, then only the maximum number or the available number of characters (up to the end of the string) are placed in the substring, and the Carry flag is set to 1. If the substring can be formed as specified, the Carry flag is cleared.

Procedure: The program exits immediately if the number of bytes to copy, the maximum length of the substring, or the starting index is 0. It also exits immediately if the starting index exceeds the length of the string. If none of these conditions holds, the program checks if the number of bytes to copy exceeds either the maximum length of the substring or the number of characters available in the string. If either is exceeded, the program reduces the number of bytes to copy appropriately. It then copies the proper number of bytes from the string to the substring. The program clears the Carry flag if the substring can be formed as specified and sets the Carry flag if it cannot.

Registers Used: All

Execution Time: Approximately 45 * NUMBER OF BYTES COPIED plus 251 cycles overhead (8080) or 46 * NUMBER OF BYTES COPIED plus 233 cycles overhead (8085). NUMBER OF BYTES COPIED is the number specified if no problems occur, or the number available or the maximum length of the substring if copying would extend beyond either the string or the substring. If, for example, NUMBER OF BYTES COPIED = 12_{10} ($0C_{16}$), the execution time is

$45 * 12 + 251 = 540 + 251 = 791$ cycles (8080)
$46 * 12 + 233 = 552 + 233 = 785$ cycles (8085)

Program Size: 85 bytes

Data Memory Required: 2 bytes anywhere in RAM for the maximum length of the substring (address MAXLEN) and an error flag (address CPYERR)

Special Cases:

1. If the number of bytes to copy is 0, the program assigns the substring a length of 0 and clears the Carry flag, indicating no errors.

2. If the maximum length of the substring is 0, the program assigns the substring a length of 0 and sets the Carry flag to 1, indicating an error.

3. If the starting index of the substring is 0, the program assigns the substring a length of 0 and sets the Carry flag to 1, indicating an error.

4. If the source string does not even reach the specified starting index, the program assigns the substring a length of 0 and sets the Carry flag to 1, indicating an error.

5. If the substring would extend beyond the end of the source string, the program places all the available characters in the substring and sets the Carry flag to 1, indicating an error. The available characters are the ones from the starting index to the end of the string.

6. If the substring would exceed its specified maximum length, the program places only the specified maximum number of characters in the substring. It sets the Carry flag to 1, indicating an error.

Entry Conditions

Base address of substring in D and E
Base address of string in H and L
Number of bytes to copy in B
Starting index to copy from in C
Maximum length of substring in A

Exit Conditions

Substring contains characters copied from string. If the starting index is 0, the maximum length of the substring is 0, or the starting index is beyond the length of the string, the substring will have a length of 0 and the Carry flag will be set to 1. If the substring would extend beyond the end of the string or would exceed its specified maximum length, only the available characters from the string (up to the maximum length of the substring) are copied into the substring; the Carry flag is set in this case also. If no problems occur in forming the substring, the Carry flag is cleared.

Examples

1. Data: String = 10'LET Y1 = R7 + X4'
($10_{16} = 16_{10}$ is the length of the string).
Maximum length of substring = 2
Number of bytes to copy = 2
Starting index = 5

   Result: Substring = 02'Y1' (2 is the length of the substring).
Two bytes from the string were copied, starting at character #5 (that is, characters 5 and 6).
Carry = 0, since no problems occur in forming the substring.

2. Data: String = 0E'8657 POWELL ST'
($0E_{16} = 14_{10}$ is the length of the string).
Maximum length of substring = $10_{16} = 16_{10}$
Number of bytes to copy = $0D_{16} = 13_{10}$
Starting index = 6

   Result: Substring = 09'POWELL ST' (09 is the length of the substring).
Carry = 1, since there were not enough characters available in the string to provide the specified number of bytes to copy.

3. Data: String = 16'9414 HEGENBERGER DRIVE'
($16_{16} = 22_{10}$ is the length of the string).
Maximum length of substring = $10_{16} = 16_{10}$
Number of bytes to copy = $11_{16} = 17_{10}$
Starting index = 6

   Result: Substring = 10'HEGENBERGER DRIV'
($10_{16} = 16_{10}$ is the length of the substring).
Carry = 1, since the number of bytes to copy exceeded the maximum length of the substring.

```
;                                                                    ;
;                                                                    ;
;                                                                    ;
;                                                                    ;
;          Title:        Copy a Substring from a String              ;
;          Name:         COPY                                        ;
;                                                                    ;
;                                                                    ;
```

```
;
;
;       Purpose:        Copy a substring from a string given a starting   ;
;                       index and the number of bytes                     ;
;                                                                         ;
;       Entry:          Register pair H = Address of source string        ;
;                       Register pair D = Address of destination string   ;
;                       Register A = Maximum length of destination        ;
;                                      string                             ;
;                       Register B = Number of bytes to copy              ;
;                       Register C = Starting index into source string    ;
;                                      Index of 1 is first character of    ;
;                                      the string.                        ;
;                                                                         ;
;                       A string is a maximum of 255 bytes long plus      ;
;                       a length byte which precedes it.                  ;
;                                                                         ;
;       Exit:           Destination string := The substring from the      ;
;                       string                                            ;
;                       If no errors then                                 ;
;                         Carry := 0                                      ;
;                       else                                              ;
;                         begin                                           ;
;                           the following conditions cause an             ;
;                           error and the Carry flag = 1:                 ;
;                           if (index = 0) or (maxlen = 0) or             ;
;                               (index > length(source)) then             ;
;                             the destination string will have a zero     ;
;                             length.                                     ;
;                           if (index + count - 1) > length(source)       ;
;                           then                                          ;
;                             the destination string becomes everything   ;
;                             from index to the end of source string.     ;
;                         end;                                            ;
;                                                                         ;
;       Registers used: All                                              ;
;                                                                         ;
;                                                                         ;
;       Time:           Approximately (45 * count) cycles plus 251        ;
;                       cycles overhead for the 8080.                     ;
;                       Approximately (46 * count) cycles plus 233        ;
;                       cycles overhead for the 8085.                     ;
;                                                                         ;
;       Size:           Program 85 bytes                                  ;
;                       Data    2 bytes                                   ;
;                                                                         ;
;
COPY:
        ;SAVE MAXIMUM LENGTH OF DESTINATION STRING
        STA     MAXLEN                  ;SAVE MAXIMUM LENGTH

        ;INITIALIZE LENGTH OF DESTINATION STRING AND ERROR FLAG
        SUB     A
        STAX    D                       ;LENGTH OF DESTINATION STRING IS ZERO
```

```
        STA       CPYERR              ;ASSUME NO ERRORS

        ;IF NUMBER OF BYTES TO COPY IS 0, EXIT WITH NO ERRORS
        ORA       B                   ;TEST NUMBER OF BYTES TO COPY
        RZ                            ;EXIT WITH NO ERRORS
                                      ; CARRY = 0

        ;IF MAXIMUM LENGTH IS 0, TAKE ERROR EXIT
        LDA       MAXLEN              ;TEST MAXIMUM LENGTH OF SUBSTRING
        ORA       A
        JZ        EREXIT              ;ERROR EXIT IF MAX LENGTH IS 0

        ;IF STARTING INDEX IS ZERO, TAKE ERROR EXIT
        MOV       A,C                 ;TEST STARTING INDEX
        ORA       A
        JZ        EREXIT              ;ERROR EXIT IF INDEX IS 0

        ;IF STARTING INDEX IS GREATER THAN LENGTH OF SOURCE
        ; STRING, TAKE ERROR EXIT
        MOV       A,M                 ;GET LENGTH OF SOURCE STRING
        CMP       C                   ;COMPARE TO STARTING INDEX
        RC                            ;ERROR EXIT IF LENGTH LESS THAN INDEX
                                      ; CARRY = 1

        ;CHECK IF COPY AREA FITS IN SOURCE STRING
        ;OTHERWISE, COPY ONLY TO END OF STRING
        ;COPY AREA FITS IF STARTING INDEX + NUMBER OF
        ; CHARACTERS TO COPY - 1 IS LESS THAN OR EQUAL TO
        ; LENGTH OF SOURCE STRING
        ;NOTE THAT STRINGS ARE NEVER MORE THAN 255 BYTES LONG
        MOV       A,C                 ;FORM STARTING INDEX + COPY LENGTH
        ADD       B
        JC        RECALC              ;JUMP IF SUM > 255
        DCR       A
        CMP       M                   ;COMPARE SUM TO STRING LENGTH
        JC        CNT1OK              ;JUMP IF MORE THAN ENOUGH TO COPY
        JZ        CNT1OK              ;JUMP IF EXACTLY ENOUGH

        ;CALLER ASKED FOR TOO MANY CHARACTERS. RETURN EVERYTHING
        ; BETWEEN INDEX AND END OF SOURCE STRING.
        ; COUNT := LENGTH(SOURCE) - INDEX + 1;
RECALC:
        MVI       A,0FFH              ;INDICATE TRUNCATION OF COUNT
        STA       CPYERR
        MOV       A,M                 ;COUNT = LENGTH - INDEX + 1
        SUB       C
        INR       A
        MOV       B,A                 ;CHANGE NUMBER OF BYTES TO COPY

        ;CHECK IF COUNT IS LESS THAN OR EQUAL TO MAXIMUM LENGTH OF
        ; DESTINATION STRING. IF NOT, SET COUNT TO MAXIMUM LENGTH
        ;IF COUNT > MAXLEN THEN
        ; COUNT := MAXLEN
CNT1OK:
        LDA       MAXLEN              ;IS MAX LENGTH LARGE ENOUGH?
        CMP       B
```

```
        JNC     CNT2OK          ;JUMP IF IT IS
        MOV     B,A             ;ELSE LIMIT COPY TO MAXLEN
        MVI     A,OFFH          ;INDICATE STRING OVERFLOW
        STA     CPYERR

        ;MOVE SUBSTRING TO DESTINATION STRING
CNT2OK:
        MOV     A,B             ;TEST NUMBER OF BYTES TO COPY
        ORA     A
        JZ      EREXIT          ;ERROR EXIT IF NO BYTES TO COPY
        MVI     B,O             ;START COPYING AT STARTING INDEX
        DAD     B
        STAX    D               ;SET LENGTH OF DESTINATION STRING
        MOV     B,A             ;RESTORE NUMBER OF BYTES

COPYLP:
        MOV     A,M             ;GET A CHARACTER FROM STRING
        INX     H               ;INCREMENT TO NEXT BYTE IN SOURCE
        INX     D               ;INCREMENT TO NEXT BYTE IN DESTINATION
        STAX    D               ;STORE CHARACTER IN SUBSTRING
        DCR     B
        JNZ     COPYLP          ;CONTINUE UNTIL DONE

        ;CHECK FOR COPY ERROR
        LDA     CPYERR          ;TEST FOR ERRORS
OKEXIT:
        ORA     A
        RZ                      ;RETURN WITH C = O IF NO ERRORS

        ;ERROR EXIT
EREXIT:
        STC                     ;SET CARRY TO INDICATE AN ERROR
        RET

        ;DATA SECTION
MAXLEN: DS      1               ;MAXIMUM LENGTH OF DESTINATION STRING
CPYERR: DS      1               ;COPY ERROR FLAG


;                                                               ;
;                                                               ;
;       SAMPLE EXECUTION                                        ;
;                                                               ;
;                                                               ;

SC8D:
        LXI     H,SSTG  ;BASE ADDRESS OF SOURCE STRING
        LXI     D,DSTG  ;BASE ADDRESS OF DESTINATION STRING
        LDA     IDX
        MOV     C,A     ;STARTING INDEX FOR COPYING
        LDA     CNT
        MOV     B,A     ;NUMBER OF CHARACTERS TO COPY
        LDA     MXLEN   ;MAXIMUM LENGTH OF SUBSTRING
        CALL    COPY    ;COPY SUBSTRING
                        ;COPYING 3 CHARACTERS STARTING AT INDEX 4
                        ; FROM '12.345E+10' GIVES '345'
```

```
        JMP      SC8D     ;LOOP FOR MORE TESTING

        ;DATA SECTION
IDX     DB       4               ;STARTING INDEX FOR COPYING
CNT     DB       3               ;NUMBER OF CHARACTERS TO COPY
MXLEN   DB       20H             ;MAXIMUM LENGTH OF DESTINATION STRING
SSTG    DB       0AH             ;LENGTH OF STRING
        DB       '12.345E+10          '  ;32-BYTE MAX LENGTH
DSTG    DB       0               ;LENGTH OF SUBSTRING
        DB       '                    '  ;32-BYTE MAX LENGTH

        END
```

Delete a Substring from a String (DELETE)

Deletes a substring from a string, given a starting index and a length. The string is a maximum of 255 bytes long and the actual characters are preceded by a byte containing the length. The Carry flag is cleared if the deletion can be performed as specified. The Carry flag is set if the starting index is 0 or beyond the length of the string; the string is left unchanged in either case. If the deletion extends beyond the end of the string, the Carry flag is set to 1 and only the characters from the starting index to the end of the string are deleted.

Procedure: The program exits immediately if either the starting index or the number of bytes to delete is 0. It also exits if the starting index is beyond the length of the string. If none of these conditions holds, the program checks to see if the string extends beyond the area to be deleted. If it does not, the program simply truncates the string by setting the new length to the starting index minus 1. If it does, the program compacts the resulting string by moving the bytes above the deleted area down. The program then determines the new string's length and exits with the Carry cleared if the specified number of bytes were deleted or with the Carry set to 1 if any errors occurred.

Registers Used: All

Execution Time: Approximately 39 * NUMBER OF BYTES MOVED DOWN + 237 cycles (8080) or 40 * NUMBER OF BYTES MOVED DOWN + 226 cycles (8085), where NUMBER OF BYTES MOVED DOWN is zero if the string can be truncated and is STRING LENGTH − STARTING INDEX − NUMBER OF BYTES TO DELETE + 1 if the string must be compacted. That is, it takes extra time when the deletion creates a "hole" in the string that must be filled by compaction.

Examples

1. STRING LENGTH = 20_{16} (32_{10})
   STARTING INDEX = 19_{16} (25_{10})
   NUMBER OF BYTES TO DELETE = 08

   Since there are exactly eight bytes left in the string starting at index 19_{16}, all the routine must do is truncate (that is, cut off the end of the string). This takes

   39 * 0 + 237 = 237 cycles (8080)
   40 * 0 + 226 = 226 cycles (8085)

2. STRING LENGTH = 40_{16} (64_{10})
   STARTING INDEX = 19_{16} (25_{10})
   NUMBER OF BYTES TO DELETE = 08

Since there are 20_{16} (32_{10}) bytes above the truncated area, the routine must move them down eight positions to fill the "hole." Thus NUMBER OF BYTES MOVED DOWN = 32_{10} and the execution time is

39 * 32 + 237 = 1248 + 237 = 1485 cycles (8080)
40 * 32 + 226 = 1280 + 226 = 1506 cycles (8085)

Program Size: 68 bytes

Data Memory Required: 1 byte anywhere in RAM for an error flag (address DELERR)

Special Cases:

1. If the number of bytes to delete is 0, the program exits with the Carry flag cleared (no errors) and the string unchanged.

2. If the string does not even extend to the specified starting index, the program exits with the Carry flag set to 1 (indicating an error) and the string unchanged.

3. If the number of bytes to delete exceeds the number available, the program deletes all bytes from the starting index to the end of the string and exits with the Carry flag set to 1 (indicating an error).

Entry Conditions

Base address of string in H and L
Number of bytes to delete in B
Starting index to delete from in C

Exit Conditions

Substring deleted from string. If no errors occur, the Carry flag is cleared. If the starting index is 0 or beyond the length of the string, the Carry flag is set and the string is unchanged. If the number of bytes to delete would go beyond the end of the string, the Carry flag is set and the characters from the starting index to the end of the string are deleted.

Examples

1. Data: String = 26'SALES FOR MARCH AND APRIL OF THIS YEAR'
   ($26_{16} = 38_{10}$ is the length of the string).
   Number of bytes to delete = $0A_{16} = 10_{10}$
   Starting index to delete from = $10_{16} = 16_{10}$

   Result: String = 1C'SALES FOR MARCH OF THIS YEAR' ($1C_{16} = 28_{10}$ is the length of the string with ten bytes deleted starting with the 16th character — the deleted material is 'AND APRIL ').
   Carry = 0, since no problems occurred in the deletion.

2. Data: String = 28'THE PRICE IS $3.00 ($2.00 BEFORE JUNE 1)' ($28_{16} = 40_{10}$ is the length of the string).
   Number of bytes to delete = $30_{16} = 48_{10}$
   Starting index to delete from = $13_{16} = 19_{10}$

   Result: String = 12'THE PRICE IS $3.00' ($12_{16} = 18_{10}$ is the length of the string with all remaining bytes deleted).
   Carry = 1, since there were not as many bytes left in the string as were supposed to be deleted.

```
;                                                                        ;
;                                                                        ;
;                                                                        ;
;                                                                        ;
;                                                                        ;
;       Title:          Delete a Substring from a String                 ;
;       Name:           DELETE                                           ;
;                                                                        ;
;                                                                        ;
;                                                                        ;
;       Purpose:        Delete a substring from a string given a         ;
;                       starting index and a length                      ;
;                                                                        ;
;       Entry:          Register pair H = Base address of string         ;
;                       Register B = Number of bytes to delete           ;
;                       Register C = Starting index into the string. An  ;
;                                    index of 1 is the first character   ;
;                                                                        ;
```

```
;                        A string is a maximum of 255 bytes long plus  ;
;                        a length byte which precedes it.               ;
;                                                                       ;
;        Exit:           Substring deleted                             ;
;                        If no errors then                             ;
;                          Carry := 0                                  ;
;                        else                                          ;
;                          begin                                       ;
;                            the following conditions cause an         ;
;                            error with Carry flag = 1:                ;
;                            if (index = 0) or (index > length(string)) ;
;                              then do not change string               ;
;                            if count is too large then                ;
;                              delete only the characters from         ;
;                              index to end of string                  ;
;                          end;                                        ;
;                                                                       ;
;        Registers used: All                                          ;
;                                                                       ;
;        Time:           Approximately 39 * (LENGTH(STRG)-INDEX-COUNT+1) ;
;                        plus 237 cycles overhead for the 8080         ;
;                        Approximately 40 * (LENGTH(STRG)-INDEX-COUNT+1) ;
;                        plus 226 cycles overhead for the 8085         ;
;                                                                       ;
;        Size:           Program 68 bytes                             ;
;                        Data    1 bytes                              ;
;                                                                       ;
;

DELETE:
        ;INITIALIZE ERROR INDICATOR (DELERR) TO 0
        SUB     A
        STA     DELERR          ;ASSUME NO ERRORS

        ;CHECK IF COUNT AND INDEX ARE BOTH NONZERO
        ORA     B               ;TEST NUMBER OF BYTES TO DELETE
        RZ                      ;RETURN WITH CARRY = 0 (NO ERRORS) IF
                                ; 0 BYTES TO DELETE
        MOV     A,C             ;TEST STARTING INDEX
        ORA     A
        STC
        RZ                      ;ERROR EXIT (CARRY = 1), IF
                                ; STARTING INDEX = 0

        ;CHECK IF STARTING INDEX WITHIN STRING
        ; ERROR EXIT IF NOT
        MOV     A,M             ;GET LENGTH
        CMP     C               ;IS INDEX WITHIN STRING?
        RC                      ;NO, TAKE ERROR EXIT

        ;BE SURE ENOUGH CHARACTERS ARE AVAILABLE
        ; IF NOT, DELETE ONLY FROM INDEX TO END OF STRING
        ; IF INDEX + NUMBER OF CHARACTERS - 1 > LENGTH(STRING) THEN
        ;    NUMBER OF CHARACTERS := LENGTH(STRING) - INDEX + 1
        MOV     A,C             ;GET INDEX
        ADD     B               ;ADD NUMBER OF CHARACTERS TO DELETE
```

```
                JC      TRUNC           ;TRUNCATE IF ·SUM > 255
                MOV     E,A             ;SAVE SUM AS STARTING INDEX FOR MOVE
                DCR     A
                CMP     M               ;COMPARE TO LENGTH
                JC      CNTOK           ;JUMP IF MORE THAN ENOUGH TO DELETE
                JZ      TRUNC           ;TRUNCATE BUT NO ERRORS (EXACTLY ENOUGH
                                        ; CHARACTERS)
                MVI     A,OFFH
                STA     DELERR          ;INDICATE ERROR - NOT ENOUGH CHARACTERS
                                        ; TO DELETE


                ;TRUNCATE STRING - NO COMPACTING NECESSARY
                ; STRING LENGTH = INDEX - 1
TRUNC:
                MOV     A,C             ;STRING LENGTH = INDEX - 1
                DCR     A
                MOV     M,A
                LDA     DELERR
                RAR                     ;CARRY = 0 IF NO ERRORS
                RET                     ;EXIT


                ;DELETE SUBSTRING BY COMPACTING
                ; MOVE ALL CHARACTERS ABOVE DELETED AREA DOWN
                ;NEW LENGTH = LENGTH - NUMBER OF BYTES TO DELETE OLD STRING
CNTOK:
                MOV     A,M
                MOV     D,A             ;SAVE OLD LENGTH
                SUB     B               ;SET NEW LENGTH
                MOV     M,A

                ;CALCULATE NUMBER OF CHARACTERS TO MOVE
                ; NUMBER = STRING LENGTH - (INDEX + NUMBER OF BYTES) + 1
                MOV     A,D             ;GET OLD LENGTH
                SUB     E               ;SUBTRACT INDEX + NUMBER OF BYTES
                INR     A               ;A = NUMBER OF CHARACTERS TO MOVE

                ;CALCULATE SOURCE AND DESTINATION ADDRESSES FOR MOVE
                ;SOURCE = BASE + INDEX + NUMBER OF BYTES TO DELETE
                ;DESTINATION = BASE + INDEX
                PUSH    H               ;SAVE STRING ADDRESS
                MVI     B,0             ;DESTINATION = BASE + INDEX
                DAD     B
                XTHL                    ;SOURCE = BASE + INDEX + NUMBER
                MVI     D,0             ; OF BYTES TO DELETE
                DAD     D               ;HL = SOURCE (ABOVE DELETED AREA)
                POP     D               ;DE = DESTINATION
                MOV     B,A             ;B = NUMBER OF CHARACTERS TO MOVE

MVLP:
                MOV     A,M             ;GET A CHARACTER
                STAX    D               ;MOVE IT DOWN
                INX     H               ;PROCEED TO NEXT CHARACTER
                INX     D
                DCR     B
                JNZ     MVLP
```

```
        ;GOOD EXIT
OKEXIT:
        ORA     A               ;CLEAR CARRY, NO ERRORS
        RET

        ;DATA
DELERR: DS      1               ;DELETE ERROR FLAG


;                                                                    ;
;                                                                    ;
;       SAMPLE EXECUTION                                             ;
;                                                                    ;
;                                                                    ;

SC8E:
        LXI     H,SSTG  ;HL = BASE ADDRESS OF STRING
        LDA     IDX
        MOV     C,A     ;C = STARTING INDEX FOR DELETION
        LDA     CNT
        MOV     B,A     ;B = NUMBER OF CHARACTERS TO DELETE
        CALL    DELETE  ;DELETE CHARACTERS
                        ;DELETING 4 CHARACTERS STARTING AT INDEX 1
                        ; FROM "JOE HANDOVER" LEAVES "HANDOVER"

        JMP     SC8E    ;LOOP FOR ANOTHER TEST

        ;DATA SECTION
IDX:    DB      1               ;STARTING INDEX FOR DELETION
CNT:    DB      4               ;NUMBER OF CHARACTERS TO DELETE
SSTG:   DB      12              ;LENGTH OF STRING
        DB      'JOE HANDOVER'

        END
```

Insert a Substring into a String (INSERT)

Inserts a substring into a string, given a starting index. The string and substring are both a maximum of 255 bytes long and the actual characters are preceded by a byte containing the length. The Carry flag is cleared if the insertion can be accomplished with no problems. The Carry flag is set if the starting index is 0 or beyond the length of the string. In the second case, the substring is concatenated to the end of the string. The Carry flag is also set if the string with the insertion would exceed a specified maximum length; in that case, the program inserts only enough of the substring to give the string its maximum length.

Procedure: The program exits immediately if the starting index or the length of the substring is 0. If neither is 0, the program checks to see if the insertion would produce a string longer than the specified maximum length. If it would, the program truncates the substring. The program then checks to see if the starting index is within the string. If not, the program simply concatenates the substring by moving it to the memory locations immediately after the end of the string. If the starting index is within the string, the program must first make room for the insertion by moving the remaining characters up in memory. This move must start at the highest address to avoid writing over any data. Finally, the program can move the substring into the open area. The program then determines the new string length and exits with the Carry flag set appropriately (to 0 if no problems occurred and to 1 if the starting index was 0, the substring had to be truncated, or the starting index was beyond the length of the string).

Registers Used: All

Execution Time: Approximately 39 * NUMBER OF BYTES MOVED + 39 * NUMBER OF BYTES INSERTED + 300 (8080) or 40 * NUMBER OF BYTES MOVED + 40 * NUMBER OF BYTES INSERTED + 288 (8085). NUMBER OF BYTES MOVED is the number of bytes that must be moved to open up space for the insertion. If the starting index is beyond the end of the string, this is 0 since the substring is simply concatenated to the string. Otherwise, this is STRING LENGTH − STARTING INDEX + 1, since the bytes at or above the starting index must be moved. NUMBER OF BYTES INSERTED is the length of the substring if no truncation occurs. It is the maximum length of the string minus its current length if inserting the substring would produce a string longer than the maximum.

Examples
1. STRING LENGTH = 20_{16} (32_{10})
   STARTING INDEX = 19_{16} (25_{10})
   MAXIMUM LENGTH = 30_{16} (48_{10})
   SUBSTRING LENGTH = 06

That is, it has been decided to insert a substring six bytes long, starting at the 25th character. Since eight bytes must be moved up (NUMBER OF BYTES MOVED = 32 − 25 + 1) and six bytes must be inserted, the execution time is approximately

$$39 * 8 + 39 * 6 + 300 = 312 + 234 + 300 = 846$$
cycles (8080)
$$40 * 8 + 40 * 6 + 288 = 320 + 240 + 288 = 848$$
cycles (8085)

2. STRING LENGTH = 20_{16} (32_{10})
   STARTING INDEX = 19_{16} (25_{10})
   MAXIMUM LENGTH = 24_{16} (36_{10})
   SUBSTRING LENGTH = 06

As opposed to Example 1, only four bytes of the substring can be inserted here without exceeding the maximum length of the string. Thus NUMBER OF BYTES MOVED = 8 and NUMBER OF BYTES INSERTED = 4. The execution time is approximately

$$39 * 8 + 39 * 4 + 300 = 312 + 156 + 300 = 768$$
cycles(8080)
$$40 * 8 + 40 * 4 + 288 = 320 + 160 + 288 = 768$$
cycles(8085)

Program Size: 103 bytes

Data Memory Required: 1 byte anywhere in RAM for an error flag (address INSERR)

Special Cases:

1. If the length of the substring (the insertion) is 0, the program exits with the Carry flag cleared (no errors) and the string unchanged.

2. If the starting index for the insertion is 0 (i.e., the insertion would start in the length byte), the program exits with the Carry flag set to 1 (indicating an error) and the string unchanged.

3. If the string with the substring inserted exceeds the specified maximum length, the program inserts only enough characters to reach the maximum

length. The Carry flag is set to 1 to indicate that the insertion has been truncated.

4. If the starting index of the insertion is beyond the end of the string, the program concatenates the insertion at the end of the string and indicates an error by setting the Carry flag to 1.

5. If the original length of the string exceeds its specified maximum length, the program exits with the Carry flag set to 1 (indicating an error) and the string unchanged.

Entry Conditions

Base address of substring in D and E
Base address of string in H and L
Maximum length of string in B
Starting index at which to insert the
    substring in C

Exit Conditions

The substring is inserted into the string. If no errors occur, the Carry flag is cleared. If the starting index or the length of the substring is 0, the Carry flag is set and the string is not changed. If the starting index is beyond the length of the string, the Carry flag is set and the substring is concatenated to the end of the string. If the string with the substring inserted would exceed the specified maximum length, the Carry flag is set and only those characters from the substring which bring the string to maximum length are inserted.

Examples

1. Data: String = 0A'JOHN SMITH' ($0A_{16} = 10_{10}$ is the length of the string).
    Substring = 08'WILLIAM ' (08 is the length of the substring).
    Maximum length of string = $14_{16} = 20_{10}$
    Starting index = 06

  Result: String = 12'JOHN WILLIAM SMITH' ($12_{16} = 18_{10}$ is the length of the string with the substring inserted).
    Carry = 0, since no problems occurred in the insertion.

2. Data: String = 0A'JOHN SMITH' ($0A_{16} = 10_{10}$ is the length of the string).
    Substring = 0C'ROCKEFELLER' ($0C_{16} = 12_{10}$ is the length of the substring).
    Maximum length of string = $14_{16} = 20_{10}$
    Starting index = 06

  Result: String = 14'JOHN ROCKEFELLESMITH' ($14_{16} = 20_{10}$ is the length of the string with as much of the substring inserted as the maximum length would allow).
    Carry = 1, since some of the substring could not be inserted without exceeding the maximum length of the string.

```
;                                                                    ;
;                                                                    ;
;                                                                    ;
;                                                                    ;
;       Title:          Insert a Substring into a String             ;
;       Name:           INSERT                                       ;
;                                                                    ;
;                                                                    ;
;                                                                    ;
;                                                                    ;
;       Purpose:        Insert a substring into a string given a     ;
;                       starting index                               ;
;                                                                    ;
;       Entry:          Register pair H = Address of string          ;
;                       Register pair D = Address of substring  to   ;
;                                      insert                        ;
;                       Register B = Maximum length of string        ;
;                       Register C = Starting index to insert the    ;
;                                      substring                     ;
;                                                                    ;
;                       A string is a maximum of 255 bytes long plus ;
;                       a length byte which precedes it.             ;
;                                                                    ;
;       Exit:           Substring inserted into string               ;
;                       If no errors then                            ;
;                         Carry = 0                                  ;
;                       else                                         ;
;                         begin                                      ;
;                           the following conditions cause the       ;
;                           Carry flag to be set:                    ;
;                           if index = 0 then                        ;
;                             do not insert the substring            ;
;                           if length(strg) > maximum length then    ;
;                             do not insert the substring            ;
;                           if index > length(strg) then             ;
;                             concatenate substg onto the end of the ;
;                             source string                          ;
;                           if length(strg)+length(substring) > maxlen ;
;                             then insert only enough of the substring ;
;                             to reach maximum length                ;
;                         end;                                       ;
;                                                                    ;
;       Registers used: All                                          ;
;                                                                    ;
;       Time:           Approximately                                ;
;                       39 * (LENGTH(STRG) - INDEX + 1) +            ;
;                       39 * (LENGTH(SUBSTG)) +                      ;
;                       300 cycles overhead for the 8080             ;
;                       Approximately                                ;
;                       40 * (LENGTH(STRG) - INDEX + 1) +            ;
;                       40 * (LENGTH(SUBSTG)) +                      ;
;                       288 cycles overhead for the 8085             ;
;                                                                    ;
;       Size:           Program 103 bytes                            ;
;                       Data     1 byte                              ;
;                                                                    ;
```

```
INSERT:
        ;INITIALIZE ERROR FLAG
        SUB     A               ;ERROR FLAG = 0 (NO ERRORS)
        STA     INSERR

        ;GET SUBSTRING AND STRING LENGTHS
        ; IF LENGTH(SUBSTG) = 0 THEN EXIT BUT NO ERROR
        LDAX    D               ;TEST LENGTH OF SUBSTRING
        ORA     A
        RZ                      ;EXIT IF SUBSTRING IS EMPTY
                                ; CARRY = 0 (NO ERRORS)

        ;IF STARTING INDEX IS ZERO, TAKE ERROR EXIT
IDX0:
        MOV     A,C             ;TEST STARTING INDEX
        ORA     A
        STC                     ;ASSUME AN ERROR
        RZ                      ;RETURN WITH ERROR IF INDEX = 0

        ;CHECK WHETHER INSERTION WILL MAKE STRING TOO LONG
        ; IF IT WILL, TRUNCATE SUBSTRING AND SET
        ; TRUNCATION FLAG.
        ;INSERTION TOO LONG IF STRING LENGTH + SUBSTRING LENGTH
        ; EXCEEDS MAXIMUM LENGTH.  REMEMBER, STRINGS CANNOT BE
        ; MORE THAN 255 BYTES LONG
CHKLEN:
        LDAX    D               ;TOTAL = STRING + SUBSTRING
        ADD     M
        JC      TRUNC           ;TRUNCATE SUBSTRING IF NEW LENGTH > 255
        CMP     B               ;COMPARE TO MAXIMUM LENGTH OF STRING
        LDAX    D               ;A = LENGTH OF SUBSTRING
        JC      IDXLEN          ;JUMP IF NEW LENGTH < MAX LENGTH
        JZ      IDXLEN          ; OR EQUAL

        ;SUBSTRING DOES NOT FIT, SO TRUNCATE IT
        ; SET ERROR FLAG TO INDICATE TRUNCATION
        ; LENGTH THAT FITS = MAXIMUM LENGTH - STRING LENGTH
TRUNC:
        MVI     A,0FFH          ;INDICATE SUBSTRING TRUNCATED
        STA     INSERR
        MOV     A,B             ;LENGTH = MAX - STRING LENGTH
        SUB     M
        RC                      ;RETURN WITH ERROR IF STRING TOO
        STC                     ; LONG INITIALLY OR ALREADY MAX
        RZ                      ; LENGTH SO NO ROOM FOR SUBSTRING

        ;CHECK IF INDEX IS WITHIN STRING. IF NOT, CONCATENATE
        ; SUBSTRING ONTO END OF STRING.
IDXLEN:
        MOV     B,A             ;B = LENGTH OF SUBSTRING
        MOV     A,M             ;GET STRING LENGTH
        CMP     C               ;COMPARE TO INDEX
        JNC     LENOK           ;JUMP IF STARTING INDEX WITHIN STRING
```

```
                ;INDEX NOT WITHIN STRING, SO CONCATENATE
                ; NEW LENGTH OF STRING = OLD LENGTH + SUBSTRING LENGTH
                MOV     C,A             ;SAVE CURRENT STRING LENGTH
                ADD     B               ;ADD LENGTH OF SUBSTRING
                MOV     M,A             ;SET NEW LENGTH OF STRING

                ;SET ADDRESSES FOR CONCATENATION
                ; DE = STRING ADDRESS + LENGTH(STRING) + 1
                ; HL = SUBSTRING ADDRESS
                XCHG                    ;HL = SUBSTRING ADDRESS
                MOV     A,C             ;DE = END OF STRING
                INR     A
                ADD     E
                MOV     E,A
                JNC     IDXL1
                INR     D
IDXL1:
                MVI     A,OFFH          ;INDICATE INSERTION ERROR
                STA     INSERR
                JMP     MVESUB          ;JUST MOVE, NOTHING TO OPEN UP

                ;OPEN UP SPACE IN SOURCE STRING FOR SUBSTRING BY MOVING
                ; CHARACTERS FROM END OF SOURCE STRING DOWN TO INDEX, UP BY
                ; SIZE OF SUBSTRING.
                ; A = LENGTH(STRING)
LENOK:
                PUSH    B               ;SAVE LENGTH OF SUBSTRING
                PUSH    D               ;SAVE ADDRESS OF SUBSTRING

                ;NEW LENGTH OF STRING = OLD LENGTH + SUBSTRING LENGTH
                MOV     E,A             ;DE = STRING LENGTH
                MVI     D,O
                ADD     B
                MOV     M,A             ;STORE NEW LENGTH OF STRING

                ;CALCULATE NUMBER OF CHARACTERS TO MOVE
                ; = STRING LENGTH - STARTING INDEX + 1
                MOV     A,E             ;GET ORIGINAL LENGTH OF STRING
                SUB     C
                INR     A               ;A = NUMBER OF CHARACTERS TO MOVE

                ;CALCULATE ADDRESS OF LAST CHARACTER IN STRING. THIS IS
                ; SOURCE ADDRESS = STRING ADDRESS + LENGTH(STRING)
                DAD     D               ;HL POINTS TO LAST CHARACTER IN STRING
                MOV     E,L             ;DE ALSO
                MOV     D,H

                ;CALCULATE DESTINATION ADDRESS
                ; = STRING ADDRESS + LENGTH(STRING) + LENGTH OF SUBSTRING
                MOV     C,B             ;BC = LENGTH OF SUBSTRING
                MVI     B,O
                DAD     B               ;HL = DESTINATION ADDRESS
                                        ;DE = SOURCE ADDRESS
                MOV     C,A             ;C = NUMBER OF CHARACTERS TO MOVE
```

```
OPNLP:
        LDAX    D                       ;GET A CHARACTER
        MOV     M,A                     ;MOVE IT UP IN MEMORY
        DCX     H                       ;INCREMENT TO NEXT CHARACTER
        DCX     D
        DCR     C
        JNZ     OPNLP                   ;CONTINUE UNTIL ALL CHARACTERS MOVED

        ;RESTORE REGISTERS
        INX     D                       ;DE = ADDRESS TO MOVE STRING TO
        POP     H                       ;HL = ADDRESS OF SUBSTRING
        POP     B                       ;B = LENGTH OF SUBSTRING

        ;MOVE SUBSTRING INTO OPEN AREA
        ; HL = ADDRESS OF SUBSTRING
        ; DE = ADDRESS TO MOVE SUBSTRING TO
        ; B = LENGTH OF SUBSTRING
MVESUB:
        INX     H                       ;INCREMENT PAST LENGTH BYTE OF SUBSTRING
MVELP:
        MOV     A,M                     ;GET A CHARACTER FROM SUBSTRING
        STAX    D                       ;INSERT IT IN OPEN AREA
        INX     H
        INX     D
        DCR     B
        JNZ     MVELP
        LDA     INSERR                  ;GET ERROR FLAG
        RAR                             ;IF INSERR <> 0 THEN CARRY = 1
                                        ; TO INDICATE ERROR
        RET

        ;DATA SECTION
INSERR: DS      1                       ;FLAG USED TO INDICATE ERROR


;                                                                       ;
;                                                                       ;
;       SAMPLE EXECUTION                                                ;
;                                                                       ;
;                                                                       ;

SC8F:
        LXI     H,STG   ;HL = BASE ADDRESS OF STRING
        LXI     D,SSTG  ;DE = BASE ADDRESS OF SUBSTRING
        LDA     IDX
        MOV     C,A     ;C = STARTING INDEX FOR INSERTION
        LDA     MXLEN
        MOV     B,A     ;B = MAXIMUM LENGTH OF STRING
        CALL    INSERT  ;INSERT SUBSTRING
                        ;RESULT OF INSERTING '-' INTO '123456' AT
                        ; INDEX 1 IS '-123456'

        JMP     SC8F    ;LOOP FOR ANOTHER TEST

        ;DATA SECTION
```

```
IDX:      DB       1               ;STARTING INDEX FOR INSERTION
MXLEN:    DB       20H             ;MAXIMUM LENGTH OF DESTINATION
STG:      DB       06H             ;LENGTH OF STRING
          DB       ´123456                        ´ ;32-BYTE MAX LENGTH
SSTG      DB       1               ;LENGTH OF SUBSTRING
          DB       ´-                             ´ ;32-BYTE MAX LENGTH

          END
```

Adds the elements of an array, producing a 16-bit sum. The array consists of up to 255 byte-length elements.

Procedure: The program clears the sum initially. It then adds elements one at a time to the less significant byte of the sum, starting at the base address. Whenever an addition produces a carry, the program increments the more significant byte of the sum.

Registers Used: AF, B, DE, HL

Execution Time: Approximately 37 cycles per byte-length element plus 57 (8080) or 51 (8085) cycles overhead

Program Size: 22 bytes

Data Memory Required: None

Special Case: An array size of 0 causes an immediate exit with the sum equal to 0.

Entry Conditions

Base address of array in H and L
Size of array in bytes in B

Exit Conditions

Sum in H and L

Example

1. Data: Array consists of
$F7_{16}$	$5A_{16}$
23_{16}	16_{16}
31_{16}	CB_{16}
70_{16}	$E1_{16}$

   Result: Sum = (H and L) = $03D7_{16}$

```
;                                                                    ;
;                                                                    ;
;                                                                    ;
;                                                                    ;
;           Title:          8-Bit Array Summation                    ;
;           Name:           ASUM8                                    ;
;                                                                    ;
;                                                                    ;
;                                                                    ;
;                                                                    ;
;           Purpose:        Sum the elements of an array, yielding a 16-bit  ;
;                           result. Maximum size is 255 bytes        ;
;                                                                    ;
;           Entry:          Register pair H = Base address of array  ;
;                           Register B = Size of array in bytes      ;
;                                                                    ;
```

```
;                                                                    ;
;          Exit:            Register pair H = Sum                     ;
;                                                                    ;
;          Registers used: AF,B,DE,HL                                ;
;                                                                    ;
;          Time:            Approximately 37 cycles per element plus  ;
;                           57 cycles overhead for the 8080           ;
;                           Approximately 37 cycles per element plus  ;
;                           51 cycles overhead for the 8085           ;
;                                                                    ;
;          Size:            Program 22 bytes                          ;
;                                                                    ;
;                                                                    ;

ASUM8:
        ;TEST ARRAY LENGTH
        ;EXIT WITH SUM = 0 IF NOTHING IN ARRAY
        XCHG                     ;SAVE BASE ADDRESS OF ARRAY
        LXI      H,0             ;INITIALIZE SUM TO 0

        ;CHECK FOR ARRAY LENGTH OF ZERO
        MOV      A,B             ;TEST ARRAY LENGTH
        ORA      A
        RZ                       ;EXIT WITH SUM = 0 IF LENGTH = 0

        ;INITIALIZE ARRAY POINTER, SUM
        XCHG                     ;RESTORE BASE ADDRESS IN H AND L
                                 ; HIGH BYTE OF SUM = 0
        SUB      A               ;A = LOW BYTE OF SUM = 0
                                 ;D = HIGH BYTE OF SUM

        ;ADD BYTE-LENGTH ELEMENTS TO SUM ONE AT A TIME
        ;INCREMENT HIGH BYTE OF SUM WHENEVER A CARRY OCCURS
SUMLP:
        ADD      M               ;ADD NEXT ELEMENT TO LOW BYTE OF SUM
        JNC      DECCNT          ;JUMP IF NO CARRY
        INR      D               ; ELSE INCREMENT HIGH BYTE OF SUM
DECCNT:
        INX      H
        DCR      B
        JNZ      SUMLP
EXIT:
        MOV      L,A             ;HL = SUM
        MOV      H,D
        RET


;                                                                    ;
;                                                                    ;
;          SAMPLE EXECUTION                                          ;
;                                                                    ;
;                                                                    ;

SC9A:
        LXI      H,BUF           ;HL = BASE ADDRESS OF BUFFER
        LDA      BUFSZ
```

```
          MOV     B,A              ;B = SIZE OF BUFFER IN BYTES
          CALL    ASUM8
                                   ;SUM OF TEST DATA IS 07F8 HEX,
                                   ; REGISTERS H AND L = 07F8H


          JMP     $C9A

          ;TEST DATA, CHANGE FOR OTHER VALUES
SIZE      EQU     010H             ;SIZE OF BUFFER IN BYTES
BUFSZ:    DB      SIZE             ;SIZE OF BUFFER IN BYTES

BUF:      DB      00H              ;BUFFER
          DB      11H              ;DECIMAL ELEMENTS ARE 0,17,34,51,68
          DB      22H              ; 85,102,119,135,153,170,187,204
          DB      33H              ; 221,238,255
          DB      44H
          DB      55H
          DB      66H
          DB      77H
          DB      88H
          DB      99H
          DB      0AAH
          DB      0BBH
          DB      0CCH
          DB      0DDH
          DB      0EEH
          DB      0FFH             ;SUM = 07F8 (2040 DECIMAL)

          END
```

Adds the elements of an array, producing a 24-bit sum. The array consists of up to 255 word-length (16-bit) elements. The elements are arranged in the usual 8080/8085 format with the less significant bytes first.

Procedure: The program clears the sum initially. It then adds elements to the less significant bytes of the sum one at a time, starting at the base address. Whenever an addition produces a carry, the program increments the most significant byte of the sum.

Registers Used: All

Execution Time: Approximately 69 (8080) or 66 (8085) cycles per 16-bit element plus 57 (8080) or 51 (8085) cycles overhead

Program Size: 28 bytes

Data Memory Required: None

Special Case: An array size of 0 causes an immediate exit with the sum equal to 0.

Entry Conditions

Base address of array in H and L
Size of array in 16-bit words in B

Exit Conditions

Most significant byte of sum in E
Middle and least significant bytes of sum in H and L

Example

1. Data: Array (in 16-bit words) consists of

$F7A1_{16}$	$5A36_{16}$
$239B_{16}$	$166C_{16}$
$31D5_{16}$	$CBF5_{16}$
$70F2_{16}$	$E107_{16}$

Result: Sum = $03DBA1_{16}$
(E) = 03_{16}
(H and L) = $DBA1_{16}$

```
;
;
;
;
;       Title:          16-Bit Array Summation
;       Name:           ASUM16
;
;
;
;
;
;       Purpose:        Sum the elements of an array, yielding a 24-bit  ;
```

```
;                           result. Maximum size is 255 16-bit elements    ;
;                                                                           ;
;           Entry:          Register pair H = Base address of array         ;
;                           Register B = Size of array in words             ;
;                                                                           ;
;           Exit:           Register A = High byte of sum                   ;
;                           Register H = Middle byte of sum                 ;
;                           Register L = Low byte of sum                    ;
;                                                                           ;
;      Registers used: All                                                  ;
;                                                                           ;
;      Time:                Approximately 69 cycles per element plus         ;
;                           57 cycles overhead for the 8080                 ;
;                           Approximately 66 cycles per element plus         ;
;                           51 cycles overhead for the 8085                 ;
;                                                                           ;
;      Size:                Program 28 bytes                                ;
;                                                                           ;
;
```

```
ASUM16:
        ;TEST ARRAY LENGTH
        ;EXIT WITH SUM = 0 IF NOTHING IN ARRAY
        XCHG                    ;SAVE BASE ADDRESS OF ARRAY
        LXI     H,0             ;INITIALIZE SUM TO 0

        ;CHECK FOR ARRAY LENGTH OF ZERO
        MOV     A,B             ;TEST ARRAY LENGTH
        ORA     A
        RZ                      ;EXIT WITH SUM = 0 IF LENGTH = 0

        ;INITIALIZE ARRAY POINTER, SUM
        XCHG                    ;MOVE BASE ADDRESS BACK TO HL
                                ; LOW, MIDDLE BYTES OF SUM = 0
        MOV     C,E             ;HIGH BYTE OF SUM = 0
                                ;C = HIGH BYTE OF SUM
                                ;D = MIDDLE BYTE OF SUM
                                ;E = LOW BYTE OF SUM

        ;ADD WORD-LENGTH ELEMENTS TO SUM ONE AT A TIME
        ;INCREMENT HIGH BYTE OF SUM WHENEVER A CARRY OCCURS
SUMLP:
        MOV     A,E             ;ADD LOW BYTES OF ELEMENT AND SUM
        ADD     M
        MOV     E,A
        INX     H
        MOV     A,D             ;ADD HIGH BYTE OF ELEMENT TO
        ADC     M               ; MIDDLE BYTE OF SUM
        MOV     D,A
        JNC     DECCNT          ;JUMP IF NO CARRY
        INR     C               ; ELSE INCREMENT HIGH BYTE OF SUM
DECCNT:
        INX     H
        DCR     B
        JNZ     SUMLP
```

```
EXIT:
        XCHG                    ;HL = MIDDLE AND LOW BYTES OF SUM
        MOV     A,C             ;A = HIGH BYTE OF SUM
        RET


;                                                                    ;
;                                                                    ;
;       SAMPLE EXECUTION                                             ;
;                                                                    ;
;                                                                    ;

SC9B:
        LXI     H,BUF           ;HL = BASE ADDRESS OF ARRAY
        LDA     BUFSZ
        MOV     B,A             ;B = SIZE OF ARRAY IN WORDS
        CALL    ASUM16

                                ;SUM OF TEST DATA IS 31FF8 HEX,
                                ; REGISTERS H AND L = 1FF8H
                                ; REGISTER A = 3

        JMP     SC9B

        ;TEST DATA, CHANGE FOR OTHER VALUES
SIZE    EQU     010H            ;SIZE OF ARRAY IN WORDS
BUFSZ:  DB      SIZE            ;SIZE OF ARRAY IN WORDS

BUF:    DW      000H            ;BUFFER
        DW      111H            ;DECIMAL ELEMENTS ARE 0,273,546,819,1092
        DW      222H            ; 1365,1638,1911,2184,2457,2730,3003,3276
        DW      333H            ; 56797,61166,65535
        DW      444H
        DW      555H
        DW      666H
        DW      777H
        DW      888H
        DW      999H
        DW      0AAAH
        DW      0BBBH
        DW      0CCCH
        DW      0DDDH
        DW      0EEEEH
        DW      0FFFFH          ;SUM = 31FF8 (204792 DECIMAL)

        END
```

Find Maximum Byte-Length
Element (MAXELM)

Finds the maximum element in an array. The array consists of up to 255 unsigned byte-length elements.

Procedure: The program exits immediately (setting Carry to 1) if the array has no elements. Otherwise, the program assumes that the element at the base address is the maximum. It then proceeds through the array, comparing the supposed maximum with each element and retaining the larger value and its address. Finally, the program clears Carry to indicate a valid result.

Registers Used: AF, B, DE, HL

Execution Time: Approximately 37 to 62 cycles per element plus 36 cycles overhead (8080) or 34 to 53 cycles per element plus 36 cycles overhead (8085). If, on the average, the program must replace the maximum in half of the iterations, the execution time is approximately $99 * \text{ARRAY SIZE}/2 + 36$ cycles (8080) or $87 * \text{ARRAY SIZE}/2 + 36$ cycles (8085).

Program Size: 22 bytes

Data Memory Required: None

Special Cases:

1. An array size of 0 causes an immediate exit with the Carry flag set to 1 to indicate an invalid result.

2. If the largest unsigned value occurs more than once, the program returns with the lowest possible address. That is, it returns with the address closest to the base address that contains the maximum value.

Entry Conditions

Base address of array in H and L
Size of array in bytes in B

Exit Conditions

Largest unsigned element in A
Address of largest unsigned element in H and L
Carry = 0 if result is valid; 1 if size of array is 0 and result is meaningless.

Example

1. Data: Array (in bytes) consists of
   35_{16} 44_{16}
   $A6_{16}$ 59_{16}
   $D2_{16}$ $7A_{16}$
   $1B_{16}$ CF_{16}

   Result: The largest unsigned element is element #2 $(D2_{16})$.
   $(A) = $ largest element $(D2_{16})$
   $(H$ and $L) = \text{BASE} + 2$ (lowest address containing $D2_{16}$)
   Carry flag $= 0$, indicating that array size is non-zero and the result is valid.

```
;                                                                          ;
;                                                                          ;
;                                                                          ;
;                                                                          ;
;          Title           Find Maximum Byte-Length Element                ;
;          Name:           MAXELM                                          ;
;                                                                          ;
;                                                                          ;
;                                                                          ;
;          Purpose:        Given the base address and size of an array,    ;
;                          find the largest element                        ;
;                                                                          ;
;          Entry:          Register pair H = Base address of array         ;
;                          Register B = Size of array in bytes             ;
;                                                                          ;
;          Exit:           If size of array not zero then                  ;
;                             Carry flag = 0                               ;
;                             Register A = Largest element                 ;
;                             Register pair H = Address of that element     ;
;                              If there are duplicate values of the largest ;
;                              element, register pair H has the address     ;
;                              nearest to the base address.                ;
;                          else                                            ;
;                             Carry flag = 1                               ;
;                                                                          ;
;      Registers used: AF,B,DE,HL                                          ;
;                                                                          ;
;          Time:           Approximately 37 to 62 cycles per byte          ;
;                          plus 36 cycles overhead for 8080                ;
;                          Approximately 34 to 53 cycles per byte          ;
;                          plus 36 cycles overhead for 8085                ;
;                                                                          ;
;          Size:           Program 22 bytes                                ;
;                                                                          ;
;                                                                          ;

MAXELM:
        ;EXIT WITH CARRY SET IF NO ELEMENTS IN ARRAY
        MOV     A,B                 ;TEST ARRAY SIZE
        ORA     A
        STC                         ;SET CARRY TO INDICATE ERROR EXIT
        RZ                          ;RETURN IF NO ELEMENTS

        ;REPLACE PREVIOUS GUESS AT LARGEST ELEMENT WITH
        ; CURRENT ELEMENT. FIRST TIME THROUGH, TAKE FIRST
        ; ELEMENT AS GUESS AT LARGEST
MAXLP:  MOV     A,M                 ;LARGEST = CURRENT ELEMENT
        MOV     E,L                 ;SAVE ADDRESS OF LARGEST
        MOV     D,H

        ;COMPARE CURRENT ELEMENT TO LARGEST
        ;KEEP LOOKING UNLESS CURRENT ELEMENT IS LARGER
```

```
MAXLP1:
        DCR     B
        JZ      EXIT
        INX     H
        CMP     M           ;COMPARE CURRENT ELEMENT, LARGEST
        JNC     MAXLP1      ;CONTINUE UNLESS CURRENT ELEMENT LARGER
        JMP     MAXLP       ;ELSE CHANGE LARGEST
EXIT:
        ORA     A           ;CLEAR CARRY TO INDICATE NO ERRORS
        XCHG                ;HL = ADDRESS OF LARGEST ELEMENT
        RET


;                                                                   ;
;                                                                   ;
;       SAMPLE EXECUTION                                            ;
;                                                                   ;
;                                                                   ;

SC9C:
        LXI     H,ARY       ;HL = BASE ADDRESS OF ARRAY
        MVI     B,SZARY     ;B = SIZE OF ARRAY IN BYTES
        CALL    MAXELM
                            ;RESULT FOR TEST DATA IS
                            ; A = FF HEX (MAXIMUM), HL = ADDRESS OF
                            ; FF IN ARY.

        JMP     SC9C        ;LOOP FOR MORE TESTING

SZARY:  EQU     10H         ;SIZE OF ARRAY IN BYTES
ARY:    DB      8
        DB      7
        DB      6
        DB      5
        DB      4
        DB      3
        DB      2
        DB      1
        DB      0FFH
        DB      0FEH
        DB      0FDH
        DB      0FCH
        DB      0FBH
        DB      0FAH
        DB      0F9H
        DB      0F8H

        END
```

Find Minimum Byte-Length
Element (MINELM)

Finds the minimum element in an array. The array consists of up to 255 unsigned byte-length elements.

Procedure: The program exits immediately (setting Carry to 1) if the array has no elements. Otherwise, the program assumes that the ele- ment at the base address is the minimum. It then proceeds through the array, comparing the supposed minimum to each element and retaining the smaller value and its address. Finally, the program clears Carry to indicate a valid result.

Registers Used: AF, B, DE, HL

Execution Time: Approximately 37 to 72 cycles per element plus 36 cycles overhead (8080) or 34 to 63 cycles per element plus 36 cycles overhead (8085). If, on the average, the program must replace the minimum in half of the iterations, the execution time is approximately 109 * ARRAY SIZE/2 + 36 cycles (8080) or 97 * ARRAY SIZE/2 + 36 cycles (8085).

Program Size: 25 bytes

Data Memory Required: None

Special Cases:

1. An array size of 0 causes an immediate exit with the Carry flag set to 1 to indicate an invalid result.

2. If the smallest unsigned value occurs more than once, the program returns with the lowest possible address. That is, it returns with the address closest to the base address that contains the minimum value.

Entry Conditions

Base address of array in H and L
Size of array in bytes in B

Exit Conditions

Smallest unsigned element in A
Address of smallest unsigned element in H and L
Carry = 0 if result is valid; 1 if size of array is 0 and result is meaningless.

Example

1. Data: Array (in bytes) consists of
35_{16} 44_{16}
$A6_{16}$ 59_{16}
$D2_{16}$ $7A_{16}$
$1B_{16}$ CF_{16}

Result: The smallest unsigned element is element #3 ($1B_{16}$).
(A) = smallest element ($1B_{16}$)
(H and L) = BASE + 3 (lowest address containing $1B_{16}$)
Carry flag = 0, indicating that array size is non-zero and the result is valid.

```
;
;
;
;
;          Title              Find Minimum Byte-Length Element           ;
;          Name:              MINELM                                     ;
;                                                                        ;
;                                                                        ;
;                                                                        ;
;          Purpose:           Given the base address and size of an array, ;
;                             find the smallest element                  ;
;                                                                        ;
;          Entry:             Register pair H = Base address of array    ;
;                             Register B = Size of array in bytes        ;
;                                                                        ;
;          Exit:              If size of array not zero then             ;
;                                Carry flag = 0                          ;
;                                Register A = Smallest element           ;
;                                Register pair H = Address of that element ;
;                                 If there are duplicate values of the smallest;
;                                 element, register pair H has the address ;
;                                 nearest to the base address.           ;
;                             else                                       ;
;                                Carry flag = 1                          ;
;                                                                        ;
;          Registers used: AF,B,DE,HL                                    ;
;                                                                        ;
;          Time:              Approximately 37 to 72 cycles per byte     ;
;                             plus 36 cycles overhead for 8080           ;
;                             Approximately 34 to 63 cycles per byte     ;
;                             plus 36 cycles overhead for 8085           ;
;                                                                        ;
;          Size:              Program 25 bytes                           ;
;                                                                        ;
;

MINELM:
        ;EXIT WITH CARRY SET IF NO ELEMENTS IN ARRAY
        MOV     A,B             ;TEST ARRAY SIZE
        ORA     A
        STC                     ;SET CARRY TO INDICATE AN ERROR EXIT
        RZ                      ;RETURN IF NO ELEMENTS

        ;REPLACE PREVIOUS GUESS AT SMALLEST ELEMENT WITH
        ; CURRENT ELEMENT.  FIRST TIME THROUGH, TAKE FIRST
        ; ELEMENT AS GUESS AT SMALLEST
MINLP:  MOV     A,M             ;SMALLEST = CURRENT ELEMENT
        MOV     E,L             ;SAVE ADDRESS OF SMALLEST
        MOV     D,H

        ;COMPARE CURRENT ELEMENT TO SMALLEST
        ;KEEP LOOKING UNLESS CURRENT ELEMENT IS SMALLER
```

```
MINLP1:
        DCR     B
        JZ      EXIT
        INX     H
        CMP     M            ;COMPARE CURRENT ELEMENT, SMALLEST
        JC      MINLP1       ;CONTINUE IF CURRENT ELEMENT LARGER
        JZ      MINLP1       ; OR SAME
        JMP     MINLP        ;ELSE CHANGE SMALLEST
EXIT:
        ORA     A            ;CLEAR CARRY TO INDICATE NO ERRORS
        XCHG                 ;HL = ADDRESS OF SMALLEST ELEMENT
        RET


;                                                                    ;
;                                                                    ;
;       SAMPLE EXECUTION                                             ;
;                                                                    ;
;                                                                    ;

SC9D:
        LXI     H,ARY        ;HL = BASE ADDRESS OF ARRAY
        MVI     B,SZARY      ;B = SIZE OF ARRAY IN BYTES
        CALL    MINELM
                             ;RESULT FOR TEST DATA IS
                             ; A = 1 HEX (MINIMUM), HL = ADDRESS OF
                             ; 1 IN ARY

        JMP     SC9D         ;LOOP FOR MORE TESTING

SZARY:  EQU     10H          ;SIZE OF ARRAY IN BYTES
ARY:    DB      8
        DB      7
        DB      6
        DB      5
        DB      4
        DB      3
        DB      2
        DB      1
        DB      0FFH
        DB      0FEH
        DB      0FDH
        DB      0FCH
        DB      0FBH
        DB      0FAH
        DB      0F9H
        DB      0F8H

        END
```

Searches an array of unsigned byte-length elements for a particular value. The elements are assumed to be arranged in increasing order. Clears Carry if it finds the value and sets Carry to 1 if it does not. Returns the address of the value if found. The size of the array is specified and is a maximum of 255 bytes.

Procedure: The program performs a binary search, repeatedly comparing the value with the middle remaining element. After each comparison, the program discards the part of the array that cannot contain the value (because of the ordering). The program retains upper and lower bounds for the part still being searched. If the value is larger than the middle element, the program discards the middle and everything below it. The new lower bound is the address of the middle element plus 1. If the value is smaller than the middle element, the program discards the middle and everything above it. The new upper bound is the address of the middle element minus 1. The program exits if it finds the value or if there is nothing left to search.

For example, assume that the array is

01_{16}, 02_{16}, 05_{16}, 07_{16}, 09_{16}, 09_{16}, $0D_{16}$, 10_{16}, $2E_{16}$, 37_{16}, $5D_{16}$, $7E_{16}$, $A1_{16}$, $B4_{16}$, $D7_{16}$, $E0_{16}$

and the value to be found is $0D_{16}$. The procedure works as follows.

In the first iteration, the lower bound is the base address and the upper bound is the address of the last element. So the result is

```
LOWER  BOUND = BASE
UPPER  BOUND = BASE + SIZE − 1 =
             BASE + 0F₁₆
GUESS = (UPPER BOUND + LOWER BOUND)/2
        (the result is truncated)
      = BASE + 7
(GUESS) = ARRAY(7) = 10₁₆ = 16₁₀
```

Since the value ($0D_{16}$) is less than ARRAY(7),

Registers Used: All

Execution Time: Approximately 123 cycles per iteration plus 57 cycles overhead (8080) or 119 cycles per iteration plus 53 cycles overhead (8085). A binary search will require on the order of $\log_2 N$ iterations, where N is the size of the array (number of elements).

Program Size: 42 bytes

Data Memory Required: None

Special Case: A size of 0 causes an immediate exit with the Carry flag set to 1. That is, the array contains no elements and the value surely cannot be found.

---

the elements beyond #6 can be discarded. The result is

```
LOWER  BOUND = BASE
UPPER  BOUND = GUESS − 1 = BASE + 6
GUESS = (UPPER BOUND + LOWER BOUND)/2 =
        BASE + 3
(GUESS) = ARRAY(3) = 07
```

Since the value ($0D_{16}$) is greater than ARRAY(3), the elements below #4 can be discarded. So the result is

```
LOWER  BOUND = GUESS + 1 = BASE + 4
UPPER  BOUND = BASE + 6
GUESS = (UPPER BOUND + LOWER BOUND)/2 =
        BASE + 5
(GUESS) = ARRAY(5) = 09
```

Since the value ($0D_{16}$) is greater than ARRAY(5), the elements below #6 can be discarded. So the result is

```
LOWER  BOUND = GUESS + 1 = BASE + 6
UPPER  BOUND = BASE + 6
GUESS = (UPPER BOUND + LOWER BOUND)/2 =
        BASE + 6
(GUESS) = ARRAY(6) = 0D₁₆
```

325

Since the value $(0D_{16})$ is equal to $ARRAY(6)$, the element has been found. If, on the other hand, the value were $0E_{16}$, the new lower bound would be $BASE + 7$ and there would be nothing left to search.

Entry Conditions

Value to find in A
Size of the array in bytes in C
Base address of array (address of smallest unsigned element) in H and L

Exit Conditions

Carry $= 0$ if the value is found; 1 if it is not found.
If the value is found, (H and L) $=$ its address.

Examples

Length of array $= 10_{16}$
Elements of array are $01_{16}, 02_{16}, 05_{16}, 07_{16}, 09_{16}, 0D_{16}, 10_{16},$
   $2E_{16}, 37_{16}, 5D_{16}, 7E_{16}, A1_{16}, B4_{16}, D7_{16}, E0_{16}$

1. Data: Value to find $= 0D_{16}$

    Result: Carry $= 0$, indicating value found
             (H and L) $=$ BASE + 6 (address containing $0D_{16}$)

2. Data: Value to find $= 9B_{16}$

    Result: Carry $= 1$, indicating value not found

```
;                                                                          ;
;                                                                          ;
;                                                                          ;
;                                                                          ;
;          Title:        Binary Search                                     ;
;          Name:         BINSCH                                            ;
;                                                                          ;
;                                                                          ;
;                                                                          ;
;          Purpose:      Search an ordered array of unsigned bytes,        ;
;                        with a maximum size of 255 elements               ;
;                                                                          ;
;          Entry:        Register pair H = Base address of array           ;
;                        Register C = Size of array                        ;
;                        Register A = Byte to find                         ;
;                                                                          ;
;          Exit:         If the value is found then                        ;
;                          Carry flag = 0                                  ;
```

```
;                           Register pair H = Address of value
;                       else
;                           Carry flag = 1
;
;       Registers used: All
;
;       Time:               Approximately 123 cycles for each iteration of
;                           the search loop plus 57 cycles overhead for
;                           8080
;                           Approximately 119 cycles for each iteration of
;                           the search loop plus 53 cycles overhead for
;                           8085
;
;                           A binary search takes on the order of log
;                           base 2 of N searches, where N is the number of
;                           elements in the array.
;
;       Size:               Program 42 bytes
;
;
BINSCH:
        ;EXIT WITH CARRY SET IF NO ELEMENTS IN ARRAY
        INR     C               ;TEST ARRAY SIZE
        DCR     C
        STC                     ;SET CARRY IF CASE SIZE IS 0
        RZ                      ;RETURN INDICATING VALUE NOT FOUND
                                ; IF SIZE IS 0

        ;INITIALIZE LOWER BOUND, UPPER BOUND OF SEARCH AREA
        ;LOWER BOUND (DE) = BASE ADDRESS
        ;UPPER BOUND (HL) = ADDRESS OF LAST ELEMENT =
        ; BASE ADDRESS + SIZE - 1
        MOV     E,L             ;LOWER BOUND = BASE ADDRESS
        MOV     D,H
        MVI     B,0             ;EXTEND SIZE TO 16 BITS
        DAD     B               ;UPPER BOUND = BASE + SIZE - 1
        DCX     H
        ;SAVE VALUE BEING SOUGHT
        MOV     C,A             ;SAVE VALUE

        ;ITERATION OF BINARY SEARCH
        ; 1. COMPARE VALUE TO MIDDLE ELEMENT
        ; 2. IF THEY ARE NOT EQUAL, DISCARD HALF THAT
        ;    CANNOT POSSIBLY CONTAIN VALUE (BECAUSE OF ORDERING)
        ; 3. CONTINUE IF THERE IS ANYTHING LEFT TO SEARCH
LOOP:
        ;HL = UPPER BOUND
        ;DE = LOWER BOUND
        ;C = VALUE TO FIND
        ;FIND MIDDLE ELEMENT
        ;MIDDLE = (UPPER BOUND + LOWER BOUND) / 2
        PUSH    H               ;SAVE UPPER BOUND
        DAD     D               ;ADD UPPER BOUND AND LOWER BOUND
        MOV     A,H             ;DIVIDE 17-BIT SUM BY 2
```

```
        RAR
        MOV     H,A
        MOV     A,L
        RAR
        MOV     L,A
        MOV     A,M             ;GET MIDDLE ELEMENT

        ;COMPARE MIDDLE ELEMENT AND VALUE
        CMP     C               ;COMPARE MIDDLE ELEMENT AND VALUE
        JNC     TOOLRG          ;JUMP IF VALUE SAME OR LARGER

        ;MIDDLE VALUE LESS THAN VALUE
        ; SO CHANGE LOWER BOUND TO MIDDLE + 1
        ; SINCE EVERYTHING BELOW MIDDLE IS EVEN SMALLER
        XCHG                    ;LOWER BOUND = MIDDLE + 1
        INX     D
        POP     H               ;RESTORE UPPER BOUND
        JMP     CONT

        ;MIDDLE VALUE GREATER THAN OR EQUAL TO VALUE
        ; SO CHANGE UPPER BOUND TO MIDDLE - 1
        ; SINCE EVERYTHING ABOVE MIDDLE IS EVEN LARGER
        ;EXIT WITH CARRY CLEAR IF VALUE FOUND
TOOLRG:
        INX     SP              ;DISCARD OLD UPPER BOUND FROM STACK
        INX     SP
        RZ                      ;IF MIDDLE VALUE SAME AS VALUE
                                ; RETURN WITH CARRY CLEAR
                                ; AND HL = ADDRESS CONTAINING VALUE
        DCX     H               ;UPPER BOUND = MIDDLE - 1

        ;CONTINUE IF THERE IS ANYTHING LEFT TO BE SEARCHED
        ;NOTHING LEFT WHEN LOWER BOUND ABOVE UPPER BOUND
CONT:
        MOV     A,L             ;FORM UPPER BOUND - LOWER BOUND
        CMP     E
        MOV     A,H
        SBB     D
        JNC     LOOP            ;CONTINUE IF ANYTHING LEFT TO SEARCH

        ;NOTHING LEFT TO SEARCH, SO COULD NOT FIND VALUE
        ;RETURN WITH CARRY SET (MUST BE OR JNC WOULD HAVE BRANCHED)
        RET


;                                                                      ;
;                                                                      ;
;       SAMPLE EXECUTION                                               ;
;                                                                      ;
;                                                                      ;

SC9E:
        ;SEARCH FOR A VALUE THAT IS IN THE ARRAY
        LXI     H,BF            ;HL = BASE ADDRESS OF ARRAY
        LDA     BFSZ
```

```
        MOV     C,A             ;C = ARRAY SIZE IN BYTES
        MVI     A,7             ;A = VALUE TO FIND
        CALL    BINSCH          ;SEARCH
                                ;CARRY FLAG = 0 (VALUE FOUND)
                                ;HL = ADDRESS OF 7 IN ARRAY

        ;SEARCH FOR A VALUE THAT IS NOT IN THE ARRAY
        LXI     H,BF            ;HL = BASE ADDRESS OF ARRAY
        LDA     BFSZ
        MOV     C,A             ;C = ARRAY SIZE IN BYTES
        MVI     A,0             ;A = VALUE TO FIND
        CALL    BINSCH          ;SEARCH
                                ;CARRY FLAG = 1 (VALUE NOT FOUND)

        JMP     SC9E            ;LOOP FOR MORE TESTS

        ;DATA
SIZE    EQU     010H            ;SIZE OF ARRAY IN BYTES
BFSZ:   DB      SIZE            ;SIZE OF ARRAY IN BYTES

BF:     DB      1               ;BUFFER
        DB      2
        DB      4
        DB      5
        DB      7
        DB      9
        DB      10
        DB      11
        DB      23
        DB      50
        DB      81
        DB      123
        DB      191
        DB      199
        DB      250
        DB      255

        END
```

Quicksort (QSORT)

Arranges an array of unsigned word-length elements into ascending order using a quicksort algorithm. Each iteration selects an element and divides the array into two parts, one consisting of elements larger than the selected element and one consisting of elements smaller than the selected element. Elements equal to the selected element may end up in either part. The parts are then sorted recursively in the same way. The algorithm continues until all parts contain either no elements or only one element. An alternative is to stop recursion when a part contains few enough elements (say, less than 20) to make a bubble sort practical.

The parameters are the array's base address, the address of its last element, and the lowest available stack address. The array can thus occupy all available memory, as long as there is room for the stack. Since the procedures that obtain the selected element, compare elements, move forward and backward in the array, and swap elements are all subroutines, they could be changed readily to handle other types of elements.

Ideally, quicksort should divide the array in half during each iteration. How closely the procedure approaches this ideal depends on how well the selected element is chosen. Since this element serves as a midpoint or pivot, the best choice would be the central value, or median. Of course, the true median is unknown. A simple but reasonable approximation is to select the median of the first, middle, and last elements.

Procedure: The program first deals with the entire array. It selects the median of the current first, middle, and last elements as a central element. It moves that element to the first position and divides the array into two parts or partitions. It then operates recursively on the

---

Registers Used: All

Execution Time: Approximately N $*$ log$_2$ N loops through PARTLP plus 2 $*$ N $+$ 1 overhead calls to SORT. Each iteration of PARTLP takes approximately 200 cycles and each overhead call to SORT takes approximately 300 cycles. Thus, the total execution time is on the order of 200 $*$ N $*$ log$_2$ N $+$ 300 $*$ (2 $*$ N $+$ 1).

Program Size: 225 bytes

Data Memory Required: 8 bytes anywhere in RAM for pointers to the first and last elements of a partition (2 bytes starting at addresses FIRST and LAST, respectively), a pointer to the bottom of the stack (2 bytes starting at address STKBTM), and the original value of the stack pointer (2 bytes starting at address OLDSP)

Special Case: If the stack overflows (i.e., comes too close to its boundary), the program exits with the Carry flag set to 1.

---

parts, dividing them into parts and stopping when a part contains no elements or only one element. Since each recursion places six bytes on the stack, the program must guard against stack overflow by checking whether the stack has reached to within a small buffer of its lowest available position.

Note that the selected element always ends up in the correct position after an iteration. Therefore, it need not be included in either partition.

Assuming that the first element is #1, the rule for choosing the middle element is:

1. If the array has an odd number of elements, take the one in the center. For example, if the array has 11 elements, take #6.

2. If the array has an even number of elements and its base address is even, take the element on the lower (base address) side of the

center. For example, if the array starts in 0300_{16} and has 12 elements, take #6.

3. If the array has an even number of elements and its base address is odd, take the element on the upper side of the center. For example, if the array starts in 0301_{16} and has 12 elements, take #7.

Entry Conditions

Base address of array in H and L
Address of last word of array in D and E
Lowest available stack address in B and C

Exit Conditions

Array sorted into ascending order, considering the elements as unsigned words. Thus, the smallest unsigned word ends up stored starting at the base address.

Carry = 0 if the stack did not overflow and the result is proper. Carry = 1 if the stack overflowed and the final array is not sorted.

Example

1. Data: Length (size) of array = $0C_{16}$
            Elements = $2B_{16}$, 57_{16}, $1D_{16}$, 26_{16},
            22_{16}, $2E_{16}$, $0C_{16}$, 44_{16},
            17_{16}, $4B_{16}$, 37_{16}, 27_{16}

   Result: The result of the first iteration is

            Selected element = median of the first (#1 = $2B_{16}$), middle (#6 = $2E_{16}$), and last (#12 = 27_{16}) elements. The selected element is therefore #1 ($2B_{16}$), and no swapping is necessary since it is already in the first position.

            At the end of the iteration, the array is

            27_{16}, 17_{16}, $1D_{16}$, 26_{16},
            22_{16}, $0C_{16}$, $2B_{16}$, 44_{16},
            $2E_{16}$, $4B_{16}$, 37_{16}, 57_{16}

            The first partition, consisting of elements less than $2B_{16}$, is 27_{16}, 17_{16}, $1D_{16}$, 26_{16}, 22_{16}, and $0C_{16}$.

            The second partition, consisting of elements greater than $2B_{16}$, is 44_{16}, $2E_{16}$, $4B_{16}$, 37_{16}, and 57_{16}.

Note that the selected element ($2B_{16}$) is now in the correct position and need not be included in either partition.

The first partition may now be sorted recursively in the same way:

Selected element = median of the first (#1 = 27_{16}), middle (#3 = $1D_{16}$), and last (#7 = $0C_{16}$) elements. Here, #4 is the median and must be exchanged initially with #1.

The final order of the elements in the first partition is

   $0C_{16}$, 17_{16}, $1D_{16}$, 26_{16},
   22_{16}, 27_{16}.

The first partition of the first partition (consisting of elements less than $1D_{16}$) is $0C_{16}$, 17_{16}. We will call this the (1,1) partition for short.

The second partition of the first partition (consisting of elements greater than $1D_{16}$) is 26_{16}, 22_{16}, and 27_{16}.

As in the first iteration, the selected element ($1D_{16}$) is in the correct position and need not be considered further.

The (1,1) partition may now be sorted recursively as follows:

Selected element = median of the first (#1 = $0C_{16}$), middle (#1 = $0C_{16}$), and last (#2 = 17_{16}) elements. Thus the selected element is the first element (#1 = $0C_{16}$), and no initial swap is necessary.

The final order is obviously the same as the initial order and the two resulting partitions contain 0 and 1 element, respectively. Thus, the next iteration concludes the recursion, and then the other partitions are sorted by the same method. Obviously, quicksort's overhead is large when the number of elements is small. This is why one might use a bubble sort once quicksort has created small enough partitions.

Note that the example array does not contain any identical elements. During an iteration, elements that are the same as the selected element are never moved. Thus, they may end up in either partition. Strictly speaking, then, the two partitions consist of elements "less than or possibly equal to the selected element" and elements "greater than or possibly equal to the selected element."

References

Augenstein, M.J., and Tenenbaum, A.M. *Data Structures and PL/I Programming.* Englewood Cliffs, N.J.: Prentice-Hall, 1979, pp. 460–71. There is also a Pascal version of this book entitled *Data Structures Using Pascal* (Englewood Cliffs, N.J.: Prentice-Hall, 1982).

Bowles, K.L. *Microcomputer Problem Solving Using Pascal.* New York: Springer-Verlag, 1977.

Knuth, D.E. *The Art of Computer Programming, Volume 3: Searching and Sorting.* Reading, Mass.: Addison-Wesley, 1973, pp. 114–23.

```
;                                                                    ;
;                                                                    ;
;                                                                    ;
;                                                                    ;
;        Title:        Quicksort                                     ;
;        Name:         QSORT                                         ;
;                                                                    ;
;                                                                    ;
;                                                                    ;
;        Purpose:      Arrange an array of unsigned words into       ;
;                      ascending order using quicksort, with a       ;
;                      maximum size of 32,767 words                  ;
;                                                                    ;
;        Entry:        Register pair H = Address of first word in the;
;                                       array                        ;
;                      Register pair D = Address of last word in the ;
;                                       array                        ;
;                      Register pair B = Lowest available stack      ;
;                                       address                      ;
;                                                                    ;
;        Exit:         If the stack did not overflow then            ;
;                        array is sorted into ascending order.       ;
```

```
;                         Carry = 0                          ;
;                    else                                    ;
;                         Carry = 1                          ;
;                                                            ;
;    Registers used: All                                     ;
;                                                            ;
;    Time:              The timing is highly data-dependent but the    ;
;                       quicksort algorithm takes approximately        ;
;                       N * log base 2 of N loops through PARTLP. There ;
;                       will be 2 * N+1 calls to SORT. The number of    ;
;                       recursions will probably be a fraction of N but ;
;                       if all data is the same, the recursion could be ;
;                       up to N. Therefore the amount of stack space    ;
;                       should be maximized. NOTE: Each recursion level ;
;                       takes 6 bytes of stack space.                   ;
;                                                            ;
;                                                            ;
;                       In the above discussion N is the number of      ;
;                       array elements.                                 ;
;                                                            ;
;    Size:              Program 225 bytes                    ;
;                       Data      8 bytes                    ;
;                                                            ;
;
QSORT:
        ;WATCH FOR STACK OVERFLOW
        ;CALCULATE A THRESHOLD TO WARN OF OVERFLOW
        ; (10 BYTES FROM THE END OF THE STACK)
        ;SAVE THIS THRESHOLD FOR LATER COMPARISONS
        ;ALSO SAVE THE POSITION OF THIS ROUTINE'S RETURN ADDRESS
        ; IN THE EVENT WE MUST ABORT BECAUSE OF STACK OVERFLOW

        PUSH    H               ;SAVE BASE ADDRESS OF ARRAY
        LXI     H,10            ;ADD SMALL BUFFER (10 BYTES) TO
        DAD     B               ; LOWEST STACK ADDRESS
        SHLD    STKBTM          ;SAVE SUM AS BOTTOM OF STACK
                                ; FOR FIGURING WHEN TO ABORT
        LXI     H,2             ;SAVE POINTER TO RETURN ADDRESS
        DAD     SP              ; IN CASE WE MUST ABORT
        SHLD    OLDSP
        POP     H               ;RESTORE BASE ADDRESS

        ;WORK RECURSIVELY THROUGH THE QUICKSORT ALGORITHM AS
        ; FOLLOWS:
        ; 1. CHECK IF THE PARTITION CONTAINS 0 OR 1 ELEMENT.
        ;     MOVE UP A RECURSION LEVEL IF IT DOES.
        ; 2. USE MEDIAN TO OBTAIN A REASONABLE CENTRAL VALUE
        ;     FOR DIVIDING THE CURRENT PARTITION INTO TWO
        ;     PARTS.
        ; 3. MOVE THROUGH THE ARRAY SWAPPING ELEMENTS THAT
        ;     ARE OUT OF ORDER UNTIL ALL ELEMENTS BELOW THE
        ;     CENTRAL VALUE ARE AHEAD OF ALL ELEMENTS ABOVE
        ;     THE CENTRAL VALUE.  SUBROUTINE COMPARE
        ;     COMPARES ELEMENTS, SWAP EXCHANGES ELEMENTS,
        ;     PREV MOVES UPPER BOUNDARY DOWN ONE ELEMENT,
```

```
        ;     AND NEXT MOVES LOWER BOUNDARY UP ONE ELEMENT.
        ;  4. CHECK IF THE STACK IS ABOUT TO OVERFLOW.  IF IT
        ;     IS, ABORT AND EXIT.
        ;  5. ESTABLISH THE BOUNDARIES FOR THE FIRST PARTITION
        ;     (CONSISTING OF ELEMENTS LESS THAN THE CENTRAL VALUE)
        ;     AND SORT IT RECURSIVELY.
        ;  6. ESTABLISH THE BOUNDARIES FOR THE SECOND PARTITION
        ;     (CONSISTING OF ELEMENTS GREATER THAN THE CENTRAL
        ;     VALUE) AND SORT IT RECURSIVELY.
SORT:
        ;SAVE BASE ADDRESS AND NUMBER OF BYTES ON STACK
        SHLD    FIRST           ;SAVE FIRST IN LOCAL AREA
        XCHG
        SHLD    LAST            ;SAVE LAST IN LOCAL AREA

        ;CHECK IF PARTITION CONTAINS 0 OR 1 ELEMENTS.
        ; IT DOES IF FIRST IS EITHER LARGER THAN (0)
        ; OR EQUAL TO (1) LAST.
PARTION:
        ;STOP WHEN FIRST >= LAST
        ;DE = ADDRESS OF FIRST
        ;HL = ADDRESS OF LAST
        MOV     A,E             ;CALCULATE FIRST - LAST
        SUB     L
        MOV     A,D
        SBB     H
        RNC                     ;IF DIFFERENCE POSITIVE, RETURN
                                ; THIS PART IS SORTED

        ;USE MEDIAN TO FIND A REASONABLE CENTRAL ELEMENT
        ;MOVE CENTRAL ELEMENT TO FIRST POSITION
        CALL    MEDIAN          ;SELECT CENTRAL ELEMENT, MOVE IT
                                ; TO FIRST POSITION
        MVI     C,0             ;BIT 0 OF REGISTER C = DIRECTION
                                ; IF IT'S 0 THEN DIRECTION IS UP
                                ; ELSE DIRECTION IS DOWN

        ;REORDER ARRAY BY COMPARING OTHER ELEMENTS WITH THE
        ; CENTRAL ELEMENT.  START BY COMPARING THAT ELEMENT WITH
        ; LAST ELEMENT.  EACH TIME WE FIND AN ELEMENT THAT
        ; BELONGS IN THE FIRST PART (THAT IS, IT IS LESS THAN
        ; THE CENTRAL ELEMENT), SWAP IT INTO THE FIRST PART IF IT
        ; IS NOT ALREADY THERE AND MOVE THE BOUNDARY OF THE
        ; FIRST PART DOWN ONE ELEMENT.  SIMILARLY, EACH TIME WE
        ; FIND AN ELEMENT THAT BELONGS IN THE SECOND PART (THAT
        ; IS, IT IS GREATER THAN THE CENTRAL ELEMENT), SWAP IT
        ; INTO THE SECOND PART IF IT IS NOT ALREADY THERE AND MOVE
        ; THE BOUNDARY OF THE SECOND PART UP ONE ELEMENT.
        ;ULTIMATELY, THE BOUNDARIES COME TOGETHER
        ; AND THE DIVISION OF THE ARRAY IS THEN COMPLETE.
        ;NOTE THAT ELEMENTS EQUAL TO THE CENTRAL ELEMENT ARE NEVER
        ; SWAPPED AND SO MAY END UP IN EITHER PART.
PARTLP:
        ;LOOP SORTING UNEXAMINED PART OF PARTITION
        ; UNTIL THERE IS NOTHING LEFT IN IT
```

```
        MOV     A,E                 ;LOWER BOUNDARY - UPPER BOUNDARY
        SUB     L
        MOV     A,D
        SBB     H
        JNC     DONE                ;EXIT WHEN EVERYTHING EXAMINED

        ;COMPARE NEXT 2 ELEMENTS.  IF OUT OF ORDER, SWAP THEM
        ;AND CHANGE DIRECTION OF SEARCH
        ; IF FIRST > LAST THEN SWAP
        CALL    COMPARE             ;COMPARE ELEMENTS
        JC      OK                  ;JUMP IF ALREADY IN ASCENDING ORDER
        JZ      OK                  ; OR IF ELEMENTS EQUAL

        ;ELEMENTS OUT OF ORDER.  SWAP THEM
        CALL    SWAP                ;SWAP ELEMENTS
        INR     C                   ;CHANGE DIRECTION

        ;REDUCE SIZE OF UNEXAMINED AREA
        ;IF NEW ELEMENT LESS THAN CENTRAL ELEMENT, MOVE
        ; TOP BOUNDARY DOWN
        ;IF NEW ELEMENT GREATER THAN CENTRAL ELEMENT, MOVE
        ; BOTTOM BOUNDARY UP
        ;IF ELEMENTS EQUAL, CONTINUE IN LATEST DIRECTION
OK:
        MOV     A,C                 ;BIT O OF C TELLS WHICH WAY TO GO
        RAR
        JNC     UP                  ;JUMP IF MOVING UP
        XCHG
        CALL    NEXT                ;ELSE MOVE TOP BOUNDARY DOWN BY
        XCHG                        ; ONE ELEMENT
        JMP     PARTLP
UP:
        CALL    PREV                ;MOVE BOTTOM BOUNDARY UP BY
                                    ; ONE ELEMENT
        JMP     PARTLP

        ;THIS PARTITION HAS NOW BEEN SUBDIVIDED INTO TWO
        ; PARTITIONS. ONE STARTS AT THE TOP AND ENDS JUST
        ; ABOVE THE CENTRAL ELEMENT.  THE OTHER STARTS
        ; JUST BELOW THE CENTRAL ELEMENT AND CONTINUES
        ; TO THE BOTTOM.  THE CENTRAL ELEMENT IS NOW IN
        ; ITS PROPER SORTED POSITION AND NEED NOT BE
        ; INCLUDED IN EITHER PARTITION
DONE:
        ;FIRST CHECK WHETHER STACK MIGHT OVERFLOW
        ;IF IT IS GETTING TOO CLOSE TO THE BOTTOM, ABORT
        ; THE PROGRAM AND EXIT
        LXI     H,O                 ;CALCULATE STKBTM - SP
        DAD     SP
        LDA     STKBTM
        SUB     L
        LDA     STKBTM+1
        SBB     H
        JNC     ABORT               ;EXIT IF STACK TOO LARGE
```

```
                ;ESTABLISH BOUNDARIES FOR FIRST (LOWER) PARTITION
                ;LOWER BOUNDARY IS SAME AS BEFORE
                ;UPPER BOUNDARY IS ELEMENT JUST BELOW CENTRAL ELEMENT
                ;THEN RECURSIVELY QUICKSORT FIRST PARTITION
                PUSH    D               ;SAVE ADDRESS OF CENTRAL ELEMENT
                LHLD    LAST
                PUSH    H               ;SAVE ADDRESS OF LAST
                XCHG
                CALL    PREV            ;CALCULATE LAST FOR FIRST PART
                XCHG
                LHLD    FIRST           ;FIRST IS SAME AS BEFORE
                CALL    SORT            ;QUICKSORT FIRST PART

                ;ESTABLISH BOUNDARIES FOR SECOND (UPPER) PARTITION
                ;UPPER BOUNDARY IS SAME AS BEFORE
                ;LOWER BOUNDARY IS ELEMENT JUST ABOVE CENTRAL ELEMENT
                ;THEN RECURSIVELY QUICKSORT SECOND PARTITION
                POP     D               ;LAST IS SAME AS BEFORE
                POP     H               ;CALCULATE FIRST FOR SECOND PART
                CALL    NEXT
                CALL    SORT            ;QUICKSORT SECOND PART
                ORA     A               ;CARRY = 0 FOR NO ERRORS
                RET

                ;ERROR EXIT
ABORT:          LHLD    OLDSP           ;TOP OF STACK IS ORIGINAL
                SPHL                    ; RETURN ADDRESS
                STC                     ;INDICATE ERROR IN SORT
                RET                     ;RETURN TO ORGINAL CALLER


                ;*******************************
                ;ROUTINE: MEDIAN
                ;PURPOSE: DETERMINE WHICH ELEMENT IN A PARTITION
                ;          SHOULD BE USED AS THE CENTRAL ELEMENT OR PIVOT
                ;ENTRY: DE = ADDRESS OF FIRST ELEMENT
                ;       HL = ADDRESS OF LAST ELEMENT
                ;EXIT:  DE IS ADDRESS OF CENTRAL ELEMENT
                ;REGISTERS USED: AF,BC,DE
                ;*******************************
MEDIAN:
                ;DETERMINE ADDRESS OF MIDDLE ELEMENT
                ; MIDDLE := ALIGNED(FIRST + LAST) DIV 2
                MOV     A,L             ;ADD ADDRESSES OF FIRST, LAST
                ADD     E               ; WITHOUT DESTROYING EITHER
                MOV     C,A             ; (MUST USE 8-BIT ADD, NOT 16-BIT)
                MOV     A,H
                ADC     D
                RAR                     ;DIVIDE UPPER BYTE OF SUM BY 2
                MOV     B,A
                MOV     A,C
                RAR                     ;DIVIDE LOWER BYTE OF SUM BY 2
                ANI     0FEH            ;CLEAR BIT 0 FOR ALIGNMENT
                MOV     C,A
                MOV     A,E             ;ALIGN MIDDLE TO BOUNDARY OF FIRST
                RAR                     ; CARRY = BIT 0 OF FIRST
```

```
        MOV     A,C
        ACI     0               ;MAKE BIT 0 OF MIDDLE SAME
        MOV     C,A             ; AS BIT 0 OF FIRST

;DETERMINE MEDIAN OF FIRST, MIDDLE, LAST ELEMENTS
;COMPARE FIRST AND MIDDLE
        PUSH    H               ;SAVE LAST
        MOV     L,C
        MOV     H,B
        CALL    COMPARE         ;COMPARE FIRST AND MIDDLE
        POP     H               ;RESTORE LAST
        JNC     MIDD1           ;JUMP IF FIRST >= MIDDLE

;WE KNOW (MIDDLE > FIRST)
; SO COMPARE MIDDLE AND LAST
        PUSH    D               ;SAVE FIRST
        MOV     E,C
        MOV     D,B
        CALL    COMPARE         ;COMPARE MIDDLE AND LAST
        POP     D               ;RESTORE FIRST
        JC      SWAPMF          ;JUMP IF LAST >= MIDDLE
        JZ      SWAPMF          ; MIDDLE IS MEDIAN

;WE KNOW (MIDDLE > FIRST) AND (MIDDLE > LAST)
; SO COMPARE FIRST AND LAST
        CALL    COMPARE         ;COMPARE FIRST AND LAST
        RNC                     ;RETURN IF LAST >= FIRST
                                ; FIRST IS MEDIAN
        JMP     SWAPLF          ;ELSE LAST IS MEDIAN, SO
                                ; SWAP LAST AND FIRST

;WE KNOW (FIRST >= MIDDLE)
; SO COMPARE FIRST AND LAST
MIDD1:
        CALL    COMPARE         ;COMPARE LAST AND FIRST
        RC                      ;RETURN IF LAST >= FIRST
        RZ                      ; FIRST IS MEDIAN

;WE KNOW (FIRST >= MIDDLE) AND (FIRST > LAST)
; SO COMPARE MIDDLE AND LAST
        PUSH    D               ;SAVE FIRST
        MOV     E,C             ;DE = MIDDLE
        MOV     D,B
        CALL    COMPARE         ;COMPARE MIDDLE AND LAST
        POP     D               ;RESTORE FIRST
        JC      SWAPLF          ;JUMP IF LAST > MIDDLE
                                ; LAST .IS MEDIAN

;MIDDLE IS MEDIAN, SWAP IT WITH FIRST
SWAPMF:
        PUSH    H               ;SAVE LAST
        MOV     L,C             ;HL = ADDRESS OF MIDDLE
        MOV     H,B
        CALL    SWAP            ;SWAP MIDDLE, FIRST
        POP     H               ;RESTORE LAST
        RET
```

```
                ;LAST IS MEDIAN, SWAP IT WITH FIRST
SWAPLF:
        CALL    SWAP            ;SWAP FIRST, LAST
        RET


                ;********************************
                ;ROUTINE: NEXT
                ;PURPOSE: MAKE HL POINT TO NEXT ELEMENT
                ;ENTRY: HL = ADDRESS OF CURRENT ELEMENT
                ;EXIT:  HL = ADDRESS OF NEXT ELEMENT
                ;REGISTERS USED: HL
                ;********************************
NEXT:
        INX     H                       ;INCREMENT TO NEXT ELEMENT
        INX     H
        RET


                ;********************************
                ;ROUTINE: PREV
                ;PURPOSE: MAKE HL POINT TO PREVIOUS ELEMENT
                ;ENTRY: HL = ADDRESS OF CURRENT ELEMENT
                ;EXIT:  HL = ADDRESS OF PREVIOUS ELEMENT
                ;REGISTERS USED: HL
                ;********************************
PREV:
        DCX     H                       ;DECREMENT TO PREVIOUS ELEMENT
        DCX     H
        RET


                ;********************************
                ;ROUTINE: COMPARE
                ;PURPOSE: COMPARE DATA ITEMS POINTED TO BY DE AND HL
                ;ENTRY: DE = ADDRESS OF DATA ELEMENT 1
                ;       HL = ADDRESS OF DATA ELEMENT 2
                ;EXIT:  IF ELEMENT 1 > ELEMENT 2 THEN
                ;            C = 0
                ;            Z = 0
                ;       IF ELEMENT 1 < ELEMENT 2 THEN
                ;            C = 1
                ;            Z = 0
                ;       IF ELEMENT 1 = ELEMENT 2 THEN
                ;            C = 0
                ;            Z = 1
                ;REGISTERS USED: AF
                ;********************************
COMPARE:
        INX     H                       ;POINT TO HIGH BYTES
        INX     D
        LDAX    D
        CMP     M                       ;COMPARE HIGH BYTES
        DCX     D                       ;POINT TO LOW BYTES
        DCX     H
        RNZ                             ;RETURN IF HIGH BYTES NOT EQUAL
        LDAX    D                       ;OTHERWISE, COMPARE LOW BYTES
        CMP     M
        RET
```

```
        ;********************************
        ;ROUTINE: SWAP
        ;PURPOSE: SWAP ELEMENTS POINTED TO BY DE,HL
        ;ENTRY: DE = ADDRESS OF ELEMENT 1
        ;          HL = ADDRESS OF ELEMENT 2
        ;EXIT:  ELEMENTS SWAPPED
        ;REGISTERS USED: AF,B
        ;********************************
SWAP:
        ;SWAP LOW BYTES
        MOV     B,M             ;GET ELEMENT 2
        LDAX    D               ;GET ELEMENT 1
        MOV     M,A             ;STORE NEW ELEMENT 2
        MOV     A,B
        STAX    D               ;STORE NEW ELEMENT 1
        INX     H
        INX     D

        ;SWAP HIGH BYTES
        MOV     B,M             ;GET ELEMENT 2
        LDAX    D               ;GET ELEMENT 1
        MOV     M,A             ;STORE NEW ELEMENT 2
        MOV     A,B
        STAX    D               ;STORE NEW ELEMENT 1
        DCX     H
        DCX     D
        RET

        ;DATA SECTION
FIRST:  DS      2               ;POINTER TO FIRST ELEMENT OF PART
LAST:   DS      2               ;POINTER TO LAST ELEMENT OF PART
STKBTM: DS      2               ;THRESHOLD FOR STACK OVERFLOW
OLDSP:  DS      2               ;POINTER TO ORIGINAL RETURN ADDRESS


;                                                                    ;
;                                                                    ;
;       SAMPLE EXECUTION                                             ;
;                                                                    ;
;                                                                    ;

SC9F:
        ;SORT AN ARRAY BETWEEN BEGBUF (FIRST ELEMENT)
        ; AND ENDBUF (LAST ELEMENT)
        ;START STACK AT 5000 HEX AND ALLOW IT TO EXPAND
        ; AS FAR AS 4F00 HEX
        LXI     SP,5000H        ;SET UP A STACK AREA
        LXI     B,4F00H         ;BC = LOWEST AVAILABLE STACK ADDRESS
        LXI     H,BEGBUF        ;HL = ADDRESS OF FIRST ELEMENT OF ARRAY
        LXI     D,ENDBUF        ;DE = ADDRESS OF LAST ELEMENT OF ARRAY
        CALL    QSORT           ; SORT
                                ;RESULT FOR TEST DATA IS
                                ; 0,1,2,3, ... ,14,15

        JMP     SC9F            ;LOOP FOR MORE TESTS
```

```
            ;DATA SECTION
BEGBUF:  DW        15
         DW        14
         DW        13
         DW        12
         DW        11
         DW        10
         DW         9
         DW         8
         DW         7
         DW         6
         DW         5
         DW         4
         DW         3
         DW         2
         DW         1
ENDBUF:  DW         0

         END
```

Tests a RAM area specified by a base address and a length in bytes. Writes the values 0, FF_{16}, AA_{16} (10101010_2), and 55_{16} (01010101_2) into each byte and checks whether they can be read back correctly. Places 1 in each bit position of each byte and checks whether it can be read back correctly with all other bits cleared. Clears the Carry flag if all tests run correctly; if it finds an error, it exits immediately, setting the Carry flag and returning the test value and the address at which the error occurred.

Procedure: The program performs the single value tests (with 0, FF_{16}, AA_{16}, and 55_{16}) by first filling the memory area and then comparing each byte with the specified value. Filling the entire area first should provide enough delay between writing and reading to detect a failure to retain data (perhaps caused by improperly designed refresh circuitry). The program then performs the walking bit test, starting with bit 7; here it writes the data into memory and attempts to read it back immediately for a comparison.

Registers Used: All

Execution Time: Approximately 754 cycles per byte tested plus 485 cycles overhead (8080) or 756 cycles per byte tested plus 481 cycles overhead (8085)

Program Size: 83 bytes

Data Memory Required: None

Special Cases:

1. An area size of 0000_{16} causes an immediate exit with no memory tested. The Carry flag is cleared to indicate no errors.

2. Since the routine changes all bytes in the tested area, using it to test an area that includes itself will have unpredictable results.

Note that Case 1 means this routine cannot be asked to test the entire memory. Such a request would be meaningless anyway since it would require the routine to test itself.

3. Testing a ROM causes a return with an error indication after the first occasion on which the test value differs from the memory's contents.

Entry Conditions

Base address of test area in H and L
Size of test area in bytes in D and E

Exit Conditions

1. If an error is found,
   Carry = 1
   Address containing error in H and L
   Test value in A.

2. If no error is found,
   Carry = 0
   All bytes in test area contain 0.

Example

1. Data: Base address $= 0380_{16}$
                 Length (size) of area $= 0200_{16}$

    Result: Area tested is the 0200_{16} bytes starting at address 0380_{16}; that is, addresses 0380_{16} through $057F_{16}$. The order of the tests is

          1. Write and read 0

2. Write and read FF_{16}
3. Write and read AA_{16} (10101010_2)
4. Write and read 55_{16} (01010101_2)
5. Walking bit test, starting with 1 in bit 7. That is, start with 10000000_2 (80_{16}) and move the 1 one position right for each subsequent test of a byte.

```
;                                                              ;
;                                                              ;
;                                                              ;
;                                                              ;
;        Title:          RAM Test                              ;
;        Name:           RAMTST                                ;
;                                                              ;
;                                                              ;
;                                                              ;
;        Purpose:        Test a RAM (read/write memory) area:  ;
;                          1. Write all 0 and test             ;
;                          2. Write all FF hex and test        ;
;                          3. Write all AA hex and test        ;
;                          4. Write all 55 hex and test        ;
;                          5. Shift a single 1 through each bit,;
;                             while clearing all other bits.   ;
;                                                              ;
;                        If the program finds an error, it exits;
;                        immediately with the Carry flag set and;
;                        indicates the test value and where the;
;                        error occurred.                       ;
;                                                              ;
;        Entry:          Register pair H = Base address of test area;
;                        Register pair D = Size of area in bytes;
;                                                              ;
;        Exit:           If there are no errors then           ;
;                          Carry flag equals 0                 ;
;                          test area contains 0 in all bytes   ;
;                        else                                  ;
;                          Carry flag equals 1                 ;
;                          Register pair H = Address of error  ;
;                          Register A = Test value             ;
;                                                              ;
;        Registers used: All                                   ;
;                                                              ;
;        Time:           Approximately 754 cycles per byte plus ;
;                        485 cycles overhead for 8080          ;
;                        Approximately 756 cycles per byte plus ;
;                        481 cycles overhead for 8085          ;
```

```
;                                                                          ;
;         Size:              Program 83 bytes                              ;
;                                                                          ;
;                                                                          ;

RAMTST:
          ;EXIT WITH NO ERRORS IF AREA SIZE IS 0
          MOV     A,D               ;TEST AREA SIZE
          ORA     E
          RZ                        ;EXIT WITH NO ERRORS IF SIZE IS ZERO

          ;FILL MEMORY WITH 0 AND TEST
          MVI     C,0
          CALL    FILCMP
          RC                        ;EXIT IF ERROR FOUND

          ;FILL MEMORY WITH FF HEX (ALL 1'S) AND TEST
          MVI     C,0FFH
          CALL    FILCMP
          RC                        ;EXIT IF ERROR FOUND

          ;FILL MEMORY WITH AA HEX (ALTERNATING 1'S AND 0'S) AND TEST
          MVI     C,0AAH
          CALL    FILCMP
          RC                        ;EXIT IF ERROR FOUND

          ;FILL MEMORY WITH 55 HEX (ALTERNATING 0'S AND 1'S) AND TEST
          MVI     C,55H
          CALL    FILCMP
          RC                        ;EXIT IF ERROR FOUND

          ;PERFORM WALKING BIT TEST. PLACE A 1 IN BIT 7 AND
          ; SEE IF IT CAN BE READ BACK.  THEN MOVE THE 1 TO
          ; BITS 6, 5, 4, 3, 2, 1, AND 0 AND SEE IF IT CAN
          ; BE READ BACK
WLKLP:
          MVI     A,10000000B       ;MAKE BIT 7 1, ALL OTHER BITS 0
WLKLP1:
          MOV     M,A               ;STORE TEST PATTERN IN MEMORY
          CMP     M                 ;TRY TO READ IT BACK
          STC                       ;SET CARRY IN CASE OF ERROR
          RNZ                       ;RETURN IF ERROR
          RRC                       ;ROTATE PATTERN TO MOVE 1 RIGHT
          CPI     10000000B
          JNZ     WLKLP1            ;CONTINUE UNTIL 1 IS BACK IN BIT 7
          MVI     M,0               ;CLEAR BYTE JUST CHECKED
          INX     H
          DCX     D                 ;DECREMENT AND TEST 16-BIT COUNTER
          MOV     A,D
          ORA     E
          JNZ     WLKLP             ;CONTINUE UNTIL MEMORY TESTED
          RET                       ;NO ERRORS (NOTE ORA E CLEARS CARRY)
```

```
;****************************************
;ROUTINE: FILCMP
;PURPOSE: FILL MEMORY WITH A VALUE AND TEST
;         THAT IT CAN BE READ BACK
;ENTRY: C = TEST VALUE
;       HL = BASE ADDRESS
;       DE = SIZE OF AREA IN BYTES
;EXIT:  IF NO ERRORS THEN
;          CARRY FLAG EQUALS 0
;       ELSE
;          CARRY FLAG EQUALS 1
;          HL = ADDRESS OF ERROR
;          DE = SIZE OF AREA IN BYTES
;          BC = BASE ADDRESS
;          A = TEST VALUE
;REGISTERS USED: ALL
;****************************************
FILCMP:
       PUSH    H               ;SAVE BASE ADDRESS
       PUSH    D               ;SAVE SIZE OF AREA

       ;FILL MEMORY WITH TEST VALUE
FILLP:
       MOV     M,C             ;FILL A BYTE WITH TEST VALUE
       INX     H               ;INCREMENT TO NEXT BYTE
       DCX     D
       MOV     A,D
       ORA     E
       JNZ     FILLP           ;CONTINUE UNTIL ENTIRE AREA FILLED

       POP     D               ;RESTORE SIZE OF AREA
       POP     H               ;RESTORE BASE ADDRESS
       PUSH    H               ;SAVE BASE ADDRESS
       PUSH    D               ;SAVE SIZE OF AREA

       ;COMPARE MEMORY AND TEST VALUE
CMPLP:
       MOV     A,M             ;GET VALUE FROM MEMORY
       CMP     C               ;IS IT THE TEST VALUE?
       JNZ     CMPER           ;NO, EXIT INDICATING AN ERROR
       INX     H
       DCX     D               ;TEST 16-BIT BYTE COUNT
       MOV     A,D
       ORA     E
       JNZ     CMPLP           ;CONTINUE UNTIL ALL BYTES COMPARED

       ;NO ERRORS FOUND, CARRY ALREADY CLEARED (BY ORA E)
       POP     D               ;DE = SIZE OF AREA IN BYTES
       POP     H               ;HL = BASE ADDRESS
       RET                     ;EXIT (ORA E LEAVES CARRY 0)

       ;ERROR EXIT, SET CARRY
       ;HL = ADDRESS OF ERROR
       ;A = TEST VALUE
```

```
CMPER:
        MOV     A,C             ;A = TEST VALUE
        POP     D               ;DE = SIZE OF AREA IN BYTES
        POP     B               ;BC = BASE ADDRESS
        STC                     ;SET CARRY INDICATING AN ERROR
        RET


;                                                               ;
;                                                               ;
;       SAMPLE EXECUTION                                        ;
;                                                               ;
;                                                               ;

SC9G:
        ;TEST RAM FROM 2000 HEX THROUGH 300F HEX
        ; SIZE OF AREA = 1010 HEX BYTES
        LXI     H,2000H         ;HL = BASE ADDRESS
        LXI     D,1010H         ;DE = NUMBER OF BYTES
        CALL    RAMTST          ;TEST MEMORY
                                ;CARRY FLAG SHOULD BE 0

        JMP     SC9G            ;LOOP FOR MORE TESTING

        END
```

Transfers control to an address selected from a table according to an index. The addresses are stored in the usual 8080/8085 format (less significant byte first), starting at address JMPTAB. The size of the table (number of addresses) is a constant LENSUB, which must be less than or equal to 128. If the index is greater than or equal to LENSUB, the program returns control immediately with the Carry flag set to 1.

Procedure: The program first checks if the index is greater than or equal to the size of the table (LENSUB). If it is, the program returns control with the Carry flag set. If it is not, the program obtains the starting address of the appropriate subroutine from the table and jumps to it.

Registers Used: AF

Execution Time: 118 cycles (8080) or 116 cycles (8085) overhead, besides the time required to execute the actual subroutine

Program Size: 21 bytes plus 2 * LENSUB bytes for the table of starting addresses, where LENSUB is the number of subroutines

Data Memory Required: None

Special Case: Entry with an index greater than or equal to LENSUB causes an immediate exit with the Carry flag set to 1.

Entry Conditions

Index in A

Exit Conditions

If (A) is greater than LENSUB, an immediate return with Carry = 1. Otherwise, control is transferred to the appropriate subroutine as if an indexed call had been performed. The return address remains at the top of the stack.

Example

1. Data: LENSUB (size of subroutine table) = 03
Table consists of addresses SUB0, SUB1, and SUB2.
Index = (A) = 02

   Result: Control transferred to address SUB2 (PC = SUB2).

```
;
;
;
;
;                Title:      Jump Table
;                Name:       JTAB
;
```

```
;
;
;
;
;
;
```

346

```
;                                                               ;
;                                                               ;
;                                                               ;
;       Purpose:        Given an index, jump to the subroutine with    ;
;                       that index in a table                   ;
;                                                               ;
;       Entry:          Register A is the subroutine number (0 to      ;
;                           LENSUB-1, the number of subroutines).;
;                           LENSUB must be less than or equal to ;
;                           128.                                ;
;                                                               ;
;       Exit:           If the routine number is valid then     ;
;                         execute the routine                   ;
;                       else                                    ;
;                         Carry flag equals 1                   ;
;                                                               ;
;       Registers used: AF                                      ;
;                                                               ;
;       Time:           118 cycles plus execution time of subroutine   ;
;                       for 8080                                ;
;                       116 cycles plus execution time of subroutine   ;
;                       for 8085                                ;
;                                                               ;
;       Size:           Program 21 bytes plus size of table (2*LENSUB) ;
;                                                               ;
;                                                               ;
;                                                               ;
        ;EXIT WITH CARRY SET IF ROUTINE NUMBER IS INVALID
        ;THAT IS, IF IT IS TOO LARGE FOR TABLE (>LENSUB - 1)
JTAB:
        CPI     LENSUB          ;COMPARE ROUTINE NUMBER, TABLE SIZE
        CMC                     ;COMPLEMENT CARRY FOR ERROR INDICATOR
        RC                      ;RETURN IF ROUTINE NUMBER TOO LARGE
                                ; WITH CARRY SET

        ;INDEX INTO TABLE OF WORD-LENGTH ADDRESSES
        ; LEAVE REGISTER PAIRS UNCHANGED SO THEY CAN BE USED FOR
        ; PASSING PARAMETERS
        PUSH    H               ;SAVE HL
        ADD     A               ;DOUBLE INDEX FOR WORD-LENGTH ENTRIES
        LXI     H,JMPTAB        ;INDEX INTO TABLE USING 8-BIT
        ADD     L               ; ADDITION TO AVOID DISTURBING
        MOV     L,A             ; ANOTHER REGISTER PAIR
        MVI     A,0
        ADC     H
        MOV     H,A             ;ACCESS ROUTINE ADDRESS

        ;OBTAIN ROUTINE ADDRESS FROM TABLE AND TRANSFER CONTROL
        ; TO IT, LEAVING ALL REGISTER PAIRS UNCHANGED
        MOV     A,M             ;MOVE ROUTINE ADDRESS TO HL
        INX     H
        MOV     H,M
        MOV     L,A
        XTHL                    ;RESTORE OLD HL, PUSH ROUTINE ADDRESS
```

```
        RET                     ;JUMP TO ROUTINE
LENSUB  EQU     3               ;NUMBER OF SUBROUTINES IN TABLE

JMPTAB:                         ;JUMP TABLE
        DW      SUB0            ;ROUTINE 0
        DW      SUB1            ;ROUTINE 1
        DW      SUB2            ;ROUTINE 2

        ;THREE TEST SUBROUTINES FOR JUMP TABLE
SUB0:
        MVI     A,1             ;TEST ROUTINE 0 SETS (A) = 1
        RET

SUB1:
        MVI     A,2             ;TEST ROUTINE 1 SETS (A) = 2
        RET

SUB2:
        MVI     A,3             ;TEST ROUTINE 2 SETS (A) = 3
       ⸍RET



;                                                               ;
;                                                               ;
;       SAMPLE EXECUTION                                        ;
;                                                               ;
;                                                               ;

SC9H:
        SUB     A               ;EXECUTE ROUTINE 0
        CALL    JTAB            ; AFTER EXECUTION, (A) = 1
        MVI     A,1             ;EXECUTE ROUTINE 1
        CALL    JTAB            ; AFTER EXECUTION, (A) = 2
        MVI     A,2             ;EXECUTE ROUTINE 2
        CALL    JTAB            ; AFTER EXECUTION, (A) = 3
        MVI     A,3             ;EXECUTE ROUTINE 3
        CALL    JTAB            ; AFTER EXECUTION, CARRY = 1
        JMP     SC9H            ;LOOP FOR MORE TESTS

        END
```

Reads a line of ASCII characters ending with a carriage return and saves them in a buffer. Defines the control characters Control H (08 hex), which deletes the latest character, and Control X (18 hex), which deletes the entire line. Sends a bell character (07 hex) to the terminal if the buffer overflows. Echoes each character placed in the buffer. Echoes non-printable characters as an up arrow or caret (^) followed by the printable equivalent (see Table 10-1). Sends a new line sequence (typically carriage return, line feed) to the terminal before exiting.

RDLINE assumes the following system-dependent subroutines:

1. RDCHAR reads a character from the terminal and puts it in the accumulator.

2. WRCHAR sends the character in the accumulator to the terminal.

3. WRNEWL sends a new line sequence to the terminal.

These subroutines are assumed to change all user registers.

RDLINE is an example of a terminal input handler. The control characters and I/O subroutines in a real system will, of course, be computer-dependent. A specific example in the listing is for a computer running the CP/M operating system with a standard Basic Disk Operating System (BDOS) accessed by calling memory address 0005_{16}. Table 10-2 lists commonly used CP/M BDOS functions. For more information on CP/M, see Thom Hogan, *Osborne CP/M User Guide,* Second Edition (Berkeley: Osborne/McGraw-Hill, 1982).

Procedure: The program starts the loop by reading a character. If the character is a carriage return, the program sends a new line sequence to the terminal and exits. Otherwise, it checks for the special characters Control H and Control X. If the buffer is not empty, Control H makes the program decrement the buffer pointer and character count by 1 and send a backspace string (cursor left, space, cursor left) to the terminal. Control X makes the program delete characters until it empties the buffer.

If the character is not special, the program determines whether the buffer is full. If it is, the program sends a bell character to the terminal. If not, the program stores the character in the buffer, echoes it to the terminal, and increments the character count and buffer pointer.

Before echoing a character or deleting one from the display, the program must determine whether the character is printable. If it is not (that is, the character is a non-printable ASCII control code), the program must display or delete two characters, the control indicator (up arrow or caret), and the printable equivalent (see Table 10-1). Note, however, that the character is stored in its non-printable form.

Registers Used: All

Execution Time: Approximately 158 (8080) or 154 (8085) cycles to place an ordinary character in the buffer, not including the execution time of RDCHAR or WRCHAR

Program Size: 160 bytes

Data Memory Required: None

Special Cases:

1. Typing Control H (delete one character) or Control X (delete the entire line) when the buffer is empty has no effect.

2. The program discards an ordinary character received when the buffer is full and sends a bell character to the terminal (ringing the bell).

349

Table 10-1. ASCII Control Characters and Printable Equivalents

Name	Hex Value	Printable Equivalent	Name	Hex Value	Printable Equivalent
NUL	00	Control @	DLE	10	Control P
SOH	01	Control A	DC1	11	Control Q
STX	02	Control B	DC2	12	Control R
ETX	03	Control C	DC3	13	Control S
EOT	04	Control D	DC4	14	Control T
ENQ	05	Control E	NAK	15	Control U
ACK	06	Control F	SYN	16	Control V
BEL	07	Control G	ETB	17	Control W
BS	08	Control H	CAN	18	Control X
HT	09	Control I	EM	19	Control Y
LF	0A	Control J	SUB	1A	Control Z
VT	0B	Control K	ESC	1B	Control [
FF	0C	Control L	FS	1C	Control \
CR	0D	Control M	GS	1D	Control]
SO	0E	Control N	RS	1E	Control ^
SI	0F	Control O	VS	1F	Control _

Table 10-2. BDOS Functions for CP/M 2.0

Function Number (Decimal in Register C)	Function Name	Input Parameters	Output Parameters
0	System Reset	None	None
1	Console Input	None	A = ASCII character
2	Console Output	E = ASCII character	None
3	Reader Input	None	A = ASCII character
4	Punch Output	E = ASCII character	None
5	List Output	E = ASCII character	None
6	Direct Console Input	E = FF_{16}	A = ASCII character or 00 if no character is available
6	Direct Console Output	E = ASCII character	None
7	Get I/O Byte	None	A = IOBYTE
8	Set I/O Byte	E = IOBYTE	None
9	Print String	DE = String Address	None
10	Read Console Buffer	DE = Buffer Address	(Data in buffer)
11	Get Console Status	None	A = 00 (no character) or A = FF_{16} (character ready)

Entry Conditions

Base address of buffer in H and L
Length (size) of buffer in bytes in A

Exit Conditions

Number of characters in the buffer in A

Examples

1. Data: Line from keyboard is 'ENTERcr'

   Result: Character count = 5 (line length)
   Buffer contains 'ENTER'
   'ENTER' is sent to terminal, followed by a
   new line sequence (typically either carriage
   return, line feed or just carriage return).
   Note that the 'cr' (carriage return) character
   does not appear in the buffer.

2. Data: Line from keyboard is 'DMcontrolHNcontrol
   XENTETcontrolHRcr'.

   Result: Character count = 5 (length of final line)
   Buffer contains 'ENTER'
   'DM BackspaceStringN BackspaceString
   BackspaceStringENTET BackspaceString
   R' is sent to terminal, followed by a new
   line sequence. The Backspace String deletes
   a character from the screen and moves the
   cursor left one space.
   The sequence of operations is as follows:

Character Typed	Initial Buffer	Final Buffer	Sent to Terminal
D	Empty	'D'	D
M	'D'	'DM'	M
Control H	'DM'	'D'	Backspace string
N	'D'	'DN'	N
Control X	'DN'	Empty	2 Backspace strings
E	Empty	'E'	E
N	'E'	'EN'	N
T	'EN'	'ENT'	T
E	'ENT'	'ENTE'	E
T	'ENTE'	'ENTET'	T
Control H	'ENTET'	'ENTE'	Backspace string
R	'ENTE'	'ENTER'	R
cr	'ENTER'	'ENTER'	New line string

What has happened is:

a. The operator types 'D', 'M'.

b. The operator sees that 'M' is wrong (it should be 'N'), types Control H to delete it, and types 'N'.

c. The operator then sees that the initial 'D' is also wrong (it should be 'E'). Since the error is not in the latest character, the operator types Control X to delete the entire line and then types 'ENTET'.

d. The operator sees that the second 'T' is wrong (it should be 'R'), types Control H to delete it, and types 'R'.

e. The operator types a carriage return to end the line.

```
;                                                              ;
;                                                              ;
;                                                              ;
;                                                              ;
;    Title:       Read a Line from a Terminal                  ;
;    Name:        RDLINE                                       ;
;                                                              ;
;                                                              ;
```

```
;                                                                      ;
;         Purpose:        Read characters from CP/M BDOS CON: device   ;
;                         until carriage return encountered. All control;
;                         characters but the following are placed in the;
;                         buffer and displayed as the equivalent printable;
;                         ASCII character preceded by a caret.         ;
;                            Control H: Delete last character          ;
;                            Control X: Delete entire line             ;
;                                                                      ;
;         Entry:          Register pair H = Base address of buffer     ;
;                         Register A = Length of buffer in bytes       ;
;                                                                      ;
;         Exit:           Register A = Number of characters in buffer  ;
;                                                                      ;
;         Registers used: All                                          ;
;                                                                      ;
;         Time:           Not applicable                               ;
;                                                                      ;
;         Size:           Program 160 bytes                            ;
;                                                                      ;
;                                                                      ;


            ;EQUATES
BELL     EQU     07H         ;BELL CHARACTER (RINGS BELL ON TERMINAL)
BSKEY    EQU     08H         ;BACKSPACE KEYBOARD CHARACTER
CR       EQU     0DH         ;CARRIAGE RETURN FOR CONSOLE
CRKEY    EQU     0DH         ;CARRIAGE RETURN KEYBOARD CHARACTER
CSRLFT   EQU     08H         ;MOVE CURSOR LEFT FOR CONSOLE
DELKEY   EQU     18H         ;DELETE LINE KEYBOARD CHARACTER
LF       EQU     0AH         ;LINE FEED FOR CONSOLE
SPACE    EQU     20H         ;SPACE CHARACTER (ALSO MARKS END OF CONTROLS)
UPARRW   EQU     5EH         ;UP ARROW OR CARET USED AS CONTROL INDICATOR

BDOS     EQU     0005H       ;BDOS ENTRY POINT
DIRIO    EQU     6           ;BDOS DIRECT I/O FUNCTION
PSTRG    EQU     9           ;BDOS PRINT STRING FUNCTION
STERM    EQU     '$'         ;CP/M STRING TERMINATOR

RDLINE:
         MOV     C,A              ;C = BUFFER LENGTH
                                  ;HL = BUFFER POINTER

         ;INITIALIZE CHARACTER COUNT TO ZERO
INIT:
         MVI     B,0              ;CHARACTER COUNT = 0

         ;READ CHARACTERS UNTIL A CARRIAGE RETURN IS TYPED
RDLOOP:
         CALL    RDCHAR           ;READ CHARACTER FROM KEYBOARD - NO ECHO

         ;CHECK FOR CARRIAGE RETURN, EXIT IF FOUND
         CPI     CRKEY
         JZ      EXITRD           ;END OF LINE IF CARRIAGE RETURN

         ;CHECK FOR BACKSPACE AND DELETE CHARACTER IF FOUND
         CPI     BSKEY
```

```
            JNZ      RDLP1           ;BRANCH IF NOT BACKSPACE
            CALL     BACKSP          ;IF BACKSPACE, DELETE ONE CHARACTER
            JMP      RDLOOP          ; THEN START READ LOOP AGAIN

            ;CHECK FOR DELETE LINE CHARACTER AND EMPTY BUFFER IF FOUND
RDLP1:
            CPI      DELKEY
            JNZ      RDLP2           ;BRANCH IF NOT DELETE LINE
DEL1:
            CALL     BACKSP          ;DELETE A CHARACTER
            JNZ      DEL1            ;CONTINUE UNTIL BUFFER EMPTY
                                     ;THIS ACTUALLY BACKS UP OVER EACH
                                     ; CHARACTER RATHER THAN JUST MOVING
                                     ; UP A LINE
            JMP      RDLOOP

            ;NOT A SPECIAL CHARACTER
            ; CHECK IF BUFFER IS FULL
            ; IF FULL, RING BELL AND CONTINUE
            ; IF NOT FULL, STORE CHARACTER AND ECHO
RDLP2:
            MOV      E,A             ;SAVE CHARACTER
            MOV      A,B             ;IS BUFFER FULL?
            CMP      C               ; COMPARE COUNT AND BUFFER LENGTH
            JC       STRCH           ;JUMP IF BUFFER NOT FULL
            MVI      A,BELL          ;FULL, RING THE TERMINAL'S BELL
            CALL     WRCHAR
            JMP      RDLOOP          ;THEN CONTINUE THE READ LOOP

            ;BUFFER NOT FULL, STORE CHARACTER
STRCH:
            MOV      A,E             ;GET CHARACTER BACK
            MOV      M,A             ;STORE CHARACTER IN BUFFER
            INX      H               ;INCREMENT BUFFER POINTER
            INR      B               ;INCREMENT CHARACTER COUNT

            ;IF CHARACTER IS CONTROL, THEN OUTPUT
            ; UP ARROW FOLLOWED BY PRINTABLE EQUIVALENT
            CPI      SPACE           ;CONTROL IF LESS THAN SPACE (20 HEX)
            JNC      PRCH            ;JUMP IF A PRINTABLE CHARACTER
            PUSH     PSW             ;SAVE CHARACTER
            MVI      A,UPARRW        ;WRITE UP ARROW OR CARET
            CALL     WRCHAR
            POP      PSW             ;RECOVER CHARACTER
            ADI      40H             ;CHANGE TO PRINTABLE FORM
PRCH:       CALL     WRCHAR          ;ECHO CHARACTER TO TERMINAL
            JMP      RDLOOP          ;THEN CONTINUE READ LOOP

            ;EXIT
            ;SEND NEW LINE SEQUENCE (USUALLY CR,LF) TO TERMINAL
            ;LINE LENGTH = CHARACTER COUNT

EXITRD:
            CALL     WRNEWL          ;ECHO NEW LINE SEQUENCE
            MOV      A,B             ;LINE LENGTH = CHARACTER COUNT
            RET
```

```
        ;************************************************
        ;ROUTINE: RDCHAR
        ;PURPOSE: READ A CHARACTER BUT DO NOT ECHO TO OUTPUT DEVICE
        ;ENTRY: NONE
        ;EXIT:   REGISTER A = CHARACTER
        ;REGISTERS USED: AF,DE
        ;************************************************
RDCHAR:
        PUSH    H                   ;SAVE HL,BC
        PUSH    B

        ;WAIT FOR CHARACTER FROM CONSOLE
RDWAIT:
        MVI     C,DIRIO             ;DIRECT CONSOLE I/O
        MVI     E,0FFH              ;INDICATE INPUT
        CALL    BDOS                ;READ CHARACTER FROM CONSOLE
        ORA     A                   ;LOOP IF NO CHARACTER (A = 0)
        JZ      RDWAIT

        POP     B                   ;RESTORE BC,HL
        POP     H
        RET                         ;RETURN WITH CHARACTER IN REGISTER A

        ;************************************************
        ;ROUTINE: WRCHAR
        ;PURPOSE: WRITE CHARACTER TO OUTPUT DEVICE
        ;ENTRY: REGISTER A = CHARACTER
        ;EXIT:   NONE
        ;REGISTERS USED: AF,DE
        ;************************************************
WRCHAR:
        PUSH    H                   ;SAVE HL,BC
        PUSH    B

        ;WRITE A CHARACTER
        MVI     C,DIRIO             ;DIRECT CONSOLE I/O
        MOV     E,A                 ;INDICATE OUTPUT - CHARACTER IN E
        CALL    BDOS                ;WRITE CHARACTER ON CONSOLE
        POP     B                   ;RESTORE BC,HL
        POP     H
        RET

        ;************************************************
        ;ROUTINE: WRNEWL
        ;PURPOSE: ISSUE NEW LINE SEQUENCE TO TERMINAL
        ;           NORMALLY, THIS SEQUENCE IS A CARRIAGE RETURN AND
        ;           LINE FEED, BUT SOME COMPUTERS REQUIRE ONLY
        ;           A CARRIAGE RETURN.
        ;ENTRY: NONE
        ;EXIT: NONE
        ;REGISTERS USED: AF,DE
        ;************************************************
WRNEWL:
        PUSH    H                   ;SAVE HL,BC
        PUSH    B
```

```
                ;SEND NEW LINE STRING TO TERMINAL
                LXI     D,NLSTRG        ;POINT TO NEW LINE STRING
                CALL    WRSTRG          ;SEND STRING TO TERMINAL

                POP     B               ;RESTORE BC, HL
                POP     H
                RET

NLSTRG: DB      CR,LF,STERM     ;NEW LINE STRING
                                ; NOTE $ (STERM) IS CP/M TERMINATOR


                ;*******************************************
                ;ROUTINE: BACKSP
                ;PURPOSE: PERFORM A DESTRUCTIVE BACKSPACE
                ;ENTRY: B = NUMBER OF CHARACTERS IN BUFFER
                ;       HL = NEXT AVAILABLE BUFFER ADDRESS
                ;EXIT:  IF NO CHARACTERS IN BUFFER
                ;           Z = 1
                ;       ELSE
                ;           Z = 0
                ;       CHARACTER REMOVED FROM BUFFER
                ;REGISTERS USED: AF,B,DE
                ;*******************************************
BACKSP:
                ;CHECK FOR EMPTY BUFFER
                MOV     A,B             ;TEST NUMBER OF CHARACTERS
                ORA     A
                RZ                      ;EXIT IF BUFFER EMPTY


                ;OUTPUT BACKSPACE STRING
                ; TO REMOVE CHARACTER FROM DISPLAY
                DCX     H               ;DECREMENT BUFFER POINTER
                PUSH    H               ;SAVE HL,BC
                PUSH    B
                MOV     A,M             ;GET CHARACTER
                CPI     20H             ;IS IT A CONTROL CHARACTER?
                JNC     BS1             ; NO, BRANCH, DELETE ONLY ONE CHARACTER
                LXI     D,BSSTRG        ; YES, DELETE 2 CHARACTERS
                                        ; (UP ARROW AND PRINTABLE EQUIVALENT)
                CALL    WRSTRG          ;WRITE BACKSPACE STRING
BS1:            LXI     D,BSSTRG
                CALL    WRSTRG          ;WRITE BACKSPACE STRING
                POP     B               ;RESTORE BC, HL
                POP     H


                ;DECREMENT CHARACTER COUNT BY 1
                DCR     B               ;ONE LESS CHARACTER IN BUFFER
                RET


                ;DESTRUCTIVE BACKSPACE STRING FOR TERMINAL
                ;MOVES CURSOR LEFT, PRINTS SPACE OVER CHARACTER, MOVES
                ; CURSOR LEFT
                ;NOTE: STERM ($) IS CP/M STRING TERMINATOR
BSSTRG: DB      CSRLFT,SPACE,CSRLFT,STERM
```

```
        ;***********************************
        ;ROUTINE: WRSTRG
        ;PURPOSE: OUTPUT STRING TO CONSOLE
        ;ENTRY: HL = BASE ADDRESS OF STRING
        ;EXIT:  NONE
        ;REGISTERS USED: AF,DE,HL
        ;***********************************
WRSTRG:
        PUSH    B               ;SAVE BC
        MVI     C,PSTRG         ;FUNCTION IS PRINT STRING
        CALL    BDOS            ;OUTPUT STRING TERMINATED WITH $
        POP     B               ;RESTORE BC
        RET


;                                                                       ;
;                                                                       ;
;       SAMPLE EXECUTION                                                ;
;                                                                       ;
;                                                                       ;


        ;EQUATES
PROMPT  EQU     '?'             ;OPERATOR PROMPT = QUESTION MARK

SC10A:
        ;READ LINE FROM TERMINAL
        MVI     A,PROMPT        ;OUTPUT PROMPT (?)
        CALL    WRCHAR
        LXI     H,INBUFF        ;HL = INPUT BUFFER ADDRESS
        MVI     A,LINBUF        ;A = LENGTH OF BUFFER
        CALL    RDLINE          ;READ LINE
        ORA     A               ;TEST LINE LENGTH
        JZ      SC10A           ;NEXT LINE IF LENGTH IS 0

        ;ECHO LINE TO CONSOLE
        MOV     B,A             ;SAVE NUMBER OF CHARACTERS IN BUFFER
        LXI     H,INBUFF        ;POINT TO START OF BUFFER
TLOOP:
        MOV     A,M             ;OUTPUT NEXT CHARACTER
        CALL    WRCHAR
        INX     H               ;INCREMENT BUFFER POINTER
        DCR     B               ;DECREMENT CHARACTER COUNT
        JNZ     TLOOP           ;CONTINUE UNTIL ALL CHARACTERS SENT
        CALL    WRNEWL          ;THEN END WITH CR,LF

        JMP     SC10A

        ;DATA SECTION
LINBUF: EQU     16              ;LENGTH OF INPUT BUFFER
INBUFF: DS      LINBUF          ;INPUT BUFFER

        END
```

Writes characters until it empties a buffer with given length and base address. Assumes the system-dependent subroutine WRCHAR, which sends the character in the accumulator to the output device.

WRLINE is an example of an output driver. The actual I/O subroutines will, of course, be computer-dependent. A specific example in the listing is for a CP/M-based computer with a standard Basic Disk Operating System (BDOS) accessed by calling address 0005_{16}.

Procedure: The program exits immediately if the buffer is empty. Otherwise, it sends characters to the output device one at a time until it empties the buffer. The program saves all temporary data in memory rather than in registers to avoid dependence on WRCHAR.

Registers Used: AF, BC, DE, HL

Execution Time: 20 cycles overhead plus 44 cycles per byte (8080) or 16 cycles overhead plus 45 cycles per byte (8085) besides the execution time of subroutine WRCHAR

Program Size: 24 bytes

Data Memory Required: None

Special Case: An empty buffer causes an immediate exit with nothing sent to the output device.

Entry Conditions

Base address of buffer in H and L
Number of characters in the buffer in A

Exit Conditions

None

Example

1. Data: Number of characters = 5
            Buffer contains 'ENTER'

   Result: 'ENTER' sent to the output device

```
;
;
;
;
;       Title:      Write a Line to an Output Device
;       Name:       WRLINE
;
;
;
```

```
;
;         Purpose:          Write characters to CP/M BDOS CON: device    ;
;                                                                        ;
;         Entry:            Register pair H = Base address of buffer     ;
;                           Register A = Number of characters in buffer  ;
;                                                                        ;
;         Exit:             None                                         ;
;                                                                        ;
;         Registers used: All                                           ;
;                                                                        ;
;         Time:             Not applicable                              ;
;                                                                        ;
;         Size:             Program 24 bytes                            ;
;                                                                        ;
;
```

```
        ;EQUATES
BDOS    EQU     0005H               ;BDOS ENTRY POINT
DIRIO   EQU     6                   ;BDOS DIRECT I/O FUNCTION
WRLINE:
        ;EXIT IMMEDIATELY IF BUFFER IS EMPTY
        ORA     A                   ;TEST NUMBER OF CHARACTERS
        RZ                          ;RETURN IF BUFFER EMPTY
        MOV     B,A                 ;B = COUNTER
                                    ;HL = BASE ADDRESS OF BUFFER

        ;LOOP SENDING CHARACTERS TO OUTPUT DEVICE
WRLLP:
        MOV     A,M                 ;GET NEXT CHARACTER
        CALL    WRCHAR              ;SEND CHARACTER
        INX     H                   ;INCREMENT BUFFER POINTER
        DCR     B                   ;DECREMENT COUNTER
        JNZ     WRLLP               ;CONTINUE UNTIL ALL CHARACTERS SENT

        RET                         ;EXIT




        ;*********************************************
        ;ROUTINE: WRCHAR
        ;PURPOSE: WRITE CHARACTER TO OUTPUT DEVICE
        ;ENTRY: REGISTER A = CHARACTER
        ;EXIT:  NONE
        ;REGISTERS USED: AF,DE
        ;*********************************************
WRCHAR:
        PUSH    H                   ;SAVE HL,BC
        PUSH    B
        MVI     C,DIRIO             ;DIRECT I/O FUNCTION
        MOV     E,A                 ;CHARACTER IN REGISTER E
        CALL    BDOS                ;OUTPUT CHARACTER

        POP     B                   ;RESTORE BC,HL
        POP     H
        RET
```

```
;                                                                    ;
;                                                                    ;
;          SAMPLE EXECUTION                                          ;
;                                                                    ;
;                                                                    ;

RCBUF     EQU       10                    ;BDOS READ CONSOLE BUFFER FUNCTION

          ;BDOS READ CONSOLE BUFFER FUNCTION USES
          ; THE FOLLOWING BUFFER FORMAT:
          ;   BYTE 0: BUFFER LENGTH (MAXIMUM NUMBER OF CHARACTERS)
          ;   BYTE 1: NUMBER OF CHARACTERS READ (LINE LENGTH)
          ;   BYTE 2 ON: ACTUAL CHARACTERS

          ;CHARACTER EQUATES
CR        EQU       0DH                   ;CARRIAGE RETURN FOR CONSOLE
LF        EQU       0AH                   ;LINE FEED FOR CONSOLE
PROMPT    EQU       '?'                   ;OPERATOR PROMPT = QUESTION MARK

SC10B:
          ;READ LINE FROM CONSOLE
          MVI       A,PROMPT              ;OUTPUT PROMPT (?)
          CALL      WRCHAR
          LXI       D,INBUFF              ;POINT TO INPUT BUFFER
          MVI       C,RCBUF               ;BDOS READ LINE FUNCTION
          CALL      BDOS                  ;READ LINE FROM CONSOLE
          MVI       A,LF                  ;OUTPUT LINE FEED
          CALL      WRCHAR

          ;WRITE LINE TO CONSOLE
          LXI       H,INBUFF+1            ;POINT TO NUMBER OF CHARACTERS IN BUFFER
          MOV       A,M                   ;GET LINE LENGTH
          INX       H                     ;POINT TO FIRST DATA BYTE
          CALL      WRLINE                ;WRITE LINE
          LXI       H,CRLF                ;OUTPUT CARRIAGE RETURN, LINE FEED
          MVI       A,2                   ;LENGTH OF CRLF STRING
          CALL      WRLINE                ;WRITE CRLF STRING

          JMP       SC10B                 ;CONTINUE

          ;DATA SECTION
CRLF      DB        CR,LF                 ;CARRIAGE RETURN, LINE FEED
LINBUF    EQU       10H                   ;LENGTH OF INPUT BUFFER
INBUFF:   DB        LINBUF                ;LENGTH OF INPUT BUFFER
          DS        LINBUF                ;DATA BUFFER

          END
```

CRC-16 Checking and Generation
(ICRC16, CRC16, GCRC16)

Generates a 16-bit cyclic redundancy check (CRC) based on the IBM Binary Synchronous Communications protocol (BSC or Bisync). Uses the polynomial $X^{16} + X^{15} + X^2 + 1$. Entry point ICRC16 initializes the CRC to 0 and the polynomial to the appropriate bit pattern. Entry point CRC16 combines the previous CRC with the CRC generated from the current data byte. Entry point GCRC16 returns the CRC.

Procedure: Subroutine ICRC16 initializes the CRC to 0 and the polynomial to a 1 in each bit position corresponding to a power of X present in the formula. Subroutine CRC16 updates the CRC for a data byte. It shifts both the data and the CRC left eight times; after each shift, it EXCLUSIVE-ORs the CRC with the polynomial if the EXCLUSIVE-OR of the data bit and the CRC's most significant bit is 1. Subroutine CRC16 leaves the CRC in memory locations CRC (less significant byte) and CRC+1 (more significant byte). Subroutine GCRC16 loads the CRC into H and L.

Registers Used:
1. ICRC16: HL
2. CRC16: None
3. GCRC16: HL

Execution Time:
1. ICRC16: 62 cycles (8080 or 8085)
2. CRC16: 153 (8080) or 154 (8085) cycles overhead plus an average of 632 (8080) or 568 (8085) cycles per data byte, assuming that the previous CRC and the polynomial must be EXCLUSIVE-ORed in half of the iterations
3. GCRC16: 26 cycles (8080 or 8085)

Program Size:
1. ICRC16: 13 bytes
2. CRC16: 42 bytes
3. GCRC16: 4 bytes

Data Memory Required: 4 bytes anywhere in RAM for the CRC (2 bytes starting at address CRC) and the polynomial (2 bytes starting at address PLY)

Entry Conditions

1. ICRC16: none

2. CRC16: data byte in A, previous CRC in memory locations CRC (less significant byte) and CRC+1 (more significant byte), CRC polynomial in memory locations PLY (less significant byte) and PLY+1 (more significant byte)

3. GCRC16: CRC in memory locations CRC (less significant byte) and CRC+1 (more significant byte)

Exit Conditions

1. ICRC16: 0 (initial CRC value) in memory locations CRC (less significant byte) and CRC+1 (more significant byte), CRC polynomial in memory locations PLY (less significant byte) and PLY+1 (more significant byte)

2. CRC16: CRC with current data byte included in memory locations CRC (less significant byte) and CRC+1 (more significant byte)

3. GCRC16: CRC in H and L

Examples

1. Generating a CRC
   a. Call ICRC16 for initialization and to start the CRC at 0.
   b. Call CRC16 repeatedly to update the CRC for each data byte.
   c. Call GCRC16 to obtain the final CRC.

2. Checking a CRC
   a. Call ICRC16 for initialization and to start the CRC at 0.
   b. Call CRC16 repeatedly to update the CRC for each data byte (including the stored CRC) for checking.
   c. Call GCRC16 to obtain the final CRC; it will be 0 if there were no errors.

Note that only ICRC16 depends on the particular CRC polynomial used. To change the polynomial, simply change the data ICRC16 loads into memory locations **PLY** (less significant byte) and **PLY+1** (more significant byte).

Reference

J.E. McNamara. *Technical Aspects of Data Communications*, 2nd ed. Billerica, Mass.: Digital Press, 1982. This book contains explanations of CRC and communications protocols.

```
;                                                                              ;
;                                                                              ;
;                                                                              ;
;                                                                              ;
;         Title:          CRC-16 Checking and Generation                       ;
;         Name:           ICRC16, CRC16, GCRC16                                ;
;                                                                              ;
;                                                                              ;
;                                                                              ;
;         Purpose:                                                             ;
;                         Synchronous Communications protocol. The CRC is      ;
;                         based on the following polynomial:                   ;
;                         (^ indicates "to the power")                         ;
;                             X^16 + X^15 + X^2 + 1                             ;
;                                                                              ;
;                         To generate a CRC:                                   ;
;                             1)  Call ICRC16 to initialize the CRC            ;
;                                 polynomial and clear the CRC.                ;
;                             2)  Call CRC16 for each data byte.               ;
;                             3)  Call GCRC16 to obtain the CRC.               ;
;                                 It should then be appended to the data,      ;
;                                 high byte first.                             ;
;                                                                              ;
```

```
;                     To check a CRC:                              ;
;                       1)  Call ICRC16 to initialize the CRC.    ;
;                       2)  Call CRC16 for each data byte and     ;
;                           the 2 bytes of CRC previously generated.;
;                       3)  Call GCRC16 to obtain the CRC. It will ;
;                           be zero if no errors occurred.        ;
;                                                                 ;
;       Entry:          ICRC16 - None                             ;
;                       CRC16  - Register A = Data byte           ;
;                       GCRC16 - None                             ;
;                                                                 ;
;       Exit:           ICRC16 - CRC, PLY initialized             ;
;                       CRC16  - CRC updated                      ;
;                       GCRC16 - H and L = CRC                    ;
;                                                                 ;
;       Registers used: ICRC16 - HL                               ;
;                       CRC16  - None                             ;
;                       GCRC16 - HL                               ;
;                                                                 ;
;                                                                 ;
;       Time:           153 cycles overhead plus 632 cycles per data ;
;                       byte for 8080                             ;
;                       154 cycles overhead plus 568 cycles per data ;
;                       byte for 8085                             ;
;                       The loop timing assumes that half the iterations;
;                       require EXCLUSIVE-ORing the CRC and the   ;
;                       polynomial.                               ;
;                                                                 ;
;       Size:           Program 59 bytes                          ;
;                       Data    4 bytes                           ;
;                                                                 ;
;                                                                 ;

CRC16:
        ;SAVE ALL REGISTERS
        PUSH    PSW
        PUSH    B
        PUSH    D
        PUSH    H

        ;LOOP THROUGH EACH DATA BIT, GENERATING THE CRC
        MVI     B,8             ;8 BITS PER BYTE
        LHLD    PLY             ;MOVE POLYNOMIAL TO DE
        XCHG
        LHLD    CRC             ;GET CURRENT CRC VALUE
CRCLP:
        MOV     C,A             ;SAVE DATA
        ANI     10000000B       ;GET BIT 7 OF DATA
        XRA     H               ;EXCLUSIVE-OR BIT 7 WITH BIT 15 OF CRC
        MOV     H,A
        DAD     H               ;SHIFT CRC LEFT
        JNC     CRCLP1          ;JUMP IF BIT 7 OF EXCLUSIVE-OR WAS 0

        ;BIT 7 WAS 1, SO EXCLUSIVE-OR CRC WITH POLYNOMIAL
        MOV     A,E             ;GET LOW BYTE OF POLYNOMIAL
        XRA     L               ;EXCLUSIVE-OR WITH LOW BYTE OF CRC
```

```
        MOV     L,A
        MOV     A,D             ;GET HIGH BYTE OF POLYNOMIAL
        XRA     H               ;EXCLUSIVE-OR WITH HIGH BYTE OF CRC
        MOV     H,A

CRCLP1:
        MOV     A,C             ;RESTORE DATA
        RAL                     ;SHIFT NEXT DATA BIT TO BIT 7
        DCR     B               ;DECREMENT BIT COUNTER
        JNZ     CRCLP           ;JUMP IF NOT THROUGH 8 BITS
        SHLD    CRC             ;SAVE UPDATED CRC

        ;RESTORE REGISTERS AND EXIT
        POP     H
        POP     D
        POP     B
        POP     PSW
        RET


        ;*********************************************
        ;ROUTINE: ICRC16
        ;PURPOSE: INITIALIZE CRC AND PLY
        ;ENTRY: NONE
        ;EXIT:   CRC AND POLYNOMIAL INITIALIZED
        ;REGISTERS USED: HL
        ;*********************************************
ICRC16:
        LXI     H,0             ;CRC = 0
        SHLD    CRC
        LXI     H,08005H        ;PLY = 8005H
        SHLD    PLY

                                ;8005H IS FOR X^16+X^15+X^2+1
                                ;A 1 IS IN EACH BIT POSITION
                                ; FOR WHICH A POWER APPEARS
                                ; IN THE FORMULA (BITS 0, 2, AND 15)
        RET


        ;*********************************************
        ;ROUTINE: GCRC16
        ;PURPOSE: GET CRC VALUE
        ;ENTRY: NONE
        ;EXIT:   REGISTER PAIR H = CRC VALUE
        ;REGISTERS USED: HL
        ;*********************************************
GCRC16:
        LHLD    CRC             ;HL = CRC
        RET

        ;DATA
CRC:    DS      2               ;CRC VALUE
PLY:    DS      2               ;POLYNOMIAL VALUE
```

```
;                                                                              ;
;                                                                              ;
;         SAMPLE EXECUTION                                                     ;
;                                                                              ;
;                                                                              ;

          ;GENERATE CRC FOR THE NUMBER 1 AND CHECK IT
SC10C:
          CALL     ICRC16             ;INITIALIZE CRC, POLYNOMIAL
          MVI      A,1                ;GENERATE CRC FOR 1
          CALL     CRC16
          CALL     GCRC16
          XCHG                        ;SAVE CRC IN REGISTER DE
          CALL     ICRC16             ;INITIALIZE AGAIN
          MVI      A,1
          CALL     CRC16              ;CHECK CRC BY GENERATING IT FOR DATA
          MOV      A,D
          CALL     CRC16              ; AND STORED CRC ALSO
          MOV      A,E
          CALL     CRC16
          CALL     GCRC16             ;CRC SHOULD BE ZERO IN HL

          ;GENERATE CRC FOR THE SEQUENCE 0,1,2,...,255 AND CHECK IT
          CALL     ICRC16             ;INITIALIZE CRC, POLYNOMIAL
          MVI      B,0                ;START DATA BYTES AT 0
GENLP:
          MOV      A,B                ;GET DATA BYTE
          CALL     CRC16              ;UPDATE CRC
          INR      B                  ;ADD 1 TO PRODUCE NEXT DATA BYTE
          JNZ      GENLP              ;BRANCH IF NOT DONE
          CALL     GCRC16             ;GET RESULTING CRC
          XCHG                        ;AND SAVE IT IN DE

          ;CHECK CRC BY GENERATING IT AGAIN
          CALL     ICRC16             ;INITIALIZE CRC, POLYNOMIAL
          MVI      B,0                ;START DATA BYTES AT 0
CHKLP:
          MOV      A,B                ;GET DATA BYTE
          CALL     CRC16              ;UPDATE CRC
          INR      B                  ;ADD 1 TO PRODUCE NEXT DATA BYTE
          JNZ      CHKLP

          ;INCLUDE STORED CRC IN CHECK
          MOV      A,D                ;INCLUDE HIGH BYTE OF STORED CRC
          CALL     CRC16
          MOV      A,E                ;INCLUDE LOW BYTE OF STORED CRC
          CALL     CRC16

          CALL     GCRC16             ;GET RESULTING CRC
                                      ;IT SHOULD BE 0

          JMP      SC10C

          END
```

Performs input and output in a device-independent manner using I/O control blocks and an I/O device table. The I/O device table is a linked list; each entry contains a link to the next entry, the device number, and starting addresses for routines that initialize the device, determine its input status, read data from it, determine its output status, and write data to it. An I/O control block is an array containing the device number, operation number, device status, and the base address and length of the device's buffer. The user must provide IOHDLR with the base address of an I/O control block and the data if only one byte is to be written. IOHDLR returns the status byte and the data (if only one byte is read).

This subroutine is an example of handling input and output in a device-independent manner. The I/O device table must be constructed using subroutines INITDL, which initializes the device list to empty, and ADDDL, which adds a device to the list.

An applications program will perform input or output by obtaining or constructing an I/O control block and then calling IOHDLR. IOHDLR uses the I/O device table to determine how to transfer control to the I/O driver.

Procedure: The program first initializes the status byte to 0, indicating no errors. It then searches the device table, trying to match the device number in the I/O control block. If it does not find a match, it exits with an error number in the status byte. If it finds a match, it checks for a valid operation and transfers control to the appropriate routine from the device table entry. That routine must end by transferring control back to the original caller. If the operation is invalid (the operation number is too large or the starting address for the routine is 0), the program returns with an error number in the status byte.

Subroutine INITDL initializes the device list, setting the initial link to 0.

Subroutine ADDDL adds an entry to the device list, making its base address the head of the list and setting its link field to the old head of the list.

Registers Used:
1. IOHDLR: All
2. INITDL: HL
3. ADDDL: DE

Execution Time:
1. IOHDLR: 359 (8080) or 348 (8085) cycles overhead plus 93 (8080) or 87 (8085) cycles for each unsuccessful match of a device number
2. INITDL: 36 cycles (8080 or 8085)
3. ADDDL: 74 (8080) or 76 (8085) cycles

Program Size:
1. IOHDLR: 95 bytes
2. INITDL: 7 bytes
3. ADDDL: 13 bytes

Data Memory Required: 5 bytes anywhere in RAM for the base address of the I/O control block (2 bytes starting at address IOCBA), the device list header (2 bytes starting at address DVLST), and temporary storage for data to be written without a buffer (1 byte at address BDATA).

Entry Conditions

1. IOHDLR: Base address of input/output control block in H and L. Data byte (if the operation is to write one byte) in A

2. INITDL: None

3. ADDDL: Base address of a device table entry in H and L

Exit Conditions

1. IOHDLR: I/O control block status byte in A if an error is found; otherwise, the routine exits to the appropriate I/O driver. Data byte in A if the operation is to read one byte

2. INITDL: Device list header (addresses DVLST and DVLST+1) cleared to indicate empty list

3. ADDDL: Device table entry added to list

Example

The example in the listing uses the following structure:

Input/Output Operations

Operation

Number	Operation
0	Initialize device
1	Determine input status
2	Read 1 byte from input device
3	Read N bytes (normally 1 line) from input device
4	Determine output status
5	Write 1 byte to output device
6	Write N bytes (normally 1 line) to output device

Input/Output Control Block

Index	Contents
0	Device number
1	Operation number
2	Status
3	Less significant byte of base address of buffer
4	More significant byte of base address of buffer
5	Less significant byte of buffer length
6	More significant byte of buffer length

Device Table Entry

Index	Contents
0	Less significant byte of link field (base address of next entry)
1	More significant byte of link field (base address of next entry)
2	Device number
3	Less significant byte of starting address of device initialization routine
4	More significant byte of starting address of device initialization routine
5	Less significant byte of starting address of input status determination routine
6	More significant byte of starting address of input status determination routine
7	Less significant byte of starting address of input driver (read 1 byte only)
8	More significant byte of starting address of input driver (read 1 byte only)
9	Less significant byte of starting address of input driver (N bytes or 1 line)
10	More significant byte of starting address of input driver (N bytes or 1 line)
11	Less significant byte of starting address of output status determination routine
12	More significant byte of starting address of output status determination routine
13	Less significant byte of starting address of output driver (write 1 byte only)
14	More significant byte of starting address of output driver (write 1 byte only)
15	Less significant byte of starting address of output driver (N bytes or 1 line)
16	More significant byte of starting address of output driver (N bytes or 1 line)

If an operation is irrelevant or undefined (such as output status determination for a keyboard or input driver for a printer), the corresponding starting address in the device table is 0.

Status Values

Value	Description
0	No errors
1	Bad device number (no such device)
2	Bad operation number (no such operation or invalid operation)
3	Input data available or output device ready
254	Buffer too small for use by CP/M BDOS function 10 (Read Console Buffer). This function requires 2 bytes for the buffer length and character count.

```
;                                                              ;
;                                                              ;
;                                                              ;
;                                                              ;
;       Title:          I/O Device Table Handler               ;
;       Name:           IOHDLR                                 ;
;                                                              ;
;                                                              ;
;                                                              ;
;                                                              ;
;       Purpose:        Perform I/O in a device-independent manner. ;
;                       This can be done only by accessing all ;
;                       devices in the same way using an I/O Control ;
;                       Block (IOCB) and a device table. The routines ;
;                       here allow the following operations:   ;
;                                                              ;
;                       Operation number  Description          ;
;                           0              Initialize device   ;
;                           1              Determine input status ;
;                           2              Read 1 byte          ;
;                           3              Read N bytes         ;
;                           4              Determine output status ;
;                           5              Write 1 byte         ;
;                           6              Write N bytes        ;
;                                                              ;
;                       Other operations that could be included are ;
;                       Open, Close, Delete, Rename, and Append, which ;
;                       would support devices such as floppy disks. ;
;                                                              ;
;                       A IOCB is an array of the following form: ;
;                                                              ;
;                       IOCB + 0 = Device number               ;
;                       IOCB + 1 = Operation number            ;
;                       IOCB + 2 = Status                       ;
;                       IOCB + 3 = Low byte of buffer address  ;
;                       IOCB + 4 = High byte of buffer address ;
;                       IOCB + 5 = Low byte of buffer length   ;
;                       IOCB + 6 = High byte of buffer length  ;
```

```
;                                                                    ;
;                        The device table is implemented as a linked ;
;                        list. Two routines maintain the list: INITDL,;
;                        which initializes the device list to empty, and ;
;                        ADDDL, which adds a device to the list.      ;
;                        A device table entry has the following form: ;
;                                                                     ;
;                        DVTBL + 0 = Low byte of link field           ;
;                        DVTBL + 1 = High byte of link field          ;
;                        DVTBL + 2 = Device number                    ;
;                        DVTBL + 3 = Low byte of device initialization ;
;                        DVTBL + 4 = High byte of device initialization;
;                        DVTBL + 5 = Low byte of input status routine  ;
;                        DVTBL + 6 = High byte of input status routine ;
;                        DVTBL + 7 = Low byte of input 1 byte routine  ;
;                        DVTBL + 8 = High byte of input 1 byte routine ;
;                        DVTBL + 9 = Low byte of input N bytes routine ;
;                        DVTBL + 10= High byte of input N bytes routine;
;                        DVTBL + 11= Low byte of output status routine ;
;                        DVTBL + 12= High byte of output status routine;
;                        DVTBL + 13= Low byte of output 1 byte routine ;
;                        DVTBL + 14= High byte of output 1 byte routine;
;                        DVTBL + 15= Low byte of output N bytes routine;
;                        DVTBL + 16= High byte of output N bytes routine;
;                                                                     ;
;         Entry:         Register pair H = Base address of IOCB       ;
;                        Register A = For write 1 byte, contains the  ;
;                                     data (no buffer is used)        ;
;                                                                     ;
;         Exit:          Register A = Copy of the IOCB status byte    ;
;                                     except contains the data for    ;
;                                     read 1 byte (no buffer is used) ;
;                        Status byte of IOCB is 0 if the operation was;
;                        completed successfully; otherwise, it contains;
;                        the error number.                            ;
;                                                                     ;
;                        Status value          Description            ;
;                             0            No errors                  ;
;                             1            Bad device number          ;
;                             2            Bad operation number       ;
;                             3            Input data available or output ;
;                                          device ready               ;
;                            254           Buffer too small for CP/M BDOS ;
;                                          function 10 (Read Console  ;
;                                          Buffer)                    ;
;                                                                     ;
; Registers used: All                                                 ;
;                                                                     ;
;         Time:          359 cycles minimum plus 93 cycles for each   ;
;                        device in the list which is not the requested;
;                        device for the 8080                          ;
;                        348 cycles minimum plus 87 cycles for each   ;
;                        device in the list which is not the requested;
;                        device for the 8085                          ;
;                                                                     ;
```

```
;       Size:          Program 115 bytes                          ;
;                      Data     5 bytes                           ;
;                                                                 ;
;                                                                 ;

            ;IOCB AND DEVICE TABLE EQUATES
IOCBDN  EQU     0           ;IOCB DEVICE NUMBER
IOCBOP  EQU     1           ;IOCB OPERATION NUMBER
IOCBST  EQU     2           ;IOCB STATUS
IOCBBA  EQU     3           ;IOCB BUFFER ADDRESS
IOCBBL  EQU     5           ;IOCB BUFFER LENGTH
DTLNK   EQU     0           ;DEVICE TABLE LINK FIELD
DTDN    EQU     2           ;DEVICE TABLE DEVICE NUMBER
DTSR    EQU     3           ;BEGINNING OF DEVICE TABLE SUBROUTINES

            ;OPERATION NUMBERS
NUMOP   EQU     7           ;NUMBER OF OPERATIONS
INIT    EQU     0           ;INITIALIZATION
ISTAT   EQU     1           ;INPUT STATUS
R1BYTE  EQU     2           ;READ 1 BYTE
RNBYTE  EQU     3           ;READ N BYTES
OSTAT   EQU     4           ;OUTPUT STATUS
W1BYTE  EQU     5           ;WRITE 1 BYTE
WNBYTE  EQU     6           ;WRITE N BYTES

            ;STATUS VALUES
NOERR   EQU     0           ;NO ERRORS
DEVERR  EQU     1           ;BAD DEVICE NUMBER
OPERR   EQU     2           ;BAD OPERATION NUMBER
DEVRDY  EQU     3           ;INPUT DATA AVAILABLE OR OUTPUT DEVICE READY
BUFERR  EQU     254         ;BUFFER TOO SMALL FOR BDOS READ CONSOLE BUFFER

IOHDLR:
            ;SAVE IOCB ADDRESS AND DATA (IF ANY)
        SHLD    IOCBA       ;SAVE IOCB ADDRESS
        XCHG                ;DE = IOCB ADDRESS
        STA     BDATA       ;SAVE DATA BYTE FOR WRITE 1 BYTE

            ;INITIALIZE STATUS BYTE TO INDICATE NO ERRORS
        LXI     H,IOCBST    ;POINT TO STATUS BYTE
        DAD     D
        MVI     M,NOERR     ;STATUS = NO ERRORS

            ;CHECK FOR VALID OPERATION NUMBER (WITHIN LIMIT)
        LXI     H,IOCBOP    ;GET OPERATION NUMBER FROM IOCB
        DAD     D
        MOV     A,M
        MOV     B,A         ;SAVE OPERATION NUMBER
        CPI     NUMOP       ;IS OPERATION NUMBER WITHIN LIMIT?
        JNC     BADOP       ;JUMP IF OPERATION NUMBER TOO LARGE

            ;SEARCH DEVICE LIST FOR THIS DEVICE
            ;DE = POINTER TO DEVICE LIST
            ;C = IOCB DEVICE NUMBER
        LXI     H,IOCBDN    ;POINT TO DEVICE NUMBER IN IOCB
```

```
            DAD      D
            MOV      C,M                  ;C = IOCB DEVICE NUMBER
            LHLD     DVLST                ;DE = FIRST ENTRY IN DEVICE LIST
            XCHG

            ;DE = POINTER TO DEVICE LIST
            ;B = OPERATION NUMBER
            ;C = REQUESTED DEVICE NUMBER
SRCHLP:
            ;CHECK IF AT END OF DEVICE LIST (LINK FIELD = 0000)
            MOV      A,D                  ;TEST LINK FIELD
            ORA      E
            JZ       BADDN                ;BRANCH IF NO MORE DEVICE ENTRIES

            ;CHECK IF CURRENT ENTRY IS DEVICE IN IOCB
            LXI      H,DTDN               ;POINT TO DEVICE NUMBER IN ENTRY
            DAD      D
            MOV      A,M                  ;COMPARE TO REQUESTED DEVICE
            CMP      C
            JZ       FOUND                ;BRANCH IF DEVICE FOUND

            ;DEVICE NOT FOUND, SO ADVANCE TO NEXT DEVICE
            ; TABLE ENTRY THROUGH LINK FIELD
            ; MAKE CURRENT DEVICE = LINK
            XCHG                          ;POINT TO LINK FIELD (FIRST WORD)
            MOV      E,M                  ;GET LOW BYTE OF LINK
            INX      H
            MOV      D,M                  ;GET HIGH BYTE OF LINK
            JMP      SRCHLP               ;CHECK NEXT ENTRY IN DEVICE TABLE

            ;FOUND DEVICE, SO VECTOR TO APPROPRIATE ROUTINE IF ANY
            ;DE = ADDRESS OF DEVICE TABLE ENTRY
            ;B = OPERATION NUMBER IN IOCB
FOUND:
            ;GET ROUTINE ADDRESS (ZERO INDICATES INVALID OPERATION)
            MOV      L,B                  ;HL = 16-BIT OPERATION NUMBER
            MVI      H,0
            DAD      H                    ;MULTIPLY BY 2 FOR ADDRESS ENTRIES
            LXI      B,DTSR
            DAD      B                    ;HL = OFFSET TO SUBROUTINE IN
                                          ; DEVICE TABLE ENTRY
            DAD      D                    ;HL POINTS TO ADDRESS OF SUBROUTINE
            MOV      A,M                  ;GET SUBROUTINE'S STARTING ADDRESS
            INX      H
            MOV      H,M
            MOV      L,A                  ;TEST STARTING ADDRESS FOR ZERO
            ORA      H
            JZ       BADOP                ;JUMP IF OPERATION INVALID (ADDRESS = 0)
            PUSH     H                    ;PUSH ADDRESS OF SUBROUTINE
            LHLD     IOCBA                ;HL = BASE ADDRESS OF IOCB
            LDA      BDATA                ;A = DATA BYTE FOR WRITE 1 BYTE
            RET                           ;GOTO SUBROUTINE

BADDN:
            MVI      A,DEVERR             ;ERROR CODE -- NO SUCH DEVICE
            JMP      EREXIT
```

```
BADOP:
        MVI     A,OPERR             ;ERROR CODE -- NO SUCH OPERATION

EREXIT:
        LHLD    IOCBA               ;POINT TO IOCB STATUS BYTE
        LXI     D,IOCBST
        DAD     D
        MOV     M,A                 ;SET STATUS BYTE IN IOCB
        RET


        ;************************************************
        ;ROUTINE: INITDL
        ;PURPOSE: INITIALIZE DEVICE LIST TO EMPTY
        ;ENTRY: NONE
        ;EXIT:   DEVICE LIST SET TO NO ITEMS
        ;REGISTERS USED: HL
        ;************************************************
INITDL:
        ;INITIALIZE DEVICE LIST HEADER TO 0 TO INDICATE NO DEVICES
        LXI     H,0                 ;HEADER = 0 (EMPTY LIST)
        SHLD    DVLST
        RET

        ;************************************************
        ;ROUTINE: ADDDL
        ;PURPOSE: ADD DEVICE TO DEVICE LIST
        ;ENTRY: REGISTER PAIR H = ADDRESS OF DEVICE TABLE ENTRY
        ;EXIT:   DEVICE ADDED TO DEVICE LIST
        ;REGISTERS USED: DE
        ;************************************************
ADDDL:
        XCHG                        ;GET CURRENT HEAD OF DEVICE LIST
        LHLD    DVLST
        XCHG                        ;TO DE
                                    ;HL = ADDRESS OF NEW DEVICE
        MOV     M,E                 ;STORE CURRENT HEAD OF DEVICE LIST
        INX     H                   ; IN LINK FIELD OF NEW DEVICE
        MOV     M,D
        DCX     H
        SHLD    DVLST               ;MAKE DVLST POINT AT NEW DEVICE
        RET

        ;DATA SECTION
IOCBA:  DS      2                   ;BASE ADDRESS OF IOCB
DVLST:  DS      2                   ;DEVICE LIST HEADER
BDATA:  DS      1                   ;DATA BYTE FOR WRITE 1 BYTE


;                                                              ;
;                                                              ;
;       SAMPLE EXECUTION                                       ;
;                                                              ;
;          This test routine sets up the CP/M console as       ;
;       device 1 and the CP/M printer as device 2. The         ;
;       routine then reads a line from the console and         ;
```

```
;           echoes it to the console and the printer.              ;
;                                                                    ;
;                                                                    ;

            ;CHARACTER EQUATES
CR          EQU     0DH                 ;CARRIAGE RETURN CHARACTER
LF          EQU     0AH                 ;LINE FEED CHARACTER

            ;CP/M EQUATES
BDOS        EQU     0005H               ;ADDRESS OF CP/M BDOS ENTRY POINT
CINP        EQU     1                   ;BDOS CONSOLE INPUT FUNCTION
COUTP       EQU     2                   ;BDOS CONSOLE OUTPUT FUNCTION
LOUTP       EQU     5                   ;BDOS LIST OUTPUT FUNCTION
RCBUF       EQU     10                  ;BDOS READ CONSOLE BUFFER FUNCTION
CSTAT       EQU     11                  ;BDOS CONSOLE STATUS FUNCTION

SC10D:
            ;INITIALIZE DEVICE LIST
            CALL    INITDL              ;DEVICE LIST IS EMPTY

            ;SET UP CONSOLE AS DEVICE 1 AND INITIALIZE IT
            LXI     H,CONDV             ;POINT TO CONSOLE DEVICE ENTRY
            CALL    ADDDL               ;ADD CONSOLE TO DEVICE LIST
            MVI     A,INIT              ;INITIALIZE OPERATION
            STA     IOCB+IOCBOP
            MVI     A,1                 ;DEVICE NUMBER = 1
            STA     IOCB+IOCBDN
            LXI     H,IOCB              ;INITIALIZE CONSOLE
            CALL    IOHDLR

            ;SET UP PRINTER AS DEVICE 2 AND INITIALIZE IT
            LXI     H,PRTDV             ;POINT TO PRINTER DEVICE ENTRY
            CALL    ADDDL               ;ADD PRINTER TO DEVICE LIST
            MVI     A,INIT              ;INITIALIZE OPERATION
            STA     IOCB+IOCBOP
            MVI     A,2                 ;DEVICE NUMBER = 2
            STA     IOCB+IOCBDN
            LXI     H,IOCB              ;INITIALIZE PRINTER
            CALL    IOHDLR

            ;LOOP READING LINES FROM CONSOLE AND ECHOING THEM TO
            ; THE CONSOLE AND PRINTER UNTIL A BLANK LINE IS ENTERED
TSTLP:
            MVI     A,1                 ;DEVICE NUMBER = 1 (CONSOLE)
            STA     IOCB+IOCBDN
            MVI     A,RNBYTE            ;OPERATION IS READ N BYTES
            STA     IOCB+IOCBOP
            LXI     H,LENBUF
            SHLD    IOCB+IOCBBL         ;SET BUFFER LENGTH TO LENBUF
            LXI     H,IOCB              ;HL = BASE ADDRESS OF IOCB
            CALL    IOHDLR              ;READ LINE FROM CONSOLE

            ;OUTPUT LINE FEED TO CONSOLE
            MVI     A,W1BYTE            ;OPERATION IS WRITE 1 BYTE
            STA     IOCB+IOCBOP
```

```
        MVI     A,LF            ;CHARACTER IS LINE FEED
        LXI     H,IOCB          ;HL = BASE ADDRESS OF IOCB
        CALL    IOHDLR          ;WRITE 1 BYTE (LINE FEED)

        ;ECHO LINE TO DEVICES 1 AND 2
        MVI     A,1
        CALL    ECHO            ;ECHO LINE TO DEVICE 1
        MVI     A,2
        CALL    ECHO            ;ECHO LINE TO DEVICE 2

        ;STOP IF LINE LENGTH IS 0
        LHLD    IOCB+IOCBBL     ;GET LINE LENGTH
        MOV     A,H             ;TEST LINE LENGTH
        ORA     L
        JNZ     TSTLP           ;JUMP IF LENGTH NOT ZERO

        JMP     SC10D           ;AGAIN

ECHO:
        ;OUTPUT LINE
        STA     IOCB+IOCBDN     ;SET DEVICE NUMBER IN IOCB
                                ;NOTE THAT ECHO WILL SEND A LINE
                                ; TO ANY DEVICE. THE DEVICE NUMBER
                                ; IS IN THE ACCUMULATOR
        MVI     A,WNBYTE        ;SET OPERATION TO WRITE N BYTES
        STA     IOCB+IOCBOP
        LXI     H,IOCB          ;HL = BASE ADDRESS OF IOCB
        CALL    IOHDLR          ;WRITE N BYTES

        ;OUTPUT CARRIAGE RETURN/LINE FEED
        MVI     A,W1BYTE        ;SET OPERATION TO WRITE 1 BYTE
        STA     IOCB+IOCBOP
        MVI     A,CR            ;CHARACTER IS CARRIAGE RETURN
        LXI     H,IOCB          ;HL = BASE ADDRESS OF IOCB
        CALL    IOHDLR          ;WRITE 1 BYTE
        MVI     A,LF            ;CHARACTER IS LINE FEED
        LXI     H,IOCB          ;HL = IOCB ADDRESS
        CALL    IOHDLR          ;WRITE 1 BYTE
        RET

        ;IOCB FOR PERFORMING I/O
IOCB    DS      1               ;DEVICE NUMBER
        DS      1               ;OPERATION NUMBER
        DS      1               ;STATUS
        DW      BUFFER          ;BUFFER ADDRESS
        DS      2               ;BUFFER LENGTH

        ;BUFFER
LENBUF  EQU     127
BUFFER  DS      LENBUF

        ;DEVICE TABLE ENTRIES
CONDV:  DW      0               ;LINK FIELD
        DB      1               ;DEVICE 1
        DW      CINIT           ;CONSOLE INITIALIZE
```

```
        DW      CISTAT              ;CONSOLE INPUT STATUS
        DW      CIN                 ;CONSOLE INPUT 1 BYTE
        DW      CINN                ;CONSOLE INPUT N BYTES
        DW      COSTAT              ;CONSOLE OUTPUT STATUS
        DW      COUT                ;CONSOLE OUTPUT 1 BYTE
        DW      COUTN               ;CONSOLE OUTPUT N BYTES
PRTDV:  DW      0                   ;LINK FIELD
        DB      2                   ;DEVICE 2
        DW      PINIT               ;PRINTER INITIALIZE
        DW      0                   ;NO PRINTER INPUT STATUS
        DW      0                   ;NO PRINTER INPUT 1 BYTE
        DW      0                   ;NO PRINTER INPUT N BYTES
        DW      POSTAT              ;PRINTER OUTPUT STATUS
        DW      POUT                ;PRINTER OUTPUT 1 BYTE
        DW      POUTN               ;PRINTER OUTPUT N BYTES

        ;**************************************
        ;CONSOLE I/O ROUTINES
        ;**************************************

        ;CONSOLE INITIALIZE
CINIT:
        SUB     A                   ;STATUS = NO ERRORS
        RET                         ;NO INITIALIZATION NECESSARY

        ;CONSOLE INPUT STATUS
CISTAT:
        PUSH    H                   ;SAVE IOCB ADDRESS
        MVI     C,CSTAT             ;BDOS CONSOLE STATUS FUNCTION
        CALL    BDOS                ;GET CONSOLE STATUS
        POP     H                   ;RESTORE IOCB ADDRESS
        ORA     A                   ;TEST CONSOLE STATUS
        JZ      CIS1                ;JUMP IF NO CHARACTER READY (A = 0)
        MVI     A,DEVRDY            ;INDICATE CHARACTER READY
CIS1:   LXI     D,IOCBST            ;STORE STATUS IN IOCB
        DAD     D
        MOV     M,A
        RET

        ;CONSOLE READ 1 BYTE
CIN:
        MVI     C,CINP              ;BDOS CONSOLE INPUT FUNCTION
        CALL    BDOS                ;READ 1 BYTE FROM CONSOLE
        RET

        ;CONSOLE READ N BYTES
CINN:
        ;READ LINE USING BDOS READ CONSOLE BUFFER FUNCTION
        ;BDOS READ CONSOLE BUFFER FUNCTION USES
        ; THE FOLLOWING BUFFER FORMAT:
        ;   BYTE 0: BUFFER LENGTH (MAXIMUM NUMBER OF CHARACTERS)
        ;   BYTE 1: NUMBER OF CHARACTERS READ (LINE LENGTH)
        ;   BYTES 2 ON: ACTUAL CHARACTERS
        XCHG                        ;DE = BASE ADDRESS OF IOCB
```

```
          LXI      H,IOCBBL         ;GET BUFFER LENGTH
          DAD      D
          MOV      A,M              ;A = BUFFER LENGTH
          SBI      3                ;BUFFER MUST BE AT LEAST 3 CHARACTERS
                                    ; TO ALLOW FOR MAX LENGTH AND COUNT
                                    ; USED BY BDOS READ CONSOLE BUFFER
          JNC      CINN1            ;JUMP IF BUFFER LONG ENOUGH
          LXI      H,IOCBST         ;SET ERROR STATUS - BUFFER TOO SMALL
          DAD      D                ; NO ROOM FOR DATA
          MVI      M,BUFERR
          RET

CINN1:    INR      A                ;ADD ONE BACK TO FIND AMOUNT OF ROOM
                                    ; IN BUFFER FOR DATA (2 BYTES OVERHEAD)
          PUSH     H                ;SAVE ADDRESS OF BUFFER LENGTH IN IOCB
          LXI      H,IOCBBA         ;GET BUFFER ADDRESS FROM IOCB
          DAD      D
          MOV      E,M              ;GET LOW BYTE OF BUFFER ADDRESS
          INX      H
          MOV      D,M              ;GET HIGH BYTE OF BUFFER ADDRESS
          PUSH     D                ;SAVE BUFFER ADDRESS
          STAX     D                ;SET MAXIMUM LENGTH IN BUFFER
          MVI      C,RCBUF          ;BDOS READ CONSOLE BUFFER FUNCTION
          CALL     BDOS             ;READ BUFFER

          ;RETURN NUMBER OF CHARACTERS READ IN IOCB
          POP      H                ;RESTORE BUFFER ADDRESS
          INX      H                ;GET NUMBER OF CHARACTERS READ
          MOV      A,M
          XCHG
          POP      H                ;GET ADDRESS OF BUFFER LENGTH IN IOCB
          MOV      M,A              ;SET BUFFER LENGTH IN IOCB
          INX      H
          MVI      M,0              ;UPPER BYTE OF LENGTH IS 0

          ;MOVE DATA TO FIRST BYTE OF BUFFER
          ;DROPPING OVERHEAD (BUFFER LENGTH, NUMBER OF CHARACTERS READ)
          ; RETURNED BY CP/M. LINE LENGTH IS NOW IN IOCB
          ORA      A                ;TEST NUMBER OF CHARACTERS READ
          RZ                        ;RETURN IF NO CHARACTERS
          MOV      B,A              ;B = NUMBER OF CHARACTERS READ
          MOV      H,D
          MOV      L,E
          INX      H                ;HL = FIRST BYTE OF DATA
                                    ; 2 BYTES BEYOND START
          DCX      D                ;DE = DESTINATION (FIRST BYTE OF BUFFER)

CIMVLP:
          MOV      A,M              ;MOVE NEXT BYTE DOWN 2 IN BUFFER
          STAX     D
          INX      H                ;INCREMENT SOURCE
          INX      D                ;INCREMENT DESTINATION
          DCR      B                ;DECREMENT COUNTER
          JNZ      CIMVLP           ;CONTINUE UNTIL DONE
          SUB      A                ;RETURN, NO ERRORS
          RET
```

```
        ;CONSOLE OUTPUT STATUS
COSTAT:
        MVI     A,DEVRDY        ;STATUS - ALWAYS READY TO OUTPUT
        RET

        ;CONSOLE OUTPUT 1 BYTE
COUT:
        MVI     C,2             ;BDOS CONSOLE OUTPUT OPERATION
        MOV     E,A             ;E = CHARACTER
        CALL    BDOS            ;OUTPUT 1 BYTE
        SUB     A               ;STATUS = NO ERRORS
        RET

        ;CONSOLE OUTPUT N BYTES
COUTN:
        LXI     D,COUT          ;DE = ADDRESS OF OUTPUT CHARACTER ROUTINE
        CALL    OUTN            ;CALL OUTPUT N CHARACTERS
        SUB     A               ;STATUS = NO ERRORS
        RET


        ;********************************************
        ;PRINTER ROUTINES
        ;********************************************

        ;PRINTER INITIALIZE
PINIT:
        SUB     A               ;NOTHING TO DO, RETURN NO ERRORS
        RET

        ;PRINTER OUTPUT STATUS
POSTAT:
        MVI     A,DEVRDY        ;STATUS = ALWAYS READY
        RET

        ;PRINTER OUTPUT 1 BYTE
POUT:
        MVI     C,LOUTP         ;BDOS LIST OUTPUT FUNCTION
        MOV     E,A             ;E = CHARACTER
        CALL    BDOS            ;OUTPUT TO PRINTER
        SUB     A               ;STATUS = NO ERRORS
        RET

        ;PRINTER OUTPUT N BYTES
POUTN:
        LXI     D,POUT          ;DE = ADDRESS OF OUTPUT ROUTINE
        CALL    OUTN            ;OUTPUT N CHARACTERS
        SUB     A               ;STATUS = NO ERRORS
        RET

        ;********************************************
        ;ROUTINE: OUTN
        ;PURPOSE: OUTPUT N CHARACTERS
        ;ENTRY: REGISTER DE = CHARACTER OUTPUT SUBROUTINE ADDRESS
        ;       REGISTER HL = BASE ADDRESS OF AN IOCB
        ;EXIT:  DATA OUTPUT
```

```
          ;REGISTERS USED: ALL
          ;**********************************************
OUTN:
          ;STORE ADDRESS OF CHARACTER OUTPUT SUBROUTINE
          XCHG
          SHLD    COSR              ;SAVE OUTPUT SUBROUTINE ADDRESS

          ;GET NUMBER OF BYTES, EXIT IF LENGTH IS 0
          ; BC = NUMBER OF BYTES
          LXI     H,IOCBBL          ;POINT TO BUFFER LENGTH IN IOCB
          DAD     D
          MOV     C,M               ;GET LOW BYTE OF BUFFER LENGTH
          INX     H
          MOV     B,M               ;AND HIGH BYTE OF BUFFER LENGTH
          MOV     A,B               ;TEST BUFFER LENGTH
          ORA     C
          RZ                        ;EXIT IF BUFFER EMPTY

          ;GET OUTPUT BUFFER ADDRESS FROM IOCB
          ; HL = BUFFER ADDRESS
          LXI     H,IOCBBA          ;POINT TO BUFFER ADDRESS IN IOCB
          DAD     D
          MOV     A,M               ;GET LOW BYTE OF BUFFER ADDRESS
          INX     H
          MOV     H,M               ;AND HIGH BYTE OF BUFFER ADDRESS
          MOV     L,A               ;HL = BUFFER ADDRESS

OUTLP:
          MOV     A,M               ;GET DATA FROM BUFFER
          PUSH    H                 ;SAVE BUFFER POINTER, CHARACTER COUNT
          PUSH    B
          CALL    DOSUB             ;OUTPUT CHARACTER
          POP     B                 ;RESTORE POINTER, COUNT
          POP     H
          INX     H                 ;POINT TO NEXT CHARACTER
          DCX     B                 ;DECREMENT AND TEST COUNT
          MOV     A,B
          ORA     C
          JNZ     OUTLP             ;CONTINUE UNTIL COUNT = 0
          RET

DOSUB:    LHLD    COSR
          PCHL                      ;GOTO ROUTINE

COSR:     DW      0                 ;ADDRESS OF CHARACTER OUTPUT SUBROUTINE

          END
```

Initializes a set of I/O ports from an array of port device addresses and data values. Examples are given of initializing the common 8080/8085 programmable I/O devices: 8251 PCI, 8253 PIT, and 8255 PPI.

This subroutine is a generalized method for initializing I/O sections. The initialization may involve data ports, data direction registers that determine whether bits are inputs or outputs, control or command registers that determine the operating modes of programmable devices, counters (in timers), priority registers, and other external registers or storage locations.

The subroutine is self-modifying, since it must change the device address in an OUT instruction. This is necessary because OUT instructions allow only direct (device) addressing, so there is no simple way to direct output to a variable device address.

Tasks the user may perform with this routine include:

1. Assigning bidirectional I/O lines as inputs or outputs.

2. Initializing output ports.

3. Enabling or disabling interrupts from peripheral chips.

4. Determining operating modes, such as whether inputs are latched, whether strobes are produced, how priorities are assigned, whether timers operate continuously or only on demand, and so forth.

5. Loading starting values into timers and counters.

6. Selecting bit rates for communications.

7. Clearing or resetting devices that are not tied to the overall system reset line.

Registers Used: All

Execution Time: 22 (8080) or 23 (8085) cycles overhead plus $61 + 57 * N$ cycles for each port, where N is the number of bytes sent

Program Size: 25 bytes plus the size of the table (at least 3 bytes per port plus 1 byte for a terminator)

Data Memory Required: None, but subroutine OUTPUT (3 bytes) must always be in RAM since the program modifies the address part of its OUT instruction.

---

8. Initializing priority registers or assigning initial priorities to interrupts or other operations.

9. Initializing vectors used in servicing interrupts, DMA requests, and other inputs.

Procedure: For each port, the program obtains the number of bytes to be sent and the device address. It then modifies the special OUT instruction and uses that instruction to send the data values to the port. This approach does not depend on the number or type of devices in the I/O section. The user may add or delete devices or change the initialization by changing the array rather than the program.

Each entry in the array consists of a series of byte-length elements in the following order:

1. Number of bytes to be sent to the port

2. 8-bit device address for the port

3. Data bytes in sequential order.

The array ends with a terminator that has 0 in its first byte.

Note that an entry may consist of an arbitrary number of bytes. The first element determines how many bytes are sent to the device address in the second element. The subsequent elements contain the data values. The terminator need consist only of a single 0 byte.

378

The actual OUT instruction is in a subroutine in data memory. The program stores the device address from the table in the second byte of that instruction before transferring control to the subroutine.

Entry Conditions

Base address of initialization array in H and L

Exit Conditions

All data values sent to appropriate ports

Example

1. Data: Array elements ᵃ.e
    3 (number of bytes for port 1)
      Port 1 device address, first value, second value, third value
    2 (number of bytes for port 2)
      Port 2 device address, first value, second value
    4 (number of bytes for port 3)
      Port 3 device address, first value, second value, third value, fourth value
    0 (terminator)

Result: Three values sent to port 1's device address
Two values sent to port 2's device address
Four values sent to port 3's device address

```
;                                                                        ;
;                                                                        ;
;                                                                        ;
;                                                                        ;
;        Title:          Initialize I/O Ports                           ;
;        Name:           IPORTS                                         ;
;                                                                        ;
;                                                                        ;
;                                                                        ;
;        Purpose:        Initialize I/O ports from an array of port     ;
;                        addresses and values                           ;
;                                                                        ;
;        Entry:          Register pair H = Base address of array        ;
;                                                                        ;
;                        The array consists of byte-length elements     ;
;                        in the following order: number of bytes to     ;
;                        be sent to the port, port device address, data ;
;                        values for the port.  This sequence is repeated ;
;                        for any number of ports. The array is terminated;
```

```
;                                  by an entry with 0 in the number of bytes.     ;
;                                  array+0 = Number of bytes for this port         ;
;                                  array+1 = Port device address                  ;
;                                  array+2 = First value for this port            ;
;                                            .                                     ;
;                                            .                                     ;
;                                  array+2+(N-1) = Last value for this port        ;
;                                            .                                     ;
;                                            .                                     ;
;                                            .                                     ;
;                                                                                  ;
;          Exit:          None                                                     ;
;                                                                                  ;
;          Registers used: All                                                     ;
;                                                                                  ;
;          Time:          22 cycles overhead plus 61 + (N * 57) cycles for;
;                         each port, where N is the number of bytes sent, ;
;                         for the 8080                                             ;
;                         23 cycles overhead plus 61 + (N * 57) cycles for;
;                         each port, where N is the number of bytes sent, ;
;                         for the 8085                                             ;
;                                                                                  ;
;          Size:          Program 25 bytes                                         ;
;                                                                                  ;
;                                                                                  ;
IPORTS:
        ;GET NUMBER OF DATA BYTES TO SEND TO CURRENT PORT
        ;EXIT IF NUMBER OF BYTES IS 0, INDICATING TERMINATOR
        MOV     A,M             ;GET NUMBER OF BYTES
        ORA     A               ;TEST FOR ZERO (TERMINATOR)
        RZ                      ;RETURN IF NUMBER OF BYTES = 0
        MOV     B,A
        INX     H               ;POINT TO PORT ADDRESS (NEXT BYTE)

        ;GET PORT ADDRESS AND PUT IT IN THE SECOND (DEVICE ADDRESS)
        ; BYTE OF AN OUT INSTRUCTION. THIS IS CODE MODIFICATION,
        ; SO THE OUT INSTRUCTION MUST BE IN RAM

        MOV     A,M             ;GET PORT ADDRESS
        STA     PORTAD          ;STORE IT IN ADDRESS BYTE OF OUT 0
        INX     H               ;POINT TO FIRST DATA VALUE (NEXT BYTE)

        ;OUTPUT DATA AND CONTINUE TO NEXT PORT
IPLP:
        MOV     A,M             ;GET NEXT DATA BYTE
        CALL    OUTPUT          ;OUTPUT DATA TO PORT
        INX     H               ;INCREMENT TO NEXT BYTE
        DCR     B               ;DECREMENT NUMBER OF BYTES
        JNZ     IPLP            ;CONTINUE UNTIL DONE

        JMP     IPORTS          ;CONTINUE WITH NEXT PORT

        ;DATA SECTION
```

```
OUTPUT:
PORTAD  EQU      OUTPUT+1              ;ADDRESS OF PORT NUMBER IN OUTPUT
                                      ; INSTRUCTION BELOW
        OUT      0                    ;OUTPUT INSTRUCTION (0 IS DUMMY ADDRESS)
        RET


;                                                                        ;
;                                                                        ;
;          SAMPLE EXECUTION                                              ;
;                                                                        ;
;                                                                        ;

        ;INITIALIZE
        ;   8253 PIT (PROGRAMMABLE INTERVAL TIMER)
        ;   8251 SERIAL INTERFACE (PROGRAMMABLE COMMUNICATION INTERFACE OR PCI)
        ;   8255 PARALLEL INTERFACE (PROGRAMMABLE PERIPHERAL INTERFACE OR PPI)

        ;ARBITRARY PORT ADDRESSES
        ;
        ;   8253 PIT ADDRESSES
PIT0    EQU      70H                  ;8253 CHANNEL 0
PIT1    EQU      71H                  ;8253 CHANNEL 1
PIT2    EQU      72H                  ;8253 CHANNEL 2
PITMDE  EQU      73H                  ;8253 MODE WORD

        ;   8251 PCI ADDRESSES
PCID    EQU      80H                  ;8251 DATA PORT
PCIC    EQU      81H                  ;8251 CONTROL/STATUS PORT

        ;   8255 PPI ADDRESSES
PPIPA   EQU      0C0H                 ;8255 PORT A
PPIPB   EQU      0C1H                 ;8255 PORT B
PPIPC   EQU      0C2H                 ;8255 PORT C
PPIC    EQU      0C3H                 ;8255 CONTROL PORT

SC10E:
        LXI      H,PINIT              ;POINT TO INITIALIZATION ARRAY
        CALL     IPORTS               ;INITIALIZE PORTS
        IN       PCID                 ;DUMMY READ TO BE SURE 8251
                                      ; IS IN CORRECT STATE

        JMP      SC10E

PINIT:
        ;INITIALIZE 8253 PIT COUNTER 0
        ;
        ;    OPERATE COUNTER SO IT GENERATES A SQUARE WAVE, DECREMENTING
        ;      THE COUNTER ON THE NEGATIVE (FALLING) EDGE OF EACH
        ;      CLOCK PULSE. THE PERIOD OF THE SQUARE WAVE IS THE
        ;      INITIAL VALUE LOADED INTO THE COUNTER.
        ;    MAKE COUNT BINARY, SET INITIAL VALUE TO 13 DECIMAL.
        ;    NOTE: 8253 RELOADS COUNTER WITH ORIGINAL COUNT AFTER EACH
        ;      SQUARE WAVE IS GENERATED.
        ;    NOTE: IF THE INITIAL VALUE IS ODD, THE PULSES ARE NOT REALLY
        ;      SQUARE.  THE OUTPUT FROM PIN 10 OF THE 8253 WILL BE HIGH
```

```
;       FOR (N+1)/2 COUNTS AND LOW FOR (N-1)/2 COUNTS, WHERE N IS
;       THE INITIAL VALUE.  IN THE PRESENT CASE, THE OUTPUT WILL
;       BE HIGH FOR 7 COUNTS AND LOW FOR 6 COUNTS.

;     THIS INITIALIZATION PRODUCES AN 8251 PCI CLOCK FOR 9600 BAUD
;       TRANSMISSION.
;     IT ASSUMES A 2 MHZ CLOCK INPUT TO PIN 9, SO A COUNT OF
;       2,000,000/153,600 = 13 WILL GENERATE A 153,600
;       (16*9600) HZ SQUARE WAVE FOR PCI PINS 9 (TRANSMIT CLOCK)
;       AND 25 (RECEIVE CLOCK). PCI IS OPERATING IN DIVIDE BY
;       16 CLOCK MODE.
DB      1                       ;OUTPUT ONE BYTE
DB      PITMDE                  ;DESTINATION IS MODE REGISTER
DB      00110110B               ;BIT 0 = 0 (BINARY COUNT)
                                ;BITS 3..1 = 011 (MODE 3 - SQUARE WAVE
                                ; RATE GENERATOR)
                                ;BITS 5,4 = 11 (LOAD 2 BYTES TO COUNTER)
                                ;BITS 7,6 = 00 (SELECT COUNTER 0)
DB      2                       ;OUTPUT TWO BYTES
DB      PIT0                    ;DESTINATION IS COUNTER 0
DB      13                      ;LOW BYTE OF COUNTER
DB      0                       ;HIGH BYTE OF COUNTER

;INITIALIZE 8251 FOR ASYNCHRONOUS SERIAL I/O.
;       RESET 8251 IN SOFTWARE BY SENDING IT 2 BYTES OF 80H,
;         FOLLOWED BY 1 BYTE OF 40H.
;       SET ASYNCHRONOUS MODE, 8-BIT CHARACTERS, NO PARITY,
;         2 STOP BITS, 16 TIMES CLOCK.
;       ENABLE TRANSMITTER AND RECEIVER, RESET ERROR
;         INDICATORS.
DB      4                       ;OUTPUT FOUR BYTES
DB      PCIC                    ;DESTINATION IS PCI CONTROL PORT
                                ;ASYNCHRONOUS MODE INSTRUCTION
DB      80H                     ;RESET 8251
DB      80H                     ; WITH 2 BYTES OF 80H
DB      40H                     ; FOLLOWED BY A RESET COMMAND
DB      11001110B               ;BITS 1,0 = 10 (16X BAUD RATE FACTOR)
                                ;BITS 3,2 = 11 (8-BIT CHARACTERS)
                                ;BIT 4 = 0 (PARITY DISABLED)
                                ;BIT 5 = 0 (DON'T CARE)
                                ;BITS 6,5 = 11 (2 STOP BITS)

                                ;ASYNCHRONOUS COMMAND INSTRUCTION
DB      00010111B               ;BIT 0 = 1 (TRANSMIT ENABLE)
                                ;BIT 1 = 1 (DATA TERMINAL READY)
                                ;BIT 2 = 1 (RECEIVE ENABLE)
                                ;BIT 3 = 0 (NO BREAK CHARACTER)
                                ;BIT 4 = 1 (ERROR RESET)
                                ;BIT 5 = 0 (NO REQUEST TO SEND)
                                ;BIT 6 = 0 (NO RESET)
                                ;BIT 7 = 0 (NOT HUNTING)

;INITIALIZE 8255 PPI (PARALLEL INTERFACE)
;
;       PORT A INPUT, PORT B OUTPUT, UPPER 4 BITS OF PORT
```

```
;           C OUTPUT, LOWER 4 BITS OF PORT C INPUT.   NO AUTOMATIC
;           HANDSHAKING SIGNALS (MODE 0 - BASIC I/O)
DB      1                    ;OUTPUT 1 BYTE
DB      PPIC                 ;DESTINATION IS PPI CONTROL PORT
DB      10010001B            ;BIT 0 = 1 (LOWER PORT C INPUT)
                             ;BIT 1 = 0 (PORT B OUTPUT)
                             ;BIT 2 = 0 (PORT B MODE IS 0)
                             ;BIT 3 = 0 (UPPER PORT C OUTPUT)
                             ;BIT 4 = 1 (PORT A INPUT)
                             ;BIT 6,5 = 00 (PORT A MODE IS 0)
                             ;BIT 7 = 1 (MODE SELECT COMMAND)

;END OF PORT INITIALIZATION DATA
DB      0                    ;TERMINATOR

        END
```

Provides a delay of between 1 and 256 milliseconds, depending on the parameter supplied. A parameter value of 0 is interpreted as 256. The user must calculate the value CPMS (cycles per millisecond) to fit a particular computer. Typical values are 2000 for a 2 MHz clock, 3000 for a 3 MHz clock, and 5000 for a 5 MHz clock.

Procedure: The program simply counts down register B for the appropriate amount of time as determined by the user-supplied constant. Extra instructions account for the CALL instruction, RET instruction, and routine overhead without changing anything.

Registers Used: AF, B

Execution Time: 1 ms * (A)

Program Size: 54 bytes

Data Memory Required: None

Special Case: (A) = 0 causes a delay of 256 ms.

Entry Conditions

Number of milliseconds to delay (1 to 256) in A

Exit Conditions

Returns after the specified delay with (A) = 0

Example

1. Data: (A) = number of milliseconds = $2A_{16}$

   Result: Software delay of $2A_{16}$ milliseconds, with proper CPMS supplied by user

---

```
;
;
;
;
;        Title:          Delay Milliseconds
;        Name:           DELAY
;
;
;        Purpose:        Delay from 1 to 256 milliseconds
;
;        Entry:          Register A = Number of milliseconds to delay.
;                                    A 0 equals 256 milliseconds.
;
;
;
```

```
;                                                                    ;
;          Exit:           Returns to calling routine after the      ;
;                          specified delay                           ;
;          Registers used: AF,B                                      ;
;                                                                    ;
;          Time:           1 millisecond * Register A                ;
;                                                                    ;
;          Size:           Program 54 bytes                          ;
;                                                                    ;
;                                                                    ;


;
;EQUATES
;CYCLES PER MILLISECOND - USER-SUPPLIED
;
CPMS      EQU      2000      ;2000 = 2 MHZ CLOCK
                            ;3000 = 3 MHZ CLOCK
                            ;5000 = 5 MHZ CLOCK
                            ;       .
                            ;       .

;NOTE: TIMING IS SPECIFIED IN THE COMMENTS.  WHEN THERE
;      ARE TWO NUMBERS SEPARATED BY COMMAS, THE
;      FIRST IS FOR THE 8080 AND THE SECOND
;      FOR THE 8085.
;
;METHOD:
; THE ROUTINE IS DIVIDED INTO 2 PARTS. THE CALL TO
; THE "DLY" ROUTINE DELAYS EXACTLY 1 LESS THAN THE
; NUMBER OF REQUIRED MILLISECONDS. THE LAST ITERATION
; TAKES INTO ACCOUNT THE OVERHEAD TO CALL "DELAY" AND
; "DLY". THIS OVERHEAD IS
;              17,18 CYCLES ==> CALL DELAY
;              17,18 CYCLES ==> CALL DLY
;               5, 4 CYCLES ==> DCR  A
;              11,12 CYCLES ==> RZ
;               5, 4 CYCLES ==> INR  A
;               7, 7 CYCLES ==> MVI  B,(CPMS/100)-1
;               0,-3 CYCLES ==> JNZ  LDLP (ADJUST FOR LAST BRANCH)
;               5, 6 CYCLES ==> RNZ
;               5, 6 CYCLES ==> RNZ
;               4, 4 CYCLES ==> NOP
;               4, 4 CYCLES ==> NOP
;              10,10 CYCLES ==> JMP  DELAY1
;              10,10 CYCLES ==> RET
;              ------
;             100,100 CYCLES OVERHEAD

DELAY:
          ;DO ALL BUT THE LAST MILLISECOND

                                   ;17,18 CYCLES FOR USER'S CALL
          CALL     DLY             ;33,34 CYCLES FOR CALL AND RETURN TO DLY
          INR      A               ;5,4 CYCLES (MAKE Z FLAG = 0)
          MVI      B,(CPMS/50)-2   ;7 CYCLES
```

```
                                    ;-----
                                    ;62,63

            ;DO LAST MILLISECOND LESS 100 CYCLES
            ; TO ALLOW FOR OVERHEAD
LDLP:
            JMP     LDLY1           ;10 CYCLES
LDLY1:      JMP     LDLY2           ;10 CYCLES
LDLY2:      JMP     LDLY3           ;10 CYCLES
LDLY3:      RZ                      ;5,6 CYCLES      (NEVER TAKEN)
            DCR     B               ;5,4 CYCLES
            JNZ     LDLP            ;10 CYCLES       (10,7 THE LAST TIME)
                                    ;---
                                    ;50 CYCLES
                                    ;(47 CYCLES THE LAST TIME)

            ;DO 38 CYCLES FOR 8080 AND 40 CYCLES FOR 8085
            ; 2 EXTRA CYCLES FOR THE 8085 ADJUSTS
            ; FOR THE "JNZ LDLP" ABOVE TAKING ONLY 7
            ; CYCLES INSTEAD OF 10 THE LAST TIME THROUGH.
            RNZ                     ;5,6 CYCLES
            RNZ                     ;5,6 CYCLES
            NOP                     ;4 CYCLES
            NOP                     ;4 CYCLES
            JMP     DELAY1          ;10 CYCLES
DELAY1:     RET                     ;10 CYCLES
                                    ;---
                                    ;38,40 CYCLES


;*****************************
;ROUTINE: DLY
;PURPOSE: DELAY ALL BUT THE LAST MILLISECOND
;ENTRY: REGISTER A = NUMBER OF MILLISECONDS TOTAL
;EXIT:   DELAY ALL BUT THE LAST MILLISECOND
;USED:   AF,B
;*****************************

DLY:
            DCR     A               ;5,4 CYCLES
            RZ                      ;5,6 CYCLES (RETURN WHEN DONE)
            MVI     B,(CPMS/50)-1   ;7 CYCLES
                                    ;---
                                    ;17 CYCLES

DLP:
            JMP     DLY1            ;10 CYCLES
DLY1:       JMP     DLY2            ;10 CYCLES
DLY2:       JMP     DLY3            ;10 CYCLES
DLY3:       RZ                      ;5,6 CYCLES   (NEVER TAKEN)
            DCR     B               ;5,4 CYCLES
            JNZ     DLP             ;10 CYCLES
                                    ;---
                                    ;50 CYCLES
```

```
                ;DO 33 CYCLES FOR 8080 AND 36 CYCLES FOR 8085
                ; EXTRA 3 CYCLES FOR THE 8085 ADJUSTS
                ; FOR THE "JNZ DLP" ABOVE TAKING ONLY 7
                ; CYCLES INSTEAD OF 10 THE LAST TIME THROUGH.
                RNZ                     ;5,6 CYCLES (NEVER TAKEN)
                RNZ                     ;5,6 CYCLES (NEVER TAKEN)
                RNZ                     ;5,6 CYCLES (NEVER TAKEN)
                NOP                     ;4 CYCLES
                NOP                     ;4 CYCLES
                JMP     DLY             ;10 CYCLES


;                                                                              ;
;               SAMPLE EXECUTION                                               ;
;                                                                              ;


SC10F:
                ;
                ;DELAY 10 SECONDS
                ; CALL DELAY 40 TIMES AT 250 MILLISECONDS EACH
                ;
                MVI     E,40            ;40 TIMES (28 HEX)
QTRSCD:
                MVI     A,250           ;250 MILLISECONDS (FA HEX)
                CALL    DELAY
                DCR     E               ;DECREMENT COUNT
                JNZ     QTRSCD          ;CONTINUE UNTIL DONE

                JMP     SC10F


                END     ;PROGRAM
```

Performs interrupt-driven input and output using an 8251 PCI (Programmable Communication Interface or USART) and single-character input and output buffers. Consists of the following subroutines:

1. INCH reads a character from the input buffer.

2. INST determines whether the input buffer is empty.

3. OUTCH writes a character into the output buffer.

4. OUTST determines whether the output buffer is full.

5. INIT initializes the 8251 PCI, the interrupt vectors, and the software flags. The flags are used to manage data transfers between the main program and the interrupt service routines.

The actual service routines are

1. RDHDLR responds to the input interrupt by reading a character from the 8251 PCI into the input buffer.

2. WRHDLR responds to the output interrupt by writing a character from the output buffer into the 8251 PCI.

Procedures

1. INCH waits for a character to become available, clears the Data Ready flag (RECDF), and loads the character into the accumulator.

2. INST sets Carry from the Data Ready flag (RECDF).

3. OUTCH waits for the output buffer to empty, stores the character in the buffer, and sets the Character Available flag (TRNDF). If no output interrupt is expected (i.e., the interrupt

---

Registers Used:

1.	INCH:	AF
2.	INST:	AF
3.	OUTCH:	AF
4.	OUTST:	AF
5.	INIT:	AF, HL

Execution Time:

1. INCH: 105 cycles (8080) or 106 cycles (8085) if a character is available
2. INST: 27 cycles (8080 or 8085)
3. OUTCH: 198 cycles (8080 or 8085) if the output buffer is empty and an output interrupt is expected; 74 (8080) or 76 (8085) additional cycles to send the data to the PCI if no output interrupt is expected
4. OUTST: 27 cycles (8080 or 8085)
5. INIT: 271 cycles (8080 or 8085)
6. RDHDLR: 95 cycles (8080) or 96 cycles (8085)
7. WRHDLR: 174 cycles (8080 or 8085) if the output buffer is full; 96 cycles (8080) or 97 cycles (8085) if the output buffer is empty

Program Size: 166 bytes

Data Memory Required: 5 bytes anywhere in RAM for the received data (address RECDAT), Receive Data flag (address RECDF), transmit data (address TRNDAT), Transmit Data flag (address TRNDF), and Output Interrupt Expected flag (address OIE)

---

has been cleared because it occurred when no data was available), OUTCH sends the data to the PCI immediately.

4. OUTST sets the Carry from the Character Available flag (TRNDF).

5. INIT clears the software flags, sets up the interrupt vectors, and initializes the 8251 PCI by placing the appropriate values in its mode and

command registers. See Subroutine 10E for more details about 8251 PCI initialization.

6. RDHDLR reads the data, saves it in the input buffer, and sets the Data Ready flag (RECDF).

7. WRHDLR determines whether data is available. If not, it simply clears the output interrupt. If data is available, the program sends it to the 8251 and clears the Character Available flag (TRNDF).

Most 8080 or 8085-based interrupt systems employ a controller that responds to interrupt acknowledgments from the CPU and contains priority, vectoring, and other management logic. The example in the listing uses the popular 8259 Programmable Interrupt Controller (PIC). The 8259 PIC latches interrupt requests from peripheral chips, blocks subsequent requests from the same and lower priority levels, and generates a CALL instruction to vector the 8080 or 8085. The service routine must send the 8259 PIC an End-of-Interrupt (EOI) command before concluding to unblock subsequent requests.

Note that when the 8259 is in its usual "edge detect" mode, it recognizes only transitions on the interrupt lines. Thus, even if an interrupt from a peripheral chip is not cleared, it will be recognized only once. The chip's interrupt output will remain active, but the 8259 PIC will not generate another processor interrupt. Beaston has described the 8259 device in detail in "Using the 8259 Programmable Interrupt Controller," Intel Application Note AP-31, Intel Corporation, Santa Clara, CA, 1977.

The special problem with the output interrupt is that it may occur when no data is available. It cannot be ignored or it will assert itself indefinitely, creating an endless loop. The solution is simply to clear the 8259 PIC interrupt by sending the device an End-of-Interrupt command.

If the 8259 PIC were not in the system, the output interrupt would have to be disabled. There is no way to clear an 8251 interrupt directly without sending data to the device; this can be done with some serial interfaces such as the Z80 SIO.

But now a new problem arises when output data becomes available. That is, since the interrupt has been cleared, it obviously cannot inform the system that the 8251 PCI is ready to transmit. The solution is to have a flag that indicates (with a 0 value) that the output interrupt has occurred without being serviced. This flag is called OIE (Output Interrupt Expected). The initialization routine clears OIE (since the 8251 surely starts out ready to transmit). The output service routine clears it when an output interrupt occurs that cannot be serviced (no data is available) and sets it after sending data to the 8251 (in case it might have been cleared). Now the output routine OUTCH can check OIE to determine whether the output interrupt has already occurred (0 indicates it has, FF hex that it has not). If no output interrupt is expected, OUTCH simply sends the data immediately.

Unserviceable interrupts occur only with output devices, since input devices always have data ready to transfer when they request service. Thus, output devices cause more initialization and sequencing problems in interrupt-driven systems than do input devices.

Entry Conditions

1. INCH: None
2. INST: None
3. OUTCH: Character to transmit in A
4. OUTST: None
5. INIT: None

Exit Conditions

1. INCH: Character in A
2. INST: Carry = 0 if input buffer empty, 1 if full
3. OUTCH: None
4. OUTST: Carry = 0 if output buffer empty, 1 if full
5. INIT: None

```
;                                                                    ;
;                                                                    ;
;                                                                    ;
;          Title:          Unbuffered Input/Output Using an 8251 PCI ;
;          Name:           SINTIO                                    ;
;                                                                    ;
;                                                                    ;
;                                                                    ;
;                                                                    ;
;          Purpose:        This program consists of five subroutines that ;
;                          perform interrupt-driven input and output using ;
;                          an 8251 USART.                            ;
;                                                                    ;
;                          INCH                                      ;
;                            Read a character                        ;
;                          INST                                      ;
;                            Determine input status (whether input   ;
;                            buffer is empty)                        ;
;                          OUTCH                                     ;
;                            Write a character                       ;
;                          OUTST                                     ;
;                            Determine output status (whether output ;
;                            buffer is full)                         ;
;                          INIT                                      ;
;                            Initialize USART and interrupt system   ;
;                                                                    ;
;          Entry:          INCH                                      ;
;                            No parameters                           ;
;                          INST                                      ;
;                            No parameters                           ;
;                          OUTCH                                     ;
;                            Register A = Character to transmit      ;
;                          OUTST                                     ;
;                            No parameters                           ;
;                          INIT                                      ;
;                            No parameters                           ;
;                                                                    ;
;          Exit:           INCH                                      ;
;                            Register A = Character                  ;
```

```
;                              INST                                     ;
;                                Carry = 0 if input buffer is empty,    ;
;                                1 if character is available            ;
;                              OUTCH                                    ;
;                                No parameters                          ;
;                              OUTST                                    ;
;                                Carry = 0 if output buffer is empty,   ;
;                                1 if it is full                        ;
;                              INIT                                     ;
;                                No parameters                          ;
;                                                                       ;
;          Registers used: INCH                                         ;
;                              AF                                       ;
;                            INST                                       ;
;                              AF                                       ;
;                            OUTCH                                      ;
;                              AF                                       ;
;                            OUTST                                      ;
;                              AF                                       ;
;                            INIT                                       ;
;                              AF,HL                                    ;
;                                                                       ;
;          Time:             INCH                                       ;
;                              105 cycles if a character is available for;
;                              8080, and 106 for 8085                   ;
;                            INST                                       ;
;                              27 cycles for 8080 and 8085              ;
;                            OUTCH                                      ;
;                              198 cycles if output buffer is not full and;
;                              output interrupt is expected for 8080 and 8085;
;                            OUTST                                      ;
;                              27 cycles for 8080 and 8085              ;
;                            INIT                                       ;
;                              271 cycles for 8080 and 8085             ;
;                            RDHDLR                                     ;
;                              95 cycles for 8080 and 96 cycles for 8085;
;                            WRHDLR                                     ;
;                              174 cycles for 8080 and 8085 if output   ;
;                              buffer is full                           ;
;                                                                       ;
;          Size:             Program 166 bytes                          ;
;                            Data       5 bytes                         ;
;                                                                       ;
;                                                                       ;
;

          ;8251 PCI (USART) EQUATES
          ; 8251 IS PROGRAMMED FOR
          ;   ASYNCHRONOUS OPERATION
          ;   16 X BAUD RATE
          ;   8-BIT CHARACTERS
          ;   2 STOP BITS
          ;ARBITRARY 8251 PCI PORT ADDRESSES
USARTDR EQU      084H              ;USART DATA REGISTER
USARTSR EQU      085H              ;USART STATUS REGISTER
USARTCR EQU      085H              ;USART CONTROL REGISTER
```

```
            ;INTERRUPT VECTORS
RDITRP   EQU      0020H              ;READ INTERRUPT VECTOR
WRITRP   EQU      0028H              ;WRITE INTERRUPT VECTOR

            ;8251 ASYNCHRONOUS MODE INSTRUCTION
MODE     EQU      11001110B          ;BITS 1,0 = 10 (16X BAUD RATE FACTOR)
                                     ;BITS 3,2 = 11 (8-BIT CHARACTERS)
                                     ;BIT 4 = 0 (PARITY DISABLED)
                                     ;BIT 5 = 0 (DON'T CARE)
                                     ;BITS 6,5 = 11 (2 STOP BITS)

            ;8251 ASYNCHRONOUS COMMAND INSTRUCTION
CMD      EQU      00010111B          ;BIT 0 = 1 (TRANSMIT ENABLE)
                                     ;BIT 1 = 1 (DATA TERMINAL READY)
                                     ;BIT 2 = 1 (RECEIVE ENABLE)
                                     ;BIT 3 = 0 (NO BREAK CHARACTER)
                                     ;BIT 4 = 1 (ERROR RESET)
                                     ;BIT 5 = 0 (NO REQUEST TO SEND)
                                     ;BIT 6 = 0 (NO RESET)
                                     ;BIT 7 = 0 (NOT HUNTING)
            ;8259 PROGRAMMABLE INTERRUPT CONTROLLER (PIC) EQUATES
            ; 8259 PIC IS PROGRAMMED FOR
            ;   SINGLE DEVICE (RATHER THAN MULTIPLE 8259'S)
            ;   FULLY NESTED MODE
            ;   ALL INTERRUPTS ENABLED
            ;   RESTART 4, ADDRESS 0020, FOR READ INTERRUPT
            ;   RESTART 5, ADDRESS 0028, FOR WRITE INTERRUPT
            ;ARBITRARY 8259 PIC PORT ADDRESSES
PIC0     EQU      90H                ;PIC PORT 1
PIC1     EQU      91H                ;PIC PORT 2

            ;8259 INITIALIZATION COMMAND WORDS ICW1 AND ICW2
ICW1     EQU      00010010B          ;BIT 0 = 0 (NOT USED)
                                     ;BIT 1 = 1 (SINGLE 8259)
                                     ;BIT 2 = 0 (VECTOR INTERVAL = 8 BYTES)
                                     ;BIT 3 = 0 (EDGE DETECT)
                                     ;BIT 4 = 1 (FIXED)
                                     ;BITS 5,6,7 = 0 (BITS 5-7 OF BASE
                                     ; ADDRESS OF RESTARTS)
ICW2     EQU      0                  ;UPPER BYTE OF BASE ADDRESS OF
                                     ; RESTARTS

            ;8259 OPERATING COMMAND WORD
EOI      EQU      00100000B          ;END OF INTERRUPT COMMAND WORD

            ;READ CHARACTER
INCH:
         CALL     INST               ;GET INPUT STATUS
         JNC      INCH               ;WAIT IF NO CHARACTER AVAILABLE
         DI                          ;DISABLE INTERRUPTS
         SUB      A
         STA      RECDF              ;INDICATE INPUT BUFFER EMPTY
         LDA      RECDAT             ;GET CHARACTER FROM INPUT BUFFER
         EI                          ;ENABLE INTERRUPTS
         RET
```

```
              ;RETURN INPUT STATUS (CARRY = 1 IF DATA AVAILABLE)
INST:
              LDA      RECDF            ;GET DATA READY FLAG
              RAR                       ;SET CARRY FROM DATA READY FLAG
                                        ; CARRY = 1 IF CHARACTER AVAILABLE
              RET

              ;WRITE CHARACTER
OUTCH:
              PUSH     PSW              ;SAVE CHARACTER TO WRITE

              ;WAIT FOR OUTPUT BUFFER TO EMPTY, STORE NEXT CHARACTER
WAITOC:
              CALL     OUTST            ;GET OUTPUT STATUS
              JC       WAITOC           ;WAIT IF OUTPUT BUFFER FULL
              DI                        ;DISABLE INTERRUPTS WHILE LOOKING AT
                                        ; SOFTWARE FLAGS
              POP      PSW              ;GET CHARACTER
              STA      TRNDAT           ;STORE CHARACTER IN OUTPUT BUFFER
              MVI      A,OFFH           ;INDICATE OUTPUT BUFFER FULL
              STA      TRNDF
              LDA      OIE              ;TEST OUTPUT INTERRUPT EXPECTED FLAG
              ORA      A
              CZ       OUTDAT           ;SEND CHARACTER IMMEDIATELY IF
                                        ; NO OUTPUT INTERRUPT EXPECTED
              EI                        ;REENABLE INTERRUPTS
              RET

              ;OUTPUT STATUS (CARRY = 1 IF OUTPUT BUFFER FULL)
OUTST:
              LDA      TRNDF            ;GET TRANSMIT FLAG
              RAR                       ;SET CARRY FROM TRANSMIT FLAG
              RET                       ; CARRY = 1 IF BUFFER FULL

              ;INITIALIZE INTERRUPT SYSTEM AND 8251 PCI
INIT:
              DI                        ;DISABLE INTERRUPTS FOR INITIALIZATION

              ;INITIALIZE SOFTWARE FLAGS
              SUB      A
              STA      RECDF            ;NO INPUT DATA AVAILABLE
              STA      TRNDF            ;OUTPUT BUFFER EMPTY
              STA      OIE              ;INDICATE NO OUTPUT INTERRUPT NEEDED
                                        ; 8251 READY TO TRANSMIT INITIALLY

              ;INITIALIZE INTERRUPT VECTORS
              LXI      H,RDHDLR
              MVI      A,OC3H           ;C3 HEX IS JMP OP CODE
              STA      RDITRP           ;STORE JUMP OP CODE FOR READ INTERRUPT
              SHLD     RDITRP+1         ;STORE JUMP ADDRESS
              LXI      H,WRHDLR
              STA      WRITRP           ;STORE JUMP OP CODE FOR WRITE INTERRUPT
              SHLD     WRITRP+1         ;STORE JUMP ADDRESS

              ;INITIALIZE 8259 INTERRUPT CONTROLLER
```

```
        MVI     A,ICW1              ;SEND FIRST WORD TO PIC PORT 0
        OUT     PIC0
        MVI     A,ICW2              ;SEND SECOND WORD TO PIC PORT 1
        OUT     PIC1

        ;INITIALIZE 8251 PCI (USART)
        MVI     A,10000000B         ;SOFTWARE RESET 8251 PCI
        OUT     USARTCR             ; BY SENDING IT 2 BYTES OF 80 HEX
        OUT     USARTCR             ; FOLLOWED BY A RESET COMMAND
        MVI     A,01000000B
        OUT     USARTCR

        MVI     A,MODE              ;OUTPUT MODE BYTE
        OUT     USARTCR
        MVI     A,CMD               ;OUTPUT COMMAND BYTE
        OUT     USARTCR
        IN      USARTDR             ;READ DATA REGISTER TO CLEAR STRAY
                                    ; DATA FROM INPUT REGISTER INITIALLY

        EI                          ;ENABLE INTERRUPTS
        RET

        ;INPUT (READ) INTERRUPT HANDLER
RDHDLR:
        PUSH    PSW                 ;SAVE AF
        IN      USARTDR             ;READ DATA FROM 8251 PCI
        STA     RECDAT              ;SAVE DATA IN INPUT BUFFER
        MVI     A,0FFH
        STA     RECDF               ;INDICATE INPUT DATA AVAILABLE
        MVI     A,EOI
        OUT     PIC0                ;CLEAR 8259 INTERRUPT
        POP     PSW                 ;RESTORE AF
        EI                          ;REENABLE INTERRUPTS
        RET

        ;OUTPUT (WRITE) INTERRUPT HANDLER
WRHDLR:
        PUSH    PSW                 ;SAVE AF
        LDA     TRNDF               ;TEST DATA AVAILABLE FLAG
        ORA     A
        JZ      NODATA              ;JUMP IF NO DATA TO TRANSMIT
        CALL    OUTDAT              ;SEND DATA TO 8251 PCI
        JMP     WRDONE

        ;IF AN OUTPUT INTERRUPT OCCURS WHEN NO DATA IS AVAILABLE,
        ; WE MUST CLEAR IT (IN THE 8259) TO AVOID AN ENDLESS
        ; LOOP. LATER, WHEN A CHARACTER BECOMES AVAILABLE, WE NEED
        ; TO KNOW THAT AN OUTPUT INTERRUPT HAS OCCURRED WITHOUT
        ; BEING SERVICED.  THE KEY TO DOING THIS IS THE OUTPUT
        ; INTERRUPT EXPECTED FLAG OIE.  THIS FLAG IS CLEARED WHEN
        ; AN OUTPUT INTERRUPT HAS OCCURRED BUT HAS NOT BEEN
        ; SERVICED.  IT IS ALSO CLEARED INITIALLY SINCE THE 8251
        ; PCI STARTS OUT READY.  OIE IS SET WHENEVER DATA IS
        ; ACTUALLY SENT TO THE PCI. THUS THE OUTPUT ROUTINE OUTCH
        ; CAN CHECK OIE TO DETERMINE WHETHER TO SEND THE DATA
        ; IMMEDIATELY OR WAIT FOR AN OUTPUT INTERRUPT.
```

```
                ;THE PROBLEM IS THAT AN OUTPUT DEVICE MAY REQUEST SERVICE
                ; BEFORE THE COMPUTER HAS ANYTHING TO SEND (UNLIKE AN
                ; INPUT DEVICE THAT HAS DATA WHEN IT REQUESTS SERVICE).
                ; THE OIE FLAG SOLVES THE PROBLEM OF AN UNSERVICED OUTPUT
                ; INTERRUPT ASSERTING ITSELF REPEATEDLY WHILE STILL
                ; ENSURING THE RECOGNITION OF OUTPUT INTERRUPTS.
NODATA:
                SUB       A
                STA       OIE                ;DO NOT EXPECT AN INTERRUPT

WRDONE:
                MVI       A,EOI              ;CLEAR 8259 INTERRUPT
                OUT       PICO
                POP       PSW                ;RESTORE AF
                EI                           ;REENABLE INTERRUPTS
                RET


                ;*************************************
                ;ROUTINE: OUTDAT
                ;PURPOSE: SEND CHARACTER TO USART
                ;ENTRY: TRNDAT = CHARACTER
                ;EXIT:  NONE
                ;REGISTERS USED: AF
                ;*************************************
OUTDAT:
                LDA       TRNDAT             ;GET DATA FROM OUTPUT BUFFER
                OUT       USARTDR            ;SEND DATA TO 8251 PCI
                SUB       A                  ;INDICATE OUTPUT BUFFER EMPTY
                STA       TRNDF
                DCR       A                  ;INDICATE OUTPUT INTERRUPT EXPECTED
                STA       OIE                ; OIE = FF HEX
                RET

                ;DATA SECTION
RECDAT  DS      1                            ;RECEIVE DATA
RECDF   DS      1                            ;RECEIVE DATA FLAG
                                             ; (0 = NO DATA, FF = DATA AVAILABLE)
TRNDAT  DS      1                            ;TRANSMIT DATA
TRNDF   DS      1                            ;TRANSMIT DATA FLAG
                                             ; (0 = BUFFER EMPTY, FF = BUFFER FULL)
OIE     DS      1                            ;OUTPUT INTERRUPT EXPECTED
                                             ; (0 = NO INTERRUPT EXPECTED,
                                             ; FF = INTERRUPT EXPECTED)


;                                                                      ;
;                                                                      ;
;          SAMPLE EXECUTION                                            ;
;                                                                      ;
;                                                                      ;


                ;CHARACTER EQUATES
ESCAPE  EQU     1BH                          ;ASCII ESCAPE CHARACTER
TESTCH  EQU     'A'                          ;TEST CHARACTER = A
```

```
SC11A:
        CALL    INIT            ;INITIALIZE 8251 PCI, INTERRUPT SYSTEM

        ;SIMPLE EXAMPLE - READ AND ECHO CHARACTERS
        ; UNTIL AN ESC IS RECEIVED
LOOP:
        CALL    INCH            ;READ CHARACTER
        PUSH    PSW
        CALL    OUTCH           ;ECHO CHARACTER
        POP     PSW
        CPI     ESCAPE          ;IS CHARACTER AN ESCAPE?
        JNZ     LOOP            ;STAY IN LOOP IF NOT

        ;AN ASYNCHRONOUS EXAMPLE
        ; OUTPUT "A" TO CONSOLE CONTINUOUSLY BUT ALSO LOOK AT
        ; INPUT SIDE, READING AND ECHOING ANY INPUT CHARACTERS
ASYNLP:
        ;OUTPUT AN "A" IF OUTPUT IS NOT BUSY
        CALL    OUTST           ;IS OUTPUT BUSY?
        JC      ASYNLP          ;JUMP IF IT IS
        MVI     A,TESTCH
        CALL    OUTCH           ;OUTPUT TEST CHARACTER

        ;CHECK INPUT PORT
        ;ECHO CHARACTER IF ONE IS AVAILABLE
        ;EXIT ON ESCAPE CHARACTER
        CALL    INST            ;IS INPUT DATA AVAILABLE?
        JC      ASYNLP          ;JUMP IF NOT (SEND ANOTHER "A")
        CALL    INCH            ;GET CHARACTER
        CPI     ESCAPE          ;IS IT AN ESCAPE?
        JZ      DONE            ;BRANCH IF IT IS
        CALL    OUTCH           ;ELSE ECHO CHARACTER
        JMP     ASYNLP          ;AND CONTINUE

DONE:
        JMP     SC11A

        END
```

Unbuffered Input/Output Using an 8255 PPI (PINTIO)

Performs interrupt-driven input and output using an 8255 PPI and single-character input and output buffers. Consists of the following subroutines:

1. INCH reads a character from the input buffer.

2. INST determines whether the input buffer is empty.

3. OUTCH writes a character into the output buffer.

4. OUTST determines whether the output buffer is full.

5. INIT initializes the 8255 PPI, the interrupt vectors, and the software flags. The flags are used to manage data transfers between the main program and the interrupt service routines.

The actual service routines are

1. RDHDLR responds to the input interrupt by reading a character from the 8255 PPI into the input buffer.

2. WRHDLR responds to the output interrupt by writing a character from the output buffer into the 8255 PPI.

Procedure

1. INCH waits for a character to become available, clears the Data Ready flag (RECDF), and loads the character into the accumulator.

2. INST sets Carry from the Data Ready flag (RECDF).

3. OUTCH waits for the output buffer to empty, stores the character in the buffer, and sets the Character Available flag (TRNDF). If no output interrupt is expected (i.e., the interrupt has been cleared because it occurred when no

---

Registers Used:

1.	INCH:	AF
2.	INST:	AF
3.	OUTCH:	AF
4.	OUTST:	AF
5.	INIT:	AF, HL

Execution Time:

1.	INCH:	102 cycles (8080) or 100 cycles (8085) if a character is available
2.	INST:	27 cycles (8080 or 8085)
3.	OUTCH:	143 cycles (8080) or 139 cycles (8085) if the output buffer is not full and an output interrupt is expected; 74 (8080) or 76 (8085) additional cycles to send the data to the 8255 PPI if no output interrupt is expected
4.	OUTST:	27 cycles (8080 or 8085)
5.	INIT:	231 cycles (8080 or 8085)
6.	RDHDLR:	95 cycles (8080) or 96 cycles (8085)
7.	WRHDLR:	171 cycles (8080) or 169 cycles (8085) if the output buffer is full; 96 cycles (8080) or 97 cycles (8085) if the output buffer is empty

Program Size: 162 bytes

Data Memory Required: 5 bytes anywhere in RAM for the received data (address RECDAT), Receive Data flag (address RECDF), transmit data (address TRNDAT), Transmit Data flag (address TRNDF), and Output Interrupt Expected flag (address OIE)

---

data was available), OUTCH sends the data to the 8255 PPI immediately.

4. OUTST sets Carry from the Character Available flag (TRNDF).

5. INIT clears the software flags, sets up the interrupt vectors, and initializes the 8255 PPI by loading its control registers and interrupt vector register. See Chapter 1 and Subroutine 10E for more details about initializing 8255 PPIs.

397

6. RDHDLR reads a character from the 8255 PPI, saves it in the input buffer, and sets the Data Ready flag (RECDF).

7. WRHDLR determines whether output data is available. If not, it simply clears the output interrupt. If data is available, WRHDLR sends it to the 8255 PPI and clears the Character Available flag (TRNDF).

Most 8080 or 8085-based interrupt systems employ a controller that responds to interrupt acknowledgments from the CPU and contains priority, vectoring, and other management logic. The example in the listing uses the popular 8259 Programmable Interrupt Controller (PIC). The 8259 latches interrupt requests from peripheral chips, blocks subsequent requests from the same and lower priority levels, and generates a CALL instruction to vector the 8080 or 8085. The service routine must send the 8259 PIC an End-of-Interrupt (EOI) command before concluding to unblock subsequent requests.

Note that when the 8259 is in its usual "edge detect" mode, it recognizes only transitions on the interrupt lines. Thus, even if an interrupt from a peripheral chip is not cleared, it will be recognized only once. The chip's interrupt output will remain active, but the 8259 PIC will not generate another processor interrupt. Beaston has described the 8259 device in detail in "Using the 8259 Programmable Interrupt Controller," Intel Application Note AP-31, Intel Corporation, Santa Clara, CA, 1977.

If the 8259 PIC were not in the system, the output interrupt would have to be disabled. There is no way to clear an 8255 PPI interrupt directly without sending data to the device; this can be done with some parallel interfaces, such as the 6820 Peripheral Interface Adapter and the 6522 Versatile Interface Adapter.

The special problem with the output interrupt is that it may occur when no data is available to send. It cannot be ignored or it will assert itself indefinitely, causing an endless loop. The solution is simply to clear the 8259 PIC interrupt by sending the device an End-of-Interrupt command.

But now a new problem arises when output data becomes available. That is, since the interrupt has been cleared, it obviously cannot inform the system that the output device is ready for data. The solution is to have a flag that indicates (with a 0 value) that the output interrupt has occurred without being serviced. This flag is called OIE (Output Interrupt Expected).

The initialization routine clears OIE (since the output device starts out ready for data). The output service routine clears it when an output interrupt occurs that cannot be serviced (no data is available) and sets it after sending data to the 8255 PPI (in case it might have been cleared). Now the output routine OUTCH can check OIE to determine whether an output interrupt is expected. If not, OUTCH simply sends the data immediately.

Unserviceable interrupts occur only with output devices, since input devices always have data ready to transfer when they request service. Thus, output devices cause more initialization and sequencing problems in interrupt-driven systems than do input devices.

Entry Conditions

1.   INCH: None
2.   INST: None
3. OUTCH: Character to transmit in A
4. OUTST: None
5.   INIT: None

Exit Conditions

1.   INCH: Character in A
2.   INST: Carry = 0 if input buffer
              empty, 1 if full
3. OUTCH: None
4. OUTST: Carry = 0 if output buffer
              empty, 1 if full
5.   INIT: None

```
;                                                                        ;
;                                                                        ;
;                                                                        ;
;                                                                        ;
;       Title:          Unbuffered Input/Output Using an 8255 PPI        ;
;       Name:           PINTIO                                           ;
;                                                                        ;
;                                                                        ;
;                                                                        ;
;                                                                        ;
;       Purpose:        This program consists of five subroutines that   ;
;                       perform interrupt-driven input and output using  ;
;                       an 8255 PPI.                                     ;
;                                                                        ;
;                       INCH                                             ;
;                         Read a character                              ;
;                       INST                                             ;
;                         Determine input status (whether input         ;
;                         buffer is empty)                              ;
;                       OUTCH                                            ;
;                         Write a character                             ;
;                       OUTST                                            ;
;                         Determine output status (whether output       ;
;                         buffer is full)                               ;
;                       INIT                                             ;
;                         Initialize 8255 PPI and interrupt system      ;
;                                                                        ;
;       Entry:          INCH                                             ;
;                         No parameters                                 ;
;                       INST                                             ;
;                         No parameters                                 ;
;                       OUTCH                                            ;
;                         Register A = Character to transmit            ;
;                       OUTST                                            ;
;                         No parameters                                 ;
;                       INIT                                             ;
;                         No parameters                                 ;
;                                                                        ;
;       Exit:           INCH                                             ;
```

```
;                                     Register A = Character                         ;
;                                   INST                                             ;
;                                     Carry = 0 if input buffer is empty,            ;
;                                     1 if character is available                    ;
;                                   OUTCH                                            ;
;                                     No parameters                                  ;
;                                   OUTST                                            ;
;                                     Carry = 0 if output buffer is                  ;
;                                     empty, 1 if it is full                         ;
;                                   INIT                                             ;
;                                     No parameters                                  ;
;                                                                                    ;
;                 Registers used:  INCH                                              ;
;                                     AF                                             ;
;                                   INST                                             ;
;                                     AF                                             ;
;                                   OUTCH                                            ;
;                                     AF                                             ;
;                                   OUTST                                            ;
;                                     AF                                             ;
;                                   INIT                                             ;
;                                     AF,HL                                          ;
;                                                                                    ;
;                 Time:             INCH                                             ;
;                                     102 cycles if a character is available for     ;
;                                     8080, and 100 for 8085                         ;
;                                   INST                                             ;
;                                     27 cycles for 8080 and 8085                    ;
;                                   OUTCH                                            ;
;                                     143 cycles if output buffer is not full and    ;
;                                     output interrupt is expected for 8080,         ;
;                                     and 139 for 8085                               ;
;                                   OUTST                                            ;
;                                     27 cycles for 8080 and 8085                    ;
;                                   INIT                                             ;
;                                     231 cycles for 8080 and 8085                   ;
;                                   RDHDLR                                           ;
;                                     95 cycles for 8080 and 96 cycles for 8085      ;
;                                   WRHDLR                                           ;
;                                     171 cycles for 8080 and 169 for 8085           ;
;                                     if output buffer is full                       ;
;                                                                                    ;
;                 Size:             Program 162 bytes                                ;
;                                   Data       5 bytes                               ;
;                                                                                    ;
;                                                                                    ;

        ;8255 PPI EQUATES
        ; 8255 PPI IS PROGRAMMED FOR
        ;   MODE 1 (STROBED INPUT AND OUTPUT)
        ;   PORT A INPUT
        ;   PORT B OUTPUT
        ;   PORT C HANDSHAKE SIGNALS
        ;ARBITRARY 8255 PPI PORT ADDRESSES
PPIA    EQU     90H                    ;PORT A DATA
```

```
PPIB        EQU     91H                 ;PORT B DATA
PPIC        EQU     92H                 ;PORT C DATA
PPICTRL     EQU     93H                 ;CONTROL PORT

            ;8255 PPI CONTROL BYTES
CTRLWRD     EQU     010110100B          ;CONTROL WORD FOR
                                        ; MODE 1, PORT A INPUT, PORT B OUTPUT
PAIE        EQU     00001001B           ;ENABLE A INTERRUPT - SET BIT 4 OF C
PAID        EQU     00001000B           ;DISABLE A INTERRUPT - CLEAR BIT 4 OF C
PBIE        EQU     00000101B           ;ENABLE B INTERRUPT - SET BIT 2 OF C
PBID        EQU     00000100B           ;DISABLE B INTERRUPT - CLEAR BIT 2 OF C


            ;8259 PROGRAMMABLE INTERRUPT CONTROLLER (PIC) EQUATES
            ; 8259 IS PROGRAMMED FOR
            ;   SINGLE DEVICE (RATHER THAN MULTIPLE 8259'S)
            ;   FULLY NESTED MODE
            ;   ALL INTERRUPTS ENABLED
            ;   RESTART 4, ADDRESS 0020, FOR READ INTERRUPT
            ;   RESTART 5, ADDRESS 0028, FOR WRITE INTERRUPT
            ;8259 PORT ADDRESSES
PIC0        EQU     0A0H                ;PIC PORT 1
PIC1        EQU     0A1H                ;PIC PORT 2

            ; INTERRUPT VECTORS
RDITRP      EQU     0020H               ;READ INTERRUPT VECTOR
WRITRP      EQU     0028H.              ;WRITE INTERRUPT VECTOR

            ;8259 INITIALIZATION COMMAND WORDS ICW1 AND ICW2
ICW1        EQU     00010010B           ;BIT 0 = 0 (NOT USED)
                                        ;BIT 1 = 1 (SINGLE 8259)
                                        ;BIT 2 = 0 (VECTOR INTERVAL = 8 BYTES)
                                        ;BIT 3 = 0 (EDGE TRIGGERED INTERRUPTS)
                                        ;BIT 4 = 1 (FIXED)
                                        ;BITS 7,6,5 = 0 (BITS 5-7 OF BASE
                                        ; ADDRESS OF RESTARTS)
ICW2        EQU     0                   ;UPPER BYTE OF BASE ADDRESS OF
                                        ; RESTARTS

            ;8259 OPERATING COMMAND WORD
EOI         EQU     00100000B           ;END OF INTERRUPT COMMAND WORD

            ;READ CHARACTER
INCH:
            CALL    INST                ;GET INPUT STATUS
            JNC     INCH                ;WAIT IF NO CHARACTER AVAILABLE
            DI                          ;DISABLE INTERRUPTS
            SUB     A
            STA     RECDF               ;INDICATE INPUT BUFFER EMPTY
            LDA     RECDAT              ;GET CHARACTER FROM INPUT BUFFER
            EI                          ;ENABLE INTERRUPTS
            RET

            ;RETURN INPUT STATUS (CARRY = 1 IF DATA AVAILABLE)
INST:
            LDA     RECDF               ;GET DATA READY FLAG
```

```
        RAR                     ;SET CARRY FROM DATA READY FLAG
                                ; CARRY = 1 IF CHARACTER AVAILABLE
        RET

        ;WRITE CHARACTER
OUTCH:
        PUSH    PSW             ;SAVE CHARACTER TO WRITE

        ;WAIT FOR OUTPUT BUFFER TO EMPTY, STORE NEXT CHARACTER
WAITOC:
        CALL    OUTST           ;GET OUTPUT STATUS
        JC      WAITOC          ;WAIT IF OUTPUT BUFFER FULL
        DI                      ;DISABLE INTERRUPTS WHILE LOOKING AT
                                ; SOFTWARE FLAGS
        POP     PSW             ;GET CHARACTER
        STA     TRNDAT          ;STORE CHARACTER IN OUTPUT BUFFER
        MVI     A,OFFH          ;INDICATE OUTPUT BUFFER FULL
        STA     TRNDF
        LDA     OIE             ;TEST OUTPUT INTERRUPT EXPECTED FLAG
        ORA     A
        CZ      OUTDAT          ;SEND CHARACTER IMMEDIATELY IF
                                ; NO OUTPUT INTERRUPT EXPECTED
        EI                      ;REENABLE INTERRUPTS
        RET
        ;OUTPUT STATUS (CARRY = 1 IF OUTPUT BUFFER FULL)
OUTST:
        LDA     TRNDF           ;GET TRANSMIT FLAG
        RAR                     ;SET CARRY FROM TRANSMIT FLAG
        RET                     ; CARRY = 1 IF BUFFER FULL

        ;INITIALIZE INTERRUPT SYSTEM AND 8255 PPI
INIT:
        DI                      ;DISABLE INTERRUPTS FOR INITIALIZATION

        ;INITIALIZE SOFTWARE FLAGS
        SUB     A
        STA     RECDF           ;NO INPUT DATA AVAILABLE
        STA     TRNDF           ;OUTPUT BUFFER EMPTY
        STA     OIE             ;INDICATE NO OUTPUT INTERRUPT NEEDED
                                ; 8255 READY TO TRANSMIT INITIALLY

        ;INITIALIZE INTERRUPT VECTORS
        LXI     H,RDHDLR
        MVI     A,OC3H          ;C3 HEX IS JMP OP CODE
        STA     RDITRP          ;STORE JUMP OP CODE FOR READ INTERRUPT
        SHLD    RDITRP+1        ;STORE JUMP ADDRESS
        LXI     H,WRHDLR
        STA     WRITRP          ;STORE JUMP OP CODE FOR WRITE INTERRUPT
        SHLD    WRITRP+1        ;STORE JUMP ADDRESS

        ;INITIALIZE 8259 INTERRUPT CONTROLLER
        MVI     A,ICW1          ;SEND FIRST WORD TO PIC PORT O
        OUT     PICO
        MVI     A,ICW2          ;SEND SECOND WORD TO PIC PORT 1
        OUT     PIC1
```

```
            ;INITIALIZE 8255 PPI
            MVI     A,CTRLWRD       ;MODE 1, A INPUT, B OUTPUT
            OUT     PPICTRL         ;INITIALIZE 8255 CONTROL PORT

            ;ENABLE 8255 PPI INTERRUPTS
            MVI     A,PAIE          ;ENABLE PORT A INTERRUPT
            OUT     PPICTRL
            MVI     A,PBIE          ;ENABLE PORT B INTERRUPT
            OUT     PPICTRL

            EI                      ;ENABLE INTERRUPTS
            RET

            ;INPUT (READ) INTERRUPT HANDLER
RDHDLR:
            PUSH    PSW             ;SAVE AF
            IN      PPIA            ;READ DATA FROM 8255 PPI
            STA     RECDAT          ;SAVE DATA IN INPUT BUFFER
            MVI     A,0FFH
            STA     RECDF           ;INDICATE CHARACTER AVAILABLE
            MVI     A,EOI           ;CLEAR 8259 INTERRUPT
            OUT     PICO
            POP     PSW             ;RESTORE AF
            EI                      ;REENABLE INTERRUPTS
            RET
            ;OUTPUT (WRITE) INTERRUPT HANDLER
WRHDLR:
            PUSH    PSW             ;SAVE REGISTER A
            LDA     TRNDF           ;TEST DATA AVAILABLE FLAG
            ORA     A
            JZ      NODATA          ;JUMP IF NO DATA TO TRANSMIT
            CALL    OUTDAT          ;SEND DATA TO 8255 PPI
            JMP     WRDONE

            ;IF AN OUTPUT INTERRUPT OCCURS WHEN NO DATA IS AVAILABLE,
            ; WE MUST CLEAR IT (IN THE 8259) TO AVOID AN ENDLESS
            ; LOOP.  LATER, WHEN A CHARACTER BECOMES AVAILABLE, WE
            ; NEED TO KNOW THAT AN OUTPUT INTERRUPT HAS OCCURRED
            ; WITHOUT BEING SERVICED.  THE KEY TO DOING THIS IS THE
            ; OUTPUT INTERRUPT EXPECTED FLAG OIE.  THIS FLAG IS
            ; CLEARED WHEN AN OUTPUT INTERRUPT HAS OCCURRED BUT HAS
            ; NOT BEEN SERVICED.  IT IS ALSO CLEARED INITIALLY SINCE
            ; THE 8255 PPI STARTS OUT READY.  OIE IS SET WHENEVER
            ; DATA IS ACTUALLY SENT TO THE PPI.  THUS THE OUTPUT
            ; ROUTINE OUTCH CAN CHECK OIE TO DETERMINE WHETHER TO
            ; SEND THE DATA IMMEDIATELY OR WAIT FOR AN OUTPUT
            ; INTERRUPT.
            ;THE PROBLEM IS THAT AN OUTPUT DEVICE MAY REQUEST SERVICE
            ; BEFORE THE COMPUTER HAS ANYTHING TO SEND (UNLIKE AN
            ; INPUT DEVICE THAT HAS DATA WHEN IT REQUESTS SERVICE).
            ; THE OIE FLAG SOLVES THE PROBLEM OF AN UNSERVICED OUTPUT
            ; INTERRUPT ASSERTING ITSELF REPEATEDLY WHILE STILL
            ; ENSURING THE RECOGNITION OF OUTPUT INTERRUPTS.
NODATA:
            SUB     A
            STA     OIE             ;DO NOT EXPECT AN INTERRUPT
```

```
WRDONE:
        MVI     A,EOI              ;CLEAR 8259 INTERRUPT
        OUT     PICO
        POP     PSW                ;RESTORE AF
        EI                         ;REENABLE INTERRUPTS
        RET


        ;*****************************************
        ;ROUTINE: OUTDAT
        ;PURPOSE: SEND CHARACTER TO 8255 PPI
        ;ENTRY: TRNDAT = CHARACTER
        ;EXIT: NONE
        ;REGISTERS USED: AF
        ;*****************************************
OUTDAT:
        LDA     TRNDAT             ;GET DATA FROM OUTPUT BUFFER
        OUT     PPIB               ;SEND DATA TO 8255 PPI
        SUB     A                  ;INDICATE OUTPUT BUFFER EMPTY
        STA     TRNDF
        DCR     A                  ;INDICATE OUTPUT INTERRUPT EXPECTED
        STA     OIE                ; OIE = FF HEX
        RET

        ;DATA SECTION
RECDAT  DS      1                  ;RECEIVE DATA
RECDF   DS      1                  ;RECEIVE DATA FLAG (0 = NO DATA,
                                   ; FF = DATA)
TRNDAT  DS      1                  ;TRANSMIT DATA
TRNDF   S       1                  ;TRANSMIT DATA FLAG
                                   ; (0 = BUFFER EMPTY, FF = BUFFER FULL)
OIE     DS      1                  ;OUTPUT INTERRUPT EXPECTED
                                   ; (0 = NO INTERRUPT EXPECTED,
                                   ; FF = INTERRUPT EXPECTED)


;                                                                  ;
;                                                                  ;
;        SAMPLE EXECUTION                                          ;
;                                                                  ;
;                                                                  ;

        ;CHARACTER EQUATES
ESCAPE  EQU     1BH                ;ASCII ESCAPE CHARACTER
TESTCH  EQU     'A'                ;TEST CHARACTER = A

SC11B:
        CALL    INIT               ;INITIALIZE 8255 PPI, INTERRUPT SYSTEM

        ;SIMPLE EXAMPLE - READ AND ECHO CHARACTERS
        ; UNTIL AN ESC IS RECEIVED
LOOP:
        CALL    INCH               ;READ CHARACTER
        PUSH    PSW
        CALL    OUTCH              ;ECHO CHARACTER
```

```
        POP     PSW
        CPI     ESCAPE          ;IS CHARACTER AN ESCAPE?
        JNZ     LOOP            ;STAY IN LOOP IF NOT

        ;AN ASYNCHRONOUS EXAMPLE
        ; OUTPUT "A" TO CONSOLE CONTINUOUSLY BUT ALSO LOOK AT
        ; INPUT SIDE, READING AND ECHOING ANY INPUT CHARACTERS
ASYNLP:
        ;OUTPUT AN "A" IF OUTPUT IS NOT BUSY
        CALL    OUTST           ;IS OUTPUT BUSY?
        JC      ASYNLP          ;JUMP IF IT IS
        MVI     A,TESTCH
        CALL    OUTCH           ;OUTPUT TEST CHARACTER

        ;CHECK INPUT PORT
        ;ECHO CHARACTER IF ONE IS AVAILABLE
        ;EXIT ON ESCAPE CHARACTER
        CALL    INST            ;IS INPUT DATA AVAILABLE?
        JC      ASYNLP          ;JUMP IF NOT (SEND ANOTHER "A")
        CALL    INCH            ;GET CHARACTER
        CPI     ESCAPE          ;IS IT AN ESCAPE?
        JZ      DONE            ;BRANCH IF IT IS
        CALL    OUTCH           ;ELSE ECHO CHARACTER
        JMP     ASYNLP          ;AND CONTINUE

DONE:
        JMP     SC11B

        END
```

Buffered Input/Output Using an 8251 PCI (SINTB)

Performs interrupt-driven input and output using an 8251 PCI and multiple-character buffers. Consists of the following subroutines:

1. INCH reads a character from the input buffer.

2. INST determines whether the input buffer is empty.

3. OUTCH writes a character into the output buffer.

4. OUTST determines whether the output buffer is full.

5. INIT initializes the buffers, the interrupt system, and the 8251 PCI.

The actual service routines are

1. RDHDLR responds to the input interrupt by reading a character from the 8251 PCI into the input buffer.

2. WRHDLR responds to the output interrupt by writing a character from the output buffer into the 8251 PCI.

Procedures

1. INCH waits for a character to become available, gets the character from the head of the input buffer, moves the head of the buffer up one position, and decreases the input buffer counter by 1.

2. INST clears Carry if the input buffer counter is 0 and sets it otherwise.

3. OUTCH waits until there is space in the output buffer (that is, until the output buffer is not full), stores the character at the tail of the buffer, moves the tail up one position, and increases the output buffer counter by 1.

Registers Used:

1. INCH: AF, C, DE, HL
2. INST: AF
3. OUTCH: AF, DE, HL
4. OUTST: AF
5. INIT: AF, HL

Execution Time:

1. INCH: Approximately 207 cycles (8080) or 210 cycles (8085) if a character is available
2. INST: 46 cycles (8080) or 47 cycles (8085)
3. OUTCH: Approximately 225 cycles (8080) or 220 cycles (8085) if the output buffer is not full and an output interrupt is expected. Approximately 157 additional cycles (8080) or 162 additional cycles (8085) if no output interrupt is expected.
4. OUTST: 34 cycles (8080 or 8085)
5. INIT: 352 cycles (8080 or 8085)
6. RDHDLR: Approximately 265 cycles (8080) or 267 cycles (8085)
7. WRHDLR: Approximately 320 cycles (8080) or 324 cycles (8085) if the output buffer is not empty, 159 cycles (8080), or 163 cycles (8085) if the output buffer is empty

Note: The approximations here are the result of the variable amount of time required to update the buffer pointers with wraparound.

Program Size: 267 bytes

Data Memory Required: 11 bytes anywhere in RAM for the heads and tails of the input and output buffers (2 bytes starting at addresses IHEAD, ITAIL, OHEAD, and OTAIL, respectively), the number of characters in the buffers (2 bytes at addresses ICNT and OCNT), and the Output Interrupt Expected flag (address OIE). This does not include the actual input and output buffers.

---

4. OUTST sets Carry if the output buffer counter is equal to the buffer's length (i.e., if the output buffer is full) and clears Carry otherwise.

5. INIT clears the buffer counters, sets both the heads and the tails of the buffers to their base addresses, sets up the interrupt vectors, and initializes the 8251 PCI by storing the appropriate values in its command and mode registers. See Subroutine 10E for more details about initializing 8251 PCIs. INIT also clears the Output Interrupt Expected flag, indicating that the PCI is initially ready to transmit data.

6. RDHDLR reads a character from the 8251 PCI. If there is room in the input buffer, it stores the character at the tail of the buffer, moves the tail up one position, and increases the input buffer counter by 1. If the buffer is full, RDHDLR simply discards the character.

7. WRHDLR determines whether output data is available. If not, it simply clears the output interrupt. If data is available, WRHDLR obtains a character from the head of the output buffer, moves the head up one position, and decreases the output buffer counter by 1.

The new problem with multiple-character buffers is the management of queues. The main program must read the data in the order in which the input interrupt service routine receives it. Similarly, the output interrupt service routine must send the data in the order in which the main program stores it. Thus, the input routines have the following requirements:

1. The main program must know whether the input buffer is empty.

2. If the input buffer is not empty, the main program must know where the oldest character is (that is, the one that was received first).

3. The input interrupt service routine must know whether the input buffer is full.

4. If the input buffer is not full, the input interrupt service routine must know where the next empty place is (that is, where it should store the new character).

The output interrupt service routine and the main program have similar requirements for the output buffer, although the roles of sender and receiver are reversed.

Requirements 1 and 3 are met by maintaining a counter ICNT. INIT initializes ICNT to 0, the interrupt service routine adds 1 to it whenever it receives a character (assuming the buffer is not full), and the main program subtracts 1 from it whenever it removes a character from the buffer. Thus, the main program can determine whether the input buffer is empty by checking if ICNT is 0. Similarly, the interrupt service routine can determine whether the input buffer is full by checking if ICNT is equal to the size of the buffer.

Requirements 2 and 4 are met by maintaining two pointers, IHEAD and ITAIL, defined as follows:

1. ITAIL contains the address of the next empty location in the input buffer.

2. IHEAD contains the address of the oldest character in the input buffer.

INIT initializes IHEAD and ITAIL to the base address of the input buffer. Whenever the interrupt service routine receives a character, it places it in the buffer at ITAIL and moves ITAIL up one position (assuming that the buffer is not full). Whenever the main program reads a character, it removes it from the buffer at IHEAD and moves IHEAD up one position. Thus, IHEAD "chases" ITAIL across the buffer with the service routine entering characters at one end (the tail) while the main program removes them from the other end (the head).

The occupied part of the buffer can start and end anywhere. If either IHEAD or ITAIL reaches the physical end of the buffer, the program simply sets it back to the base address, thus providing wraparound. That is, the occupied part of the buffer could start near the end (say, at byte #195 of a 200-byte buffer) and continue back past the beginning (say, to byte #10).

Then IHEAD would be BASE+194, ITAIL would be BASE+9, and the buffer would contain 15 characters occupying addresses BASE+194 through BASE+199 and BASE through BASE+8.

Entry Conditions

1. INCH: None
2. INST: None
3. OUTCH: Character to transmit in A
4. OUTST: None
5. INIT: None

Exit Conditions

1. INCH: Character in A
2. INST: Carry = 0 if input buffer empty, 1 if not empty
3. OUTCH: None
4. OUTST: Carry = 0 if output buffer not full, 1 if full
5. INIT: None

```
;                                                                    ;
;                                                                    ;
;                                                                    ;
;           Title:         Buffered Input/Output Using an 8251 PCI   ;
;           Name:          SINTB                                     ;
;                                                                    ;
;                                                                    ;
;                                                                    ;
;           Purpose:       This program consists of five subroutines that ;
;                          perform interrupt-driven input and output ;
;                          an 8251 USART.                            ;
;                                                                    ;
;                          INCH                                      ;
;                            Read a character                        ;
;                          INST                                      ;
;                            Determine input status (whether input   ;
;                            buffer is empty)                         ;
;                          OUTCH                                      ;
;                            Write a character                       ;
;                          OUTST                                      ;
;                            Determine output status (whether output ;
;                            buffer is full)                          ;
;                          INIT                                      ;
;                            Initialize 8251 PCI and interrupt system ;
;                                                                    ;
;           Entry:         INCH                                      ;
```

```
;                                  No parameters                              ;
;                                INST                                         ;
;                                  No parameters                              ;
;                                OUTCH                                        ;
;                                  Register A = Character to transmit         ;
;                                OUTST                                        ;
;                                  No parameters                              ;
;                                INIT                                         ;
;                                  No parameters                              ;
;                                                                             ;
;           Exit:                INCH                                         ;
;                                  Register A = Character                     ;
;                                INST                                         ;
;                                  Carry = 0 if input buffer is empty,        ;
;                                  1 if character is available                ;
;                                OUTCH                                        ;
;                                  No parameters                              ;
;                                OUTST                                        ;
;                                  Carry = 0 if output buffer is              ;
;                                  empty, 1 if it is full                     ;
;                                INIT                                         ;
;                                  No parameters                              ;
;                                                                             ;
;           Registers used: INCH                                             ;
;                                  AF,C,DE,HL                                 ;
;                                INST                                         ;
;                                  AF                                         ;
;                                OUTCH                                        ;
;                                  AF,DE,HL                                   ;
;                                OUTST                                        ;
;                                  AF                                         ;
;                                INIT                                         ;
;                                  AF,HL                                      ;
;                                                                             ;
;           Time:                INCH                                         ;
;                                  Approximately 207 cycles if a character is ;
;                                  available for 8080, and 210 for 8085       ;
;                                INST                                         ;
;                                  46 cycles for 8080, 47 for 8085            ;
;                                OUTCH                                        ;
;                                  Approximately 225 cycles (8080) or 223     ;
;                                  cycles (8085) if output buffer is not full ;
;                                  and output interrupt is expected           ;
;                                OUTST                                        ;
;                                  34 cycles for 8080 and 8085                ;
;                                INIT                                         ;
;                                  352 cycles for 8080 and 8085               ;
;                                RDHDLR                                       ;
;                                  265 cycles for 8080, 267 for 8085          ;
;                                WRHDLR                                       ;
;                                  320 cycles for 8080 and 324 for 8085       ;
;                                  if output buffer is not empty              ;
;                                                                             ;
;           Size:                Program 267 bytes                           ;
;                                Data    11 bytes plus buffers                ;
```

```
;
;
            ;8251 PCI (USART) EQUATES
            ; 8251 IS PROGRAMMED FOR
            ;   ASYNCHRONOUS OPERATION
            ;   16 X BAUD RATE
            ;   8-BIT CHARACTERS
            ;   2 STOP BITS
            ;ARBITRARY 8251 PCI PORT ADDRESSES
USARTDR EQU      0B4H                ;USART DATA REGISTER
USARTSR EQU      0B5H                ;USART STATUS REGISTER
USARTCR EQU      0B5H                ;USART CONTROL REGISTER

            ;8251 ASYNCHRONOUS MODE INSTRUCTION
MODE    EQU      11001110B           ;BITS 1,0 = 10 (16X BAUD RATE FACTOR)
                                     ;BITS 3,2 = 11 (8-BIT CHARACTERS)
                                     ;BIT 4 = 0 (PARITY DISABLED)
                                     ;BIT 5 = (DON'T CARE)
                                     ;BITS 6,5 = 11 (2 STOP BITS)

            ;8251 ASYNCHRONOUS COMMAND INSTRUCTION
CMD     EQU      00010111B           ;BIT 0 = 1 (TRANSMIT ENABLE)
                                     ;BIT 1 = 1 (DATA TERMINAL READY)
                                     ;BIT 2 = 1 (RECEIVE ENABLE)
                                     ;BIT 3 = 0 (NO BREAK CHARACTER)
                                     ;BIT 4 = 1 (ERROR RESET)
                                     ;BIT 5 = 0 (NO REQUEST TO SEND)
                                     ;BIT 6 = 0 (NO RESET)
                                     ;BIT 7 = 0 (NOT HUNTING)

            ;8259 PROGRAMMABLE INTERRUPT CONTROLLER (PIC) EQUATES
            ; 8259 IS PROGRAMMED FOR
            ;   SINGLE DEVICE (RATHER THAN MULTIPLE 8259'S)
            ;   FULLY NESTED MODE
            ;   ALL INTERRUPTS ENABLED
            ;   RESTART 4, ADDRESS 0020, FOR READ INTERRUPT
            ;   RESTART 5, ADDRESS 0028, FOR WRITE INTERRUPT
            ;ARBITRARY 8259 PIC PORT ADDRESSES
PICO    EQU      0A0H                ;PIC PORT 1
PIC1    EQU      0A1H                ;PIC PORT 2

            ; INTERRUPT VECTORS
RDITRP  EQU      0020H               ;READ INTERRUPT VECTOR
WRITRP  EQU      0028H               ;WRITE INTERRUPT VECTOR

            ;8259 INITIALIZATION COMMAND WORDS ICW1 AND ICW2
ICW1    EQU      00010010B           ;BIT 0 = 0 (NOT USED)
                                     ;BIT 1 = 1 (SINGLE 8259)
                                     ;BIT 2 = 0 (VECTOR INTERVAL = 8 BYTES)
                                     ;BIT 3 = 0 (NOT USED)
                                     ;BIT 4 = 1 (MUST BE 1)
                                     ;BITS 7,6,5 = 0 (BITS 5-7 OF BASE
                                     ; ADDRESS OF RESTARTS)
ICW2    EQU      0                   ;UPPER BYTE OF BASE ADDRESS OF
                                     ; RESTARTS
```

```
           ;8259 OPERATING COMMAND WORD
EOI        EQU      00100000B          ;END OF INTERRUPT COMMAND WORD

           ;READ CHARACTER
INCH:
           CALL     INST               ;GET INPUT STATUS
           JNC      INCH               ;WAIT IF NO CHARACTER AVAILABLE
           DI                          ;DISABLE INTERRUPTS
           LXI      H,ICNT             ;REDUCE INPUT BUFFER COUNT BY 1
           DCR      M
           LHLD     IHEAD              ;GET CHARACTER FROM HEAD OF INPUT BUFFER
           MOV      C,M
           CALL     INCIPTR            ;MOVE HEAD POINTER UP 1
           SHLD     IHEAD
           MOV      A,C                ;REGISTER A = CHARACTER READ
           EI                          ;REENABLE INTERRUPTS
           RET

           ;RETURN INPUT STATUS (CARRY = 1 IF INPUT DATA AVAILABLE)
INST:
           LDA      ICNT               ;TEST INPUT BUFFER COUNT
           ORA      A
           RZ                          ;RETURN, CARRY = 0, IF BUFFER EMPTY
           STC                         ;SET CARRY TO INDICATE DATA AVAILABLE
           RET                         ;RETURN, CARRY = 1, IF DATA AVAILABLE

           ;WRITE CHARACTER
OUTCH:
           PUSH     PSW                ;SAVE CHARACTER TO OUTPUT

           ;WAIT UNTIL OUTPUT BUFFER NOT FULL, STORE NEXT CHARACTER
WAITOC:
           CALL     OUTST              ;GET OUTPUT STATUS
           JC       WAITOC             ;WAIT IF OUTPUT BUFFER FULL
           DI                          ;DISABLE INTERRUPTS WHILE LOOKING AT
                                       ; BUFFER, INTERRUPT STATUS
           LXI      H,OCNT             ;INCREASE OUTPUT BUFFER COUNT BY 1
           INR      M
           LHLD     OTAIL              ;POINT AT NEXT EMPTY BYTE IN BUFFER
           POP      PSW                ;GET CHARACTER
           MOV      M,A                ;STORE CHARACTER AT TAIL OF BUFFER
           CALL     INCOPTR            ;MOVE TAIL POINTER UP 1
           SHLD     OTAIL
           LDA      OIE                ;TEST OUTPUT INTERRUPT EXPECTED FLAG
           ORA      A
           CZ       OUTDAT             ;OUTPUT CHARACTER IMMEDIATELY IF
                                       ; OUTPUT INTERRUPT NOT EXPECTED
           EI                          ;REENABLE INTERRUPTS
           RET

           ;OUTPUT STATUS (CARRY = 1 IF OUTPUT BUFFER FULL)
OUTST:
           LDA      OCNT               ;GET OUTPUT BUFFER COUNT
           CPI      SZOBUF             ;IS OUTPUT BUFFER FULL?
           CMC                         ;COMPLEMENT CARRY
           RET                         ;CARRY = 1 IF BUFFER FULL, 0 IF NOT
```

```
        ;INITIALIZE 8251 PCI, INTERRUPT SYSTEM
INIT:
        DI                              ;DISABLE INTERRUPTS FOR INITIALIZATION

        ;INITIALIZE BUFFER COUNTERS AND POINTERS, INTERRUPT FLAG
        SUB     A
        STA     ICNT            ;INPUT BUFFER EMPTY
        STA     OCNT            ;OUTPUT BUFFER EMPTY
        STA     OIE             ;INDICATE NO OUTPUT INTERRUPT EXPECTED
        LXI     H,IBUF          ;INPUT HEAD/TAIL POINT AT FIRST
        SHLD    IHEAD           ; CHARACTER OF INPUT BUFFER
        SHLD    ITAIL
        LXI     H,OBUF          ;OUTPUT HEAD/TAIL POINT AT FIRST
        SHLD    OHEAD           ; CHARACTER OF OUTPUT BUFFER
        SHLD    OTAIL

        ;INITIALIZE INTERRUPT VECTORS
        LXI     H,RDHDLR
        MVI     A,0C3H          ;REGISTER A = JMP OP CODE
        STA     RDITRP          ;STORE JUMP OP CODE FOR READ INTERRUPT
        SHLD    RDITRP+1        ;STORE JUMP ADDRESS
        LXI     H,WRHDLR
        STA     WRITRP          ;STORE JUMP OP CODE FOR WRITE INTERRUPT
        SHLD    WRITRP+1        ;STORE JUMP ADDRESS

        ;INITIALIZE 8259 INTERRUPT CONTROLLER
        MVI     A,ICW1
        OUT     PIC0            ;SEND FIRST WORD TO PIC PORT 0
        MVI     A,ICW2
        OUT     PIC1            ;SEND SECOND WORD TO PIC PORT 1

        ;INITIALIZE 8251 PCI (USART)
        MVI     A,80H           ;SOFTWARE RESET 8251 PCI
        OUT     USARTCR         ; BY SENDING IT 2 BYTES OF 80 HEX
        OUT     USARTCR         ; FOLLOWED BY A RESET COMMAND
        MVI     A,40H
        OUT     USARTCR

        MVI     A,MODE          ;OUTPUT MODE BYTE
        OUT     USARTCR
        MVI     A,CMD           ;OUTPUT COMMAND BYTE
        OUT     USARTCR
        IN      USARTDR         ;READ DATA REGISTER TO CLEAR STRAY
                                ; DATA FROM INPUT REGISTER INITIALLY

        EI                      ;ENABLE INTERRUPTS
        RET

        ;INPUT (READ) INTERRUPT HANDLER
RDHDLR:
        PUSH    PSW             ;SAVE REGISTERS
        PUSH    B
        PUSH    D
        PUSH    H
```

```
              IN        USARTDR        ;READ DATA FROM 8251 PCI
              MOV       C,A            ;SAVE DATA IN REGISTER C
              LXI       H,ICNT         ;ANY ROOM IN INPUT BUFFER?
              MOV       A,M
              CPI       SZIBUF
              JNC       XITRH          ;JUMP IF NO ROOM IN INPUT BUFFER
              INR       M              ;INCREMENT INPUT BUFFER COUNT
              LHLD      ITAIL          ;STORE CHARACTER AT TAIL OF INPUT BUFFER
              MOV       M,C
              CALL      INCIPTR        ;INCREMENT TAIL POINTER
              SHLD      ITAIL

XITRH:        POP       H              ;RESTORE REGISTERS
              POP       D
              POP       B
              MVI       A,EOI          ;CLEAR 8259 INTERRUPT
              OUT       PICO
              POP       PSW
              EI                       ;REENABLE INTERRUPTS
              RET

              ;OUTPUT (WRITE) INTERRUPT HANDLER
WRHDLR:
              PUSH      PSW            ;SAVE REGISTERS
              PUSH      B
              PUSH      D
              PUSH      H

              LDA       OCNT           ;TEST OUTPUT BUFFER COUNT
              ORA       A
              JZ        NODATA         ;JUMP IF NO DATA TO TRANSMIT
              CALL      OUTDAT         ;ELSE OUTPUT DATA TO 8251 PCI
              JMP       WRDONE

              ;IF AN OUTPUT INTERRUPT OCCURS WHEN NO DATA IS AVAILABLE,
              ; WE MUST CLEAR IT TO AVOID AN ENDLESS LOOP. WHEN THE
              ; NEXT CHARACTER IS READY, IT MUST BE SENT IMMEDIATELY
              ; SINCE NO INTERRUPT WILL OCCUR.  THIS STATE, IN WHICH AN
              ; OUTPUT INTERRUPT HAS OCCURRED BUT HAS NOT BEEN SERVICED,
              ; IS INDICATED BY CLEARING OIE (OUTPUT INTERRUPT EXPECTED
              ; FLAG).
NODATA:
              SUB       A
              STA       OIE            ;DO NOT EXPECT AN INTERRUPT

WRDONE:
              POP       H              ;RESTORE REGISTERS
              POP       D
              POP       B
              MVI       A,EOI          ;CLEAR 8259 INTERRUPT
              OUT       PICO
              POP       PSW
              EI                       ;REENABLE INTERRUPTS
              RET
```

```
        ;****************************************
        ;ROUTINE: OUTDAT
        ;PURPOSE: SEND CHARACTER TO 8251 PCI
        ;ENTRY: TRNDAT = CHARACTER
        ;EXIT:  NONE
        ;REGISTERS USED: AF,DE,HL
        ;****************************************
OUTDAT:
        LHLD    OHEAD
        MOV     A,M             ;GET DATA FROM HEAD OF OUTPUT BUFFER
        OUT     USARTDR         ;SEND DATA TO 8251 PCI
        CALL    INCOPTR         ;INCREMENT HEAD POINTER
        SHLD    OHEAD
        LXI     H,OCNT          ;DECREMENT OUTPUT BUFFER COUNT
        DCR     M
        MVI     A,OFFH          ;EXPECT AN OUTPUT INTERRUPT
        STA     OIE
        RET


        ;****************************************
        ;ROUTINE: INCIPTR
        ;PURPOSE: INCREMENT POINTER INTO INPUT
        ;        BUFFER WITH WRAPAROUND
        ;ENTRY: HL = POINTER
        ;EXIT:  HL = POINTER INCREMENTED WITH WRAPAROUND
        ;REGISTERS USED: AF,DE,HL
        ;****************************************
INCIPTR:
        INX     H               ;INCREMENT POINTER
        LXI     D,EIBUF         ;COMPARE POINTER, END OF BUFFER
        MOV     A,L
        CMP     E
        RNZ                     ;RETURN IF LOW BYTES NOT EQUAL
        MOV     A,H
        CMP     D
        RNZ                     ;RETURN IF HIGH BYTES NOT EQUAL
        LXI     H,IBUF          ;IF POINTER AT END OF BUFFER,
        RET                     ; SET IT BACK TO BASE ADDRESS


        ;****************************************
        ;ROUTINE: INCOPTR
        ;PURPOSE: INCREMENT POINTER INTO OUTPUT
        ;        BUFFER WITH WRAPAROUND
        ;ENTRY: HL = POINTER
        ;EXIT:  HL = POINTER INCREMENTED WITH WRAPAROUND
        ;REGISTERS USED: AF,DE,HL
        ;****************************************
INCOPTR:
        INX     H               ;INCREMENT POINTER
        LXI     D,EOBUF         ;COMPARE POINTER, END OF BUFFER
        MOV     A,L
        CMP     E
        RNZ                     ;RETURN IF LOW BYTES NOT EQUAL
        MOV     A,H
        CMP     D
```

```
                RNZ                         ;RETURN IF HIGH BYTES NOT EQUAL
                LXI      H,OBUF             ;IF POINTER AT END OF BUFFER,
                RET                         ; SET IT BACK TO BASE ADDRESS

                ;DATA SECTION
IHEAD:          DS       2                  ;POINTER TO OLDEST CHARACTER IN INPUT
                                            ; BUFFER (NEXT CHARACTER TO READ)
ITAIL:          DS       2                  ;POINTER TO NEWEST CHARACTER IN INPUT
                                            ; BUFFER (LAST CHARACTER READ)
ICNT:           DS       1                  ;NUMBER OF CHARACTERS IN INPUT BUFFER
OHEAD:          DS       2                  ;POINTER TO OLDEST CHARACTER IN OUTPUT
                                            ; BUFFER (LAST CHARACTER WRITTEN)
OTAIL:          DS       2                  ;POINTER TO NEWEST CHARACTER IN OUTPUT
                                            ; BUFFER (NEXT CHARACTER TO SEND)
OCNT:           DS       1                  ;NUMBER OF CHARACTERS IN OUTPUT BUFFER
SZIBUF          EQU      10                 ;SIZE OF INPUT BUFFER
IBUF:           DS       SZIBUF             ;INPUT BUFFER
EIBUF           EQU      $                  ;END OF INPUT BUFFER
SZOBUF          EQU      10                 ;SIZE OF OUTPUT BUFFER
OBUF:           DS       SZOBUF             ;OUTPUT BUFFER
EOBUF           EQU      $                  ;END OF OUTPUT BUFFER
OIE:            DS       1                  ;OUTPUT INTERRUPT EXPECTED
                                            ; (0 = NO INTERRUPT EXPECTED,
                                            ; FF = INTERRUPT EXPECTED)

;                                                                           ;
;                                                                           ;
;               SAMPLE EXECUTION                                            ;
;                                                                           ;
;                                                                           ;

                ;CHARACTER EQUATES
ESCAPE          EQU      1BH                ;ASCII ESCAPE CHARACTER
TESTCH          EQU      'A'                ;TEST CHARACTER = A

SC11C:
                CALL     INIT               ;INITIALIZE 8251 PCI, INTERRUPT SYSTEM

                ;SIMPLE EXAMPLE - READ AND ECHO CHARACTERS
                ; UNTIL AN ESC IS RECEIVED
LOOP:
                CALL     INCH               ;READ CHARACTER
                PUSH     PSW
                CALL     OUTCH              ;ECHO CHARACTER
                POP      PSW
                CPI      ESCAPE             ;IS CHARACTER AN ESCAPE?
                JNZ      LOOP               ;STAY IN LOOP IF NOT

                ;AN ASYNCHRONOUS EXAMPLE
                ; OUTPUT "A" TO CONSOLE CONTINUOUSLY BUT ALSO LOOK AT
                ; INPUT SIDE, READING AND ECHOING ANY INPUT CHARACTERS
ASYNLP:
                ;OUTPUT AN "A" IF OUTPUT IS NOT BUSY
                CALL     OUTST              ;IS OUTPUT BUSY?
                JC       ASYNLP             ;JUMP IF IT IS
```

```
        MVI     A,TESTCH
        CALL    OUTCH                   ;OUTPUT CHARACTER

        ;CHECK INPUT PORT
        ;ECHO CHARACTER IF ONE IS AVAILABLE
        ;EXIT ON ESCAPE CHARACTER
        CALL    INST            ;IS INPUT DATA AVAILABLE?
        JC      ASYNLP          ;JUMP IF NOT (SEND ANOTHER "A")
        CALL    INCH            ;GET CHARACTER
        CPI     ESCAPE          ;IS IT AN ESCAPE CHARACTER?
        JZ      DONE            ;BRANCH IF IT IS
        CALL    OUTCH           ;ELSE ECHO CHARACTER
        JMP     ASYNLP          ;AND CONTINUE

DONE:
        JMP     SC11C

        END
```

Maintains a time-of-day 24-hour clock and a calendar based on a real-time clock interrupt generated from an 8253 Programmable Interval Timer (PIT). Consists of the following subroutines:

1. CLOCK returns the base address of the clock variables.

2. ICLK initializes the clock interrupt and the clock variables.

3. CLKINT updates the clock after each interrupt (assumed to be spaced one tick apart).

Procedures

1. CLOCK loads the base address of the clock variables into registers H and L. The clock variables are stored in the following order (lowest address first): ticks, seconds, minutes, hours, days, months, less significant byte of year, more significant byte of year.

2. ICLK initializes the 8253 PIT, the interrupt system, and the clock variables. The arbitrary starting time is 00:00.00, January 1, 1980. A real application would clearly require outside intervention to load or change the clock.

3. CLKINT decrements the remaining tick count by 1 and updates the rest of the clock if necessary. Of course, the number of seconds and minutes must be fewer than 60 and the number of hours must be fewer than 24. The day of the month must be less than or equal to the last day

---

Registers Used:
1. CLOCK: HL
2. ICLK: AF, HL
3. CLKINT: None

Execution Time:
1. CLOCK: 20 cycles (8080 or 8085)
2. ICLK: 269 cycles (8080 or 8085)
3. CLKINT: 103 cycles (8080) or 105 cycles (8085) if only TICK must be decremented; 522 cycles (8080) or 510 cycles (8085) maximum if changing to a new year

Program Size: 187 bytes

Data Memory Required: 8 bytes anywhere in RAM for the clock variables (starting at address CLKVAR)

---

for the current month; an array of the last days of each month begins at address LASTDY.

If the month is February (that is, month 2), the program checks to see if the current year is a leap year. This involves determining whether the two least significant bits of memory location YEAR are both 0s. If the current year is a leap year, the last day of February is the 29th, not the 28th.

The month number may not exceed 12 December) or a carry to the year number is necessary. The program must reinitialize the variables properly when carries occur; that is, TICK to DTICK; seconds, minutes, and hours to 0; day and month to 1 (meaning the first day and January, respectively).

Entry Conditions

1. CLOCK: None
2. ICLK: None
3. CLKINT: None

Exit Conditions

1. CLOCK: Base address of clock variables in H and L
2. ICLK: None
3. CLKINT: None

Examples

These examples assume that the tick rate is DTICK Hz (less than 256 Hz—typical values would be 60 Hz or 100 Hz) and that the clock and calendar are saved in memory locations

TICK	Ticks before a carry, counted down from DTICK
SEC	Seconds (0 to 59)
MIN	Minutes (0 to 59)
HOUR	Hour of day (0 to 23)
DAY	Day of month (1 to 28, 29, 30, or 31)
MONTH	Month of year (1 through 12)
YEAR and YEAR+1	Current year

1. Data: March 7, 1982, 11:59.59 P.M. and 1 tick left
(TICK) = 1

(SEC) = 59   (DAY) = 07
(MIN) = 59   (MONTH) = 03
(HOUR) = 23   (YEAR) = 1982

Result: March 8, 1982, 12:00.00 A.M. and DTICK ticks
(TICK) = DTICK

(SEC) = 0   (DAY) = 08
(MIN) = 0   (MONTH) = 03
(HOUR) = 0   (YEAR) = 1982

2. Data: Dec. 31, 1982, 11:59.59 P.M. and 1 tick left
(TICK) = 1

(SEC) = 59   (DAY) = 31
(MIN) = 59   (MONTH) = 12
(HOUR) = 23   (YEAR) = 1982

Result: Jan. 1, 1983, 12:00.00 A.M. and DTICK ticks
(TICK) = DTICK

(SEC) = 0   (DAY) = 1
(MIN) = 0   (MONTH) = 1
(HOUR) = 0   (YEAR) = 1983

```
;                                                              ;
;                                                              ;
;        Title:       Real-Time Clock and Calendar             ;
;        Name:        CLOCK                                    ;
;                                                              ;
;                                                              ;
;                                                              ;
;                                                              ;
;        Purpose:     This program maintains a time-of-day 24-hour ;
;                     clock and a calendar based on a real-time clock ;
;                     interrupt from an 8253 programmable timer. ;
;                                                              ;
```

```
;                       CLOCK                                        ;
;                         Returns base address of clock variables   ;
;                       ICLK                                         ;
;                         Initializes 8253 timer and clock interrupt;
;                                                                    ;
;       Entry:          CLOCK                                        ;
;                         None                                       ;
;                       ICLK                                         ;
;                         None                                       ;
;                                                                    ;
;       Exit:           CLOCK                                        ;
;                         Register HL = Base address of time variables;
;                       ICLK                                         ;
;                         None                                       ;
;                                                                    ;
;       Registers used: All                                         ;
;                                                                    ;
;       Time:           CLOCK                                        ;
;                         20 cycles                                  ;
;                       ICLK                                         ;
;                         269 cycles                                 ;
;                       CLKINT                                       ;
;                         If decrementing tick only: 103 cycles for ;
;                         8080, 105 cycles for 8085                  ;
;                         Maximum if changing to a new year:  522   ;
;                         cycles for 8080, 510 cycles for 8085      ;
;                                                                    ;
;       Size:           Program 187 bytes                            ;
;                       Data      8 bytes                            ;
;                                                                    ;
;                                                                    ;

        ;   8253 PROGRAMMABLE INTERVAL TIMER (PIT)
        ;
        ;INITIALIZE COUNTER 0 OF 8253 PIT AS 100 HZ SQUARE WAVE
        ; GENERATOR FOR USE IN TIME-OF-DAY CLOCK.
        ;SQUARE WAVE IS GENERATED FROM PIN 10 OF THE 8253, WHICH
        ; IS CONNECTED TO PIN 21 OF AN 8259 PROGRAMMABLE
        ; INTERRUPT CONTROLLER (PIC).
        ;THE CLOCK INTERRUPT IS THUS TIED TO RESTART VECTOR 3.
        ;WE ASSUME A 4 MHZ CLOCK INTO PIN 18 OF THE 8253, SO THAT
        ; A COUNTER VALUE OF 4,000,000/100 = 40,000 IS NEEDED TO
        ; GENERATE A 100 HZ SQUARE WAVE.

        ;ARBITRARY PORT ADDRESSES FOR 8253 PIT
PIT0    EQU     0B0H            ;8253 COUNTER 0
PIT1    EQU     0B1H            ;8253 COUNTER 1
PIT2    EQU     0B2H            ;8253 COUNTER 2
PITMDE  EQU     0B3H            ;8253 CONTROL WORD REGISTER

        ;8253 PIT MODE BYTE, COUNTER VALUE
PITCTRL EQU     00110110B       ;BIT 0 = 0 (BINARY MODE)
                                ;BITS 3..1 = 011 (MODE 3 - SQUARE WAVE
                                ; GENERATOR)
                                ;BITS 5,4 = 11 (LOAD 2 BYTES TO COUNTER)
                                ;BITS 7,6 = 00 (PROGRAM COUNTER 0)
```

```
PITCNT   EQU       40000           ;COUNTER VALUE = 40000

         ;DEFAULT TICK VALUE (100 HZ REAL-TIME CLOCK)
DTICK    EQU       100             ;DEFAULT TICK VALUE

         ;8259 PROGRAMMABLE INTERRUPT CONTROLLER (PIC) EQUATES
         ; 8259 IS PROGRAMMED FOR
         ;   SINGLE DEVICE (RATHER THAN MULTIPLE 8259'S)
         ;   FULLY NESTED MODE
         ;   ALL INTERRUPTS ENABLED
         ;   RESTART 3, ADDRESS 0018, FOR CLOCK INTERRUPT
         ;ARBITRARY 8259 PIC PORT ADDRESSES
PIC0     EQU       0B4H            ;PIC PORT 1
PIC1     EQU       0B5H            ;PIC PORT 2

         ;INTERRUPT VECTOR
CLKITRP  EQU       0018H           ;CLOCK INTERRUPT VECTOR

         ;8259 INITIALIZATION COMMAND WORDS ICW1 AND ICW2
ICW1     EQU       00010010B       ;BIT 0 = 0 (NOT USED)
                                   ;BIT 1 = 1 (SINGLE 8259)
                                   ;BIT 2 = 0 (VECTOR INTERVAL = 8 BYTES)
                                   ;BIT 3 = 0 (NOT USED)
                                   ;BIT 4 = 1 (MUST BE 1)
                                   ;BITS 7,6,5 = 0 (BITS 5-7 OF BASE
                                   ; ADDRESS OF RESTARTS)
ICW2     EQU       0               ;UPPER BYTE OF BASE ADDRESS OF
                                   ; RESTARTS

         ;8259 OPERATING COMMAND WORD
EOI      EQU       00100000B       ;END OF INTERRUPT COMMAND WORD


         ;RETURN BASE ADDRESS OF CLOCK VARIABLES
CLOCK:
         LXI       H,CLKVAR        ;GET BASE ADDRESS OF CLOCK VARIABLES
         RET

         ;INITIALIZE 8253 PIT COUNTER 0 AS A CLOCK INTERRUPT
ICLK:
         DI                        ;DISABLE INTERRUPTS
         MVI       A,0C3H          ;C3 HEX IS JMP OP CODE
         STA       CLKITRP         ;STORE JUMP AT INTERRUPT ADDRESS
         LXI       H,CLKINT
         SHLD      CLKITRP+1       ;STORE JUMP ADDRESS

         ;INITIALIZE 8259 INTERRUPT CONTROLLER
         MVI       A,ICW1
         OUT       PIC0            ;SEND FIRST WORD TO PORT 0
         MVI       A,ICW2
         OUT       PIC1            ;SEND SECOND WORD TO PORT 1

         ;INITIALIZE 8253 PROGRAMMABLE INTERVAL TIMER
         MVI       A,PITCTRL       ;OUTPUT CONTROL WORD
         OUT       PITMDE
         LXI       H,PITCNT        ;OUTPUT INITIAL COUNT IN 2 BYTES
```

```
        MOV     A,L
        OUT     PITO
        MOV     A,H
        OUT     PITO

        ;INITIALIZE CLOCK VARIABLES TO ARBITRARY VALUE
        ;JANUARY 1, 1980 00:00.00
        ;A REAL CLOCK WOULD NEED OUTSIDE INTERVENTION
        ; TO SET OR CHANGE VALUES
        LXI     H,TICK
        MVI     M,DTICK         ;INITIALIZE TICKS
        INX     H
        SUB     A               ;A = 0
        MOV     M,A             ;SECOND = 0
        INX     H
        MOV     M,A             ;MINUTE = 0
        INX     H
        MOV     M,A             ;HOUR = 0
        INR     A               ;A = 1
        INX     H
        MOV     M,A             ;DAY = 1 (FIRST)
        INX     H
        MOV     M,A             ;MONTH = 1 (JANUARY)
        LXI     H,1980
        SHLD    YEAR            ;YEAR = 1980

        EI
        RET

        ;SERVICE CLOCK INTERRUPT
CLKINT:
        PUSH    PSW             ;SAVE AF, HL
        PUSH    H
        LXI     H,TICK          ;SUBTRACT 1 FROM TICK COUNT
        DCR     M
        JNZ     EXIT1           ;JUMP IF TICK COUNT NOT ZERO
        MVI     M,DTICK         ;SET TICK COUNT BACK TO DEFAULT

        ;SAVE REMAINING REGISTERS
        PUSH    B               ;SAVE BC, DE
        PUSH    D

        MVI     B,0             ;0 = DEFAULT FOR SECONDS, MINUTES, HOURS

        ;INCREMENT SECONDS
        INX     H               ;POINT AT SECONDS
        INR     M               ;INCREMENT TO NEXT SECOND
        MOV     A,M
        CPI     60              ;SECONDS = 60?
        JC      EXIT0           ;EXIT IF LESS THAN 60 SECONDS
        MOV     M,B             ;ELSE SECONDS = 0

        ;INCREMENT MINUTES
        INX     H               ;POINT AT MINUTES
        INR     M               ;INCREMENT TO NEXT MINUTE
        MOV     A,M
```

```
        CPI       60                  ;MINUTES = 60?
        JC        EXITO               ;EXIT IF LESS THAN 60 MINUTES
        MOV       M,B                 ;ELSE MINUTES = 0

        ;INCREMENT HOUR
        INX       H                   ;POINT AT HOUR
        INR       M                   ;INCREMENT TO NEXT HOUR
        MOV       A,M
        CPI       24                  ;HOURS = 24?
        JC        EXITO               ;EXIT IF LESS THAN 24 HOURS
        MOV       M,B                 ;ELSE HOUR = 0

        ;INCREMENT DAY
        XCHG                          ;DE = ADDRESS OF HOUR
        LXI       H,LASTDY-1
        LDA       MONTH               ;GET CURRENT MONTH
        MOV       C,A                 ;REGISTER C = MONTH
        MVI       B,0
        DAD       B                   ;POINT AT LAST DAY OF MONTH
        XCHG                          ;HL = ADDRESS OF HOUR
        INX       H                   ;POINT AT DAY
        MOV       A,M                 ;GET DAY
        INR       M                   ;INCREMENT DAY
        XCHG                          ;DE = ADDRESS OF DAY
        MOV       B,A                 ;REGISTER B = DAY
        CMP       M                   ;IS CURRENT DAY END OF MONTH?
        XCHG                          ;HL = ADDRESS OF DAY
        JC        EXITO               ;EXIT IF NOT AT END OF MONTH

        ;DETERMINE IF THIS IS END OF FEBRUARY IN A LEAP
        ; YEAR (YEAR DIVISIBLE BY 4)
        MOV       A,C                 ;GET MONTH
        CPI       2                   ;IS THIS FEBRUARY?
        JNZ       INCMTH              ;JUMP IF NOT, INCREMENT MONTH
        LDA       YEAR                ;IS IT A LEAP YEAR?
        ANI       00000011B
        JNZ       INCMTH              ;JUMP IF NOT

        ;FEBRUARY OF A LEAP YEAR HAS 29 DAYS, NOT 28 DAYS
        MOV       A,B                 ;GET DAY
        CPI       29
        JC        EXITO               ;EXIT IF NOT 1ST OF MARCH

INCMTH:
        MVI       B,1                 ;DEFAULT IS 1 FOR DAY AND MONTH
        MOV       M,B                 ;DAY = 1

        INX       H
        INR       M                   ;INCREMENT MONTH
        MOV       A,C                 ;GET OLD MONTH
        CPI       12                  ;WAS OLD MONTH DECEMBER?
        JC        EXITO               ;EXIT IF NOT
        MOV       M,B                 ;ELSE
                                      ; CHANGE MONTH TO 1 (JANUARY)
```

```
              ;INCREMENT YEAR
              LHLD     YEAR
              INX      H
              SHLD     YEAR

EXIT0:
              ;RESTORE REGISTERS
              POP      D                    ;RESTORE DE, BC
              POP      B
EXIT1:
              POP      H                    ;RESTORE HL
              MVI      A,EOI                ;CLEAR 8259 INTERRUPT
              OUT      PICO
              POP      PSW                  ;RESTORE AF
              EI                            ;REENABLE INTERRUPTS
              RET                           ;RETURN

              ;ARRAY OF LAST DAYS OF EACH MONTH
LASTDY:
              DB       31                   ;JANUARY
              DB       28                   ;FEBRUARY (EXCEPT LEAP YEARS)
              DB       31                   ;MARCH
              DB       30                   ;APRIL
              DB       31                   ;MAY
              DB       30                   ;JUNE
              DB       31                   ;JULY
              DB       31                   ;AUGUST
              DB       30                   ;SEPTEMBER
              DB       31                   ;OCTOBER
              DB       30                   ;NOVEMBER
              DB       31                   ;DECEMBER

              ;CLOCK VARIABLES
CLKVAR:
TICK:         DS       1                    ;TICKS LEFT IN CURRENT SECOND
SEC:          DS       1                    ;SECONDS
MIN:          DS       1                    ;MINUTES
HOUR:         DS       1                    ;HOURS
DAY:          DS       1                    ;DAY (1 TO NUMBER OF DAYS IN A MONTH)
MONTH:        DS       1                    ;MONTH 1 = JANUARY .. 12 = DECEMBER
YEAR:         DS       2                    ;YEAR


;                                                                      ;
;                                                                      ;
;             SAMPLE EXECUTION                                         ;
;                                                                      ;
;                                                                      ;

              ;CLOCK VARIABLE INDEXES
TCKIDX        EQU      0                    ;INDEX TO TICK
SECIDX        EQU      1                    ;INDEX TO SECOND
MINIDX        EQU      2                    ;INDEX TO MINUTE
HRIDX         EQU      3                    ;INDEX TO HOUR
DAYIDX        EQU      4                    ;INDEX TO DAY
```

```
MTHIDX  EQU     5                   ;INDEX TO MONTH
YRIDX   EQU     6                   ;INDEX TO YEAR

SC11D:
        CALL    ICLK                ;INITIALIZE CLOCK

        ;INITIALIZE CLOCK TO 2/7/83 14:00:00 (2 PM, FEB. 7, 1983)
        CALL    CLOCK               ;HL = ADDRESS OF CLOCK VARIABLES
        DI                          ;DISABLE INTERRUPTS WHILE
                                    ; INITIALIZING CLOCK
        INX     H                   ;SKIP TICK VARIABLE
        MVI     M,0                 ;SECONDS = 0
        INX     H
        MVI     M,0                 ;MINUTES = 0
        INX     H
        MVI     M,14                ;HOUR = 14 (2 PM)
        INX     H
        MVI     M,7                 ;DAY = 7
        INX     H
        MVI     M,2                 ;MONTH = 2 (FEBRUARY)
        LXI     D,1983
        INX     H
        MOV     M,E                 ;YEAR = 1983
        INX     H
        MOV     M,D
        EI                          ;REENABLE INTERRUPTS

        ;WAIT FOR CLOCK TO BE 2/7/83 14:01:20 (2:01.20 PM, FEB.
        ; 7, 1983)
        ;
        ;NOTE: MUST BE CAREFUL TO EXIT IF CLOCK IS ACCIDENTALLY
        ; SET AHEAD.  IF WE CHECK ONLY FOR EQUALITY, WE MIGHT
        ; NEVER FIND IT.  THUS WE HAVE >= IN TESTS BELOW, NOT
        ; JUST =.

        ;WAIT FOR YEAR >= 1983
        CALL    CLOCK               ;HL = BASE ADDRESS OF CLOCK VARIABLES
        PUSH    H                   ;SAVE BASE ADDRESS
        LXI     D,YRIDX
        DAD     D                   ;HL = ADDRESS OF LOW BYTE OF YEAR
        LXI     D,1983              ;DE = YEAR TO WAIT FOR
WAITYR:
        ;OBTAIN CURRENT YEAR, DISABLING INTERRUPTS SINCE IT IS 2 BYTES
        DI                          ;DISABLE INTERRUPTS WHILE PICKING UP
                                    ; 2-BYTE YEAR
        MOV     C,M                 ;GET LOW BYTE OF YEAR
        INX     H
        MOV     B,M                 ;GET HIGH BYTE OF YEAR
        DCX     H
        EI                          ;REENABLE INTERRUPTS

        ;COMPARE CURRENT YEAR AND 1983
        MOV     A,C
        CMP     E
        MOV     A,B
```

```
        SBB     D
        JC      WAITYR          ;JUMP IF YEAR NOT >= 1983
        ;WAIT FOR MONTH >= 2
        POP     H               ;HL = BASE ADDRESS OF CLOCK VARIABLES
        LXI     D,MTHIDX
        DAD     D               ;POINT AT MONTH
        MVI     B,2
        CALL    WAIT            ;WAIT FOR FEBRUARY OR LATER

        ;WAIT FOR DAY >= 7
        DCX     H               ;POINT AT DAY
        MVI     B,7
        CALL    WAIT            ;WAIT FOR 7TH OR LATER

        ;WAIT FOR HOUR >= 14
        DCX     H               ;POINT AT HOUR
        MVI     B,14
        CALL    WAIT            ;WAIT FOR 2 PM OR LATER

        ;WAIT FOR MINUTE >= 1
        DCX     H               ;POINT AT MINUTE
        MVI     B,1
        CALL    WAIT            ;WAIT FOR 2:01 OR LATER

        ;WAIT FOR SECOND >= 20
        DCX     H               ;POINT AT SECOND
        MVI     B,20
        CALL    WAIT            ;WAIT FOR 2:01.20 OR LATER

        ;DONE
HERE:
        JMP     HERE            ;IT IS NOW TIME OR LATER

        ;**********************************
        ;ROUTINE: WAIT
        ;PURPOSE: WAIT FOR VALUE POINTED TO BY HL
        ;         TO BECOME GREATER THAN OR EQUAL TO VALUE IN B
        ;ENTRY: HL = ADDRESS OF VARIABLE TO WATCH
        ;       B = VALUE TO WAIT FOR
        ;EXIT:  WHEN B >= (HL)
        ;REGISTERS USED: AF
        ;**********************************
WAIT:
        MOV     A,M             ;GET PART OF CLOCK TIME
        CMP     B               ;COMPARE TO TARGET
        JC      WAIT            ;WAIT IF TARGET NOT REACHED
        RET

        END
```

Appendix A **8080/8085 Instruction Set**

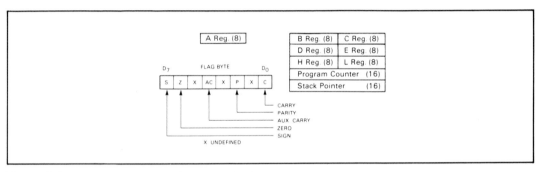

Figure A-1. 8080/8085 Internal register organization

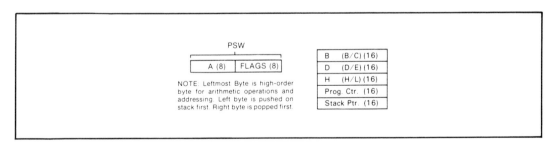

Figure A-2. 8080/8085 Register pair organization

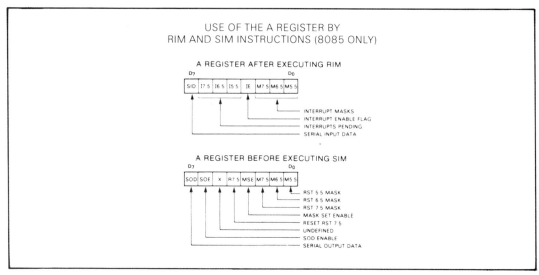

Figure A-3. 8085 RIM and SIM instructions

Table A-1. 8080/8085 Instructions in Alphabetical Order

INSTRUCTION		OBJECT CODE	BYTES	CYCLES		INSTRUCTION		OBJECT CODE	BYTES	CYCLES	
				8085	8080A					8085	8080A
ACI	DATA	CE YY	2	7	7	MOV	M,REG	01110sss	1	7	7
ADC	REG	10001XXX	1	4	4	MOV	REG,M	01ddd110	1	7	7
ADC	M	8E	1	7	7	MVI	REG,DATA	00ddd110 YY	2	7	7
ADD	REG	10000XXX	1	4	4	MVI	M,DATA	36 YY	2	10	10
ADD	M	86	1	7	7	NOP		00	1	4	4
ADI	DATA	C6 YY	2	7	7	ORA	REG	10110XXX	1	4	5
ANA	REG	10100XXX	1	4	4	ORA	M	B6	1	7	7
ANA	M	A6	1	7	7	ORI	DATA	F6 YY	2	7	7
ANI	DATA	E6 YY	2	7	7	OUT	PORT	D3 YY	2	10	10
CALL	LABEL	CD ppqq	3	18	17	PCHL		E9	1	6	5
CC	LABEL	DC ppqq	3	9/18	11/17	POP	RP	11XX0001	1	10	10
CM	LABEL	FC ppqq	3	9/18	11/17	PUSH	RP	11XX0101	1	12	11
CMA		2F	1	4	4	RAL		17	1	4	4
CMC		3F	1	4	4	RAR		1F	1	4	4
CMP	REG	10111XXX	1	4	4	RC		D8	1	6/12	5/11
CMP	M	BE	1	7	7	RET		C9	1	10	10
CNC	LABEL	D4 ppqq	3	9/18	11/17	RIM		20	1	4	
CNZ	LABEL	C4 ppqq	3	9/18	11/17	RLC		07	1	4	4
CP	LABEL	F4 ppqq	3	9/18	11/17	RM		F8	1	6/12	5/11
CPE	LABEL	EC ppqq	3	9/18	11/17	RNC		D0	1	6/12	5/11
CPI	DATA	FE YY	2	7	7	RNZ		C0	1	6/12	5/11
CPO	LABEL	E4 ppqq	3	9/18	11/17	RP		F0	1	6/12	5/11
CZ	LABEL	CC ppqq	3	9/18	11/17	RPE		E8	1	6/12	5/11
DAA		27	1	4	4	RPO		E0	1	6/12	5/11
DAD	RP	00XX1001	1	10	10	RCC		0F	1	4	4
DCR	REG	00XXX101	1	4	5	RST	N	11XXX111	1	12	11
DCR	M	35	1	10	10	RZ		C8	1	6/12	5/11
DCX	RP	00XX1011	1	6	5	SBB	REG	10011XXX	1	4	4
DI		F3	1	4	4	SBB	M	9E	1	7	7
EI		FB	1	4	4	SBI	DATA	DE YY	2	7	7
HLT		76	1	4	4	SHLD	ADDR	22 ppqq	3	16	16
IN	PORT	DB YY	2	10	10	SIM		30	1	4	
INR	REG	00XXX100	1	4	5	SPHL		F9	1	6	5
INR	M	34	1	10	10	STA	ADDR	32 ppqq	3	13	13
INX	RP	00XX0011	1	6	5	STAX	RP	000X0010	1	7	7
JC	LABEL	DA ppqq	3	7/10	10	STC		37	1	4	4
JM	LABEL	FA ppqq	3	7/10	10	SUB	REG	10010XXX	1	4	4
JMP	LABEL	C3 ppqq	3	10	10	SUB	M	96	1	7	7
JNC	LABEL	D2 ppqq	3	7/10	10	SUI	DATA	D6 YY	2	7	7
JNZ	LABEL	C2 ppqq	3	7/10	10	XCHG		EB	1	4	4
JP	LABEL	F2 ppqq	3	7/10	10	XRA	REG	10101XXX	1	4	4
JPE	LABEL	EA ppqq	3	7/10	10	XRA	M	AE	1	7	7
JPO	LABEL	E2 ppqq	3	7/10	10	XRI	DATA	EE YY	2	7	7
JZ	LABEL	CA ppqq	3	7/10	10	XTHL		E3	1	16	18
LDA	ADDR	3A ppqq	3	13	13						
LDAX	RP	000X1010	1	7	7						
LHLD	ADDR	2A ppqq	3	16	16						
LXI	RP,DATA16	00XX0001 YYYY	3	10	10						
MOV	REG,REG	01dddsss	1	4	5						

Object Code:
ddd   Destination register — same coding as xxx
nnn   Restart number 000 to 111
ppqq   A 16-bit memory address
sss   Source register — same coding as xxx
x   Register pair 0 = BC
       1 = DE

xx   Register pair 00 = BC
                      01 = DE
                      10 = HL
                      11 = SP or (if PUSH/POP) PSW

xxx   Register 111 = A
                000 = B
                001 = C

010 = D
011 = E
100 = H
101 = L

yy   An 8-bit binary data unit
yyyy   A 16-bit binary data unit
*8085 instructions only

Table A-2. Summary of the 8080A/8085 Instruction Set

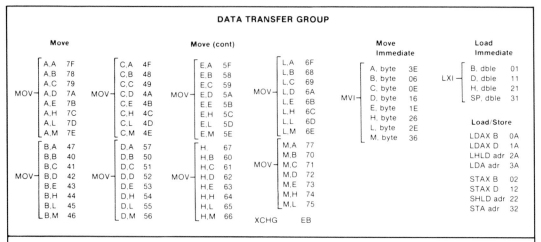

byte = constant, or logical/arithmetic expression that evaluates to an 8-bit data quantity. (Second byte of 2-byte instructions).	* = all flags (C, Z, S, P, AC) affected.
dble = constant, or logical/arithmetic expression that evaluates to a 16-bit data quantity. (Second and Third bytes of 3-byte instructions).	** = all flags except CARRY affected. (exception: INX and DCX affect no flags).
adr = 16-bit address (Second and Third bytes of 3-byte instructions).	† = only CARRY affected.

Table A-2. (Continued)

BRANCH CONTROL GROUP			

Jump		Call		Return		Restart	
JMP adr	C3	CALL adr	CD	RET	C9	0	C7
JNZ adr	C2	CNZ adr	C4	RNZ	C0	1	CF
JZ adr	CA	CZ adr	CC	RZ	C8	2	D7
JNC adr	D2	CNC adr	D4	RNC	D0	RST 3	DF
JC adr	DA	CC adr	DC	RC	D8	4	E7
JPO adr	E2	CPO adr	E4	RPO	E0	5	EF
JPE adr	EA	CPE adr	EC	RPE	E8	6	F7
JP adr	F2	CP adr	F4	RP	F0	7	FF
JM adr	FA	CM adr	FC	RM	F8		
PCHL	E9						

I/O AND MACHINE CONTROL			

Stack Ops		Input/Output		Control		New Instructions (8085 Only)	
	B	C5	OUT byte	D3	DI	F3	
PUSH	D	D5	IN byte	DB	EI	FB	RIM	20
	H	E5					SIM	30
	PSW	F5			NOP	00	
					HLT	76	
POP	B	C1					
	D	D1					
	H	E1					
	PSW*	F1					
XTHL	E3						
SPHL	F9						

byte	constant, or logical/arithmetic expression that evaluates to an 8-bit data quantity. (Second byte of 2-byte instructions)	*	all flags (C, Z, S, P, AC) affected
dble	constant, or logical/arithmetic expression that evaluates to a 16-bit data quantity. (Second and Third bytes of 3-byte instructions)	**	all flags except CARRY affected. (exception: INX and DCX affect no flags)
adr	16-bit address (Second and Third bytes of 3-byte instructions)	†	only CARRY affected

Table A-3. 8080/8085 Operation Codes in Numerical Order

Code	Mnemonic	Operand		Code	Mnemonic	Operand
00	NOP			80	ADD	B
01	LXI	B,dble		81	ADD	C
02	STAX	B		82	ADD	D
03	INX	B		83	ADD	E
04	INR	B		84	ADD	H
05	DCR	B		85	ADD	L
06	MVI	B,byte		86	ADD	M
07	RLC			87	ADD	A
08	---			88	ADC	B
09	DAD	B		89	ADC	C
0A	LDAX	B		8A	ADC	D
0B	DCX	B		8B	ADC	E
0C	INR	C		8C	ADC	H
0D	DCR	C		8D	ADC	L
0E	MVI	C,byte		8E	ADC	M
0F	RRC			8F	ADC	A
10	---			90	SUB	B
11	LXI	D,dble		91	SUB	C
12	STAX	D		92	SUB	D
13	INX	D		93	SUB	E
14	INR	D		94	SUB	H
15	DCR	D		95	SUB	L
16	MVI	D,byte		96	SUB	M
17	RAL			97	SUB	A
18	---			98	SBB	B
19	DAD	D		99	SBB	C
1A	LDAX	D		9A	SBB	D
1B	DCX	D		9B	SBB	E
1C	INR	E		9C	SBB	H
1D	DCR	E		9D	SBB	L
1E	MVI	E,byte		9E	SBB	M
1F	RAR			9F	SBB	A
20	RIM*			A0	ANA	B
21	LXI	H,dble		A1	ANA	C
22	SHLD	adr		A2	ANA	D
23	INX	H		A3	ANA	E
24	INR	H		A4	ANA	H
25	DCR	H		A5	ANA	L
26	MVI	H,byte		A6	ANA	M
27	DAA			A7	ANA	A
28	---			A8	XRA	B
29	DAD	H		A9	XRA	C
2A	LHLD	adr		AA	XRA	D
2B	DCX	H		AB	XRA	E
2C	INR	L		AC	XRA	H
2D	DCR	L		AD	XRA	L
2E	MVI	L,byte		AE	XRA	M
2F	CMA			AF	XRA	A
30	SIM*			B0	ORA	B
31	LXI	SP,dble		B1	ORA	C
32	STA	adr		B2	ORA	D
33	INX	SP		B3	ORA	E
34	INR	M		B4	ORA	H
35	DCR	M		B5	ORA	L
36	MVI	M,byte		B6	ORA	M
37	STC			B7	ORA	A
38	---			B8	CMP	B
39	DAD	SP		B9	CMP	C
3A	LDA	adr		BA	CMP	D
3B	DCX	SP		BB	CMP	E
3C	INR	A		BC	CMP	H
3D	DCR	A		BD	CMP	L
3E	MVI	A,byte		BE	CMP	M
3F	CMC			BF	CMP	A
40	MOV	B,B		C0	RNZ	
41	MOV	B,C		C1	POP	B
42	MOV	B,D		C2	JNZ	adr
43	MOV	B,E		C3	JMP	adr
44	MOV	B,H		C4	CNZ	adr
45	MOV	B,L		C5	PUSH	B
46	MOV	B,M		C6	ADI	byte
47	MOV	B,A		C7	RST	0
48	MOV	C,B		C8	RZ	
49	MOV	C,C		C9	RET	
4A	MOV	C,D		CA	JZ	adr
4B	MOV	C,E		CB	---	
4C	MOV	C,H		CC	CZ	adr
4D	MOV	C,L		CD	CALL	adr
4E	MOV	C,M		CE	ACI	byte
4F	MOV	C,A		CF	RST	1
50	MOV	D,B		D0	RNC	
51	MOV	D,C		D1	POP	D
52	MOV	D,D		D2	JNC	adr
53	MOV	D,E		D3	OUT	byte
54	MOV	D,H		D4	CNC	adr
55	MOV	D,L		D5	PUSH	D
56	MOV	D,M		D6	SUI	byte
57	MOV	D,A		D7	RST	2
58	MOV	E,B		D8	RC	
59	MOV	E,C		D9	---	
5A	MOV	E,D		DA	JC	adr
5B	MOV	E,E		DB	IN	byte
5C	MOV	E,H		DC	CC	adr
5D	MOV	E,L		DD	---	
5E	MOV	E,M		DE	SBI	byte
5F	MOV	E,A		DF	RST	3
60	MOV	H,B		E0	RPO	
61	MOV	H,C		E1	POP	H
62	MOV	H,D		E2	JPO	adr
63	MOV	H,E		E3	XTHL	
64	MOV	H,H		E4	CPO	adr
65	MOV	H,L		E5	PUSH	H
66	MOV	H,M		E6	ANI	byte
67	MOV	H,A		E7	RST	4
68	MOV	L,B		E8	RPE	
69	MOV	L,C		E9	PCHL	
6A	MOV	L,D		EA	JPE	adr
6B	MOV	L,E		EB	XCHG	
6C	MOV	L,H		EC	CPE	adr
6D	MOV	L,L		ED	---	
6E	MOV	L,M		EE	XRI	byte
6F	MOV	L,A		EF	RST	5
70	MOV	M,B		F0	RP	
71	MOV	M,C		F1	POP	PSW
72	MOV	M,D		F2	JP	adr
73	MOV	M,E		F3	DI	
74	MOV	M,H		F4	CP	adr
75	MOV	M,L		F5	PUSH	PSW
76	HLT			F6	ORI	byte
77	MOV	M,A		F7	RST	6
78	MOV	A,B		F8	RM	
79	MOV	A,C		F9	SPHL	
7A	MOV	A,D		FA	JM	adr
7B	MOV	A,E		FB	EI	
7C	MOV	A,H		FC	CM	adr
7D	MOV	A,L		FD	---	
7E	MOV	A,M		FE	CPI	byte
7F	MOV	A,A		FF	RST	7

*8085 Only

Table A-4. 8080/8085 Branch Control Instructions

Flag Condition	Jump		Call		Return	
Zero=True	JZ	CA	CZ	CC	RZ	C8
Zero=False	JNZ	C2	CNZ	C4	RNZ	C0
Carry=True	JC	DA	CC	DC	RC	D8
Carry=False	JNC	D2	CNC	D4	RNC	D0
Sign=Positive	JP	F2	CP	F4	RP	F0
Sign=Negative	JM	FA	CM	FC	RM	F8
Parity=Even	JPE	EA	CPE	EC	RPE	E8
Parity=Odd	JPO	E2	CPO	E4	RPO	E0
Unconditional	JMP	C3	CALL	CD	RET	C9

Table A-5. 8080/8085 Accumulator Operations

	Code	Function
XRA A	AF	Clear A and Clear Carry
ORA A	B7	Clear Carry
CMC	3F	Complement Carry
CMA	2F	Complement Accumulator
STC	37	Set Carry
RLC	07	Rotate Left
RRC	0F	Rotate Right
RAL	17	Rotate Left Thru Carry
RAR	1F	Rotate Right Thru Carry
DAA	27	Decimal Adjust Accum

Table A-6. 8080/8085 Register Pair and Stack Operations

| | PSW (A/F) | Register Pair | | | SP | PC | Function |
		B (B/C)	D (D/E)	H (H/L)			
INX		03	13	23	33		Increment Register Pair
DCX		0B	1B	2B	3B		Decrement Register Pair
LDAX		0A	1A	7E(1)			Load A Indirect (Reg. Pair holds Adrs)
STAX		02	12	77(2)			Store A Indirect (Reg. Pair holds Adrs)
LHLD				2A			Load H/L Direct (Bytes 2 and 3 hold Adrs)
SHLD				22			Store H/L Direct (Bytes 2 and 3 hold Adrs)
LXI		01	11	21	31	C3(3)	Load Reg. Pair Immediate (Bytes 2 and 3 hold immediate data)
PCHL						E9	Load PC with H/L (Branch to Adrs in H/L)
XCHG			EB				Exchange Reg. Pairs D/E and H/L
DAD		09	19	29	39		Add Reg. Pair to H/L
PUSH	F5	C5	D5	E5			Push Reg. Pair on Stack
POP	F1	C1	D1	E1			Pop Reg. Pair off Stack
XTHL				E3			Exchange H/L with Top of Stack
SPHL					F9		Load SP with H/L

Notes: 1. This is MOV A,M. 2. This is MOV M,A. 3. This is JMP.

Table A-7. 8080/8085 Restart
Instructions and Inputs

Name	Code	Restart Address
RST 0	C7	0000_{16}
RST 1	CF	0008_{16}
RST 2	D7	0010_{16}
RST 3	DF	0018_{16}
RST 4	E7	0020_{16}
TRAP	Hardware* Function	0024_{16}
RST 5	EF	0028_{16}
RST 5.5	Hardware* Function	$002C_{16}$
RST 6	F7	0030_{16}
RST 6.5	Hardware* Function	0034_{16}
RST 7	FF	0038_{16}
RST 7.5	Hardware* Function	$003C_{16}$

*NOTE: The hardware functions refer to the on-chip
Interrupt feature of the 8085 only

Table A-8. 8080/8085 Assembler Reference

Operators	
( )	
NUL	
LOW, HIGH	
*, /, MOD, SHL, SHR	
+, —	
NOT	
AND	
OR, XOR	

Constant Definition

0BDH, 1AH	Hex
105D, 105	Decimal
72O, 72Q	Octal
11011B, 00110B	Binary
'TEST', 'A' 'B'	ASCII

Pseudo Instruction

General:	Relocation:
ORG	ASEG	NAME
END	DSEG	STKLN
EQU	CSEG	STACK
SET	PUBLIC	MEMORY
DS	EXTRN	
DB		
DW		

Macros:
| MACRO |
| ENDM |
| LOCAL |
| REPT |
| IRP |
| IRPC |
| EXITM |

Conditional Assembly:
| IF |
| ELSE |
| ENDIF |

Appendix B **Programming Reference for the 8255 PPI**

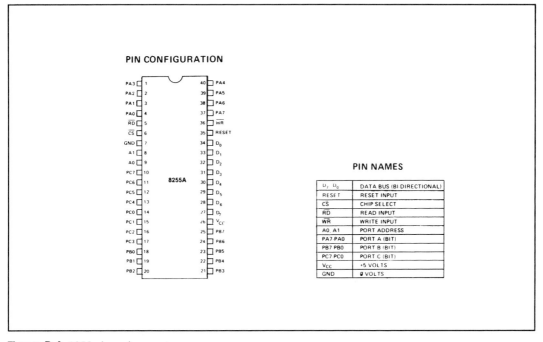

PIN CONFIGURATION

8255A

PA3	1	40	PA4
PA2	2	39	PA5
PA1	3	38	PA6
PA0	4	37	PA7
$\overline{RD}$	5	36	$\overline{WR}$
$\overline{CS}$	6	35	RESET
GND	7	34	D_0
A1	8	33	D_1
A0	9	32	D_2
PC7	10	31	D_3
PC6	11	30	D_4
PC5	12	29	D_5
PC4	13	28	D_6
PC0	14	27	D_7
PC1	15	26	V_{CC}
PC2	16	25	PB7
PC3	17	24	PB6
PB0	18	23	PB5
PB1	19	22	PB4
PB2	20	21	PB3

PIN NAMES

D_7, D_0	DATA BUS (BI DIRECTIONAL)
RESET	RESET INPUT
$\overline{CS}$	CHIP SELECT
$\overline{RD}$	READ INPUT
$\overline{WR}$	WRITE INPUT
A0, A1	PORT ADDRESS
PA7 PA0	PORT A (BIT)
PB7 PB0	PORT B (BIT)
PC7 PC0	PORT C (BIT)
V_{CC}	+5 VOLTS
GND	0 VOLTS

Figure B-1. 8255 pin assignments

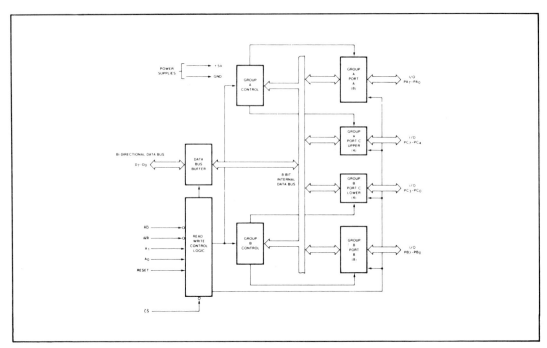

Figure B-2. Block diagram of the 8255 Programmable
Peripheral Interface (PPI)

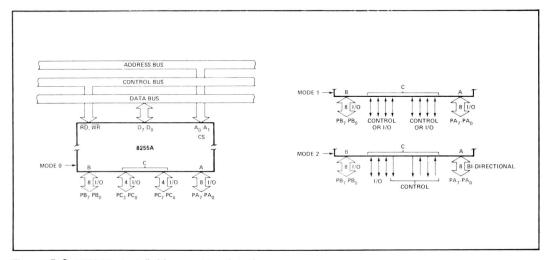

Figure B-3. 8255 Mode definitions and bus interface

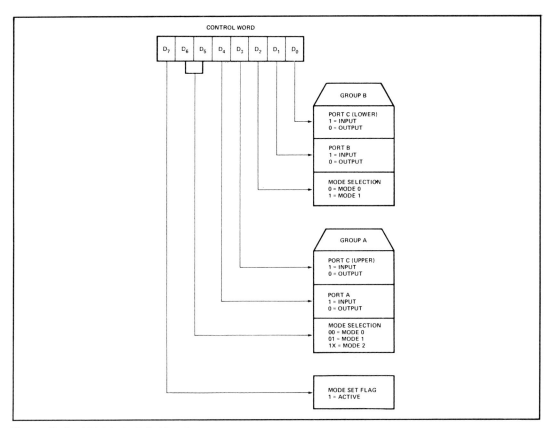

Figure B-4. 8255 Mode definition format

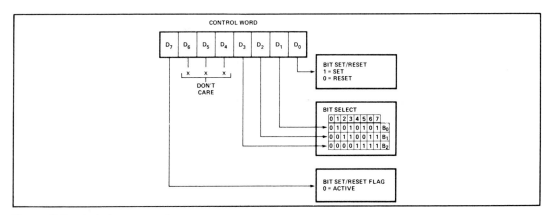

Figure B-5. 8255 Bit set/reset format

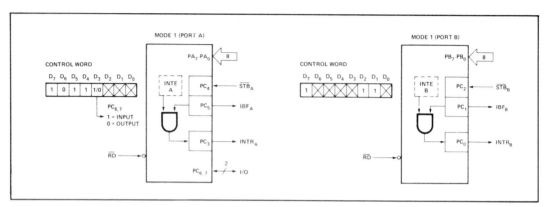

Figure B-6. 8255 Mode 1 input

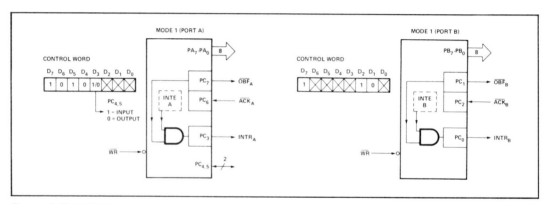

Figure B-7. 8255 Mode 1 output

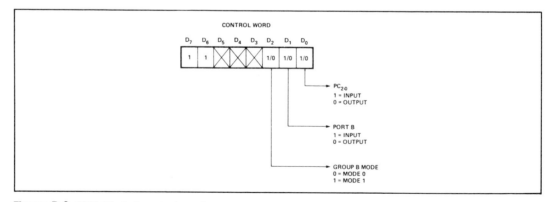

Figure B-8. 8255 Mode 2 control word

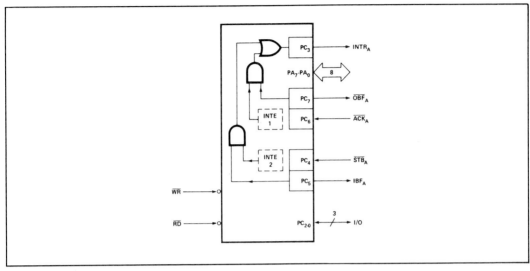

Figure B-9. 8255 Bidirectional mode (Mode 2)

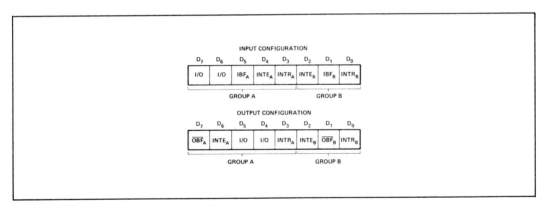

Figure B-10. 8255 Mode 1 status word format

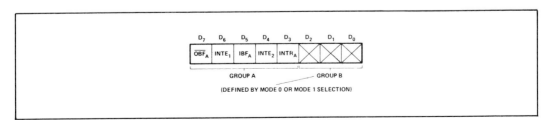

Figure B-11. 8255 Mode 2 status word format

Table B-1. 8255 PPI Operations

8255A BASIC OPERATION

A_1	A_0	$\overline{RD}$	$\overline{WR}$	$\overline{CS}$	INPUT OPERATION (READ)
0	0	0	1	0	PORT A ⇒ DATA BUS
0	1	0	1	0	PORT B ⇒ DATA BUS
1	0	0	1	0	PORT C ⇒ DATA BUS
					OUTPUT OPERATION (WRITE)
0	0	1	0	0	DATA BUS ⇒ PORT A
0	1	1	0	0	DATA BUS ⇒ PORT B
1	0	1	0	0	DATA BUS ⇒ PORT C
1	1	1	0	0	DATA BUS ⇒ CONTROL
					DISABLE FUNCTION
X	X	X	X	1	DATA BUS ⇒ 3-STATE
1	1	0	1	0	ILLEGAL CONDITION
X	X	1	1	0	DATA BUS ⇒ 3-STATE

Table B-2. 8255 Mode 0 Port Definitions

MODE 0 Port Definition

A		B		GROUP A			GROUP B	
D_4	D_3	D_1	D_0	PORT A	PORT C (UPPER)	#	PORT B	PORT C (LOWER)
0	0	0	0	OUTPUT	OUTPUT	0	OUTPUT	OUTPUT
0	0	0	1	OUTPUT	OUTPUT	1	OUTPUT	INPUT
0	0	1	0	OUTPUT	OUTPUT	2	INPUT	OUTPUT
0	0	1	1	OUTPUT	OUTPUT	3	INPUT	INPUT
0	1	0	0	OUTPUT	INPUT	4	OUTPUT	OUTPUT
0	1	0	1	OUTPUT	INPUT	5	OUTPUT	INPUT
0	1	1	0	OUTPUT	INPUT	6	INPUT	OUTPUT
0	1	1	1	OUTPUT	INPUT	7	INPUT	INPUT
1	0	0	0	INPUT	OUTPUT	8	OUTPUT	OUTPUT
1	0	0	1	INPUT	OUTPUT	9	OUTPUT	INPUT
1	0	1	0	INPUT	OUTPUT	10	INPUT	OUTPUT
1	0	1	1	INPUT	OUTPUT	11	INPUT	INPUT
1	1	0	0	INPUT	INPUT	12	OUTPUT	OUTPUT
1	1	0	1	INPUT	INPUT	13	OUTPUT	INPUT
1	1	1	0	INPUT	INPUT	14	INPUT	OUTPUT
1	1	1	1	INPUT	INPUT	15	INPUT	INPUT

Table B-3. Summary of 8255 Operating Modes

Mode Definition Summary

	MODE 0		MODE 1		MODE 2
	IN	OUT	IN	OUT	GROUP A ONLY
PA_0	IN	OUT	IN	OUT	←——→
PA_1	IN	OUT	IN	OUT	←——→
PA_2	IN	OUT	IN	OUT	←——→
PA_3	IN	OUT	IN	OUT	←——→
PA_4	IN	OUT	IN	OUT	←——→
PA_5	IN	OUT	IN	OUT	←——→
PA_6	IN	OUT	IN	OUT	←——→
PA_7	IN	OUT	IN	OUT	←——→
PB_0	IN	OUT	IN	OUT	——
PB_1	IN	OUT	IN	OUT	——
PB_2	IN	OUT	IN	OUT	——
PB_3	IN	OUT	IN	OUT	——
PB_4	IN	OUT	IN	OUT	—— MODE 0
PB_5	IN	OUT	IN	OUT	—— OR MODE 1
PB_6	IN	OUT	IN	OUT	—— ONLY
PB_7	IN	OUT	IN	OUT	——
PC_0	IN	OUT	$INTR_B$	$INTR_B$	I/O
PC_1	IN	OUT	IBF_B	$\overline{OBF}_B$	I/O
PC_2	IN	OUT	$\overline{STB}_B$	$\overline{ACK}_B$	I/O
PC_3	IN	OUT	$INTR_A$	$INTR_A$	$INTR_A$
PC_4	IN	OUT	$\overline{STB}_A$	I/O	$\overline{STB}_A$
PC_5	IN	OUT	IBF_A	I/O	IBF_A
PC_6	IN	OUT	I/O	$\overline{ACK}_A$	$\overline{ACK}_A$
PC_7	IN	OUT	I/O	$\overline{OBF}_A$	$\overline{OBF}_A$

Appendix C **ASCII Character Set**

	MSD	0	1	2	3	4	5	6	7
LSD		000	001	010	011	100	101	110	111
0	0000	NUL	DLE	SP	0	@	P	`	p
1	0001	SOH	DC1	!	1	A	Q	a	q
2	0010	STX	DC2	"	2	B	R	b	r
3	0011	ETX	DC3	#	3	C	S	c	s
4	0100	EOT	DC4	$	4	D	T	d	t
5	0101	ENQ	NAK	%	5	E	U	e	u
6	0110	ACK	SYN	&	6	F	V	f	v
7	0111	BEL	ETB	'	7	G	W	g	w
8	1000	BS	CAN	(	8	H	X	h	x
9	1001	HT	EM	)	9	I	Y	i	y
A	1010	LF	SUB	*	:	J	Z	j	z
B	1011	VT	ESC	+	;	K	[	k	}
C	1100	FF	FS	,	<	L	\	l	¦
D	1101	CR	GS	–	=	M	]	m	{
E	1110	SO	RS	•	>	N	^	n	~
F	1111	SI	US	/	?	O	_	o	DEL

Glossary

A

Absolute address. An address that identifies a storage location or an I/O device without the use of a base, offset, or other factor. *See also* Effective address, Relative offset.

Absolute addressing. An addressing mode in which the instruction contains the actual address required for its execution, as opposed to modes in which the instruction contains a relative offset or identifies a base register.

Accumulator. A register that is the implied source of one operand and the destination of the result in most arithmetic and logical operations.

Active transition. The edge on a strobe line that sets an indicator. The alternatives are a negative edge (1 to 0 transition) or a positive edge (0 to 1 transition).

Address. The identification code that distinguishes one memory location or I/O port from another and that can be used to select a specific one.

Addressing mode. The method for specifying the addresses to be used in executing an instruction. Common addressing modes are direct, immediate, indexed, indirect, and relative.

Address register. A register that contains a memory address.

Address space. The total range of addresses to which a particular computer may refer.

ALU. *See* Arithmetic-logic unit.

Arithmetic-logic unit (ALU). A device that can perform a variety of arithmetic and logical functions; function inputs select which one the device performs during a particular cycle.

Arithmetic shift. A shift operation that keeps the sign (most significant) bit the same. In a right shift, this results in copies of the sign bit moving right (called *sign extension*).

Arm. Allow, but usually refers specifically to interrupts. *See* Enable.

Array. A collection of related data items, usually stored in consecutive memory addresses.

445

ASCII (American Standard Code for Information Interchange). A 7-bit character code widely used in computers and communications.

Assembler. A computer program that converts assembly language programs into a form (machine language) that the computer can execute directly. The assembler translates mnemonic operation codes and names into their numerical equivalents and assigns locations in memory to data and instructions. A popular CP/M assembler is MAC from Digital Research.

Assembly language. A computer language in which the programmer can use mnemonic operation codes, labels, and names to refer to their numerical equivalents.

Asynchronous. Operating without reference to an overall timing source, that is, at irregular intervals.

Autodecrementing. The automatic decrementing of an address register as part of the execution of an instruction that uses it.

Autoincrementing. The automatic incrementing of an address register as part of the execution of an instruction that uses it.

Automatic mode (of a peripheral chip). An operating mode in which the peripheral chip produces control signals automatically without specific program intervention.

Auxiliary carry. *See* Half-carry.

B

Base address. The address in memory at which an array or table starts. Also called *starting address* or *base*.

Baud. A measure of the rate at which serial data is transmitted; bits per second, including both data bits and bits used for synchronization, error checking, and other purposes. Common baud rates are 110, 300, 600, 1200, 2400, 4800, 9600, and 19,200.

Baud rate generator. A device that generates the proper time intervals between bits for serial data transmission.

BCD (Binary-Coded Decimal). A representation of decimal numbers in which each decimal digit is coded separately into a binary number.

Bidirectional. Capable of transporting signals in either direction.

Binary-coded decimal. *See* BCD.

Binary search. A search method that divides the set of items to be searched into two equal (or nearly equal) parts in each iteration. The part containing the item being sought is then determined and used as the set in the next iteration. Each iteration of a binary search thus halves the size of the set being searched. This method assumes an ordered set of items.

BIOS (Basic Input/Output System).   The part of CP/M that allows the operating system to use the I/O devices for a particular computer. The computer manufacturer or dealer typically supplies the BIOS; Digital Research, the originator of CP/M, provides only a sample BIOS with comments.

Bit test.   An operation that determines whether a bit is 0 or 1. Usually refers to a logical AND operation with an appropriate mask.

Block.   An entire group or section, such as a set of registers or a section of memory.

Block comparison (or *block compare*).   A search that extends through a block of memory until either the item being sought is found or the entire block is examined.

Block move.   Moving an entire set of data from one area of memory to another.

Block search.   *See* Block comparison.

Boolean variable.   A variable that has only two possible values, which may be represented as true and false or as 1 and 0. *See also* Flag.

Borrow.   A bit that is set to 1 if a subtraction produces a negative result and to 0 if it produces a positive or zero result. The borrow is commonly used to subtract numbers that are too long to be handled in a single operation.

Bounce.   To move back and forth between states before reaching a final state. Usually refers to mechanical switches that do not open or close cleanly, but rather move back and forth between positions for a while before settling down.

Branch instruction.   *See* Jump instruction.

Breakpoint.   A condition specified by the user under which program execution is to end temporarily, used as an aid in debugging programs. The specification of the conditions under which execution will end is referred to as *setting breakpoints* and the deactivation of those conditions is referred to as *clearing breakpoints.*

BSC (Binary Synchronous Communications or Bisync).   An older line protocol often used by IBM computers and terminals.

Bubble sort.   A sorting technique that works through the elements of an array consecutively, exchanging an element with its successor if they are out of order.

Buffer.   Temporary storage area generally used to hold data before it is transferred to its final destination.

Buffer empty.   A signal that is active when all data entered into a buffer or register has been transferred to its final destination.

Buffer full. A signal that is active when a buffer or register is completely occupied with data that has not been transferred to its final destination.

Buffer index. The index of the next available address in a buffer.

Buffer pointer. A storage location that contains the next available address in a buffer.

Bug. An error or flaw in a program.

Byte. A unit of eight bits. May be described as consisting of a high nibble or digit (the four most significant bits) and a low nibble or digit (the four least significant bits).

Byte-length. A length of eight bits per item.

C

Call (a subroutine). Transfers control to a subroutine while retaining the information required to resume the current program. A call differs from a jump or branch in that a call remembers the previous position in the program, whereas a jump or branch does not.

Carry. A bit that is 1 if an addition overflows into the succeeding digit position.

Carry flag. A flag that is 1 if the last operation generated a carry from the most significant bit and 0 if it did not.

CASE statement. A statement in a high-level computer language that directs the computer to perform one of several subprograms, depending on the value of a variable. That is, the computer performs the first subprogram if the variable has the first value specified, etc. The **ON GOTO** statement serves a similar function in **BASIC**.

Central processing unit (CPU). The control section of the computer, the part that controls its operations, fetches and executes instructions, and performs arithmetic and logical functions.

Checksum. A logical sum that is included in a block of data to guard against recording or transmission errors. Also referred to as *longitudinal parity* or *longitudinal redundancy check* (LRC).

Circular shift. *See* Rotate.

Cleaning the stack. Removing unwanted items from the stack, usually by adjusting the stack pointer.

Clear. Set to zero.

Clock. A regular timing signal that governs transitions in a system.

Close (a file).   To make a file inactive. The final contents of the file are the last information the user stored in it. The user must generally close a file after working with it.

Coding.   Writing instructions in a computer language.

Combo chip.   See Multifunction device.

Command register.   See Control register.

Comment.   A section of a program that has no function other than documentation. Comments are neither translated nor executed, but are simply copied into the program listing.

Complement.   Invert. *See also* One's complement, Two's complement.

Concatenation.   Linking together, chaining, or uniting in a series. In string operations, concatenation refers to the placing of one string after another.

Condition code.   See Flag.

Control (or *command*) *register.*   A register whose contents determine the state of a transfer or the operating mode of a device.

CP/M (Control Program/Microcomputer).   A widely used disk operating system for 8080/8085-based computers developed by Digital Research (Pacific Grove, CA).

Cyclic redundancy check (CRC).   An error-detecting code generated from a polynomial that can be added to a block of data or a storage area.

D

Data accepted.   A signal that is active when the most recent data has been transferred successfully.

Data direction register.   A register that determines whether bidirectional I/O lines are being used as inputs or outputs.

Data-link control.   Conventions governing the format and timing of data exchange between communicating systems. Also called a *protocol.*

Data-link controller.   A chip that performs all or most of the functions required by a protocol. The 8273 programmable protocol controller is a data-link controller in the 8080/8085 family.

Data ready.   A signal that is active when new data is available to the receiver. Same as *valid data.*

DDCMP (Digital Data Communications Message Protocol). A protocol that supports any method of physical data transfer (synchronous or asynchronous, serial or parallel).

Debounce. Convert the output from a contact with bounce into a single, clean transition between states. Debouncing is most commonly applied to outputs from mechanical keys or switches that bounce back and forth before settling into their final positions.

Debounce time. The amount of time required to debounce a change of state.

Debugger. A systems program that helps users locate and correct errors in their programs. Some versions are referred to as dynamic debugging tools or DDTs. A popular CP/M debugger is SID (Symbolic Instruction Debugger) from Digital Research.

Debugging. Locating and correcting errors in a program.

Device address. The address of a port associated with an I/O device.

Diagnostic. A program that checks the operation of a device and reports its findings.

Digit shift. A shift of one BCD digit position or four bit positions.

Direct addressing. An addressing mode in which the instruction contains the address required for its execution.

Disable (or *disarm*). Prevent an activity from proceeding or a signal (such as an interrupt) from being recognized.

Disarm. Usually refers specifically to interrupts. *See* Disable.

Double word. When dealing with microprocessors, a unit of 32 bits.

Driver. *See* I/O driver.

Dump. A facility that displays the contents of an entire section of memory or group of registers on an output device.

Dynamic allocation (of memory). The allocation of memory for a subprogram from whatever is available when the subprogram is called. An alternative is *static allocation* of a fixed area of storage to each subprogram. Dynamic allocation often reduces overall memory usage because subprograms can share areas; it does, however, generally require additional execution time and overhead spent in memory management.

E

EBCDIC (Expanded Binary-Coded Decimal Interchange Code).   An 8-bit character code used in large IBM computers.

Echo.   To reflect transmitted information back to the transmitter or send back to a terminal the information received from it.

Editor.   A program that manipulates text material and allows the user to make corrections, additions, deletions, and other changes. A popular CP/M editor is ED from Digital Research.

Effective address.   The actual address used by an instruction to fetch or store data.

EIA RS-232.   *See* RS-232.

Enable (or arm).   Allow an activity to proceed or a signal (such as an interrupt) to be recognized.

Endless loop or *jump-to-self instruction.*   An instruction that transfers control to itself, thus executing indefinitely (or until a hardware signal interrupts it).

Error-correcting code.   A code that the receiver can use to correct errors in messages; the code itself does not contain any additional message.

Error-detecting code.   A code that the receiver can use to detect errors in messages; the code itself does not contain any additional message.

Even parity.   A 1-bit error-detecting code that makes the total number of 1 bits in a unit of data (including the parity bit) even.

EXCLUSIVE-OR function.   A logical function that is true if either of its inputs is true, but not both inputs. It is thus true if its inputs are not equal (that is, if one of them is a logic 1 and the other is a logic 0).

Extend (a number).   Add digits to a number to conform to a format without changing its value. For example, one may extend an 8-bit unsigned result with zeros to fill a 16-bit word.

External reference.   The use in a program of a name that is defined in another program.

F

F (flag) register.   *See* Flag register.

Field.   A set of one or more positions within a larger unit, such as a byte, word, or record.

File.   A collection of related information that is treated as a unit for purposes of storage or retrieval.

Fill.   To place values in storage areas not previously in use, initializing memory or storage.

Flag (or condition code or status bit).   A single bit that indicates a condition within the computer, often used to choose between alternative instruction sequences.

Flag (software).   An indicator that is either on or off and can be used to decide between two alternative courses of action. *Boolean variable* and *semaphore* are other terms with the same meaning.

Flag register.   A register that holds all the flags. Also called the *(processor) status register.*

Free-running mode.   An operating mode for a timer in which it indicates the end of a time interval and then starts another of the same length. Also called a *continuous mode.*

Function key.   A key that causes a system to perform a function (such as clearing the screen of a video terminal) or execute a procedure.

G

Global variable.   A variable that is defined in more than one section of a computer program, rather than only locally.

H

Half carry.   A flag used in 8-bit computers to indicate whether there was a carry from the less significant (4-bit) digit.

Handshake.   An asynchronous transfer in which sender and receiver exchange signals to establish synchronization and to indicate the status of the data transfer. Typically, the sender indicates that new data is available and the receiver reads the data and indicates that it is ready for more.

Hardware stack.   A stack that the computer manages automatically when executing instructions that use it.

Head (of a queue).   The location of the item most recently entered into a queue.

Header, queue.   *See* Queue header.

Hexadecimal (or hex).   Number system with base 16. The digits are the decimal numbers 0 through 9, followed by the letters A through F (representing 10 through 15 decimal).

Hex code. *See* Object code.

High-level language. A programming language that is aimed toward the solution of problems, rather than being designed for convenient conversion into computer instructions. A compiler or interpreter translates a program written in a high-level language into a form that the computer can execute. Common high-level languages include Ada, BASIC, C, COBOL, FORTRAN, and Pascal.

I

Immediate addressing. An addressing mode in which the data required by an instruction is part of the instruction. The data immediately follows the operation code in memory.

Index. A data item used to identify a particular element of an array or table.

Indexed addressing. An addressing mode in which the address is modified by the contents of an index register to determine the effective address (the actual address used).

Indexed indirect addressing. *See* Preindexing.

Index register. A register that can be used to modify memory addresses.

Indirect addressing. An addressing mode in which the effective address is the contents of the address included in the instruction, rather than the address itself.

Indirect indexed addressing. *See* Postindexing.

Indirect jump. A jump instruction that transfers control to the address stored in a register or memory location, rather than to a fixed address.

Input/output control block (IOCB). A group of storage locations that contains the information required to control the operation of an I/O device. Typically included in the information are the addresses of routines that perform operations such as transferring a single unit of data or determining device status.

Input/output control system (IOCS). A set of computer routines that controls the performance of I/O operations.

Instruction. A group of bits that defines a computer operation and is part of the instruction set.

Instruction cycle. The process of fetching, decoding, and executing an instruction.

Instruction execution time. The time required to fetch, decode, and execute an instruction.

Instruction fetch. The process of addressing memory and reading an instruction into the CPU for decoding and execution.

Instruction length. The amount of memory needed to store a complete instruction.

Instruction set. The set of general-purpose instructions available on a given computer. The set of inputs to which the CPU will produce a known response when they are fetched, decoded, and executed.

Interpolation. Estimating values of a function at points between those at which the values are already known.

Interrupt. A signal that temporarily suspends the computer's normal sequence of operations and transfers control to a special routine.

Interrupt-driven. Dependent on interrupts for its operation; may idle until it receives an interrupt.

Interrupt flag. A bit in the input/output section that is set when an event occurs that requires servicing by the CPU. Typical events include an active transition on a control line and the exhaustion of a count by a timer.

Interrupt mask (or interrupt enable). A bit that determines whether interrupts will be recognized. A mask or disable bit must be cleared to allow interrupts, whereas an enable bit must be set.

Interrupt request. A signal that is active when a peripheral is requesting service, often used to cause a CPU interrupt. *See also* Interrupt flag.

Interrupt service routine. A program that performs the actions required to respond to an interrupt.

Interrupt vector. An address to which an interrupt directs the computer, usually the starting address of a service routine.

Inverted borrow. A bit that is set to 0 if a subtraction produces a negative result and to 1 if it produces a positive or 0 result. An inverted borrow can be used like a true borrow, except that the complement of its value (i.e., 1 minus its value) must be used in the extension to longer numbers.

IOCB. *See* Input/output control block.

IOCS. *See* Input/output control system.

I/O device table. A table that establishes the correspondence between the logical devices to which programs refer and the physical devices that are actually used in data transfers. An I/O device table must be placed in memory in order to run a program that refers to logical devices on a computer with a particular set of actual (physical) devices. The I/O device table may, for example, contain the starting addresses of the I/O drivers that handle the various devices.

I/O driver.   A computer program that transfers data to or from an I/O device, also called a *driver* or *I/O utility*. The driver must perform initialization functions and handle status and control, as well as physically transfer the actual data.

Isolated input/output.   An addressing method for I/O ports that uses a decoding system distinct from that used by the memory section. I/O ports thus do not occupy memory addresses.

J

Jump instruction (or branch instruction).   An instruction that places a new value in the program counter, thus departing from the normal one-step incrementing. Jump instructions may be conditional; that is, the new value may be placed in the program counter only if a condition holds.

Jump table.   A table consisting of the starting addresses of executable routines, used to transfer control to one of them.

L

Label.   A name attached to an instruction or statement in a program that identifies the location in memory of the machine language code or assignment produced from that instruction or statement.

Latch.   A device that retains its contents until new data is specifically entered into it.

Leading edge (of a binary pulse).   The edge that marks the beginning of a pulse.

Least significant bit.   The rightmost bit in a group of bits, that is, bit 0 of a byte or a 16-bit word.

Library program.   A program that is part of a collection of programs and is written and documented according to a standard format.

LIFO (last-in, first-out) memory.   A memory that is organized according to the order in which elements are entered and from which elements can be retrieved only in the order opposite of that in which they were entered. *See also* Stack.

Linearization.   The mathematical approximation of a function by a straight line between two points at which its values are known.

Linked list.   A list in which each item contains a pointer (or *link*) to the next item. Also called a *chain* or *chained list*.

List.   An ordered set of items.

Logical device.   The input or output device to which a program refers. The actual or physical device is determined by looking up the logical device in an I/O device table—a table containing actual I/O addresses (or starting addresses for I/O drivers) corresponding to the logical device numbers.

Logical shift.   A shift operation that moves zeros in at the end as the original data is shifted.

Logical sum.   A binary sum with no carries between bit positions. *See also* Checksum, EXCLUSIVE-OR function.

Longitudinal parity.   *See* Checksum.

Longitudinal redundancy check (LRC).   *See* Checksum.

Lookup table.   An array of data organized so that the answer to a problem may be determined merely by selecting the correct entry (without any calculations).

Low-level language.   A computer language in which each statement is translated directly into a single machine language instruction.

M

Machine language.   The programming language that the computer can execute directly with no translation other than numeric conversions.

Maintenance (of programs).   Updating and correcting computer programs that are in use.

Majority logic.   A combinational logic function that is true when more than half the inputs are true.

Mark.   The 1 state on a serial data communications line.

Mask.   A bit pattern that isolates one or more bits from a group of bits.

Maskable interrupt.   An interrupt that the system can disable.

Memory capacity.   The total number of different memory addresses (usually specified in bytes) that can be attached to a particular computer.

Memory-mapped I/O.   An addressing method for I/O ports that uses the same decoding system used by the memory section. The I/O ports thus occupy memory addresses.

Microcomputer.   A computer that has a microprocessor as its central processing unit.

Microprocessor. A complete central processing unit for a computer constructed from one or a few integrated circuits.

Mnemonic. A memory jogger; a name that suggests the actual meaning or purpose of the object to which it refers.

Modem (modulator/demodulator). A device that adds or removes a carrier frequency, thereby allowing data to be transmitted on a high-frequency channel or received from such a channel.

Modular programming. A programming method whereby the overall program is divided into logically separate sections or *modules.*

Module. A part or section of a program.

Monitor. A program that allows the computer user to enter programs and data, run programs, examine the contents of the computer's memory and registers, and utilize the computer's peripherals. *See also* Operating system.

Most significant bit. The leftmost bit in a group of bits, that is, bit 7 of a byte or bit 15 of a 16-bit word.

Multifunction device. A device that performs more than one function in a computer system; the term commonly refers to devices containing memory, input/output ports, timers, etc. Popular multifunction devices in the 8080/8085 family are the 8155 or 8156 RAM/I/O/Counter-Timer, the 8355 ROM/I/O, and the 8755 EPROM (erasable PROM)/I/O.

Multitasking. Executing many tasks during a single period of time, usually by working on each one for a specified part of the period and suspending tasks that must wait for input, output, the completion of other tasks, or external events.

Murphy's Law. The famous maxim that "whatever can go wrong, will."

N

Negate. To find the two's complement (negative) of a number.

Negative edge (of a binary pulse). A 1 to 0 transition.

Negative flag. *See* Sign flag.

Negative logic. Circuitry in which a logic zero is the active or ON state.

Nesting. Constructing programs in a hierarchical manner with one level contained within another, and so forth. The nesting level is the number of transfers of control required to reach a particular part of a program without ever returning to a higher level.

Nibble. A unit of four bits. A byte (eight bits) may be described as consisting of a high nibble (four most significant bits) and a low nibble (four least significant bits).

Nine's complement. The result of subtracting a decimal number from a number having nines in all digit positions.

Non-maskable interrupt. An interrupt that cannot be disabled from within the CPU.

Non-volatile memory. A memory that retains its contents when power is removed.

No-op (or *no operation*). An instruction that does nothing except increment the program counter.

Normalization (of numbers). Adjusting a number into a regular or standard format. A typical example is the scaling of a binary fraction to make its most significant bit 1.

O

Object code (or object program). The program that is the output of a translator program, such as an assembler—usually a machine language program ready for execution.

Odd parity. A 1-bit error-detecting code that makes the total number of 1 bits in a unit of data (including the parity bit) odd.

One's complement. A bit-by-bit logical complement of a number, obtained by replacing each 0 bit with a 1 and each 1 bit with a 0.

One-shot. A device that produces a pulse output of known duration in response to a pulse input. A timer operates in a *one-shot mode* when it indicates the end of a single interval of known duration.

Open (a file). To make a file ready for use. The user generally must open a file before working with it.

Operating system (OS). A computer program that controls the overall operations of a computer and performs such functions as assigning places in memory to programs and data, scheduling the execution of programs, processing interrupts, and controlling the overall input/output system. Also known as a monitor, executive, or master-control program, although the term *monitor* is usually reserved for a simple operating system with limited functions.

Operation code (op code). The part of an instruction that specifies the operation to be performed.

OS. *See* Operating system.

Overflow (of a stack). Exceeding the amount of memory allocated to a stack.

Overflow, two's complement. *See* Two's complement overflow.

P

Packed decimal. A binary-coded-decimal format in which each byte contains two decimal digits.

Page. A subdivision of the memory. In byte-oriented computers, a page is generally a 256-byte section of memory in which all addresses have the same eight most significant bits *(or page number)*. For example, page C6 would consist of memory addresses C600 through C6FF.

Paged address. The identifier that characterizes a particular memory address on a known page. In byte-oriented computers, this is usually the eight least significant bits of a memory address.

Page number. The identifier that characterizes a particular page of memory. In byte-oriented computers, this is usually the eight most significant bits of a memory address.

Parallel interface. An interface between a CPU and input or output devices that handle data in parallel (more than one bit at a time). The 8255 Programmable Peripheral Interface is a parallel interface in the 8080/8085 family.

Parameter. An item that must be provided to a subroutine or program for it to be executed.

Parity. A 1-bit error-detecting code that makes the total number of 1 bits in a unit of data, including the parity bit, odd (odd parity) or even (even parity). Also called *vertical parity* or *vertical redundancy check* (VRC).

Passing parameters. Making the required parameters available to a subroutine.

PCI. *See* Programmable Communication Interface.

Peripheral ready. A signal that is active when a peripheral can accept more data.

Physical device. An actual input or output device, as opposed to a logical device.

Pointer. A storage place that contains the address of a data item rather than the item itself. A pointer tells where the item is located.

Polling. Determining which I/O devices are ready by examining the status of one device at a time.

Polling interrupt system. An interrupt system in which a program determines the source of a particular interrupt by examining the status of potential sources one at a time.

Pop. Remove an operand from a stack.

Port. The basic addressable unit of the computer's input/output section.

Positive edge (of a binary pulse). A 0 to 1 transition.

Postdecrementing. Decrementing an address register after using it.

Postincrementing. Incrementing an address register after using it.

Postindexing. An addressing mode in which the effective address is determined by first obtaining the base address indirectly and then indexing from that base address. The "post" refers to the fact that the indexing is performed after the indirection.

Power fail interrupt. An interrupt that informs the CPU of an impending loss of power.

PPI. *See* Programmable Peripheral Interface.

Predecrementing. Decrementing an address register before using it.

Preincrementing. Incrementing an address register before using it.

Preindexing. An addressing mode in which the effective address is determined by indexing from the base address and then using the indexed address indirectly. The "pre" refers to the fact that the indexing is performed before the indirection. Of course, the array starting at the given base address must consist of addresses that can be used indirectly.

Priority interrupt system. An interrupt system in which some interrupts have precedence over others; that is, they will be serviced first or can interrupt the others' service routines.

Processor status word (PSW). An 8080/8085 register pair consisting of the accumulator (more significant byte) and the flags (less significant byte).

Program counter (PC register). A register that contains the address of the next instruction to be fetched from memory.

Programmable Communication Interface (PCI). In 8080/8085 terminology, refers specifically to the 8251 serial interface chip, a popular family USART (synchronous/asynchronous serial interface).

Programmable I/O device. An I/O device that can have its mode of operation determined by loading registers under program control.

Programmable peripheral chip (or *programmable peripheral interface*). A chip that can operate in a variety of modes; its current operating mode is determined by loading control registers under program control. In 8080/8085 terminology, programmable peripheral interface refers specifically to the 8255 parallel interface chip.

Programmable timer. A device that can handle a variety of timing tasks, including the generation of delays, under program control. The 8253 programmable interval timer is a programmable timer in the 8080/8085 family.

Program relative addressing. A form of relative addressing in which the base address is the program counter. Use of this form of addressing makes it easy to move programs from one place in memory to another.

Programmed input/output. Input or output performed under program control without using interrupts or other special hardware techniques.

Protocol. *See* Data-link control.

Pseudo-operation (or *pseudo-op* or *pseudo-instruction*). An assembly language operation code that directs the assembler to perform some action but does not result in the generation of a machine language instruction.

PSW. *See* Processor status word.

Pull. Remove an operand from a stack. Same as *pop.*

Push. Store an operand in a stack.

Q

Queue. A set of tasks, storage addresses, or other items that are used in a first-in, first-out manner; that is, the first item entered in the queue is the first to be used or removed.

Queue header. A set of storage locations describing the current location and status of a queue.

R

RAM. *See* Random-access memory.

Random-access (read/write) memory (RAM). A memory that can be both read and altered (written) in normal operation.

Read-only memory (ROM). A memory that can be read but not altered in normal operation.

Ready for data. A signal that is active when the receiver can accept more data.

Real-time. In synchronization with the actual occurrence of events.

Real-time clock. A device that interrupts a CPU at regular time intervals.

Real-time operating system. An operating system that can act as a supervisor for programs that have real-time requirements. May also be referred to as a *real-time executive* or *real-time monitor*.

Reentrant. A program or routine that can be executed concurrently while the same routine is being interrupted or otherwise held in abeyance.

Refresh. Rewriting data into a memory before its contents are lost. Dynamic RAMs must be refreshed periodically (typically every few milliseconds) or they will lose their contents spontaneously.

Register. A storage location inside the CPU.

Register indirect addressing. An addressing mode in which a register contains the address required to execute the instruction.

Register pair. In 8080/8085 terminology, two 8-bit registers that can be referenced as a 16-bit unit.

Relative addressing. An addressing mode in which the address specified in the instruction is the offset from a base address.

Relative offset. The difference between the actual address to be used in an instruction and the current value of the program counter.

Relocatable. Can be placed anywhere in memory without changes; that is, a program that can occupy any set of consecutive memory addresses.

Return (from a subroutine). Transfers control back to the program that originally called the subroutine and resumes its execution.

ROM. *See* Read-only memory.

Rotate. A shift operation that treats the data as if it were arranged in a circle, that is, as if the most significant and least significant bits were connected either directly or through a Carry bit.

Row major order. Storing elements of a multidimensional array in memory by changing the indexes starting with the rightmost first. That is, if a typical element is A(I,J,K) and the elements begin with A(0,0,0), the order is A(0,0,0), A(0,0,1),..., A(0,1,0), A(0,1,1),... The opposite technique (changing the leftmost index first) is called *column major order*.

RS-232 (or *EIA RS-232*). A standard interface for the transmission of digital data, sponsored by the Electronic Industries Association of Washington, D.C. It has been partially superseded by RS-449.

S

Scheduler. A program that determines when other programs should be started and terminated.

Scratchpad. An area of memory that is generally easy and quick to use for storing variable data or intermediate results.

SDLC. (Synchronous Data Link Control). The successor protocol to BSC for IBM computers and terminals.

Semaphore. See Flag.

Serial. One bit at a time.

Serial interface. An interface between a CPU and input or output devices that handle data serially. The 8251 Programmable Communication Interface is a popular serial interface chip in the 8080/8085 family. *See also* UART.

Setpoint. The value of a variable that a controller is expected to maintain.

Shift instruction. An instruction that moves all the bits of the data by a certain number of bit positions, just as in a shift register.

Signed number. A number in which one or more bits represent whether the number is positive or negative. A common format is for the most significant bit to represent the sign (0 = positive, 1 = negative).

Sign extension. The process of copying the sign (most significant) bit to the right as in an arithmetic shift. Sign extension preserves the sign when two's complement numbers are being divided or normalized.

Sign flag. A flag that contains the most significant bit of the result of the previous operation. It is sometimes called a *negative flag,* since a value of 1 indicates a negative signed number.

Sign function. A function that is 0 if its parameter is positive and 1 if its parameter is negative.

Size (of an array dimension). The distance in memory between elements that are ordered consecutively in a particular dimension; the number of bytes between the starting address of an element and the starting address of the element with an index one larger in a particular dimension but the same in all other dimensions.

Software delay. A program that has no function other than to waste time.

Software interrupt. See Trap.

Software stack. A stack that is managed by means of specific instructions, as opposed to a hardware stack which the computer manages automatically.

Source code (or source program). A computer program written in assembly language or in a high-level language.

Space. The zero state on a serial data communications line.

Stack. A section of memory that can be accessed only in a last-in, first-out manner. That is, data can be added to or removed from the stack only through its top; new data is placed above the old data and the removal of a data item makes the item below it the new top.

Stack pointer. A register that contains the address of the top of a stack.

Standard (or 8,4,2,1) BCD. A BCD representation in which the bit positions have the same weight as in ordinary binary numbers.

Standard teletypewriter. A teletypewriter that operates asynchronously at a rate of ten characters per second.

Start bit. A 1-bit signal that indicates the start of data transmission by an asynchronous device.

Static allocation (of memory). Assignment of fixed storage areas for data and programs; an alternative is *dynamic allocation* in which storage areas are assigned at the time they are needed.

Status register. A register whose contents indicate the current state or operating mode of a device.

Status signal. A signal that describes the current state of a transfer or the operating mode of a device.

Stop bit. A 1-bit signal that indicates the end of data transmission by an asynchronous device.

String. An array (set of data) consisting of characters.

String functions. Procedures that allow the programmer to operate on data consisting of characters rather than numbers. Typical functions are insertion, deletion, concatenation, search, and replacement.

Strobe. A signal that identifies or describes another set of signals and that can be used to control a buffer, latch, or register.

Subroutine. A subprogram that can be executed (called) from more than one place in a main program.

Subroutine call. The process whereby a computer transfers control from its current program to a subroutine while retaining the information required to resume the current program.

Subroutine linkage.   The mechanism whereby a computer retains the information required to resume its current program after it completes the execution of a subroutine.

Suspend (a task).   Halt execution and preserve the status of a task until some future time.

*Synchronization (*or *sync) character.*   A character that is used only to synchronize the transmitter and the receiver.

Synchronous.   Operating according to an overall timing source or clock, that is, at regular intervals.

Systems software.   Programs that perform administrative functions or aid in the development of other programs but do not actually perform any of the computer's workload.

T

Tail (of a queue).   The location of the oldest item in the queue, that is, the earliest entry.

Task.   A self-contained program that can serve as part of an overall system under the control of a supervisor.

Task status.   The set of parameters that specifies the current state of a task. A task can be suspended and resumed as long as its status is saved and restored.

Teletypewriter.   A device containing a keyboard and a serial printer that is often used in communications and with computers. Also referred to as a Teletype (a registered trademark of Teletype Corporation of Skokie, Illinois) or TTY.

Ten's complement.   The result of subtracting a decimal number from zero (ignoring the negative sign), the nine's complement plus one.

Terminator.   A data item that has no function other than to signify the end of an array.

Threaded code.   A program consisting of subroutines, each of which automatically transfers control to the next one upon its completion.

Timeout.   A period during which no activity is allowed to proceed; an inactive period.

Top of the stack.   The address containing the item most recently entered into the stack.

Trace.   A debugging aid that provides information about a program while the program is being executed. The trace usually prints all or some of the intermediate results.

Trailing edge (of a binary pulse).   The edge that marks the end of a pulse.

Translate instruction. An instruction that converts its operand into the corresponding entry in a table.

Transparent routine. A routine that operates without interfering with the operations of other routines.

Two's complement overflow. A situation in which a signed arithmetic operation produces a result that cannot be represented correctly—that is, the magnitude overflows into the sign bit.

True borrow. See Borrow.

True comparison. A comparison that finds the two operands to be equal.

Two's complement. A binary number that, when added to the original number in a binary adder, produces a zero result. The two's complement of a number may be obtained by subtracting the number from zero or by adding 1 to the one's complement.

Two's complement overflow. A situation in which a signed arithmetic operation produces a result that cannot be represented correctly— that is, the magnitude overflows into the sign bit.

U

UART (Universal Asynchronous Receiver/Transmitter). An LSI device that acts as an interface between systems that handle data in parallel and devices that handle data in asynchronous serial form.

Underflow (of a stack). Attempting to remove more data from a stack than has been entered into it.

Unsigned number. A number in which all the bits are used to represent magnitude.

USART (Universal Synchronous/Asynchronous Receiver/Transmitter). An LSI device (such as the 8251 PCI) that can serve as either a UART or a USRT.

USRT (Universal Synchronous Receiver/Transmitter). An LSI device that acts as an interface between systems that handle data in parallel and devices that handle data in synchronous serial form.

Utility. A general-purpose program, usually supplied by the computer manufacturer or part of an operating system, that executes a standard or common operation such as sorting, converting data from one format to another, or copying a file.

V

Valid data.   A signal that is active when new data is available to the receiver.

Vectored interrupt.   An interrupt that produces an identification code (or *vector*) that the CPU can use to transfer control to the appropriate service routine. The process whereby control is transferred to the service routine is called *vectoring*.

Volatile memory.   A memory that loses its contents when power is removed.

W

Walking bit test.   A procedure whereby a single 1 bit is moved through each bit position in an area of memory and a check is made as to whether it can be read back correctly.

Word.   The basic grouping of bits that a computer can process at one time. When dealing with microprocessors, the term often refers to a 16-bit unit of data.

Word boundary.   A boundary between 16-bit storage units containing two bytes of information. If information is being stored in word-length units, only pairs of bytes conforming to (aligned with) word boundaries contain valid information. Misaligned pairs of bytes contain one byte from one word and one byte from another.

Word-length.   A length of 16 bits per item.

Wraparound.   Organization in a circular manner as if the ends were connected. A storage area exhibits wraparound if operations on it act as if the boundary locations were contiguous.

Write-only register.   A register that the CPU can change but cannot read. If a program must determine the contents of such a register, it must save a copy of the data placed there.

Z

Zero flag.   A flag that is 1 if the last operation produced a result of zero and 0 if it did not.

Zoned decimal.   A binary-coded decimal format in which each byte contains a single decimal digit.

Index

469

Other Osborne/McGraw-Hill Publications

Douglas P. Barnes
7341 Jefferson St.
Harrisburg PA 17111
717-564-2742